Y0-BRV-527

Death and Dying
SOURCEBOOK

Health Reference Series

First Edition

Death and Dying
SOURCEBOOK

Basic Consumer Health Information for the Layperson about End-of-Life Care and Related Ethical and Legal Issues, Including Chief Causes of Death, Autopsies, Pain Management for the Terminally Ill, Life Support Systems, Insurance, Euthanasia, Assisted Suicide, Hospice Programs, Living Wills, Funeral Planning, Counseling, Mourning, Organ Donation, and Physician Training; Along with Statistical Data, a Glossary, and Listings of Sources for Further Help and Information

Edited by
Annemarie S. Muth

615 Griswold • Detroit, MI 48226

Bibliographic Note

Because this page cannot legibly accommodate all the copyright notices, the Bibliographic Note portion of the Preface constitutes an extension of the copyright notice.

Beginning with books published in 1999, each new volume of the *Health Reference Series* will be individually titled and called a "First Edition." Subsequent updates will carry sequential edition numbers. To help avoid confusion and to provide maximum flexibility in our ability to respond to informational needs, the practice of consecutively numbering each volume will be discontinued.

Edited by Annemarie S. Muth

Health Reference Series

Karen Bellenir, *Series Editor*
Peter D. Dresser, *Managing Editor*
Joan Margeson, *Research Associate*
Dawn Matthews, *Verification Assistant*
Margaret Mary Missar, *Research Coordinator*
Jenifer Swanson, *Research Associate*

Omnigraphics, Inc.

Matthew P. Barbour, *Vice President, Operations*
Laurie Lanzen Harris, *Vice President, Editorial Director*
Thomas J. Murphy, *Vice President, Finance and Comptroller*
Peter E. Ruffner, *Senior Vice President*
Jane J. Steele, *Marketing Consultant*

Frederick G. Ruffner, Jr., Publisher

© 2000, Omnigraphics, Inc.

Library of Congress Cataloging-in-Publication Data

Library of Congress Cataloging-in-Publication Data

Death and dying sourcebook : basic consumer health information for the layperson about end-of-life care and related ethical and legal issues ... / edited by Annemarie S. Muth.— 1st ed.
p. cm.
Includes bibliographical references and index.
ISBN 0-7808-0230-6 (lib. bdg. : alk. paper)
1. Death. 2. Terminal care. I. Muth, Annemarie.

R726.8 .D3785 1999
362.1'75—dc21

99-044810

∞

This book is printed on acid-free paper meeting the ANSI Z39.48 Standard. The infinity symbol that appears above indicates that the paper in this book meets that standard.

Printed in the United States

Table of Contents

v

Part III: Health Care Options for the Terminally III

Part IV: End-of-Life Medical Care: Issues and Innovations

Part V: Approaching Death

Part VI: Final Arrangements

Part VII: Bereavement

Part VIII: Additional Help and Information

Preface

About This Book

Although more than 2 million people die each year in the United States, little information is available on how to prepare for death. Americans, who live longer today than ever before, tend to put off dealing with the unpleasant issues of death and dying until confronted personally. Even the medical profession, bent on curing patients, is often at a loss when faced with treating the physical and emotional pain of the dying.

This book provides the reader with timely information on the medical, legal, and ethical issues related to death and dying in the United States. Documents selected from a wide variety of government and private organizations that offer advice on such topics as selecting the right health care facility, Medicare and Medicaid, patients' rights, advance directives, innovations in hospice care, pain management, physician-assisted suicide, funeral costs, and the grieving process are included. A glossary and resource directory offer additional help and information.

How to Use This Book

This book is divided into parts and chapters. Parts focus on broad areas of interest. Chapters are devoted to single topics within a part.

Part I: Death and Dying Statistics in the United States presents mortality and life expectancy statistics by age, sex, ethnicity, and race;

the 10 leading causes of death; mortality in long-term care facilities; homicide in the workplace; and autopsy statistics.

Part II: Attitudes toward Death and Dying looks at a variety of religious and cultural attitudes on death and dying in the United States; the different coping strategies employed by men and women faced with a life-threatening disease; an account of one man's dying from his daughter's perspective; and the National Hospice Organization's stand on euthanasia and physician-assisted suicide.

Part III: Health Care Options for the Terminally Ill gives statistics and information on health conditions among the elderly; Medicare, Medicaid, and private long-term care insurance; how to select the right nursing home or home care provider; the National Hospice Organization; patients' rights in health care facilities; and living wills and durable power of attorney.

Part IV: End-Of-Life Medical Care: Issues and Innovations profiles the shortcomings and advances in the care of the dying, including a look at the effectiveness of the intensive care unit; the status of physician training in end-of-life care; involving the patient in decisions about his or her own medical treatment; improving palliative care to prevent suicide among terminally ill patients; assisting the family caregiver; the myth of cost-saving in end-of-life care; and increasing hospice eligibility.

Part V: Approaching Death describes the common discomforts of the dying patient and how the physician can provide relief; physical and spiritual dimensions of the dying process; and how the physician determines that a patient has died and what follows.

Part VI: Final Arrangements advises consumers on purchasing funeral, cremation, and burial goods and services; discusses wills, insurance, probate, and veteran benefits; and explains the ethical and legal issues involved in organ and tissue donation.

Part VII: Bereavement looks at the stages of mourning, including the stages of grief in children and how parents cope with the loss of a child, and bereavement services provided by a hospice program.

Part VIII: Additional Help and Information provides a glossary of medical and legal terminology related to death and dying and a list of government and private agencies and online sites that may be contacted for further information.

Bibliographic Note

This volume contains documents and excerpts from publications issued by the following U.S. government agencies: Administration on Aging (AoA), Agency for Health Care Policy and Research (AHCPR), Centers for Disease Control and Prevention (CDC), Federal Trade Commission (FTC), Health Care Financing Administration (HCFA), National Cancer Institute (NCI), National Center for Health Statistics (NCHS), National Institute for Occupational Safety and Health (NIOSH), National Institute of Neurological Disorders and Stroke (NINDS), National Institute of Nursing Research (NINR), National Institutes of Health (NIH), Office of Minority Health (OMH), U.S. Department of Health and Human Services (DHHS), U.S. General Accounting Office (GAO), and U.S. General Services Administration (GSA).

In addition, this volume contains copyrighted documents from the following organizations and individuals: American Association of Retired Persons (AARP); American Health Care Association (AHCA); Americans for Better Care of the Dying (ABCD); Center for Intercultural Relations; Gary Hickerson, M.S.S.W.; National Association for Home Care (NAHC); National Hospice Organization (NHO); North Central Florida Hospice, Inc.; Physicians for Compassionate Care (PCC); and George Soros, Project on Death in America. Copyrighted articles from *American Demographics, Archives of Internal Medicine, Community Care, Critical Care Nursing Quarterly, Death & Dying, Human Life News, Journal of the American Medical Association, Medical Economics, The New England Journal of Medicine, OMEGA,* and *Science News* are also included.

Full citation information is provided on the first page of each chapter. Every effort has been made to secure all necessary rights to reprint the copyrighted material. If any omissions have been made, please contact Omnigraphics to make corrections for future editions.

Acknowledgements

In addition to the many organizations and agencies that contributed the material included in this book, thanks go to Joan Margeson for her tireless efforts in tracking down documents and Dawn Matthews for her verification assistance.

Note from the Editor

This book is part of Omnigraphics' *Health Reference Series*. The series provides basic information about a broad range of medical concerns. It is not intended to serve as a tool for diagnosing illness, in prescribing treatments, or as a substitute for the physician/patient relationship. All persons concerned about medical symptoms or the possibility of disease are encouraged to seek professional care from an appropriate health care provider.

Our Advisory Board

The *Health Reference Series* is reviewed by an Advisory Board comprised of librarians from public, academic, and medical libraries. We would like to thank the following board members for providing guidance to the development of this series:

Nancy Bulgarelli, William Beaumont Hospital Library, Royal Oak, MI

Karen Imarasio, Bloomfield Township Public Library, Bloomfield Township, MI

Karen Morgan, Mardigian Library, University of Michigan-Dearborn, Dearborn, MI

Rosemary Orlando, St. Clair Shores Public Library, St. Clair Shores, MI

Health Reference Series *Update Policy*

The inaugural book in the *Health Reference Series* was the first edition of *Cancer Sourcebook* published in 1992. Since then, the *Series* has been enthusiastically received by librarians and in the medical community. In order to maintain the standard of providing high-quality health information for the lay person, the editorial staff at Omnigraphics felt it was necessary to implement a policy of updating volumes when warranted.

Medical researchers have been making tremendous strides, and the challenge to stay current with the most recent advances is one our editors take seriously. Each decision to update a volume will be made on an individual basis. Some of the considerations will include how much new information is available and the feedback we receive from people who use the books. If there's a topic you would like to see added to the update list, or an area of medical concern you feel has not been adequately addressed, please write to:

Editor
Health Reference Series
Omnigraphics, Inc.
615 Griswold
Detroit, MI 48226

The commitment to providing on-going coverage of important medical developments has also led to some technical changes in the *Health Reference Series*. Beginning with books published in 1999, each new volume will be individually titled and called a "First Edition." Subsequent updates will carry sequential edition numbers. To help avoid confusion and to provide maximum flexibility in our ability to respond to informational needs, the practice of consecutively numbering each volume will be discontinued.

Part One

Death and Dying Statistics in the United States

Chapter 1

Patterns of Death: Overview

The National Center for Health Statistics (NCHS), Centers for Disease Control and Prevention, announces the first release of data from the latest National Mortality Followback Survey—the first study since the 1980s to examine detailed patterns of mortality by supplementing the information provided through death certificates with interviews of next of kin. The survey allows for the examination of trends in mortality, differences by income and education, risk factors and causes of death, and health care utilization in the last year of life.

Highlights of the data show

Where death occurs. The majority of deaths (56 percent) occur in a hospital, clinic, or medical center; 19 percent in a nursing home; and some 21 percent of people died at home.

Who gets health care. While 10 percent of decedents were reported to have never visited a doctor during the last year of life, an almost equal number made 50 or more visits.

Who pays for health care. Medicare was the principal source of payment for the largest number of decedents (46 percent). Private

From "New Study of Patterns of Death in the United States," [Online] February 23, 1998. Available: http://www.cdc.gov/nchswww/releases/98facts/ 98sheets/93nmfs.htm. Produced by the CDC's National Center for Health Statistics (NCHS). For complete contact information, please refer to Chapter 60, "Resources."

insurance paid most of the medical expenses for about 20 percent; about 10 percent of people paid for their own medical care; and Medicaid was the source of payment for another 10 percent. Over half of the decedents were covered by private insurance or HMO and about three-quarters by Medicare.

Who needs health care. Almost 200,000 decedents needed but had not received health care, primarily for problems in paying bills or in finding or getting treatment.

What diseases people have. One-quarter of decedents have had a heart attack and about an equal number had angina. Over 40 percent were reported to have had hypertension. Other frequent conditions were cancer and arthritis, each reported for about one-third of decedents. Fifteen percent suffered from some type of memory impairment.

How their last year of life was. Illness or injury kept one in 10 in bed most of their last year of life. About half of decedents were reported to have had a functional limitation due to physical or mental conditions during their last year of life. Some 58 percent of those with limitations received help at home from a spouse; daughters provided care for 46 percent and 31 percent received help from visiting nurses. In the last year of life, 39 percent of decedents took pain medication.

How many smoked or used drugs or alcohol. Slightly more than half of all decedents smoked cigarettes at some point during their lives. About one-quarter of all decedents used alcohol during their last year of life; 29 percent of drinkers used alcohol every day. About 2 percent used marijuana during their last year of life and less than 1 percent were reported to have used other types of illicit drugs.

What circumstances were related to homicide, suicide, or fatal motor vehicle crashes. For those who died of homicide, suicide, or unintentional injuries, 19 percent had an alcoholic beverage within 4 hours of death and 17 percent had taken drugs or medication within 24 hours of death. Of the 36,000 firearm related deaths, almost three-quarters (72 percent) involved the use of handguns. One-third of decedents involved in fatal motor vehicle crashes were reported to not have been wearing safety belts.

The 1993 National Mortality Followback Survey (NMFS) is the latest in a series of followback surveys that supplement information

4

on the death records of a sample of United States citizens who die in a given year with telephone or in-person interviews of the next of kin or other persons familiar with the decedent's life history. The 1993 survey is based on almost 23,000 records of individuals aged 15 years or over who died in 1993. All states (with the exception of South Dakota where state law restricts the use of death certificate information) and the District of Columbia participated in the survey.

Chapter 2

Death in the Hospital

Advances in medical science during the last half century mean people survive many acute illnesses that previously would have resulted in death. The majority of deaths in the United States occur in health care institutions, although in geriatric[1] and hospice practices a larger percentage of individuals die at home. For the last quarter century, the medical, legal, and lay literature have discussed the appropriate use of technology and palliation in the care of dying patients. For many, death comes either as a gradual decline from chronic illness or as an acute exacerbation in the context of significant disease. Increasingly, the importance of a systematic approach to care of dying patients has been recognized.[2-4]

Despite the substantial literature addressing care of dying patients, the medical management of dying has not been implemented in an organized way. Optimal decision making for a patient has been outlined,[5] yet patients often die with many distressing symptoms and problems.[6-8] An organized approach to the care of dying individuals may not be used.

To better understand current care for dying patients, we developed a chart review instrument that addresses clinical and other aspects of the dying process. We reviewed the medical records of patients

From "Death in the Hospital," by Sarah J. Goodlin, Gary S. Winzelberg, Joan M. Teno, Marie Whedon, and Joanne Lynn, in *Archives of Internal Medicine,* Vol. 158, No. 14, pp. 1570-2, July 27, 1998. © 1998 by the American Medical Association, 515 N. State St., Chicago, IL 60610. All rights reserved. Reprinted with permission.

dying in the 2 major teaching hospitals associated with our medical school. Our goals were to identify a reference point from which we can begin to improve performance of our health care system, and to which others could compare care for dying patients in other systems.

Results

Overall, 70 patients (68%) were men and 34 were women. The patients from the Veterans' Affairs hospital were predominantly male. Age ranged from 28 to 97 years (mean [+ or -] SD, 68.9 [+ or -] 12.6 years). Most patients (63 [61%]) were admitted from home, although 36 (35%) were transferred from another hospital. Primary diagnosis is listed in Table 2.1. Fifty-three patients (51%) were hospitalized with a clinical picture consistent with the terminal stage of the illness, 34 patients (33%) were hospitalized with an acute, potentially reversible illness (including acute cardiovascular events and infectious processes), and 17 patients (16%) were hospitalized with an acute illness or complication in the face of chronic disease (e.g., pneumonia in the presence of chronic lung disease).

Advance care directives were present for 49 patients (47%), with 45 (43%) having a "living will" and 36 (35%) having a durable power

Table 2.1. Primary Diagnoses

Diagnosis	No.
Solid tumor	35
Lymphoma, leukemia	11
Ischemic heart disease	13
Chronic pulmonary disease	10
Infectious processes	6
Stroke	6
Congestive heart failure	5
Liver disease	5
Renal failure	3
Acquired immunodeficiency syndrome	3
Dissecting aortic aneurysm	2
Valvular heart disease	2
Trauma	2
Other	3

of attorney for health care. By the time of death, 92 patients (89%) had a do-not-resuscitate (DNR) order. For 35 patients (42% of those with a DNR), the rationale given in the record for the DNR order was that death appeared imminent. The number of days between a DNR status and death ranged from 0 to 90 (median, 5 days; mean, 11 days). Thirty-three percent of DNR orders were written within 2 days of death and 10% were written on the day of death. Forty-eight percent of patients had an order or a progress note specifying comfort measures only (CMO). Almost all patients (98%) with CMO status had a DNR order. Of those patients admitted in the terminal stage of their illness, 30 (57%) had a CMO status.

Table 2.2. lists symptoms documented within the final 48 hours of life. There were no significant differences in rates of symptoms or treatments between the 2 institutions. Dyspnea was documented for more than half of the patients, as was restlessness or agitation. Pain was documented for almost half of the patients, although pain was

Table 2.2. Symptoms within 48 Hours of Death Expressed as Prevalence*

Symptoms	All Cases, % (N = 104)
Dyspnea	51
Pain	47
Severe pain[†]	12
Anxiety	26
Restlessness	51
Nausea	19
Anorexia	19
Fever	28
Incontinence	18
Confusion	34
Bed bound	68

(*)There were no significant differences in prevalence of symptoms for patients with a do-not-resuscitate order, or for patients for whom a decision was made to provide comfort measures only.

(†)Severe pain was described as severe, excruciating, or worst (a pain score of 8 on a scale of 0-10).

characterized as "severe" in only 12% of the records. Anxiety and confusion were present in one third of patients. Patients with CMO status did not differ significantly from the entire group in prevalence of symptoms documented. We could not consistently discern the extent to which symptoms were relieved in the medical records.

Almost all patients had a DNR status by the time of death; those with DNR did not differ from those without in the rate of interventions. Almost all patients received intravenous fluids and medications. Narcotics were given to nearly all patients as they died. Half of the patients received antibiotics and 60% had blood samples taken within

Table 2.3a. Interventions within 48 Hours of Death Expressed as Prevalence* (continued in Table 2.3b).

Intervention	All Cases (N = 104)	DNR (N = 92)
Resuscitation	12	6
Ventilatory support	27	23[†]
Intubation	28	24[†]
Intensive care unit	40	34[†]
Antibiotics	55	55
Intravenous fluids	71	89
Intravenous medications	93	97
Central line	42	40
Enteral tube	36	35
Narcotics	85	88
Weight taken	54	48[†]
Blood samples taken	64	60
Radiography	44	40
Restraints	19	18
Foley catheter	77	80
Bereavement	23	25
Chaplain	22	25
Social work	23	26
Arterial line	28	23

2 days of death. Only 8 had no tube attached (i.e., no intravenous line, endotracheal tube, arterial line, or Foley catheter). Almost one fifth of patients were restrained within 2 days of death. More than half were weighed in their last 2 days.

Patients with a CMO status had significantly lesser rates of some interventions (Table 2.3.), including resuscitation (P = .02), ventilation (P = .001), care in the intensive care unit (P =.001), antibiotic therapy (P = .009), venopuncture (P < .001), radiography (P < .001), and arterial lines (P < .001). Patients with a CMO status also had better documentation of bereavement efforts in their records.

Table 2.3b. Interventions within 48 Hours of Death Expressed as Prevalence* (continued from Table 2.3a).

Intervention	CMO (N = 48)
Resuscitation	5[†]
Ventilatory support	11[‡]
Intubation	13[†]
Intensive care unit	22[‡]
Antibiotics	32[†]
Intravenous fluids	42
Intravenous medications	92
Central line	35
Enteral tube	23
Narcotics	94
Weight taken	26[‡]
Blood samples taken	14[‡]
Radiography	25[‡]
Restraints	10
Foley catheter	79
Bereavement	35[†]
Chaplain	35
Social work	27
Arterial line	9[†]

(*)DNR indicates patients with a do-not-resuscitate order; CMO, patients with an order or a progress note stating that comfort measures only are to be given. All data are presented as percentages.

([†])<.05.

([‡])<.001.

Comment

Important first steps in improving the care for the dying are to characterize current care and to identify opportunities for improvement. We report our effort to understand current care for individuals in the final 48 hours of life in our hospitals through a retrospective chart review.

The retrospective review limited us to documented information. Errors in documentation may include underreporting of symptoms, omission of report of response of symptoms to treatment, and misinterpretation of clinical presentation when a patient report of symptoms was not used. Systematic patient assessment tools were not used to record symptoms. Rates of interventions were high, and to some extent this may reflect insurance and aggressiveness of care criteria required for patients in acute care hospitals. The DNR order would not necessarily relate to a plan of care, particularly when it reflected advance care preferences of a patient.

Others[10] state goals of treatment for the terminally ill including relief of pain and suffering, support of the patient and family, comfort, and dignity (copies of the chart review instrument are available from Dr. Goodlin). Use of a chart review tool documented rates of symptom prevalence in hospitalized patients that suggest that these goals are not consistently reached. The rate of pain is consistent with that documented in surveys of individuals and chart review in the SUPPORT study.[9,11] In a palliative care service the rates of symptoms in dying patients can be substantially reduced with careful medical management.[12] The order to provide CMO appears to be associated with limitation of interventions that might prolong life. A CMO status was designated for only half of the patients who appeared to have been admitted in the terminal stage of their illness. In our hospitals there were no organized approaches to palliative care or enhancement of comfort in the form of reduced symptoms for those patients with a CMO status. Some interventions, such as weighing the patient, seem unlikely to enhance comfort in any situation. Other interventions, such as bereavement support and chaplaincy, were documented at rates lower than expected.

Conclusions

Information on which to base improvement of care for dying individuals can be obtained through a brief retrospective chart review. Pain, dyspnea, restlessness, and other symptoms were prevalent in our sample within 48 hours of death. While patients in whom a decision was made to provide CMO received less aggressive care, they did not appear to have more comfort than other patients. There were no clear, systematic approaches to dying patients discerned from the medical records that we reviewed at both institutions. We believe that evaluation and testing of processes of care for dying patients herein and elsewhere are necessary to begin the improvement of care.

References

1. P. A. Sanger, D. E. Easterling, D. A. Kindig, et al., "Changes in the Location of Death after Passage of Medicare's Prospective Payment System," *New England Journal of Medicine* 320: 433-9 (1989).

2. T. R. Fried and M. R. Gillick, "Medical Decision-Making in the Last Six Months of Life: Choices about Limitation of Care," *Journal of the American Geriatric Society* 42: 303-7 (1994).

3. S. H. Wanzer, D. D. Federman, S. J. Aderstein, et al., "The Physician's Responsibility toward Hopelessly Ill Patients: A Second Look," *New England Journal of Medicine* 320: 844-9 (1989).

4. American Board of Internal Medicine Committee on Evaluation of Clinical Competence, *Caring for the Dying: Identification and Promotion of Physician Competencies, An Educational Resource Document* (Philadelphia, Pa: American Board of Internal Medicine, 1996).

5. J. Lynn and J. M. Teno, "Good Care of the Dying Patient," *Journal of the American Medical Association* 275: 474-8 (1996).

6. The Hastings Center, *Guidelines on the Termination of Life-Sustaining Treatment and the Care of the Dying* (Bloomington: Indiana University Press, 1987).

7. R. P. Mogielnicki, W. A. Nelson, and J. A. Dulac, "A Study of the Dying Process in Elderly Hospitalized Males," *Journal of Cancer Education* 5: 135-45 (1990).

8. J. M. Hockley, R. Dunlop, and R. J. Davies, "Survey of Distressing Symptoms in Dying Patients and Their Families in

Hospital and the Response to a Symptom Control Team," *British Medical Journal* 296: 1715-7 (1988).

9. The SUPPORT Principal Investigators, "A Controlled Trial to Improve Care for Seriously Ill Hospitalized Patients," *Journal of the American Medical Association* 274: 1591-8 (1995).

10. M. Angel, "The Quality of Mercy," *New England Journal of Medicine* 306: 55 (1982).

11. World Health Organization Expert Committee, *Cancer Pain Relief and Palliative Care* (Geneva, Switzerland: World Health Organization, 1990) Technical Report Series 804.

12. K. Turner, R. Chye, G. Aggarwal, J. Philip, A. Skeels, and J. N. Lickiss, "Dignity in Dying: A Preliminary Study of Patients in the Last Three Days of Life," *Journal of Palliative Care* 12: 7-13 (1996).

— by Sarah J. Goodlin,
Gary S. Winzelberg,
Joan M. Teno,
Marie Whedon,
and Joanne Lynn

Dr. Goodlin is a Faculty Scholar, Open Society Institute, Project on Death in America, New York, NY. Reprints: Sarah J. Goodlin, M.D., Center for the Evaluative Clinical Sciences, Dartmouth Medical School, Hanover, NH 03755.

Chapter 3

Predictors of Death in Long-Term Care Facilities

For most of this century the hospital has been the dominant site of death for the elderly. However, research on where people die documents that this changed during the 1980s when long-term care institutions emerged as dominant sites of death for the elderly. Medicare's prospective payment system (PPS) may have augmented this change (Gaumer and Stavins, 1992). Deaths in the hospital setting consume greater quantities of resources than those in long-term care institutions (Brooks and Smyth-Staruch, 1984; Merrill and Mor, 1993). Thus, the cost saving incentives encouraged by the PPS fostered more rapid discharge of ill patients (Mor, Stalker, Gralla, et al., 1988; Shaughnessy and Kramer, 1990) and may have influenced this shift in the site of death.

Previous research addressing these changes is limited. Studies have primarily examined nursing homes as sites of death for the elderly (e.g., Brooks and Smyth-Staruch, 1984; Merrill and Mor, 1993). Other long-term care institutions remain to be investigated, for example, board and care homes. Board and care homes are an important institutional component caring for the elderly. The National Association of Residential Care Facilities (NARCF) estimates that

From "Predictors of Mortality in Board and Care Homes," by Nicholas G. Castle, Ph.D., in *Omega: Journal of Death and Dying,* Vol. 36, No. 1, pp. 77-87, 1997-98. Supported in part by the Agency for Health Care Policy and Research (AHCPR) Institutional National Research Award (# HS 00011). © 1997 by Baywood Publishing Co., Inc., 26 Austin Ave., Amityville, NY 11701. Reprinted with permission.

there were 41,196 licensed board and care facilities with a total of 513,550 board and care beds in the U.S. in 1987 (Newcomer and Grant, 1989). A large proportion of these beds (70%) are filled by elders (Mor, Sherwood, and Gutkin, 1986).

Demographic factors are often associated with mortality in the elderly. For example, being male, nonwhite, medically indigent, and poorly educated are predictors and/or correlates of death (Engle and Graney, 1993; Lewis, Leake, Clark, and Leal-Sotelo, 1990; Lewis, Kane, Cretin, and Clark, 1985). Functional status is also associated with mortality. Elderly with poor physical and/or mental functioning are more likely to die than other elders (Engle and Graney, 1993; Lewis, et al., 1990; Liu and Manton, 1984; Rovner, German, Brant, Clark, Burton, and Foistein, 1991). Specific diseases, such as cancer, also shorten the life expectancy of the elderly (Engle and Graney, 1993; McMillan, Mentnech, Lubitz, McBean, and Russell, 1990; Mor, 1987).

The probability of mortality may also be influenced by facility factors. For example, because of time demands or concerns with medical proficiency, a facility with less clinical staff may have higher mortality rates in comparison to a facility with more clinical staff. Studies of "small area variation" (e.g., Wennberg, 1973; Wennberg, Barnes, and Zubkoff, 1982; Wennberg, Freeman, and Culp, 1987) also attest to the strong impact facility factors have on clinical decision making.

The purpose of this research is to determine demographic, functional, disease, and facility predictors and/or correlates of death for the elderly residing in board and care facilities. In a period when more appropriate targeting of services is paramount, profiling these factors has policy relevance in that it provides a means of distinguishing and prioritizing eligibility for services.

Data and Methods

Data

The data used in this investigation come from the Office of the Assistant Secretary for Planning and Evaluation (ASPE) data on the effect of regulation on the quality of care in board and care homes collected in the fall of 1993. This evaluation was undertaken in ten states selected for variation in regulatory oversight of board and care facilities (limited versus extensive). The degree of regulatory oversight was determined from requirements for personnel training, staffing standards, inspection processes, and enforcement mechanisms. The states selected with limited regulatory oversight were Arkansas, Georgia, Illinois, Kentucky, and Texas. The states selected with extensive regulatory oversight were California, Florida, New Jersey, Oklahoma, and Oregon.

A probability sample of counties within these states was selected. Within these selected counties, board and care homes were identified. The process of identifying board and care homes included contact with hospital discharge planners, mental health case workers, building inspectors, and Ombudsmen. The "yellow pages" and newspaper advertisements were also reviewed. A board and care home was defined as "a nonmedical community-based facility that provides shelter (room), food (board), and twenty-four-hour supervision/protective oversight, as well as some additional services or personal care to residents" (Hawes, Mor, Wildfire, et al., 1995, p. 5). A further probability sample of those facilities identified was selected. The sample was stratified by size (small, medium, and large) and licensure status (licensed/unlicensed). Board and care homes licensed for special populations, such as children, the mentally ill, and substance abuse facilities, were excluded from the sampling frame.

The final sample consisted of 512 board and care homes, 386 of which were licensed and 126 unlicensed. A survey instrument was given to the director (facility operator) of each facility. In addition, 1,138 staff and 3,257 residents (or their proxies) were interviewed. The residents were chosen according to fixed target sample sizes according to the size of the facility.

The survey instrument was used to collect facility characteristics, health, and socioeconomic characteristics of the residents. For example, during interviews with the residents or their proxies, the need for assistance with activities of daily living (ADLs: bathing, toileting, transferring, eating, locomotion, and dressing) was obtained. Both bladder and bowel incontinence for the preceding fourteen days were also identified. Cognitive status was ascertained using the Short Blessed Scale (Katzman, Brown, Fuld, Schechter, and Schimmel, 1983) or the Cognitive Performance Scale (Morris, Fries, Mehr, et al., 1994). Facility characteristics collected included ownership, bed size, occupancy rate, case-mix, and staffing. Further details of this study are given elsewhere (Hawes, et al., 1995).

The subject of this investigation is the mortality of residents in board and care homes. Questions concerning deaths were asked at the facility level; that is, questions concerning the numbers of residents who had died during the previous twelve months were obtained for each facility. Therefore, the facility level file is used in this analysis.

Analytic Approach

For the proportion of deaths in each facility the logit value in a multiple regression analysis is used. The logit value transforms the range of the dependent variable from 0-1 to an unbounded range, and may normalize the dependent variable.

No previous studies could be identified that specifically addressed the mortality of board and care residents. Therefore, it was unclear which factors were most significant for analysis. Several studies have characterized the characteristics of nursing home residents and nursing facilities that were associated with mortality (e.g., Engle and Graney, 1993; Lewis, et al., 1990; Liu and Manton, 1984); these are used as a guide for this analysis. As resident characteristics, the proportion of residents greater than sixty-five years, chair- or bed-fast, urinary incontinent, having substance abuse problems, who are HIV positive, and with mental illness(es) are used. Facility characteristics used are: bed size, ownership, occupancy rate, whether the facility is part of a chain, staffing levels of RNs, LPNs, and nurse aides, staff turnover (in previous 6 months), number of health and social services provided, and the proportion of private pay residents. Also included are whether the facility was affiliated or attached to a nursing home and whether or not the facility is licensed—factors not included in previous nursing home studies that may also influence mortality rates in board and care homes. Licensure may be a proxy for overall quality which may be related to mortality rates. Those facilities affiliated or attached to a nursing home may be more likely to use resources from that nursing home, thereby possibly reducing mortality rates. Resident transfers to other facilities, such as psychiatric hospitals, acute care hospitals, and nursing homes are controlled for because these may also affect mortality rates: a facility that transfers "sick" residents may have a low mortality rate simply because these residents die elsewhere.

Insufficient data were present in twenty-five (5%) cases resulting in an unweighted analytic sample of 486 board and care facilities, and a weighed sample of 11,936 facilities. Comparisons between the missing cases and the analytic sub-sample show no significant differences for any of the independent variables. In most cases information for the independent variables in this analytic sample are available. Missing cases represented between 0 to 5% for all of these variables, with the exception of proportion of private pay residents (14%). All missing values for the independent variables are adjusted using mean substitution.

The unit of our analysis is the individual facility. However, since the sampling design relied on complex, multi-stage cluster sampling, all analyses were performed with the Software for Survey Data Analysis (SUDAAN). This was specifically developed to analyze this type of data and appropriately weights cases and adjusts the standard errors to account for the sampling strategy (Shah, Barnwell, Hunt, and LaVange, 1995). The result is a more precise comparison of the differences between groups in the populations of interest (Mor, Intrator, Fries, et al., in press). SUDAAN is commonly used in health services research, for example to analyze the National Health Interview Survey (Kovar, Gitti, and Chyba, 1992).

Results

Table 3.1. presents descriptive statistics of the independent predictor and the dependent variables. During the previous twelve months an average of 14 percent of board and care residents died. The resident population is quite old: 72 percent are sixty-five years old or greater. Nine percent of residents are chair-or bed-fast and 23 percent are urinary incontinent. Many residents also have mental illnesses (28%). During the previous twelve months, 10 percent of the residents were transferred to an acute care hospital at least once, 9 percent were transferred to a psychiatric hospital, and 17 percent were transferred to a nursing home.

As for the facility characteristics, most of the board and care homes are for-profit (73%), and the average size is twenty beds. The average occupancy rate is 80 percent. Seventy-five percent of facilities are licensed. The average number of RNs, LPNs, and nurse aides (per 100 residents) is 2.19, 2.15, and 33, respectively. An average of 2.2 health services are provided by the facility and 0.93 health services are provided by others. An average of 3.86 social services are provided by the facility and 1.88 are provided by others.

Other descriptive statistics (not shown) show that 55 percent of the board and care residents are seventy-five years or older, 17 percent are between sixty-five to seventy-four, and 28 percent are younger than sixty-five. Sixty-four percent of residents are female and 36 percent are male. The age and gender distributions are not uniform, however. Males are generally younger than females. Forty-nine percent of males are younger than sixty-five, 16 percent are between sixty-five to seventy-four, and 35 percent are seventy-five years or older. For females, 21 percent are younger than sixty-five, 14 percent are between sixty-five to seventy-four, and 65 percent are seventy-five or older. Despite the fact that males are more likely to die at a younger age than females, because of the dissimilar age and gender distributions in this sample, approximately equal proportions of males and females die. These rates are 34 percent for males and 40 percent for females.

Table 3.1. Descriptive Statistics of the Dependent and Independent Variables[a]

Variables	Mean (or %)	Standard Deviation
Dependent Variable:		
1. Average mortality rate	14%	2%
Independent Variables:		
1. Residents greater than sixty-five years	72%	4.3%
2. Residents chair- or bed-fast	9%	2%
3. Residents urinary incontinent	23%	3%
4. Residents with mental illness	28%	3%
5. Residents with substance abuse problems	7%	8%
6. Residents with HIV	0.5%	5%
7. Transfers to a psychiatric hospital	9%	1%
8. Transfers to an acute care hospital	10%	1%
9. Transfers to a nursing home	17%	1%
10. Bed size	20	3
11. For-profit	73%	—
12. Occupancy rate	0.80	0.01
13. Licensed facilities	75%	—
14. Number of health services provided by facility	2.2	0.06
15. Number of health services provided by others	0.93	0.07
16. Number of social services provided by facility	3.86	0.06
17. Number of social services provided by others	1.88	0.13
18. Private pay residents	0.54	0.03
19. RNs per 100 residents	2.19	0.49
20. LPNs per 100 residents	2.15	0.36
21. Nurse aides per 100 residents	33	3
22. Staff turnover (previous 6 months)	9%	18%
23. Visit from Ombudsman (past 12 months)	1.7	0.9
24. Part of a chain	32%	—
25. Affiliated or attached to a nursing home	12%	—

[a]*N=511 facilities*
Total weighted N=11,936

Parameter estimates and standard errors are presented for the multiple regression model in Table 3.2. Twelve variables are significant for mortality rates. As the proportion of residents older than sixty-five years of age increases, as the proportion of residents who are chair- or bed-fast increases, and as the proportion of residents with

Table 3.2. Multiple Regression Estimates

	Mortality Rate[a]
Residents greater than sixty-five years	0.001 (0.00)**
Residents chair- or bed-fast	0.001 (0.00)**
Residents urinary incontinent	0.02 (0.04)
Residents with substance abuse problems	0.02 (0.05)
Residents with HIV	0.69 (0.24)*
Private pay residents	-0.04 (0.05)
Transfers to a psychiatric hospital	0.01 (0.10)
Transfers to an acute care hospital	0.02 (0.03)
Transfers to a nursing home	-0.05 (0.02)**
Bed size	-0.002 (0.00)**
For-profit	-0.09 (0.05)*
Part of a chain	-0.09 (0.02)**
Affiliated or attached to a nursing home	-0.14 (0.06)**
Occupancy rate	-0.11 (0.08)
Licensed facilities	0.02 (0.03)
Number of health services provided by facility	-0.01 (0.01)
Number of health services provided by others	-0.05 (0.01)***
Number of social services provided by facility	0.04 (0.01)*
Number of social services provided by others	-0.02 (0.01)*
RNs per 100 residents	0.00 (0.00)
LPNs per 100 residents	-0.00 (0.01)
Nurse aides per 100 residents	0.00 (0.00)
Staff turnover	0.02 (0.07)
Visit from Ombudsman (past 12 months)	-0.04 (0.02)**
R^2	0.18
$N=$	486
Total weighted $N=$	11,936

[a]*Standard errors given in parentheses*
Significant at $p < .05$
**Significant at $p < .01$*
***Significant at $p < .001$*

HIV increases, mortality rates likewise increase. Alternatively, increases in transfers to nursing homes, increases in the bed size, not-for-profit ownership, non-chain membership, and non-affiliation or non-attachment to a nursing home, decrease mortality rates. As the number of health services provided other than by the facility increase and as the number of social services provided other than by the facility increase, the mortality rates also decrease. As the number of social services provided by the facility increases, the mortality rates increase. Finally, as visits by Ombudsmen increase, mortality rates decrease.

Discussion

In this investigation the effect of demographic, functional, disease, and facility predictors and/or correlates of death for the elderly residing in board and care facilities are studied. Twelve factors are found to be significant: residents older than sixty-five, chair- or bed-fast, HIV positive, transfer to a nursing home, bed size, chain membership, affiliated or attached to a nursing home, number of health services provided by others, number of social services provided by the facility, number of social services provided by others, and visits from Ombudsmen.

Some of these results parallel factors that are important for the mortality of nursing home residents. For example, as the acuity level of residents increase, mortality is more likely. ADLs are often used as acuity measures in nursing home investigations (Castle and Banaszak-Holl, 1997). An ADL scale was not available for this analysis, but older age and chair- or bed-fast residents are highly correlated with acuity.

As the size of the board and care facility increases, the mortality rate decreases. This also parallels results found for nursing homes (Davis, 1991). It is often assumed that the effect of size is due to both economies of scale and economies of scope. That is, larger facilities are able to provide both more services (economies of scale) and a wider variety of services (economies of scope) per resident. The results showing that as the number of health services provided by others increases and as the number of social services provided by others increases, residents are less likely to die would appear to corroborate this. But because which services are provided is unknown it is impossible to determine whether economies of scale or economies of scope is most important.

It is difficult to explain why residents are less likely to die as the number of social services provided by others increases, while as the number of social services provided by the board and care facility increases, residents are more likely to die. Clearly, these service provisions require further investigation.

For-profit nursing homes approach resident care in a way that is different from that of not-for-profit facilities (Davis, 1991). In some areas of resident care, prevalence of pressure ulcers and psychiatric care, for example, for-profit nursing homes perform less well than not-for-profits (Davis, 1991). On the other hand, the rates of urethral catheterization are lower in for-profit nursing homes (Zinn, Aaronson, and Rosko, 1993). The result showing residents are more likely to die in for-profit board and care homes may be an indication that for-profit and not-for-profit board and care homes are also dissimilar.

The for-profit/not-for-profit dichotomy is sometimes used to deride for-profit nursing homes (Davis lists several of these studies). However, whether these facilities are actually worse than not-for-profit facilities is not as clear cut as these studies would have us believe (Davis, 1991). The same may be true for board and care homes. Therefore, although the results suggest residents are more likely to die in for-profit board and care homes, this should be interpreted with caution.

Recent evidence would suggest that chain membership is important when examining care processes in the nursing home setting (Castle and Banaszak-Holl, 1997). It may be that when a facility is a member of a chain certain economies of scale are achieved. For example, the purchasing of equipment and supplies may be less expensive. These cost savings may then free-up resources that are used for other purposes, although these other purposes do not always include resident care and cost savings may be used to increase profits (Castle and Banaszak-Holl, 1997). This study shows that board and care homes that are members of chains have lower mortality rates than their non-chain counterparts. Thus, chain membership may also be an important variable in board and care homes.

Staffing factors produced results unlike those found in nursing homes. Increasing numbers of LPNs, RNs, and nurse aides generally decrease mortality rates in nursing homes (Spector and Takada, 1991). It is curious that a similar pattern was not found in this investigation. However, these nurses are uniformly used in very low numbers in board and care homes and were not subject to much variability in the data; a "floor effect" may have reduced the likelihood of finding statistical significance.

Because Ombudsmen are the quality "watch-dogs" of the long-term care industry, it was expected that their visits would be positively correlated with death rates. However, it was found that as visits from Ombudsmen increase, mortality rates decrease. It is proposed that these visits may prompt board and care facilities to alter their behavior toward their sickest residents. For example, these residents may be transferred to other institutions. In this way facilities can minimize the number of high care residents and use the same staff resources with the remaining resident population. But no data to support this proposition are available and complaints to Ombudsmen from board and care residents need to be investigated more thoroughly.

Due to data limitations only the overall mortality rate in board and care facilities in the previous twelve months could be assessed. Obviously, resident level data would provide a more accurate picture of resident deaths. The retrospective nature of the study is also problematic for the purposes of examining mortality. Deaths occurring in a twelve-month period are enumerated and are combined with cross-sectional data on current health status and facility factors. It is plausible that these cross-sectional factors changed during the twelve months that are reflected in the mortality data. This is most likely for the death status measures used. To the extent that this occurs, the significant associations in the analysis would represent a consequence of the dependent variable, rather than predict its occurrence. This limitation is endemic to all cross-sectional research in health services that examine past events based on current data.

Despite these limitations, findings indicate that deaths in board and care homes are frequent and some predictors are dissimilar to those found in other long-term care settings. However, examinations of mortality in these facilities are rare. More research effort is needed to advance our understanding of these deaths to improve our ability to assure that board and care homes are as competent as possible.

References

Brooks, C. H., and K. Smyth-Staruch. 1984. Hospice home care cost savings to third-party insurers. *Medical Care* 22:691-703.

Castle, N. G., and J. C. Banaszak-Holl. 1997. Top management team characteristics and innovation in nursing homes. *The Gerontologist* 37(5):572-80.

Davis, M. A. 1991. On nursing home quality: A review and analysis. *Medical Care Review* 48: 129-66.

Engle, F., and M. Graney. 1993. Predicting outcomes of nursing home residents: Death and discharge home. *Journal of Gerontology* 48: 5269-75.

Gaumer, G. L., and J. Stavins. 1992. Medicare use in the last ninety days of life. *Health Services Research* 26(6):725-42.

Hawes, C., V. Mor, J. Wildfire, et al. 1995. Executive summary: Analysis of the effect of regulation on the quality of care in board and care homes. *Research Triangle Institute and Brown University report to the Office of the Assistant Secretary of Planning and Evaluation Office of Aging.*

Katzman, R., T. Brown, P. Fuld, R. Schechter, and H. Schimmel. 1983. Validation of a short orientation-memory-concentration test of cognitive impairment. *American Journal of Psychiatry* 140:734-9.

Kovar, M. G., J. E. Gitti, and M. M. Chyba. 1992. The longitudinal study of aging: 1984-90. National Center for Health Statistics, *Vital Health Statistics* 1(28).

Lewis, M. A., B. Leake, V. Clark, and M. Leal-Sotelo. 1990. Changes in case mix and outcomes of readmissions to nursing homes between 1980 and 1984. *Health Services Research* 24:713-28.

Lewis, M. A., R. Kane, S. Cretin, and V. Clark. 1985. The immediate and subsequent outcomes of nursing home care. *American Journal of Public Health* 75:758-61.

Liu, K., and K. G. Manton. 1984. The characteristics and utilization pattern of an admission cohort of nursing home patients. *The Gerontologist* 24:70-6.

McMillan, A., R. Mentnech, J. Lubitz, A. M. McBean, and D. Russell. 1990. Trends and patterns in place of death for Medicare enrollees. *Health Care Financing Review* 12:1-7.

Merrill, D. M., and V. Mor. 1993. Pathways to hospital death among the oldest old. *Journal of Aging and Health* 5:516-35.

Mor, V., O. Intrator, B. E. Fries, C. Phillips, J. Teno, J. Hiris, and C. Hawkes. In press. Changes of hospitalization associated with introducing the resident assessment instrument. *Journal of the American Geriatric Society.*

Mor, V., M. Z. Stalker, R. Gralla, H. I. Scher, C. Cimma, D. Park, A. M. Flaherty, M. Kiss, P. Nelson, L. Laliberte, R. Schwartz, P. A. Marks, and H. F. Oettgen. 1988. Day hospital as an alternative to inpatient care for cancer patients: A random assignment trial. *Journal of Clinical Epidemiology* 41(8):771-85.

Mor, V., S. Sherwood, and C. Gutkin. 1986. A national study of residential care for the aged. *The Gerontologist* 26:405-17.

Mor, V. 1987. *Hospice care systems: Structure, process, costs, and outcome*. New York: Springer.

Morris, J. N., B. E. Fries, D. R. Mehr, C. Hawes, C. Phillips, V. Mor, and L. A. Lipsitz. 1994. MDS Cognitive Performance Scale. *Journal of Gerontology: Medical Sciences* 49(4):M174-M182.

Newcomer, R., and L. Grant. 1989. Residential care facilities: Understanding their role and improving their effectiveness. Unpublished manuscript.

Rovner, B. W., P. S. German, L. J. Brant, R. Clark, L. Burton, and M. F. Folstein. 1991. Depression and mortality in nursing homes. *Journal of the American Medical Association* 265: 993-6.

Shah, S. V., B. G. Barnwell, P. N. Hunt, and L. M. LaVange. 1995. *SUDAAN User's Manual,* Release 6.0. Research Triangle Park, NC: Research Triangle Institute.

Shaughnessy, P. W., and A. M. Kramer. 1990. The increased needs of patients in nursing homes and patients receiving home health care. *New England Journal of Medicine* 322:21-7.

Spector, W., and H. A. Takada. 1991. Characteristics of nursing homes that affect resident outcomes. *Journal of Aging and Health* 3:427-54.

Wennberg, J. E. 1973. Small area variations in health care delivery. *Science* 182:1102-8.

Wennberg, J. E., B. Barnes, and M. Zubkoff. 1982. Professional uncertainty and the problem of supplier-induced demand. *Social Science and Medicine* 16:811-24.

Wennberg, J. E., J. L. Freeman, and W. J. Culp. 1987. Are hospital services rationed in New Haven or over-utilized in Boston? *Lancet* 78:1185-8.

Zinn, J. S., W. E. Aaronson, and M. D. Rosko. 1993. Variations in the outcomes of care provided in Pennsylvania nursing homes: Facility and environmental correlates. *Medical Care* 31(6):475-87.

— by Nicholas G. Castle, Ph.D.

Nicholas G. Castle, Ph.D., is the Director of Health Outcomes Research, AtlantiCare Health System, Egg Harbor Township, NJ 08234.

Chapter 4

Life Expectancy at Birth

For years of birth beginning with 1940, Table 4.1a-c, shown on the following pages, lists life expectancy at birth for the following variables:

- All Races
- White
- Black
- Male and female combined
- Male
- Female

The statistics were produced by the Centers for Disease Control and Prevention (CDC), National Center for Health Statistics (NCHS).

From "Advance Report of Final Mortality Statistics, 1995," by R. N. Anderson, K. D. Kochanek, and S. L. Murphy, in *Monthly Vital Statisitcs Report,* Vol. 45, No. 11, Supp. 2, p. 19 [Online] 1997. Available: http://www.cdc.gov:80/nchswww/datawhstatab/pubd/4511s2.htm. Produced by the CDC's National Center for Health Statistics (NCHS). For complete contact information, please refer to Chapter 60, "Resources."

Table 4.1a. (Continued in Table 4.1b.) Life Expectancy at Birth by Race and Sex: United States, 1940, 1950, 1960, and 1970-95

Yr	All Races			White			All Other					
							Total			Black		
	M/F	M	F	M/F	M	F	M/F	M	F	M/F	M	F
95	75.8	72.5	78.9	76.5	73.4	79.6	71.9	67.9	75.7	69.6	65.2	73.9
94	75.7	72.4	79.0	76.5	73.3	79.6	71.7	67.6	75.7	69.5	64.9	73.9
93	75.5	72.2	78.8	76.3	73.1	79.5	71.5	67.3	75.5	69.2	64.6	73.7
92	75.8	72.3	79.1	76.5	73.2	79.8	71.8	67.7	75.7	69.6	65.0	73.9
91	75.5	72.0	78.9	76.3	72.9	79.6	71.5	67.3	75.5	69.3	64.6	73.8
90	75.4	71.8	78.8	76.1	72.7	79.4	71.2	67.0	75.2	69.1	64.5	73.6
89	75.1	71.7	78.5	75.9	72.5	79.2	70.9	66.7	74.9	68.8	64.3	73.3
88	74.9	71.4	78.3	75.6	72.2	78.9	70.8	66.7	74.8	68.9	64.4	73.2
87	74.9	71.4	78.3	75.6	72.1	78.9	71.0	66.9	75.0	69.1	64.7	73.4
86	74.7	71.2	78.2	75.4	71.9	78.8	70.9	66.8	74.9	69.1	64.8	73.4
85	74.7	71.1	78.2	75.3	71.8	78.7	71.0	67.0	74.8	69.3	65.0	73.4
84	74.7	71.1	78.2	75.3	71.8	78.7	71.1	67.2	74.9	69.5	65.3	73.6
83	74.6	71.0	78.1	75.2	71.6	78.7	70.9	67.0	74.7	69.4	65.2	73.5

Table 4.1b. (Continued in Table 4.1c.) Life Expectancy at Birth by Race and Sex: United States, 1940, 1950, 1960, and 1970-95

Yr	All Races			White			All Other					
							Total			Black		
	M/F	M	F	M/F	M	F	M/F	M	F	M/F	M	F
82	74.5	70.8	78.1	75.1	71.5	78.7	70.9	66.8	74.9	69.4	65.1	73.6
81	74.1	70.4	77.8	74.8	71.1	78.4	70.3	66.2	74.4	68.9	64.5	73.2
80	73.7	70.0	77.4	74.4	70.7	78.1	69.5	65.3	73.6	68.1	63.8	72.5
79	73.9	70.0	77.8	74.6	70.8	78.4	69.8	65.4	74.1	68.5	64.0	72.9
78	73.5	69.6	77.3	74.1	70.4	78.0	69.3	65.0	73.5	68.1	63.7	72.4
77	73.3	69.5	77.2	74.0	70.2	77.9	68.9	64.7	73.2	67.7	63.4	72.0
76	72.9	69.1	76.8	73.6	69.9	77.5	68.4	64.2	72.7	67.2	62.9	71.6
75	72.6	68.8	76.6	73.4	69.5	77.3	68.0	63.7	72.4	66.8	62.4	71.3
74	72.0	68.2	75.9	72.8	69.0	76.7	67.1	62.9	71.3	66.0	61.7	70.3
73	71.4	67.6	75.3	72.2	68.5	76.1	66.1	62.0	70.3	65.0	60.9	69.3
72[1]	71.2	67.4	75.1	72.0	68.3	75.9	65.7	61.5	70.1	64.7	60.4	69.1

[1]Deaths based on a 50-percent sample.

Table 4.1c. (Continued from Table 4.1b.) Life Expectancy at Birth by Race and Sex: United States, 1940, 1950, 1960, and 1970-95

Yr	All Races			White			All Other							
							Total			Black		
	M/F	M	F	M/F	M	F	M/F	M	F	M/F	M	F
71	71.1	67.4	75.0	72.0	68.3	75.8	65.6	61.6	69.8	64.6	60.5	68.9
70	70.8	67.1	74.7	71.7	68.0	75.6	65.3	61.3	69.4	64.1	60.0	68.3
60	69.7	66.6	73.1	70.6	67.4	74.1	63.6	61.1	66.3	---	---	---
50	68.2	65.6	71.1	69.1	66.5	72.2	60.8	59.1	62.9	---	---	---
40	62.9	60.8	65.2	64.2	62.1	66.6	53.1	51.5	54.9	---	---	---

- - - Data not available.

Chapter 5

Leading Causes of Death in the United States

Table 5.1a-f, presented on the following pages, provides statistical information from the Centers for Disease Control and Prevention (CDC) about leading causes of death in the United States, based on preliminary records for 1996.

Data are shown for:

- All ages
- 5-14 years
- 15-24 years
- 25-44 years
- 45-64 years
- 65 years and over

From "Births and Deaths: United States, 1996," by S. J. Ventura, K. D. Peters, J. A. Martin, and J. D. Maurer, in *Monthly Vital Statistics Report,* Vol. 46, No. 1, supp. 2, pp. 32-.3 [Online] 1997. Available: http://www.cdc.gov:80/nchswww/datawh/statab/pubd/leadcod.htm. Produced by the CDC's National Center for Health Statistics (NCHS). For complete contact information, please refer to Chapter 60, "Resources."

Table 5.1a. (continued in Table 5.1b.) Deaths and Death Rates for the 10 Leading Causes of Death in Specified Age Groups: United States, Preliminary 1996

[Data are based on a continuous file of records received from the states. Rates per 100,000 population in specified group. Figures are based on weighted data rounded to the nearest individual, so categories may not add to totals.]

Rank[1]	Cause of Death and Age (Based on Ninth Revision, International Classification of Diseases, 1975)	Number	Rate
	All Ages[2]		
. . .	All causes	2,322,421	875.4
1	Diseases of heart	733,834	276.6
2	Malignant neoplasms, including neoplasms of lymphatic and hematopoietic tissues	544,278	205.2
3	Cerebrovascular diseases	160,431	60.5
4	Chronic obstructive pulmonary diseases and allied conditions	106,146	40.0
5	Accidents and adverse effects	93,874	35.4
. . .	Motor vehicle accidents	43,449	16.4
. . .	All other accidents and adverse effects	50,425	19.0
6	Pneumonia and influenza	82,579	31.1

Table 5.1b. (continued in Table 5.1c.) Deaths and Death Rates for the 10 Leading Causes of Death in Specified Age Groups: United States, Preliminary 1996

Rank[1]	Cause of Death and Age (Based on Ninth Revision, International Classification of Diseases, 1975)	Number	Rate
7	Diabetes mellitus	61,559	23.2
8	Human immunodeficiency virus infection	32,655	12.3
9	Suicide	30,862	11.6
10	Chronic liver disease and cirrhosis	25,135	9.5
. . .	All other causes (residual)	451,068	170.0
	1-4 years		
. . .	All causes	5,947	38.3
1	Accidents and adverse effects	2,155	13.9
. . .	Motor vehicle accidents	834	5.4
. . .	All other accidents and adverse effects	1,321	8.5
2	Congenital anomalies	633	4.1
3	Malignant neoplasms, including neoplasms of lymphatic and hematopoietic tissues	440	2.8
4	Homicide and legal intervention	395	2.5
5	Diseases of heart	207	1.3
6	Pneumonia and influenza	167	1.1
7	Human immunodeficiency virus infection	149	1.0
8	Septicemia	74	0.5
9	Benign neoplasms, carcinoma in situ, and neoplasms of uncertain behavior and unspecified nature	71	0.5
10	Certain conditions originating in the perinatal period	69	0.4
. . .	All other causes (residual)	1,587	10.2
	5-14 years		
. . .	All causes	8,465	22.0

Table 5.1c. (continued in Table 5.1d.) Deaths and Death Rates for the 10 Leading Causes of Death in Specified Age Groups: United States, Preliminary 1996

Rank[1]	Cause of Death and Age (Based on Ninth Revision, International Classification of Diseases, 1975)	Number	Rate
1	Accidents and adverse effects	3,521	9.2
. . .	Motor vehicle accidents	2,002	5.2
. . .	All other accidents and adverse effects	1,519	4.0
2	Malignant neoplasms, including neoplasms of lymphatic and hematopoietic tissues	1,035	2.7
3	Homicide and legal intervention	513	1.3
4	Congenital anomalies	456	1.2
5	Diseases of heart	341	0.9
6	Suicide	305	0.8
7	Human immunodeficiency virus infection	174	0.5
8	Chronic obstructive pulmonary diseases and allied conditions	147	0.4
9	Pneumonia and influenza	136	0.4
10	Benign neoplasms, carcinoma in situ, and neoplasms of uncertain behavior and unspecified nature	99	0.3
. . .	All other causes (residual)	1,738	4.5
	15-24 years		
. . .	All causes	32,699	90.3
1	Accidents and adverse effects	13,872	38.3
. . .	Motor vehicle accidents	10,624	29.3
. . .	All other accidents and adverse effects	3,248	9.0
2	Homicide and legal intervention	6,548	18.1
3	Suicide	4,369	12.1
4	Malignant neoplasms, including neoplasms of lymphatic and hematopoietic tissues	1,642	4.5

Table 5.1d. (continued in Table 5.1e.) Deaths and Death Rates for the 10 Leading Causes of Death in Specified Age Groups: United States, Preliminary 1996

Rank[1]	Cause of Death and Age (Based on Ninth Revision, International Classification of Diseases, 1975)	Number	Rate
5	Diseases of heart	920	2.5
6	Human immunodeficiency virus infection	420	1.2
7	Congenital anomalies	387	1.1
8	Chronic obstructive pulmonary diseases and allied conditions	230	0.6
9	Pneumonia and influenza	197	0.5
10	Cerebrovascular diseases	174	0.5
. . .	All other causes (residual)	3,940	10.9
	25-44 years		
. . .	All causes	148,904	177.8
1	Accidents and adverse effects	26,554	31.7
. . .	Motor vehicle accidents	14,528	17.3
. . .	All other accidents and adverse effects	12,026	14.4
2	Human immunodeficiency virus infection	22,795	27.2
3	Malignant neoplasms, including neoplasms of lymphatic and hematopoietic tissues	22,147	26.4
4	Diseases of heart	16,261	19.4
5	Suicide	12,536	15.0
6	Homicide and legal intervention	9,261	11.1
7	Chronic liver disease and cirrhosis	4,230	5.1
8	Cerebrovascular diseases	3,418	4.1
9	Diabetes mellitus	2,520	3.0
10	Pneumonia and influenza	1,972	2.4
. . .	All other causes (residual)	27,210	32.5

Table 5.1e. (continued in Table 5.1f.) Deaths and Death Rates for the 10 Leading Causes of Death in Specified Age Groups: United States, Preliminary 1996

Rank[1]	Cause of Death and Age (Based on Ninth Revision, International Classification of Diseases, 1975)	Number	Rate
	45-64 years		
. . .	All causes	380,396	708.0
1	Malignant neoplasms, including neoplasms of lymphatic and hematopoietic tissues	132,805	247.2
2	Diseases of heart	102,510	190.8
3	Accidents and adverse effects	16,332	30.4
. . .	Motor vehicle accidents	7,659	14.3
. . .	All other accidents and adverse effects	8,673	16.1
4	Cerebrovascular diseases	15,526	28.9
5	Chronic obstructive pulmonary diseases and allied conditions	12,849	23.9
6	Diabetes mellitus	12,678	23.6
7	Chronic liver disease and cirrhosis	10,718	19.9
8	Human immunodeficiency virus infection	8,443	15.7
9	Suicide	7,717	14.4
10	Pneumonia and influenza	5,646	10.5
. . .	All other causes (residual)	55,172	102.7
	65 years and over		
. . .	All causes	1,717,218	5,071.4
1	Diseases of heart	612,886	1,810.0
2	Malignant neoplasms, including neoplasms of lymphatic and hematopoietic tissues	386,092	1,140.2
3	Cerebrovascular diseases	140,938	416.2
4	Chronic obstructive pulmonary diseases and allied conditions	91,624	270.6
5	Pneumonia and influenza	73,968	218.4

Table 5.1f. (continued from Table 5.1e.) Deaths and Death Rates for the 10 Leading Causes of Death in Specified Age Groups: United States, Preliminary 1996

Rank[1]	Cause of Death and Age (Based on Ninth Revision, International Classification of Diseases, 1975)	Number	Rate
6	Diabetes mellitus	46,194	136.4
7	Accidents and adverse effects	30,564	90.3
. . .	Motor vehicle accidents	7,539	22.3
. . .	All other accidents and adverse effects	23,025	68.0
8	Nephritis, nephrotic syndrome, nephrosis	20,955	61.9
9	Alzheimer's disease	20,848	61.6
10	Septicemia	17,340	51.2
. . .	All other causes (residual)	275,809	814.5

[1]Rank based on number of deaths.
[2]Includes deaths under 1 year of age.
NOTES: Data are subject to sampling and/or random variation.

Chapter 6

Infant, Fetal, and Perinatal Mortality

Infant Mortality

All figures are for the United States.

Infant Mortality Rate (deaths per 1,000 live births): 7.2 (1996)
Source: *Monthly Vital Statistics Report, Vol. 46, No. 1 Supplement*

International Ranking for the United States: 25th (1993)
Source: *Health, United States: 1996-97*

Ten Leading Causes of Infant Death:
Congenital Anomalies: 6,463
Pre-Term/Low Birthweight: 3,706
Sudden Infant Death Syndrome (SIDS): 2,906
Respiratory Distress Syndrome: 1,368
Problems Related to Complications of Pregnancy: 1,212
Complications of Placenta, Cord, and Membrane: 892

From "Infant Mortality," [Online] June 4, 1998. Available: http://www.cdc.gov/nchswww/fastats/infmort.htm. And from "Update on Risk Factors for Infant Mortality," [Online] September 1, 1998; and "Infant Mortality Rates, Fetal Mortality Rates, and Perinatal Mortality Rates, According to Race: United States, Selected Years 1950-96," [Online] September 30, 1998; available: http://www.cdc.gov:80/nchswww/. Produced by the CDC's National Center for Health Statistics (NCHS). For complete contact information, please refer to Chapter 60, "Resources."

Accidents: 772
Perinatal Infections: 747
Pneumonia/Influenza: 469
Intrauterine Hypoxia and Birth Asphyxia: 429
Source: *Monthly Vital Statistics Report, Vol. 46, No. 1 Supplement*

Update on Risk Factors for Infant Mortality

In 1996 the infant mortality rate declined to 7.3 deaths per 1,000 live births, the lowest rate ever recorded and a decline of 3 percent from 1995. Infants with low birthweight, born preterm, or in multiple births have a higher risk of dying in the first year of life. Babies born to teenagers and to women in their forties and to mothers who did not complete high school, were unmarried, did not receive timely prenatal care, or smoked during pregnancy also have higher infant mortality rates.

A new report from the National Center for Health Statistics, Centers for Disease Control and Prevention, presents infant mortality statistics from the latest linked birth/infant death data set to identify factors that impact infant mortality or survival. The report is a special analysis of birth and death information provided through the nation's vital statistics system and follows up an earlier report released last February.

Birthweight is one of the most important predictors of an infant's subsequent health and survival. In 1996, 7.4 percent of infants were low birthweight, defined as less than 2,500 grams (5 lbs, 8 oz); however, 64 percent of all infant deaths were among low birthweight babies. Survival of low birthweight infants has improved however. The largest declines (8 to 10 percent) in bodyweight-specific infant mortality rates from 1995-96 were for infants born weighing 750-1,250 grams and 1,500-1,999 grams.

The infant mortality rate for male infants was 8.0 in 1996, 21 percent higher than the rate of 6.6 for females. Babies born in multiple births have an infant mortality rate 5 times that of single births. Infant mortality rates are highest for teenagers and for women in their 40s and lowest for women in their 20s and early 30s. The infant mortality rate was nearly twice as high for unmarried women as for married women. In general, infant mortality declined with increasing education of the mother. Mothers who had not completed high school had infant mortality rates which were twice that of women with a college education.

Analysis of the vital statistics data also showed that mortality rates varied considerably by race of mother. In 1996 the overall infant mortality rate from the linked file was 7.3 deaths per 1,000 live births. Mortality rates were lowest for infants born to Asian and Pacific Islander mothers (5.2), followed by white (6.1), American Indian (10.0), and black (14.1) mothers. The mortality rate for infants of Hispanic mothers (6.1) was similar to the rate for non-Hispanic white mothers (6.0) and ranged from 5.0 for infants of Central and South American mothers to 8.6 for infants of Puerto Rican mothers.

For infants of American Indian mothers, death rates were highest in the postneonatal period with death rates from sudden infant death syndrome and accidents more than 3 times the rate for white infants. For black infants, disorders related to short gestation and low birthweight was the leading cause of death, with black infants more than 4 times as likely to die from this cause as white infants.

"Infant Mortality Statistics from the 1996 Period Linked Birth/ Infant Death Data Set" by Marian F. MacDorman and Jonnae O. Atkinson is based on information from the death certificate linked to the corresponding birth certificate for each infant under 1 year of age who died in 1996.

The purpose of the linkage is to use the additional information from the birth certificate to conduct more detailed analyses of infant mortality patterns to provide better information for prevention, research, and medical care. Birth and death certificates are linked by the state vital statistics offices where the original records are filed and reported to NCHS through the National Vital Statistics System. Copies of the report are available from NCHS.

Infant, Fetal, and Perinatal Mortality, by Race

Tables 6.1–6.5, beginning on the next page present infant, fetal, and perinatal mortality for all races, for White children and mothers, and for Black children and mothers.

Table 6.1. All Races

[Data are based on the National Vital Statistics System]

Race and Year	Infant[1]	Neonatal[1]		Post-Neonatal[1]	Fetal Mortality Rate[2]	Late Fetal Mortality Rate[3]	Perinatal Mortality Rate[4]
		Under 28 Days	Under 7 Days				
All Races	Deaths per 1,000 Live Births						
1950[5]	29.2	20.5	17.8	8.7	18.4	14.9	32.5
1960[5]	26.0	18.7	16.7	7.3	15.8	12.1	28.6
1970	20.0	15.1	13.6	4.9	14.0	9.5	23.0
1980	12.6	8.5	7.1	4.1	9.1	6.2	13.2
1985	10.6	7.0	5.8	3.7	7.8	4.9	10.7
1988	10.0	6.3	5.2	3.6	7.5	4.5	9.7
1989	9.8	6.2	5.1	3.6	7.5	4.5	9.6
1990	9.2	5.8	4.8	3.4	7.5	4.3	9.1
1991	8.9	5.6	4.6	3.4	7.3	4.1	8.7
1992	8.5	5.4	4.4	3.1	7.4	4.1	8.5
1993	8.4	5.3	4.3	3.1	7.1	3.8	8.1
1994	8.0	5.1	4.2	2.9	7.0	3.7	7.9
1995	7.6	4.9	4.0	2.7	7.0	3.6	7.6
1996	7.3	4.8	3.8	2.5	6.9	3.6	7.4

Table 6.2. Race of Child: White

[Data are based on the National Vital Statistics System]

Race and Year	Infant[1]	Neonatal[1]		Post-Neonatal[1]	Fetal Mortality Rate[2]	Late Fetal Mortality Rate[3]	Perinatal Mortality Rate[4]
		Under 28 Days	Under 7 Days				
Race of Child:[6] White	Deaths per 1,000 Live Births						
1950[5]	26.8	19.4	17.1	7.4	16.6	13.3	30.1
1960[5]	22.9	17.2	15.6	5.7	13.9	10.8	26.2
1970	17.8	13.8	12.5	4.0	12.3	8.6	21.0
1980	11.0	7.5	6.2	3.5	8.1	5.7	11.9

45

Table 6.3. Race of Mother: White

[Data are based on the National Vital Statistics System]

Race and Year	Infant[1]	Neonatal[1]		Post-Neonatal[1]	Fetal Mortality Rate[2]	Late Fetal Mortality Rate[3]	Perinatal Mortality Rate[4]
		Under 28 Days	Under 7 Days				
Race of Mother:[7] White	Deaths per 1,000 Live Births						
1980	10.9	7.4	6.1	3.5	8.1	5.7	11.8
1985	9.2	6.0	5.0	3.2	6.9	4.5	9.5
1988	8.4	5.3	4.3	3.1	6.4	4.0	8.3
1989	8.1	5.1	4.2	2.9	6.4	4.0	8.2
1990	7.6	4.8	3.9	2.8	6.4	3.8	7.7
1991	7.3	4.5	3.7	2.8	6.2	3.7	7.4
1992	6.9	4.3	3.5	2.6	6.2	3.7	7.2
1993	6.8	4.3	3.5	2.5	6.1	3.4	6.9
1994	6.6	4.2	3.4	2.4	6.0	3.3	6.7
1995	6.3	4.1	3.3	2.2	5.9	3.3	6.5
1996	6.1	4.0	3.2	2.1	5.9	3.3	6.4

Table 6.4. Race of Child: Black

[Data are based on the National Vital Statistics System]

Race and Year	Infant[1]	Neonatal[1]		Post-Neonatal[1]	Fetal Mortality Rate[2]	Late Fetal Mortality Rate[3]	Perinatal Mortality Rate[4]
		Under 28 Days	Under 7 Days				
Race of Child:[6] Black	Deaths per 1,000 Live Births						
1950[5]	43.9	27.8	23.0	16.1	32.1	—	—
1960[5]	44.3	27.8	23.7	16.5	—	—	—
1970	32.6	22.8	20.3	9.9	23.2	—	34.5
1980	21.4	14.1	11.9	7.3	14.4	8.9	20.7

47

Table 6.5. Race of Mother: Black

[Data are based on the National Vital Statistics System]

Race and Year	Infant[1]	Neonatal[1]		Post-Neonatal[1]	Fetal Mortality Rate[2]	Late Fetal Mortality Rate[3]	Perinatal Mortality Rate[4]
		Under 28 Days	Under 7 Days				
Race of Mother:[7] Black	Deaths per 1,000 Live Births						
1980	22.2	14.6	12.3	7.6	14.7	9.1	21.3
1985	19.0	12.6	10.8	6.4	12.8	7.2	17.9
1988	18.5	12.1	10.3	6.5	13.0	6.9	17.1
1989	18.6	11.9	10.1	6.7	13.1	6.8	16.8
1990	18.0	11.6	9.7	6.4	13.3	6.7	16.4
1991	17.6	11.2	9.4	6.3	12.8	6.4	15.7
1992	16.8	10.8	9.0	6.0	13.3	6.4	15.4
1993	16.5	10.7	9.0	5.8	12.8	5.8	14.7
1994	15.8	10.2	8.6	5.6	12.5	5.8	14.3
1995	15.1	9.8	8.2	5.3	12.7	5.7	13.8
1996	14.7	9.6	7.8	5.1	12.5	5.5	13.3

Notes to the Tables

— Data not available.

[1]Infant (under 1 year of age), neonatal (under 28 days), early neonatal (under 7 days), and postneonatal (28-365 days).

[2]Number of fetal deaths of 20 weeks or more gestation per 1,000 live births plus fetal deaths.

[3]Number of fetal deaths of 28 weeks or more gestation per 1,000 live births plus late fetal deaths.

[4]Number of late fetal deaths plus infant deaths within 7 days of birth per 1,000 live births plus late fetal deaths.

[5]Includes births and deaths of persons who were not residents of the 50 states and the District of Columbia.

[6]Infant deaths are tabulated by race of decedent; live births and fetal deaths are tabulated by race of child.

[7]Infant deaths are tabulated by race of decedent; fetal deaths and live births are tabulated by race of mother.

NOTES: Infant mortality rates in this table are based on infant deaths from the mortality file (numerator) and live births from the natality file (denominator). Inconsistencies in reporting race for the same infant between the birth and death certificate can result in underestimated infant mortality rates for races other than white or black. Infant mortality rates for minority population groups are available from the national linked files of live births and infant deaths.

SOURCES: Centers for Disease Control and Prevention, National Center for Health Statistics: *Vital Satistics of the United States, Vol. II, Mortality, Part A,* for data years 1950-96. Public Health Service. Washington. U.S. Government Printing Office; Peters, K. D., K. D. Kochanek, and S. L. Murphy. *Report of Final Mortality Statistics, 1996. Monthly Vital Statistics Report; Vol. 45.* Hyattsville, Maryland: 1998; and data computed by the Division of Health and Utilization Analysis from data compiled by the Division of Vital Statistics.

Chapter 7

Men's and Women's Health Facts

Men's Health

All figures are for the United States.

Leading Cause of Death (overall): Heart Disease (1996)
Leading Cause of Death (25-44 Year Olds): Accidents and adverse effects (1996)
Number of Deaths From Prostate Cancer: 34,123 (1996)
Source: *National Vital Statistics Reports, Vol. 47, No. 9*

Most Common Chronic Condition: Chronic Sinusitis (1995)
Most Common Acute Condition: Influenza (1995)
Source: *Vital and Health Statistics Series 10, No. 199*

Number of Annual Office Visits to Physicians (all ages): 300 million (1996)
Number of Annual Hospital Outpatient Department Visits: 26 million (1996)
Number of Annual Emergency Department Visits: 42 million (1996)
Source: *Vital and Health Statistics Series 13, No. 134*

From "Men's Health," [Online] January 29, 1999 and "Women's Health," [Online] May 28, 1998. Available: http://www.cdc.gov/nchswww/fastats.htm. Produced by the CDC's National Center for Health Statistics (NCHS). For complete contact information, please refer to Chapter 60, "Resources."

Number of Hospital Discharges (Inpatients): 12.1 million (1996)
Number of Surgical Procedures Performed Annually: 16 million (1996)
Source: *Advance Data 301*

Women's Health

All figures are for the United States.

Leading Cause of Death (overall): Heart Disease
Source: *Monthly Vital Statistics Report, Vol. 46, No. 1 Supplement 2*

Leading Cause of Death (25-44 Year Olds): Cancer (1995)
Number of Deaths From Breast Cancer: 44,209 (1995)
Source: *Monthly Vital Statistics Report, Vol. 45, No. 11 Supplement 2*

Most Common Chronic Condition: Chronic Sinusitis (1994)
Most Common Acute Condition: Influenza (1994)
Source: *Vital and Health Statistics Series 10, No. 193*

Number of Annual Office Visits to Physicians (all ages): 416.3 million (1995)
Number of Annual Hospital Outpatient Department Visits: 41 million (1995)
Number of Annual Emergency Department Visits: 50 million (1995)
Source: *Vital and Health Statistics Series 13, No. 129*

Number of Hospital Discharges (Inpatients): 18.6 million (1995)
Number of Surgical Procedures Performed Annually: 40.8 million (1995)
Source: *Advance Data 291*

Chapter 8

African American, Asian, Hispanic, and Native American Health

African American Health Facts

All figures are for the United States.

Births Annually: 596,039 (1996)
Birth Rate: 70.8 births per 1,000 population (1996)
Percent of Births to Teenagers: 22.9 (1996)
Percent of Births to Unmarried Mothers: 69.8 (1996)
Percent Low Birthweight: 13.0 (1996)
Percent of Births by Cesarean Delivery: 21.7 (1996)
Percent of Mothers Receiving Prenatal Care in First Trimester: 71.3 (1996)
Deaths Annually: 281,790 (1996)
Age-Adjusted Death Rate: 737.8 deaths per 100,000 population (1996)
Infant Mortality Rate: 14.2 infant deaths per 1,000 live births (1996)
Source: *Monthly Vital Statistics Report, Vol. 46, No. 1 Supplement*

Excerpted from "African American Health Facts," "Asian or Pacific Islanders Health Facts," "Hispanic American Health Facts," and "American Indian Health Facts," [Online] 1998. Available: http://www.cdc.gov/nchswww/fastats.htm. Produced by the CDC's National Center for Health Statistics (NCHS). For complete contact information, please refer to Chapter 60, "Resources."

Asian and Pacific Islanders Health Facts

All figures are for the United States.

Births Annually: 158,447 (1995)
Birth Rate: 65.6 births per 1,000 women ages 15-44 (1995)
Deaths Annually: 27,742 (1995)
Age-Adjusted Death Rate: 293.2 deaths per 100,000 population (1995)
Source: *Monthly Vital Statistics Report, Vol. 45, No. 11 Supplement 2*

Hispanic American Health Facts

All figures are for the United States.

Births Annually: 697,829 (1996)
Birth Rate: 104 births per 1,000 women ages 15-44 (1996)
Percent of Births to Teenagers: 17.4 (1996)
Percent of Births to Unmarried Mothers: 40.9 (1996)
Percent Low Birthweight: 6.3 (1996)
Percent of Births by Cesarean Delivery: 19.9 (1996)
Percent of Mothers Receiving Prenatal Care in First Trimester: 70.8 (1996)
Deaths Annually: 95,173 (1996)
Age-Adjusted Death Rate: 365.7 deaths per 100,000 population (1996)
Source: *Monthly Vital Statistics Report, Vol. 46, No. 1 Supplement*

Native American Health Facts

All figures are for the United States.

Births Annually: 38,456 (1996)
Birth Rate: 69.8 births per 1,000 women ages 15-44 (1996)
Deaths Annually: 10,251 (1996)
Age-Adjusted Death Rate: 462.6 deaths per 100,000 population (1996)
Source: *Monthly Vital Statistics Report, Vol. 46, No. 1 Supplement*

Chapter 9

Hispanic Death Rates

Hispanics have low death rates from cancer and heart disease. Their secret weapons may be beans, rice, and a strong family life.

Hispanic Americans are less likely than non-Hispanic whites to have health insurance, and they are more likely to live in poverty. Yet a recent study shows that they are also less likely to succumb to the nation's biggest killers.

Hispanics are less likely than non-Hispanics to die of cancer, heart disease, suicide, or motor-vehicle accidents, all of which fall in the top-ten causes of death for Americans. They are more likely than non-Hispanics to die of pneumonia or influenza, cirrhosis of the liver, diabetes, and homicide. But cancer and heart disease are far more common causes of death, so the overall death rate for Hispanics is lower than for other Americans.

Paul D. Sorlie, a statistician and epidemiologist at the National Institutes of Health, led a team that compared national survey data for 40,000 Hispanics with 660,000 non-Hispanics between 1979 and 1987. "Hispanics are not immune to the detrimental effects of poverty," says Sorlie. "Our data show that poverty is very detrimental." Experts also warn against interpreting the study as a sign that Hispanics have generally good health. Mexican Americans are three times as likely as the average American to have Type II diabetes, and Hispanic

From "Why Do Hispanics Have Lower Death Rates?" by Patricia Braus, in *American Demographics,* May 1994, [Online]. Available: http:// www.demographics.com/publications/ad/94_ad/9405_ad/ad583.htm. © 1997 by Cowles Business Media. Reprinted with permission.

children as a whole are more likely to catch common childhood diseases preventable by immunization, according to Antonio Furino and Eric Munoz, authors of an earlier report. But the fact remains: for Hispanic men in all income groups and for Hispanic women in most income groups, death rates are lower than for non-Hispanics.

Sorlie's research challenges many notions about health care, including the idea that people with better access to medical care will live longer. No one knows for sure why Hispanics have lower death rates, "but a lot of what people do in their lives has an impact on health," says Norman J. Johnson, a Census Bureau statistician and coauthor of the study.

The reasons for lower Hispanic death rates may have to do with lifestyle factors like diet and family structure. Because the term "Hispanic" encompasses a wide range of cultures, there is no such thing as a single Hispanic diet. But many people from Spanish-speaking cultures eat a lot of beans and rice, which are known as healthy low-fat ways to get protein and carbohydrates.

Hispanics also tend to eat a lot of fatty foods like lard and high-fat milk products, says Sorlie. Unhealthy food may contribute to Hispanics higher-than-average rate of diabetes, says Benjamin Bradshaw, a demographer at the University of Texas in San Antonio. He says that a diet high in refined sugar may also contribute to diabetes.

Hispanics may have lower death rates because they tend to live in extended families. Numerous studies have suggested that people with extensive social support networks recover more quickly from certain types of illness than do those without such support.

It could even be as simple as having a good start in life. Data collected in southern California show that Hispanic mothers are less likely than non-Hispanic white mothers to have low-birth-weight babies, even though they are poorer and less likely to get regular medical care.

Whatever the cause, something about traditional Hispanic culture has a positive effect on health. The mortality study finds that foreign-born Hispanic Americans have even lower death rates, on average, than those born in the U.S.

For more information, see "Mortality by Hispanic Status in the United States," *Journal of the American Medical Association* (Vol. 270, No. 20). Reprints are available from Paul D. Sorlie, National Heart, Lung, and Blood Institute, Room 3A10, Federal Building, Bethesda, MD 20892.

— by Patricia Braus

Patricia Braus is a contributing editor of *American Demographics*.

Chapter 10

Strokes and the South

In some parts of the South, the death risk from stroke is twice as high as the national average. After 50 years of research, doctors still don't know why.

Southerners have a reputation for doing things in a slow, low-key way. Yet most of the Southeast is marred by a life-threatening condition that is usually associated with high levels of stress. Since the 1940s, doctors have known that the risks of having a stroke and dying of a stroke are well above the national average in a broad swath of the Deep South.

Recently, researchers have identified a hot zone within the 8- to 11-state region long known as the "stroke belt." Within this "stroke buckle" (an area covering the coastal plains of North Carolina, South Carolina, and Georgia), the stroke death rate is about twice as high as in the rest of the country.

"The nation should be outraged" by the loss of life in the region, says George Howard, a professor of biostatistics and epidemiology at Bowman Gray School of Medicine in Winston-Salem, North Carolina. "If any single other factor, such as an environmental element or a food additive, was causing this many deaths every year, there would be a major outcry." He estimates that 1,000 of the approximately 160,000 U.S. stroke deaths each year occur because of the added risk in the stroke belt.

From "Strokes and the South," by Patricia Braus, in *American Demographics*, May 1998, [Online]. Available: http://www.demographics.com/publications/ad/98_ad/9805_ad/ad98057.htm. © 1998 by Primedia Intertec, 745 Fifth Ave., New York, NY 10151. All rights reserved. Reprinted with permission.

The national death rate for stroke decreased more than 50 percent from the early 1970s to the early 1990s, thanks to better treatments for hypertension and increased knowledge of stroke and its risk factors. Yet this rate stopped declining in the 1990s, and now it may be increasing again. Solving the mystery of the stroke belt could give physicians ways to drive stroke mortality rates down even further.

Blacks and Stroke

Stroke is an injury to brain tissue resulting from a blocked or burst blood vessel. About 500,000 Americans suffer a stroke each year, and it is the nation's third leading cause of death. Caring for afflicted Americans may cost $30 billion a year, according to Metropolitan Life's Statistical Bulletin. Strokes primarily occur among the elderly. Almost two-thirds (64 percent) of stroke sufferers are women, mainly because women tend to live longer than men. Still, 28 percent of strokes occur in people under age 65.

The stroke belt is more of an idea than an actual territory with rigid boundaries. While Howard describes the stroke belt as encompassing 8 states, the National Heart, Lung and Blood Institute says there are 11 states where the death rate due to stroke is more than 10 percent above the national average. Florida is not included in either definition of the stroke belt. The most likely reason is that Florida is populated largely by migrants from the Northeast and Midwest, where stroke rates are lower.

Another oddity that puzzles researchers is the stroke belt's movement. The zone of highest risk for stroke appears to be shifting west, even as the highest stroke areas remain along the Carolina and Georgia coasts. This may be due to a higher rate of decline in stroke deaths in the easternmost areas of the belt, says Dr. Richard Gillum, special assistant for cardiovascular epidemiology at the Centers for Disease Control (CDC) in Atlanta.

One sure reason for the South's higher stroke death rates is its high concentration of black residents. Slightly more than half of African Americans live in the South, and blacks in the U.S. have one of the highest stroke death rates in the world. The stroke rate is about twice as high among blacks aged 35 to 74 as it is among whites in the same age group, according to Kenneth Gaines, chief of neurology for the Field Neuroscience Institute at Michigan State University in Saginaw.

African Americans have a higher prevalence of high blood pressure than whites, according to Gaines, and high blood pressure is widely considered the most significant risk factor for a stroke. Diabetes and obesity are other risk factors for stroke. Black people overall are more likely to suffer from the risk factor of diabetes, and black women are more likely than white women to be obese.

The South's higher percentage of African Americans does not entirely account for the regional differences in stroke rates. The stroke rate is also higher among white men and women in the South, says Gillum. But the link between blacks and stroke is a significant and under-studied part of the problem, according to many researchers.

Various small studies suggest that blood in black people may coagulate differently than blood in whites. One clinical trial currently underway is exploring the possibility that African Americans may respond differently to drugs that are used to prevent stroke. There is even evidence that the tendency toward high blood pressure, which is endemic among African Americans, is present in childhood. A 1976 study found that black children aged 5 to 14 already had higher blood pressure than white children the same ages.

One problem in evaluating stroke in blacks is the relative scarcity of data about African Americans, heart disease, and stroke. Until recently, most of the data on stroke risks were collected in communities that had few black residents. "The studies that we rely on most—it wasn't that they excluded African Americans," says Gaines. "They were just not there."

Uncommon Factors

Yet black Southerners are not alone in their added risk of stroke. One study found that the risk of stroke for white men aged 45 to 74 was 39 percent higher in the Southeast than it was in the Northeast. White women in the same age group were 59 percent more likely to have a stroke in the Southeast than in the Midwest.

Whites and blacks in the stroke belt and stroke buckle regions share more than an address. Both groups are likely to have low incomes and low educational attainment, both of which are often linked to increased risk of chronic health problems. Within the stroke buckle, 35 percent of an 8,001-person sample earned less than $10,000 per year, compared with 24 percent among a nearly 400,000-person sample of other Americans. Poor people are less likely than more affluent individuals to have regular contact with a doctor, and are more likely to die from a stroke, according to Howard. But poverty and education alone don't account for the added stroke risk. In a 1997 study, Howard and others evaluated the known risk factors faced by people with a low socioeconomic level, and found that these factors alone did not account for the stroke belt's higher risk.

Another area that could be important is access to medical care. Southerners are less likely than other Americans to take preventive measures that protect their health. Yet preventive activities such as monitoring blood pressure and taking daily medication are effective ways to cut the risk of stroke. The issue of access to a doctor should be investigated, particularly in rural areas where doctors may be located a long way from patients, says Gillum.

Food is another area researchers have considered in a region known for high-cholesterol delicacies like fried chicken. Southerners eat less fruit than other Americans and also have a lower consumption of calcium. Low levels of calcium have been documented as a possible stroke risk factor. Some researchers have compared the southern diet to the Japanese diet: both are higher in sodium and carbohydrates than diets in other American regions, and both the southern U.S. and Japan have relatively high rates of stroke. But again, this single factor could not explain the entire difference, according to researchers.

One possible answer to the mystery may be a gene or genes that predispose an individual to develop stroke. Such a gene has not been found, but it may emerge in the future, says Howard. Because the stroke buckle is an area where people tend to live for generations, a stroke gene would be more common there.

Environmental factors, such as minerals in southern soil or drinking water, may also have something to do with the stroke belt, says Howard. However, studies have yet to definitively link soil or any other substance to the Southeast's high stroke rates.

The failure to find a satisfactory explanation for the stroke belt has driven researchers to speculate. "It's sort of like Sherlock Holmes. If all the common things have been discussed, you look at the uncommon things," says Howard. While the speculation continues, the relative lack of research frustrates Howard and other researchers. "If I were a black man, I'd be furious," he says.

Stroke Therapy Improves

While the stroke belt has persisted, the outlook for stroke victims has brightened over the last three decades. This is due to better prevention and new medication. Screening and treatment for high blood pressure are generally credited with the dramatic reduction in national stroke death rates from [the] 1960s through the mid-1990s. This reduction occurred within and outside of the stroke belt.

The number of strokes has not necessarily gone down, according to Dr. William H. Barker, associate professor of preventive medicine and gerontology at the University of Rochester School of Medicine and Dentistry. But individuals who have a stroke are less likely to have the most serious type of stroke, according to a 1997 study coauthored by Barker that examined data on more than 1,000 northwestern stroke patients between 1967 and 1985. "More people are surviving after a stroke," he says.

Controlling high blood pressure appears to dramatically lessen one's risk of a fatal stroke, because hypertension-related strokes are more likely to be massive intra-cerebral hemorrhages, Barker and his colleague reported in their study. Such strokes have a higher fatality rate than the far more common "ischemic" strokes, which occur when constriction or obstruction in a blood vessel reduces blood supply to an organ.

Treatment for stroke improved with the 1996 introduction of the first drug therapy for ischemic stroke. "Stroke had no [drug therapies] until that time," says Thomas Brott, chairman of the American Heart Association's stroke council and a professor of neurology at the University of Cincinnati College of Medicine. The treatment, called tissue plasminogen activator (tPA), increases the likelihood of a complete or near-complete recovery in 30 to 50 percent of ischemic stroke patients, Brott says.

Yet tPA is not a miracle drug. It must be administered within three hours of a stroke. This can be impossible when people are unsure they are having a stroke. "People don't get to the hospital soon enough because they don't recognize symptoms soon enough," says Brott. In addition, the drug can be harmful if the stroke is the less-common hemorrhagic type. This means a patient must have a high-tech CT scan to determine the type of stroke before tPA can be administered.

As a result of these limits on treatment with tPA, only a fraction of individuals who have a stroke receive treatment with the drug. Between 5,000 and 10,000 patients a year now receive tPA, says Brott. But the availability of the drug makes education about stroke even more important, within and outside the stroke belt. If stroke symptoms become more recognizable, people who have a stroke will be more likely to be treated within the three-hour window demanded by tPA.

Successful efforts to prolong the lives of stroke patients are transforming the nature of stroke. Stroke is increasingly less likely to be an acute problem resulting in rapid death and more likely to be a chronic illness. This can be seen in the number of stroke patients who are discharged from the hospital instead of dying there. The number of men discharged from the hospital after a stroke increased 26 percent between 1988 and 1995, according to the *Statistical Bulletin*. Improved rates of survival mean there will be greater demands for care in the future, says Barker.

Such care is already costly, because recovery from stroke involved an average six-day hospital stay in 1995. The average in-hospital charge for a stroke patient was $11,010 in the U.S. in 1995, although regional differences are substantial, according to the *Bulletin*. Hawaii had the highest average cost for treating a stroke patient ($19,890), while Maine had the lowest average cost ($5,920). Even in the least costly states, strokes cost millions and create immeasurable human hardship. Stroke is the leading cause of serious neurological disability in adults, according to the *Bulletin*.

Efforts to understand high rates of stroke may result in better treatment, more effective prevention efforts, and less suffering nationwide. But population trends suggest that the number of strokes will increase unless things change dramatically. "We have to come up with something better for stroke management," says Gillum of the CDC. "We must either redouble our efforts at hypertension control or have some kind of a breakthrough." Until then, strokes will be an unfortunate by-product of an aging population. Without a breakthrough, "the number of strokes is going to go through the ceiling," says Howard.

Taking It Further

For a complete description of the "stroke buckle," see George Howard et al., "Evaluation of Social Status as a Contributing Factor to the Stroke Belt Region of the United States," in the journal, *Stroke,* Vol. 28, No. 5, May 1997, published by the American Heart Association (AHA); single copies are $15; telephone Collete at the Scientific Publishing Division, (214) 706-1201. For an extensive catalog of AHA publications, contact its national headquarters in Dallas, Texas; telephone (214) 706-1179, or go to Internet address, http://www.amhrt.org. See also Kenneth Gaines, "Regional and Ethnic Differences in Stroke in the Southeastern United States Population," published in the journal, *Ethnicity and Disease,* Vol. 7, Spring/Summer 1997; single copies are $12.95; telephone (785) 843-1221; fax: (785) 843-1274; or e-mail orders@allenpress.com. For more on the cost of treating stroke, see

Margaret Mushinski, "Variations in Average Charges for Strokes and TIAs: United States, 1995," in the *Statistical Bulletin,* Vol. 78, No. 4, October-December 1997, published by Metropolitan Life; single copies are available from Mushinski at telephone (212) 685-5014; fax (212) 685-7987.

—by Patricia Braus

Patricia Braus is a contributing editor of *American Demographics.*

Chapter 11

Homicide in the Workplace

NIOSH Data

Data from the National Traumatic Occupational Fatalities (NTOF) Surveillance System indicate that 9,937 workplace homicides occurred during the 13-year period from 1980 through 1992, with an average workplace homicide rate of 0.70/100,000 workers (Table 11.1.) [National Institute for Safety and Health (NIOSH) 1995]. Over the course of the 1980s, workplace homicides decreased; but in the 1990s, the numbers began to increase, surpassing machine-related deaths and approaching the number of workplace motor-vehicle-related deaths. Although the 1992 figure was lower than that for 1991, it exceeded the 1990 figure and did not include 1992 data for New York City and the state of Connecticut. NTOF is an ongoing, death-certificate-based census of traumatic occupational fatalities in the United states, with data from all 50 states and the District of Columbia. NTOF includes information for all workers aged 16 or older who died from an injury or poisoning and for whom the certifier noted a positive response to the *injury at work?* item on the death certificate. For additional discussion of the NTOF system and the limitations of death certificates for the study of workplace homicide, see Castillo and Jenkins (1994).

From "Homicide in the Workplace," in *Violence in the Workplace,* [Online] July 16, 1996. Available: http://www.cdc.gov/niosh/violhomi.html. Produced by the CDC's National Institute for Occupational Safety and Health (NIOSH). For complete contact information, please refer to Chapter 60, "Resources."

Sex

The majority (80%) of workplace homicides during 1980-92 occurred among male workers. The leading cause of occupational injury death varied by sex, with homicides accounting for 11% of all occupational injury deaths among male workers and 42% among female workers [NIOSH 1995]. The majority of female homicide victims were

Table 11.1. Workplace Homicides in the United States, 1980-92*

Year	Number	Rate[†]
1980	929	0.96
1981	944	0.94
1982	859	0.86
1983	721	0.72
1984	660	0.63
1985	751	0.70
1986	672	0.61
1987	649	0.58
1988	699	0.61
1989	696	0.59
1990	725	0.61
1991	875	0.75
1992	757	0.64
Total	9,937	0.70

Source: NIOSH (1995).

*Data not available for New York City and Connecticut.

†Per 100,000 workers.

employed in retail trade (46%) and service (22%) industries (Table 11.2.). A large number of male homicide victims were employed not only in retail trade (36%) and service (16%) industries but in public administration (11%) and transportation/communication/public utilities (11%) (Table 11.2.). Although homicide is the leading cause of occupational injury death among female workers, male workers have more than three times the risk of work-related homicide (Table 11.3.).

Table 11.2. Workplace Homicides by Industry and Sex— United States 1980-92*

Industry	Homicides (% of Total)[†]	
	Male Worker	**Female Worker**
Retail trade	36.1	45.5
Services	16.0	22.2
Public administration	10.5	2.9
Transportation/communication/public utilities	10.6	3.8
Manufacturing	7.0	4.9
Construction	4.1	0.6
Agriculture/forestry/fishing	2.7	0.6
Finance/insurance/real estate	2.4	6.8
Wholesale trade	1.7	1.1
Mining	0.6	0.1
Not classified	8.5	11.7

Source: NIOSH (1995).
*Data for New York City and Connecticut were not available for 1992.
[†]Percentages add to more than 100% because of rounding.

Age

The age of workplace homicide victims ranged from 16 (the youngest reported in NTOF) to 93 during 1980-92. The largest number of workplace homicides occurred among workers aged 25 to 34, whereas the rate of workplace homicide increased with age (Table 11.3.). The highest rates of workplace homicide occurred among workers aged 65 and older; the rates for these workers were more than twice those for workers aged 55-64 (Table 11.3.). This pattern held true for both male and female workers.

Table 11.3. Workplace Homicides by Age Group and Sex—United States, 1980-92*

Age Group	Male Workers		Female Workers		All Workers	
	Number	Rate[†]	Number	Rate[†]	Number	Rate
16-19	242	0.55	102	0.25	344	0.41
20-24	796	0.87	285	0.35	1,081	0.62
25-34	2,020	0.89	591	0.33	2,611	0.65
35-44	1,841	0.99	423	0.28	2,265	0.68
45-54	1,344	1.04	293	0.29	1,637	0.71
55-64	1,055	1.22	191	0.31	1,246	0.84
65+	620	2.59	115	0.71	735	1.83
Total[‡]	7,935	—	2,001	—	9,937	—
Average	—	1.01	—	0.32	—	0.70

Source: NIOSH (1995)
*Data for New York City and Connecticut were not available for 1992.
[†]Rates are per 100,000 workers.
[‡]Totals include victims for whom age data were missing (17 male workers) and 1 worker whose sex was not reported.

Race

Although the majority of workplace homicide victims were white (73%), black workers (1.39/100,000) and workers of other races (1.87/100,000) had the highest rates of work-related homicide (Table 11.4.).

Geographic Distribution

During 1980-92, the largest number of homicides and the highest rates per 100,000 workers occurred in the South (N=4,819; rate=1.02/100,000) and the West (N=2,278; rate= 0.79/100,000) (Table 11.5.). Note that during the early years of the NTOF data collection effort, four states—Louisiana, Nebraska, Oklahoma, and New York—were unable to provide data on work-related homicides. In addition, data for 1992 were unavailable from New York City and Connecticut.

Homicide was the leading cause of occupational injury death over the 13-year period in Alabama, Connecticut, the District of Columbia, Michigan, and South Carolina. Although complete data for the period are not available for New York, estimates and data for recent years indicate that homicide was also the leading cause of occupational injury death in that state.

In the document *Fatal Injuries to Workers in the United States, 1980-1989: A Decade of Surveillance* (Jenkins, et al., 1993), all occupational injury deaths were analyzed for 1980 through 1989. Geographic differences in the leading causes of death were examined by mapping the state-specific, cause-specific rates in relation to the average cause-specific rate for all states combined. This analysis revealed that most (N=45) states had workplace homicide rates within one standard deviation above or below the average workplace homicide rate (Jenkins, et al., 1993).

Method of Homicide

Between 1980 and 1992, 76% of work-related homicides were committed with firearms, and another 12% resulted from wounds inflicted by cutting or piercing instruments (Table 11.6.). During this period, the number of firearm-related homicides declined then gradually increased, with the number of firearm-related workplace homicides in 1991 exceeding that in 1980. The number declined slightly in 1992, but data for this year are incomplete. Firearms accounted for an increasing percentage of the total workplace homicides over the 13-year period: 74% in 1980 and 84% in 1991. Firearms were used in 79% of the workplace homicides in 1992, but data are missing for New York City and Connecticut for this year.

Table 11.4. Workplace Homicides by Race—United States, 1980-92*

Race/Ethnicity of Victims	Number	% of Total	Rate†
White (includes Hispanic)	7,239	72.8	0.59
Black	1,938	19.5	1.39
Other	760	7.6	1.87

Source: NIOSH (1995)
*Data for New York City and Connecticut were not available for 1992.
†Per 100,000 workers

Table 11.5. Workplace Homicides by Bureau of the Census Geographic Region—United States, 1980-92*

Region	Number	% of Total	Rate†
North Central	1,797	18.1	0.50
Northeast	1,043	10.5	0.35
South	4,819	48.5	1.02
West	2,278	22.9	0.79

Source: NIOSH (1995).
*Data for New York City and Connecticut were not available for 1992.
†Per 100,000 workers.

Table 11.6. Workplace Homicides by Method—United States, 1980-92*

Method	Number	% of Total
Firearm	7,590	76.4
Cutting or piercing instrument	1,231	12.4
Strangulation	185	1.9
All other methods	931	9.4

Source: NIOSH (1995).
*Data for New York City and Connecticut were not available for 1992.

Industry and Occupation

During the 13-year period 1980-92, the greatest number of deaths occurred in the retail trade (3,774) and service (1,713) industries, whereas the highest rates per 100,000 workers occurred in retail trades (1.6), public administration (1.3), and transportation/communication/public utilities (0.94) (Table 11.7.).

At the more detailed levels of industry (Table 11.8.), the largest number of deaths occurred in grocery stores (N=330), eating and drinking places (N=262), taxicab services (N=138), and justice/public order

Table 11.7. Workplace Homicides by Industry—United States, 1980-92*

Industry	Number	% of Total	Rate†
Retail trade	3,774	38.0	1.60
Public administration	889	8.9	1.30
Transportation/ communication/ public utilities	917	9.2	0.94
Agriculture/forestry/ fishing	222	2.2	0.50
Mining	45	0.5	0.40
Service	1,713	17.2	0.38
Construction	335	3.4	0.37
Finance/insurance/ real estate	327	3.3	0.35
Wholesale trade	155	1.6	0.27
Manufacturing	650	6.5	0.24
Not classified	910	9.1	—

Source: NIOSH (1995).
Data for New York City and Connecticut were not available for 1992.
†*Per 100,000 workers.*

71

establishments (N=137). Taxicab services had the highest rate of work-related homicide during the 3-year period 1990-92 (41.4/ 100,000). This rate was nearly 60 times the national average rate of work-related homicides (0.70/100,000). This figure was followed by rates for liquor stores (7.5), detective/protective services (7.0), gas service stations (4.8), and jewelry stores (4.7) (Table 11.8.). The rates show an increase from the previously published rates for 1980-89 for taxicab services, detective/protective services, grocery stores, and jewelry stores. Rates decreased in liquor stores, gasoline service stations,

Table 11.8. Workplace homicides in high-risk industries— United States, 1980-89 and 1990-92*,†

Industry	1980-89		1990-92	
	Number	Rate	Number	Rate
Taxicab services	287	26.9	138	41.4
Liquor stores	115	8.0	30	7.5
Gas service stations	304	5.6	68	4.8
Detective/protective services	152	5.0	86	7.0
Justice/public order establishments	640	3.4	137	2.2
Grocery stores	806	3.2	330	3.8
Jewelry stores	56	3.2	26	4.7
Hotels/motels	153	1.5	33	0.8
Barber shops	14	1.5	4	‡
Eating/drinking places	734	1.5	262	1.5

Source: NIOSH (1995). Data for 1980-89 from Castillo and Jenkins (1994).
*Data for New York City and Connecticut were not available for 1992.
†Rates are per 100,000 workers.
‡Rate was not calculated because of the instability of rates based on small numbers.

justice/public order establishments, and hotels/motels; they remained the same in eating and drinking places.

When detailed occupations were analyzed for 1990-92 (Table 11.9.), the highest homicide rates were found for taxicab drivers/chauffeurs (22.7), sheriffs/bailiffs (10.7), police and detectives—public service (6.1), gas station/garage workers (5.9), and security guards (5.5). Compared with previously published data for the 7-year period 1983-89, these data indicate that rates increased more than two and a half times for sales counter clerks and nearly two times for motor vehicle and boat sales workers and sales workers in other commodities (includes workers in jewelry, food, sporting goods, book, coin, and other retail stores). Homicide rates for taxicab drivers and security guards were one and a half times higher during the early 1990s than they had been during 1983-89. However, some rates decreased: for 1990-92, the rate for hotel clerks was less than half the 1983-89 rate, and the rate for police and detectives was two-thirds the 1983-89 rate. During 1990-92, an extraordinary number of homicides (N=372) occurred among sales supervisors and proprietors, who had double the number of deaths in any other single category during both periods.

Bureau of Labor Statistics Data

Information from the Bureau of Labor Statistics (BLS) Census of Fatal Occupational Injuries (CFOI) Program identifies the same high-risk demographic and occupational groups as NIOSH NTOF data and allows description of the circumstances of workplace homicides for the period 1992-94. According to the BLS data, 73% to 82% of the homicides occurred during a robbery or other crime, whereas only 9% to 10% were attributed to business disputes, and only 4% to 6% were attributed specifically to coworkers or former employees (Table 11.10.). A shift occurred in the *robbery and other crimes* category with the creation of the new *security guard in line of duty* category, but the distribution of the circumstances has remained fairly stable during the 3 years in which data have been collected. The CFOI system uses multiple sources, including administrative documents from federal and state agencies (e.g., death certificates, medical examiner records, workers' compensation reports, and regulatory agency reports) as well as news reports and followup questionnaires to business establishments (Windau and Toscano 1994).

The BLS described a number of the robberies as occurring while workers were locking up at night or making money drops or pickups, but these were not specifically quantified. Also, homicide appeared

Table 11.9. Workplace Homicides in High-Risk* Occupations—United States, 1983-89 and 1990-92[†]

Occupation	1983-89		1990-92	
	No.	Rate[‡]	No.	Rate
Taxicab driver/chauffeur	197	15.1	140	22.7
Sheriff/bailiff	73	10.9	36	10.7
Police/detective-public services	267	9.0	86	6.1
Hotel clerk	29	5.1	6	2.0
Gas station/garage worker	83	4.5	37	5.9
Security guard	160	3.6	115	5.5
Stock handler/bagger	189	3.1	95	3.5
Supervisor/proprietor, sales	662	2.8	372	3.3
Supervisor, police/detective	12	2.2	0	§
Barber	14	2.2	4	§
Bartender	49	2.1	20	2.3
Correctional institution officer	19	1.5	3	§
Salesperson, motor vehicle/boat	21	1.1	17	2.0
Salesperson, other commodities	98	1.0	73	1.7
Sales counter clerk	13	1.2	18	3.1
Fire fighter	18	1.4	8	1.3
Logging occupation	4	§	6	2.3
Butcher/meatcutter	11	0.6	12	1.5

Source: NIOSH (1995). Data for 1988-89 from Castillo and Jenkins (1994).
*High-risk occupations have workplace homicide rates that are twice the average rate during one or both time periods.
[†]Data for New York City and Connecticut were not available for 1992.
[‡]Rates are per 100,000 workers.
§Rate was not calculated because of the instability of rates based on small numbers.

to be primarily an urban problem, with eight of the largest metropolitan areas accounting for nearly half of the workplace homicides in 1993 (Toscano and Weber 1995). The self-employed accounted for 24% to 27% of the homicides documented by the CFOI program for 1992-94, whereas this group accounted for only about 9% of the workforce during those years (BLS 1993, 1994b, 1995).

Discussion

Despite differences in data collection and the resulting total number of homicides reported by the NTOF and CFOI fatality surveillance systems, the ranking of high-risk industries and occupations is consistent, with taxicab drivers/chauffeurs, law enforcement and security personnel, and retail trade workers experiencing the greatest risks and the largest numbers of workplace homicides. Findings about

Table 11.10. Circumstances of Workplace Homicides—United States, 1992-94

Circumstance	Homicides (% of Total)*		
	1992	**1993**	**1994**
	N=1,004	**N=1,063**	**N=1,071**
Robbery/other crime	82	75	73
Business dispute/work associate	9	10	9
Coworker/former coworker	4	6	5
Customer/client	5	4	4
Police in line of duty	6	6	7
Security guard in line of duty	†	5	7
Personal dispute/acquaintance	4	4	4

Source: BLS (1994b, 1995), Windau and Toscano (1994).
*Percentages add to more than %100 because of rounding.
†This category was not included in 1992.

75

the distributions by demographic characteristics are also remarkably similar (Windau and Toscano 1994; Toscano and Weber 1995; Castillo and Jenkins 1994).

Differences in leading causes of occupational injury death by sex can be attributed at least in part to variations in employment patterns (Jenkins 1994). For example, homicide is the leading cause of occupational injury death for female workers because they are exposed less frequently than male workers to hazards such as heavy machinery and work at elevations. The same is also true for differences among industries in leading causes of death. Workers in retail trade, services, and finance/insurance/real estate are not exposed to the same kinds of hazards as workers in construction, agriculture/forestry/ fishing, mining, or transportation/communication/public utilities. These factors are extremely important to the future direction of occupational safety and health as employment patterns shift from traditional heavy industry to retail trade and service sectors. Workplace homicide must be addressed to continue the trends of decreasing numbers and rates of occupational injury deaths (Jenkins, et al., 1993; Stout, et al., 1996).

Elevated rates of workplace homicide among workers aged 65 and older may be attributable to a number of factors, including a decreased ability to survive injury or the perception that such workers are softer targets (Jenkins, et al., 1992).

Regional data for homicides in the general population show a similar pattern to those in the workplace, with crude homicide rates being highest in the South and the West (O'Carroll and Mercy 1989).

The percentage of work-related homicides attributed to firearms (76%) is slightly higher than that found in the general population, where 71% of the 1993 murders with victims aged 18 or older were committed with firearms (FBI 1994).

Changes in the risk of workplace homicide in specific industry and occupation groups between the 1980s and the early 1990s may be attributable to a number of factors, including increased recognition and recording of cases as work-related, changes in training or other work practices, increased levels of crime in certain settings, and the distribution of resources in response to perceived levels of crime. The shift in risk for public police officers and private security guards is particularly noteworthy, as the data indicate a decline in rates among public police officers and a dramatic increase among private security guards. We do not know the extent to which these findings are attributable to efforts among public police forces to reduce risks through training and use of protective equipment, the employment of private security guards by businesses and communities that had previously relied solely on public safety personnel, and the level of training and background of private security officers. However, further research is warranted.

The circumstances of workplace homicides differ substantially from those portrayed by the media and from homicides in the general population. For the most part, workplace homicides are not the result of disgruntled workers who take out their frustrations on coworkers or supervisors, or of intimate partners and other relatives who kill loved ones in the course of a dispute; rather, they are mostly robbery-related crimes.

Chapter 12

Autopsy Statistics

Current Trends in Autopsy Frequency

In approximately 14% of the 2,089,378 deaths reported in the United States in 1985, an autopsy was performed. Recent reports indicate that the frequency of autopsy has been declining and that the decline may have adversely affected the accuracy of determining the underlying cause of death. To assess the recent variation in autopsy frequency, mortality data collected by the National Center for Health Statistics, CDC, for the period 1980-1985 were analyzed. During that time, the proportion of deaths involving an autopsy gradually declined from 17% to 14%. Within each year, however, autopsy frequency varied substantially by cause of death.

For this analysis, cause of death was grouped into six general categories: natural causes, unintentional injuries and poisonings, suicide, homicide, external causes with undetermined intent, and unknown or unspecified causes. These groups correspond to the codes in the International Classification of Diseases, Ninth Revision (ICD-9).

The proportion of autopsies performed ranged from 12% among natural deaths to 97% among homicide deaths. Deaths with unknown autopsy status were enumerated separately and excluded from the

From "Current Trends Autopsy Frequency—United States, 1980-1985," *Morbidity and Mortality Weekly Report,* Vol. 37, No. 12, pp. 191-4, April 1, 1988 [Online]. Available: http://www.cdc.gov/epo/mmwr/preview/mmwrhtml/00000003.htm. Produced by the Centers for Disease Control and Prevention (CDC). For complete contact information, please refer to Chapter 60, "Resources."

calculations. Although 12% of all records lacked autopsy data, the proportion of records without autopsy data varied from 2% among homicide deaths to 13% among natural deaths. In general, larger autopsy percentages are associated with smaller percentages of missing data.

Autopsies for natural deaths declined at least 0.5% every year during the period 1980-1985, from 13% in 1980 to 10% in 1985. In contrast, the frequency of autopsies for deaths caused by unintentional injuries and poisoning increased from 46% to 51%, and the frequency among suicide deaths increased from 48% to 52%. Similarly, autopsies among deaths due to external causes of undetermined intent increased from 79% to 84%. The frequency of autopsy among homicide deaths was consistently high over this period (between 96% and 97%). The number of autopsies for deaths of unknown or unspecified cause fluctuated between 28% and 32%.

The distribution of cause of death for all autopsies has changed. In 1980, natural deaths accounted for 70% of all autopsies. By 1985, natural deaths accounted for 66% of all autopsies.

Autopsies for natural deaths or deaths occurring among patients under the care of a physician are usually performed at the hospital where the death occurred and with the permission of the decedent's next of kin. If the death is sudden, unexpected, or due to external causes, local statutes may require an autopsy. This autopsy is either requested by a coroner or performed by a medical examiner, depending upon the local medicolegal system. Since deaths due to other than natural causes require medicolegal investigation in most states, the number of autopsies performed was examined by type of medicolegal jurisdiction in the state. In 1980, 15 states had coroner systems; 18 states and the District of Columbia had medical examiner systems, and 17 states had both medical examiner systems and coroner systems. Approximately 44% of all deaths during the period 1980-1985 occurred in states with both medical examiners and coroners (a mixed medicolegal system); 29% of deaths occurred in states with a medical examiner system; the remaining 27% occurred in states with a coroner system. The percentage of deaths in which an autopsy was performed during this six-year period was greatest among states with a mixed medicolegal system, 16%. States with a medical examiner system had autopsies performed in 15% of deaths and states with coroners, 14%. States with a coroner system had the highest proportion of death records that did not indicate whether an autopsy was performed, 16%, and states with mixed systems had the smallest, 10%.

When autopsy frequency was examined by medicolegal system and cause of death, states with a medical examiner system had the highest autopsy frequency for deaths due to unintentional injuries and poisoning, homicide, suicide, undetermined intent, and unknown causes. States with mixed systems had higher autopsy frequencies for deaths due to unintentional injuries and poisoning, suicide, and undetermined intent than did states with coroners. The same pattern of annual trends was observed for each medicolegal system. Reported by: Surveillance and Programs Br, Div of Environmental Hazards and Health Effects, Center for Environmental Health and Injury Control. Editorial Note: Death certificates are the principal source of mortality statistics for the United States. Several studies, however, have raised questions concerning the accuracy of the recorded cause of death, and some investigators have advocated improving these statistics by performing more autopsies. Current data show a decline in the proportion of autopsy for natural causes of death and an increase in autopsy proportions for medicolegal deaths (homicides, suicides, and deaths caused by unintentional injuries and poisoning). As a result, 34% of autopsies performed in 1985 involved deaths due to other than natural causes, compared to 30% of autopsies performed in 1980.

State and local laws vary, but medical examiners and coroners typically have the legal authority to order autopsies for traumatic, sudden, or unexpected deaths. A more accurate picture of the frequency of autopsy among deaths outside of the medicolegal system would require separating the sudden or unexpected deaths from other natural deaths.

Part Two

Attitudes toward Death and Dying

Chapter 13

Reflections on Death in America

My father died at home in 1963. He was terminally ill. Although he agreed to an operation, he didn't particularly want to survive it because he was afraid that the combination of the illness and the operation would invade and destroy his autonomy as a human being. Unfortunately, that in fact is what happened. After the operation he had very little time left. I'm afraid I kind of wrote him off at that point. I was there when he died, yet I let him die alone. I could see him, but I wasn't at his bedside. The day after he died, I went into the office. I didn't talk about my father's death. So I kind of denied his dying, I certainly didn't participate in it. Afterwards, I read Kubler-Ross and learned that I might have maintained contact with him if I tried. Had I read Kubler-Ross earlier I would have probably held his hand, because I did love him. I just didn't know that it might make a difference. I forgave myself because I did not know any better.

My mother's death was more recent. She had joined the Hemlock Society and had at hand a means of doing away with herself. I asked her if she needed my help; I offered it, although I wasn't particularly keen to do it. But I would have helped her because I felt that I owed it to her. At the point of decision, however, she did not want to take her own life, and I'm glad she didn't. Her decision gave the family a

Excerpted from: "Reflections on Death in America," by George Soros [Online] 1998. Available: http://www.soros.org/death/reflections.html. Produced by Project on Death in America (PDIA), Open Society Institute, 400 W. 59th St., New York, NY 10019. For complete contact information, please refer to Chapter 60, "Resources." Reprinted with permission.

chance to rally around and be there as she prepared to die. And this time we did maintain good contact right to the end.

She had this experience, which is described in Kubler-Ross, of walking up to the gates of heaven, and I was accompanying her. She told me she was worried that she might drag me with her. So I reassured her that I was firmly ensconced on this earth and she should not worry. Her dying was really a very positive experience for all of us because of the way she handled herself and the way the family, not just me but particularly my children, could participate in it.

These two personal experiences made me realize that there is a need to better understand the experience of dying. In my initial research in the issue I was assisted by a friend, Patricia Prem, who as a social worker had dealt professionally with dying. She brought together the people who helped create the Project on Death in America. She is on the Project's advisory board now, as are Susan Block of Harvard Medical School, Robert Burt of Yale Law School, Robert Butler of Mt. Sinai, Joanne Lynn of George Washington University, Velvet Miller of the New Jersey State Department of Human Resources, David Rothman of Columbia's College of Physicians and Surgeons, Attorney William D. Zabel, and Kathleen M. Foley who is the chief of pain service at the Memorial Sloan-Kettering Cancer Center and Director of the Project on Death in America.

The mission of the Project is to promote a better understanding of the experiences of dying and bereavement and by doing so help transform the culture surrounding death. To do this, the Project will support initiatives in research, scholarship, the humanities and the arts, as well as innovations in the provision of care, public education, professional education, and public policy. I have committed $5 million a year to the Project's work for the first three years. The board has decided to use the money in two ways: by developing its own programs and by holding itself open for grant applications.

The first major program is to establish a number of faculty scholarships. We hope to identify outstanding faculty and clinicians who are committed to the Project's goals and to support them in their work of developing new models for the care of the dying and new approaches to the education of health professionals about the care of dying patients and their families. The scholars, who will receive two- to three-year fellowships for projects that explore critical aspects of the care of the dying, will become the academic leaders on this issue, the role models, and mentors to future generations of health professionals. Each year the project will select ten faculty scholars. In three years, we will have a leader and role model in place in one-fourth of the country's medical schools.

In opening up for grant applications our areas of interest are broad enough to cover every aspect of the culture of dying. They include the epidemiology, ethnography, and history of dying and bereavement in the [United States]; the physical, emotional, spiritual, and existential components of dying and bereavement; new service-delivery models for the dying and their family and friends; separate educational programs for the public and the health care professionals; and the shaping of governmental and institutional policy. Personally I hope that the ratio between research and action will be heavily weighed toward action.

Now, let us look briefly at what we want to transform and why. We will begin with a small matter, the name of our project. It took a considerable amount of discussion to rid ourselves of clever euphemisms and settle on a name that states our purpose directly, even starkly: the Project on Death in America. In America, the land of [the] perpetually young, growing older is an embarrassment, and dying is a failure. Death has replaced sex as the taboo subject of our times. People compete to appear on talk shows to discuss the most intimate details of their sex lives, but they have nothing to say about dying, which in its immensity dwarfs the momentary pleasures of sex. Only our preoccupation with violence breaks through this shroud of silence. Killing yes; dying no.

Even doctors, especially doctors, don't like to think about death. A recent federal pamphlet for physicians on HIV infection never even mentions that AIDS is a fatal disease. It recommends making arrangements for the care of the children when the patient becomes sick, but says nothing about the need for long-term plans for when the patient dies. It is easier to find descriptions of the way people die and what can be done to ease their death in the medical textbooks of the turn of the century than in today's voluminous literature on the treatment and cure of diseases.

This emphasis on treating disease, instead of providing care, has altered the practice of medicine. People live longer, surviving four or five illnesses before dying. But the health care bill grows with every illness. Our success has also brought other unintended consequences. We have created a medical culture that is so intent on curing disease and prolonging life that it fails to provide support in that inevitable phase of life—death. Advances in high technology interventions have contributed to this weakness in our medical system, deluding doctors and patients alike into believing that the inevitable can be delayed almost indefinitely.

The reality of death and the perceptions of the participants—the dying person, the doctor, the family members—are separated by a wide gap. We need to bring [them] into closer alignment. Doctors who are on a first-name basis with disease must reacquaint themselves with the patient. They must recognize that, by focusing exclusively on conquering disease and prolonging life, they abandon the dying when, in their own words, there is nothing more to be done. They must come to terms with their own death in order to provide proper care for the dying.

Eighty percent of people die in hospitals, yet, for most people, hospitals are not a good place to die. Hospitals are set up to take care of acute illnesses, and dying is not an illness. It doesn't belong to an official medical category, it has no DRG [diagnosis-related group] that would permit reimbursement for the hospital and the physician. If you go to a hospital to die, the doctors have to find something wrong with you, something to treat, like pneumonia or dehydration, or they cannot admit you. They hook you up to tubes and machines and try to fix a condition that isn't fixable. The need to arrive at a reimbursable diagnosis changes the reality. The doctors and nurses are working to prolong life, instead of preparing a patient for death. The ideal of a peaceful death is impossible in such an alien setting, under such extreme conditions.

A peaceful death is more likely to be achieved at home in familiar surroundings that are more conducive to the comfort and ritual of leave taking from family and friends. Both my parents died at home. In my mother's case, after I accompanied her to the gates of heaven and left her in good hands, she lost consciousness and lingered for another seven to ten days before dying. I visited her regularly to see if there was any sign of communication or consciousness, but there wasn't. She died at home, because we could afford to keep her there with round-the-clock nurses attending to her. We weren't forced by lack of financial resources to put her into a hospital where medical intervention may well have kept her much longer in a state of limbo between living and dying. Just by giving her food, the process could have been unnecessarily prolonged.

Only twenty percent of people die in their own home, in a nursing home, or in a hospice. Hospices offer the kind of palliative care that should be routine procedure in every institution that cares for the dying.

Proper care includes the control of pain and other symptoms as well as attention to the psychological and spiritual needs of the patient. To provide this care, hospices employ teams of doctors, nurses, social workers, and bereavement counselors. But the hospice alternative, unfortunately, is not available to the majority of dying patients. Medicare coverage is limited. As a result, most hospice programs deliver care to the dying in their own home, restricting custodial services to only four hours a day. This requires the presence of a family member who doesn't work, who is physically able, and who is willing to assume the responsibilities for care the rest of the time.

The recommendations that follow from these observations are obvious. First and foremost, doctors, nurses, and other health professionals need better training in the care of the dying, especially in the relief of pain. Health professionals also need training in alleviating the psychological, emotional, and existential suffering that may accompany dying. Physical pain is what people fear most about dying. A dying person in pain cannot think about anything else, leaving no room for coming to terms with death, for reviewing one's life, putting one's affairs in order, for saying good-bye. Therefore, pain relief must come first. Doctors often under-medicate their dying patients for fear of turning them into drug addicts.

Second, hospitals must be required to develop and adopt a comprehensive DRG for terminal care. This single change would go a long ways toward removing the hypocrisy that now surrounds a hospitals' treatment of the dying and freeing doctors and nurses to provide the kind of care that doesn't rely on technology—such as the simple act of paying attention to a dying person, holding their hand, listening, and comforting them.

Third, we must increase the availability of hospice services for terminally ill patients removing restrictions on admittance and enhancing reimbursement regulations. We should consider laws that permit next of kin to decide to forego life sustaining medical interventions even when a patient's wishes are not known. The government may have to help family members financially so that they can take care of dying persons at home by the least expensive means. These are only a few of the approaches to transforming the culture of dying that our project will be exploring in the months to come.

How much will all this cost? Can we afford to care for the dying properly? The number of people dying in the United States currently stands at 2.2 million [dollars] annually. Increases in cancer and AIDS deaths and the aging of the baby boomers will cause this figure to climb faster than the population. Today 1 in 8 Americans is 65 years or older. In 30 to 40 years, 1 in 5 will be in that age group. The average life expectancy for those reaching age 65 is already 81 for men and 85 for women. The fear is that the dying of the elderly will drain the national treasury. Like most fears, this one is based on a myth, the popular perception that elderly, terminally ill patients consume enormous amounts of resources shortly before they die.

It is true that nearly half of all medical expenses are incurred in the last six months of peoples' lives. But it is also true that medical expenditures in the last year of life are lower for people 80 years and older than for those in younger age groups.

Aggressive, life-prolonging interventions, which may at times go against the patient's wishes, are much more expensive than proper care for the dying.

This brings me to that hotly debated subject, physician-assisted suicide and euthanasia. This is the one aspect of dying that is talked about everywhere—on television, in public forums, in newspaper headlines, and serious journal articles. Voters in Oregon just approved a law that makes it the first state to lift the prohibition against physician-assisted suicide.

As the son of a mother who was a member of the Hemlock Society, and as a reader of Plato's Phaedra, I cannot but approve. But I must emphasize that I am speaking in my personal capacity and not on behalf of the Board of the Project on Death in America. There are members of the Board who take a different position and the Board as a whole wants to steer clear of the issue because it feels it has plenty to do before opening that Pandora's box. Instead of getting embroiled in the debate on physician-assisted suicide and euthanasia, they want to support the training of health care professionals, enabling them to provide humane, compassionate care to the dying, including improved physician-patient communication, patient-centered care, better physician judgment on withdrawing or withholding care, and familiarity with the principles and practices of palliative care.

As founder of the project, I respect their judgment. I believe in personal autonomy; I believe people should be allowed to determine their own end. But I also recognize that legalizing euthanasia could have unintended consequences, leading to all kind of abuses. The issues need to be carefully weighed, but I accept that this is not the first priority of the Project. Very few terminally ill patients would avail themselves of the opportunity even if euthanasia were legalized. After all, my mother refused my help and I am glad she did. The Project on Death in America concerns itself with the vast majority of people who are not looking for physician-assisted suicide and they have their work cut out for them.

In conclusion, let me tell you how I came to terms with my own death—a subject I gave a lot of thought to in my youth. I spent years thinking about it. Building on my insight that there is always a divergence between ideas and facts I came to the conclusion that it is the idea of my death which I cannot accept because it is a total denial of my consciousness. The fact of dying, when it comes, may be much more acceptable, especially if it comes at the end of a long life. The insight that the idea is not the same as the fact, made the idea more bearable.

I am sure that I would not find the argument persuasive if I had to confront the fact of my death here and now but as an idea I find it both convincing and comforting. I wonder whether it has the same effect on you when you hear it for the first time.

As people come to terms with death, recognizing it as a fact of life, then the demand for physician-assisted suicide, as well as for unnecessary medical interventions, will drop. That is one way I hope our efforts will influence the culture of dying.

Chapter 14

Religious and Cultural Perspectives

Increasingly our towns, cities, and villages are changing into multiethnic and multicultural communities. Already, some 160 different ethnic and linguistic groups exist in the country, each with its own understanding of health and illness, its own attitudes towards pain and suffering, its own concepts and beliefs on death and dying. It's imperative to the care giver in our multicultural society to become more aware of these different notions, concepts, and beliefs as they shape different people's and cultures' attitude toward death and dying, expressions of grief and mourning, and their ways of coping with loss and suffering.

Though there are, of course, many similarities between dying and grief practices of people and cultures and religions all around the world, the differences, too, are many, and often extreme. It's these differences that are the main focus of this [chapter]. Among them, three stand out very forcefully:

1. American *individualism* versus other cultures' *group-orientation*. In the latter, families play a powerful role in the healing of and caring for the dying patient; in preparing people for death, and in the rituals associated with death and dying.

Excerpted from "Death and Dying: A Cross-Cultural Perspective," by Gottfried Oosterwal, Ph.D., Litt.D., Director, Center for Intercultural Relations, 4534 Hillcrest Dr., P. O. Box 133, Berrien Springs, MI 49103. For complete contact information, please refer to Chapter 60, "Resources." Reprinted with permission.

Table 14.1a. (continued in Table 14.1b.) Cultural Differences and Similarities Relating to Pain, Treatment, and Death

Ethnic Groups	Behavior Re: Symptoms	Treatments Preferred	Support System	Belief Re: Death	Behavior Re: Death
Native American	May/may not be expressive	Holistic; purification; medicine man, helps with journey, not with cure	Family; shaman; tribal group	Part of cycle; return to ancestors; two souls, two choices	Some wail, some quiet; use bells; mourning; restraints; ceremonies
Anglo American	From vocal to stoic; some demanding	From Western medicine to alternative and holistic	Nuclear family and friends	Afterlife; judgement, then Heaven/Hell	Controlled; taboo subject
African American	Emotional; need very clear instructions	Prayer; folk medicine; magic; pica; miracle cures	Extended family; friends; church	Protestants believe in God's ability to heal	Very emotional
Hispanic/ Latino	What will be.... Don't talk much about illness, death, or dying; need very clear instructions	Curanderos used first; want priest at deathbed; miracle cures; herbs; cupping	Strong patriarchal family; church	Heaven/Hell; believe in contact with dead; 90% Catholic; illness/death—God's will	Very emotional; fascinated with death
Asian American (general) Chinese Japanese Korean Indo-Chinese	Extremely modest re: the body; may refuse meds at first, need second request; *saving face is vital*	Some believe Western medicine may interfere with their spirit; self-healing highly valued	Patriarchal family; wife and children expected to provide all care	Part of life; need items for the death journey; Taoist; Buddhist; Shinto; ancestor worship	Need member of the family present; want to keep body in home as long as possible

Table 14.1b. (continued from Table 14.1a.) Cultural Differences and Similarities Relating to Pain, Treatment, and Death

Ethnic Groups	Behavior Re: Symptoms	Treatments Preferred	Support System	Belief Re: Death	Behavior Re: Death
S. Asian, Indian, Pakistani	Don't discuss personal things with others easily	Acupuncture; herbs; coining; cupping; folk remedies	—	Reincarnation; Nirvana; Hindu; Islam; Animist	Women beat breasts; men jump, cry without tears and chant
Filipino	Emotional; accepting	Folk and Western medicine	Extended family	90% Catholic	Detailed rituals; very emotional
Jewish	Emotional; demanding; anxious	Attention; sympathy; good medicine	Family	Many do not believe in Heaven/Hell	—
Arab, Mid. Eastern	Women emotional; men demanding and emotional; look down on women medical personnel	—	Extended family; Islam	Transition; see God; resurrection; judgement; Paradise/Hell	Express grief openly; stay with deceased until transported
Italian	Emotional; appropriate	—	Extended family	Catholic; atheist/agnostic	—

2. In most non-Western cultures, a clear distinction is made between *biological* and *social* death. There, death occurs not only at one point of time; it is seen and experienced as a process. That's also why death is accompanied by so many ceremonies and activities that are processual: double or even triple funerals; special taboos and restrictions during interim periods; etc.

3. Unlike in the USA, in most non-Western cultures, the process of death and dying is embedded in *rituals*. These include prayers and incantations, chanting and readings (from holy writings); candles and flowers; ritual washings; wailing, crying and confessing; special foods and drinks; etc. The purpose of these rituals is to overcome fear, uncertainty, and anxiety; provide standardized ways of dealing with unpleasant emotions; confirm a sense of belonging; reassert basic values; protect from harm and evil, and other.

Buddhist Attitudes toward Death

The Four Noble Truths:

1. To exist is to suffer.
2. The cause is the natural tendency to desire, to thirst.
3. There is a way to overcome suffering.
4. The way is to follow the eightfold path: right intention, speech, conduct, livelihood, effort, mindfulness, and contemplation.

Focus: Liberation, illumination, peace—Nirvana
Scripture: The Dharma (teaching)

Buddhism is a faith, a body of philosophy and wisdom, and a group of practices meant to relieve humankind of material, spiritual, and psychological suffering and to resolve the inevitable contradictions of life . . . Buddhism's concern is not God or the *why* of life but rather *how* humans shall exist in this universe and give value to every breath drawn. (Ed., *The Long Search,* 1978, p. 84.)

"It is crucial to understand that Buddha did not die to desire itself, for one cannot live without desires, but to his attachment to desire. Ultimately, there exists only an ever-changing combination of . . . matter, sensations, perceptions, mental formations, consciousness . . . at death, according to Buddha, life-stream continues . . . Any particular so-called death is seen as one of a succession of deaths." It is believed the goal of achieving oneness with the universe may take several cycles of rebirth. All things are seen as impermanent, in constant change, and one is to focus on a dynamic becoming: Be here now. . . Be here . . . Be . . .

Buddhist Rituals surrounding Death

Death rituals vary greatly, but the following are generally agreed upon:

1. The thoughts and mental condition of the dying person are of primary importance, and to assure that the person feels at peace,

2. The person should be surrounded by family, relatives, friends, and monks who will assist the person's state of mind by

3. Reciting Buddhist *sutras* (scriptures) and repeat *mantras* during the dying process and even afterwards.

In some traditional Buddhist settings:

1. The body is taken by the male members of the family and washed;

2. The body is then wrapped in burial clothes,

3. The thumbs and big toes are tied together in hair from a deceased member of the family;

4. A *coin* is placed inside the mouth and at the head.

5. A *vase* is placed holding a flower so the dead may still worship Buddha.

6. From *death until cremation, the body lies in state.*

7. Family and friends come to pay respects, in some traditions no outward signs of sympathy are shown, in some there is loud crying.

8. The *body is never left alone.*

9. Relatives do all the cooking.

10. Some Buddhists believe "that the conscious soul remains in or around the body for up to three days, after which the body is

cremated. On the seventh day after a person has died, monks are invited to the deceased's house to chant from the sacred texts . . . to drive away the ghost of the dead, and . . . to confer merit upon the soul of the dead person. This, it is believed, will make the dead person's passing from the material to the spiritual world easier. It also helps the living to be purged of any fear of the ghost or of personally dying. This ritual leads one to the awareness that human life will continue through myriad lifetimes until everyone reaches *nirvana.*" (Kramer, 1988)

Hindu Attitudes toward Death

"When it comes to death, Some to the womb return,—Embodied souls, to receive another body; Others pass into a lifeless stone In accordance with their works . . ." Katha Upanishad, VI: 17-18

Focus: Realization of the Supreme Self through devotion and surrender (*bhakti yoga*), and final liberation from birth and death . . .

In India, there seems to be a preoccupation with death and what happens after death. Death is seen on the streets and in the railway stations, and is a frequent topic in sacred texts and stories.

"When the body dies, the Self (Atman) does not die! The secret of death is to realize the Supreme Self hidden in the heart, not by preaching, not by sacrifice, but through meditation and grace." (Kramer, 1988) When one realizes the Self, one is liberated from life's *karma* (action) and from *samsara* (the endless round of birth, death, and rebirth).

Hindu Rituals surrounding Death

1. Before death, the son and relatives put water, taken, if possible, from the Ganges River into the mouth of the dying person (relieving thirst and providing a blessing from the Ganges which will bring peace).

2. Family and friends sing devotional prayers and chant *Vedic mantras.*

3. If a monk is present, he recites *mantras* in order to revive the person; if unsuccessful, he will pronounce the person dead.

4. Prior to cremation, the body is washed and anointed, the hair (and beard) trimmed, and [the body is] clothed in new or clean clothes.

5. Relatives and mourners, who carry the body to the cremation site, chant verses.

6. The body is placed on a funeral pyre (if in India). If the deceased is a man, his widow sits in vigil beside him, then is asked to rise up.

7. The eldest son walks around the pyre three times, each time pouring sacred water on the deceased. He then sets fire to the wood with a torch that has been blessed.

8. Relatives and mourners chant *Vedic mantras* to quicken the soul's release.

Three different burial practices are used in India—cremation, burial, and outside disintegration. "Hindus believe that cremation is most spiritually beneficial to the departed soul. It is believed that as long as the physical body remains visible, because of the astral body's lingering attachment, the soul remains nearby for days or months. The corpse is therefore burned so that the soul can begin its journey as soon as possible."

"When the mourners return home, they are obliged to ceremonially bathe themselves, again recite *mantras* and offer a libation at the family altar, a practice which is continued for ten days. Three days after the death, the eldest son returns to the cremation spot, takes the remaining bones, and buries them or casts them into a river." (Kramer, 1988, pp. 27-39)

Islamic Attitudes toward Death

"There is no other God but Allah, and Muhammad is his prophet."

Focus: Submission to the will of Allah
Scripture: The Holy Qur'an

"To the biblical account of creation the Qur'an adds not only the announcement of death's inevitability, but also the Day of Resurrection. Creation, death, and resurrection are therefore each sacred, and inexorably linked from the beginning. . . . Allah's creation is too wonderful to end with death . . . these stages have no meaning until one completes the full cycle—through them the soul itself develops. Life then is a preparation for the soul to pass through the stage of death, and to be fit to progress in the life after death." (Kramer, 1988)

It is believed there will be a day of judgment, and Muslims who have not lived up to the will of Allah, and unbelievers, will be burned in Hell. Once the soul separates from the body, believers will journey through seven layers of heaven to live in Paradise.

Islamic Rituals surrounding Death

Tradition dictates the following:

1. A person who is actively dying should be positioned on her or his back, with the head facing Mecca.

2. The room is perfumed, and anyone who is unclean or is menstruating has to leave the room.

3. The dying person is encouraged to confess all earthly sins.

4. The name of Allah "in the heart" means the person is ready to go into the next world.

5. When dead, the person's mouth and eyes should be closed, the feet tied together, the body covered with a sheet (Note: a prayer may be said at this time, but it as not proper to quote from or read the Qur'an; often a teacher, an *Imam* [ee-MOM], will lead the prayer. Prayers are to be recited in a standing position.)

6. The body is to be gently cleaned, perfumed, and then wrapped in *white* cotton *by the family.*

7. Embalming is not practiced.

8. The deceased is then placed in a plain wooden coffin and carried to the place of burial.

9. The bearers repeat . . . . : "God is great. God is Merciful."

10. The body is taken from the coffin and lowered into a six-foot-deep grave.

11. All those present cover the body with flowers and dirt, and pour over it blessed rose water. (Kramer, 1988, pp. 157-65)

Jewish Attitudes toward Death

"Hear, O Israel, the Lord is our God, the Lord is one." Deut. 6:4 *(shema)*

Focus: To worship God, and to live responsibly in the world as God's Chosen People

Scripture: The Torah, the Hebrew Bible

In Jewish tradition, both life and death are from God, so death is not seen as a punishment but a sacred and natural part of God's creation. At death, both the body and the soul go back to their source. There is a wide range of beliefs about what that means: Some believe that there is no afterlife, some believe in the resurrection of the body and the immortality of the soul. Many believe in a judgment, with the deceased going either to Heaven or Hell. And it is believed that the dead will be raised again at the coming of the Messiah.

"In the Hebrew Bible, the word death is used in at least three ways: as biological cessation, as a power which opposes God's creation, and as a metaphor for anything which leads a person away from God." Great value is placed on diligently searching for "meaning in life despite its absurdities." (Kramer, 1988)

Jewish Rituals surrounding Death

1. A person who is about to die must be constantly attended.

2. At death, the dying person is to make confession (no rabbi needs to be present), and special prayers are offered, including the *shema*.

3. The body is never left unattended from death until the funeral.

4. A son, or the nearest relative, closes the eyes and mouth and extends the arms and hands to the side of the body.

5. The body is to be washed and dressed in a white linen or shroud.

6. Embalming is not practiced, so the deceased is buried as quickly as possible after the death in a pine box.

7. At the gravesite, at the end of the service, the relatives recite a mourner's prayer (*kaddish*), a prayer to life, praising God: "The Lord gives and the Lord takes away; blessed be the name of the Lord."

8. The rabbi then recites the rest of the *kaddish*. (It is expected that the relatives will recite the *kaddish* prayer regularly during the first year of mourning.)

9. The casket is lowered into the ground, and the mourners throw handfuls of dirt on it to mark the final farewell.

10. The next seven days are set aside for intense mourning by the family, including thinking, praying, and reading from the Mishnah and Zohar. The only exception is on the sabbath, the day of joy. (Kramer, 1988, pp. 122-36)

Native American Attitudes toward Death

"Today is a good day to die." Chief Crazy Horse, Sioux warrior
North American Indian cultures and beliefs about dying vary greatly. This information from the traditions of the Yaqui and the Lakota Sioux serves as one example.

Sioux warriors began each day with the words *ho ka hey* (it's a good day to die), expressing willingness to surrender to death fearlessly, at any time. The Yaqui Indian sorcerer warrior, Don Juan Matus, practiced the sacred art of dying, treating death as if it were a constant companion, focusing on the link between life and death without remorse.

To the North American Indians, nature is sacred and life is lived with much ritual. Mother Earth is seen as a respected vehicle through which the Great Spirit flows; each day and each creature is sacred. The sacred pipe used by the First Americans represents oneness with all who share in ceremonies involving the pipe: the bowl is seen as the earth itself, the feathers that hang from the stem represent the eagle and other "wingeds", the stem is wood and represents all that grows on the earth.

It is believed there are two souls, one the spirit or breath *(ni)*, or vital force of the body. At death, the life breath and the body decays back to the elements. The second soul, called the "free" soul *(nagi)*, leaves the body during sickness or dreams. At death, this free soul migrates to the land of the dead. However, first the free soul lingers with the loved one, then is freed after one year. There is a time of judgment and the good persons go to a good place with *ni*, and the evil persons are pushed over a cliff and their spirits return to the earth. These doomed spirits continue to contribute to the evil forces which threaten the well-being of the living. The innate power *(sicun)*, given by the supernaturals at birth returns to the supernaturals at a person's death.

Native American Rituals surrounding Death

1. A lock of hair is cut, and ritualistically blessed and purified

over the smoke, wrapped in buckskin and laid in a special place within the tipi.

2. The pipe is lit, smoked, and passed (toward the east) around the circle of mourners, and prayers are offered.

3. A bundle is made of the deceased's body, taken away from the camp and left on a scaffold with some of the person's possessions.

4. The soul is believed to stay with the loved ones, but only for six months to a year.

5. A second ceremony is then performed called the "Releasing of the Soul." (The entire community is present for this. Buffalo are killed, food is prepared, tribal leaders assembled)

6. The sacred pipe is readied, the bowl placed over the smoke so that the smoke passes through the stem-end which is pointed toward heaven, and the soul is released . . . when the soul bundle leaves the lodge, the soul is released and departs on the spirit path. (Kramer, 1988, pp. 169-75)

From Kramer, Kenneth. 1988. *The Sacred Art of Dying*. NY: Paulist Press.

For Further Study and Reference

Doka, K. J., and J. D. Morgan, eds. 1993. *Death and Spirituality*. New York: Baywood.

Eisenbruch, M. 1984. Cross-cultural aspects of bereavement. *Cult Med Psychiatry* 8: 315-47.

Hertz, R. *Death and the Right Hand*. 1980. London: Cohen and West.

Humphreys, S. C., and H. King, eds. 1981. *Mortality and Immortality: The Anthropology and Archeology of Death*. London: Academic Press.

Irish, D. P., K. F. Lundquist, and V. J. Nelsen, eds. 1993. *Ethnic Variations in Dying, Death and Grief*. Washington D.C.: Taylor and Franers.

Kramer, K. 1988. *The Sacred Art of Dying.* New York: Paulist Press.

Parks, C. M. 1975. *Bereavement.* Penguin, Hammondsworth.

Parry, J. K., and A. S. Ryan, eds. 1995. *A Cross-Cultural Look at Death, Dying and Religion.* Nelson-Hall.

Parry, J. K. 1990. *Social Work with the Terminally Ill: A Transcultural Perspective.* Springfield, Ill.: Charles C. Thomas.

Platt, L. A., and V. R. Persico. 1992. *Grief in Cross-Cultural Perspective: A Casebook.* New York: Garland.

Rosenblatt, P., R. Walsh, and D. Jackson. 1976. *Grief and Mourning in Cross-Cultural Perspective.* New Haven, Conn.

— by Gottfried Oosterwal, Ph.D., Litt.D.

Gottfried Oosterwal is the director of the Center for Intercultural Relations, providing worldwide training, consulting, and research for business, health care, education, and service in a multicultural setting.

Chapter 15

A Death in the Family

On the morning of September 12, 1997, my 86-year-old father awoke to a world turned suddenly strange and threatening. He sat up confused and lost, his words to his wife of 56 years jumbled and hard to decipher. Distraught at his sudden inability to communicate, he crawled back to the safety of his bed, drawing the covers over his head. He had suffered an acute stroke, affecting mainly his speech at this point. But within another day, the damage done by this one episode would render him unable to swallow and speak, or to move his left arm and leg. Within 3 weeks, he would be dead from pneumonia brought on not only by complications of the stroke, but mistakes made in his care by various medical personnel during his brief but intense illness.

What ensued in the next few weeks for him, and for my family, was the gradual unfolding of a nightmare. It was an education we would rather not have had of a medical community caught at a strange crossroads of being both on the cutting edge of miracle cures but apparently still lacking understanding in pain control and end-of-life care. The whole medical system seemed caught up in cost-saving measures, endangering the very lives it espouses to save.

From "A Death in the Family," by Elenor K. Schoen, in *HUMAN LIFE News*, pp. 6-9, 11, June 1998. © June 1998 by HUMAN LIFE of Washington, 2725 152nd Ave. NE, Redmond, WA 98052. For complete contact information, please refer to Chapter 60, "Resources." Reprinted with permission.

A Dying Father and an Ailing Medical System

Before the morning of my father's sudden illness, I had never witnessed someone going through the immediate aftermath of a stroke. The afflicted person is transformed. My elderly father, who just the day before seemed rather frail and bent over, now seemed to have such a surge of adrenaline and strength. All the agitation was a condition of the swelling and bleeding in his brain caused by the initial stroke episode which continued to spread the damage. With difficulty, we got my father to the emergency room of a local hospital. Before he suffered paralysis, he did not seem to understand who we were or what anyone was saying to him. A sufferer from an apparently slow-moving version of Alzheimer's disease for the past 10-15 years, my Dad now had the added loss brought on by cerebral hemorrhaging. As the agitation grew worse, he was placed in restraints, even after paralysis to his left side set in. His left hand was badly bruised in his struggles to get out of bed and leave the hospital, which must have seemed in his confusion to be a frightening place. Drugs were administered by IV to calm his distress. However, some seemed to heighten both agitation and cause him to hallucinate.

My family now began our bedside vigils. Our need to be there was intensified by the knowledge that this particular hospital had recently laid off nursing staff. At night, the ratio of nurses to patients on this floor specializing in acute care was 1 nurse to 10 patients. As Dad was in no condition to push a call button for help, and his family could not be there overnight, the doctor asked my mother to hire a "sitter" to be with my father during the night. This extra help by a freelance LPN was not covered by my parents' medical insurance. The added help ran up an additional $1,000 fee for the week he was first hospitalized. Considering all the other expenses entailed in his care, the extra money needed for him to receive necessary nursing care in an acute patient ward of a large metropolitan hospital shocked us.

The Reality of Patient Rights

The lack of nurses heightened our realization that we must be full-time advocates for my father's care. As a family, we are fairly sophisticated in our medical knowledge owing to our various vocational choices and college training. However, under the present circumstances, we were confused and overwhelmed by the questions we were being asked about Dad's medical treatment.

We were given conflicting information about how close to death my father was at the time. Some of the nurses we spoke with, who had experience in dealing with elderly stroke victims, felt that any diagnosis at this point was terribly premature until the brain swelling subsided. A hospice nurse, who was a friend of ours, agreed with them, saying that cerebral swelling can take months to recede. Until then, the patient's condition is not stabilized enough to really test damage caused by the stroke. The effectiveness of therapy at this point was uncertain.

But the doctors at the hospital seemed convinced that my father was probably going to die very soon. If he did survive, he would be unable to regain use of his paralyzed limbs, as well as his ability to swallow or speak, they told us. In combination with his age and previous memory problems, they had no hope of real recovery. Recovery should have been apparent early on—in the first 48 hours—we were told.

The lack of agreement among the various medical professionals we talked with made it difficult to know who to believe and what to do. We felt we were being rushed to make decisions which could profoundly affect my father's condition, for better or worse, at a time when everything seemed so unpredictable. We continued to insist on comfort care, battling infection and pneumonia with antibiotics, and keeping him as tranquil as possible. We did agree that they should not "code" my father to be resuscitated—which in itself was a painful decision to make.

To Treat or Not to Treat

After Dad had been on an IV which provided both medicine as well as some basic nutrients and hydration—which was not life-sustainable for the long haul—the time had come to make the first big decision as to whether a feeding tube should be placed in his stomach. We assured the attending physician that our main concern was for my father's comfort. We were not expecting a cure, after hearing the doctors' consensus that this was unrealistic. However, we did feel that it seemed too premature to assume that death was imminent. The rule in medicine is that immediately after a major health emergency, the patient is stabilized—introducing food and water, if this is possible—before deciding on further treatment.

Nutrition and hydration wouldn't really stop the destructive process of the stroke. Starvation and dehydration would most likely kill my father at this point before any further complications of the stroke would. So with our urging, the physician at the hospital agreed to have the stomach tube inserted. But he returned to his view that it did not look good for the future. The family responded to his pessimism by saying that as long as Dad appeared to struggle for life, we would care for him—no matter the long- or short-term prognosis, despite his physical or mental state. At this point in his illness, "care" for us meant food and water until he could no longer absorb this sustenance because of imminent death.

The Real Cost of Discharging Patients Prematurely

Once we decided in favor of palliative care for Dad, we were appalled to learn that after only one week of hospitalization following a major stroke, my father was to be discharged to a nursing facility off the premises. The hospital was quite insistent on this point, even though he had just barely beaten back an attack of pneumonia and seemed in a very precarious state. We were told that we now needed to find a nursing home where he might continue his care and receive therapy for the paralysis.

This caught us by surprise. The opinion had been that a feeding tube was useless treatment because he was close to death. Now it appeared he was deemed to be in good enough health to be discharged for therapy. Or was he? It seemed so baffling and contradictory. How could they be talking about the same patient who was apparently both ready to die and ready for therapy? Were we trying to bring him back or let him go? Was he getting better or failing? And should all families be required to have medical degrees before placing a relative in the hospital?

There was no question in our minds that my father was in very frail health. We watched him struggle with the first of three attacks of pneumonia during these final weeks of his life. Pneumonia was hardly the "old man's friend," as it was often portrayed when the infection supposedly acted as a release at the end of a long illness. The lung infection caused my father a great deal of discomfort. His temperature and blood pressure shot up, and his respiration was labored, as if he were running up a very steep hill. They fought off the first two of these attacks successfully with antibiotics.

The sedatives however, continued to cause problems, adding to his misery with delusional periods. The drug therapy caused him to swing back and forth between heavy sleeping and episodes of agitation and restlessness. We continued to plead that they try to adjust the sedatives, or try something different. We had always understood that it was possible to keep patients comfortable, no matter the amount of pain or agitation they were encountering.

But now, added to all this, the hospital was demanding that we send him off by ambulance to a strange bed in a nursing home. We feared setbacks, rather than recovery for my father. Our fears, unfortunately, were realized.

Seeking a Nursing Home and Keeping Your Physician

It is a well-known fact that Alzheimer's sufferers find unfamiliar environments upsetting. Previously, my parents' physician had warned my mother not to change residences as Dad was acclimated to their apartment and would find any change traumatic. If this were the case while he was in relatively good health, one can only imagine the confusion he was suffering after his stroke, being moved every week. In a three-week period, my father was transferred to four different care facilities. It was our task to help set this misery for him in motion by frantically trying to locate an available bed, providing sub-acute, long-term care.

Considering the frequency of patients being discharged to nursing homes, long-term (and even short-term) nursing beds are very hard to find, especially on the kind of short notice hospitals tend to give patients and their families.

In fact, this entire experience forced the family to observe at close range an endless stream of built-in problems that did more to endanger the health and healing of the patient than it did to improve them. The next glitch to appear contradicted what we had always believed about "primary" physicians.

We learned to our dismay that doctors don't necessarily follow their patients who are transferred to nursing centers. Physicians only visit *some* of the care facilities where their patients are sent. Since we could find few available nursing home beds that our doctor visited, which the family could reach easily, we looked for a good facility close to home so we could continue our constant monitoring.

Being able to maintain the relationship with one's primary doctor throughout an illness, and final dying process, should be the rule rather than the exception, or so we had thought. Most patients try to pick a primary physician whom they trust and hopefully agree with philosophically. However, with the established procedure of discharging patients so quickly, it is a rarity to keep a relationship going with one's primary physician. My father was in the care of three primary doctors in a three-week period, plus several other physicians in various supporting or temporary roles.

Besides the obvious inconvenience of switching doctors mid-illness, this shipping of patients around to different locations to be cared for by different medical personnel, increases the patient's risk factor, as we found out. With each new facility my Dad was moved to, and with each new doctor he encountered, we literally had to start all over again in explaining the circumstances of his illness and re-establish the level of care we wished him to receive. His medical records followed him, but not the one person who really understood his history. This forced the family even more into a role of playing "primary physician"—Dad's primary advocate for care.

We finally located a bed in a nearby nursing facility, choosing another physician who would visit Dad there. As medical director, he visited the facility once a week, which we appreciated owing to the fact that we had heard that most doctors may only visit nursing homes as often as once a month.

In this new location, Dad drifted in and out of sleep, but eventually became quite agitated. The nursing staff had loosened the restraints on his arms hoping to make him more comfortable. But Dad took this opportunity to yank out his feeding tube. The doctor predicted that if we put the stomach tube back in, my father would probably pull it out later. Once again, we faced the feeding tube dilemma.

The doctor started turning up the pressure on us to stop nutrition and hydration. If we chose not to reintroduce food and water, he told us, they would heavily sedate Dad until he died. This was supposed to be reassuring, but we were not comforted by his suggestion, nor the rather exasperated way he responded to our questioning and our feeling that this was too drastic a move right now.

In our battle fatigue, we began to think that maybe if death were imminent, this might be the best we could do at this juncture. But as our hospice friend explained, this dying process might not take merely a day or two, as we had thought, but a matter of weeks. The stroke, bad as it was, would not in itself cause death at this point. However, stopping all nutrition and hydration would. The parent of a close friend of mine, who also suffered a paralyzing stroke, survived 20 days without benefit of nutrition and hydration before her death. The description of her death was a sobering reality check.

The doctor persisted to the point of giving us an ultimatum. If the physician sent Dad back to yet another hospital to have the tube reinserted, we would lose this nursing home bed and have to start the search all over again. But we were more committed than ever to the idea that my father's death would be God's call, not ours. We would care for him until God decided to take him home. We realized, sadly, that this was going to be a long, uphill battle against the prevailing attitude in medicine.

It wasn't as if we were asking for high-tech miracles, or trying to kid ourselves that Dad would recuperate fully to the point where he was before his stroke. We had decided at the first hospital that he should not be resuscitated. No one would attempt CPR. No one would prolong his agony in intensive care if he were to suddenly have another stroke or heart attack. There was a limit to our expectations for Dad's condition. He had suffered a major health setback with this stroke. Resuscitation would only bring him back in worse shape. We had discussed this with our parents before, and we felt we had a pretty good idea when "enough was enough." We all must die at some point, and if it appears that it is time, then we shouldn't fight the inevitable. But we felt that even taking all of that into consideration, we were still not at this point. He wasn't dying yet.

Even tube feeding and hydration has its limitations. We understood that as death approaches, and the body begins to shut down, food and water cannot be processed by it. It causes more pain than comfort. But Dad didn't appear to be in his final hours. So my father was shipped off, once again, to another hospital, to have the feeding tube reinserted.

Another Hospital, Another Nursing Home

At the second hospital, there was a much better nurse-to-patient ratio. But even with this, my father suffered from a worsening problem of skin made raw and bleeding owing to the apparent infrequency of his diaper being changed. This was obviously a cause of discomfort for him. At the same time, the doctor also cut back on his sedation, explaining that sometimes patients can be more agitated if left on heavy drug treatment for long periods.

This was the first time we began to see what appeared to be a little improvement in Dad's responsiveness. Although the doctors had predicted otherwise, my father briefly communicated with us. He seemed to be attempting to read a sign on a wall opposite his bed. He counted out loud, apparently measuring how well his brain was working once we explained to him about his recent stroke. When my sister whistled to him from the doorway, he turned and commented: "Oh, are you still here?" And when my mother entered the room, he blew kisses in her direction. For a very brief moment during the whole miserable period, Dad seemed to be his old self again. But it was not meant to last. After his short stay at this hospital, it was time to find another nursing home again. With this final transfer to another facility, Dad appeared to lose ground rapidly.

Into the Valley of Death

It was also at the second hospital that they discovered that the first feeding tube had been placed improperly, going through a portion of the intestine before entering the stomach. This might explain some of Dad's agitation. The tube probably formed a blockage in the intestine, causing my father a good deal of pain, prompting him to yank out the feeding tube. A nurse then tried to place a temporary tube in the original opening. His abdomen began to swell, followed by constant attacks of diarrhea. We later surmised that the temporary tube never reached its proper destination in the stomach, having been placed only as far as the entrance into the intestine. Even after making a new incision for the second tube, the old sight probably continued to cause a problem.

In this second nursing home, during the final three days of his life, the food from the tube backed up from the intestine into the stomach, causing vomiting. He aspirated some of this into his lungs, causing a final bout of pneumonia. Death followed a long day of pain, the cause of the pain remaining undiagnosed. His final physician, a weekend substitute who never saw my father, gave directions by phone to the nurses and medics attending Dad. The doctor increased the dosage of painkiller. When we left him around 11 p.m., he seemed to be resting peacefully. Nevertheless, the call came at 1 a.m., after we had spent a long day by his side. The attending nurse observed that he had taken four deep breaths and then expired. The struggle was over for him, and for his beleaguered family.

My father's death certificate indicated that the pneumonia was the primary cause of his dying, with the misplacement of the stomach tube listed as a contributing factor.

In the aftermath, complete peace of mind has been hard to come by. We collectively felt that the system failed Dad when he needed it most. We were not asking for a cure, but for simple comfort care. For all the medical expertise available, this seemed an elusive goal.

A Call to Recognize an Ailing System

In retelling this story, it is not my purpose to condemn medicine or those who practice it. We still have an excellent health care system in this country, far better than other countries. But the emphasis in the U.S. seems focused more on the financial aspects of medicine rather than on caring for the sick and vulnerable in our society.

It is also very apparent that knowledge of treatment for end-of-life care is an area sadly lacking among most of our health care professionals. From a technical standpoint as far as finding cures go, we are advancing steadily in our ability to cure many diseases. But the most basic knowledge of pain control and palliative care for those suffering acute or life-threatening illness is an area where we fail more often than not in treatment.

To their credit, more and more professionals in the medical community admit to this deficiency in their knowledge. The American Medical Association has sponsored a series of classes for their membership all over the country to provide continuing education on these areas of concern—pain management, palliative care issues, better communication between doctors and patients, end-of-life care, hospice, and care directives. There is an increasing awareness that this is an important missing link in helping to prevent "physician-assisted suicide" as a solution for the dying. Hospice is the one hopeful presence on this front. It would be good to examine how best we can utilize the wisdom and experience gained by this outreach to the terminally ill. Possibly hospice care could be extended to those who are not yet in the dying process. At least the option might be taken under consideration until the rest of the medical profession advances in knowledge of both pain control and comfort care for seriously ill or dying patients.

With Oregon's assisted suicide law in place, we are becoming increasingly more pragmatic toward dealing with care for the elderly or those suffering long-term illness. The effect of sanctioning this "final solution" has led to a discussion of extending such assisted suicide treatment to those who are not terminally ill. We can point to the Netherlands as an example of where this sort of thinking leads. It was recently reported that, of the 130,000 Dutch people who have died there on a yearly basis, about 25,000 lives are terminated through direct or indirect euthanasia. One-fourth of the practicing physicians in Holland have reported that they have ended a patient's life, with or without his or her knowledge or approval. Widespread fear of physicians and hospitals is becoming increasingly obvious as 10,000 Dutch citizens carry wallet cards stating that they do not wish to be euthanized.

In talking with others about my family's experience, it is apparent that treatment of older people "who will die soon anyway" causes a reluctance in the medical community to test or treat the elderly aggressively or even adequately. This reticence in treating ailing older adults—whether they are suffering a life-threatening illness or not—leaves an impression that the health care establishment isn't particularly interested in caring for these people.

We are fostering a world which encourages giving up on anyone whose apparent "quality of life" does not measure up to prevailing standards. Such underlying notions—combined with hospital and nursing facilities which espouse using fewer staff, or less-trained staff, in order to cut costs, or prematurely discharging patients in order to retain more insurance-paid fees—only lead me to believe that it will become increasingly more risky to either work in, or be a patient in, our medical institutions.

Health Care Alert

Patient rights. Medical ethics hails involvement by patients and their families as an improvement over the more paternalistic mentality of the past—where the doctor's decision was considered sacred in determining treatment protocol. However, this new concept of rights can be fraught with problems and complications. Rights theory for the patient revolves around the notion of "informed consent." This means that the patient and/or family member has a right to make decisions concerning health care once they are told by the physician, in understandable language, what the prognosis is, and what options are available. This seems reasonable enough, except that it assumes the following:

- The patient or family member either understands what is being said, or feels comfortable in asking questions of the doctor;

- The physician takes the time to explain everything completely, and is not attempting to sway the decision in a certain direction by either giving incomplete, or incorrect, information;

- The patient or family member is truly competent in making a decision—meaning that they are neither too ill nor too depressed to understand the choices presented;

- There is no stress applied to make a hasty decision, or one that favors the wishes of the physician, the family, or the medical insurer over the desire or need of the patient;

- The patient doesn't live in Oregon where "assisted suicide" is an inexpensive and permanent solution to all one's health care problems.

"Informed consent" can be a rather elusive goal when ill patients or traumatized family members are consulted about medical decisions. Add to this the recent cost-cutting measures by providers, and patient rights become an endangered theory.

Prematurely discharging patients. This practice arose out of the creation of the DRG (diagnosis-related group). Established in the 1970s, the DRG was designed for use by reimbursement agencies, such as Medicare. It is "a system of classifying patients according to diagnosis, length of hospital stay and therapy received," as the literature states. Instead of depending on after-the-fact reimbursement, it is a prospective payment system (PPS) which revolves around a pre-existing classification and payment schedule of diseases and patient recuperation time. A hospital is allotted a certain amount of money for each patient according to the DRG profile, which is not affected by the actual length of time the treatment takes for the particular patient. By discharging patients early, and therefore reducing outlay of expense, the hospital retains more of the pre-set payment it will receive for each patient's stay. Because this is often a truly premature discharge, the patient is readmitted soon after to complete treatment, for which the hospital will receive another DRG-based payment.

Keeping your doctor once you transfer to a nursing facility. Doctors do not generally visit every nursing facility in the area, especially if there are many such facilities. In some cases, these doctors—besides visiting their own patients in the nursing home—may also visit other patients whose personal physicians no longer see them. They may also function as medical directors of one or more nursing centers. Nursing home staff report that patients are lucky if they see their doctors more often than once a month. The less scrupulous visiting physicians may do nothing more than wave from the doorway of a patient's room, or glance at a chart and leave.

Cutbacks in nursing staff. Cost-cutting measures in health care have recently favored reducing the numbers of RNs in hospitals and nursing homes, using instead LPNs or the even lesser trained aides and "patient care assistants" who do the work once performed by more extensively-trained registered nurses. This leaves patients short-changed, as far as quality of care goes, and puts them at higher risk for mistakes or undiagnosed problems going unchecked. The more training nurses have, the more likely they will detect health problems in their patients early, averting serious, expensive setbacks for both patient and hospital.

There has been an overall downsizing in not only nursing personnel at hospitals and nursing facilities but in other clinical staff as well. This reduction in employees means fewer medical staff per patient in general, which leaves remaining personnel stressed out and overworked. This is not good for the patients, the staff, or the anxiety level of the public toward the increasing signs of decline in health care delivery in this country.

—by Elenor K. Schoen

Elenor K. Schoen is the Associate Editor of *HUMAN LIFE News* and Director of Publications and Research. HUMAN LIFE of Washington is a nonprofit, pro-life educational organization.

Chapter 16

Gender Differences in Coping with Life-Threatening Disease

Coping has emerged over the past several decades as an important variable influencing the outcomes of difficult life situations. Research has been directed not only toward identifying the infinite ways in which individuals cope with life situations, but also toward identifying factors that influence coping strategies used, and the effectiveness of such strategies in managing the demands of a situation. The context within which coping occurs is considered to be extremely important in understanding coping responses[1]. Accordingly, coping can, and should, be expected to vary depending on the context in which the coping response occurs. A context of particular interest to social scientists and health care researchers is the experience of coping with chronic and life-threatening illness. Knowledge of how individuals deal with the demands of such illnesses should contribute to the understanding of diverse responses to illness and to the development of interventions to help individuals cope more effectively with illness and its consequences.

Although a growing body of research on coping with chronic or life-threatening illness has emerged, very little of this research has focused

Excerpted from "Coping Strategies Used by HIV Infected Women," by Alice Demi, D.N.S., F.A.A.N.; Linda Moneyham, D.N.S.; Richard Sowell, P.h.D., F.A.A.N.; and Leland Cohen, Ph.D., in *Omega: Journal of Death and Dying,* Vol. 35, No. 4, pp. 377-91, 1997. Funded by the Centers for Disease Control and Prevention Cooperative Agreement # U64/CCU408293. © 1997 by Baywood Publishing Co., Inc., 26 Austin Ave., Amityville, NY 11701. Reprinted with permission.

on the context of HIV/AIDS. The few studies that address coping with HIV infection have tended to focus on either gay/bisexual males or intravenous drug users (IVDU)[2-13]. Much less attention has been directed toward studying the coping responses of HIV infected women; in fact, only one published study was found that focused on coping responses of HIV infected women, and that study focused on women with identified psychiatric illness[14]. This disparity in attention is not surprising since, until recently, the rate of HIV infection among women was extremely low, and was confined primarily to IV drug users and sex partners of IV drug users[15]. Currently, however, more attention is directed to women in general since women are now one of the fastest growing subgroups among those infected with HIV[16].

Research related to coping in general, and research related specifically to gay/bisexual males' coping with HIV may not be relevant to women who are infected with HIV, because of the different contexts within which they experience their illness. Factors that affect the context of women's experiences with HIV include not only the stigma and fear of contagion associated with the disease (as is experienced by all HIV infected persons) but also the factors associated with being a woman and with the women's socioeconomic status. HIV infected women tend to be of minority status, to live in poverty, to have limited education, to be single heads of households, and to have young dependent children[17,18].

Background

While earlier conceptualizations of coping defined coping in terms of traits or general dispositions with cross situational stability[19-21], more recent conceptualizations of coping responses recognize coping as being specific to the context in which the coping occurs[1,22,23]. Research has demonstrated that individual coping responses vary significantly across and within situations and that coping also changes as the nature of the stressful encounter changes over time [24-27]. There is also evidence that individuals employ a variety of coping strategies simultaneously in order to deal with a stressful situation[24], and that coping effectiveness is a function of the appropriateness, or fit, of the strategies used with respect to the demands of the situation[1].

To date, a major portion of the work on coping has focused on creating a typology of various coping responses and developing valid measures of coping responses. A number of typologies are evident in the coping measures which have been developed. One of the more popular measures is Lazarus and Folkman's Ways of Coping which conceptualizes coping as being of two major types[1]: 1)problem-focused coping which is focused toward the prevention or management of the situation causing the distress; and 2) emotion-focused coping which is focused toward managing and regulating emotional distress arising from the situation. In studies of the factor structure of the Ways of Coping scale two forms of problem-focused coping (confrontive coping and planful problem solving) and six forms of emotion-focused coping (distancing, escape-avoidance, accepting responsibility, self-control, seeking social support, and positive reappraisal) were identified[25,27,28]. A major criticism of this measure of coping is that validation was carried out primarily with healthy middle class adults and college students [24,25,27]. While there is consistent evidence of reliability for the scale, factor analysis of the dimensional structure of the scale revealed that the factor structure, as well as items comprising each factor, varied somewhat across studies and populations.

Billings and Moos[29,30] identified two major categories of coping similar to those identified by Lazarus and Folkman[1]: 1) approach coping which includes both cognitive and behavioral strategies aimed at dealing directly with the problem; and 2) avoidance coping which includes strategies aimed at managing stress symptoms by avoidance of the problem. Pearlin and Schooler developed a similar conceptualization of coping and identified three major categories of coping [22]: 1) responses directed toward modifying the situation; 2) responses directed toward controlling the meaning of the situation; and 3) responses directed toward controlling stress symptoms.

Another conceptualization of coping was developed by Jalowiec, Murphy, and Powers[31]. Although they originally included only problem-oriented and affective-oriented coping categories in their measure of coping, after testing their scale they found that coping is more multidimensional than the problem-oriented/affective-oriented categories conceptualized by previous researchers. Consequently, Jalowiec revised the scale so that it included eight dimensions of coping: confrontive; evasive; optimistic; fatalistic; emotive; palliative; supportant; and self-reliant[32].

The ongoing work on coping suggests that coping is much more complex than originally thought, with numerous types of coping strategies and subcategories possible. The number of potential subcategories of coping appears to be infinite, and it seems almost impossible to identify one typology that can capture all possible strategies relevant for the myriad contexts in which coping occurs. The context of chronic and life-threatening illness may require coping strategies not reflected in the major categories of coping identified so far. The findings of studies that have examined coping effectiveness in the context of chronic illness suggest that some coping strategies are more effective in maintaining health and a sense of well-being than others. Repeatedly, avoidance coping strategies have been found to be ineffective in coping with chronic illness[33-36]. Likewise, emotion-focused forms of coping have been shown to be related to poor adjustment to chronic illness[37-40]. In contrast, other strategies such as cognitive restructuring[39], information seeking[39], problem orientation[40-42], positive thinking[43], confronting and maintaining control[40,44,45], optimism[13,40,44], and level of hope[45] have been shown to support adaptation to chronic illness.

Studies indicate that HIV infected men use a variety of coping strategies, some of which are not clearly explicated in commonly used coping typologies. A study of long-term survivors of AIDS[46] revealed strategies including denial, vigilance regarding health care, and multiple other cognitive and behavioral strategies. Another study found that HIV positive gay men cope with the threat of AIDS by developing a fighting spirit, using refraining, planning a course of action, and seeking social support[48]. Although the research on the coping with HIV is limited, findings tend to suggest that coping styles are related to well-being. For example, an active coping style was associated with natural killer cell cytotoxicity in asymptomatic HIV positive gay men[4], while helpless avoidance coping was related to psychological distress[3]. A study comparing the coping strategies of HIV positive and HIV negative gay and bisexual men found that HIV positive men used positive attitudes and avoidance of AIDS significantly more than HIV negative men, and that HIV positive men used more coping strategies than HIV negative men[5].

The one study of HIV infected women by Commerford and associates compared coping strategies of fifteen women IVDU with fourteen non-IVDU, all of whom were patients at a psychiatric clinic, and found no difference in coping strategies[14]. Furthermore none of the coping strategies were related to a decrease in depression or anxiety. These findings may be the result of the small sample size or the select nature of the participants: all were experiencing severe psychiatric distress, and their ability to cope was overwhelmed.

The review of the literature revealed a major gap in knowledge about the coping responses of women infected with HIV. The instruments commonly used to study coping have been validated on white, middle income, well educated, healthy, men and women, who are very different from the people who were the target of this study—minority, low income, women with limited education, and having a life-threatening disease. Since coping is believed to be context specific, it is likely that the instruments developed for other groups and other stressful events would not be valid or reliable for this group. Thus, the purpose of this study was to describe the coping strategies used by women to deal with the experience of being infected with HIV and to develop a typology of coping strategies relevant to this population.

Methods

Sample

The sample of 264 HIV infected women was recruited from eight AIDS/HIV treatment sites serving both urban and non-urban clients in a southeastern state over a fourteen-month period in 1993-94. Participants were recruited by female research assistants who had training in recruitment and interview techniques. Criteria for selection of the participants included: 1) age fifteen or older; 2) verified HIV positive status (by HIV sero-testing); 3) English speaking; and 4) no evidence of dementia (as reported by medical care provider at HIV clinic). Sampling resulted in 185 (70%) participants from urban areas, and seventy-nine (30%) participants from non-urban areas. Participants ranged in age from fifteen to sixty-four years of age, with a mean age of thirty-four. The majority were African Americans (82%). Although 41 percent of the participants had not graduated from high school, 34 percent held a high school diploma, and 25 percent had some post-secondary education. While the majority of the participants had children (82%), only 25 percent were married or living with a partner. Household income was under $10,000 for seventy percent of the participants; 10 percent reported incomes over $20,000. Only 21 percent were employed in paid jobs. The demographic characteristics of the sample reflected the demographic characteristics of the public health clinic population from which the majority of the sample was drawn.

Measurement

The questions about coping were included in a semi-structured interview which covered a variety of topics related to stressors, resistance factors, and adaptational outcomes. Interviews generally lasted from one to two hours. The women were paid $30.00 for the interview. The following questions were asked to elicit participants' coping strategies: "How have you been dealing with being HIV positive?" and "What is most helpful to you in dealing with being HIV positive?"

Content analysis was used to analyze and interpret the verbatim data. Two of the investigators with expertise in coping theory independently coded the individual items and identified major categories of coping. After independently reviewing the data, the investigators met to compare categorizations and create a coding schema. Three investigators, including the two who developed the coding schema, independently coded the data according to the established categories. Agreement between at least two of the three coders was required to retain an item in a category.

Findings

In response to each of the two questions, many of the participants reported more than one coping strategy. In these instances, each coping strategy was bracketed by panel members and categorized independently. A total of 663 items were identified; eighty-six of these items were not codable as coping strategies, such as "I'm coping real well" or "I'm not dealing with this at all." The remaining 577 items were coded into eight categories: seeking/using support, spirituality, avoidance/denial, managing the illness/promoting health, focusing on the here and now, positive thinking, focusing on others, and information seeking. At least two of the three panel members agreed with the coding of 516 items, for an agreement rate of 89.4 percent. The coping categories are described in detail in the following section. The number of items in each category is listed in Table 16.1.

Seeking/Using Support

Seeking/using support was the most commonly reported coping strategy; 163 items (31.6%) were coded into this category. This category consisted of strategies to solicit emotional and instrumental support from various groups of people including two major groups: 1) close significant others such as family and friends; and 2) others from whom they sought HIV-specific support such as health care professionals and others with HIV.

Seeking/using support from significant others consisted of five major strategies: 1) talking to others; 2) seeking love, caring, and a feeling of emotional closeness; 3) seeking acceptance; 4) being with others; and 5) seeking instrumental support. The most commonly stated strategy was talking to trusted significant others about being HIV positive or about their concerns related to their illness; the next most commonly stated strategy was seeking demonstrations of love and caring by others. Participants also sought demonstrations of acceptance from others. Many reported that just being in the presence of significant others was helpful to them and gave them strength and the ability to go on. Seeking instrumental support consisted of seeking financial assistance or help with specific tasks or problems. HIV specific support involved seeking out opportunities to interact with others with HIV infection, sharing commonalities in dealing with the disease, and attending support group meetings.

Examples of seeking/using support of significant others include: "I go to my family for emotional support"; "I ask my family for help"; and "I spend time with friends who love and care for me." Examples of seeking/using support of other HIV infected persons include: "I seek out people who are dealing with the same problem"; and "I listen to other people talk about how they cope with HIV."

Spirituality

Spirituality was the second most commonly reported coping strategy with ninety-five items (18.4%) coded into this category. Many stated specifically that God or the Lord helped them cope, while a few stated that Jesus was the one who helped them. Some who used this

Table 16.1. Coping Categories and Number and Percent of Items Coded in Each Category[a]

Category	No. of Items	Percent
Seeking/using support	163	31.6
Spirituality	95	18.4
Avoidance	81	15.6
Focusing on here and now	46	8.9
Managing the illness/promoting health	46	8.9
Positive thinking	38	7.4
Focusing on others	24	4.7
Information seeking	23	4.5
Total	**516**	**100.0**

[a]*Number of participants was 264; some participants reported more than one coping strategy.*

coping mechanism reported that they "put it in the hands of the Lord" and this relieved them of the need to deal with it in other ways. Bible reading and church attendance were reported by a few participants. Examples of spirituality based coping included: "Talking to the Lord about it helps"; "I put my HIV in the hands of the Almighty"; "I read the Bible a lot and go to church"; and "I just pray a lot."

Avoidance/Denial

The third most common coping strategy was avoidance/denial with eighty-one items (15.6%) coded into this category. The avoidance/denial coping category consisted of both cognitive and behavioral strategies for coping with their HIV infection.

Avoidance consisted of five strategies: control of thoughts, control of cues, control of information, distraction, and normalizing. Avoidance ranged from passive avoidance by keeping busy and productive to active attempts to avoid all thoughts and reminders of the illness. Control of thoughts was used to avoid thinking about or worrying about HIV, while control of cues was used to avoid people, situations, or other triggers that reminded them that they were infected with HIV, and control of information was used to conceal their HIV status. Distraction served to redirect thoughts from their HIV infection to other people or other activities. A common distraction strategy was keeping busy. Another type of distraction strategy was the use of alcohol or drugs to block out thoughts about their illness. Normalizing was evident in the participants' efforts to carry on their lives as if nothing was wrong with them, and to live life as they had prior to diagnosis of HIV. Examples of avoidance include: "I try to get into things that are active and time consuming"; "I stay busy"; and "I try to live my life as if there is nothing wrong with me." Examples of information control included: "I try to stay clear of people"; and "I felt like I could not tell anyone."

Denial consisted of two related strategies: 1) denial of the existence of their illness; and 2) denial of the impact of the illness on their lives. Denial strategies were intricately intertwined with avoidance strategies, and often existed concurrently. Denial ranged from the participant's total refusal to believe she was infected with HIV to minimizing the impact of the illness on herself, either presently or in the future. Denial included feelings of disbelief, doubt, and skepticism about the illness. Examples of denial included: "I tried all I could to believe it was a lie"; and "I go through stages of thinking it is something else, for example, Lupus."

Managing the Illness

Forty-six items (8.9%) were coded as managing the illness and included such strategies as practicing healthy habits, avoiding bad habits (such as using drugs or alcohol, or engaging in unsafe sex), seeking and obtaining medical care, complying with their medical regimen or taking an active part in their medical regimen. The participants' level of involvement in managing the illness varied from minor changes in habits to major life-style changes. Examples of managing the illness included: "I am taking my care serious"; "I don't drink or do drugs since I found out"; "I live and eat right"; and "going to the doctor."

Focusing on the Here and Now

Focusing on the here and now was evident in forty-six (8.9%) items. Here and now focused coping included strategies that ranged from plodding along and taking it one day at a time to living as fully as possible in their remaining time. Examples of this strategy included: "I take it one day at a time"; "I take mornings as they come and nights as they fall"; and "I'm living each day as if it was my last here on earth."

Positive Thinking

Positive thinking was evident in thirty-eight items (7.4%). Positive thinking as a coping strategy was expressed consistently in very similar ways that indicated an effort to look at the bright side of things, and to reframe attitudes from negative perspectives to positive ones. Examples of this strategy included: "I have a positive outlook"; "I keep a good frame of mind"; "I live with it positively." Some stated there was nothing they could do other than to think positively. Others indicated that they made conscious efforts to reframe their thoughts from a negative to a positive outlook. The emphasis in this category was on the women's thought processes as a coping strategy.

Focusing on Others

Focusing on others was a less frequently reported coping strategy and was evident in twenty-four items (4.7%). Focusing on others as a coping strategy included directing their attention to others through providing care to family members or to others whom they perceived as less fortunate than themselves and finding meaning in life through responsibility for the care of others. Examples of this strategy included: "I think about my kids more than myself"; "Feeling that I am helping someone else helps me to feel good about myself"; "I concentrate on my family"; and "I take care of others and don't think about myself."

Information Seeking

Twenty-three items (3.5%) were coded as information seeking and included active attempts to gain knowledge about HIV infection, its treatment, and how others coped with the illness. Such strategies included asking questions of health care professionals and others, reading HIV related material, attending educational programs, and watching talk shows that dealt with HIV. Examples of this strategy included: "I try to stay informed and up to date about it"; "I ask lots of questions"; "I read all I can about it"; and "I educate myself."

Participants' Most Frequently Reported Coping Strategies

The responses of participants were reviewed to identify the most commonly used coping strategies. The analysis by participants' responses followed the same pattern as the analysis by items, with Seeking/Using Support being the most commonly used strategy, with 51.5 percent of the women reporting using this strategy, followed in descending order by Spirituality, Avoidance/Denial, Focusing on the Here and Now, Managing the Illness/Promoting Health, Positive Thinking, Focusing on Others, and Information Seeking (see Table 16.2.).

Table 16.2. Coping Strategies and Number and Percent of Participants Reporting Use of Each Strategy

Strategy	No. of Participants[a]	%
Seeking/using support	136	51.5
Spirituality	91	34.5
Avoidance/denial	74	28.0
Focusing on here and now	60	22.7
Managing the illness/promoting health	41	15.5
Positive thinking	36	13.6
Focusing on others	28	10.6
Information seeking	16	6.0

[a]The number of participants was 264. Some participants reported more than one coping strategy.

Discussion

Our findings indicate that HIV infected women employ a variety of coping strategies to deal with the various manifestations of the disease and the effect that it has on their lives. However, it is difficult to compare the coping strategies of the women in this study with the coping strategies of PWAs in other studies because of the diverse methods and instruments used to assess coping, and the varying conceptualizations of coping strategies. For example, Folkman, et al., used a shortened version of the Ways of Coping Scale, and the categories traditionally associated with this scale: self-controlling, cognitive escape-avoidance, behavioral escape-avoidance, distancing, planful problem solving, seeking social support, and positive reappraisal[12]. Taylor and associates used a scale derived from Lazarus' Ways of Coping Scale and, through factor analysis, identified five coping strategies used by HIV positive and negative men to cope with AIDS or the threat of AIDS; positive attitude, personal growth/helping others, seeking social support, fatalism, and avoidance of AIDS[5]. Reed and associates also used an adaptation of the Ways of Coping Scale and identified six coping strategies: community involvement/ spiritual growth, active cognitive coping, avoidance and self-blame, seeking social support, realistic acceptance, and seeking information[49]. Fleishman developed a simple three variable categorization: avoidance coping, positive coping, and seeking social support[3].

Several researchers used qualitative approaches to assess coping strategies of PWAs. Jue identified numerous coping strategies that long-term AIDS survivors utilized: social support, positive attitude, humor, remaining active, seeking information, practicing healthy habits, being assertive, psychotherapy, and spirituality[50]. McCain and Gramling identified three coping processes: living with dying, fighting the sickness, and getting worn out[51].

In general, the coping strategies identified in this study are similar to the coping strategies reported in other studies of HIV infected people, despite the use of diverse data collection instruments and methods. For example, avoidance/denial was reported in numerous studies[3,5,9,36,47,49], as was seeking/using social support[3,48,9]. Other strategies such as focusing on the here and now[51,52], positive thinking[5,52], information seeking[52], and managing the illness[52] were reported less often.

In this study spirituality was the second most commonly reported coping strategy. Interestingly, only two previous studies of coping with HIV infection specifically identified spirituality as a coping strategy[49,51]. This difference between the findings of previous studies of coping with HIV and this study may be because the participants in this study were primarily African-American women who were from a southern state; other research has shown that in the southern United States and particularly in African-American households, religion and spirituality are strongly emphasized[53]. Another explanation for this finding may be that in other studies spirituality items were placed in other categories.

Surprisingly, what was not seen in this study was the fighting spirit reported by several authors in studies of HIV infected men[48,51]. These women managed their illness and promoted their health through their daily activities; they did not report these actions in a way that indicated a fighting spirit or an overwhelming vigilance about their health care, but rather demonstrated an ongoing commitment to follow their medical regime and to do whatever they could to maintain their health.

A coping strategy relatively unique to this study was Focusing on Others. This difference may be related to the fact that all of the participants were women, and women have traditionally focused more on caring for others than caring for themselves, often to the neglect of themselves [54]. Women have learned from early childhood that they are to be the care providers, and they are often rewarded for this behavior. Thus, focusing on others has been incorporated into a characteristic and automatic coping strategy.

Limitations

Some limitations of the present study should be noted. The women who participated in the study were largely African American with low incomes. The overwhelming majority received their health care at public health clinics in a Southern state. Thus these women may not be representative of women from different ethnic groups, or other economic classes, or other areas of the country, or of women who received health care from the private sector, or women who were not in the health care system at all.

Another limitation of the study was that the methodology required conscious recall of coping strategies; the strategies elicited were perhaps those the women were most consciously aware of and those they used most frequently. However, it is likely that they used many other coping strategies, some that they did not recall at the moment they were interviewed, and others that they were not consciously aware that they used. Further, it is likely that more verbal women reported more coping strategies than less verbal women. While the methodology may not have tapped the full scope of coping strategies, nevertheless, the findings shed light on the most commonly recalled conscious strategies.

Directions for Research

Additional information is needed about coping strategies used by HIV infected women to manage their illness. Important questions to consider are the following. What coping strategies are related to outcomes? Are different coping strategies used at different stages of the illness? Do coping strategies change over time as the disease progresses? Does urban or rural residence influence the coping strategies used? Does age influence the coping strategies used? The findings of this study were used to develop a structured questionnaire which has been tested and is currently being used to address those questions.

Summary

The major contribution of this study is in the explication of salient, yet little recognized differences in the coping strategies used by men and women facing a similar chronic and life-threatening illness. Understanding the diversity in coping strategies may be useful in planning interventions to help women cope more effectively with HIV infection and the effects it has on their lives. Further research is necessary to determine whether some coping strategies are more effective in coping with HIV infection, and whether some strategies are more effective at various points in the continuum of illness.

References

1. R. S. Lazarus and S. Folkman, *Stress and Coping,* Springer, New York, 1984.

2. W. L. Earl, C. J. Martindale, and D. Cohn, Adjustment: Denial in the Styles of Coping with HIV Infection, *Omega: Journal of Death and Dying,* 24:1, pp. 35-47, 1991-92.

3. J. A. Fleishman and B. Fogel, Coping and Depressive Symptoms among People with AIDS, *Health Psychology* 13:2, pp. 156-169, 1994.

4. K. Goodkin, N. Blaney, D. Feaster, M. Fletcher, et al., Active Coping Style Is Associated with Natural Killer Cell Cytotoxicity in Asymptomatic HIV-1 Seropositive Homosexual Males, *Journal of Psychosomatic Research,* 36, pp. 635-650, 1992.

5. S. E. Taylor, M. E. Kemeny, L. G. Aspinwall, S. G. Schneider, R. Rodriguez, and M.Herbert, Optimism, Coping, Psychological Distress, and High-Risk Sexual Behavior among Men at Risk for Acquired Immunodeficiency Syndrome (AIDS), *Journal of Personality and Social Psychology* 63:3, pp. 460-473, 1992.

6. S. E. Taylor, M. E. Kemeny, S. G. Schneider, and L. G. Aspinwall, Coping with the Threat of AIDS, in *The Social Psychology of HIV Infection,* J. B. Pryor and G. D. Reeder (eds.), Lawrence Erlbaum Associates, Hillsdale, New Jersey, pp. 305-332, 1993.

7. T. M. Wolf, P. M. Balson, E. V. Morse, P. M. Simon, et al., Relationship of Coping Style to Affective State and Perceived Social Support in Asymptomatic and Symptomatic HIV-Infected Persons: Implications for Clinical Management, *Journal of Clinical Psychology,* 52, pp. 171-173, 1991.

8. T. M. Wolf, P. W. Dralle, E. V. Morse, P. M. Simon, et al., A Biopsychosocial Examination of Symptomatic and Asymptomatic HIV-Infected Patients, *International Journal of Psychiatry in Medicine,* 21, pp. 263-279, 1991.

9. L. A. Kurdek and G. Siesky, The Nature and Correlates of Psychological Adjustment in Gay Men with AIDS-Related Conditions, *Journal of Applied Social Psychology,* 20, pp. 846-860, 1990.

10. S. S. Swartzberg, Vitality and Growth in HIV-Infected Gay Men, *Social Science and Medicine,* 38, pp. 593-602, 1994.

11. D. J. Martin, Coping with AIDS and AIDS-Risk Reduction Efforts among Gay Men, *AIDS Education and Prevention,* 5, pp. 104-120, 1993.

12. S. Folkman, M. Chesney, L. Pollack, and T. Coates, Stress, Control, Coping and Depressive Mood in Human Immunodeficiency Virus Positive and Negative Gay Men in San Francisco, *Journal of Nervous and Mental Disorders,* 181, pp. 409-416. 1993.

13. K. I. Pakenham, M. R. Dadds, and D. J. Terry, Relationships between Adjustment to HIV and Both Social Support and Coping, *Journal of Consulting and Clinical Psychology,* 62, pp. 1,194-1,203, 1994.

14. M. C. Commerford, E. Gular, D. A. Orr, and M. Reznikoff, Coping and Psychological Distress in Women with HIV/AIDS, *Journal of Community Psychology,* 22, pp. 224-230, 1994.

15. Centers for Disease Control and Prevention, *HIV/AIDS Surveillance Report: Year-End Edition,* Author, Atlanta, 1991.

16. Centers for Disease Control and Prevention, *Morbidity and Mortality Weekly Reports,* 44, pp. 8 1-84, 135, 1995.

17. V. T. Shayne and B. J. Kaplan, Double Victims: Poor Women and AIDS, *Women and Health,* 17, pp. 21-37, 1991.

18. M. Pizzi, Women, HIV Infection and AIDS: Tapestries of Life, Death, and Empowerment, *American Journal of Occupational Therapy,* 46, pp. 1,021-1,026, 1992.

19. G. E. Valliant, Natural History of Male Psychological Health, Vol. 5: The Relation of Choice of Ego Mechanisms of Defense to Adult Adjustment, *Archives of General Psychology,* 33, pp. 535-545, 1976.

20. S. M. Miller, When Is a Little Information a Dangerous Thing? Coping with Stressful Events by Monitoring vs. Blunting, in *Coping and Health,* S. Levine and H. Ursine (eds.), Plenum, New York, 1980.

21. H. W. Krohne and J. Rogner, Repression-Sensitization as a Central Construct in Coping Research, in *Achievement, Stress, and Anxiety,* H. W. Krohne and L. Laux (eds.), Hemisphere, Washington, D.C., 1982.

22. L. I. Pearlin and C. Schooler, The Structure of Coping, *Journal of Health & Social Behavior,* 19, pp. 2-21, 1978.

23. A. Jalowicc, *Psychometric Results on the 1987 Jalowiec Coping Scale,* Loyola University, Chicago, 1991.

24. S. Folkman and R. S. Lazarus, An Analysis of Coping in a Middle-Aged Community Sample, *Journal of Health and Social Behavior,* 21, pp. 219-239, 1980.

25. S. Folkman, R. S. Lazarus, C. Dunkel-Schetter, A. DeLongis, and R. Gruen, Dynamics of a Stressful Encounter: Cognitive Appraisal, Coping, and Encounter Outcomes, *Journal of Personality and Social Psychology,* 50, pp. 992-1,003, 1986.

26.   S. Folkman, R. S. Lazarus, R. J. Gruen, and A. DeLongis, Appraisal, Coping, Health Status, and Psychological Symptoms, *Journal of Personality and Social Psychology*, 50, pp. 571-579, 1986.

27.   S. Folkman and R. S. Lazarus, If It Changes It Must be a Process: Study of Emotion and Coping during Three Stages of a College Examination, *Journal of Personality and Social Psychology*, 48, pp. 150-170, 1985.

28.   S. Folkman, R. S. Lazarus, S. Pimley, and J. Novacek, Age Differences in Stress and Coping Processes, *Psychology of Aging*, 2, pp. 171-184, 1987.

29.   A. G. Billings and R. H. Moos, The Role of Coping Responses and Social Resources in Attenuating the Stress of Life Events, *Journal of Behavioral Medicine*, 4, pp. 139-157, 1981.

30.   A. G. Billings and R. H. Moos, Coping, Stress, and Social Resources among Adults with Unipolar Depression, *Journal of Personality and Social Psychology*, 46, pp. 877-891, 1984.

31.   A. Jalowiec, S. P. Murphy, and M. J. Powers, Psychometric Assessment of the Jalowiec Coping Scale, *Nursing Research*, 33, pp. 157-161, 1984.

32.   A. Jalowiec, *The Revised Jalowiec Coping Scale,* unpublished manuscript, Loyola University, Chicago, 1987.

33.   H. Feifel, S. Strack, and V. T. Nagy, Coping Strategies and Associated Features of Chronically Ill Patients, *Psychosomatic Medicine*, 49, pp. 616-625, 1987.

34.   C. D. Sherbourne, L. S. Meredith, W. Rogers, and J. E. Ware, Social Support and Stressful Life Events: Age Differences in Their Effects on Health-Related Quality of Life among the Chronically Ill, *Quality of Life Research*, 1, pp. 235-246, 1992.

35.   N. E. White, J. M. Richter, and C. Fry, Coping, Social Support, and Adaptation to Chronic Illness, *Western Journal of Nursing Research*, 14, pp. 211-224, 1992.

36.   S. Namir, D. L. Wolcott, I. F. Fawzy, and M. J. Alumbaugh, Coping with AIDS: Psychological and Health Implications, *Journal of Applied Social Psychology* 17, pp. 309-328, 1987.

37. M. M. Arklie, The Relationship between Stress, Coping, and Quality of Life in Middle-Aged Adults with a Chronic Illness, *Dissertation Abstracts International,* 50, 8920652B, 1990.

38. C. H. Bombadier, C. D'Amico, and J. S. Jordan, The Relationship of Appraisal and Coping to Chronic Illness Adjustment, *Behavior Research and Therapy,* 28, pp. 297-304, 1990.

39. B. J. Felton, T. A. Revenson, and G. A. Hinrichsen, Stress and Coping in the Explanation of Psychosocial Adjustment among Chronically Ill Adults, *Journal of Social Science and Medicimie,* 18, pp. 889-898, 1984.

40. G. R. Perry, Loneliness and Coping among Tertiary-Level Adult Cancer Patients in the Home, *Cancer Nursing,* 13, pp. 293-302, 1990.

41. I. L. Janis and J. Rodin, Attribution, Control, and Decision-Making: Social Psychology and Health, in *Health Psychology: A Handbook,* G. Stone, F. Cohen, and N. Adler (eds.), Jossey-Bass, San Francisco, pp. 487-531, 1979.

42. J. W. Worden and H. J. Sobel, Ego Strength and Psychosocial Adaptation to Cancer, *Journal of Psychosomatic Medicine,* 40, pp. 585-591, 1978.

43. G. Forsyth, K. Delaney, and M. Gresham, Vying for a Winning Position: Management Styles of the Chronically Ill, *Research in Nursing and Health,* 1, pp. 181-188, 1984.

44. S. Penckofer, A. Jalowiec, N. Fink, and L. Hutson-Danekas, Coping Responses of Coronary Artery Bypass Patients and Their Spouses, *Circulation* (Supplement), 84, p. 11-135, 1991.

45. K. A. Herth, The Relationship between Level of Hope and Level of Coping Response and Other Variables in Patients with Cancer, *Oncology Nursing Forum,* 16, pp. 67-72, 1989.

46. R. H. Remien, J. G. Rabkin, J. B. Williams, and L. Katoff, Coping Strategies and Health Beliefs of AIDS Longterm Survivors, *Journal of Psychology and Health,* 6:4, pp. 335-345, 1992.

47. J. Catalan, I. Klimes, A. Day, A. Garrod, et al., The Psychosocial Impact of HIV Infection in Gay Men: A Controlled Investigation and Factors Associated with Psychiatric Morbidity, *Journal of British Psychology* 161, pp. 774-778, 1992.

48. J. Leserman, D. O. Perkins, and D. L. Evans, Coping with the Threat of AIDS: The Role of Social Support, *American Journal of Psychology,* 149, pp. 1,514-1,520, 1992.

49. G. M. Reed, M. E. Kemeny, S. E. Taylor, H. J. Wang, and B. Visscher, Realistic Acceptance as a Predictor of Decreased Survival Time in Gay Men with AIDS, *Health Psychology,* 13, pp. 299-307, 1994.

50. S. Jue, Psychosocial Issues of AIDS Long-Term Survivors, *Families in Society: The Journal of Contemporary Human Services,* pp. 324-332, June 1994.

51. N. McCain and L. Gramling, Living with Dying: Coping with HIV Disease, *Issues in Mental Health Nursing,* 13, pp. 271-284, 1992.

52. R. Weitz, Uncertainty and the Lives of Persons with AIDS, *Journal of Health and Social Behavior,* 30, pp. 270-281, 1989.

53. R. J. Taylor and L. M. Chatters, Religious Life, in *Life in Black America,* J. S. Jackson (ed.), Sage Publications, Newbury Park, pp. 105-123, 1991.

54. S. Reverby, *Ordered to Care: The Dilemma of American Nursing 1850-1945,* Cambridge University Press, New York, 1987.

— by Alice Demi, D.N.S., F.A.A.N.;
Linda Moneyham, D.N.S.;
Richard Sowell, P.h.D., F.A.A.N.;
and Leland Cohen, Ph.D.

Direct reprint requests to: Alice S. Demi, School of Nursing, Box 4019, Georgia State University, Atlanta, GA 30302-4019.

Chapter 17

Opposing the Legalization of Euthanasia and Assisted Suicide

The National Hospice Organization (NHO) was formed in 1978 to promote the principles and concepts of the hospice program of care for terminally ill patients and their families. Over the past decade, NHO has championed the ideals of relief [from] suffering, freedom of choice, and death with dignity. The nation's hospice programs currently provide compassionate, terminal care to more than 390,000 patients and families each year. NHO's membership includes more than 2,200 hospice programs and more than 4,000 hospice professionals. In November 1996, NHO reaffirmed a resolution rejecting the practice of voluntary euthanasia and assisted suicide. This paper is offered as background information in support of this position.

NHO defines hospice as a coordinated program of palliative medicine and supportive services provided in both the home and inpatient settings that provides for physical, psychological, social, and spiritual care for dying persons and their families. Services are provided by a medically directed, interdisciplinary team of professionals and volunteers. Hospice recognizes dying as part of the normal process of living and focuses on maintaining the quality of remaining life. Hospice affirms life and neither hastens nor postpones death. Hospice exists in the hope and belief that through appropriate care and the promotion

From "Statement of the National Hospice Organization Opposing the Legalization of Euthanasia and Assisted Suicide," [Online]. Available: http://www.nho.org/pasposition.htm. © 1997 by the National Hospice Organization, 1901 N. Moore St., Ste. 901, Arlington, VA 22209. For complete contact information, please refer to Chapter 60, "Resources." Reprinted with permission.

of a caring community sensitive to their needs, patients and families may be free to obtain a degree of mental and spiritual preparation for death.

The concept of hospice care emerged in this country in response to the unmet needs of dying patients and their families for whom traditional medical care was no longer effective, appropriate, or desired. Hospice has become an effective alternative to there being "nothing else to do:"

- Skilled, intensive palliative care controls physical symptoms and facilitates the relief of the psychological, social, spiritual, and financial pain of terminal illness.

- Hospice is unique in its focus on the patient/family as the unit of care.

- Hospice care helps assure patients and families that everything possible has been done to control the patient's disease and its symptoms.

- Hospice care offers respite care for the patient so that the family can be revitalized. Hospice care supports the opportunity for the anticipatory grief work that aids the bereavement process.

- Hospice care continues as bereavement support for the patient's family after the patient's death to normalize their grief so that they may return to leading full and productive lives.

For the purpose of this paper, the term euthanasia will mean an act which intentionally and directly causes a patient's death. This definition of euthanasia encompasses active euthanasia, voluntary euthanasia, aid-in-dying, and in some settings, physician-assisted suicide. The term "assisted suicide" is most commonly used to represent an act in which a patient is given the means and specific instructions to take his or her own life. Withholding or withdrawing life-sustaining therapies or unintentionally hastening death through treatments aimed at controlling symptoms does not constitute either euthanasia or assisted suicide. The purpose of these acts is comfort of the patient, not ending the patient's life; thus these acts neither intentionally nor directly cause a patient's death. The position taken in this paper against the legalization of euthanasia applies to both euthanasia and assisted suicide.

The ethical pitfalls in legalizing euthanasia are evident in all aspects of medical ethics: autonomy, beneficence, justice, and integrity of the health care professional. Patient autonomy/self-determination is the most touted rationale for the legalization of euthanasia. Indeed, patients must have the right to choose their own care. The National Hospice Organization supports a patient's right to choose palliative care and a patient's right to refuse unwanted medical attention including the provision of artificially supplied hydration and nutrition. Patients must be allowed to accept or refuse therapy based on informed consent. Central to all good health care, informed consent implies that the patient has been told of the care alternatives available and of the probable consequences of the choice they make.

One must question whether the choice of euthanasia is fully informed or truly voluntary. The proponents of change in the legal status of these practices often paint a stark picture in which a patient's choice is between painful existence devoid of value on the one hand and voluntary euthanasia or assisted suicide on the other.

Family members, health care providers, and society frequently exert subtle or overt pressures upon terminally ill patients to consent to excessive disease-oriented therapy which can be discontinued should the patient so desire. Terminally ill patients may similarly be pressured to consent to euthanasia if it becomes an acceptable legal option; however, there is no return from the choice of euthanasia.

Physicians have the right and the responsibility to advise patients whether the therapy they request is beneficial. Euthanasia lacks beneficence in many ways. An act which directly kills the patient, by definition, causes the most basic form of medical harm, death. Since its primary effect is death and only secondarily the relief of suffering, euthanasia does not allow for the inaccuracies in diagnosis and prognosis commonly experienced with patients labeled as "terminal." Patients who choose euthanasia rather than aggressive palliative care forfeit the opportunity to correct errors in prognosis or to benefit from skilled, intensive symptom control. Aggressive palliative care can improve the quality and quantity of remaining life. Previously unobtainable goals may become attainable, and some patients can even return to disease-oriented therapy if that is their desire. Euthanasia forecloses these options.

Beyond physical and psychological comfort, spiritual comfort is an important goal of hospice care. Patients who opt for euthanasia may miss the opportunity to transcend their suffering and find meaning in their lives for themselves and their survivors. Patient autonomy should not totally override the beneficence needs of the patient's family and community. Anticipatory grief work, which has value to both patient and family, would be truncated by the expedience of euthanasia.

The request for euthanasia also can aggravate the family's sense of failure to obtain adequate palliative care for their loved one. There is a fine but important distinction between withholding or withdrawing treatments that sustain life and providing treatments that directly end it. The critical issue is the intent or goal of the therapy. Euthanasia is different in kind, not degree, from treatments that allow death to occur or even those which unintentionally hasten it. No patient need die in pain. Although the ideal goal of palliative care is to maximize comfort and function, effective symptom control in some patients causes forfeiture of cognitive function, discontinuation of eating and drinking, suppression of cough reflex, and depression of respiration. These unintended consequences may hasten the death caused by the underlying disease; they do not of themselves directly cause death.

Family members can often use this final period of peaceful, pharmacologically-induced sleep to begin to separate from their loved one in preparation for the time of actual physical death. This type of intensive symptom control is ethically acceptable and distinctly different from the administration of a drug whose primary intent is to end life. Achievement of comfort through intensive symptom control prior to death is less of a burden to the family and the caregivers than having to directly cause death as the only way to relieve the patient's suffering.

Hospice has done much to restore public trust in the health care delivery system. Even in families who fully accept euthanasia as beneficent, having to resort to an act that directly causes death leaves room for corrosive doubt regarding the completeness and expertise of care rendered prior to the request for euthanasia. The very presence of euthanasia as an option can erode trust that the health care delivery system will do everything possible to relieve suffering prior to terminating life. Euthanasia may be offered to patients disguised as the most compassionate care while, in fact, it represents an impersonal act of isolation. Distrust with the health care system already delays initial contact and decreases patient compliance with appropriate medical care leading to increased morbidity and mortality. The maleficence of euthanasia thus encompasses probable harm to the patient, the patient's family, and society at large.

Justice issues of equal access to care and allocation of limited resources apply more to the probable abuse of, rather than to the proposed use of legalized euthanasia. If euthanasia were to be legalized, policies and procedures would have to be enacted to assure ready access to euthanasia services by all interested patients. Such universal access is not yet available for general medical care let alone hospice. Of greater concern is the potential of euthanasia being recommended to those patients whose disease, family system, financial status, or community resources denies them access to appropriate medical care including hospice care. Euthanasia could become a penalty for being too sick, too isolated, or too poor. It is for these reasons that the National Hospice Organization supports improved access to hospice care for terminally ill patients and their families, including those who have expressed a desire for assistance with suicide.

Legalization of euthanasia would also abort ongoing efforts to enhance the quantity and quality of palliative care. The administrative and financial requirements of developing and maintaining euthanasia as a component of the health care delivery system could competitively diminish the support needed to increase access to appropriate health care for the terminally ill. The scientific, ethical, and emotional energy that will be required to establish euthanasia as a safe and effective therapeutic option for the small number of terminally ill patients who might choose it is an unjustifiable drain on the use of that energy to advance the art and science of the more applicable and already proven option of end-of-life care.

The ethical dilemma created for health care professionals caused by legalizing euthanasia is its contradiction with their professional codes and standards. More importantly, even if these standards should change, clinicians have the right to their own beliefs and values. Patients are not the only moral agents in this process. Ethical decisions are bilateral, not unilateral.

Health care professionals traditionally have had the option to transfer patients to another professional's care if the patient requests something with which only the latter professional can comply. If transfer is not possible and the clinical situation is imminently life-threatening, the initial health care professional's autonomy would defer to the patient's. Causing death lacks the moral universality of saving life to justify such deference. It is the health care professional's right and responsibility to refuse to perform procedures which he or she deems will cause more harm than good to the patient, their family, or society.

Legalization of euthanasia would put undue pressure upon physicians, the vast majority of whom oppose euthanasia, to perform an act which they feel is wrong. Merely diagnosing patients as terminal so that they might be eligible for euthanasia, would co-opt a physician's personal opposition to participating in euthanasia.

Beyond the immediate ethical pitfalls mentioned above, legalization of euthanasia has a high risk for over-expansion and corruption resulting in even more personal and social harm. The failure of policies, procedures, rules, and regulations to guarantee the safety and efficacy of the care currently being rendered to terminally ill patients in this country offers little security that proposed administrative "safeguards" will protect the public from such potential dangers.

Provision of euthanasia to competent, terminally ill adults can be expected to be extended to incompetent adults through advance directives. Definitions of terminal illness and unbearable suffering may broaden and stray from the limitations of the current debate. Extending euthanasia to non-terminally ill patients with even vaguer definitions of quality of life engender the specter of the expansion of euthanasia as a cost-effective alternative to rehabilitative or custodial care for the disabled, frail, elderly, and poor.

Laws are symbols of what society values. Legalization of euthanasia would devalue life and would add to the growing decay of social and moral values. Allowing unpreventable death to occur with dignity and comfort is quite different from accepting euthanasia as an expeditious way out of difficult situations for individuals or society.

Hospice is an ethically sound model of compassionate, cost-effective, quality assured, patient/family oriented, terminal care. Hospice must be expanded to reach more eligible patients. Public and professional education must be increased and appropriate reimbursement must be secured. Alternatives to traditional home settings must be created and inpatient care must be expanded to reach patients and families for whom home care will remain impossible.

Through appropriate and timely application, hospice can truly improve the quality of life for all terminally ill patients and their families. Hospice must tell its story loudly and clearly, so that society will know that there are other ways of dealing with the fears that have led to the request for euthanasia. The call for euthanasia is a call for hospice to accelerate its evolution and expand its influence so that all terminally ill patients may live as fully and comfortably as possible.

Part Three

Health Care Options for the Terminally Ill

Chapter 18

Projected Health Conditions among the Elderly

Summary and Implications

During the next 3 to 4 decades, we can expect a very dramatic increase both in the number of elderly persons and in the proportion of elderly persons in the population. Changes in the overall population 65 and over and in the population 65 to 74 years of age will be muted until 2010, but the arrival of the large baby-boom cohorts at age 65 will trigger the large increases in the number and percentage of elderly in the next half century. The record large proportion of elderly persons now in the population, 13 percent, will rise to perhaps 20 percent by the year 2030, and the number of elderly is expected to double by that year. These prospective demographic changes have given rise to a general concern about the social, economic, and physical "health" of our nation's population.

The most rapid increases in the number and share of persons 85 years and over will occur between 2030 and 2050, when the baby-boom cohort reaches these ages. The cumulative growth of the population 85 years and over from 1995 to 2050 is expected to be over 400 percent, and the group should make up nearly 5 percent of the population in 2050 as compared with 1.4 percent today. These figures are

From "Projected Health Conditions Among the Elderly," [Online] January 1997. Available: http://www.aoa.dhhs.gov/stats/aging21/health.html. Produced by the U.S. Department of Health and Human Services, Administration on Aging (AoA). For complete contact information, please refer to Chapter 60, "Resources."

143

drawn from the Bureau of the Census' middle series of projections. Considering the whole range of this set of projections, they essentially encompass the other leading "competitive" projections.

These changes will be brought about mainly by historical and prospective shifts in the number of births, birth rates, and the level and age pattern of death rates. The volume and age pattern of net immigration will be important in affecting the numbers too, but will be secondary in influencing the age distribution, that is, the share of elderly persons in the population.

The rapid growth of the elderly, particularly the oldest old, represents in part a triumph of the efforts to extend human life, but these age groups also require a disproportionately large share of special services and public support. There will be large increases by 2030 in the numbers requiring special services in housing, transportation, recreation, and education, as well as in health and nutrition. There will also be large increases in some very vulnerable groups, such as the oldest old living alone, older women, elderly racial minorities living alone and with no living children, and elderly unmarried persons with no living children and no siblings. These are also groups with high percentages living in poverty or with low incomes. The number of persons requiring formal care (mainly nursing home care) and informal care (mainly care at home) will rise sharply even if the share of persons at each age remains unchanged. Accordingly, there will be a large increase in the numbers participating in various entitlement programs such as Social Security and Medicare.

Living alone presents an additional risk, and the risk mounts when the person living alone has no children or siblings. These characteristics are more common among those 85 years and over as compared with those under age 85. At ages 65 and over only 2 percent of the population have these characteristics in combination, but at ages 85 and over perhaps 6 percent have them.

The outlook for the longevity and health of the elderly is not altogether clear. There will probably be a substantial increase in life expectancy, even at the older ages, but there are also likely to be large increases in the number of persons with poor health and disabilities, including Alzheimer's disease (and in persons requiring nursing home care and home care), if only because of the massive population increases projected to occur. If disability ratios fall sharply or mortality rates at the higher ages rise, or if both occur, the numbers of disabled persons could fall, but this now appears very unlikely.

Accompanying these general changes will be shifts in the racial/ Hispanic composition of the elderly population. As compared with 15 percent today, in 2050, about one-third of the elderly will be other than non-Hispanic white. The rapid growth of these groups, in particular, will "color" the demand for special services. To the extent that these groups have distinctive social and economic characteristics (e.g., living arrangements, number of living children, income, education, and knowledge of English) that affect their risk of requiring formal and informal support, these services may require a different structure and orientation.

Most of the survivors at the highest ages are women and, in particular, widowed women. This will remain the prevailing sex-marital balance because its principal causes (the premature death of men, including married men, and the very low remarriage rates of elderly women) are expected to persist. The imbalance of the sexes and the low percent of married women have been associated with reduced income, greater poverty, poorer health, and greater risk of institutionalization of older women.

The need and cost of support of dependent elderly can be mitigated by substituting home care for nursing home care and family, friends, and neighbors as caregivers for private caregivers; by working energetically to reduce the death rates of married men in mid-life; and in other ways. Some groups in our society have gone further than others in the use of family members, friends, and neighbors as caregivers.

The prospective changes in age structure and in labor force participation will lead to shifts in the balance of nonworkers to workers and, more specifically, the balance of OASDI beneficiaries to covered workers. The latter ratio is expected to increase from 31 beneficiaries per 100 covered workers in 1995 to 51 in 2050. The prospective increase in these balances can be offset by future rises in the birth rate, the volume of immigration, labor force participation ratios, worker productivity, and death rates at the older ages, and by reduced unemployment and underemployment. These are not all likely to occur, or to occur in sufficient degree to obviate the need to deal directly with the demographic and socioeconomic changes associated with aging into the 21st century.

We have noted that, during the next 3 to 4 decades, there will be a very significant increase in the number of elderly persons, particularly the older aged; a sharp increase in the share of elderly persons in the population; and changes in the overall age composition of the elderly population. These changes will be brought about mainly by historical and prospective shifts in birth rates and declines in death rates, particularly at the older ages. Moreover, there will be large increases in the numbers of some very vulnerable groups, such as the

145

oldest old living alone, especially women; elderly racial minorities living alone and with no living children; and unmarried elderly persons with no living children or siblings. We turn now to the specific basis for a large part of the demand for both formal and informal support and special services, namely health conditions among the elderly.

Predicting health conditions is difficult because it requires consideration of prospective developments in medical diagnosis and treatment, in lifestyle and behavior patterns, in community actions related to health, in the health delivery system, in the possibility of the reduction and control of various existing diseases and of the emergence of new diseases, in the state of the economy, and in other related factors.

There is a wide divergence of views held by experts in these areas. An additional difficulty of predicting health conditions among the elderly is the differing approaches in measuring recent changes in morbidity. In this report we choose from the great variety of materials on health projections to present one combination of data on these topics from several sources that we hope will provide reasonable and useful projections in the areas of:

- life expectancy;
- health status;
- disability; and
- nursing home and home care usage

Life Expectancy

First, we consider the expected course of life expectancy at birth and at age 65 underlying the new population projections of the Bureau of the Census (Table 18.1.). The most optimistic series, the high series, posits an increase in life expectancy at birth by 2050 to 86 years for males and 92 years for females. At age 65, the figures are 25 years and 30 years, respectively. These projections imply considerable increases over the current figures of 72.5 and 15.5 for males, and 79.3 and 19.2 for females. The middle series shows smaller, yet substantial, increases to 80 and 20 for males and 84 and 22 for females in life expectancy at birth and at age 65, respectively. Life expectancy at age 85 is also projected to increase, especially in the high series.

The inference that might be drawn from these projections is that there could be much progress in extending the average length of life and that a larger proportion of the population is likely to survive to the very advanced ages. Note that these projections are independent

146

of any assumptions regarding the extension of human life span. Higher life expectancy is expected for blacks and Hispanics as well as whites, but convergence between white and black mortality is not anticipated. The Office of the Actuary of the SSA has published an alternative set of projections of life expectancy for use in cost projections of the Social Security system. They closely resemble those of the Bureau of the Census but are, on the whole, more conservative.

Health Status

For many scholars, as well as the general public, the basic question is: Will people live well during these added years of life or will they be physically dependent on others because of serious health problems? More generally, how healthy will the elderly population be? First, we consider some projections of self-reported health status, which is a simple, yet rather informative measure of health, known to be associated with longevity. Projections of respondent-assessed health status for 2030 were prepared jointly by the University of Illinois at Chicago and the University of Chicago (Table 18.2.). About 10 percent of the elderly reported themselves to be in poor health in 1990. Blacks reported poor health almost twice as often as whites and others. There is a general tendency for the proportion reporting fair or poor health to increase with advancing age. Assuming that essentially the same proportion of each race group falls in each health category in 2030 as in 1990, the numbers of elderly with poor health are projected to increase sharply from 1990 to 2030, paralleling the population increase. From 1.0 to 1.4 million blacks would be in poor health in 2030, implying well over a doubling or even tripling of the number reported in 1990.

Disability

Of critical importance are the number and proportion of our elderly population that will be disabled. We first consider the series of projections of disabled persons prepared by Kunkel and Applebaum (1992). Even when they assume reduced disability ratios, albeit with increased longevity (the high series of life expectancy), the number of disabled persons at all levels of disability would grow rapidly between 1986 and 2040. According to this series of projections, the number of those severely or moderately disabled would more than triple during this period. Even if longevity improves more moderately (middle mortality series) and disability ratios are held constant, the

Table 18.1a. (continued in Table 18.1b.) Life Expectancy at Birth, Age 65, and Age 85, by Sex and Race/Hispanic Origin: 1995 and 2050

(Projections are based on the low, middle, and high series of the U.S. Bureau of the Census.)

Age, Sex, and Race	1995	2050		
		Middle Series	Low Series	High Series
ALL RACES				
Male				
Birth	72.5	79.7	70.9	86.4
65	15.5	20.3	15.3	25.2
85	5.2	6.8	5.2	11.1
Female				
Birth	79.3	84.3	78.8	92.3
65	19.2	22.4	19.1	29.9
85	6.5	9.4	6.6	14.9
WHITE				
Male				
Birth	73.6	82.0	72.4	86.8
65	15.7	21.6	15.8	26.0
Female				
Birth	80.1	85.9	79.9	92.6
65	19.4	23.6	19.6	30.2

Table 18.1b. (Continued from Table 18.1a.) Life Expectancy at Birth, Age 65, and Age 85, by Sex and Race/Hispanic Origin: 1995 and 2050

(Projections are based on the low, middle, and high series of the U.S. Bureau of the Census.)

Age, Sex, and Race	1995	2050		
		Middle Series	**Low Series**	**High Series**
BLACK				
Male				
Birth	64.8	70.8	63.0	81.2
65	13.6	16.5	13.8	21.6
Female				
Birth	74.5	79.7	74.0	89.8
65	17.6	20.3	17.7	27.6
HISPANIC ORIGIN[1]				
Male				
Birth	74.9	84.4	73.1	85.5
65	18.5	25.6	18.4	26.1
Female				
Birth	82.2	89.6	81.7	91.4
65	21.8	27.9	21.7	29.4

SOURCE: U.S. Bureau of the Census (1996a).
[1]Persons of Hispanic origin may be of any race.
Table compiled by the National Aging Information Center

number of disabled persons would nearly triple. Moreover, there is the possibility of a combination of high life expectancy with increased disability ratios. These assumptions result in a massive increase in the projected number of moderately or severely disabled elderly persons by 2040. The number would grow from about 5.1 million in 1986 to 22.6 million in 2040, or nearly 350 percent; the elderly population overall would grow by only 175 percent.

The projections of the population with Activities of Daily Living (ADL) limitations and, among these, the severely disabled, prepared by Manton and Liu on the basis of the 1982 National Long-Term Care

Table 18.2. Self-Reported Health Status of Persons 65 Years and Over, by Race: 1989 to 1991 and 2030

(Numbers in thousands. Projections are based on highest and lowest population series of U.S. Bureau of the Census.)

Series and Year	Excellent, Very Good, or Good Health	Poor Health		
		All Groups	Other than Black	Black
2030				
Lowest Series	41,382	5,488	4,501	987
Highest Series	55,057	7,590	6,223	1,367
Percent of Population	71	10	9	16
1989-1991				
Number	22,359	2,904	2,499	411
Percent of Population	71.6	9.3	8.7	16.4

SOURCE: 2030 data—National Center for Health Statistics, Centers for Disease Control and Prevention, January, 1996. Unpublished study. 1989-91 data—National Center for Health Statistics, National Health Interview Study.

Survey and the 1977 National Nursing Home Survey, represent an alternative set of figures on disability (Table 18.3.). The differences between these figures strongly underline the risk of error in projections of disability, a set of health conditions which are subject to wide interpretation. Manton and Liu projected that there would be 2.8 million severely disabled persons in 2040, whereas the lowest projection of the wide range of projections prepared by Kunkel and Applebaum is 7.6 million. The total from the former source for all persons with ADL limitations in 2040 is 14.4 million, whereas the lowest figure from the latter source for moderate or severe disability

Table 18.3. Projections of the Noninstitutional Population 65 Years and Over with ADL Limitations: 1990 to 2040

(Number in thousands. Based on sample data for past years.)

Year	Number		Percent of Population[1]	
	With ADL Limitations	**Severely Disabled**	**With ADL Limitations**	**Severely Disabled**
1990	6,029	1,123	18.8	3.5
1995	6,712	1,265	19.3	3.6
2000	7,262	1,384	20.0	3.8
2020	10,118	1,927	19.2	3.7
2040	14,416	2,806	21.4	4.2

SOURCE: Calculated on the basis of projections of the U.S. population prepared by the U.S. Social Security Administration and preliminary data from the 1982 National Long-Term Care Survey. See K. Manton and K. Liu (1984).
[1]Base includes the institutional population.
Table compiled by the National Aging Information Center

Table 18.4. Persons 65 Years and Over and 85 Years and Over Residing in a Nursing Home, by Sex and Assumptions as to Residency Ratios: 1985 and 2030

(Numbers in thousands. Projections are based on highest and lowest series of U.S. Census Bureau population projections.)

Age and Sex	1985	2030			
		Stable Ratios		6.5% Decrease in Ratios/ Decade	
		Lowest Series	Highest Series	Lowest Series	Highest Series
65 AND OVER					
Total	1,317	2,634	3,497	1,964	2,674
Male	334	720	995	501	761
Female	983	1,914	2,502	1,463	1,913
% Female	74.6	72.7	71.5	74.5	71.5
% of Population	4.6	4.5	4.5	3.4	3.4
85 AND OVER					
Total	597	1,213	2,419	936	1,863
Male	112	257	530	181	380
Female	485	956	1,889	755	1,483
% Female	81.2	78.8	78.1	80.7	79.4
% of Population	22.0	21.8	21.8	16.8	16.8

SOURCE: National Center for Health Statistics, Centers for Disease Control and Prevention, January, 1996. Unpublished study. Table compiled by the National Aging Information Center.

is 14.8 million and the highest figure is 22.6 million. However, all sets of data suggest that the number of persons who will be disabled will increase sharply.

Among those included in the severely disabled category are those with clinically diagnosed Alzheimer's disease. A team of researchers (Evans, et al., 1992) has compiled a set of projections of persons with this condition. These analysts expect 10.2 million cases (middle series) at ages 65 and over by 2050, and possibly 14.3 million cases (high series) by 2040, as compared with about 3.8 million (both middle and high series) in 1990. There is the expected progression in numbers of cases with increasing age, a pattern that intensifies with the passage of time. By 2040, most of these cases, some 70 percent, occur among ages 85 and over. The number of cases at these ages will increase by over 300 percent, as compared with 25 to 50 percent for ages 65 to 74. This change reflects the entry of the baby-boom cohorts into the highest ages by 2040.

Nursing Home Usage

Serious health or disabling conditions usually lead to residence in a nursing home because of the grave difficulties of home management of the patient. This outcome is all the more likely when social, financial, and housing resources are limited. Like Alzheimer's disease, nursing home residence is most common at the highest ages. In 1985, according to the National Nursing Home Survey, at ages 65 and over, the percent of the population in nursing homes was only 5 percent, but for ages 85 and over, the figure was 22 percent (Table 18.4.). A wide gap of this magnitude is likely to continue for the indefinite future. The very high concentration of women in nursing homes, with increasing proportions of women in older age groups as age increases, is also likely to continue, if only because of the continuation of the difference in mortality between the sexes.

The projections of a joint team from the University of Illinois and the University of Chicago indicate that, if residency ratios remain unchanged, the number of persons residing in nursing homes will double or triple by 2030 (Rivlin and Wiener, 1988). The number could rise by over 300 percent for those aged 85 and over. Even if residency ratios decrease by 6.5 percent per decade to 2030, as the report of the team assumes in one projection series, the number of residents of nursing homes will increase at the least by 57 percent. Contrary to the general view, there is considerable turnover in nursing homes and residents often are discharged after short periods. Discharges because of death account for one-quarter to one-third of the total discharges in any year. An average resident, particularly one discharged to a residence or other similar arrangement, stays only a few months. Hence, one realistic indicator of the demand for nursing home services is the number of persons residing in nursing homes at any time during a year. Rivlin and Weiner (1988) have prepared projections of persons requiring home health care and nursing home care that incorporate this "flow" concept. Their projected estimates for 1986 to 1990 and their projections for years 2001 to 2005 and 2016 to 2020 reflect the increase in the number and proportion of persons in nursing homes with increasing age, and the transfer of disabled persons from home health care to nursing home care with increasing age. The projections show no net temporal rise in the proportion of those requiring nursing home care or home care at ages 65 and over and at ages 85 and over between 1986 to 1990 and 2016 to 2020, but they do show substantial percentage increases in the number requiring care in this period, with the larger increase occurring for nursing home care than home care and at ages 85 and over than at ages 65 and over.

Chapter 19

The State of Long-Term Care

Introduction

Long-term care is an increasingly important and rapidly changing component of today's health care delivery system. Four out of every ten people turning age 65 will use a nursing home at some point in their lives, and many will need home care and other related services as well. As the population ages, the need for these services will continue to grow, particularly for women. Long-term care services are essential to many younger populations as well—children with disabilities, people with mental health problems, people with Alzheimer's disease, people with acquired immunodeficiency syndrome (AIDS), and others.

The increasing need for these services is creating significant budget concerns for federal and state governments, as well as straining family finances. Combined Medicare and Medicaid outlays have been growing dramatically. About 40 percent of long-term care costs are paid by the federal/state Medicaid program. Although the Medicare program accounts for only a small share of total expenditures, its share has been growing. Despite rising government expenditures, out-of-pocket payments continue to be a large source of financing for long-term care.

From "AHCPR Research on Long-Term Care," [Online] February 22, 1996. Available: http://www.ahcpr.gov/research/longterm.htm. Produced by the U.S. Department of Health and Human Services, Agency for Health Care Policy and Research (AHCPR). For complete contact information, please refer to Chapter 60, "Resources."

As a result, for many individuals who have chronic care needs, long-term care remains a catastrophic cost.

These financial pressures, combined with similar pressures related to acute care, are fueling unprecedented changes in the health care marketplace. Long-term care providers are diversifying and combining forces to maintain and expand market share as the influence of managed care spills into the long-term care market. Pressures to reduce costs have pushed sicker and more disabled persons into lower levels of care. These market and delivery system changes, in turn, are underscoring questions about the appropriateness, cost, and quality of services delivered in each of these settings and are prompting increased interest and concern on the part of consumers, providers, and federal and state governments charged with regulating and paying for these services. In recent years, for example, Congress has considered prospective payment systems for nursing home and home health agency payments under the Medicare program, as well as proposals to diminish the federal role in the Medicaid program. Many states are exploring managed care options for the elderly and disabled under Medicaid.

As they consider how to respond to these cost pressures and market changes, purchasers, providers, consumers, and policymakers will need answers to fundamental questions in six broad areas:

- Use, cost, and financing.
- Access and quality of care.
- Organization and delivery of care.
- Consumer and care giver behavior.
- Special populations.
- Data development and methodology.

As the leading federal agency charged with supporting and conducting health services research, the Agency for Health Care Policy and Research (AHCPR) has undertaken and funded important studies in each of these areas of long-term care research. The following sections highlight selected findings. The bibliographies that follow provide citations for these findings as well as a complete listing of long term-care research conducted and funded by AHCPR since 1990.

Use, Cost, and Financing

The growing cost of long-term care has stimulated policymakers to develop new approaches to control public expenditures and also has altered market strategies for providing that care. Accurate estimates of use and cost and identification of factors that influence care decisions provide the basis for designing new public policies and new market strategies to meet demand with fewer resources.

AHCPR's research has documented the high use of care by, and expenditures for, elderly and long-term care populations in general and the significant overlap of long-term and acute care:

- In 1987, per capita health care expenditures (in 1992 dollars) for the elderly living in the community were over $6,000 compared with $1,700 for the nonelderly. Per capita expenditures for nursing home residents were about $29,000 (Cohen, Carlson, and Potter, 1995).

- Nursing home residents are also important users of hospitals. About 9 percent of all Medicare hospital admissions are transfers from nursing homes. About 28 percent had one or more hospital visits during their nursing home stay. (Murtaugh and Freiman, 1995; Freiman and Murtaugh, 1995).

Nursing home costs represent about 70 percent of long-term care expenditures, as well as a large part of AHCPR long-term care research. Studies such as the following document the likelihood of nursing home use, reliance on government funds, and characteristics of users:

- About 43 percent of persons turning age 65 will use a nursing home before they die. About 20 percent of users will spend 5 or more years there (Kemper and Murtaugh, 1991). Of those turning 65, 17 percent can expect to use a nursing home and receive Medicaid reimbursement (Spillman and Kemper, 1995).

- More than 70 percent of nursing and personal care home residents are women and two-thirds of them are widowed or divorced. About 40 percent are demented and about 59 percent require assistance with four or more Activities of Daily Living (ADLs) (Lair and Lefkowitz, 1990).

- About 10 percent of residents in nursing and personal care homes are under age 65 (Lair, 1992) and 11 percent do not need help with ADLs (Lair and Lefkowitz, 1990).

Other studies estimate the rate of nursing home use by age and functional status, and, for users, expenses per day and source of

157

payment (Feinleib, Cunningham, and Short, 1994; Short, Feinleib, and Cunningham, 1994). Examples of additional studies include a model of hospital discharges to nursing homes (Roberge, Grant No. HS07953), predictors of long stays in nursing homes (Muller, Grant No. HS06672), and a comparison of nursing home admissions in urban and rural areas (Netzer, Grant No. HS000088). Differences in long-term care use and expenditures among African-American, Hispanic, and white populations have also been studied (Pourat, Grant No. HS08034; Proctor, Grant No. HS06406; Wallace, Grant No. HS07672).

AHCPR studies have also contributed to our knowledge of home care use and expenditures, as these examples illustrate:

- Nearly 6 million persons used home health services in 1987 (Altman and Walden, 1993).

- The most frequently used home care services are home health aides and homemakers, providers that frequently are not covered by either public or private insurance (Altman and Walden, 1993).

- Women were twice as likely to use home care as men. Those persons aged 85 and older, widows, those living alone, and those having difficulties with basic daily activities were the most likely to have a home care visit (Altman and Walden, 1993; Short and Leon, 1990).

Generally, home care is provided to a less functionally dependent population, compared with nursing home care, but policies have been designed to try to encourage home care use in lieu of nursing homes, as AHCPR studies have shown:

- Married persons are half as likely as unmarried persons to be admitted to a nursing home; having at least one daughter or sibling reduces those chances by about one-fifth (Freedman, 1996).

- Generous home care programs increase the likelihood that unmarried persons will live independently rather than live in shared housing or enter a nursing or personal care home (Pezzin, Kemper, and Reschovsky, 1996). Evidence was not found that these interventions displaced informal care (Kemper and Pezzin, 1996).

Although there is little evidence that subsidized home care reduces aggregate long-term care costs, one study suggests that if home care services were more tightly targeted to appropriate individuals, the potential for program-level cost savings might be significantly improved (Greene, Lovely, Miller, and Ondrich, 1995).

Studies of the financing of long-term care have analyzed the impact of waiting periods, coinsurance, and deductibles on coverage and the percentage of lifetime cost that is covered (Kemper, Spillman, and Murtaugh, 1991; Short, Kemper, Cornelius, and Walden, 1992). The impact on public costs has also been studied (Short and Kemper, 1994). Another study found that between 12 and 23 percent of persons would be ineligible for private long-term care insurance because of underwriting criteria if everyone applied at age 65 (Murtaugh, Kemper, and Spillman, 1995).

Access and Quality of Care

Concern for controlling the cost of long-term care has increased interest in ways to reduce home care costs by targeting home care programs to those who need the most care. AHCPR studies have contributed to this debate with estimates of the number of persons with long-term care needs and the numbers that are eligible under different criteria. Studies have also contributed to questions of appropriateness of nursing home placements:

- About 20 percent of the elderly living in the community (5.4 million persons) in 1987 had difficulty with at least one instrumental or basic ADL (Leon and Lair, 1990). About 4 million of these persons need human help with these activities (Stone and Murtaugh, 1990). About one-fourth of those needing human help are cognitively impaired, and about one-half receive help with just ADLs (Spector, 1991).

- A conservative estimate is that 15 percent of nursing home residents could be cared for at lower levels of care (Spector, Reschovsky, and Cohen, 1996).

- About one million persons aged 65 and older living in the community would be eligible under criteria of needing active or standby help with three or more ADLs. The number would increase as much as 70 percent if eligibility were included for cognitively impaired persons, depending how that was defined (Spector, 1991). Other criteria are also potentially important, such as the need for complex medical treatments (Kemper, 1992).

One study illustrated the tradeoffs of changing targeting criteria and the difficulties of establishing criteria using simple eligibility measures such as ADLs and cognitive impairment (Spector and Kemper, 1994). Another study found less access to nursing home care for Medicaid-covered persons as opposed to private payers (Reschovsky, 1996).

AHCPR research has also made major contributions to the understanding of what factors affect the quality of long-term care services. The Agency sponsored development of guidelines for prevention and treatment of pressure sores, detection and prevention of depression, prevention of incontinence, and assessment of Alzheimer's disease—all common problems faced by long-term care patients. These guidelines have been adapted by the American Medical Directors Association for use in long-term care facilities. Evaluations of the implementation of guidelines have also been funded, including a study of the implementation of the AHCPR urinary incontinence guideline (Watson, Grant No. HS08491).

In addition to sponsoring development of clinical guidelines, AHCPR has researched clinical factors associated with important clinical problems facing long-term care patients. Studies include risk of pressure sores (Spector, 1994); behavior problems (Spector and Jackson, 1994); basic functioning in daily activities (Spector, 1995; Spector and Takada, 1991); and sensory impairments (Laforge, Spector, and Sternberg, 1992).

A number of additional studies have focused on long-term care quality. A study currently underway is looking at the difference in outcomes for home health care patients in urban and rural areas and examining differences in both the quantity and quality of care (Shaughnessy, Grant No. HS08031). One study developed a nursing home quality information system (Harrington, Grant No. HS07574), while another study has tested a facility-level outcome quality assurance system (Caro, Grant No. HS07585). Other research includes an analysis of consumer preferences for restraints versus other protocols for preventing falls (Mion, Grant No. HS06923) and a study of psychoactive drug regulations (Maloney, Grant No. HS07954).

Organization and Delivery of Care

The changing dynamics of the health care system have affected how long-term care is organized and delivered, and the major questions focus on how these changes have affected quality, access, and cost. The Agency has been engaged in a number of studies in which the organization of care and the structure of long-term care industries and markets have been the focus. The results of some of these studies follow:

- Cost-based reimbursement increases the number of registered nurses, but reduces the number of practical nurses compared with flat-rate reimbursement. Higher reimbursement levels encourage the employment of practical nurses (Cohen and Spector, 1996).

- Higher professional nursing staff levels and lower turnover of staff improve nursing home outcomes (Cohen and Spector, 1996; Spector and Takada, 1991).

- Nursing facilities with few private pay residents are associated with negative outcomes (Spector and Takada, 1991).

- For-profit nursing homes have lower operating costs (Cohen and Dubay, 1990) but higher hospitalization rates than nonprofits (Freiman and Murtaugh, 1993).

- Case management can reduce cost per participant and maintain quality if the agency has power to authorize public payments, maintains an average expenditure cap, and provides the case management services itself (Kemper, 1990).

Another study developed a theoretical framework for explaining the existence of nonprofit nursing home ownership in a market for long-term care characterized by less information for consumers than providers and the underprovision of quality (Hirth, Grant No. HS06934). This study received the Kenneth Arrow Health Economics Award in 1994.

Additional AHCPR-funded research includes the changing structure of the home care industry, clients, and outcomes (Peters, Grant No. HS08892); a comparison of unlicensed and licensed home care providers (Estes, Grant No. HS06860); State variation in nursing home and home health markets (Harrington, Grant No. HS06174); the dynamics of the hospice industry (Hamilton, Grant No. HS06619); a comparison of social HMOs and risk-based Medicare HMOs (Dowd, Grant No. HS07171); and the supply of special care units for Alzheimer's patients in nursing homes (Leon, Potter, Cunningham, 1990; 1991).

Consumer and Caregiver Behavior

Studies of caregiving behavior provide a basis for understanding the dynamics of home care demand and supply and help guide long-term

161

care policies. Because long-term care is generally a family decision, research encompasses not only the disabled person but also the family and other informal caregivers. AHCPR has conducted a number of studies on consumer and family responses to long-term care needs. Findings from these efforts indicate that:

- About 95 percent of noninstitutionalized elderly persons in need of long-term care rely on family members and friends for help with activities of daily living. About 70 percent of the combined community and institutional population receiving long-term care rely entirely on private resources (Spillman and Kemper, 1992).

- Publicly-provided formal home care results in only small reductions in the overall amount of care provided by informal caregivers (Pezzin, Kemper, and Reschovky, 1996) while enabling elderly persons with disabilities to live more independently and to reduce their probability of institutionalization (Kemper and Pezzin, 1996).

- The effectiveness of alternative government long-term care policies, such as caregiver allowances and other cash incentives designed to promote family care, depends critically on whether transferred resources are targeted to the elderly person or the caregiver (Pezzin and Schone, 1997).

Other studies have reached the following conclusions:

- Caregivers of elders with greater care needs are more likely to take unpaid leave, reduce work hours, or rearrange their work schedules to assume elder care responsibilities. Being female, white, and in fair-to-poor health also increased the likelihood of the caregiver requiring accommodation in his or her work (Stone and Short, 1990).

- Major determinants of caregiver attrition are the degree of dependence of the frail elderly care recipient and the need for help on demand (Boaz and Muller, 1991).

Other research has attempted to quantify the relationships between employment, caregiving hours, and financial assistance from the adult children (Boaz and Muller, 1992).

Special Populations

Long-term care services are required by several different populations, and the needs of these populations vary. In addition to the elderly, many of the long-term care users are younger persons with physical disabilities; persons with developmental disabilities (DD); and persons with chronic diseases such as diabetes, emphysema, and AIDS. AHCPR studies of special populations indicate the following:

- About 95 percent of the facilities for the mentally retarded are community based, but they represent only about 60 percent of the beds because of large state institutions (Beauregard and Potter, 1992).

- About half of persons with DD in institutions are admitted after they are past the age of 40. About two-thirds of persons with DD aged 65 or older are in nursing homes or other long-term care facilities that are not specially designated for DD (Altman, 1995a).

- The most ADL-disabled persons tend to reside in state institutions, and the least disabled tend to reside in small private or public facilities (Cunningham and Mueller, 1990).

- The type of services needed are very similar across age groups, although the reasons for these needs differ (Altman, 1995a).

AHCPR has funded a substantial amount of research that examines service use, costs, and Medicaid coverage of HIV-infected patients. Those studies have determined the following:

- Home care use is the greatest among persons with AIDS, compared with persons at less advanced stages, such as HIV+ status (Buchanan, 1995).

- HIV-infected persons covered under Medicaid are more likely to receive paraprofessional help than those covered by private insurance (Fleishman, 1997).

- The course of functional loss is variable and episodic, which suggests the need for flexible and responsive systems for authorizing and managing in-home services for persons with HIV (Crystal and Sambamoorthi 1996).

Other HIV-related research includes a study of access to home care and use (Hanley, Grant No. HS06404), resource use in chronic care facilities (Blustein, Grant No. HS00034), and models to predict service intensity and visit-related costs (Payne, Grant No. HS06843). One other study looked at the effects of case-managed home care on the health of AIDS caregivers (Reynolds, Grant No. HS06971).

Data Development and Methodological Studies

AHCPR has also been an important contributor to the infrastructure of long-term care research through its survey activities. Over the years, AHCPR surveys have been a major source of data for policy and basic research in long-term care:

- The 1987 National Medical Expenditure Survey (NMES) included data for persons living in the community, persons institutionalized in nursing and personal care homes, and persons in intermediate care facilities for the mentally retarded.

- The 1996 Medical Expenditure Panel Survey (MEPS) provides population-based information on the consumers of health care, the services used (including home care), and expenditures made regardless of insurer. The nursing home component of MEPS provides information on a nationally representative sample of nursing homes and their residents.

- The HIV Cost and Services Utilization Study (HCSUS) is a national sample of persons with HIV infection who are in treatment. Long-term care issues that can be addressed include utilization of home health care and nursing facility care, case management services, and patterns and correlates of health-related quality of life, including functional status. The AIDS Cost and Services Utilization Study (ACSUS), the predecessor of HCSUS, was also funded by the Agency.

The development of national estimates of long-term care use and expenditures from the institutional component of NMES and other large data sets involves many methodological issues, some of which in themselves have contributed to the statistical and measurement literature. Research staff have contributed to methodological studies in diverse ways using statistical methods to develop nationally representative estimates of measurement issues. In addition, AHCPR has funded projects to improve research methodologies for studying long-term care populations.

Examples of statistical and measurement studies include the following:

- Problems of nonresponse in the development of year-long profiles of nursing home residents and their movement in and out of other settings (Cohen and Potter, 1990).

- Imputation and weights for national estimates (Cohen and Potter, 1993; Cohen, Potter, and Flyer, 1994).

- Episode-based estimates of nursing home length of stay, which include short-term hospitalizations (Short, Cunningham, and Mueller, 1990).

- Development of a nationally representative sample of decedents who used nursing homes during their lives (Carlson, Kemper, and Murtaugh, 1995).

Other papers have focused on the measurement of disability and cognitive impairment with national data (Altman, 1994; Spector, 1990), and the measurement of ADL change (Mathiowetz and Lair, 1994). Research has also been funded to improve methods to study duration in nursing homes with multiple outcomes using hierarchical duration models (Morris, Grant No. HS07306; Morris, Norton, and Zhou, 1994).

Chapter 20

Medicare and Medicaid

The Health Care Financing Administration (HCFA) administers Medicare, the nation's largest health insurance program, which covers 39 million Americans.

Medicare provides health insurance to people age 65 and over, those who have permanent kidney failure, and certain people with disabilities.

Who's Eligible for Medicare?

Generally, you are eligible for Medicare if you or your spouse worked for at least 10 years in Medicare-covered employment and you are 65 years old and a citizen or permanent resident of the United States. You might also qualify for coverage if you are a younger person with a disability or with chronic kidney disease.

Here are some simple guidelines. You can get Part A at age 65 without having to pay premiums if:

- You are already receiving retirement benefits from Social Security or the Railroad Retirement Board.

Excerpted from "What is Medicare?" and "Medicare Amounts for 1999" [Online] September 1998. Available: http://www.medicare.gov. And from "Overview of Medicaid Program," "Medicaid Eligibility," "Medicaid Services," and "The Medicaid Program," [Online] 1996. Available: http://www.hcfa.gov/medicaid. Produced by the U.S. Department of Health and Human Services' Health Care Financing Administration (HCFA). For complete contact information, please refer to Chapter 60, "Resources."

- You are eligible to receive Social Security or Railroad benefits but have not yet filed for them.

- You or your spouse had Medicare-covered government employment.

If you are under 65, you can get Part A without having to pay premiums if:

- You have received Social Security or Railroad Retirement Board disability benefits for 24 months.

- You are a kidney dialysis or kidney transplant patient.

While you do not have to pay a premium for Part A if you meet one of those conditions, you must pay for Part B if you want it. The Part B monthly premium in 1999 is $45.50. It is deducted from your Social Security, Railroad Retirement, or Civil Service Retirement check.

If you have questions about your eligibility for Medicare Part A or Part B, or if you want to apply for Medicare, call the Social Security Administration. The toll-free telephone number is: 1- 800-772-1213. The TTY-TDD number for the hearing and speech impaired is 1-800-325-0778. You can also get information about buying Part A as well as part B if you do not qualify for premium-free part A.

Enrollment

Enrollment in Medicare is handled in two ways: either you are enrolled automatically or you have to apply. Here's how it works.

Automatic Enrollment

If you are not yet 65 and already getting Social Security or Railroad Retirement benefits, you do not have to apply for Medicare. You are enrolled automatically in both Part A and Part B and your Medicare card is mailed to you about 3 months before your 65th birthday. If you do not want Part B, follow the instructions that come with the card.

If you are disabled, you will be automatically enrolled in both Part A and Part B of Medicare beginning in your 25th month of disability. Your card will be mailed to you about 3 months before you are entitled to Medicare.

Applying for Medicare

You need to apply for Medicare if you are not receiving Social Security or Railroad Retirement Benefits 3 months before you turn 65, or if you require regular dialysis or kidney transplant. That's the beginning of your 7-month initial enrollment period. By applying early, you'll avoid a possible delay in the start of your Part B coverage. You apply by contacting any Social Security Administration office or, if you or your spouse worked for the railroad, the Railroad Retirement Board.

If you do not enroll during this 7-month period, you'll have to wait to enroll until the next general enrollment period. General enrollment periods are held January 1 to March 31 of each year, and Part B coverage starts the following July.

Don't put off enrolling. If you wait 12 or more months to sign up, your premiums generally will be higher. Part B premiums go up 10 percent for each 12 months that you could have enrolled but did not. The increase in the Part A premium (if you have to pay a premium) is 10 percent no matter how late you enroll for coverage.

Under certain circumstances, however, you can delay your Part B enrollment without having to pay higher premiums. If you are age 65 or over and have group health insurance based on your own or your spouse's current employment, or if you are disabled and have group health insurance based on your current employment or the current employment of any family member, you have a choice:

- You may enroll in Part B at any time while you are covered by the group health plan; or,

- You can enroll in Part B during the 8-month enrollment period that begins the month employment ends or the month you are no longer covered under the employer plan, whichever comes first.

If you enroll in Part B while covered by an employer plan or during the first full month when not covered by that plan, your coverage begins the first day of the month you enroll. You also have the option of delaying coverage until the first day of the following 3 months. If you enroll during any of the 7 remaining months of the special enrollment period, your coverage begins the month after you enroll.

If you do not enroll by the end of the 8-month period, you'll have to wait until the next general enrollment period, which begins January 1 of the next year.

Even if you continue to work after you turn 65, you should sign up for Part A of Medicare. Part A may help pay some of the costs not covered by the employer plan. It may not, however, be advisable to sign up for Part B if you have health insurance through your employer. You would have to pay the monthly Part B premium, and the Part B benefits may be of limited value to you as long as the employer plan was the primary payer of your medical bills. Moreover, you would trigger your 6-month Medigap open enrollment period (see Medigap Insurance).

Medigap Insurance

Though Medicare covers many health care costs, you will still have to pay Medicare's coinsurance and deductibles. There are also many medical services that Medicare does not cover.

You may want to buy a Medicare supplemental insurance (Medigap) policy. Medigap is private insurance that is designed to help pay your Medicare cost-sharing amounts. There are 10 standard Medigap policies, and each offers a different combination of benefits.

The best time to buy a policy is during your Medigap open enrollment period. For a period of 6 months from the date you are first enrolled in Medicare Part B and are age 65 or older, you have a right to buy the Medigap policy of your choice. That is your open enrollment period.

You cannot be turned down or charged higher premiums because of poor health if you buy a policy during this period. Once your Medigap open enrollment period ends, you may not be able to buy the policy of your choice. You may have to accept whatever Medigap policy an insurance company is willing to sell you.

If you have Medicare Part B but are not yet 65, your 6-month Medigap open enrollment period begins when you turn 65. However, several states (Connecticut, Maine, Massachusetts, Minnesota, New Jersey, New York, Oklahoma, Oregon, Pennsylvania, Virginia, Washington, and Wisconsin) require at least a limited Medigap open enrollment period for Medicare beneficiaries under 65.

Your state health insurance assistance program can answer questions about Medicare and other health insurance. The services are free. You can get help in deciding whether you need more insurance and, if so, what kind and how much to buy. [In the State of Michigan, contact the Insurance Deparment, Consumer Services Division at 517-373-0240.] Free copies of the *Guide to Health Insurance for People with Medicare* are also available from the assistance office.

Your state assistance program can also provide you with information about Medicare SELECT, another type of Medicare supplemental health insurance sold by insurance companies and HMOs throughout most of the country. Medicare SELECT is the same as standard Medigap insurance in nearly all respects. The only difference between Medicare SELECT and standard Medigap insurance is that each insurer has specific hospitals, and in some cases specific doctors, that you must use, except in an emergency, in order to be eligible for full benefits. Medicare SELECT policies generally have lower premiums than other Medigap policies because of this requirement. Medicare SELECT is explained in more detail in the *Guide to Health Insurance for People with Medicare.*

Suspected violations of the laws governing the marketing and sales of Medigap and other types of insurance policies should generally be reported to your state insurance department. [See above for the State of Michigan's Insurance Department telephone number.] If you believe you have been a victim of Medigap fraud, you can also call the federal toll-free number for registering such complaints. The number is 1-800-638-6833, or TTY/TDD 1-800-820-1202 for the hearing or speech impaired.

Copy of Initial Enrollment Package

[Below (pp. 171-180) is a copy of the Medicare Initial Enrollment Package which is mailed to seniors who have applied for Medicare coverage. The package offers information about Parts A and B Medicare coverage, supplemental insurance, hospital and in-home services, assistance for low-income beneficiaries, and the Medicare Card, as well as references to package enclosures. The contents of the enrollment package have been reprinted here to give seniors an idea of what to expect when they apply for Medicare.]

A message about Medicare from the Health Care Financing Administration—Nancy-Ann DeParle, Administrator.

Welcome to Medicare! You have been enrolled automatically in Part A and Part B of the Medicare program because you are a Social Security beneficiary. Part A helps pay for hospital expenses and Part B helps pay for medical expenses, such as doctor visits. This package will help you learn about the Medicare program. It contains your red, white, and blue Medicare card. Your Medicare card shows that you have hospital insurance (Part A) and medical insurance (Part B).Your card also shows the dates your coverage begins. Your Part A is free. There is a monthly premium for your Part B medical insurance. In

1999, Part B costs you $45.50 each month. If your income is low, your state may pay your Part B monthly premium. Read the section, "Assistance for Low-Income Medicare Beneficiaries," in the enclosed booklet. You have three important decisions to make:

1. Do you want to keep Medicare Part B?

2. If you keep Medicare Part B, how do you want to receive your Medicare-covered services?

3. Do you need supplemental insurance to pay for services and products that Medicare does not cover?

1) Decision: Do you need Part B?

Before you make a decision, you should read the information about Part B in the enclosed booklet, *What You Need to Know about Medicare and Other Health Insurance.* You must keep Part B if you want to be able to join any of the Medicare managed care plans (such as HMOs), Medicare medical savings accounts, or other Medicare health insurance options. If you do not keep Part B, you will only be eligible to receive Medicare hospital coverage.

If you are turning 65 or are older, you can delay taking your Part B medical insurance if: (1) you or your spouse (of any age) continue to work and (2) you are covered under a group health plan from that current employment.

If you are under age 65 and disabled, you can delay your Part B if (1) you, or any member of your family is currently working, *and* (2) you have group health plan coverage from that current employment.

You can find out how your group health plan works together with Medicare by contacting your employer or health benefits representative.

IMPORTANT: If you do not have group health plan coverage based on current employment and you delay taking Part B, your monthly premium may be higher. Your premium **will increase by 10 percent** for each 12 months that you could have had Part B, but did not take it. For example, if you delayed your Part B for 12 months at the current rate, you may have to pay $50.10 each month for Part B, instead of $45.50. If you do not keep Part B now, you will only have a chance to sign up for Part B once a year—between January 1 and March 31. Your Part B insurance will start the following July. If you choose to delay taking Part B because you currently

172

have group health plan coverage, you may be able to avoid paying this higher premium by signing up for Part B while you have this group coverage or within eight months after the employment ends or the group health coverage ends, whichever comes first.

If you want to keep Part B, cut out the enclosed card and keep it with you. No further action is necessary. Your premium will begin to be deducted from your Social Security payment the month your Part B starts. If you do not get monthly Social Security benefits, you will receive a bill every three months for your Part B. **Do not send any money now.**

If you do not want to keep Part B, sign the enclosed form and check the block after "I do not want medical insurance." Return the entire form in the enclosed envelope. Do this before the date shown on the card so you will not owe a monthly premium. We will send you a new card that shows you have Part A only.

2) Decision: How do you want to receive your services?

3) Decision: Do you need supplemental insurance?

The enclosed booklet provides some information to help you answer these two questions. It gives you more details about Part B, supplemental insurance, and Medicare health insurance options, such as managed care. It also lists additional resources to help you get the information that you need.

If you have any questions or need more information, you can call Social Security at 1-800-772-1213.

Medicare Has More to Offer

Medicare allows you to choose the way you receive your benefits. You have been enrolled automatically in the Original Medicare Plan, which is the traditional payment-per-service arrangement. **If you want to stay with the Original Medicare Plan, you don't have to do anything.** The basic benefits of this plan are described below.

Starting in 1999, Medicare offers more ways to receive your benefits through other health plan choices. Choices that may be available in your area include Medicare Managed Care Plans, such as Health Maintenance Organizations, Preferred Provider Organizations, or Provider Sponsored Organizations. In addition, Private Fee-For-Service Plans and Medicare Medical Savings Account Plans may be available in your area. One of the new health plan choices might

173

be right for you. The choice is yours. No matter what you decide, you are still in the Medicare program.

Your copy of *Medicare & You* will explain the Original Medicare Plan and other Medicare health plans in detail. It also will explain how to enroll in other health plan options, if you are interested. If you don't have a computer, your local public library or senior center may be able to help you find this information.

All Medicare health plans must provide at least the basic Medicare covered services.

Medicare Covered Services

Hospital Insurance (Part A)

Medicare hospital insurance helps pay for necessary medical care and services furnished by Medicare-certified hospitals, skilled nursing facilities, home health agencies, and hospices.

The number of days that Medicare covers care in hospitals and skilled nursing facilities is measured in benefit periods. A benefit period begins on the first day you receive services as a patient in a hospital or skilled nursing facility and ends after you have been out of the hospital or skilled nursing facility and have not received skilled care in any other facility for 60 days in a row. There is no limit to the number of benefit periods you can have.

Inpatient Hospital Care

Medicare Part A helps pay for up to 90 days of inpatient hospital care in each benefit period. Covered services include your semi-private room and meals, general nursing services, operating and recovery room costs, intensive care, drugs, laboratory tests, X-rays, and all other necessary medical services and supplies.

Skilled Nursing Facility Care

You may need inpatient skilled nursing or rehabilitation services after a hospital stay. If you meet certain conditions, Part A helps pay for up to 100 days in a participating skilled nursing facility in each benefit period. Medicare pays all approved charges for the first 20 days; you pay a coinsurance amount for days 21 through 100. Covered services include your semi-private room and meals, skilled nursing services, rehabilitation services, drugs, and medical supplies.

Home Health Care

If you meet certain conditions, Medicare pays the full approved cost of covered home health care services. This includes part-time or intermittent skilled nursing services prescribed by a physician for treatment or rehabilitation of homebound patients. The only amount you pay for home health care is a 20 percent coinsurance charge for medical equipment such as a wheelchair or walker.

Hospice Care

Medicare helps pay for hospice care for terminally ill beneficiaries who select the hospice care benefit. There are no deductibles, but you pay limited costs for drugs and inpatient respite care.

Medical Insurance (Part B)

Medicare Part B helps pay for doctor's services, outpatient hospital services (including emergency room visits), ambulance transportation, diagnostic tests, laboratory services, some preventive care like mammography and Pap smear screening, outpatient therapy services, durable medical equipment and supplies, and a variety of other health services. Part B also pays for home health care services for which Part A does not pay.

Medicare Part B pays 80 percent of approved charges for most covered services. You are responsible for paying a $100 deductible per calendar year and the remaining 20 percent of the Medicare approved charge. You will have to pay limited additional charges if the doctor who cares for you does not accept assignment. This means the doctor does not agree to accept the Medicare approved charge for services.

Services Medicare Does Not Cover

Medicare Part A does not pay for convenience items such as telephones and televisions provided by hospitals or skilled nursing facilities, private rooms (unless medically necessary), or private duty nurses.

The only type of nursing home care Medicare pays for is skilled nursing facility care for rehabilitation, such as recovery time after a hospital discharge. Medicare does not pay if you need only custodial services (help with daily living activities like bathing, eating, or getting dressed).

Medicare Part B usually does not pay for most prescription drugs, routine physical examinations, or services not related to treatment of illness or injury. Part B does not pay for dental care or dentures, cosmetic surgery, routine foot care, hearing aids, eye examinations, or eyeglasses.

Except for certain limited cases in Canada and Mexico, Medicare does not pay for treatment outside the United States.

The Original Medicare Plan

This is the traditional payment-per-service arrangement. You have been enrolled automatically in this option. This plan includes all Medicare covered services listed above.

Carriers and Fiscal Intermediaries

Private insurance organizations called Medicare carriers and fiscal intermediaries handle claims under the Original Medicare Plan. Carriers handle medical insurance (Part B) claims. Fiscal intermediaries handle all hospital insurance (Part A) claims. *Medicare & You* gives more information about how to contact your carrier or fiscal intermediary. The Social Security Administration does not handle claims for Medicare payment.

The Original Medicare Plan with a Supplemental Policy

Many private insurance companies sell Medicare Supplemental Insurance Policies (Medigap or Medicare SELECT) to help fill the coverage gaps in the Original Medicare Plan. If you remain in the Original Medicare Plan, you may want to consider buying one of these 10 standard policies for extra benefits. These policies help pay Medicare's coinsurance amounts and deductibles, and other out-of-pocket costs for health care.

The federal government does not sell these types of policies. You should read the publication called *Guide to Health Insurance for People with Medicare* before you buy a supplemental policy. For a free copy, call the Medicare hotline at 1-800-638-6833. Your state insurance department also has information available to help you.

Do not delay. When you first enroll in Part B at age 65 or older, you have a 6-month Medigap open enrollment period. During that time your health status cannot be used as a reason either to refuse you a policy or to charge you more than all other open enrollment applicants. (The insurer may make you wait up to 6 months for coverage of a pre-existing condition.) If you try to enroll later, you may be denied a policy or charged a higher rate.

At age 65, Medigap open enrollment is available to beneficiaries who are enrolled in Part B. If you are under age 65, contact your state insurance department for information about open enrollment.

Other Medicare Health Plan Choices

In addition to the plans explained above, you may have other Medicare health plan choices available to you. To be eligible for these other health plan choices, you must:

- Have both Part A (hospital insurance) and Part B (medical insurance).

- Continue to pay the monthly Part B premium.

- Live in the plan's service area (the counties in which the plan is offered).

- Not have permanent kidney failure (End-Stage Renal Disease).

The following types of plans may be options for you.

Medicare Managed Care Plans

You may choose to get your Medicare coverage through a managed care plan. Medicare Managed Care Plans may include Health Maintenance Organizations (HMOs), HMOs with a Point-of-Service option (POS), Provider Sponsored Organizations (PSOs), and Preferred Provider Organizations (PPOs). These types of plans involve a specific group of doctors, hospitals, and other providers who provide your care as a member of the plan.

Medicare Managed Care Plans provide all services covered by both Part A and Part B. Most offer a variety of additional benefits, like preventive care, prescription drugs, dental care, hearing aids, eyeglasses, and other items not covered by the Original Medicare Plan. Costs for these extra benefits vary among plans.

Other Choices

In addition to the Original Medicare Plan and Medicare Managed Care Plans, other Medicare health plan choices may be available in your area. These include Private Fee-for-Service Plans, Medicare Medical Savings Account (MSA) Plans, and Religious Fraternal Benefit Plans. These plans provide all services covered by both Part A and Part B. Some offer a variety of additional benefits.

Your copy of *Medicare & You* will explain all of these health plan choices. For information about which ones are available in your area, look on the Internet at www.medicare.gov.

Other Insurance Sometimes Pays before Medicare

Some people who have Medicare have other insurance (not including Medigap policies) that must pay before Medicare pays its share of your bill. Your other insurance pays first if:

- (a) You are 65 or older; (b) you or your spouse are currently working at an employer with 20 or more employees; and (c) you have group health insurance based on that employment.

- (a) You are under age 65 and are disabled; (b) you or any member of your family is currently working at an employer with 100 or more employees; and (c) you have group health insurance based on that employment.

- You have Medicare because of permanent kidney failure.

- You have an illness or injury that is covered under workers' compensation, the federal black lung program, no-fault insurance, or any liability insurance.

If you match any of these descriptions and you have other insurance along with Medicare, your other insurance will often be the first payer on your health claims. Tell your doctor, hospital, and all other providers of services about your other insurance. Your claims can then be sent to the right insurer first.

Assistance for Low-Income Beneficiaries

If you have a low income and limited resources, your state may pay your Medicare costs, including premiums, deductibles, and coinsurance. To qualify:

- You must be entitled to Medicare hospital insurance (Part A).

- Your annual income level must be at or below the national poverty guidelines.

- and You cannot have resources such as bank accounts or stocks and bonds worth more than $4,000 for one person or $6,000 for a couple (your home and first car don't count).

If your income is just above the poverty guidelines, you may qualify for help with paying your Part B premiums. If you think you qualify, contact your state or local welfare, social service, or Medicaid agency. The contact number is available on the Internet at www.medicare.gov. Ask about the Qualified Medicare Beneficiary (QMB) program, the Medicare Buy-In program, the Specified Low-Income Medicare Beneficiary (SLMB) program, or the Qualifying Individual (QI) program.

If you have young children in your care, you also should ask about your state's Child Health Program to help pay their health care costs.

For More Information

Up-to-date information about Medicare is available on the Internet at the web site www.medicare.gov. If you don't have a computer, your local public library or senior center may be able to help you find this information.

If you have questions about how to enroll in Medicare, call Social Security's toll-free number, 1-800-772-1213, any business day from 7:00 a.m. to 7:00 p.m. The lines are busiest early in the week and early in the month, so it is best to call at other times. People who are deaf or hard of hearing may call a toll-free TTY number, 1-800-325-0778, between 7:00 a.m. and 7:00 p.m. on business days. When you call, have your Social Security number handy.

These calls are all treated confidentially. Some calls may be monitored by a second customer representative to make sure you are receiving accurate information and courteous service.

If you have any questions about what Medicare covers, call the Medicare carrier that processes Medicare claims in your area. The name and number are listed in *Medicare & You.*

If you want to order free publications, like the *Guide to Health Insurance for People with Medicare,* call the Medicare hotline at 1-800-638-6833. Audio-tapes in English and Spanish, and Spanish copies of *Medicare & You* are also available by calling this number.

If you believe you have been discriminated against because of your race, color, sex, national origin, disability, or age, call the DHHS Office for Civil Rights at 1-800-368-1019 or 1-800-537-7697 (TTY/TDD).

179

Your Medicare Card

Once enrolled, you'll receive a Medicare card imprinted with your name and Medicare claim number. It shows what coverage you have (Part A, Part B, or both) and the date your coverage started.

Show your card whenever you get medical care. This will assure that a claim for payment is sent to Medicare. Make sure to use your exact name and claim number. If you are married, your spouse will have his or her own card and claim number. Never let anyone else use your Medicare card, and keep the number as safe as you would a credit card number. Take your card with you when you travel, and have it handy when you call about a Medicare claim. If you lose your card, contact the Social Security Administration right away.

Medicare Amounts for 1999

Inpatient Hospital Insurance (Part A)

- Deductible—$768 (Per Benefit Period)

- Coinsurance—$192 a day for the 61st-90th day each benefit period. $384 a day for the 91st-150th day for each lifetime reserve day (total of 60 lifetime reserve days—non-renewable).

- Skilled Nursing Facility Coinsurance—$96.00 a day for the 21st-100th day each benefit period.

Hospital Insurance (Part A) Premium

- $309 per month [NOTE: This premium is paid only by individuals who are not otherwise eligible for premium-free hospital insurance.]

- $339.90 must be paid by those who must pay a premium surcharge for late enrollment.

- In addition, there is a Part A premium of $170 for those individuals having 30 or more Quarters of Coverage. These individuals must pay a premium plus surcharge total of $187 for late enrollment.

Supplementary Medical Insurance (SMI) Part B Deductible

- $100 per year

Part B Monthly Premium

- $45.50—1999 ($43.80—1997 and 1998)

Overview of Medicaid Program

Title XIX of the Social Security Act is a program which provides medical assistance for certain individuals and families with low incomes and resources. The program, known as Medicaid, became law in 1965 as a jointly funded cooperative venture between the federal and state governments to assist states in the provision of adequate medical care to eligible needy persons. Medicaid is the largest program providing medical and health-related services to America's poorest people. Within broad national guidelines which the federal government provides, each of the states:

1. establishes its own eligibility standards;

2. determines the type, amount, duration, and scope of services;

3. sets the rate of payment for services; and

4. administers its own program.

Thus, the Medicaid program varies considerably from state to state, as well as within each state over time.

Medicaid Eligibility

NOTE: The Medicaid eligibility requirements listed below are accurate at present. However, they are expected to change somewhat in the near future as states implement the new welfare reform bill which was signed into law on August 22, 1996.

States have some discretion in determining which groups their Medicaid programs will cover and the financial criteria for Medicaid eligibility. To be eligible for federal funds, states are required to provide Medicaid coverage for most individuals who receive federally assisted income maintenance payments, as well as for related groups not receiving cash payments. Some examples of the mandatory Medicaid eligibility groups are:

- recipients of Aid to Families with Dependent Children (AFDC);

- Supplemental Security Income (SSI) recipients (or in states using more restrictive criteria—aged, blind, and disabled individuals who meet criteria which are more restrictive than those of the SSI program and which were in place in the state's approved Medicaid plan as of January 1, 1972);

- infants born to Medicaid-eligible pregnant women. Medicaid eligibility must continue throughout the first year of life so long as the infant remains in the mother's household and she remains eligible, or would be eligible if she were still pregnant;

- children under age 6 and pregnant women who meet the state's AFDC financial requirements or whose family income is at or below 133 percent of the federal poverty level. (The minimum mandatory income level for pregnant women and infants in certain states may be higher than 133 percent, if as of certain dates the state had established a higher percentage for covering those groups.) States are required to extend Medicaid eligibility until age 19 to all children born after September 30, 1983, in families with incomes at or below the federal poverty level. This phases in coverage, so that by the year 2002, all poor children under age 19 will be covered. Once eligibility is established, pregnant women remain eligible for Medicaid through the end of the calendar month ending 60 days after the end of the pregnancy regardless of any change in family income. States are not required to have a resource test for these poverty level related groups. However, any resource test imposed can be no more restrictive than that of the AFDC program for infants and children and the SSI program for pregnant women;

- recipients of adoption assistance and foster care under Title IV-E of the Social Security Act;

- certain Medicare beneficiaries (described later); and

- special protected groups who lose cash assistance because of the cash program's rules, but who may keep Medicaid for a period of time. Examples are: persons who lose AFDC or SSI payments due to earnings from work or increased Social Security benefits; and two-parent, unemployed families whose AFDC cash assistance time is limited by the state and who are provided a full 12 months of Medicaid coverage following termination of cash assistance.

States also have the *option* to provide Medicaid coverage for other "categorically needy" groups. These optional groups share characteristics of the mandatory groups, but the eligibility criteria are somewhat more liberally defined. Examples of the optional groups that states may cover as categorically needy (and for which they will receive federal matching funds) under the Medicaid program are:

- infants up to age one and pregnant women not covered under the mandatory rules whose family income is below 185 percent of the federal poverty level (the percentage to be set by each state);

- certain aged, blind, or disabled adults who have incomes above those requiring mandatory coverage, but below the federal poverty level;

- children under age 21 who meet income and resources requirements for AFDC, but who otherwise are not eligible for AFDC;

- institutionalized individuals with income and resources below specified limits;

- persons who would be eligible if institutionalized but are receiving care under home and community-based services waivers;

- recipients of state supplementary payments; and

- TB-infected persons who would be financially eligible for Medicaid at the SSI level (only for TB-related ambulatory services and TB drugs).

Medically Needy Eligibility Groups

The option to have a "medically needy" program allows states to extend Medicaid eligibility to additional qualified persons who may have too much income to qualify under the mandatory or optional categorically needy groups. This option allows them to "spend down" to Medicaid eligibility by incurring medical and/or remedial care expenses to offset their excess income, thereby reducing it to a level below the maximum allowed by that state's Medicaid plan. States may also allow families to establish eligibility as medically needy by paying monthly premiums to the state in an amount equal to the difference between family income (reduced by unpaid expenses, if any, incurred for medical care in previous months) and the income eligibility standard.

Eligibility for the medically needy program does not have to be as extensive as the categorically needy program. However, states which elect to include the medically needy under their plans are required to include certain children under age 18 and pregnant women who except for income and resources would be eligible as categorically needy. They may choose to provide coverage to other medically needy persons: aged, blind, and/or disabled persons; certain relatives of children deprived of parental support and care; and certain other financially eligible children up to age 21. In 1995, there were 40 medically needy programs which provided at least some services to recipients.

Amplification on Medicaid Eligibility

Coverage may start retroactive to any or all of the 3 months prior to application if the individual would have been eligible during the retroactive period. Coverage generally stops at the end of the month in which a person's circumstances change. Most states have additional "state-only" programs to provide medical assistance for specified poor persons who do not qualify for the Medicaid program. No federal funds are provided for state-only programs.

Medicaid does not provide medical assistance for all poor persons. Even under the broadest provisions of the federal statute (except for emergency services for certain persons), the Medicaid program does not provide health care services, even for very poor persons, unless they are in one of the groups designated above. Low income is only one test for Medicaid eligibility; assets and resources are also tested against established thresholds. As noted earlier, categorically needy persons who are eligible for Medicaid may or may not also receive cash assistance from the AFDC program or from the SSI program. Medically needy persons who would be categorically eligible except for income or assets may become eligible for Medicaid solely because of excessive medical expenses.

States may use more liberal income and resources methodologies to determine Medicaid eligibility for certain AFDC-related and aged, blind, and disabled individuals under section 1902(r)(2) of the Social Security Act. The more liberal income methodologies cannot result in the individual's income exceeding the limits prescribed for federal matching (for those groups which are subject to these limits).

Significant changes were made in the Medicare Catastrophic Coverage Act (MCCA) of 1988 which affected Medicaid. Although much of the MCCA was repealed, the portions affecting Medicaid remain in effect. The law also accelerated Medicaid eligibility for some nursing home patients by protecting assets for the institutionalized person's spouse at home at the time of the initial eligibility determination after

184

institutionalization. Before an institutionalized person's monthly income is used to pay for the cost of institutional care, a minimum monthly maintenance needs allowance is deducted from the institutionalized spouse's income to bring the income of the community spouse up to a moderate level.

Medicaid-Medicare Relationship

The Medicare program (Title XVIII of the Social Security Act) provides hospital insurance (HI), also known as Part A coverage and supplementary medical insurance (SMI), which is known as Part B coverage. For persons aged 65 and older (and for certain disabled persons) who have insured status under Social Security or Railroad Retirement, coverage for HI is automatic. Coverage for SMI, however, requires payment of a monthly premium. Some aged and/or disabled persons are covered under both the Medicaid and Medicare programs.

For Medicare beneficiaries who are also fully eligible for Medicaid, Medicare coverage is supplemented by health care services that are available under the state's Medicaid program. If a person is a Medicare beneficiary, payments for any services covered by Medicare are made by the Medicare program before any payments are made by the Medicaid program. Medicaid is always "payer of last resort." As each state elects, services such as eyeglasses, hearing aids, and nursing facility care not covered by Medicare may be provided by the Medicaid program.

Limited Medicaid benefits are available for certain qualified disabled working individuals (QDWIs), who have earnings sufficiently high to preclude entitlement to Medicare coverage except if the individual purchases coverage, and whose earnings are less than 200 percent of the federal poverty level (FPL). State Medicaid programs must pay the HI premium for QDWIs with income less than 150 percent of the FPL, and may pay some or all of the HI premium for QDWIs with earnings between 150 and 200 percent of the FPL. Medicaid does not pay SMI premiums for these individuals.

For certain poor Medicare recipients known as "Qualified Medicare Beneficiaries" (QMBs) (those beneficiaries with incomes below the federal poverty level and with resources at or below twice the standard allowed under the SSI program), the Medicaid program pays the Medicare premiums and cost-sharing expenses for Medicare HI and SMI. For "Specified Low-Income Medicare Beneficiaries" (SLMBs) (those like QMBs, but with slightly higher incomes), the Medicaid program pays only the SMI premiums.

Medicaid Services

Title XIX of the Social Security Act requires that in order to receive federal matching funds, certain basic services must be offered to the categorically needy population in any state program:

- inpatient hospital services;

- outpatient hospital services;

- physician services;

- medical and surgical dental services;

- nursing facility (NF) services for individuals aged 21 or older;

- home health care for persons eligible for nursing facility services;

- family planning services and supplies;

- rural health clinic services and any other ambulatory services offered by a rural health clinic that are otherwise covered under the state plan;

- laboratory and x-ray services;

- pediatric and family nurse practitioner services;

- federally-qualified health center services and any other ambulatory services offered by a federally-qualified health center that are otherwise covered under the state plan;

- nurse-midwife services (to the extent authorized under state law); and early and periodic screening, diagnosis, and treatment (EPSDT) services for individuals under age 21.

If a state chooses to include the medically needy population, the state plan must provide, as a minimum, the following services:

- prenatal care and delivery services for pregnant women;

- ambulatory services to individuals under age 18 and individuals entitled to institutional services;

- home health services to individuals entitled to nursing facility services; and

- if the state plan includes services either in institutions for mental diseases or in intermediate care facilities for the mentally retarded (ICF/MRs), it must offer either of the following to each of the medically needy groups: the services contained in 42 CFR sections 440.10 through 440.50 and 440.165 (to the extent that nurse-midwives are authorized to practice under state law or regulations); or the services contained in any seven of the sections in 42 CFR 440.10 through 440.165.

States may also receive federal funding if they elect to provide other optional services. The most commonly covered optional services under the Medicaid program include:

- clinic services;
- nursing facility services for [those] under age 21;
- intermediate care facility/mentally retarded services;
- optometrist services and eyeglasses;
- prescribed drugs;
- TB-related services for TB-infected persons;
- prosthetic devices; and
- dental services.

States may provide home and community-based care waiver services to certain individuals who are eligible for Medicaid. The services to be provided to these persons may include case management, personal care services, respite care services, adult day health services, homemaker/home health aide, habilitation, and other services requested by the state and approved by HCFA.

Amount and Duration of Medicaid Services

Within broad federal guidelines, states determine the amount and duration of services offered under their Medicaid programs. The amount, duration, and scope of each service must be sufficient to reasonably achieve its purpose. States may place appropriate limits on a Medicaid service based on such criteria as medical necessity or utilization control. For example, states may place a reasonable limit on the number of covered physician visits or may require prior authorization to be obtained prior to service delivery.

Health care services identified under the EPSDT program as being "medically necessary" for eligible children must be provided by Medicaid, even if those services are not included as part of the covered services in that state's plan.

With certain exceptions, a state's Medicaid plan must allow recipients freedom of choice among health care providers participating in

Medicaid. States may provide and pay for Medicaid services through various prepayment arrangements, such as a health maintenance organization (HMO). In general, states are required to provide comparable services to all categorically needy eligible persons.

There is an important exception related to home and community-based services "waivers" under which states offer an alternative health care package for persons who would otherwise be institutionalized under Medicaid. States are not limited in the scope of services they can provide under such waivers so long as they are cost effective (except that, other than as a part of respite care, they may not provide room and board for such recipients).

Payment for Medicaid Services

Medicaid operates as a vendor payment program, with payments made directly to the providers. Providers participating in Medicaid must accept the Medicaid reimbursement level as payment in full. Each state has relatively broad discretion in determining (within federally-imposed upper limits and specific restrictions) the reimbursement methodology and resulting rate for services, with three exceptions: (1) for institutional services, payment may not exceed amounts that would be paid under Medicare payment rates; (2) for disproportionate share hospitals (DSHs), different limits apply; and (3) for hospice care services, rates cannot be lower than Medicare rates.

States may impose nominal deductibles, coinsurance, or copayments on some Medicaid recipients for certain services. Emergency services and family planning services must be exempt from such copayments. Certain Medicaid recipients must be excluded from this cost sharing: pregnant women, children under age 18, hospital or nursing home patients who are expected to contribute most of their income to institutional care, and categorically needy HMO enrollees.

The amount of total federal outlays for Medicaid has no set limit (cap); rather, the federal government must match whatever the individual state decides to provide, within the law, for its eligible recipients. However, reimbursement rates must be sufficient to enlist enough providers so that Medicaid care and services are available under the plan at least to the extent that such care and services are available to the general population in that geographic area.

States must augment payment to qualified hospitals that provide inpatient services to a disproportionate number of Medicaid recipients and/or other low-income persons under what is known as the disproportionate share hospital (DSH) program. Legislation passed in 1991 has curtailed some states DSH payments.

The portion of the Medicaid program which is paid by the federal government, known as the Federal Medical Assistance Percentage (FMAP), is determined annually for each state by a formula that compares the state's average per capita income level with the national average. By law, the FMAP cannot be lower than 50 percent nor greater than 83 percent. The wealthier states have a smaller share of their costs reimbursed. The federal government also shares in the state's expenditures for administration of the Medicaid program. Most administrative costs are matched at 50 percent for all states. However, higher matching rates (75, 90, and 100 percent) are authorized by law for certain functions and activities.

Medicaid Trends

Initially, Medicaid was a medical care extension of federally funded income maintenance programs for the poor, with an emphasis on the aged, the disabled, and dependent children and their mothers. Over time, however, Medicaid has been diverging from a firm tie to eligibility for cash programs. Recent legislation ensures Medicaid coverage to an expanded number of low-income pregnant women, poor children, and some Medicare beneficiaries who are not eligible for any cash assistance program, and would not have been eligible for Medicaid under earlier Medicaid rules. Legislative changes focus on enhanced outreach toward specific groups of pregnant women and children, increased access to care, and improved quality of care. Legislation also continued specific benefits beyond the normal run of Medicaid eligibility and placed some restrictions on states' ability to limit some services.

In addition to the increase in numbers of beneficiaries from new legislation, the most pronounced Medicaid service-related trends in recent years have been the continued sharp increase in expenditures for intensive acute care and for home health and nursing facility services for the aged and disabled.

The most significant trend in service delivery is the rapid growth in managed care enrollment within Medicaid. In 1995, almost a quarter of all Medicaid recipients were enrolled in managed care plans. One vehicle for the expansion of managed care, and of new eligibility groups, is the 1915(b) waiver process which allows states increased flexibility to research health care delivery alternatives while controlling program costs. Another vehicle is the section 1115(b) waiver authority which permits states to implement managed care delivery systems within prescribed parameters.

Medicaid Statistics

Who Does Medicaid Serve?

For 1995, Medicaid served the following populations:

- 18.7 million children;
- 7.6 million adults who care for these children;
- 4.4 million elderly; and
- 5.9 million blind and disabled.

(Some beneficiaries are included in more than one category.)

The 18.7 million children served by Medicaid represent one out of every five children in the nation. About one-third of all babies born in the United States are covered by Medicaid.

The number of Medicaid beneficiaries under age 21 has risen from 9.8 million in 1985 to 18.7 million in 1995.

Although the number of Medicaid elderly beneficiaries has increased from 3.1 million in 1985 to 4.4 million in 1995, the payments for these beneficiaries have more than doubled.

Medicaid covered 6 million people with disabilities in 1995. Medicaid blind and disabled beneficiaries increased from 3.0 million in 1985 to 5.8 million in 1995. Payments have increased from $13 billion in 1985 to $49 billion in 1995.

A growing number of states are using the authority available under current law to design and launch a wide variety of Medicaid health care reform demonstrations. The states have used this flexibility to cover more of the working poor, expand managed care enrollment, and test other innovations in the financing and delivery of services for parts or all of their Medicaid populations.

What Services Does the Medicaid Program Purchase?

All states cover a minimum set of services including hospital, physician, and nursing home services. States have the option of covering an additional 31 services including prescription drugs, hospice care, and personal care services. States' flexibility in designing their Medicaid program is highlighted by the fact that over 50 percent of Medicaid benefit payments in 1995 were for optional services and populations selected by the states.

Medicaid is the largest insurer of long term care for all Americans, including the middle class. Medicaid covers 68 percent of nursing home residents and over 50 percent of nursing home costs.

Medicaid covers skilled nursing facility care, intermediate care facilities for the mentally retarded and developmentally disabled, and home and community based services. Although most long term care spending is for institutional care, Medicaid has made great strides in shifting the delivery of services to home and community settings.

How Much Does Medicaid Cost?

Medicaid expenditures for health care in 1995 amounted to $152 billion. The states paid $66 billion (43%) and the federal government paid $86 billion (57%). The federal government contributes between 50% and 80% of the payments made under each state's program. That percentage varies depending on the average per capita income in each state. States and the federal government spent an average of about $3,700 per Medicaid eligible in 1995.

Expenditures vary among beneficiary categories and from state to state. The largest number of Medicaid beneficiaries are AFDC children—47%, but they account for only 15% of the dollars paid out. Conversely, only 27% of beneficiaries are aged, blind, or disabled, yet they account for 72% of the payments made.

Medicaid Serves as a Vehicle for State Health Reform

Freedom-of-choice waivers allow states to enroll Medicaid beneficiaries in cost-effective managed care programs. Currently 45 states operate FOC waiver programs.

The number of Medicaid beneficiaries in managed care programs reached 11.6 million in 1995.

States are using the 1115 waiver authority to conduct demonstration projects aimed at testing large-scale Medicaid program innovations.

Chapter 21

Private Long-Term Care Insurance

Long-term care is a major concern of American families. Studies have shown that Americans rank long-term care second, behind saving for retirement, when prioritizing financial needs. Unfortunately, many Americans do not want to think about needing long-term care and, therefore, fail to plan for it. Others wrongly assume that Medicare or standard health insurance policies will cover the costs of long-term care services. As a result of this failure to plan, tens of thousands of Americans are impoverished each year by the costs of long-term care.

The best time to plan for long-term care is before it is needed. Start thinking about long-term care when you plan for retirement. If you are already retired, it is not too late to begin planning for potential care needs.

Private long-term care insurance is an excellent way to finance long-term care. This [chapter] will guide you through the important process of selecting the right long-term care insurance policy. This [chapter] provides information on long-term care services [and] what to look for in a long-term care insurance policy. [Chapter 59 includes a glossary of terms.]

From "What Consumers Need to Know about Private Long-Term Care Insurance," [Online] undated. Available: http://www.ahca.org/info/what.htm. Produced by American Health Care Association (AHCA), 1201 L St. NW, Washington, DC 20005. For complete contact information, please refer to Chapter 60, "Resources." Reprinted with permission.

Finding a good policy will take some effort, but the effort will be worthwhile. Here are some steps to take when considering the decision to purchase a long-term care insurance policy:

- Talk to your financial planner or insurance agent about whether long-term care insurance makes sense for you.

- Ask your financial advisor to recommend a company and a policy.

- Check with insurance rating services to make sure the insurance company you are considering is financially secure.

- Call your state insurance department and ask about the company and its record in your state.

- Make sure your insurance agent is licensed to sell long-term care insurance in your state.

- Review all the details and options of the policy. Do not rely just on the marketing materials or outline of coverage.

- Make sure you understand all the provisions before you purchase any policy.

- Ask your insurance agent questions. Seek guidance from the state insurance commission office, the Area Agency on Aging, or local senior centers. Discuss policies with friends, family, and others whose opinions you respect. Take time when choosing a policy, and don't allow yourself to be pressured into making quick decisions. And remember: Never pay cash.

The decision to purchase long-term care insurance is not a simple one, but thorough investigation and thoughtful planning now can offer you and your family financial protection for the future, and, most importantly, peace of mind.

Defining Long-Term Care

Long-term care includes a range of nursing, social, and rehabilitative services for people who need ongoing assistance. Most people in long-term care facilities are older, but many young people need long-term care during an extended illness or after an accident.

Assistance with routine personal needs such as bathing, dressing, eating, toileting, and taking medicine is the most common long-term care service. Long-term care facilities also provide skilled nursing and rehabilitative care, which is ordered by a physician and supervised by skilled medical personnel such as a nurse or licensed therapist.

Long-Term Care Is Offered in a Variety of Settings

Nursing facilities are the primary settings for people who require medical care daily or intermittently. You must have a physician specify needed services in a written treatment plan for admission to a nursing facility. Many nursing facility stays are short periods of recuperation from an acute medical episode such as a hip fracture or surgery.

Assisted living facilities or residential care facilities provide general supervision, housekeeping services, medical monitoring, and planned social, recreational, and spiritual activities for people who are still independent and ambulatory. Assisted living facilities do not provide medical care.

Facility care services include skilled nursing care, speech, physical, or occupational therapy, facility health aides, or help from facility makers. Sometimes, family members, or caregivers, provide most of the care with the help of facility aides and skilled professionals.

Adult day care services are available in many communities, providing personal care, skilled care, and recreational services.

Financial Issues and Long-Term Care

The cost of long-term care varies by the level of care needed, the setting where the care is provided, and geographic location. Nursing facilities, assisted living facilities, and facility care services provide different levels of care to different resident populations; therefore, costs are not comparable.

On average, round-the-clock long-term care services in a nursing facility cost $40,000 per year, or $112 per day.

Assisted living costs vary dramatically—anywhere from $900 to $3000 per month depending on room size, amenities provided, and services required.

Facility care, if needed daily, also can be quite expensive. In 1996, an average facility care visit from a registered nurse (RN) cost $99. RN visits for facility care typically do not exceed 2-4 hours per day, so care is not round-the-clock.

Eight hours of adult day care can cost an average of $45 per day.

Nursing Facility Care: About one third of the costs of nursing facility care are paid directly by individuals and their families. Two government programs may pay for some of your care.

195

Medicare, a health insurance program for people age 65 or older, only covers skilled facility care and up to 100 days of skilled care in a nursing facility if you are admitted after a three-day hospitalization (not required if you are an HMO member) and your physician prescribes skilled care in your treatment plan. Many people think that Medicare is the primary payer of nursing facility stays, but Medicare accounts for only 9 percent of nursing facility expenditures.

Medicaid, a program for the poor, pays for approximately 52 percent of the nation's nursing facility care, but only for people who have spent almost all their assets and become impoverished. Due to lack of planning for long-term care, Medicaid is the source of payment for nearly 70 percent of people in nursing facilities!

Unless you have long-term care insurance, qualify under limited conditions for Medicare coverage, or become poor, you will pay out of your savings for nursing facility services.

Assisted Living: About 90 percent of the nation's assisted living services are paid for with private funds. The Supplemental Security Income, Older Americans Act, and Social Services Block Grant programs pay for some assisted living services, while about one-fifth of the states allow the federal Medicaid program to pay for some service components.

Facility Care: Private funds pay for about 46 percent of facility care costs; Medicare covers 32 percent; Medicaid, 22 percent.

Adult Day Care: There are some out-of-pocket expenses for adult day care; however, the majority of funding comes from public sources either the state exclusively, or, in some states, Medicare and Medicaid. Private donations from corporations and charitable groups such as the United Way also supplement the costs of adult day care.

When to Buy Long-Term Care Insurance

Because long-term care insurance premiums are based on age at the time of purchase, the younger you are when you purchase a policy, the less expensive the annual premium. These premiums for most policies stay level each year as you age. If you buy at age 55 a policy that cost $800 per year, you will continue to pay the same premium. However, if you wait until you are 65, the same policy will cost you $1,700 per year.

What to Look for in a Policy

The best policy for you depends on several factors, including your family arrangement, your financial situation, your preferences regarding long-term care choices, and the level of risk you are willing to accept. There is no one best company or one best policy for everyone. You should select a policy that meets your needs.

Before you buy a policy, make sure you know the product you are buying and from whom you are buying it. Be sure your agent is licensed to sell insurance in your state and has received specific training on long-term care insurance. Consult friends, consumer guides, and information from your state's insurance counseling program or local agency on aging.

Selecting a Good Company

More than 115 companies now offer long-term care insurance products, according to the Health Insurance Association of America. Contact your state insurance commissioner's office for a list of companies authorized to sell long-term care insurance in your state.

Investigate the financial health of any insurance company that you are considering. Look for ratings from insurance rating services, such as Moody's or A.M. Best. The insurance company should be rated in one of the top two categories by at least two services and have no low ratings. You can find these rating services in the reference section of your library, or you may call Moody's at 212-553-0300, or A.M. Best at 908-439-2200.

Finding a Policy

Long-term care insurance is sold in the form of individual policies, individual policies through an organization, and group policies. An individual policy is sold directly to you, usually by insurance agents or financial planners. You have tremendous flexibility selecting the company, the policy, and the amount of coverage.

Some individual policies are sold through groups, such as an association or organization. Although you do not have a choice of companies, you have the advantage that the organization selected a good company and policy to offer you. But you may have fewer choices in the amount of coverage and options in the policy.

A group policy is usually offered through your employer, who contracts for the insurance plan. Group policies may cost less than comparable individual policies, but your choices are also limited.

Selecting A Policy

The most important factor in selecting a policy is the set of conditions required to qualify for coverage. Buying a policy that covers long-term care services will not help if you do not qualify for benefits. Many policies require a policyholder to have an acute medical condition before he or she can qualify for benefits. The best policies are not contingent on an acute medical condition: They will pay for the long-term care of a person with a physical or cognitive impairment.

People who have a physical impairment need assistance with the activities of daily living (ADLs) feeding, dressing, transferring, bathing, taking medications, and toileting. Policies differ in the number of impairments a person must have before they qualify for benefits. Avoid policies that require physical impairment due to a medical condition, or that require assistance with ADLs to be medically necessary.

People who are cognitively impaired have Alzheimer's disease or other forms of dementia. A policy's definition of cognitive impairment should never refer to the activities of daily living. People with dementia usually can perform ADLs if prompted, but often exhibit inappropriate or bizarre behavior.

Another important factor is which entity or gatekeeper decides whether or not you qualify for benefits. Most policies require your physician to certify the reasons you need long-term care services. Some policies require your physician to write a treatment plan. Some insurance companies offer a care (or case) manager to determine if you qualify or continue to qualify for benefits. Some care managers also help you find and monitor long-term care services available in your community.

How Much Insurance to Buy

Most long-term care insurance policies pay a maximum fixed dollar amount for each day you receive covered services. When you buy a policy, you decide the value of the fixed dollar amount and the length of time your benefits will run. For example, if you buy a policy that pays $100 per day for three years, the policy value is $109,500 a figure that is computed by multiplying 365 days times 3 years for the maximum number of days multiplied by $100, the amount the policy will pay per day. Remember that no policy guarantees to cover all costs of long-term care without a limit.

Because most retirement income is fixed and may not keep pace with inflation, your ability to afford premiums may diminish. Buying too much insurance may mean that you cannot afford to pay the premium later. The four components used to determine how much insurance to buy are:

- Benefit Amount
- Inflation Adjustment
- Benefit Period
- Deductible Period

Benefit Amount is the maximum fixed dollar amount that a policy will pay each day. A potential purchaser of long-term care insurance usually has the option to choose a daily benefit amount ranging from $40 per day to $200 per day for nursing facility coverage. Most policies offer a daily benefit for facility care that is equal to half of the nursing facility daily benefit, while some allow you to select the benefit amount you want for facility care. To determine the benefit amount best for you, find out today's cost of a nursing facility of your choice, then decide how much from your income you could afford to spend per day. Couples, likely to need the entire income for the other spouse, should figure that no income will go to cover long-term care costs. The difference between the cost of a good nursing facility and the amount from your income is the benefit amount you should buy. Generally, this is 80 percent to 100 percent of today's long-term care cost.

Inflation Adjustment is the increase of the benefit amount to cover the effect of inflation. The cost of long-term care services increases every year due to inflation. A policy paying $100 per day will cover most of the cost of a nursing facility today. However, this same policy probably will cover only a fraction of the cost in future years unless you buy inflation protection.

There are several optional policy features. The best, and most expensive, is an inflation adjustment that increases the benefit amount by a certain percentage (usually 5 percent) compounded for the life of the policyholder including while you are receiving benefits. In other words, the benefit amount increases 5 percent annually over what the policy would pay the previous year.

Instead of a compounded rate, you can buy a simple rate inflation adjustment, which increases the benefit amount by 5 percent of the original benefit, instead of the previous year's benefit amount. The difference is small in a short period of time, but quite substantial over a long period of time.

Policies may limit the length of time the inflation adjustment will increase the benefit amount. Some policies limit the increase of the benefit amount to a specific number of years generally about 20 or until the policy doubles, which is about 16 years for a compounded rate of inflation, and 20 years for a simple rate. Some policies

199

will increase the benefit amount until the policyholder reaches a specific age.

Any limit on the benefit amount increase will reduce the cost of the inflation adjustment option. You may want to consider an inflation adjustment restriction, if the option would not leave you without inflation protection. If you are 60 years old and expect to live into your nineties, a policy that stopped increasing the benefit amount after 20 years would leave you with 10 or more years without any inflation adjustment to your benefit amount. Meanwhile, the cost of long-term care has continued to increase. It is worth it to pay a little extra to ensure that you are protected. However, if you are 70 and believe you will need long-term care by the time you are 80, you could save some money by buying a policy that has a simple rate inflation adjustment for 20 years.

A few policies allow you to purchase additional benefit amounts in future years. However, you will buy these additional amounts at the higher premium based on age. You may want to consider this option if you are under age 50. However, for older ages, this option is substantially more expensive than the automatic annual inflation adjustment option.

Ask your financial advisor to compare various inflation options and the resulting premiums. You should select the inflation option that is best for your situation.

Benefit Period is the length of time the policy will pay for covered services. Policies offer benefit periods ranging from two years to an unlimited benefit period. You should first determine the benefit amount before you consider the benefit period. Many people worry about the potential of a very long stay in a nursing facility. However, there is a very small probability (less than 8 percent) that you will stay more than five years in a nursing facility. The primary consideration is how much you can afford in premiums. The average length of stay in a nursing facility is two-and-a-half years. If all you can afford is two years of coverage, it probably will be adequate. If you can afford a longer benefit period, you should buy it.

Deductible Period, also called the elimination period, is the number of days that you pay for covered services before the policy pays. Consumer advisors recommend a deductible period between 20 days and 100 days. Policies with longer deductible periods have lower premiums, but you will have to pay for needed services until you meet the deductible. The length of the deductible period you should buy depends on the assets you have available to pay for services during the deductible period and how much you can afford in premiums.

Services Covered by Long-Term Care Insurance

The most important service a policy should cover is custodial or personal care. A good long-term care insurance policy will cover all levels of care, especially personal care, and all settings, including facility care, community adult day care, assisted living facilities, and nursing facilities. Policies usually differentiate between nursing facility care and facility care. Under facility care, most policies include the community services of adult day care and respite care (temporary overnight care to relieve family caregivers). Most policies pay a different benefit amount for facility care, usually amounting to half the nursing facility daily benefit. However, many are now offering equal benefit amounts or the option to choose a benefit amount.

Assisted living facility services are usually covered under facility care. If a policy requires you to purchase facility care services from a facility health agency, it may not cover assisted living facility care because the facility provides the service, not a facility health agency. Some policies cover assisted living facilities under nursing facility benefits. If you are interested in assisted living facilities, make sure you know how the policy handles the service.

Services Not Covered by Long-Term Care Insurance

Like all insurance policies, long-term care insurance contains limitations and exclusions. Without limitations and exclusions, premiums would be unaffordable. In general, the following conditions are NOT covered:

- Health problems you had before you purchased the policy (some insurance companies exclude coverage for pre-existing conditions for six months);

- Mental and nervous disorders or diseases, other than Alzheimer's disease and related dementia;

- Alcohol and drug addiction;

- Illnesses caused by an act of war;

- Illnesses resulting from intentionally self-inflicted injury;

- Attempted suicide; and

- Treatment already paid for by the government.

Other Available Options

Some policies offer a nonforfeiture benefit, which provides a return of some premiums paid or a reduced benefit if the policyholder stops paying the premium after some period of time. You should consider the likelihood of not being able to pay your premium if the premium increases or your income decreases. Because this benefit significantly increases the cost of the premium, carefully review the available nonforfeiture benefit options. For policies that offer a reduced benefit for the premiums paid, it is usually preferable to have a policy that will pay the full benefit amount for a shorter benefit period.

On the other hand, if your financial situation is secure, and you foresee no risk of losing your coverage because you cannot pay the premium, you might choose a lower premium with no nonforfeiture benefit. It is helpful to keep in mind the comparison between investment and insurance. If you are considering long-term care insurance as an investment, paying a higher premium now and having some protection against lapsing in the future makes sense. The other option for those seeking an investment, rather than pure insurance, is to purchase a life insurance policy with a long-term care rider or accelerated death benefits, or to invest the additional premium amount in a high-return investment.

The Cost of Long-Term Care Insurance

The cost of a long-term care insurance policy primarily depends on your age. The older you are when you purchase a policy, the higher your premium. The annual premium for a low-option policy for a person at age 50 is about $400. This same policy for a 65-year-old person is about $1,100 per year; for a person age 79, the policy would cost more than $4,300. Of course, the younger person pays the premium for a longer period of time. However, if long-term care is needed at age 85 in each of these cases, the 50-year-old person would have paid a total of $14,175 for long-term care insurance, compared to the 79-year-old person paying $26,232. In addition, the 50-year-old will receive a higher benefit amount from the inflation adjustment. Simply, the earlier you buy the policy, the less expensive it will be in the long run.

Of course, there is nothing you can do about your age. But you can control the premium by controlling the amount and options you purchase in a policy. Higher daily benefits and special features, such as inflation protection and nonforfeiture benefits, increase your premium.

Studies of the cost of long-term care insurance show a three-fold difference from a low-option policy to a high-option policy in every age category.

The following chart will help you compare the premiums of different insurance policies. Indicate the amount of insurance and the option you select for each policy.

Table 21.1. Comparison of Total Premiums Paid by Issue Age

Issue Age	Annual Premium	No. of Years Paying Premium	Total Premiums Paid at Age 85
50	$405	35	$14,175
65	$1,086	20	$20,000
79	$4,372	6	$26,232

Table 21.2. Comparing Cost of Policies

	Policy A	Policy B	Policy C
Annual Premiums	_____	_____	_____
Benefit Amount	_____	_____	_____
Nursing Facility	_____	_____	_____
Facility Care	_____	_____	_____
Inflation Adjustment	_____	_____	_____
Annual Percent	_____	_____	_____
Simple/Compounded	_____	_____	_____
Time Period	_____	_____	_____
Benefit Period	_____	_____	_____
Nursing Facility	_____	_____	_____
Facility Care	_____	_____	_____
Deductible Period	_____	_____	_____
Special Features	_____	_____	_____
_____	_____	_____	_____
_____	_____	_____	_____
_____	_____	_____	_____

Premium Increases

Most premiums for long-term care are level. After you have purchased a policy, the premiums do not automatically increase as you get older. However, level premiums do not mean that the premium will never increase. It means that the company cannot raise the premiums due to increased age or the health of an individual policyholder. The insurance company may raise premium rates for an entire class of people in the state, with permission from the state insurance commission.

Policy Cancellation

The best policy to buy is guaranteed renewable, meaning that the insurance company cannot cancel the policy for any reason, except if you do not pay the premium. Most companies selling individual policies clearly state that the policy is guaranteed renewable.

Some policies provide lapse protection for individuals who develop dementia. Thus, if a person who has regularly paid premiums for years develops Alzheimer's disease or some other condition affecting mental health, and forgets to pay the premium, coverage will not be canceled. Some companies offer to notify a third party if a premium is not paid on time.

Health Status

All insurance companies ask questions regarding your current health status. The better companies will medically underwrite the policy by asking you to complete a medical history form and supply the name of your physician. The insurance company may contact you or your physician to verify your answers or clarify your medical conditions. If you have medical conditions in your history or have current medical programs, the company may refuse to insure you. Medical underwriting is not an exact science. Therefore, if you are denied a policy, appeal the decision. Ask the company why it refused to insure you.

At the time you submit a claim, a few companies will claim that you failed to disclose your entire medical history when purchasing a policy, and state they would not have sold that policy to you if they had known your full medical history. This procedure, known as post claims underwriting, is illegal in many states. Be sure to purchase a policy from a company that asks the detailed medical questions up front.

A good company will sell a long-term care insurance policy only to people who are reasonably healthy and at relatively low risk of needing long-term care in the near future. Some companies will not sell to a person over age 85, or will sell only a lower benefit policy to people between 80 and 85 years of age.

Some companies require a waiting period for any pre-existing conditions. Regardless of these consequences, you should fully disclose your medical conditions.

Reviewing the Policy

You should review the actual policy before buying. If your agent will not leave a sample policy for you to review at your leisure, then find a new agent. After you buy, you have a right to review the policy for 30 days with the option to cancel for a full refund.

Complaints

If you have any complaints regarding the agent or the company that sold you long-term care insurance, write to the consumer affairs or insurance department in your state. Your complaint will trigger an investigation, which could help you, as well as other consumers. The policy should explain how to file a complaint, where to get information from your insurance company, and how to appeal a claim denial.

Switching Policies

There might be situations in which canceling an existing policy and buying a new one makes sense. You should carefully compare the increased premiums to the added benefits of the new policy. Remember that your premium is based on your age at the time you initially purchase a policy.

Insurance companies introduce new products about every two or three years. Ask your agent about the company's record regarding policy upgrades. Many companies automatically notify existing policyholders and offer the new policy at a higher premium. Some companies automatically upgrade existing policies to new policies. However, some companies do not always notify policyholders of newer, better products, and require you to buy the improved policy as though you were a new buyer.

Conclusion

Long-term care insurance can protect your assets and provide you with peace of mind. You and your financial advisor should discuss whether long-term care insurance is right for you. If long-term care insurance fits your needs, purchase from a reputable company a policy that offers benefits that cover physical or cognitive impairment. Carefully consider how much insurance and the options you need. There is no one best policy. However, with a little research, you will find a policy that fits your needs at a premium you can afford.

For More Information

Your state Insurance Commissioner's office

Your local Area Agency on Aging

American Association of Retired Persons
(or your local AARP chapter)
601 E St., NW
Washington, DC 20049
(202) 434-2277

Health Insurance Association of America
555 13th St. NW
Washington, DC 20004
(202) 824-1600

National Association for Home Care
519 C St., NE
Washington, DC 20002
(202) 547-7424

United Seniors Health Cooperative
1331 H St., NW
Washington, DC 20005
(202) 393-6222

Chapter 22

Nursing Home Statistics

All figures are for the United States.

Number of Nursing Homes: 16,700 (1995)
Percent Change Since 1985: -13%
Number of Residents: 1.5 million (1995)
Number of Beds Available: 1.8 million (1994)
Percent Change Since 1985: +9% (1995)
Source: *Advance Data 280*

Americans Less Likely to Use Nursing Home Care Today

Dramatic changes in the nursing home industry have taken place over the past decade, especially because of growth in home health care, according to findings from the latest survey of nursing homes in America released today by HHS [the Department of Health and Human Services].

The 1995 survey shows there are fewer, but larger, nursing homes offering long-term care today than 10 years ago. At the same time,

---

Excerpted from "Nursing Home Care," [Online] May 27, 1998. Available: http://www.cdc.gov/nchswww/fastats/nursingh.htm; and from "Americans Less Likely to Use Nursing Home Care Today," [Online] January 23, 1997. Available: http://www.cdc.gov/nchswww/releases/97news/nurshome.htm. Produced by the CDC's National Center for Health Statistics (NCHS). For complete contact information, please refer to Chapter 60, "Resources."

despite the growth in the number of older Americans who make up the largest proportion of nursing home residents, there has been only a slight increase in the number of residents and an actual decline in the occupancy rates.

The 1995 survey also showed that nursing homes are more likely to be operated as part of a chain, when comparing the 1995 survey with the previous survey conducted in 1985.

"Americans who need long-term care have more choices today. Many more are able to stay in their homes and still receive the care they need," said HHS Secretary Donna E. Shalala. She attributed this shift to the rapid growth in home health care as well as the advances in medical technology that permit people to postpone institutional care and opt for less costly home-based alternatives.

However, Secretary Shalala said, "Nursing homes remain a critical component of health care in this country and are essential for those who need intensive, 24-hour medical care. Wherever care is provided, we must ensure that it is appropriate and high quality."

Since 1985, the number of nursing homes decreased by 13 percent while the number of beds increased by 9 percent. The number of nursing home residents was up only 4 percent between 1985 and 1995, despite an 18-percent increase in the population aged 65 years and over. Prior to the 1995 survey, utilization rates had kept pace with the increase in the elderly population.

About 1.5 million residents were receiving care in 16,700 nursing homes in 1995. Nearly 1.8 million beds were available for use and these facilities operated at about 87 percent of their capacity. Almost 90 percent of the residents in the 1995 survey were aged 65 years and over. More than 35 percent were aged 85 years and over. Residents were also predominantly white (88 percent) and female (72 percent).

Most nursing homes (66 percent) are operated for profit and over half are operated as part of chains. Chain-affiliated homes increased from 41 to 55 percent between 1985 and 1995. While there was a 23-percent drop in the number of proprietary homes over the past decade, the total number of beds in proprietary homes increased by almost 3 percent, resulting in fewer, but larger, homes.

Overall, some 1.3 million full-time equivalent employees (FTEs) were working in nursing homes. The largest single category—almost 1 million FTEs—provide nursing services.

The 1995 National Nursing Home Survey is the fourth survey conducted by the National Center for Health Statistics, Centers for Disease Control and Prevention, since the early 1970s to track and profile the use of nursing homes.

The report, "An Overview of Nursing Homes and Their Current Residents: Data from the 1995 National Nursing Home Survey," is available from the National Center for Health Statistics, 6525 Belcrest Rd., Hyattsville, MD 20782, and can be downloaded from the NCHS home page on the Internet at http://www.cdc.gov/nchswww/default.htm.

For questions about NCHS, please contact the NCHS Office of Public Affairs (301) 436-7551, or via e-mail at nchsquery@cdc.gov.

Chapter 23

Selecting a Nursing Home

The selection of nursing home care for a loved one or friend is often a difficult task. To do the job right, one must be prepared for the time-consuming effort of gathering the many facts needed to help in the decision-making process. Finding the right facility is all-important to a loved one's well-being. The facility selected will be the person's home and community sometimes for the remainder of the person's life. However, through rehabilitative efforts, nearly one-half of the patients of a proficient nursing home can be discharged to live independently once again.

What Is a Nursing Home?

The term "nursing home" is a widely misused and misunderstood term. The term has been defined as anything from a rest home to an acute care hospital. This is confusing to anyone who needs to know the type of facility to select that will best meet their needs and what the appropriate level of care should be.

Nursing homes are primarily designed to meet the needs of persons convalescing from illness or to provide long-term nursing supervision for persons with chronic medical problems. A nursing home is not a hospital and does not provide the acute care provided in a

Excerpted from "The Nursing Home Information Site," by Gary Hickerson, M.S.S.W. [Online]. Available: http://www.angelfire.com/tn/NursingHome/ index.html. © 1996, 1997, 1998, 1999 by The Nursing Home Information Site. All rights reserved. Reprinted with permission.

hospital setting. The goal of nursing home care is to provide care and treatment to restore or maintain the patient's highest level of physical, mental, and social well-being. To help the reader better understand the various levels of care available, included below are definitions of nursing facilities:

- A Skilled Nursing Facility (SNF) is a facility that is required to provide continuous (24-hour) nursing supervision by registered or licensed vocational nurses. Commonly referred to as "nursing homes" or "convalescent hospitals," these facilities normally care for the incapacitated person in need of long- or short-term care and assistance with many aspects of daily living (walking, bathing, dressing, eating). At a minimum, SNFs provide medical, nursing, dietary, pharmacy, and activity services.

- An Intermediate Care Facility (ICF) is a facility that is required to provide 8 hours of nursing supervision per day. Because of their physical appearance, these facilities are often confused with the SNFs. Intermediate care, however, is less extensive than skilled nursing care and generally serves patients who are ambulatory and need less supervision and care. Licensed nurses are not always immediately available in an ICF. At a minimum, ICFs provide medical, intermittent nursing, dietary, pharmacy, and activity services.

- A Skilled Nursing Facility for special disabilities is a facility that provides a "protective" or "security" environment to persons with mental disabilities. Many of these facilities will have "locked" or "security" areas where patients reside for their own protection or the protection of others in the facility. Some SNFs have a designated number of beds for long-term mental patients.

Licensing and Certification

All state governments require that nursing homes be licensed. The licensing requirements establish acceptable practices for care and services. State inspectors visit nursing homes at least once a year to determine their compliance with state standards and their qualifications to receive Medicare and Medicaid reimbursement. Most nursing homes are certified to participate in both the federal Medicare and Medicaid (Medi-Cal in California) programs. Some have been approved to provide both skilled nursing and intermediate care services.

Who Owns and Manages Nursing Homes?

Some nursing homes are operated as nonprofit corporations. They are sponsored by religious, charitable, fraternal, and other groups or run by government agencies at the federal, state, or local levels. But many nursing homes are businesses operated for profit. They may be owned by individuals or corporations. Sometimes they are part of a chain of nursing homes.

Final responsibility for the operation of a nursing home lies with its governing body. It is the legal entity licensed by the state to operate the facility. The governing body sets policies, adopts rules, and enforces them for the healthcare and safety of patients. The person in charge of the day-to-day management is called the administrator.

Who Directs Care?

A person in a nursing home must be under the care of a physician. If the person's personal physician will not continue to provide care, a new physician must be chosen. It is the physician's obligation to evaluate a patient's needs and to prescribe a program of medical care for the patient's health and well-being. A nursing home is not free to initiate any form of medical treatment, medication, restraint, special diet, or therapy without the consent of a physician.

Before a person is admitted to a nursing home, a complete physical examination should be completed. The results of this examination will determine whether skilled nursing care or intermediate care is required, the patient's diagnosis, the duration of the illness or need for nursing home care, what treatments are indicated, and the patient's rehabilitation potential.

What about Financing?

Nursing home care is expensive. Although prices vary, the basic charge for a double-bed room in a typical nursing home is in the range of $20,000 to $50,000 a year. Homes in rural areas tend to be slightly less expensive than those in cities. The cost of medications and physician visits are not included in the basic charge. Also, special treatments such as physical, occupational, and speech therapy often add to the cost. There are also possible additional charges for drugs, laundry, haircuts, and extra services.

Three out of four patients are dependent upon government assistance through Medicare and/or Medicaid. Other sources of financial aid might be available to the patient from private health insurance (possibly supplemental Medicare insurance, called Medigap). However, Medicare will partially pay for the first 100 days of skilled nursing home care and nothing for care in an intermediate care nursing facility. Medigap policies typically pay only a portion of the daily costs and then only for a limited number of days. Long-term or catastrophic care insurance is designed to provide benefits for this type of care.

Eligibility for Medicaid (Medi-Cal in California) is contingent upon the amount of a patient's (and spouse's) income and personal and real property. To receive nursing home services under the Medicaid (Medi-Cal) program, certain medical requirements must also be met. Financial assets accumulated by the patient and spouse could be exhausted through prolonged care in a skilled nursing facility. Therefore, it is extremely important to plan ahead by determining all of the benefits available under Medicare and Medicaid. Medicaid generally pays a daily rate that is significantly lower than private-pay residents. Hence, Medicaid residents are less preferred by nursing homes. Some nursing homes do accept Medicaid residents or retain residents whose personal resources have been depleted and who have become Medicaid recipients.

Federal and state laws are intended to limit discrimination against Medicaid beneficiaries yet they often face discrimination in admissions to nursing homes or the services they receive.

Most states determine Medicaid eligibility using the combined assets and income of a couple. A Medicaid applicant must deplete a spouse's income and assets before receiving coverage. Impoverishment of the spouse of a nursing home resident who is on Medicaid is not uncommon. Consult your state's policies as they relate to spousal assets and income.

Advance Planning

If you think you will need a nursing home at some time in the foreseeable future—for yourself or a relative—it will pay to plan ahead. Many good nursing homes have long waiting lists, and the chances of getting placed in the home of your choice will be greatly enhanced if placement is made on a waiting list prior to the actual time of need. Also, this will give a prospective patient time to get mentally adjusted to the idea of the change.

Unfortunately, the choice of a nursing home is often made in a crisis atmosphere when time is short and minds are troubled. Selecting a home is an important decision—one that deserves foresight and careful clear-headed consideration.

Here are some things you can do in advance that will help you in deciding on a nursing home:

- Make a point of learning about nursing homes. Watch for articles in newspapers and magazines and for television programs that deal with nursing homes. Also, pick up brochures on the subject from social service agencies, senior centers, or your local health department.

- Find out what nursing homes are located in your community and learn what you can about them. If you have friends or relatives who are familiar with the homes, ask for their opinions on them. If you know people who live in nursing homes, pay them a visit and gather some firsthand impressions.

- If your county has published a nursing home guide, you can probably start by making a list of possible homes in your area. Or you may check with the State Department of Health Services' Licensing Field Office and ask to see the latest "Health Facilities Directory." Your local Agency on Aging will also be able to help.

- Each county has an ombudsman program that provides volunteer problem solving for relatives and patients in nursing homes. It may be helpful to contact your local ombudsman office for information about a particular nursing home. The ombudsman program, federally mandated, is designed to provide information to the public about nursing homes in a particular area and to resolve complaints on behalf of the nursing home residents. The ombudsman should be listed in the local government section of your telephone book. Your physician also may be able to suggest some nursing homes you might consider.

Nursing home inspection reports completed by the State Department of Health Services are also available to the public at the field offices. You may wish to review the latest inspection reports for various homes on your list before making actual visits to the facilities. Be sure to check for noncompliance pertaining to patient care, staff adequacy, and facility cleanliness and maintenance.

Selection of a Nursing Home

When you have compiled a list of the places that seem most appropriate, you should make a personal visit to each one. It is best to make an appointment with the administrator and take along a copy of the nursing home checklist.

When you do visit a home, there are a number of services and other matters that should be observed and evaluated:

- Location—Consider the home's location. It is not always possible, but it is preferable that the home be convenient for friends, relatives, and your doctor, as well as appealing to you. The home should be reasonably close to a hospital in case of a medical emergency.

- Facility Size—A large home may have more activities while a smaller home might be more personal. Decide which is best for your needs. You should also consider the quality—not just the quantity—of the services and activities offered.

- Visiting Hours—Find out whether the visiting hours are convenient. Often the best arrangement is one that allows visitors to come anytime.

- Financing—It is very important to check with the facility regarding what services Medicaid (Medi-Cal) or Medicare covers. Make sure you find out what extra costs are involved in addition to the basic daily room rate. Often extra charges are made for professional services beyond basic nursing care (also for things such as television and toiletries). Some homes only provide the bare minimum in the way of services.

- Room Selection—Find out whether attention is paid to roommate and room selection—two factors that can be very important to your happiness. You do not need to feel committed to your first roommate. If you are dissatisfied, see if you can change. Also, see if you can bring some of your own furniture.

- Bedhold—Ask if they reserve a bed if you need to be transferred to a hospital. Medicaid will pay for 7 days of bedhold. Medicare and private-pay residents will have to pay for each day the bed is held but not more than the regular daily rate. Sometimes if hospital stay is extended, you can make an agreement with the nursing home.

- Valuables—Find out how valuables are protected. Theft is sometimes a problem in nursing homes. If at all possible, you should leave valuable items with friends or relatives.

- Grievance Procedure—Ask whether patients have some sort of grievance procedure. Find out if there is a patients' council and a way that patients can be involved in decision making.

- Volunteers—Find out if community volunteers are used at the home. Active community involvement by individuals and groups of volunteers can greatly extend the amount of patient services available and help reduce the isolation and loneliness that many nursing home patients feel.

- Morale—See how the patients' morale appears to be. Do they have privacy and respect? Do they have access to things like television and radio? Be sure you take into consideration what you are comfortable with when making your selection.

- Food—Check the food being served. Make a visit at the time of the midday meal which is often the main meal. Ask the other patients about the quality of the food. Is the dining room atmosphere attractive, pleasant, and clean, the cold food cold? Is some food available at times other than mealtimes? Do they supply food for special diets?

Nursing Home Admission Agreements

Once you have made a selection of a nursing home, you will want to review and be sure you thoroughly understand the home's contract or financial agreement. If you have questions, ask a lawyer or the local long-term-care ombudsman in your area (check in phone book). Since this agreement constitutes a legal contract, it is advisable to have a lawyer review the agreement before signing it. Free legal assistance is usually available to senior citizens. You can find out about this from your Area Agency on Aging (listed in your phone book) or from someone at the Senior Center. NEVER SIGN A LEGAL DOCUMENT THAT YOU DO NOT UNDERSTAND.

Your admission papers should include the following items:

- The agreement stating the terms and conditions, the daily room rate, and what services are covered by it. States set licensing standards requiring nursing homes to provide a basic set of services (such as nursing and personal care, meals, activities). These are supposed to be covered by the basic rate.

- A list of optional services and the charges for them. The facility must provide an itemized bill. Such optional services could include

217

choice of meals, laundry, toiletry items, special trips, etc. If you are a Medicaid recipient, you should receive a special list of optional services (Medicaid pays for laundry and hair trims, for example).

- A copy of each Patient's Bill of Rights.

- A statement about eligibility for Medicaid.

- A statement that the nursing home is or is not Medicare and Medicaid certified.

Illegal Actions

Certified nursing homes may not require Medicaid-eligible persons to make contributions, donations, or gifts as a condition of admission or continued stay in a nursing home. Private-paying individuals do not have this protection. When certified nursing homes sign with the Medicaid program, they agree to accept Medicaid payment as "payment in full." If you become eligible for Medicaid, then the nursing home will receive payment for care and may not discharge the patient on the grounds of "nonpayment." Certified nursing homes may not transfer or discharge you when your private funds have been exhausted and you become eligible for Medicaid unless the home does not participate in the Medicaid or Medicare program. If someone treats you in this manner check with a lawyer or ombudsman.

Resources

While in a nursing home, most problems can be worked out with the nurses, the staff, or the resident council. If they cannot, discuss the problems with family members. Persons who experience problems with nursing homes may obtain assistance from the nursing home ombudsman, a person in your state or local office on aging who is designated to investigate complaints and take corrective action on behalf of nursing home residents. Federal law guarantees your right to seek help from an ombudsman without fear of retaliation.

Making a Smooth Transition

Be prepared to make the transition into a nursing home [as] easy as possible. Such a change may affect the whole family and it will take some time to adjust to the new living arrangements. Some nursing homes have a social worker or nurse specialist who conducts preadmission group sessions for family members. You can make the resident more comfortable by accompanying him or her on moving day, and by helping choose familiar items to bring along—family photos or favorite decorative items to make the room more attractive.

The frequency of visits to the resident is an individual decision, but keep in mind that the presence of family members greatly helps to create a more personal atmosphere in the nursing home. Family visits offer reassurance to the resident that someone still cares. In fact, those residents whose families are involved in their care usually have higher morale and receive better care from the staff. Taking the resident out occasionally is also helpful.

Nursing Home Checklist

The following is a checklist of points to consider when selecting a nursing home. Refer to it as you talk with staff members and tour a home. It can also help you in comparing different homes.

Administration

1. Does the nursing home have the required current license from the state or letter of approval from a licensing agency?

2. Is the home certified to participate in the Medicare and Medicaid programs?

3. Do staff members show patients genuine interest and affection?

4. Do patients look well cared for and generally content?

5. Are patients allowed to wear their own clothes, decorate their rooms, and keep a few prized possessions on hand?

6. Is there a written statement of patients' rights? Is this statement displayed where it can be seen?

General Physical Considerations

Comfort

1. Is the nursing home clean and orderly?

2. Are toilet and bathing facilities easy for handicapped patients to use?

3. Is the home well lighted?

4. Is the home reasonably free of unpleasant odors?

5. Are rooms well ventilated and kept at a comfortable temperature?

Safety

1. Are there wheelchair ramps where necessary?

2. Are there grab bars in toilet and bathing facilities?

3. Are there handrails on both sides of the hallways?

4. Is there an automatic sprinkler system and automatic emergency lighting?

5. Are there portable fire extinguishers?

6. Are exit doors unobstructed and unlocked from inside and easily accessible?

7. Are emergency evacuation plans posted in prominent locations?

8. Are there smoke detectors and fire alarms on every floor?

9. Is there a fire station near the home?

Medical, Dental, and Pharmaceutical Services

1. In case of medical emergencies, is a physician available at all times, either on staff or on call?

2. Does the home have an arrangement with an outside dental service to provide patients with dental care?

3. Are pharmaceutical services supervised by a qualified pharmacist?

4. Does the home have arrangements with a nearby hospital for quick transfer of patients in an emergency?

Nursing Services

1. Is at least one registered nurse (RN) or licensed practical nurse (LPN) on duty day and night?

2. Are nurse call buttons located at each patient's bed and in toilet and bathing facilities?

Food Services

1. Is the kitchen clean and reasonably tidy?

2. Are at least three meals served each day?

3. Are patients given enough food?

4. Are special meals prepared for patients on therapeutic or other diets?

5. Do patients who need help receive it, whether in the dining room or in their own rooms?

Rehabilitation Therapy, Social Service, and Patient Activities

1. Is there a full-time program of physical therapy for patients who need it?

2. Are there special services available to aid patients and their families?

3. Does the nursing home have a varied program of recreational, cultural, and intellectual activities for patients?

4. Are activities offered for patients who are relatively inactive or confined to their rooms?

Patients' Rooms

1. Is a married couple allowed to share a room?

2. Do all rooms have a window to the outside?

3. Is there a curtain or screen available to provide privacy for each bed whenever necessary?

4. Does each patient have a reading light, a comfortable chair, and a closet and chest of drawers for personal belongings?

Responsibilities

1. Once a patient is admitted, will the nursing home assume responsibility for taking the patient to medical appointments or other outside community activities?

2. Is the nursing home clear about what responsibilities should be assumed and/or kept by the family?

Financing of Long-Term Care

There are three basic ways to pay for long-term care in a nursing home: Medicare, Medicaid, or private pay (out of pocket or by using long-term care insurance).

Medicare is the federal program offered to those who are needing a skilled level of care after a 3-day hospital stay. Skilled care is best described by the type of care you need due to a hip fracture or stroke—therapy on a daily basis.

Medicare is limited in the number of days it will pay—up to 100. Medicare pays 100% for the first 20 days (after the 3 day hospital stay and if skilled care is needed), beginning on day 21-100 there is a copayment required with Medicare. Most Seniors have a Medicare Supplement policy. Medicare supplements will pay in conjunction with Medicare. Once Medicare stops paying for care, most supplements will not continue to pay.

If you have exhausted Medicare payments the only other options are Medicaid and paying out of pocket (private pay). Medicaid is available for those individuals that are low income or have limited resources. Medicaid is the state welfare program and has limitations as to the amount of assets you can own and the amount of income you may receive each month before you are eligible.

The federal government has instituted restrictions on the transferring of assets out of an estate to qualify for Medicaid. There is a look-back period of 36 months or 60 months if a trust has been established. A law was passed in 1996 making it a crime to shift assets to become eligible for Medicaid.

In 1996, the average cost for a year in a nursing home averaged between $36,000 and $50,000. This can be financially devastating. Especially if a patient stays the average of 3 years or even longer. Some patients have spent more than $100,000 or even $500,000 on long-term care expenses.

Besides paying out of your own pocket you can purchase long-term care insurance. This insurance must be purchased prior to needing long-term care. The eligibility for the insurance is based on your current health. Therefore if you are already ill, you probably will not be insurable.

Most financial planners recommend that LTC insurance be purchased in your late 50s or early 60s. In this range the cost is quite affordable and your health is probably still pretty good. The premiums are based on your age, health, and the type of plan that you purchase.

LTC Insurance Benefit Considerations

When purchasing LTC Insurance you must make three main decisions:

1. Daily Benefit—the amount of money you will receive from the insurance company on a daily basis for your care. You usually can select between $50 and $250 per day. Find out what the current cost of care is in your area and it will help you make the decision as to what daily benefit you want. (also see inflation protection below).

2. Benefit Period—the length of time you will receive payments from the insurance company once you need care. You usually can select a specific number of years (2,3,4,5,) or lifetime plans are also available. The average length of stay in a nursing home is 2 1/2 to 3 years. Note: A three-year plan will be less expensive than a lifetime plan.

3. Elimination Period (deductible)—the number of days that you will be responsible for paying for your care before the insurance begins to pay. This works like most insurance deductibles except it is stated in a number of days instead of dollars. Most plans have a variety of options like 0 days, 20 days, 60 days, or 100 days. Be sure to check if this deductible is once in a lifetime or if it can repeat.

Also, there are three optional decisions that can be added to your plan:

1. Inflation Protection—this ties back to your daily benefit and allows it to grow on an annual basis to help keep your plan in step with inflation. It is built into your original premium and therefore will increase your annual premium. You may have choices of 5% simple or 5% compounded. You do not have to add this to your plan - but it is certainly recommended if you are younger when you buy your policy.

2. Home Health Care Coverage—some policies will also give you the option of receiving insurance benefits in your own home. This options will allow you greater choice as to where your

care can be paid for by the insurance. It may cover community care like Adult Day Care Centers and Assisted Living Facilities as well as care in the home. This option will increase your premium.

3. Nonforfeiture—this option provides some form of paid-up benefit if the policy should lapse. This option increases your base premium.

I hope this will give you some direction when comparing LTC policies. Always look for a strong and reputable company and also make sure your agent is knowledgeable about long-term care issues as well. Shop around and educate yourself and use your best judgment when selecting a plan. Look for plans that are Tax Qualified.

If you live in Alabama, Georgia, Florida, Indiana, Kentucky, Missouri, South Carolina, Tennessee or Virginia you can call a toll free number to receive a quote for long-term care insurance: 1-800-229-7141, Long Term Care Insurance Division of National HealthCare Corporation, Murfreesboro, Tennessee. They are licensed with a number of companies and based on your age, current health condition, and the type of plan you want they can send a quote.

For individuals living in other states, contact several insurance companies in your area and compare quotes using the above information as a guide.

Helpful Advice for Family Members

- Make sure you understand the importance of someone having Legal and Medical Powers of Attorney for the patient. This will allow someone else to legally make decisions and act on your family member's behalf if they should ever become incompetent. It can also avoid family conflicts over who should speak for your family member in the future.

- Become informed about Medicare and Medicaid. Have a working knowledge of what each program covers and pays for. Know the appeals process and how to challenge a nursing home's decision regarding coverage limitations.

- Know your family member's physician. Schedule an appointment at their office to discuss and review your family member's case. Be familiar with their office hours and schedule for visiting their patients.

- Become educated about your family member's diagnosis/disease. Be aware of the complications, treatment options, and later stages.

- Appreciate your family member the way he or she is now. Allow for recurring periods of grieving for yourself and other family members as the patient's condition deteriorates/advances.

- Realize the nursing home will not be like home. It is a group living facility. You have been used to seeing your family member in a home setting with 1:1 attention and care. In the nursing home they will be assigned to a nurse aid who has 8 to 10 other patients to care for. There will be times in which your family member may have to wait awhile until their needs are seen to. Be patient with the staff. Imagine how it would have been at home to try and care for several individuals with varying needs and health problems.

- Be nice to the nursing home staff. The staff want to make you happy with the care they provide. If there are problems, you need to voice them immediately. But don't be overly critical. No one wants to care for a patient when it appears that the family is always looking out for problems and is critical. Compliment the staff a hundred times for every one time you present a concern. Remember: No one will be able to take as good of care of your family member as you did (or think you can)!

- Realize that each person reacts differently to changes and stresses in their life. Your family member's mood or behavior may change greatly related to being placed in a nursing home. This is a time of adjustment for them as well as you and other family members. Give each other time to adjust and be supportive of each others needs. Key: Don't expect others to react the same way you do!

- Take time for yourself. If you have been caring for your family member for any period of time you now need time for yourself. Participate in enjoyable activities. Take a vacation. If you don't take care of yourself, you won't be able to see after your family member. Notice I said "see" them, not "take care" of them. The nursing home is to provide for their care. You can help provide for your family member's emotional needs by seeing them. If you don't trust the nursing home in providing care for your family member, your family member needs to be somewhere else!

Would you leave your child with someone you didn't trust in providing for their needs? The key is trust, which leads to the next point.

- Human beings make mistakes and nursing homes employ human beings. When mistakes occur report them immediately to the staff. Nursing homes want to have happy satisfied patients and families. Don't expect perfection. You will always be disappointed. Instead, expect your family member to have all their basic needs met in a timely and professional manner.

- Give yourself permission to do only what you can reasonably manage, i.e., visiting, calling, taking gifts. Be open with your family member and explain your needs in regards to personal time and commitments. Don't feel guilty not being present for all holidays, especially if you previously were not present for all holidays.

- Adapt gift giving. Encourage useful gifts such as, easy to remove clothing, slippers, socks, audio tapes of favorite music or family members singing/talking, photo albums, subscriptions to magazines, or calling cards for long distance calls. Allow the family member to join in gift giving. You could buy the gift and allow them to wrap it.

- Last, ASK FOR HELP AND SUPPORT WHEN YOU NEED IT! Develop a bulletin board for listing tasks and responsibilities. If someone ever asks, "What can we do to help?" you can respond with a specific idea.

Patients' Rights

Patients' rights. Nothing is as important as an individual's rights! Make sure you know your or your loved ones' rights.

Nursing facilities are required to meet a number of requirements relating to provision of services, residents' rights, and administration.

In general, to the extent needed to fulfill all plans of care, a nursing facility must provide, or arrange for the provision of:

- nursing and related services and specialized rehabilitative services to attain or maintain the highest practicable physical, mental, and psychosocial well-being of each resident;

- medically-related social services to attain or maintain the highest practicable physical, mental, and psychosocial well-being of each resident;

- pharmaceutical services (including procedures that assure the accurate acquiring, receiving, dispensing and administering of all drugs and biologicals) to meet the needs of each resident;

- dietary services that assure that the meals meet the daily nutritional and special dietary needs of each resident;

- an on-going program, directed by a qualified professional, of activities designed to meet the interests and the physical, mental, and psychosocial well-being of each resident;

- routine dental services (to the extent covered under the state plan) and emergency dental services to meet the needs of each resident; and

- treatment and services required by mentally ill and mentally retarded residents not otherwise provided or arranged for (or required to be provided or arranged for) by the state.

Resident rights. Each nursing facility resident has a right to a dignified existence, self-determination and communication with and access to persons and services inside and outside the facility. A facility must protect the rights of each resident. The resident has the right to exercise his or her rights as a resident of the facility and as a citizen or resident of the United States.

- The resident has the right to be free of interference, coercion, discrimination, and reprisal from the facility in exercising his/her rights.

- In the case of a resident who has been adjudged incompetent by a court, the rights of the resident are exercised by a person appointed to act on the person's behalf.

- In the case of a resident who has not been adjudged incompetent by the court, any legal-surrogate designated in accordance with state law may exercise the resident's rights to the extent provided by state law.

- The facility must inform the resident both orally and in writing, in a language that the resident understands, of his/her rights and all rules and regulations concerning resident conduct and responsibilities during his/her stay in the facility. This notice must be made prior to or upon admission and during the person's stay. Receipt of the information must be acknowledged in writing.

- The resident has the right to access all records pertaining to himself or herself, including current clinical records within 24 hours (excluding weekends and holidays). At the cost of the community standard, the individual has a right to a copy of the records or any portion of the records.

- The resident has the right to be fully informed, in language that he/she can understand, of his/her total health status.

- The resident has the right to refuse treatment; to refuse to participate in experimental research; and to formulate an advance directive.

- The facility must inform each Medicaid resident, in writing: The items and services that are included in the facility payment for which the resident may not be charged and those other items and services that the facility offers, for which the resident may be charged, and the cost for those services. The resident must be informed when changes are made to the items, services, and costs.

- The facility must furnish a written description of legal rights.

- The facility must inform each resident of the name, specialty, and way of contacting the physician responsible for his/her care.

- The facility must prominently display, in the facility, written information and provide applicants for admission, oral and written information about how to apply for and use Medicare and Medicaid benefits, and how to receive refunds for previous payments covered by such benefits.

- A facility must immediately inform the resident; consult with the resident's physician; and, if known, notify the resident's legal representative or an interested family member when there is:

  1. an accident involving the resident which results in injury and has the potential for requiring physician intervention;

  2. a deterioration in health, mental, or psychosocial status in either life-threatening conditions or clinical complications;

  3. a need to change treatment significantly; or

  4. a decision to transfer or discharge the resident from the facility.

The resident has the right to manage his or her financial affairs, and the facility may not require residents to deposit their personal funds with the facility. If a resident does deposit funds with the facility, regulations specify how those moneys will be treated and protected.

Services Included in the Medicare and Medicaid Payment

During the course of a covered Medicare or Medicaid stay, facilities may not charge a resident for the following categories of items and services:

- Nursing services.

- Dietary services.

- An activities program.

- Room/bed maintenance services.

- Routine personal hygiene items and services, as required, to meet the needs of residents, including, but not limited to: hair hygiene supplies, comb., brush, bath soap, disinfecting soaps or specialized cleansing agents, when indicated to treat special skin problems or to fight infection, razor, shaving cream, toothbrush, toothpaste, denture adhesive, denture cleaner, dental floss, moisturizing lotion, tissues, cotton balls, cotton swabs, deodorant, incontinence care and supplies, sanitary napkins, and related supplies, towels, washcloths, hospital gowns, over-the-counter drugs, hair and nail hygiene services, bathing, and basic personal laundry.

- Medically-related social services.

Items and Services That May Be Charged to Residents' Funds

General categories and examples of items and services that the facility may charge to residents' funds if they are requested by a resident, if the facility informs the resident that there will be a charge and if payment is not made by Medicaid or Medicare:

- Telephone.

- Television/radio for personal use.

- Personal comfort items, including smoking materials, notions and novelties, and confections.

- Cosmetic and grooming items and services in excess of those for which payment is made under Medicaid or Medicare.

- Personal clothing.

- Personal reading materials.

- Gifts purchased on behalf of a resident.

- Flowers and plants.

- Social events and entertainment offered that are not part of the activities program.

- Noncovered special care services, such as privately hired nurses or aides.

- Private room, except when therapeutically required (for example, isolation for infection control).

- Specially prepared or alternative food requested instead of the food generally prepared by the facility.

The facility must not charge a resident (or his/her representative) for any item or service not requested by the resident.

Where to Find the Ombudsman

There are more than 800 state and local ombudsmen throughout the U.S. Almost all state ombudsmen are housed in state agencies on aging. Their mission is to protect the health, safety, welfare, and rights of the elderly in nursing homes. The local ombudsman can provide assistance with useful advice on finding a good nursing home, assisting with admissions, investigating complaints, quality of care issues, financial information, Medicaid eligibility, residents' rights, Social Security information, estate problems, and/or alternative care options.

—by Gary Hickerson, M.S.S.W.

Chapter 24

Home and Hospice Care Statistics

Home care in the United States is a diverse and dynamic service industry. More than 20,000 providers deliver home care services to some 8 million individuals who require such services because of acute illness, long-term health conditions, permanent disability, or terminal illness. Annual expenditures for home care were $40 billion in 1997 and are expected to total $42 billion in 1998.[1]

Home Care Providers

The first home care agencies were established in the 1880s. Their number grew to some 1,100 by 1963 and to more than 20,000 currently. Home health agencies, home care aide organizations, and hospices are known collectively as "home care organizations."

Medicare-Certified Agencies

Home care agencies of various types have been providing high-quality, inhome services to Americans for more than a century. However, Medicare's enactment in 1965 greatly accelerated the industry's growth. Medicare made home care services, primarily skilled nursing

Excerpted from "Basic Statistics about Home Care," [Online] November 1997. Available: http://www.nahc.org/Consumer/hcstats.html. Produced by the National Association for Home Care (NAHC), 228 Seventh St. SE, Washington, DC 20003. For complete contact information, please refer to Chapter 60, "Resources." Reprinted with permission.

and therapy of a curative or restorative nature, available to the elderly. In 1973, these services were extended to certain disabled younger
Americans. Between 1967 and 1985, the number of agencies certified
to participate in the Medicare program more than tripled, from 1,753
to 5,983. In the mid-1980s, the number of Medicare-certified home
care agencies leveled off at around 5,900 as a result of increasing
Medicare paperwork and unreliable payment policies. These problems
led to a lawsuit brought against the Health Care Financing Administration (HCFA) in 1987 by a coalition of members of the U.S. Congress led by Reps. Harley Staggers (D-WV) and Claude Pepper (D-FL),
consumer groups, and the National Association for Home Care (NAHC).
The successful conclusion of this lawsuit gave NAHC the opportunity to
participate in rewriting the Medicare home care payment policies. Following these revisions, annual outlays for Medicare's home health benefit increased significantly and the number of Medicare-certified home
health agencies rose to more than 10,000. More recently, the number
declined to 9,655. NAHC believes the recent decline in agencies is the
direct result of changes in Medicare home health reimbursement enacted
as part of the Balanced Budget Act of 1997 (BBA).

The number of hospital-based and freestanding proprietary agencies has grown faster than any other type of certified agency since
the coverage clarifications. Freestanding proprietary agencies now
comprise 46% and hospital-based agencies 27% of all certified agencies. This differs markedly from the industry composition in the early
1980s, when public health agencies dominated the ranks of certified
agencies and proprietary and hospital-based agencies combined accounted for only one-fourth of the total.

Medicare-Certified Hospices

Medicare added hospice benefits in October 1983, 10 years after
the first hospice was established in the United States. Hospices provide palliative medical care and supportive social, emotional, and
spiritual services to the terminally ill and their families. The number of Medicare-certified hospices has grown from 31 in January 1984
to 2,287 in September 1998 (for a separate fact sheet with detailed
information on hospices, please contact the Hospice Association of
America, 202-546-4759).

Non-Medicare-Certified Agencies

The noncertified home care agencies, home care aide organizations,
and hospices that remain outside Medicare do so for a variety of reasons.

Some do not provide the kinds of service that Medicare covers. For example, home care aide organizations that do not provide skilled nursing care are not eligible to participate in Medicare.

Home Care Expenditures and Utilization

National Expenditures

HCFA projects the national expenditure for health care will total $1,147 billion in 1998.[2] In the past few years, growth in health care spending has slowed. Health spending grew at an average annual rate of 5.3% in 1997 and 1998, maintaining a slowed growth trend begun in 1996. In part, this slowdown in the rate of spending for health care has been attributed to the growing influence of managed care as a payment mechanism and to the relatively low inflation rates for the economy as a whole. For the early part of the next decade (2001-2007), HCFA projects an average annual national health spending growth rate of 7.5%.

Table 24.1. provides the estimated 1996 national expenditures for personal health care by type. Personal health care is a subset of total health spending and includes spending for health care goods and services used by individuals. Of the $907 billion attributed to personal health care spending in 1996, 62% was for hospital care and physician services and only a small fraction (3%) was spent on home care.

Total home care spending is difficult to estimate due to limitations of data sources. Home care spending was estimated to total $40 billion in 1997. Based on the prior year's trends, NAHC estimates total spending for home care of $42 billion in 1998. However, some spending for home care services is not included in the national health accounts data, for example, payments made by consumers to independent providers and payments to hospital-based agencies by sources other than Medicare and Medicaid.

Health Care Prices

Information on the average cost to consumers of home care by visit type was collected through the National Medical Expenditure Survey (NMES) in 1987. These figures were updated by NAHC using the Medicare rates of growth in per-visit charges. Table 24.2. shows that on average a home care visit cost $48 in 1987 and $75 in 1997. HCFA estimates the 1997 average benefit payment per Medicare home health visit at $67.

Table 24.1. Personal Health Care Expenditures, 1996

	Percent
Total personal health care	100
Hospital care	40
Physicians' services	22
Nursing home care	9
Drugs and other medical nondurables	10
Other professional services	6
Dentists' services	5
Home care	3
Other personal health care	3
Vision products and other medical durables	2

Source: Levit, K.R., et al., "National Health Spending Trends in 1996," *Health Affairs* (January/February 1998): 35-51.

Table 24.2. Average Cost per Home Care Visit, 1987 and 1997

	1987	1997[a]
Average	$48	$75
Nurse	62	96
Therapist	57	89
Home care aide	34	53
Homemaker	33	51
Other[b]	56	87

Sources: Altman, B., and D. Walden. 1993. "Home Health Care: Use, Expenditures and Sources of Payment." *National Medical Expenditure Survey Research Findings* 15, Publication No. 93-0040, Agency for Health Care Policy and Research (AHCPR), Rockville, MD: Public Health Service.

Notes: [a]*Updated by the average annual rate of increase of Medicare per-visit charges, which was 4.5% between 1987 and 1996 (HCFA, Office of Information Services).*
[b]*Includes social workers and other professionals.*

Medicare Home Health

Medicare is the largest single payer of home care services. In 1996, Medicare spending accounted for nearly 40% of total home care expenditures. Other public funding sources for home care include Medicaid, the Older Americans Act, Title XX Social Services Block Grants, the Veterans' Administration, and Civilian Health and Medical Program of the Uniformed Services (CHAMPUS). Private insurance comprised only a small portion of home care payments. Close to one-fourth of home care service is financed through out-of-pocket payments (see Table 24.3.).

Prior to BBA enactment, the home health benefit represented a small but growing portion of Medicare spending—less than 9% of total benefit payments in 1997. However, since BBA implementation, home health has experienced a dramatic downturn, and in 1998 made up only 6.2% of total Medicare outlays (see Table 24.4.). About 42% of the estimated $210 billion 1998 Medicare benefit payments will go to hospitals and approximately 15% to physicians. Hospice payments will account for 1% of the total Medicare benefit payments in 1998.

In 1997, HCFA estimated 38.5 million aged and disabled persons were enrolled in the Medicare program. An estimated 3.4 million enrollees received fee-for-service home health services in 1997, representing a greater than 40% rise from the number of home health

Table 24.3. Sources of Payment for Home Care 1996

Source of Payment	Percent
Total	100.0
Medicare	38.7
Medicaid	27.2
Private insurance	12.2
Out-of-pocket	20.5
Other and unknown	1.3

Source: AHCPR, Center for Cost and Financing Studies, National Medical Expenditure Survey data (aligned to National Health Accounts Data), December 1997.

Note: Figures may not add to 100.0% due to rounding.

Table 24.4. Medicare Benefit Payments, 1998 (estimated) and 1999 (projected)

	1998		1999	
	Amount ($ mil.)	% of Total	Amount ($ mil.)	% of Total
Total Medicare Benefit Payments*	**$210,136**	**100.0**	**$222,002**	**100.0**
Part A				
Hospital care	88,236	42.0	88,310	39.8
Skilled nursing facility	13,408	6.4	13,835	6.2
Home health agency**	12,790	6.1	6,171	2.8
Hospice	2,080	1.0	2,181	1.0
Managed care	17,807	8.5	20,493	9.2
Total	**$134,321**	**64.0**	**$130,990**	**59.0**
Part B				
Physician	31,595	15.0	32,967	14.8
Durable medical equipment	4,246	2.0	4,214	1.9
Carrier lab	4,779	2.3	4,306	1.9
Hospital	10,625	5.1	11,082	5.0
Home health**	273	0.1	8,420	3.8
Intermediary lab	1,683	0.8	1,765	0.8
Other intermediary	4,228	2.0	4,744	2.1
Managed care	14,132	6.7	18,793	8.5
Total	**$75,815**	**36.1**	**$91,012**	**41.0**

Source: HCFA, Office of the Actuary, unpublished estimates for the President's fiscal year 2000 budget (December 1998).

*Notes: *Medicare Part A totals do not include peer review organizations (PROs). Figures may not add to totals due to rounding.*

**Home health outlays do not include the transfer of funds between the trust funds.

recipients in 1990. Table 24.5. shows the growth over time in the Medicare home health benefit. For the period 1990-1997, Medicare home health expenditures increased from $3.9 billion to an estimated $17.2 billion. Most of the rise in spending occurred as a result of the increase in visits, which increased from 70 million in 1990 to an estimated 270 million in 1997. Growth in the Medicare home health benefit between 1990 and 1996 can be attributed to specific court decisions, legislative expansions of the benefit, and to a number of socio-demographic trends, which had fostered growth in the program from the beginning.

The BBA (PL 105-33) introduced a new per-beneficiary limit, designed to reduce growth in Medicare home health expenditures, that restricts payments to agencies under Medicare to the lowest of the agency's actual, allowable costs, its aggregate per-visit cost limits, or its aggregate per-beneficiary annual limit. The Lewin Group estimated that 90% of agencies would have costs that exceed BBA limits in 1998 by an average of 32% without a change in Medicare practice patterns.[3] These reductions have resulted in agency closures throughout the country (contact NAHC for more information).

Table 24.5. Medicare Fee-For-Service Home Health Outlays, Clients, and Visits for Selected Years, 1967-1997

Year	Outlays ($ mil.)	Clients (1,000s)	Visits (1,000s)
1967	$46	n/a	n/a
1980	662	957	22,428
1985	1,773	1,589	39,742
1990	3,860	1,940	69,532
1991	5,566	2,223	99,183
1992	7,724	2,523	132,494
1993	10,198	2,868	168,029
1994	13,269	3,175	220,495
1995	15,976	3,457	266,261
1996	17,266	3,583	283,936
1997	17,241	3,370	269,919

Source: HCFA, Office of the Actuary and Bureau of Data Management and Strategy.

Note: The 1990 to 1997 data was updated June 1998.

Medicare hospice expenditures have grown from $112 million in 1987 to an estimated $2.2 billion in 1998. An estimated 338,273 beneficiaries received hospice services under Medicare in 1996.

Medicaid Home Care

As in the case of Medicare, home health services represent a relatively small part of total Medicaid payments. Table 24.6. shows that close to half of the $117 billion in Medicaid benefit payments in fiscal year (FY) 96 went for hospital and skilled nursing facility services.

Table 24.6. Medicaid Expenditures, by Type of Service, Fiscal Years 1994, 1995, and 1996

Fiscal Year	1994	1995	1996
Total Vendor Payments ($ bil.)	**$108.3**	**$120.1**	**$117.1**
	Percent of Total		
Nursing facility services	25.0	24.2	24.2
Inpatient services	26.1	24.0	22.3
General hospitals	24.2	21.9	20.6
Mental hospitals	1.9	2.1	1.7
Other care	8.6	10.0	8.6
Intermediate care facility (MR) services[a]	7.7	8.6	7.1
Prescribed drugs	8.2	8.1	8.5
Home health services[b]	6.5	7.8	9.0
Physician services	6.6	6.1	5.7
Outpatient hospital services	5.9	5.5	5.3
Clinic services	3.5	3.6	3.6
Laboratory and radiological services	1.1	1.0	0.9
Early and periodic screening	0.9	1.0	1.2

Source: HCFA, Division of Medical Statistics. Data are from the Form HCFA-2082.

Notes: [a]"MR" indicates facilities for persons with mental retardation.

[b]Includes home health, personal care, and home and community-based waiver payments.

Home care services comprised 9% of the payments. Hospice is an optional Medicaid service that is currently offered by 42 states. Payments for hospice services were estimated at $319 million in FY96.

Table 24.7. shows the growth in the Medicaid home health benefit since FY75. Between FY96 and FY97, expenditures increased from $10.6 billion to $12.2 billion, an increase of 15%.

Managed Care

Health care services in the United States are increasingly financed through managed care organizations. A managed care organization, including health maintenance organizations, typically finances health care services through a negotiated prepaid rate to health care providers. A fully capitated contract specifies a lump sum payment per enrollee to cover all care provided through the plan, but there are many variations. In contrast, traditional health insurance pays providers based on the number of services delivered with few limitations on which providers would be paid, a payment arrangement commonly termed fee-for-service.

Table 24.7. Medicaid Home Health Expenditures and Recipients, for Selected Years, 1975-1997

Fiscal Year	Vendor Payments ($ mil.)	Recipients (1000s)
1975	70	343
1980	332	392
1985	1,120	535
1990	3,404	719
1991	4,101	812
1992	4,888	926
1993	5,601	1,067
1994	7,049	1,376
1995	9,406	1,639
1996	10,583	1,633
1997	12,237	1,861

Source: HCFA, Division of Medicaid Statistics. Data are derived from Form HCFA-2082.

Managed care is most prevalent in the employer-based health insurance market. Three out of four workers with health insurance received health insurance through a managed care plan in 1995.[4] Managed care enrollment has increased among Medicaid enrollees, particularly in states that have federal waivers to convert their Medicaid program to a managed care program. As of June 30, 1996, 40% of all Medicaid beneficiaries were enrolled in managed care.[5] Medicare managed care has increased at a slower pace. As of August 1997, about 14% of Medicare beneficiaries were part of Medicare managed care.[6]

The increasingly competitive health care market has created incentives for home care agencies to enter managed care provider networks. However, little is known about the extent to which home care agencies have entered into managed care arrangements. A preliminary study conducted for HCFA compared patient outcomes and total expenditures for Medicare home health clients who received services through Medicare managed care and a group who received services through fee-for-service Medicare home health. The authors found the managed care clients used less home health resources but also had less favorable outcomes on average than their Medicare fee-for-service counterparts, suggesting the need for further research on the relationship between volume of home care services and outcomes.[7]

Home Care Recipients

Based on a need for assistance in performing basic life activities known as activities of daily living or instrumental activities of daily living, research from the Disability Statistics Rehabilitation Research and Training Center indicates that as of 1994, approximately 16% of the U.S. population aged 65 and over and approximately 2.5% of U.S. population ages 18-64 could benefit from home care services.[8] Most receive services from so-called informal caregivers—family members, friends, or others who provide services on an unpaid basis.

The NMES findings indicate that 5.9 million individuals, roughly 2.5% of the U.S. population, received formal home care services in 1987. Of these recipients, nearly half were older than 65, and the amount of home care they used tended to increase with age. About 40% of the home care recipients had functional limitations in one or more activities of daily living. Age and functional disability are likely predictors of the need for home care services. By projecting the NMES estimate forward based on Census Bureau population projections, NAHC estimates that 8 million people received home care services in 1998.

A more recent survey, conducted by the National Center for Health Statistics (NCHS), profiled persons discharged from home health agencies in 1995-96 and collected information on client diagnoses.[9] Table 24.8. shows two-thirds of discharges were over age 65 and 64% were women.

Table 24.8. Percent of Home Health Discharges by Age, Sex, Race, and Marital Status, 1995-96

Characteristic	Percent
Age	
under 45 years	19.5
45-54 years	5.9
55-64 years	8.4
65-69 years	10.8
70-74 years	13.2
75-79 years	12.4
80-84 years	14.2
85 years and older	15.4
Unknown	*
Gender	
Male	36.5
Female	63.5
Race	
White	62.8
Black	7.4
Other	2.6
Unknown	27.2
Marital status at discharge	
Married	37.0
Widowed	24.6
Divorced or separated	5.0
Single or never married	18.4
Unknown	15.0

Source: National Center for Health Statistics (NCHS) *Advance Data* No. 297, April 16, 1998.

Note: Percentages based on a national sample representing 7,775,700 home health patients discharged from October 1995 to September 1996.

*Figure does not meet standard of reliability or precision

Medicare home health utilization by principal diagnosis is similar to the NCHS data. In the HCFA data, diseases of the circulatory system accounted for almost 30% of the Medicare beneficiaries admitted to home care in 1996. Medicare home health patients with neoplasms comprised 6.8% of all the program's home care admissions; endocrine, nutritional and metabolic diseases, and immunity disorders accounted for 9.1%. Diseases of the respiratory system made up 8.1%; diseases of the musculoskeletal system comprised 10.2%; and injury and poisoning accounted for 10.5%.

Many hospital patients are discharged to home care services for continued rehabilitative care. As hospital stays shortened in the early 1980s, the percentage of Medicare patients discharged to home health care increased from 9.1% in 1981 to 17.9% in 1985. More recently, the Medicare Payment Advisory Commission (MedPAC) estimated that 16% of Medicare hospital patients used home health care within 30 days of discharge in FY96.

Caregivers

Informal Caregivers

Estimates indicate that almost three-quarters of elderly persons with severe disabilities receiving home care services in 1989 relied solely on family members or other unpaid help.[10] Eight of 10 of these informal caregivers provide unpaid assistance for an average of four hours a day, seven days a week. Three-quarters of informal caregivers are female, and nearly one-third are over age 65. A 1996 telephone survey of U.S. households estimated there were 22 million U.S. households with at least one member who provided some level of unpaid assistance to a spouse, relative, or other person older than age 50.[11]

Formal Caregivers

Formal caregivers include professionals and paraprofessionals who provide inhome health care and personal care services, and are compensated for the services they provide. The Bureau of Labor Statistics (BLS) and HCFA provide data on these employees. However, agency definitions and methods of counting are different. BLS provides an occupational classification for "home health care services," which excludes hospital-based and public agency workers. Its method of counting is "number of employees." HCFA limits its statistics to employees of certified home health agencies. Furthermore, its survey presents data on full-time equivalents (FTEs).

In Table 24.9., BLS estimates that more than 500,000 persons were employed in home health care agencies, with the exclusions described above. HCFA recorded 372,453 FTEs employed in Medicare-certified agencies as of September 1998. The HCFA FTE counts show a decline of 43,000 FTEs since December 1997. Using either method, the largest numbers of employees are home care aides and registered nurses.

The 1996 number of employees data by job category presented in Table 24.9 is based on the Current Population Survey, which is conducted every three years. However, BLS also collects monthly information on employment for all workers, which includes home care services. BLS monthly statistics present data at an aggregate level combining all job titles. Table 24.10. shows the calendar year home care services employment for 1993-1998, based on BLS monthly statistics. During the period 1993-1997, home care employment grew from 510,000 employees to 713,000 employees—a 7.9% average annual rate of growth. However, in 1998, total home care employment declined by 7.2%.[12]

Table 24.9. Numbers of Home Health Care Workers, 1996, and Medicare-Certified Agency FTEs, 1998

Type of Employee	Number of Employees[a]	Number of FTEs[b]
RNs	134,443	132,796
LPNs	47,651	27,775
Physical therapists	11,236	13,619
Home care aides	318,124	124,218
Occupational therapists	4,344	3,574
Speech pathologists	3,304	1,985
Social workers	8,995	6,895
Other	137,303	61,591
Totals	665,400	372,453

Sources: [a]U.S. Department of Labor, Bureau of Labor Statistics (BLS), National Industry-Occupation Employment Matrix, data for 1996. Excludes hospital-based and public agencies.

[b]*Unpublished data on FTEs in Medicare-certified home health agencies as of September 1998 from the HCFA Center for Information Systems, Health Standards and Quality Bureau.*

243

Table 24.10. Home Health Care Services Total Employment, 1993-1998

Year	Total Number of Employees
1993	510,000
1994	596,000
1995	656,000
1996	695,000
1997	713,000
1998	662,000

Sources: U.S. Department of Labor, BLS: Establishment Data, 1999. BLS online.

Note: Excludes hospital-based and public home care agency employees. All numbers are as of December of the corresponding year.

Cost Effectiveness

In many cases, home care is a cost-effective service, not only for individuals recuperating from a hospital stay but also for those who, because of a functional or cognitive disability, are unable to take care of themselves. Table 24.11. compares the average Medicare charges on a per-day basis for hospital and skilled nursing facility to the average Medicare charge for a home health visit. The following section lists some examples of cost-effective home care. However, it should be noted that cost-effectiveness is not the only rationale for home care. In fact, the best argument for home care is that it is a humane and compassionate way to deliver health care and supportive services. Home care reinforces and supplements the care provided by family members and friends and maintains the recipient's dignity and independence, qualities that are all too often lost even in the best institutions. Furthermore, home care allows patients to take an active role in their care, becoming members of a multidisciplinary health care team.[13] Several research studies conducted in the past several years have compared inpatient care to home care costs for a specific group of patients. The cost savings data for six of these studies are summarized in Table 24.12. The information has been aggregated at a monthly level for purposes of comparison.

Table 24.11. Comparison of Hospital, SNF [Skilled Nursing Facility], and Home Health Medicare Charges, 1995-1997

	1995	1996	1997
Hospital charges per day	$1,909	$2,071	$2,121
Skilled nursing facility charges per day	401	443	454
Home health charges per visit	84	86	88

Sources: The 1995 and 1996 hospital and SNF Medicare charge data are from the *Annual Statistical Supplement, 1997,* to the Social Security Bulletin, Social Security Administration (December 1997). Home care information from HCFA, Office of Information Services.

Note: Additional years are projected using consumer price index forecasts from the Bureau of Labor Statistics' web site and "The Economic and Budget Outlook: Fiscal Years 1999-2008" Congressional Budget Office web site (January 1998).

Table 24.12. Cost of Inpatient Care Compared to Home Care, Selected Conditions

Conditions	Per-Patient Per-Month Hospital Costs	Per-Patient Per-Month Home Care Costs
Low birth weight[a]	$26,190	$330
Ventilator-dependent adults[b]	21,570	7,050
Oxygen-dependent children[c]	12,090	5,250
Chemotherapy for children with cancer[d]	69,870	55,950
Congestive heart failure among the elderly[e]	1,758	1,605
Intravenous antibiotic therapy for cellulitis, osteomyelitis, others[f]	12,510	4,650

Sources:

[a]Casiro, O. G., McKenzie, M. E., McFayden, L., Shapiro, C., Seshia M. M. K., MacDonald, N., Moffat, M., and Cheang, M.S. "Earlier Discharge with Community-Based Intervention for Low Birth Weight Infants: A Randomized Trial." *Pediatrics,* 1993, 92(1), 128-34.

Continued on next page.

Table 24.12. Cost of Inpatient Care Compared to Home Care, Selected Conditions [continued from previous page]

Sources: [continued]

[b]Bach, J. R., Intinola, P., Alba, A. S., and Holland, I. E. "The Ventilator-Assisted Individual: Cost Analysis of Institutionalization vs. Rehabilitation and In-Home Management." *Chest,* 1992, 101(1), 26-30.

[c]Field, A. I., Rosenblatt, A., Pollack, M. M., and Kaufman, J. "Home Care Cost-Effectiveness for Respiratory Technology-Dependent Children." *American Journal of Diseases of Children,* 1991, 145, 729-33.

[d]Close, P., Burkey, E., Kazak, A., Danz, P., and Lange, B. "A Prospective Controlled Evaluation of Home Chemotherapy for Children with Cancer." *Pediatrics,* 1995, 95(6), 896-900. Note: The study found that the daily charges for chemotherapy were $2,329±627 in the hospital and $1,865±833 at home. These charges were multiplied by 30 days reflecting the above per-patient per-month costs.

[e]Rich, M. W., Beckham, V., Wittenberg, C., Leven, C., Freedland, K., and Carney, R. M. "A Multidisciplinary Intervention to Prevent the Readmission of Elderly Patients with Congestive Heart Failure." *The New England Journal of Medicine,* 1995, 333(18), 1190-5.

[f]William, D. N., et al. "Safety, Efficacy, and Cost Savings in an Outpatient Intravenous Antibiotic Program." *Clinical Therapy,* 1993, 15, 169-79, cited in Williams, D. "Reducing Costs and Hospital Stay for Pneumonia with Home Intravenous Cefotaxime Treatment: Results with a Computerized Ambulatory Drug Delivery System." *The American Journal of Medicine,* 1994, 97(2A), 50-5.

Note: The estimated hospital cost/day/patient is $417 and the estimated savings/day/patient is $262. These costs were multiplied by 30 days, reflecting the above patient per-month costs.

Endnotes

1. Health Care Financing Administration, Office of the Actuary, National Health Statistics Group, unpublished data on hospital-based and non-hospital-based home health expenditures, 1960-1997. NAHC based its 1998 projection on the 4.8% average annual rate of growth in freestanding home health expenditures from 1996-1998.

2. S. Smith, M. Freeland, S. Heffler, D. McKusick, et al., "The Next Ten Years of Health Spending: What Does the Future Hold?" *Health Affairs* 17, no. 5 (1998).

3. The Lewin Group, "An Impact Analysis for Home Health Agencies of the Medicare Home Health Interim Payment System of the 1997 Balanced Budget Act," (Washington, DC: National Association for Home Care, August 11, 1998).

4. Gail A. Jensen, M.A. Morrisey, S. Gaffney, and D. K. Liston, "The New Dominance of Managed Care: Insurance Trends in the 1990s," *Health Affairs* 16, no. 1 (January/February 1997):136.

5. Health Care Financing Administration, "Managed Care in Medicare and Medicaid," *Fact Sheet* (February 20, 1998).

6. Ibid.

7. P. W. Shaughnessy, R.E. Schlenker, D. F. Hittle, et al., *A Study of Home Health Care Quality and Cost under Capitated and Fee-For-Service Payment Systems, Vol. 1: Summary* (Denver: Center for Health Policy Research, 1994).

8. U.S. Department of Education, National Institute on Disability and Rehabilitation Research, Disability Statistics Rehabilitation Research and Training Center, University of California, San Francisco, "Disability Statistics Abstract," no. 17 (November 1996).

9. Barbara J. Haupt, National Center for Health Statistics, "An Overview of Home Health and Hospice Care Patients: 1996 National Home and Hospice Care Survey," *Advance Data,* no. 297 (April 16, 1998).

10. U.S. Bipartisan Commission on Comprehensive Health Care, *The Pepper Commission Final Report: A Call for Action,* S. Prt. 101-114 (Washington, DC: Government Printing Office, 1990).

11. National Alliance for Caregiving and the American Association for Retired Persons, *Family Caregiving in the U.S.: Findings from a National Survey* (Washington, DC: Author, 1997).

12. Bureau of Labor Statistics, online (1/11/99).

13. P. Sheldon and M. Bender, "High-Technology in Home Care," *Community Health Nursing and Home Health Nursing* 3 (1994): 507-519.

Chapter 25

Selecting a Home Care Provider

What is Home Care?

"Home care" is a simple phrase that encompasses a wide range of health and social services. These services are delivered at home to recovering, disabled, chronically, or terminally ill persons in need of medical, nursing, social, or therapeutic treatment and/or assistance with the essential activities of daily living.

Generally, home care is appropriate whenever a person prefers to stay at home but needs ongoing care that cannot easily or effectively be provided solely by family and friends. More and more older people, electing to live independent, non-institutionalized lives, are receiving home care services as their physical capabilities diminish. Younger adults who are disabled or recuperating from acute illness are choosing home care whenever possible. Chronically ill infants and children are receiving sophisticated medical treatment in their loving and secure home environments. Adults and children diagnosed with terminal illness also are being cared for at home, receiving compassion and maintaining dignity at the end of life. As hospital stays decrease, increasing numbers of patients need highly skilled services when they return home. Other patients are able to stay at home to begin with, receiving safe and effective care in the comfort of their own homes.

Who Provides Home Care

Home care services are usually provided by home care organizations but may also be obtained from registries and independent providers. Home care organizations include home health agencies; hospices; homemaker and home care aide (HCA) agencies; staffing and private-duty agencies; and companies specializing in medical equipment and supplies, pharmaceuticals, and drug infusion therapy. Several types of home care organizations may merge to provide a wide variety of services through an integrated system.

Home care services generally are available 24 hours a day, seven days a week. Depending on the patient's needs, these services may be provided by an individual or a team of specialists on a part-time, intermittent, hourly, or shift basis. Following are descriptions of the various types of home care providers.

Home Health Agencies

The term home health agency often indicates that a home care provider is Medicare certified. A Medicare-certified agency has met federal minimum requirements for patient care and management and therefore can provide Medicare and Medicaid home health services. Individuals requiring skilled home care services usually receive their care from a home health agency. Due to regulatory requirements, services provided by these agencies are highly supervised and controlled. Some agencies deliver a variety of home care services through physicians, nurses, therapists, social workers, homemakers and HCAs, durable medical equipment and supply dealers, and volunteers. Other home health agencies limit their services to nursing and one or two other specialties. For cases in which an individual requires care from more than one specialist, home health agencies coordinate a caregiving team to administer services that are comprehensive and efficient. Personnel are assigned according to the needs of each patient. Home health agencies recruit and supervise their personnel; as a result, they assume liability for all care.

Hospices

Hospice care involves a core interdisciplinary team of skilled professionals and volunteers who provide comprehensive medical, psychological, and spiritual care for the terminally ill and support for patients' families. Hospice care also includes the provision of related medications, medical supplies, and equipment. It is based primarily in the home, enabling families to remain together. Trained hospice professionals are available 24 hours a day to assist the family in caring for the patient, ensure that the patient's wishes are honored, and keep the patient comfortable and free from pain. Most hospices are Medicare certified and licensed according to state requirements.

Homemaker and Home Care Aide Agencies

Homemaker and HCA agencies employ homemakers or chore workers, HCAs, and companions who support individuals through meal preparation, bathing, dressing, and housekeeping. Personnel are assigned according to the needs and wishes of each client. Some states require these agencies to be licensed and meet minimum standards established by the state. Most homemaker and HCA agencies recruit, train, and supervise their personnel and thus are responsible for the care rendered.

Staffing and Private-Duty Agencies

Staffing and private-duty agencies generally are nursing agencies that provide individuals with nursing, homemaker, HCA, and companion services. Most states do not require these agencies to be licensed or meet regulatory requirements. Some staffing and private-duty agencies assign nurses to assess their clients' needs to ensure that personnel are properly assigned and provide ongoing supervision. These agencies recruit their own personnel. Again, responsibility for patient care rests with each agency.

Pharmaceutical and Infusion Therapy Companies

Pharmaceutical and infusion therapy companies specialize in the delivery of drugs, equipment, and professional services for individuals receiving intravenous or nutritional therapies through specially placed tubes. These companies employ pharmacists who prepare solutions and arrange for delivery to patients. Nurses also are hired to teach self-administration in patients' homes. Some pharmaceutical and infusion therapy companies are home health agencies, certified by Medicare. In addition, some states require these organizations to be licensed. Each company assumes responsibility for personnel and the services rendered.

Durable Medical Equipment and Supply Dealers

Durable medical equipment and supply dealers provide home care patients with products ranging from respirators, wheelchairs, and walkers, to catheter and wound care supplies. These dealers employ staff who deliver and, when necessary, install these products as well as instruct patients on their proper in-home use. Durable medical equipment and supply dealers usually do not provide physical care for patients, but there are a few exceptions. Some dealers offer pharmacy and infusion services, where a nurse administers medication and nutritional formulas to patients and teaches them the proper techniques for self-administration. Some companies also provide respiratory therapy services to help individuals use breathing equipment. Durable medical equipment and supply dealers that bill the Medicare program are required to meet federal minimum standards. Some states require that these organizations be licensed. Each dealer is liable for its personnel and the services provided to patients.

Registries

Registries serve as employment agencies for home care nurses and aides by matching these providers with clients and collecting finder's fees. These organizations usually are not licensed or regulated by government. Registries are not required to screen or background-check the caregivers, but some do undertake these tasks routinely. In addition, although not legally required to, some registries offer procedures for patients to file complaints. Clients select and supervise the work of a registry-referred provider. They also pay the provider directly and must comply with all applicable state and federal labor, health, and safety laws and regulations, including payroll tax and social security withholding requirements.

Independent Providers

Independent providers are nurses, therapists, aides, homemakers and chore workers, and companions who are privately employed by individuals who need such services. Aides, homemakers, chore workers, and companions are not required to be licensed or to meet government standards except in cases where they receive state funding. In this arrangement, the responsibility for recruiting, hiring, and supervising the provider rests with the client. Finding back-up care in the event that the provider fails to report to work or fulfill job requirements is the client's responsibility. Clients also pay the provider directly and must comply with all applicable state and federal labor, health, and safety requirements.

What Types of Services Do Home Care Providers Deliver?

Home care providers deliver a wide variety of health care and supportive services, ranging from professional nursing and HCA care to physical, occupational, respiratory, and speech therapies. They also may provide social work and nutritional care and laboratory, dental, optical, pharmacy, podiatry, x-ray, and medical equipment and supply services. Services for the treatment of medical conditions usually are prescribed by an individual's physician. Supportive services, however, do not require a physician's orders. An individual may receive a single type of care or a combination of services, depending on the complexity of his or her needs. Home care services can be provided by the following professionals, paraprofessionals, and volunteers.

Physicians visit patients in their homes to diagnose and treat illnesses just as they do in hospitals and private offices. They also work with home care providers to determine which services are needed by patients, which specialists are most suitable to render these services, and how often these services need to be provided. With this information, physicians prescribe and oversee patient plans of care. Under Medicare, physicians and home health agency personnel review these plans of care as often as required by the severity of patient medical conditions at least once every 62 days. The interdisciplinary team reviews the care plans for hospice patients and their families at least once a month, or as frequently as patient conditions and/or family circumstances require.

Registered nurses (RNs) and licensed practical nurses (LPNs) provide skilled services that cannot be performed safely and effectively by nonprofessional personnel. Some of these services include injections and intravenous therapy, wound care, education on disease treatment and prevention, and patient assessments. RNs may also provide case management services. RNs have received two or more years of specialized education and are licensed to practice by the state. LPNs have one year of specialized training and are licensed to work under the supervision of registered nurses. The intricacy of a patient's medical condition and required course of treatment determine whether care should be provided by an RN or can be provided by an LPN.

Physical therapists (PTs) work to restore the mobility and strength of patients who are limited or disabled by physical injuries through the use of exercise, massage, and other methods. PTs often alleviate pain and restore injured muscles with specialized equipment. They also teach patients and caregivers special techniques for walking and transfer.

Social workers evaluate the social and emotional factors affecting ill and disabled individuals and provide counseling. They also help patients and their family members identify available community resources. Social workers often serve as case managers when patients' conditions are so complex that professionals need to assess medical and supportive needs and coordinate a variety of services.

Speech language pathologists work to develop and restore the speech of individuals with communication disorders; usually these disorders are the result of traumas such as surgery or stroke. Speech therapists also help retrain patients in breathing, swallowing, and muscle control.

Occupational therapists (OTs) help individuals who have physical, developmental, social, or emotional problems that prevent them from performing the general activities of daily living (ADLs). OTs instruct patients on using specialized rehabilitation techniques and equipment to improve their function in tasks such as eating, bathing, dressing, and basic household routines.

Dietitians provide counseling services to individuals who need professional dietary assessment and guidance to properly manage an illness or disability.

HCAs/home health aides assist patients with ADLs such as getting in and out of bed, walking, bathing, toileting, and dressing. Some aides have received special training and are qualified to provide more complex services under the supervision of a nursing professional.

Homemaker and chore workers perform light household duties such as laundry, meal preparation, general housekeeping, and shopping. Their services are directed at maintaining patient households rather than providing hands-on assistance with personal care.

Companions provide companionship and comfort to individuals who, for medical and/or safety reasons, may not be left at home alone. Some companions may assist clients with household tasks, but most are limited to providing sitter services.

Volunteers meet a variety of patient needs. The scope of a volunteer's services depends on his or her level of training and experience. Volunteer activities include, but are not limited to providing companionship, emotional support, and counseling and helping with personal care, paperwork, and transportation.

Who Pays for Home Care Services?

Home care services can be paid for directly by the patient and his or her family members or through a variety of public and private sources. Hospice care generally is provided regardless of the patient's and/or family's ability to pay. Public third-party payors include Medicare, Medicaid, the Older Americans Act, the Veterans Administration, and Social Services block grant programs. Some community organizations, such as local chapters of the American Cancer Society, the Alzheimer's Association, and the National Easter Seal Society, also provide funding to help pay for home care services. Private third-party payors include commercial health insurance companies, managed care organizations, CHAMPUS, and workers' compensation.

Self-Pay

Home care services that fail to meet the criteria of third-party payors must be paid for "out of pocket" by the patient or other party. The patient and home care provider negotiate the fees.

Public Third-Party Payers

- Medicare—Most Americans older than 65 are eligible for the federal Medicare program. If an individual is homebound, under a physician's care, and requires medically necessary skilled nursing or therapy services, he or she may be eligible for services provided by a Medicare-certified home health agency. Depending on the patient's condition, Medicare may pay for intermittent skilled nursing; physical, occupational, and speech therapies; medical social work; HCA services; and medical equipment and supplies. The referring physician must authorize and periodically review the patient's plan of care. With the exception of hospice care, the services the patient receives must be intermittent or part-time and provided through a Medicare-certified home health agency for reimbursement.

  Hospice services are available to individuals who are terminally ill and have a life expectancy of six months or less; there is no requirement for the patient to be homebound or in need of skilled nursing care. A physician's certification is required to qualify an individual for the Medicare Hospice Benefit. The physician also must re-certify the individual at the beginning of each six-month benefit period. In turn, the patient is required

255

to sign a statement indicating that he or she understands the nature of the illness and of hospice care. By signing this statement, the patient surrenders his or her rights to other Medicare benefits related to terminal illness.

* Medicaid—Administered by the states, Medicaid is a joint federal-state medical assistance program for low-income individuals. Each state has its own set of eligibility requirements; however, states are only mandated to provide home health services to individuals who receive federally assisted income maintenance payments, such as Social Security Income and Aid to Families with Dependent Children (AFDC), and individuals who are "categorically needy." Categorically needy recipients include certain aged, blind, and/or disabled individuals who have incomes that are too high to qualify for mandatory coverage but below federal poverty levels. Individuals younger than 21 who meet income and resources requirements for AFDC, yet otherwise are ineligible for AFDC, also qualify as categorically needy. Under federal Medicaid rules, coverage of home health services must include part-time nursing, HCA services, and medical supplies and equipment. At the state's option, Medicaid also may cover audiology; physical, occupational, and speech therapies; and medical social services. Hospice is a Medicaid-covered benefit in 38 states. The Medicaid hospice benefit covers the same range of services that Medicare does.

* Older Americans Act (OAA)—Enacted by Congress in 1965, the OAA provides federal funds for state and local social service programs that enable frail and disabled older individuals to remain independent in their communities. This funding covers HCA, personal care, chore, escort, meal delivery, and shopping services for individuals with the greatest social and financial need who are 60 years of age and older. Increasingly, individuals who can afford to pay for some of these services are being asked to contribute in proportion to their income. Individuals often request the services they need through an Area Agency on Aging, which will provide them directly or in cooperation with local organizations.

* Veterans Administration—Veterans who are at least 50% disabled due to a service-related condition are eligible for home health care coverage provided by the Veterans Administration (VA). A physician must authorize these services, which must be

delivered through the VA's network of hospital-based home care units. The VA does not cover nonmedical services provided by HCAs.

- Social Services Block Grant Programs—Each year states receive federal social services block grants for state-identified service needs. The government allocates these funds on the basis of the state's population and within a federal limit. Portions of the funding often are directed into programs providing HCA and homemaker or chore worker services. Individuals should contact their state health departments and local offices on aging for additional information.

- Community Organizations—Some community organizations, along with state and local governments, provide funds for home health and supportive care. Depending on an individual's eligibility and financial circumstances, these organizations may pay for all or a portion of the needed services. Hospital discharge planners, social workers, local offices on aging, and the United Way are excellent sources for information about community resources.

Private Third-Party Payers

- Commercial Health Insurance Companies—Commercial health insurance policies typically cover some home care services for acute needs, but benefits for long-term services vary from plan to plan. Commercial insurers, including Blue Cross and Blue Shield and others, generally pay for skilled professional home care services with a cost-sharing provision. Such policies occasionally cover personal care services. Most commercial and private insurance plans will cover comprehensive hospice services, including nursing, social work, therapies, personal care, medications, and medical supplies and equipment. Cost-sharing varies with individual policies, but often is not required.

Individuals sometimes find it necessary to purchase Medigap insurance or long-term care insurance policies, for additional home care coverage.

- Medigap insurance is designed to bridge some of the gaps in Medicare coverage. Some Medigap policies offer at-home recovery benefits, which pay for some personal care services

257

when the policyholder is receiving Medicare-covered skilled home health services. The policyholder's physician must order this personal care in conjunction with the skilled services. Home care coverage in Medigap policies is not designed to cover extended long-term care. This type of coverage is most helpful to individuals recovering from acute illness, injuries, or surgery.

- Long-term care insurance primarily was intended to protect individuals from the catastrophic expense of a lengthy stay in a nursing home. However, as the public need and preference for home care has grown, private long-term care insurance policies have expanded their coverage of personal care, companionship, and other in-home services. Considerable care should be taken in selecting a long-term care insurance policy, as home care benefits vary greatly among plans. Consumers should be aware of limitations on coverage, such as prior hospitalization requirements, and pre-existing condition exclusions. Some policies may only pay for services that are already covered by Medicare.

- Managed Care Organizations—Managed care organizations (MCOs) and other group health plans sometimes include coverage for home care services. MCOs contracting with Medicare must provide the full range of Medicare-covered home health services available in a particular geographic area. Medicare beneficiaries who are enrolled with an MCO may elect their hospice benefit from the hospice of their choice. These organizations only pay for services that are pre-approved.

- CHAMPUS—On a cost-shared basis the Civilian Health and Medical Program of the Uniformed Services (CHAMPUS) covers skilled nursing care and other professional medical home care services for dependents of active military personnel and military retirees and their dependents and survivors. CHAMPUS offers a comprehensive hospice benefit to its terminally ill beneficiaries, which covers nursing, social work and counseling services, therapies, personal care, medications, and medical supplies and equipment.

- Workers' Compensation—Any individual requiring medically necessary home care services as a result of injury on the job is eligible to receive coverage through workers' compensation.

What Are the Standard Billing and Payment Practices?

When services are covered by Medicare and/or Medicaid, home care providers must bill their fees directly to the payor to Medicare or Medicaid. Providers often will bill other third-party payors directly as well. Any uncovered costs are later billed to the client. However, if a client receives services from a registry or independent provider, he or she must pay the provider directly. Later the client may file for reimbursement from the insurance company if the services qualify as covered benefits. Payment options are detailed below.

Home Health Agencies

Medicare, Medicaid, and most private insurance plans pay for services that home health agencies deliver. Payment from these sources depends on whether the care is medically necessary and the individual meets specific coverage criteria. Individuals may opt to pay out of pocket for services that are not covered by other sources. Some agencies receive special funding from state and local governments and community organizations to cover the costs of needed care when other options are not available.

Hospices

Coverage for hospice care is available through Medicare, Medicaid programs in 38 states, and most private insurance plans. If insurance coverage is insufficient or unavailable, the patient and his or her family may pay for services out of pocket. Most hospices may provide free services to individuals who have limited or no financial resources.

Homemaker and Home Care Aide Agencies

Individual consumers usually pay for services from homemaker and HCA agencies. However, some states contract with these agencies to deliver personal care and homemaker services within their social services and medical assistance programs. On rare occasions, commercial insurers may pay for a portion or all of the costs of these services. Some agencies draw assistance from charitable community funds when other sources of payment are not available.

Staffing and Private-Duty Agencies

Typically, the individual or his or her commercial insurance carrier pays for services provided by staffing and private-duty agencies, provided that the insurance policy's coverage requirements are met. Some staffing agencies contract with state Medicaid programs to provide nursing and personal care services.

Pharmaceutical and Infusion Therapy Companies

Pharmaceutical and infusion therapy supplies and services are almost always paid for by commercial insurance companies and Medicaid. Medicare covers the cost of nutritional supplements and certain medications when the situation meets strict coverage criteria.

Durable Medical Equipment and Supply Dealers

Fees for durable medical equipment and supplies are usually covered by Medicare, Medicaid, and commercial insurance programs, provided that the products are ordered by a physician and are medically necessary to treat an illness or injury.

Registries

The individual client generally pays for registry services. In some cases, commercial insurance companies may reimburse a portion or all of these costs.

Independent Providers

Usually the individual pays for services rendered by independent providers. Some commercial insurance policies will provide reimbursement if the services qualify as covered benefits.

How Do I Find Home Care Services?

Finding the home care provider best suited for your needs requires research, but it is time well spent. Important factors include the quality of care, availability of needed services, personnel training and expertise, and coverage provided by the payor. Before starting a search, it is important to determine which types of services you need. You may wish to consult with your physician, a hospital discharge planner, or a social service organization, such as an Area Office on Aging, for assistance in evaluating your needs. Once you've completed this assessment, you will be able to identify the type of home care provider most appropriate to assist you.

Fortunately most communities have a variety of providers to choose from. Your physician or hospital discharge planner can help you locate home care providers in your area. Contact your state's departments of health, aging, and social services to obtain a list of licensed agencies. In addition, most state home care and hospice associations maintain directories of existing home care organizations and can assist you in identifying an appropriate provider.

Home care providers also are listed in the yellow pages under "home care," "hospice," or "nurses." If your community has information and referral services available through an Area Agency on Aging or a local chapter of the United Way, check with them. Your place of religious worship may also have information about local home care providers.

How Do I Select the Right Home Care Provider?

Once you acquire the names of several providers, you will want to learn more about their services and reputations. Following is a checklist of questions to ask providers and other individuals who may know about the provider's track record. Their insight will help you determine which provider is best for you or your loved one:

1. How long has this provider been serving the community?

2. Does this provider supply literature explaining its services, eligibility requirements, fees, and funding sources? Many providers furnish patients with a detailed "Patient Bill of Rights" that outlines the rights and responsibilities of the providers, patients, and caregivers alike. An annual report and other educational materials also can provide helpful information about the provider.

3. How does this provider select and train its employees? Does it protect its workers with written personnel policies, benefits packages, and malpractice insurance?

4. Are nurses or therapists required to evaluate the patient's home care needs? If so, what does this entail? Do they consult the patient's physicians and family members?

5. Does this provider include the patient and his or her family members in developing the plan of care? Are they involved in making care plan changes?

6. Is the patient's course of treatment documented, detailing the specific tasks to be carried out by each professional caregiver? Does the patient and his or her family receive a copy of this plan, and do the caregivers update it as changes occur? Does this provider take time to educate family members on the care being administered to the patient?

7. Does this provider assign supervisors to oversee the quality of care patients are receiving in their homes? If so, how often do these individuals make visits? Who can the patient and his or her family members call with questions or complaints? How does the agency follow up on and resolve problems?

8. What are the financial procedures of this provider? Does the provider furnish written statements explaining all of the costs and payment plan options associated with home care?

9. What procedures does this provider have in place to handle emergencies? Are its caregivers available 24 hours a day, seven days a week?

10. How does this provider ensure patient confidentiality?

11. In addition, ask the home care provider to supply you with a list of references, such as doctors, discharge planners, patients or their family members, and community leaders who are familiar with the provider's quality of service.

Contact each reference and ask:

1. Do you frequently refer clients to this provider?

2. Do you have a contractual relationship with this provider? If so, do you require the provider to meet special standards for quality care?

3. What sort of feedback have you gotten from patients receiving care from this provider, either on an informal basis or through a formal satisfaction survey?

4. Do you know of any clients this provider has treated whose cases are similar to mine or my loved one's? If so, can you put me in touch with these individuals?

Where Can I Find Additional Information about a Provider's Services?

To determine the caliber of a Medicare-certified provider, you can review its Medicare Survey Report. For assistance in obtaining this document, contact your state's health department or health insurance counseling program, which offers free information specifically about the Medicare home health benefit. These offices also can direct you to the state's Medicare hot line for information about the quality of services provided by Medicare-certified home health agencies and hospices in your area.

In addition, many states require home care providers to earn a license to operate. To obtain a license, a provider must meet the basic legal and operating standards imposed by the state department of health. Your state health department can provide you with information on its licensed providers.

Last, several professional organizations have established standards to define quality in home care services. Through a voluntary process, many home care providers seek accreditation from these organizations to signify that they have met national standards for quality care. Home care accrediting agencies include the Accreditation Commission for Home Care, Inc., the Community Health Accreditation Program, the Joint Commission on Accreditation of Healthcare Organizations, the National Committee for Quality Assurance, and the National HomeCaring Council. Consider contacting one or more of these organizations for information about their accredited members.

What If a Problem Develops?

If you invest some time and follow the steps outlined in this brochure, you most likely will receive high-quality, safe, and effective home care. If a problem develops, however, or if you would like to issue a complaint, notify the home care provider's chief supervisor or administrator, the state health department or state Medicare hot line, and/or the local Better Business Bureau.

Although rare, cases of fraud do exist in some health care operations. These fraudulent activities waste valuable health care dollars. If you suspect fraud, even on the slightest scale, you should report these activities to your state department of health. If a case involves the delivery of Medicare home care services, contact the Office of the Inspector General hot line at 800/HHS-TIPS.

What Are My Rights as a Patient?

Federal law requires that all individuals receiving home care services be informed of their rights as a patient. Following is a model patient bill of rights the National Association for Home Care (NAHC) has developed, based on the patient rights currently enforced by law.

Home care patients have the right to:

- be fully informed of all his or her rights and responsibilities by the home care agency;

- choose care providers;

- appropriate and professional care in accordance with physician orders;

- receive a timely response from the agency to his or her request for service;

- be admitted for service only if the agency has the ability to provide safe, professional care at the level of intensity needed;

- receive reasonable continuity of care;

- receive information necessary to give informed consent prior to the start of any treatment or procedure;

- be advised of any change in the plan of care, before the change is made;

- refuse treatment within the confines of the law and to be informed of the consequences of his or her action;

- be informed of his or her rights under state law to formulate advanced directives;

- have health care providers comply with advance directives in accordance with state law requirements;

- be informed within reasonable time of anticipated termination of service or plans for transfer to another agency;

- be fully informed of agency policies and charges for services, including eligibility for third-party reimbursements;

- be referred elsewhere, if denied service solely on his or her inability to pay;

- voice grievances and suggest changes in service or staff without fear of restraint or discrimination;

- a fair hearing for any individual to whom any service has been denied, reduced, or terminated, or who is otherwise aggrieved by agency action. The fair hearing procedure shall be set forth by each agency as appropriate to the unique patient situation (i.e., funding source, level of care, diagnosis);

- be informed of what to do in the event of an emergency; and

- be advised of the telephone number and hours of operation of the state's home health hot line, which receives questions and complaints about Medicare-certified and state-licensed home care agencies.

NAHC's affiliate, the Hospice Association of America, has developed the following model bill of rights for all individuals receiving hospice care. It also is based on the patient rights currently enforced by law.

Hospice patients have the right to:

- receive care of the highest quality;

- have relationships with hospice organizations that are based on ethical standards of conduct, honesty, dignity, and respect;

- in general, be admitted by a hospice organization only if it is assured that all necessary palliative and supportive services will be provided to promote the physical, psychological, social, and spiritual well-being of the dying patient. However, an organization with less than optimal resources may admit the patient if a more appropriate hospice organization is not available, but only after fully informing the client of its limitations and the lack of suitable alternative arrangements;

- be notified in writing of their rights and obligations before their hospice care begins. Consistent with state laws, the patient's family or guardian may exercise the patient's rights when the patient is unable to do so. Hospice organizations have an obligation to protect and promote the rights of their patients;

- be notified in writing of the care the hospice organization will furnish, the types of caregivers who will furnish the care, and the frequency of the services that are proposed to be furnished;

- be advised of any change in the plan of care before the change is made;

- participate in the planning of the care and in planning changes in the care, and to be advised that they have the right to do so;

- refuse services and to be advised of the consequences of refusing care;

- request a change in caregiver without fear of reprisal or discrimination;

- confidentiality with regard to information about their health, social, and financial circumstances and about what takes place in the home;

- expect the hospice organization to release information only as consistent with its internal policy, required by law, or authorized by the client;

- be informed of the extent to which payment may be expected from Medicare, Medicaid, or any other payor known to the hospice organization;

- be informed of any charges that will not be covered by Medicare, and the charges for which he or she may be liable;

- receive this information orally and in writing within 15 working days of the date the hospice organization becomes aware of any changes in charges;

- have access, on request, to all bills for service the patient has received regardless of whether they are paid out of pocket or by another party;

- be informed of the hospice's ownership status and its affiliation with any entities to whom the patient is referred;

- be informed of the procedure they can follow to lodge complaints with the hospice organization about the care that is, or fails to be, furnished, and regarding a lack of respect for property;

- know about the disposition of such complaints;

- voice grievances without fear of discrimination or reprisal for having done so; and

- be told what to do in the case of an emergency.

Chapter 26

National Hospice Organization

The Basics of Hospice

hos'pis

The term "hospice" (from the same linguistic root as "hospitality") can be traced back to early Western Civilization when it was used to describe a place of shelter and rest for weary or sick travelers on long journeys. The term was first applied to specialized care for dying patients in 1967, at St. Christopher's Hospice in a residential suburb of London. Today, the term "hospice" refers to a steadily growing concept of humane and compassionate care which can be implemented in a variety of settings—in patients' homes, hospitals, nursing homes, or freestanding inpatient facilities.

The Hospice Philosophy

Hospice is a special kind of care designed to provide sensitivity and support for people in the final phase of a terminal illness. Hospice care seeks to enable patients to carry on an alert, pain-free life and to manage other symptoms so that their last days may be spent with dignity and quality at home or in a home-like setting.

From "General Information," [Online]. Available: http://www.nho.org. © 1999 by the National Hospice Organization, 1901 Moore St., Ste. 901, Arlington, VA 22209. For complete contact information, please refer to Chapter 60, "Resources." Reprinted with permission.

How Hospice Works

Hospice services are available to persons who can no longer benefit from curative treatment; the typical hospice patient has a life expectancy of six months or less. Most receive care at home. Services are provided by a team of trained professionals—physicians, nurses, counselors, therapists, social workers, aides, and volunteers—who provide medical care and support services not only to the patient, but to the patient's family and caregivers. The patient is usually referred to hospice by the primary physician. Referrals can also be made by family members, friends, clergy, or health professionals.

How Hospice Differs from Other Types of Healthcare

Hospice offers palliative, rather than curative, treatment. Under the direction of a physician, hospice uses sophisticated methods of pain and symptom control that enable the patient to live as fully and comfortably as possible.

Hospice treats the person, not the disease. The interdisciplinary hospice team is made up of professionals who can address the medical, emotional, psychological, and spiritual needs of the patients and their loved ones.

Hospice emphasizes quality, rather than length, of life. Hospice neither hastens nor postpones death: it affirms life and regards dying as a normal process. The hospice movement stresses human values that go beyond the physical needs of the patient.

Hospice considers the entire family, not just the patient, the "unit of care." Patients and their families are included in the decision-making process, and bereavement counseling is provided after the death of their loved one.

Hospice offers help and support to the patient and family on a 24-hours-a-day, seven-days-a-week basis. For hospice patients and their loved ones, help is just a phone call away. Patients routinely receive periodic in-home services of a nurse, home health aide, social worker, volunteer, and other members of the hospice interdisciplinary team.

Who Pays for Hospice Care?

Studies have shown hospice care to be no more costly—and frequently less expensive—than conventional care during the last six months of life. This is because less high-cost technology is used, and family, friends, and volunteers provide much of the day-to-day patient care at home.

Hospice care is a covered benefit under most private insurance plans, including HMOs and managed care organizations. In addition, hospice is a covered Medicare benefit, and in most states is a covered Medicaid benefit.

The Medicare Hospice benefit covers:

- Nursing services on an intermittent basis
- Physician services
- Drugs, including outpatient drugs for pain relief and symptom management
- Physical, occupational, and speech-language therapy
- Home health aide and homemaker services
- Medical supplies and appliances
- Short-term inpatient care, including respite care
- Medical social services
- Spiritual, dietary, and other counseling
- Continuous care at home during periods of crisis
- Trained volunteers
- Bereavement services

Hospices also rely upon grants and community support for both donations and volunteer staff. While each hospice has its own policies concerning payment for care, it is a principle of hospice to offer services based upon need, rather than the ability to pay.

Hospice in America—Remarkable Growth

The first hospice program in the United States began serving patients in 1974. Today, over 3,000 hospice programs in all fifty states, the District of Columbia, and Puerto Rico offer comprehensive hospice care. It is estimated that hospice programs serve over 450,000 terminally ill persons and their families each year.

The National Hospice Organization is the largest nonprofit membership organization devoted **exclusively** to hospice. NHO is dedicated to promoting and maintaining quality care for terminally ill persons and their families, and to integrating hospice into the U.S. healthcare system.

As the representative of hospice providers and caregivers, NHO actively addresses the following areas of concern:

- Quality of care
- Research and evaluation
- Licensure and reimbursement
- Ethics
- Public information and referral
- Legislation
- Education

The 20 Most Commonly Asked Questions about Hospice

1. When should a decision about entering a hospice program be made—and who should make it?

At any time during a life-limiting illness, it's appropriate to discuss all of a patient's care options, including hospice. By law the decision belongs to the patient.

Understandably, most people are uncomfortable with the idea of stopping aggressive efforts to "beat" the disease. Hospice staff members are highly sensitive to these concerns and always available to discuss them with the patient and family.

2. Should I wait for our physician to raise the possibility of hospice, or should I raise it first?

The patient and family should feel free to discuss hospice care at any time with their physician, other healthcare professionals, clergy, or friends.

3. What if our physician doesn't know about hospice?

Most physicians know about hospice. If your physician wants more information about hospice, it is available from the National Council of Hospice Professionals Physician Section, medical societies, State Hospice Organizations, or NHO's Hospice Information Line (800) 658-8898.

In addition, physicians and all others can also obtain information on hospice from the American Cancer Society, the American Association of Retired Persons, and the Social Security Administration.

4. Can a hospice patient who shows signs of recovery be returned to regular medical treatment?

Certainly. If the patient's condition improves and the disease seems to be in remission, patients can be discharged from hospice and return to aggressive therapy or go on about their daily life.

If the discharged patient should later need to return to hospice care, Medicare and most private insurance will allow additional coverage for this purpose.

5. What does the hospice admission process involve?

One of the first things the hospice program will do is contact the patient's physician to make sure he or she agrees that hospice care is appropriate for this patient at this time. (Most hospices have medical staff available to help patients who have no physician.)

The patient will be asked to sign consent and insurance forms. These are similar to the forms patients sign when they enter a hospital.

The so-called "hospice election form" says that the patient understands that the care is palliative (that is, aimed at pain relief and symptom control) rather than curative. It also outlines the services available. The form Medicare patients sign also tells how electing the Medicare hospice benefit affects other Medicare coverage.

6. Is there any special equipment or changes I have to make in my home before hospice care begins?

Your hospice provider will assess your needs, recommend any equipment, and help make arrangements to obtain any necessary equipment. Often the need for equipment is minimal at first and increases as the disease progresses.

In general, hospice will assist in any way it can to make home care as convenient, clean, and safe as possible.

7. How many family members or friends does it take to care for a patient at home?

There's no set number. One of the first things a hospice team will do is to prepare an individualized care plan that will, among other things, address the amount of caregiving needed by the patient. Hospice staff visit regularly and are always accessible to answer medical questions, provide support, and teach caregivers.

8. Must someone be with the patient at all times?

In the early weeks of care, it's usually not necessary for someone to be with the patient all the time. Later, however, since one of the most common fears of patients is the fear of dying alone, hospice generally recommends someone be there continuously.

While family and friends do deliver most of the care, hospices provide volunteers to assist with errands and to provide a break and time away for primary caregivers.

9. How difficult is caring for a dying loved one at home?

It's never easy and sometimes can be quite hard. At the end of a long, progressive illness, nights especially can be very long, lonely, and scary. So, hospices have staff available around the clock to consult by phone with the family and make night visits if appropriate.

To repeat: Hospice can also provide trained volunteers to provide "respite care," to give family members a break and/or provide companionship to the patient.

10. What specific assistance does hospice provide home-based patients?

Hospice patients are cared for by a team of physicians, nurses, social workers, counselors, hospice certified nursing assistants, clergy, therapists, and volunteers—and each provides assistance based on his or her own area of expertise. In addition, hospices provide medications, supplies, equipment, and hospital services, related to the terminal illness, and additional helpers in the home, if and when needed.

11. Does hospice do anything to make death come sooner?

Hospice neither hastens nor postpones dying. Just as doctors and midwives lend support and expertise during the time of child birth, hospice provides its presence and specialized knowledge during the dying process.

12. Is caring for the patient at home the only place hospice care can be delivered?

No. Although 90% of hospice patient time is spent in a personal residence, some patients live in nursing homes or hospice centers.

13. How does hospice "manage pain"?

Hospice believes that emotional and spiritual pain are just as real and in need of attention as physical pain, so it can address each. Hospice nurses and doctors are up to date on the latest medications and devices for pain and symptom relief. In addition, physical and occupational therapists can assist patients to be as mobile and self sufficient as they wish, and they are often joined by specialists schooled in music therapy, art therapy, massage, and diet counseling.

Finally, various counselors, including clergy, are available to assist family members as well as patients.

14. What is hospice's success rate in battling pain?

Very high. Using some combination of medications, counseling and therapies, most patients can attain a level of comfort that is acceptable to them.

15. Will medications prevent the patient from being able to talk or know what's happening?

Usually not. It is the goal of hospice to have the patient as pain free and alert as possible. By constantly consulting with the patient, hospices have been very successful in reaching this goal.

16. Is hospice affiliated with any religious organization?

No. While some churches and religious groups have started hospices (sometimes in connection with their hospitals), these hospices serve a broad community and do not require patients to adhere to any particular set of beliefs.

17. Is hospice care covered by insurance?

Hospice coverage is widely available. It is provided by Medicare nationwide, by Medicaid in 42 states, and by most private insurance providers. To be sure of coverage, families should, of course, check with their employer or health insurance provider.

18. If the patient is eligible for Medicare, will there be any additional expense to be paid?

Medicare covers all services and supplies for the hospice patient related to the terminal illness. In some hospices, the patient may be required to pay a 5 percent or $5 "copayment" on medication and a 5 percent co-payment for respite care. You should find out about any co-payment when selecting a hospice.

19. If the patient is not covered by Medicare or any other health insurance, will hospice still provide care?

The first [task of hospice is to assist] families in finding out whether the patient is eligible for any coverage they may not be aware of. Barring this, most hospices will provide for anyone who cannot pay using money raised from the community or from memorial or foundation gifts.

20. Does hospice provide any help to the family after the patient dies?

Hospice provides continuing contact and support for caregivers for at least a year following the death of a loved one. Most hospices also sponsor bereavement groups and support for anyone in the community who has experienced a death of a family member, a friend, or similar losses.

Hospice Fact Sheet

Following are the most up-to-date figures available from the National Hospice Organization.

Hospice Count

As of April 1998, NHO has knowledge of approximately 3,200 operational or planned hospice programs in all 50 states, the District of Columbia, and Puerto Rico. In the 1990s, annual growth of new hospices has averaged around eight percent. In the past five years, growth has averaged nearly 17 percent.

Patient Count

NHO estimates that 495,000 patients were served by hospice in the U.S. in 1997. In the last five years annual growth in the number of hospice patients nationwide has averaged 16 percent.

Medical Coverage

Currently, nearly eighty percent of hospices are Medicare-certified.

In 1994, Medicare spent $1.2 billion of its roughly $200 billion budget on hospice services.

Currently, hospice is covered under Medicaid in 42 states plus the District of Columbia.

In 1993, Medicaid spent $129 million on hospice services.

Coverage for hospice is provided to more than 80 percent of employees in medium and large businesses. Eighty-two percent of managed care plans offer hospice services. In addition, most private insurance plans include a hospice benefit.

In 1995, the Federal Register published the authorization of a hospice benefit under CHAMPUS (the Civilian Health and Medical Program of the Uniformed Services).

Organizational Structure and Admissions

Approximately 26 percent of hospices are independent community-based organizations; 27 percent are divisions of hospitals; 19 percent are divisions of home health agencies; five percent are divisions of hospice corporations; one percent are divisions of nursing homes; and 18 percent are "other" or not identified.

Approximately 65 percent of hospices are nonprofit; four percent are government organizations; 16 percent are for-profit; and 15 percent are "other" or unidentified.

In 1995, 50.1 percent of hospices reported operational budgets of less than $500,000; 18.7 percent had budgets between $500,001 and $1 million; 19.3 percent reported between $1-3 million budgets; nine percent between $3-7 million; and three percent have budgets larger than $7 million.

In 1995, 98 percent of hospice programs admitted persons with non-cancer diagnoses. Ninety- seven percent admitted persons with AIDS. Eighty-six percent admitted terminally ill children.

In 1995, 60 percent of hospices admitted patients without primary caregivers; another 27 percent admitted patients without caregivers on a case-by-case basis.

In 1995, 53 percent of hospices admitted individuals requiring "high-tech" therapies; an additional 39 percent admitted patients needing "high-tech" services on a case-by-case basis.

In 1995, 76 percent of hospice programs admitted patients without requiring DNR orders. In some states, the Patient Self Determination Act makes it a violation of federal law to require a DNR order as part of the admission criteria.

Patient Information (1995 NHO Census)

Sixty percent of hospice patients had cancer; six percent heart-related diagnoses; four percent had AIDS; one percent renal (kidney) diagnoses; two percent Alzheimer's; and twenty-seven percent "other." In 1995, hospices cared for about one out of every two cancer deaths in America.

In 1995 the average length of stay (ALOS) for all patients admitted to a hospice program of care was 61.5 days.

The 1995, sources of payment (presented as a percentage of patients) for hospice services are as follows: Medicare, 65.3 percent; private insurance, 12 percent; Medicaid, 7.8 percent; indigent (nonreimbursed) care, 4.2 percent; other, 10.7 percent.

In 1995, 52 percent of hospice patients were male; 48 percent female. Of male patients, 71 percent were 65 or older; 17.2 percent were 50-64; ten percent were 18-49; and one percent were 17 or younger. Of the female patients, 74 percent were 65 or older; 16.7 percent were 50-64; 8.6 percent were 18-49; and one percent were 17 or younger.

Consistent with other health care census statistics, in 1995, 83 percent of hospice patients were white; eight percent were African American; three percent Hispanic; and six percent were identified as "other."

In 1995, 77 percent of hospice patients died in their own personal residence; 19 percent died in an institutional facility; and 4 percent in other settings.

Costs, Savings, and Revenue

There is no nationwide standard on what the cost of caring for a hospice patient is. The closest determination is Medicare per diem rates which for FY 1997 are currently around $94.17 per day for home care and $418.93 per day for general inpatient care.

More than 90 percent of hospice care hours are provided in patient's homes, thus substituting for more expensive multiple hospitalizations.

The National Hospice Organization

NHO was founded in 1978 as a nonprofit public-benefit charitable organization advocating for the needs of terminally ill persons in America. NHO is the largest independent national nonprofit membership organization devoted exclusively to the promotion of hospice care in the U.S.

As of April, 1998, NHO's membership included 2,200 hospice programs, 48 state hospice organizations (plus the District of Columbia), and 4,900 individuals.

Karen A. Davie is president of the organization. The current board chairperson is David Simpson of Hospice of the Western Reserve in Cleveland, Ohio. NHO is located at 1901 N. Moore St., Ste. 901, Arlington, VA 22209. Phone: (703) 243-5900; Fax: (703) 525-5762; E-mail: drsnho@cais.com; National Hospice Organization Website: www.nho.org.

Miscellaneous

A nationwide Gallup Survey conducted for NHO in fall 1996 indicated:

- Nine out of ten adults would prefer to be cared for at home if terminally ill with six months or less to live. The majority of adults would be interested in a comprehensive program of care, such as hospice.

- Belief in whether or not it should be legal for a physician to participate in assisted suicide was split, however, men are more likely than women to feel it should be legal.

- Only 35 percent of the adults surveyed reported, if terminally ill, they would ask their doctor to help end their life.

- When asked to name their greatest fear associated with death, respondents most cited "being a burden to family and friends;" "pain" was the second most common fear.

- Most adults (62%) believe it would take a year or more to adjust to the death of a loved one, yet few (10%) of the general public have ever participated in a bereavement program of grief counseling following the death of a loved one.

- Nearly 90% of adults believe it is the family's responsibility to care for the dying.

There is no current mandatory nationwide hospice accreditation or "seal of approval," although many programs are certified voluntarily by Medicare and accredited by JCAHO (the Joint Commission on Accreditation of Healthcare Organizations) or CHAP (Community Health Accreditation Program). Additionally, as of April, 1998, 43 states have hospice licensure laws. Forty-two states have Medicaid Hospice Benefits. These statistics are representative of all fifty states, Puerto Rico, and the District of Columbia.

For More Information

To find the hospice nearest you for a loved one, or to obtain additional information about hospice, call the toll-free NHO Hospice Information Line at (800) 658-8898. You can also use our on-line referral database to search for a hospice program near you.

You can also submit a request for a General Information Packet via e-mail. Please include your name and mailing address. Please note that this e-mail address is to request a General Information Packet only. If you have a specific question, view the NHO Staff Roster to determine who might be able to assist you with your question.

Chapter 27

Hospital Patients' Rights

Clinical Center Patient's Bill of Rights

Members of the staff of this hospital have a responsibility to make sure that the patient receives information necessary to make decisions about participation in any research procedure; that care is given in a manner consistent with the patient's beliefs; and that those rights basic to human dignity are observed.

This bill of rights for Clinical Center patients, given to all patients here since 1977, has been adapted from a similar document developed by the American Hospital Association for use by general hospitals:

1. The patient has the right to considerate and respectful care.

2. The patient has the right to know, by name, the physician responsible for coordinating his or her care at the Clinical Center.

3. The patient has the right to obtain from his or her physician complete current information about diagnosis, treatment, and prognosis in easily understandable terms. If it is medically inadvisable to give such information to patients, it will be given to a legally authorized representative.

Excerpted from "Clinical Center Patient's Bill of Rights," in the Clinical Center *Medical Staff Handbook*, November 20, 1995 [Online]. Available: http://ww.cc.nih.gov/ccc/aboutcc/msh/bill.html. Produced by the National Institutes of Health.

4. The patient has the right to receive from his or her physician information necessary to give informed consent to the start of any procedure or treatment. Except in emergencies, this will include, but not necessarily be limited to, a description of the specific procedure or treatment, any risks involved, and the probable duration of any incapacitation. When there are alternatives to therapeutically designed research protocols, the patient has the right to know about them. The patient also has the right to know the name of the person responsible for directing the procedures or treatment.

5. The patient has the right to refuse to participate in research, to refuse treatment to the extent permitted by law, and to be informed of the medical consequences of these actions, including possible dismissal from the study and discharge from the institution. If discharge would jeopardize the patient's health, he or she has the right to remain under Clinical Center care until discharge or transfer is medically advisable.

6. The patient has the right to be transferred to another facility when his or her participation in the Clinical Center study is terminated, providing the transfer is medically permissible, the patient has been informed of the needs for and alternatives to such a transfer, and the facility has agreed to accept the patient.

7. The patient has the right to privacy concerning the medical care program. Case discussion, consultation, examination, and treatment are confidential and will be conducted discreetly. The patient has the right to expect that all communications and records pertaining to care will be treated as confidential to the extent permitted by law.

8. The patient has the right to routine services whenever hospitalized at the Clinical Center in connection with the active protocol for which he or she is eligible; these services will generally include diagnostic procedures and medical treatment deemed necessary and advisable by the professional staff. Complicating chronic conditions will be noted, reported to the patient, and treated as necessary, without the assumption of long-term responsibility for their management. The patient may be returned for long-term or definitive care of these conditions to the referring physician or to other medical resources as appropriate.

9. The patient has the right to expect that medical information about him or her discovered at the Clinical Center as well as an account of his or her medical program here will be communicated to the referring physician.

10. The patient has the right to know in advance what appointment times and physicians are available and where to go for continuity of care provided by the Clinical Center when such care is required under the study for which the patient was admitted.

[For more information on patient rights, see Chapter 23, "Selecting a Nursing Home," and Chapter 25, "Selecting a Home Care Provider."]

Chapter 28

Advance Directives

You can decide in advance what medical treatment you want to receive if you become physically or mentally unable to communicate your wishes.

Your Rights as a Patient

As an adult in a hospital, skilled nursing facility, or other health care setting, you have the right to:

- Keep your personal and medical records private,

- Know what kind of medical treatment you will receive, and

- Tell people ahead of time what type of treatment you want, or don't want, in case you lose the ability to speak for yourself.

You can do this by preparing an **Advance Directive.**

From "Advance Directives," [Online] July 7, 1998. Available: http://www.medicare.gov/publications/advdir.htm. Publication No. HCFA 02175, produced by the Health Care Financing Administration (HCFA), U.S. Department of Health and Human Services. And excerpted from "Orders Not to Attempt Cardiac Resuscitation," in The Clinical Center *Medical Staff Handbook*, [Online] November 20, 1995. Available: http://www.cc.nih.gov/ccc/aboutcc/msh/nocpr.html. Produced by the National Institutes of Health (NIH).

What Is an Advance Directive?

Generally, an Advance Directive is a written document that tells people how to make your medical decisions when you can't make them for yourself. An Advance Directive can also designate someone else to make medical decisions for you.

Common Advance Directives are:

- a Living Will
- a Durable Power of Attorney For Health Care

A Living Will is a written document that generally states the kind of medical care you want (or do not want) in case you become unable to make your own decisions. It's called a Living Will because it takes effect while you are still living. While most states have their own Living Will forms, you might also be able to write a personal statement of your preferences for treatment.

A Durable Power of Attorney for Health Care is a signed, dated, and witnessed paper that authorizes someone else to make your medical decisions if you are unable to make them for yourself. This can include instructions about any treatment you want to avoid, [for example, cardiac resuscitation, as described below.]

Orders Not to Attempt Cardiac Resuscitation

An official DNR [Do Not Resuscitate] policy statement [should include] several of the following key points:

1. The senior physician caring for the patient documents in a progress note the discussion with the patient and/or surrogate and family, indications, and the rationale for the DNR.

2. An order is placed in the MIS system by the senior attending physician and a DNR sticker is placed on the front of the patient's chart.

3. An emergency DNR order may be written when there is a sudden decline in the patient's condition. This is documented in the patient's chart and in MIS and must be cosigned by the senior physician as soon as possible.

In the absence of an order not to attempt resuscitation, the patient care staff will make all efforts at resuscitation if the patient has a cardiac arrest.

Which Is Better: A Living Will or a Durable Power of Attorney for Health Care?

In some states, laws may make it better to have one, the other, or both. The decision is up to you. But remember, a Living Will doesn't allow you to name someone to make your medical decisions, if that is what you want. Check with your attorney or you may want to consult the State Attorney General offices listed at the end of this article.

Federal law requires hospitals, skilled nursing facilities, hospices, home health agencies, and managed care plans to give their patients who are covered by Medicare or Medicaid information about Advance Directives.

The law is intended to increase your control over medical treatment decisions. However, health care providers only have to provide information about the laws for the state in which they are located. Laws governing Advance Directives differ from state to state. Also, the laws on honoring Advance Directives from one state to another aren't clear. If you live in one state, but travel to other states frequently, you may want to consider having your Advance Directive meet the laws of other states. A good source of information is the Office of the State Attorney General.

Points to Consider:

- You don't have to have an Advance Directive if you don't want one.

- If you have an Advance Directive:

   1. Tell your family. Make sure they know where it is located.

   2. Tell your lawyer.

   3. Tell your doctor. Make sure the Advance Directive is part of your medical records.

- If you have a Durable Power of Attorney, give a copy of the original to that person.

- Keep a small card in your purse or wallet that notifies Emergency Medical Services (EMS) providers of your wishes. (EMS generally refers to ambulance companies and paramedics).

However, in an emergency situation, EMS staff don't have much time to look for, or to evaluate different types of documentation. They

285

may only acknowledge cards issued by the state's EMS Program, and only when the cards are signed by your personal physician.

Canceling an Advance Directive

You may change or cancel your Advance Directive at any time. Any change or cancellation should be written, signed, and dated. Give copies to your doctor and to anyone else to whom you may have given copies of the original. Some states allow you to change an Advance Directive by oral statement. To check the laws that apply to your state, contact the organizations listed at the end of this article.

If you want to cancel an Advance Directive while you are in the hospital, notify your doctor, your family, and others who may need to know. Even without a change in writing, telling your doctor directly about your wishes generally will carry more weight than a Living Will or Durable Power of Attorney as long as you can decide and communicate for yourself.

For Additional Information

Preparing an Advance Directive lets your physician and other health care provider know the kind of medical care you want, or don't want, if you become incapacitated. It also relieves your family and friends of the responsibility of making decisions regarding life-prolonging actions.

If you need help in preparing an Advance Directive, or if you would like more information about it, you may want to contact a lawyer. You may also consult your State Attorney General's Office, the State Office on Aging, or an Insurance Counseling Program for Medicare beneficiaries. Those numbers are at the end of this article.

Each state has its own laws and regulations regarding Advance Directives.

The numbers in the left columns are for the agencies that issue cards advising Emergency Medical Service personnel that you have an Advance Directive. The numbers in the middle column are for the offices that determine the Advance Directive laws for that state, and how they will work with the laws of other states. The numbers in the right column are for general insurance counseling services for Medicare beneficiaries.

Calls to 800 numbers are free only when made within the respective state.

Table 28.1a. (continued in Table 28.1b.) Important Contacts for Information about Advance Directives

State	Emergency Medical Service	Office of the Attorney General	Insurance Counseling Program
AL	(334)206-5383	(334)242-7300	(334)242-5743 (800)243-5463
AK	(907)465-3027	(907)465-3600	(907)269-3680 (800)478-6065
AS	011684-633-1869	(684)633-4163	xxxxxxxx
AZ	(602)255-1170	(602)542-4266	(602)542-6588 (800)432-4040
AR	(501)661-2262	(501)682-2007	(501)371-2785 x 356 (800)852-5494
CA	(916)322-4336	(916)324-5437	(916)322-3887 (800)434-0222
CO	(303)692-2980	(803)866-3052	(303)894-7499 (800)544-9181
CT	(860)509-7406	(860)808-5318	(860)424-5245 (800)994-9422
DE	(302)739-6637	(302)577-3838	(302)739-6266 (800)336-9500
DC	(202)645-5628	(202)727-6248	(202)676-3900
FL	(850)487-1911	(904)487-1963	(850)414-2060 (800)963-5337
GA	(404)657-6700	(404)656-4585	(404)657-5334 (800)669-8387
GU	011671-735-7303	(671)475-3324	(671)475-0262/0263
HI	(808)733-9210	(808)586-1282	(808)586-7299
ID	(208)334-4000	(208)334-2400	Boise: (800)247-4422 Pocatello: (800)488-5764 Twin Falls: (800)448-5731 Lewiston: (800)448-5725
IL	(217)785-2080	(312)814-2503	(217)785-9021 (800)548-9034
IN	(317)232-3980	(317)233-4386	(317)233-3475 (800)452-4800

Table 28.1b. (continued in Table 28.1c.) Important Contacts for Information about Advance Directives

State	Emergency Medical Service	Office of the Attorney General	Insurance Counseling Program
IA	(515)281-3239	(515)281-3053	(515)281-6867 (800)351-4664
KS	(913)296-7296	(913)296-2215	(316)337-6010 (800)860-5260
KY	(502)564-8963	(502)564-7600	(502)564-7372
LA	(504)342-4881	(504)342-7013	(504)342-5301 (800)259-5301
ME	(207)287-3953	(207)626-8800	(207)623-1797 (800)750-5353
MD	(410)706-5074	(410)576-6300	(410)767-1074 (800)243-3425
MA	(617)753-8300	(617)727-2200	(617)727-7750 (800)882-2003
MI	(517)241-3020	(517)373-1110	800-803-7174
MN	(612)627-5424	(612)296-6196	(612)333-2433 (800)333-2433
MS	(601)987-3880	(601)359-3692	(601)359-4956 (800)948-3090
MO	(573)751-6356	(573)751-3321	(573)893-7900 (800)390-3330
MT	(406)444-4458	(406)444-2026	(406)444-7781 (800)332-2272
NE	(402)471-0124	(402)471-2682	(402)471-2201
NV	(702)687-3065	(702)687-4170	(702)486-4602 (800)307-4444
NH	(603)271-4568	(603)271-3658	(603)271-3944 (800)852-3388
NJ	(609)633-7777	(609)292-4925	(609)588-3139 (800)792-8820
NM	(505)476-7000	(505)827-6000	(505)827-7640 (800)432-2080

Table 28.1c. (continued in Table 28.1d.) Important Contacts for Information about Advance Directives

State	Emergency Medical Service	Office of the Attorney General	Insurance Counseling Program
NY	(518)402-0996	(518)474-7330	(212)869-3850 NYC (212)333-5511 NYC (800)333-4114
NC	(919)733-2285	(919)716-6400	(919)733-0111 (800)443-9354
ND	(701)328-2388	(701)328-2210	(800)247-0560
NMI	(670)235-9110	(670)664-2341	(607)234-6011
OH	(614)466-9447	(614)466-3376	(614)644-3399 (800)686-1578
OK	(405)271-4027	(405)521-3921	(405)521-6628 (800)763-2828
OR	(503)731-4011	(503)378-6002	(503)947-7984 (800)722-4134
PA	(717)787-8741	(717)787-3391	(717)783-8975 (800)783-7067
PR	(787)766-1733	(787)721-7700	(787)721-8590
RI	(401)222-2401	(401)274-4400	(401)222-2880 (800)322-2880
SC	(803)737-7204	(803)734-3970	(803)253-6177 (800)868-9095
SD	(605)773-4031	(605)773-3215	(605)773-3656 (800)822-8804
TN	(615)741-2584	(615)741-6474	(616)242-0438 (800)525-2816
TX	(512)834-6740	(512)463-2191	(512)424-6840 (800)252-9240
UT	(801)538-6435	(801)538-1326	(801)538-3910
VT	(802)863-7310	(802)828-3171	(802)748-5182 (800)642-5119
VA	(804)371-3500	(804)786-2071	(804)662-9333 (800)552-3402
VI	(809)776-7708	(809)774-5666	(809)778-6311-2338

Table 28.1d. (continued from Table 28.1c.) Important Contacts for Information about Advance Directives

State	Emergency Medical Service	Office of the Attorney General	Insurance Counseling Program
WA	(360)705-6745	(360)753-6200	(800)397-4422
WV	(304)558-3956	(304)558-2021	(304)558-3317
WI	(608)266-9781	(608)266-1221	(608)267-3201 (800)242-1060
WY	(307)777-6004	(307)777-7841	(307)856-6880 (800)856-4398

AS=American Samoa
GU=Guam
NMI=North Mariana Islands
PR=Puerto Rico
VI=Virgin Islands

Part Four

End-of-Life Medical Care: Issues and Innovations

Chapter 29

Hospital Care of Acute Stroke

Delivery systems for acute stroke hospital care are relatively primitive compared to systems for state-of-the-art emergency cardiac care. In part, this reflects the nihilistic attitude toward acute stroke care fostered by years of providing only supportive therapy.[1] The recent approval of intravenous t-PA for selected patients with ischemic stroke of less than 3 hours' duration has exposed these deficiencies and mandates changes in the hospital care system. Importantly, although the immediate impetus stems from thrombolysis and brain ischemia, these long-delayed changes in hospital stroke care will also benefit patients with subarachnoid and intracerebral hemorrhage.

Pertinent to acute stroke intervention are aggressive stroke teams with a paging and response algorithm modeled after the "Code Blue" concept used in acute myocardial infarction (AMI).[2,3] Pilot studies using stroke teams have been conducted in tertiary centers, usually related to clinical trials, with dramatic reductions in diagnostic and treatment delays.[4-6] However, it probably will not be feasible to develop comprehensive acute stroke teams in many community hospitals. Some hospitals may not be equipped to care for more severe or

From "Hospital Care of Acute Stroke," by Anthony J. Furlan, M.D., in the Proceedings of a National Symposium on Rapid Identification and Treatment of Acute Stroke, December 12-13, 1996 [Online]. Available: http://www.ninds.nih.gov/healinfo/disorder/stroke%20proceedings/furlan.htm. Presented by the National Institute of Neurological Disorders and Stroke (NINDS), National Institutes of Health. For complete contact information, please refer to Chapter 60, "Resources."

complex stroke patients, for example those with intracerebral or sub-arachnoid hemorrhage. Availability of neurologists, neurosurgeons, interventional neuroradiologists, and other specialists may be limited in outlying regions.

Comprehensive regional stroke centers for patients with complex, resource-intensive cerebrovascular disorders should be identified and linked to outlying community hospitals via stroke networks. The National Stroke Association has developed guidelines for the identification of comprehensive stroke centers. However, transfer of acute stroke patients to a regional stroke center would preclude treatment in many patients. Even when 911 is called, the mean time to emergency department (ED) arrival for acute stroke patients is 2.6 hours.[4-6] If the system is accessed through the family doctor or by family transport to the ED, the mean arrival time exceeds 5 hours. Hence, therapy is precluded in many stroke patients simply because of late arrival at the hospital.

To address these concerns, minimal qualifications must be established for physicians and hospitals treating patients with acute stroke. The recommended target for intravenous t-PA in acute ischemic stroke is a door-to-drug time of less than 60 minutes, which is close to the average time for starting thrombolysis after AMI.[7,8] To achieve this ambitious goal, hospitals should develop an acute stroke plan designed to reduce management delays to a minimum. The National Stroke Association's Emergency Response System Organization at Sites (ERSOS) guidelines provide a detailed template for implementing a comprehensive acute stroke hospital care delivery system.[9] Using templates, hospital stroke plans can be tailored to fit local needs but should include four basic elements outlined in the following sections.

Resource Utilization

As the hospital entry point for both ambulance patients and walk-ins, the ED is the common denominator for most acute stroke patients. On-site and en route communication with emergency medical services (EMS) by telemetry, radio, or telephone permits mobilization of the stroke team preferably through a dedicated beeper. An accurate prehospital diagnosis of stroke by EMS personnel using a simplified stroke scale is feasible although less precise than a diagnosis of AMI since there is no simple test like the electrocardiogram for confirmation.[10,11]

Preprinted ED stroke order sheets and prepackaged specimen tubes ensure that all necessary chemistries and tests are done before treatment is started. Coagulation studies are essential. The ED should be able to test the activated clotting time (ACT), activated partial thromboplastin time (APTT), and international normalization ratio (INR) on-site and have STAT laboratory access. A 12-lead electrocardiogram machine and electrocardiogram technician should be immediately available. Training the ED nursing staff to perform a 12-lead electrocardiogram and establishing a critical pathway protocol that includes an electrocardiogram as part of the initial evaluation of vital signs in patients with possible stroke will minimize diagnostic delays.

The essential imaging technology for acute stroke is CT. Although more than 90% of hospitals with at least 200 beds have CT scanners,[12] personnel and transportation delays consume 1 hour or more between ED and CT in most hospitals. Some hospitals with active stroke programs have a CT scanner in the ED. CT results should be available to the treating physician within 45 minutes of patient arrival at the ED. This can only be accomplished if there is effective integration between the ED, radiology services, and patient transport.

Diagnostic emergency cerebral angiography is required in selected stroke patients and should be available within 60 minutes of presentation to the ED. Neurointerventional procedures such as aneurysm coiling, angioplasty, and intraarterial thrombolysis require special expertise and imaging technology and should be performed at regional comprehensive stroke centers. Intraoperative angiography, stereotactic devices, and microneurosurgical equipment are necessary at comprehensive centers performing complex aneurysm and vascular malformation surgery.

A number of diagnostic technologies are available at comprehensive stroke centers but, although desirable, are not mandatory for all patients with acute stroke. These technologies include emergency carotid ultrasound and transcranial Doppler, magnetic resonance imaging (MRI, MR angiography, diffusion and perfusion MRI, echoplanar MRI), single photon emission computer tomography, positron emission tomography, and transesophageal echocardiography.

After the physician has written an order for a thrombolytic drug to be administered, the agent must be obtained, properly reconstituted, and administered. Stocking the thrombolytic drug in the ED instead of in a central pharmacy significantly decreases the delay to therapy. Use of a thrombolytic drug cart, kit, or tackle box to stock the drug, checklists, standing orders, flow sheets, and adjunctive equipment including intravenous tubing, needles, blood tubes, and tape is one of the most efficient ways to organize the ED team.

A number of novel concepts have recently been developed to focus the attention and efforts of hospital ED staff on treating patients with chest pain in an expedited fashion. The most popular of these ideas is the chest pain center. Most hospitals that have developed chest pain centers have dedicated one or more monitored beds in the ED to the rapid evaluation and treatment of patients with suspected AMI. Some hospitals have dedicated a section of the ED as a clinical decision unit, where patients can be observed for up to 24 hours. This approach can reduce the cost of ruling out an AMI by up to 80% by not admitting all patients to the coronary care unit. A similar approach could potentially reduce acute stroke admissions and costs.

Hospitals lacking any intensive care capabilities should not manage patients with acute stroke. Hemorrhagic stroke often requires management in an intensive care unit (ICU) with neurosurgical input. High-risk therapies like thrombolysis and complications such as cerebral edema also necessitate that many ischemic stroke patients have access to intensive care. The utility of stroke units has been demonstrated through shortened length of stay and lower mortality, but not consistently by a better neurological outcome.[13,14] However, dedicated stroke units, or even neurological intensive care units, may not be cost-effective in all hospital settings. Hospitals can adapt medical or surgical intensive care beds for acute stroke. Also, many acute stroke patients require only intermediate level neurological monitoring that can be accomplished in stepped units with lower staffing levels than an ICU (e.g., nurse:patient ratio of 1:4 versus 1:2).

Stroke Expertise

New approaches and attitudes toward stroke will require neurological retraining beginning with residency programs. Physicians treating acute stroke must have some neurological experience and must learn the selection criteria for thrombolysis, including the NIH Stroke Scale (NIHSS).[15] The ability to read CT scans, recognize the early signs of brain ischemia, and distinguish hemorrhagic from nonhemorrhagic stroke is essential. Minimum stroke training and continuing medical education (CME) requirements for neurologists, neurosurgeons, family practitioners, internists, emergency medicine physicians, and radiologists must be established by the appropriate national organizations.

A comprehensive stroke team incorporates 24-hour access to a neurologist, neurosurgeon, and interventional neuroradiologist capable of diagnosing and managing any cerebrovascular problem. Subarachnoid and intracerebral hemorrhage require neurosurgical expertise. In outlying hospitals, access to neurological and neurosurgical expertise may require networked telecommunication and transportation links.

In the majority of cases of AMI, the ED physician makes the decision to administer thrombolytic therapy without further consultation. It is typically faster to treat with thrombolytic agents in the ED than to transfer the patient to an ICU. A minority of hospitals require the ED physician to consult with a cardiologist or the patient's primary care physician before administering a thrombolytic drug. Consultation remains essential in patients with relative contraindications or in whom the diagnosis is unclear, but in the majority of cases of AMI, consultation only delays the administration of thrombolytic therapy. An analogous situation could pertain to the treatment of acute ischemic stroke, but first there must be improved neurological training for nurses, ED physicians, internists, and family practitioners as well as some standardization of stroke diagnostic and treatment protocols.

Experienced ED physicians can interpret electrocardiograms of patients with chest pain with nearly the same level of accuracy as cardiologists; however, cardiologists are more likely to be correct in the evaluation of difficult electrocardiograms.[16] By contrast, many ED physicians receive no formal training in brain CT interpretation. Early signs of infarction on CT have been linked to an increased risk of hemorrhage complicating thrombolysis but are easily missed even by experienced radiologists.[17] CT misdiagnosis is an infrequent problem in full-service hospitals with 24-hour access to radiologists, but could be a major problem in outlying community hospitals.

Transmission of an electrocardiogram to a cardiologist by a facsimile machine can provide backup interpretive assistance for the ED physician in difficult cases without significantly delaying care. Teleradiology links could provide similar services for interpreting CT scans in the ED. However, unlike the electrocardiogram in AMI, CT is normal in most patients with early ischemic stroke and the diagnosis ultimately rests on clinical neurological expertise. ED physicians, internists, and family practitioners must therefore receive sufficient neurological training during residency and through CME to be able to diagnose and treat acute stroke.

Guidelines, Algorithms, and Critical Pathways

Identification and prioritization of patients with AMI or acute stroke are challenges in every busy ED. Only 4-5% of patients with chest pain who present to the ED are candidates for thrombolytic therapy.[18,19] Similarly, recent stroke thrombolysis trials suggest that fewer than 5% of screened patients are eligible for therapy.[15] Therefore, triage nurses may have to screen 25 patients to find one stroke patient who is eligible for urgent treatment. This low yield greatly reduces the incentive for nursing and medical staff to immediately evaluate every patient who arrives at the ED with suspected stroke symptoms. Ambulatory patients pose a particular problem, since their presentation to the ED may not be as dramatic as that of patients who arrive by ambulance. If registration is required for ambulatory patients prior to seeing a triage nurse, there is a further delay, particularly when the ED is busy and overcrowded.

Guidelines, algorithms, and critical pathways are important tools for minimizing delays and enhancing the triage of patients with acute stroke. Guidelines for the treatment of acute ischemic stroke have been published and recently were supplemented for thrombolysis.[20,21] Similar guidelines have been published for subarachnoid and intracerebral hemorrhage.[22,23] The thrombolysis guidelines set a promising new trend since they were jointly developed by the American Heart Association Stroke Council and the American Academy of Neurology. Guidelines improve the process of care although by themselves are insufficient to implement changes in physician behavior.[24-27]

Critical pathways build on guidelines by identifying the optimal sequencing of medical management decisions and thereby enhance efficiency in the process of care.[28] Integrated critical pathways have both area-specific (ED, angiography suite, ICU, regular nursing floor) and diagnosis-specific (ischemic stroke, subarachnoid hemorrhage, intracerebral hemorrhage) components. Critical pathways are often implemented by nursing personnel as they assure the continuity of care in different locations and by different medical specialists. They are also important tools for quality assurance.[29]

Algorithms are tools that physicians use to organize the process of making diagnostic and treatment decisions. Evidence-based algorithms for stroke have been developed but have not been widely adopted.[30,31] Algorithms are controversial since they cannot take into account all of the variables and options involved in clinical decision-making and therefore run the risk of creating "cookbook" medicine. Algorithms should not be used as surrogates for neurological expertise but can provide some guidance in clinical decision-making.

Quality Improvement

The ultimate goal of any hospital acute stroke plan is to improve patient outcome. Therefore, quality improvement is an essential component of any hospital acute stroke plan, and is becoming even more important as hospitals and physicians seek to justify health care expenditures.

Community-based attempts to assess quality of care and outcomes in acute stroke have emphasized costs, length of stay, and in-hospital mortality rather than long-term disability or handicap. Available models rely heavily on coma and level of consciousness (LOC) to predict risk of death from stroke. Coma and LOC on admission are very important in predicting mortality after intracerebral hemorrhage and subarachnoid hemorrhage,[32,33] but LOC alone is insufficient to predict mortality after brain infarction[34-36] and thrombolysis does not reduce ischemic stroke mortality.

Many stroke outcome models reflect the trend toward creating "minimal clinical data sets" by relying on a few easily extracted physiological variables that show statistical correlation but have no clear relevance to quality of care.[37] Skepticism about outcomes research was highlighted by Iezzoni, et al.,[38] who compared 11 different severity-adjusted models assessing stroke mortality and found that 25% of the hospitals were ranked differently, either "better" or "worse," depending on which particular model was used.

Previously there has been little pressure on physicians or hospitals to systematically change the way they examine stroke patients or record essential data.[39] The omission by statistical models of stroke outcome variables validated in peer-reviewed medical literature reflects the fact that such data are not routinely collected by physicians and recorded in the medical record in a standardized format. Furthermore, measures of treatment efficacy used in clinical trials, such as stroke scales (NIHSS) and functional measures of stroke outcome at 90 days (Barthel index or modified Rankin scale), have not been the standard of care in the community setting.

It is doubtful whether short-term stroke mortality can be used to meaningfully compare quality of care between hospitals. Most of the variation in mortality between hospitals reflects not quality of care but systematic differences in unmeasured or unobserved patient characteristics, inadequacy of the fit of the model, and random error.[40] Short-term mortality models cannot normalize for all of the known and unknown variables affecting outcome in different patient populations regardless of how much clinical information is available. Alternatives include process analysis, which could be linked with critical pathways, functional assessment, and patient satisfaction.

Attempts to work with neurological specialty societies to develop algorithms for stroke care have met with limited success.[41] Problems included imprecise data collection and coding, and consensus difficulties due to lack of agreement over appropriate practice criteria. As expensive and dangerous new therapies like thrombolysis emerge, research on community-based stroke outcomes is urgently needed.[42] A clinically relevant national stroke database created with community physician compliance in mind would greatly facilitate this effort.

References

1. Biller, J., and B. B. Love. 1991. Nihilism and stroke therapy. *Stroke* 22:1105-7.

2. Gomez, C. R., M. D. Malkoff, C. M. Sauer, et al. 1994. Code Stroke. An attempt to shorten inhospital therapeutic delays. *Stroke* 25:1920-3.

3. A Working Group on Emergency Brain Resuscitation. 1995. Emergency brain resuscitation. *Ann Intern Med* 122:622-7.

4. Barsan, W. G., T. G. Brott, J. P. Broderick, et al. 1993. Time of hospitalization in patients with acute stroke. *Arch Intern Med* 153:2558-61.

5. Bratina, P., L. Greenberg, W. Pasteur, et al. 1995. Current emergency department management of stroke in Houston, Texas. *Stroke* 26:409-14.

6. Lyden, P. D., K. Rapp, T. Babcock, et al. 1994. Ultra-rapid identification, triage, and enrollment of stroke patients into clinical trials. *J Stroke Cerebrovasc Dis* 2:106-13.

7. Kereiakes, D. J., W. D. Weaver, J. L. Anderson, et al. 1990. Time delays in the diagnosis and treatment of acute myocardial infarction: A tale of eight cities. *Am Heart J* 120:773-80.

8. Rogers, W. J., L. J. Bowlby, N. C. Chandra, et al. 1994. Treatment of myocardial infarction in the United States (1990 to 1993). Observations from the National Registry of Myocardial Infarction. *Circulation* 90(4):2103-14.

9. Houser, G., and J. Spilker. 1995. The NSA Clinical Trials Acceleration Program (CTAP). In: Grotta, J., L. P. Miller, and A. M. Buchan, eds. *Ischemic Stroke. Recent Advances in Understanding and Therapy. International Business Communications, USA* 3(7):107-43.

10. Kothari, R., W. Barsan, T. Brott, et al. 1995. Frequency and accuracy of prehospital diagnosis of acute stroke. *Stroke* 26:937-41.

11. Kothari, R., K. Hall, J. Broderick, et al. 1996. Early stroke recognition: A prehospital stroke scale. *Stroke* 27:171.

12. American Hospital Association Statistics. 1992. Chicago: American Hospital Association 214 (Table 12A).

13. Indredavik, B., F. Bakke, R. Solberg, et al. 1991. Benefit of a stroke unit: A randomized controlled trial. *Stroke* 22:1026-31.

14. Kalra, L. 1994. The influence of stroke unit rehabilitation on functional recovery from stroke. *Stroke* 25(4):821-5.

15. The National Institute of Neurological Disorders and Stroke rt-PA Stroke Study Group. 1995. Tissue plasminogen activator for acute ischemic stroke. *N Engl J Med* 333:1581-7.

16. Kudenchuk, P. J., M. T. Ho, W. D. Weaver, et al. 1991. Accuracy of computer interpreted electrocardiography in selecting patients for thrombolytic therapy. *J Am Coll Cardiol* 17(7):1486-91.

17. Hacke, W., M. Kaste, C. Fieschi, et al. (for the ECASS Study Group). 1995. Intravenous thrombolysis with recombinant tissue plasminogen activator for acute hemispheric stroke. *JAMA* 274:1017-26.

18. Ornato, J. P. 1990. The earliest thrombolytic treatment of acute myocardial infarction: Ambulance or emergency department? *Clin Cardiol* 13(Supplement VIII):27-31.

19. Ornato, J. P. 1991. Problems faced by the urban emergency department in providing rapid triage and intervention for the patient with suspected acute myocardial infarction. *Heart Lung* 20:584-8.

20. Adams, H. P., T. G. Brott, R. M. Crowell, et al. 1994. Guidelines for the management of patients with acute ischemic stroke: A statement for healthcare professionals from a special writing group of the Stroke Council, American Heart Association. *Stroke* 25:1901-14.

21. Adams, H. P., T. G. Brott, A. J. Furlan, et al. 1996. Guidelines for thrombolytic therapy for acute stroke: A supplement to the

guidelines for the management of patients with acute ischemic stroke. A statement for healthcare professionals from a special writing group of the Stroke Council, American Heart Association. *Circulation* 94:1167-74.

22. Mayberg, M. R., H. H. Batjer, R. Dacey, et al. 1994. Guidelines for the management of subarachnoid hemorrhage. *Stroke* 25:2315-28.

23. National Stroke Association Consensus Statement. 1993. Stroke: The first six hours. *J Stroke Cerebrovasc Dis* 3:133-44.

24. Lomas, J. 1993. Making clinical policy explicit. Legislative policy making and lessons for developing practice guidelines. *Int J Technol Assess Health Care* 9(1):11-25.

25. Lomas, J., M. Enkin, G. M. Anderson, et al. 1991. Opinion leaders vs. audit and feedback to implement practice guidelines. *JAMA* 265:2202-7.

26. Haynes, R. B. 1990. Loose connections between peer-reviewed clinical journals and clinical practice. *Ann Intern Med* 113:724-8.

27. Lomas, J. 1993. Diffusion, dissemination, and implementation: Who should do what? *Ann NY Acad Sci* 703:226-35.

28. Pearson, S. D., D. Goulart-Fisher, and T. M. Lee. 1995. Critical pathways as a strategy for improving care: Problems and potential. *Ann Intern Med* 1123:941-8.

29. Ringel, S. P., and R. L. Hughes. 1996. Evidence-based medicine, critical pathways, practice guidelines, and managed care. *Arch Neurol* 53:867-71.

30. Brown, R. D., B. A. Evans, D. O. Wiebers, et al. 1994. Transient ischemic attack and minor ischemic stroke: An algorithm for evaluation and treatment. *Mayo Clin Proc* 69:1027-39.

31. Bowen, J., and C. Yaste. 1994. Effect of a stroke protocol on hospital costs of stroke patients. *Neurology* 44:1961-4.

32. Tuhrim, S., and T. R. Price. 1988. Prediction of intracerebral hemorrhage survival. *Ann Neurol* 24:258-63.

33. Broderick, J. P., T. G. Brott, J. E. Duldner, et al. 1993. Volume of intracerebral hemorrhage. A powerful and easy-to-use predictor of 30 day mortality. *Stroke* 24:987-93.

34. Sacco, R. L., T. Shi, M. C. Zamanillo, et al. 1994. Predictors of mortality and recurrence after hospitalized cerebral infarction in an urban community. *Neurology* 44:626-34.

35. Chambers, B. R., J. W. Norris, B. L. Shurvell, et al. 1987. Prognosis of acute stroke. *Neurology* 37:221-5.

36. Bounds, J. V., D. O. Wiebers, J. P. Whisnant, et al. 1981. Mechanisms and timing of deaths from cerebral infarction. *Stroke* 12:474-7.

37. Ruttiman, U. E. 1994. Statistical approaches to development and validation of predictive instruments. *Crit Care Clinics* 10:19-36.

38. Iezzoni, L. I., M. Shartz, A. S. Ash, et al. 1995. Using severity-adjusted stroke mortality rates to judge hospitals. *Int J Qual Health Care* 7:81-94.

39. Fink, A., and R. H. Brook. 1989. The condition of the literature on differences in hospital mortality. *Med Care* 27:15-36.

40. Normand, S. T., M. E. Glickman, R. G. Sharma, et al. 1996. Using admission characteristics to predict short-term mortality from myocardial infarction in elderly patients. Results from the Cooperative Cardiovascular Project. *JAMA* 275:1322-8.

41. Lanska, D. 1995. A public/private partnership in the quest for quality: Development of cerebrovascular disease practice guidelines and review criteria. *Am J Med Quality* 10:100-6.

42. Blumenthal, D., and A. M. Epstein. 1996. The role of physicians in the future of quality management. *N Engl J Med* 335:1328-31.

— by Anthony J. Furlan, M.D.,
The Cleveland Clinic Foundation

Chapter 30

Effectiveness of the Intensive Care Unit

Introduction

A Consensus Development Conference was held at the National Institutes of Health on March 7-9, 1983, to discuss issues related to the practice of critical care medicine.

NIH Consensus Development Conferences bring together investigators in the biomedical sciences, practicing physicians and other health professionals, and representatives of the public to provide a scientific assessment of medical technologies and to develop a consensus statement on their safety and effectiveness.

On the first two days of the meeting, a Consensus Development Panel and members of the audience heard scientific presentations from a distinguished group of medical scientists. The panel then considered the following questions:

1. Is there empirical evidence that intensive care units (ICUs) cause a decrease in patient morbidity or mortality? Which patients are most likely to benefit from intensive care?

2. What skills are essential for personnel in a critical care unit? How should this personnel be trained and organized to assure the best care for patients most in need?

From "Critical Care Medicine. NIH Consensus Statement Online," [Online] March 7-9, 1983. Available: http://odp.od.nih.gov/consensus/cons/035/ 035_statement.htm. Produced by the National Institutes of Health (NIH). For complete contact information, please refer to Chapter 60, "Resources."

3. What special technology and therapeutic interventions should be routinely available for the most effective ICU function?

4. How is a hospital's critical care delivery system best structured: one large multispecialty unit or multiple small subspecialty units?

5. How has the development of ICUs affected the traditional functions of a hospital?

6. What direction should critical care research follow?

Members of this panel included biomedical investigators, critical care physicians, other medical specialists, nurses, a biostatistician, and a jurist.

Critical Care Medicine (CCM) is a multidisciplinary and multiprofessional medical/nursing field concerned with patients who have sustained or are at risk of sustaining acutely life-threatening single or multiple organ system failure due to disease or injury. These conditions necessitate prolonged minute-to-minute therapy or observation in an intensive care unit (ICU) which is capable of providing a high level of intensive therapy in terms of quality and immediacy.

In its broadest meaning, CCM includes management at the scene of onset of critical illness or injury, during transportation, in the emergency department, during surgical intervention in the operating room, and finally in the ICU. However, this consensus report is limited to CCM as it relates to the adult patient's management in the ICU. The report focuses not only on units that offer the full range of CCM but also on units providing a narrower range of critical care services. However, pediatric and neonatal CCM, the care of patients with burns, and all forms of extra-hospital care are not addressed in this report. Although these units are excluded from this report, valuable similarities with other ICUs in their organization and structure should not be ignored.

While critical care may be considered a higher level of management than intensive care, the two terms are used synonymously in this report.

Is there empirical evidence that intensive care units cause a decrease in patient morbidity or mortality? Which patients are most likely to benefit from intensive care?

The estimation of the efficacy of ICUs with respect to mortality and morbidity can be made only in the context of the patient populations admitted, the objectives for admission, the interventions which are being employed and the alternate patient management systems to which comparisons could be made. Mortality and morbidity may refer to events occurring in the ICU, hospital, or during a longer period of followup. Uniform goals and results for all ICUs are not attainable or desirable.

Historically, intensive care units were organized to serve specific purposes such as rhythm monitoring, the care of postoperative patients, airway maintenance and mechanical ventilation for patients with reversible neurological disease. The highly favorable outcomes derived from such specialized care served as the stimulus for establishing large numbers of such units. Over the past two decades, the availability of physical resources, nursing staff, and related specialized procedures, as well as patients' expectations, have resulted in an expansion of the original indications for admission to categories of patients for whom the achievable benefits are less clear.

There is empirical evidence that interventions commonly restricted to areas designated as intensive, coronary, or critical care units result in a decrease in mortality or morbidity. However, evidence for such a benefit can be considered unequivocal for only a portion of the heterogeneous patient populations currently admitted to such units. For a larger proportion of patients, evidence is equivocal but the weight of clinical opinion is that ICU care improves survival. It is recognized, however, that for some patients the risk of iatrogenic illnesses associated with ICU care may outweigh any potential benefit.

This spectrum of ICU effectiveness for different patients can be better understood by considering some typical patient categories.

First is the patient with acute reversible disease for whom the probability of survival without ICU intervention is low, but the survival probability with such interventions is high. Common clinical examples include the patient with acute reversible respiratory failure due to drug overdose, or with cardiac conduction disturbances resulting in cardiovascular collapse but amenable to pacemaker therapy. Because survival for many of these patients without such life-support interventions is uncommon, the observed high survival rates constitute unequivocal evidence of reduced mortality for this category of ICU patients. These patients clearly benefit from ICU care.

Another group consists of patients with a low probability of survival without intensive care whose probability of survival with intensive care may be higher—but the potential benefit is not as clear. Clinical examples include patients with septic or cardiogenic shock. The weight of clinical opinion is that ICUs reduce mortality for many of these patients, though this conviction is supported only by uncontrolled or poorly controlled studies. Often these studies do not allow one to distinguish between ICU effectiveness and the effects of patient selection and/or differences in cointerventions that do not require the ICU.

A third category is patients admitted to the ICU, not because they are critically ill, but because they are at risk of becoming critically ill. The purposes of intensive care in these instances are to prevent a serious complication or to allow a prompt response to any complication that may occur. It is presumed that the prompt response to a potentially fatal complication made possible by continuous monitoring plus the concentration of specialized personnel in the ICU increases the probability of a favorable outcome. The risk of complication may be high (as in the patient with an acute myocardial infarction and complex ventricular ectopy) or low (as in the patient with myocardial infarction suspected because of chest pain in the absence of electrocardiographic abnormalities). Also, the differences in probability of a favorable outcome following a complication inside rather than outside the ICU may be large (as in the patient with postcraniotomy intracranial bleeding) or small (as in the patient with gastrointestinal bleeding). The strength of evidence supporting the effectiveness of the ICU varies with the probability of a complication and with the difference in expected outcome inside and outside the ICU. When the risk of complication is high and the potential gain large, a decrease in mortality is likely. Similarly, when the risk is low and the potential gain small, an observable decrease in mortality is unlikely. These patients are not likely to benefit from ICU care.

The risk of iatrogenic morbidity and mortality for all patients must be included in consideration of ICU effectiveness. Complications associated with major interventions are not infrequent despite the concentration of skilled personnel in the intensive care unit. More subtle ill effects, including anxiety and psychiatric disturbances, are common and may increase the incidence of complications for which patients are monitored (e.g., ventricular arrhythmias in the coronary patient). Technical difficulties, errors in interpretation, increasing interventions induced by continuous monitoring, facilitated by immediate availability of personnel and equipment, are potential hazards for the monitored patient. Iatrogenic illness rates in the ICU are not known with any precision. This gap in our knowledge contributes substantially to our uncertainty about the effectiveness of ICU care.

A difficult clinical problem in the allocation of ICU resources is the disposition of patients with a very low probability of survival despite optimal ICU care.

It is not medically appropriate to devote limited ICU resources to patients without reasonable prospect of significant recovery when patients who need those services, and who have a significant prospect of recovery from acutely life-threatening disease or injury are being turned away due to lack of capacity. It is inappropriate to maintain ICU management of a patient whose prognosis has resolved to one of persistent vegetative state, and it is similarly inappropriate to employ ICU resources where no purpose will be served but a prolongation of the natural process of death.

Coronary care units (CCUs) deserve separate consideration as they represent the largest group of specialized intensive care units. These units appear to have improved survival of patients hospitalized with acute myocardial infarction. This change relates to the traditional function of CCUs; i.e., observations of cardiac rhythm, prompt recognition of life threatening arrhythmias, and appropriate drug and electrical cardioversion therapy. Since mortality within the first 24 hours following infarction is due primarily to ventricular fibrillation and since this arrhythmia (or "warning arrhythmia") is more likely to be treated successfully in monitored units than in general services, the assumption is made that the current relatively low hospital mortality from myocardial infarction is due to CCUs.

Considerable knowledge of the natural history and pathophysiology of acute myocardial infarction has accrued as a result of CCUs. Much of this relates to risk stratification based on clinical observations, demographic and hemodynamic factors, and characterizations of electrocardiographic phenomena, etc. Principles of therapy have evolved which reflect the heterogeneous nature of the disease; e.g., short-term, nonintervention care for low risk patients; aggressive, invasive medical/surgical therapy for high risk patients or for those who develop complications of myocardial infarction such as cardiogenic shock. The use of high risk procedures such as coronary angiography or intra-aortic balloon counterpulsation in patients with acute myocardial infarction requires a fine degree of judgment since the short- and long-term benefits have not yet been clarified.

In characterizing the effectiveness of CCU and ICU care it should be recognized that this is subject to ongoing change due to the interaction between trends in the natural history of those diseases leading to admission and improvements in available technology. For example, within two decades, potent antiarrhythmic agents, pulmonary artery catheters, computerized cardiac output measurements, and intra-aortic balloon pumps have all been introduced to the coronary care unit. During the same period, a major national improvement has developed in the control of hypertension and interest in cardiac fitness. From another less complex perspective, the apparently "fixed" mortalities of respiratory failure, from poliomyelitis and idiopathic respiratory distress syndrome of the newborn, have been changed dramatically by the introduction of intermittent positive pressure ventilation and continuous positive airway pressure, respectively. In both instances, a single maneuver, not previously considered for use in those diseases, changed outcome almost overnight. For these reasons, decisions as to which patients may benefit must be subject to ongoing revision, based on continuously updated data. Considerations as to whom to exclude from access to intensive care should not ignore this changing picture.

What skills are essential for personnel in a critical care unit? How should this personnel be trained and organized to assure the best care for patients most in need?

Essential skills for an ICU. The skills essential for ICU personnel depend on the level of responsibilities and mission of that unit. For example, a CCU will require distinctly different skills from those required in a trauma unit. Skills required of a nurse or primary physician may be different from those required of the director of the ICU.

Once the mission of the ICU is established and the boundaries of expertise in the ICU are defined, certain specific skills may be omitted. For example, if the hospital lacks an active neurosurgical program, skills unique to a neurosurgery unit can be excluded and patients requiring this expertise will by necessity be triaged elsewhere.

Some personnel skills are generic to any ICU:

- *Decision-Making Skills.* Clear lines of authority must be established for decision making. Certain decisions will be made as policy of the ICU with exceptions depending on the needs of the individual patient. Qualified personnel other than physicians may make life-saving decisions about interventions without prior consultation with the responsible physician. For each patient, medical management decisions should be made by a physician-coordinator who may delegate decision-making responsibility to other members of the ICU health care team and consultants. The physician-coordinator may be either an ICU-based physician or another physician credentialed by the hospital; but in the case of every patient the physician-coordinator will be explicitly designated.

- *Equipment Skills.* Qualified personnel must be available to inspect, maintain, and calibrate equipment used for monitoring and life support. All ICUs should be capable of arrhythmia monitoring and have equipment immediately available for cardiopulmonary resuscitation. Other equipment skills will differ depending on the mission of the ICU. For example, intracranial pressure monitoring may be important in a neurological unit, whereas such skills would not be required in a CCU.

- *Procedure Skills.* For a CCU and an intermediate CCU, arrhythmia detection and treatment and resuscitation skills are the basic procedural necessities. At the other end of the spectrum, a large medical/surgical ICU usually would have the procedural abilities of placing and maintaining arterial lines, placing and maintaining pulmonary artery catheters and central venous lines, inserting endotracheal tubes and managing mechanical ventilation, providing cardioversion and cardiopulmonary resuscitation, placing enteral tubes and hyperalimentation catheters, etc. Some procedures might be the function of personnel in the ICU while other procedural functions might be better provided by a specialized team (e.g., nutritional support team and hemodialysis team).

- *Administrative Skills.* In each ICU, there should be a policy for assuring continuity of patient care and the availability of both appropriate logistic support and experienced personnel for each shift.

- *Teaching and Training Skills.* A continuing teaching and training program is essential for each ICU to acquire and maintain skills and will be described in the following section.

Personnel Training

The general principle is that all involved personnel should be trained to do their jobs with emphasis on competence in their area of critical care medicine. The medical director and nursing director of the ICU should coordinate and/or participate in the various teaching programs for ICU personnel.

Depending on the categories of patients admitted and level of care provided in a specific ICU, there may be one or more physicians of one or several disciplines working in the unit. ICU experience should be part of most house staff training programs. In addition, those who seek special competence in critical care medicine should participate in structured ICU training programs under the direction of established professionals in appropriate disciplines. The ICU Director should be trained in a specialty of importance to the type of patients in the unit. Additional training in critical care medicine and/or another appropriate subspecialty is also desired.

Registered nurses must have significant postgraduate clinical experience prior to ICU training. Usually this should be at least one year in duration. This training and education should include a comprehensive orientation program, followed by on-the-job training with a preceptor. After significant ICU experience, each nurse should have the opportunity to participate in continuing education in critical care courses. If licensed practical nurses are used, adequate training must be provided that will be appropriate to the job performance required.

Depending upon the categories of patients, respiratory therapists should be integral members of the critical care team in order to provide respiratory care and related services. These personnel should have initial orientation followed by on-the-job training and, in addition, a regular lecture program on ICU patient problems and their respiratory care.

Other personnel categories that may be involved in the ICU but do not provide nursing interventions include paramedics, nurses' aides, unit clerks, physiotherapists, laboratory technicians, biomedical electronics technicians, clinical engineers, pharmacists, dietitians, social workers, data managers, and clergy. They should all have access to appropriate teaching programs that will vary in content depending on the individual's profession and the goals and objectives of the ICU.

Organization of ICU Personnel

General considerations. An ICU combines the capacity to provide needed care and technology with a potential to do great harm. Any organizational structure must, therefore, match technology with the correct blend of personnel to guarantee safe application of invasive monitoring and insure that generated data are correct, interpretation of derived data appropriate, and therapy safely employed. The organizational structure will vary depending on the overall mission of the hospital. There should be risk stratification for patients leading to distribution among units—matching the appropriate units with the necessity for intervention or monitoring. Within each ICU, organization should be structured to insure proper care of the total patient.

Physician staff. The ICU should be directed by a physician with demonstrated competence in the areas necessary for provision of critical care. These areas generally include a broad base in physiology, pharmacology, the continuum of disease, cardiopulmonary function, and the associated intervention skills. He or she must recognize the need for teamwork, specialty consultation, and have demonstrated administrative and leadership skills. Competence, availability, demonstrated interest and ability in promoting harmonious interaction of various members of the health care team rather than departmental affiliation should guide this selection.

Other physicians (ICU attending physicians), as credentialed by the hospital, may assume day-to-day unit and patient management responsibilities. All ICU physicians should demonstrate maintenance of clinical competence and skills through regular ICU practice. The role of the ICU physician may range, depending on unit and hospital type, from absolute control of patient management through coordinator to consultant. The medical director or designate should have final authority over admission and discharge of patients from the ICU.

The medical and nursing directors assume ultimate responsibility for the safety and appropriateness of services provided by the ICU. To this end, unstable clinical situations requiring minute-to-minute titration of therapy, such as a delicate balance of multiorgan failure, require that the ICU medical director or his/her designee direct patient care. This places even greater emphasis on the need to communicate regularly and frequently with primary physicians, family, and others involved in the current and future care of the patient.

Any hospital with a level II or III unit (level I units have in-unit physicians) should have immediately available, in hospital, 24 hours a day, a physician credentialed by the hospital as competent in life support and airway and ventilator management. Where house staff programs exist, trainees must occupy appropriately supervised roles in patient care that add to the quality and clarity of care.

Nursing personnel. Nurses are the key element in critical care. They provide continuity while physicians and other health professionals come and go. The organizational structure must support rather than detract from this role. The same considerations in selecting a medical director apply to selection of the unit nursing director. Nursing management and nursing practice decisions should be made by the nursing director. The organizational structure should promote and require that nurses and physicians work together as colleagues at all levels—especially the medical director and nursing director. Clerical and administrative support are necessary to prevent distraction of the nurse from direct patient care functions. The nurse coordinates the activity of all other allied health personnel at the bedside. Staffing patterns should be keyed to level of patient illness rather than a fixed nurse-to-patient ratio. Nursing staff capabilities must match the spectrum of patients cared for in the unit.

What special technology and therapeutic interventions should be routinely available for the most effective ICU function?

Effective intensive care units will have special technology, therapeutic capabilities, and personnel that are determined by the types of patients treated in the units. An ICU's technology and therapeutic capabilities must be based on an analysis of the reasons for which the unit was developed. This analysis should lead to clearly written guidelines for the care of patients in the ICU, defining clinical expertise needed, size of unit(s) needed, teaching versus nonteaching status, and commitment, if any, to research activities.

Incorporation of any technology and therapeutic capability must support the ultimate function of the ICU, which is to provide high-quality care to patients who sustain or are at risk of developing potentially reversible severe illness. Thus, every ICU should have a well-trained team whose expertise matches the specific clinical problems that must be treated. This team must develop admission and continuing stay requirements, discharge criteria, and protocols that define the clinical scope of the ICU. In addition, policies for triage must be formally established and practiced.

An ICU, regardless of location, must have the following minimal technological capabilities:

1. Cardiopulmonary resuscitation

2. Airway management, including endotracheal intubation and assisted ventilation

3. Oxygen delivery systems and qualified respiratory therapists or registered nurses to deliver oxygen therapy

4. Continual electrocardiographic monitoring

5. Emergency temporary cardiac pacing

6. Access to rapid and comprehensive laboratory services including but not limited to arterial blood gas analysis, electrolyte

determinations, hemograms, measurement of cardiac enzymes, renal function studies, microbiologic studies, fluoroscopy, and other radiologic studies

7. Access to nutritional support services to advise on both enteral and parenteral nutritional techniques

8. Titrated therapeutic interventions with infusion pumps

9. Based on determination of the ICU patient composition, technological capability must be available to support therapeutic interventions that are commonly accepted medical practice. For example, an ICU that manages shock syndromes needs hemodynamic monitoring capability techniques to allow for the rational diagnostic categorization and subsequent therapy of patients with shock syndromes

10. Portable life-support equipment for use in patient transport, both within the hospital and for transfer

Should the above minimal capabilities not be available, patient stabilization and referral procedures should be implemented. Furthermore, health care providers must be conscious of their obligation not to use investigational therapy or technology without defined protocols and appropriate informed patient consent.

How is a hospital's critical care delivery system best structured: One large multispecialty unit or multiple small subspecialty intensive care units?

The nature of the hospital, the degree of subspecialty expertise available within the institution, the patient population being treated, and whether the institution is a referral center, a community hospital, or a teaching hospital, are all issues that must be taken into account to determine the best structure for its critical care delivery system.

In many hospitals, a multispecialty ICU is most practical and allows better aggregation of ICU resources (technology, physicians, nurses, and allied health personnel). In other hospitals, it is appropriate to combine one or more multispecialty units with one or more subspecialty units. Thus, the spectrum of ICUs today ranges from multispecialty to specific purpose ICUs.

In addition, there is diversity in the staffing and organizational structure in ICUs across institutions. These differences are identified below and grouped into levels representing current practices in hospitals. The levels are distinguished by differences in availability of certain human and technical resources and by the frequency of performance of certain interventions such as continuous ventilatory therapy. Suggested nurse-patient ratios are presented with some flexibility because the presence of other personnel such as respiratory therapists and temporal variations in patient mix may influence individual unit requirements. In many Level I and Level II ICUs, for example, continuous availability of on-site respiratory therapists will facilitate better patient care. The organization and scope of aggregated ICU resources integrated with patients who have special needs should occur in one or more of the following levels:

- *Level I.* This is a comprehensive and multisystem critical care unit. A physician-director or qualified designee is immediately available to the unit at all times. The nurse-patient ratio is 1:1 or greater depending on the severity of the patients' conditions. Measurement and derivation of all necessary invasive and noninvasive monitoring is accessible. There is a teaching and research obligation.

- *Level II.* This unit is a multipurpose or a specific purpose unit. Examples include respiratory ICU, neuro ICU, coronary care unit, mixed medical/surgical unit, etc. A physician-director or qualified designee is available in the hospital. This unit can perform therapeutic interventions based on invasive and non-invasive monitoring and has a nurse-patient ratio of 1:1 or 1:2 or 1:3 depending on the severity of the patients' conditions.

- *Level III.* This unit provides for limited use of invasive monitoring and therapeutic interventions such as assisted ventilation. A physician-director or his/her designee must be readily available. In-hospital coverage must be available from a physician who is credentialed by the hospital in life support and airway and ventilator management. Nurse-patient ratio is 1:2 or 1:3 or 1:4 depending on the severity of the patients' conditions.

- *Level IV.* This is a specialty care unit but does not meet the definition of an ICU. This unit provides noninvasive monitoring for those patients who may have arrhythmias and the potential for complications. A unit director or designee is provided and will respond as needed. Arrhythmia monitoring and basic CPR skills are provided. The nurse-patient ratio is 1:4 or 1:5 depending on the severity of the patients' conditions. This ratio does not apply if the number of patients is less than four.

Larger hospitals might have several units (Level I or II and Level IV as intermediate care, for example). Transfer among units and to the general service adds additional risk; the level of care during transfer must not be less than that provided prior to initiation of transfer.

The ability to administer each level effectively becomes increasingly difficult if the unit is too large. Ordinarily, intensive care units should not be larger than 12 beds. If there is a need for more intensive care beds, development of additional ICUs must be considered, either general or specific purpose units. Where possible, institutions with more than one unit should place them in close proximity and adjacent to needed support services.

Admission criteria must be based on the sound judgment and clinical expertise of practicing physicians who feel there is a reasonable probability that admission will benefit the patient. Once in the ICU, the medical and nursing directors or their designees are responsible for evaluating admission and determining a patient's need to stay in the unit.

How Has the Development of Intensive Care Units Affected the Traditional Functions of a Hospital?

The primary impact of the development of intensive care units in a hospital is that such units have enabled the hospital to provide more complete and higher-quality services to the community. It has also enabled the hospital to more economically group its resources so that similar types of seriously ill patients can benefit equally.

The delivery of high-quality service from ICUs has made it necessary for hospitals to evaluate and expand many of the ancillary areas that support these services. Specifically, hospitals that have developed such units have added more comprehensive laboratory, radiology, nutrition, biomedical engineering, respiratory therapy, psychological, and social work services, among others. Such expansions of support operations have added complexity to the day-to-day functions of institutions, resulting in the need for more refined organizational structures throughout hospitals. This in turn has necessitated the development of more controlled communication systems to ensure availability of needed medical information and continuity of patient care services.

ICUs have also added prestige and enhanced the communities' good will toward the institutions in which they are based. This good will has often taken the form of financial and volunteer support as well as general moral support.

But while the ICUs have improved patient care, day-to-day operations, and institutional prestige, they also have added pressures and stresses to hospital personnel both within and outside of the ICUs. For example, movement of patients into ICUs has had undesirable effects upon the general medical surgical units of the hospital.

First, there has been, in many hospitals, a reduction in appreciation for the continued care given and the possibilities for effective patient care on the general floors. The aura of urgency associated with critically ill patients tends to reinforce the perception of personnel from the general services that they are not as important in the care chain.

A more serious result of the formation of ICUs has been the removal from general services of the more acutely ill, thus reducing the experience of the general staff in caring for such patients.

Nursing care in the ICU has an emphasis opposite from such care in general services. The effectiveness of the ICU nurse is his/her knowledge of all the details necessary to care for one or two patients while the effectiveness of the general service nurse rests upon his or her ability to direct care delivery by others to numerous patients. This contradiction in nursing practice techniques may not be fully understood by the physicians who tend to equate the quantity of nursing care with quality. As the physician becomes more reluctant to use the general services for patients who are acutely ill, but not critically ill, the general services staff is deprived of the opportunity to gain and maintain skills which ultimately must be exercised on behalf of the post-ICU patient. These problems are recognized by hospitals and require ongoing programs to deal with them.

Beyond these issues, the development of ICUs has motivated hospitals to better focus on their mission in the community and to work with other institutions to insure a more rational approach to patient care services. Further, the nature of ICU medicine has precipitated the need for hospitals to develop protocols and statements on ethical issues.

Advancing technology requires ICU personnel to become more expert in evaluation of medical devices and much more active in staff training to insure that relevant medical practices and capabilities are provided in the highest-quality manner.

In general, ICUs have had many positive effects on hospitals but cause pressures and stresses which must be dealt with continuously.

What Direction Should Critical Care Research Follow?

Directions for Critical Care Research

The national cost of ICU care is in excess of 15 percent of hospital costs, and is between $10 and $20 billion annually. Although the cost of ICU-related research is high, the panel believes that substantial savings—greatly in excess of research costs—can be gained by better defining indications for ICU admission and the use of monitoring technology and interventions.

Intensive care related research readily falls into one of four groups:

1. Natural history, risk, and outcome research, directed at broad questions of utilization and efficacy

2. Research focused on specific ICU technology and application, and therapeutic interventions

3. Human resource research

4. Disease entity research, ranging from basic studies of etiologic mechanisms to specific clinical therapeutic trials

Natural History, Risk, and Outcome Research

The combination of life-threatening diseases, finite resources, invasive therapeutic and monitoring techniques, and high costs makes the need for adequate data on which to base decisions a high priority.

Such research is aimed at determining how ICUs can be used for the maximum benefit of the ICU population. This research should include procedures for "triaging" patients so that admission is not denied to patients who can most benefit from an ICU as well as excluding patients who have no reasonable chance to benefit. Research aimed at developing accurate outcome predictors as a function of initial presenting condition, diagnosis, and other ongoing prognostic variables should be encouraged.

Patients being monitored require sensitive predictors of potential complications, whereas patients being considered for intervention need specific predictors of success for the range of possible interventions.

ICU Technology and Applications and Therapeutic Interventions

A highly expensive component of intensive care is the monitoring technology. It is easy to assume a proportional relationship between quantity of information and quality of care, but this is not necessarily true. Indeed it has been suggested that, since there is a natural tendency to respond to abnormal data with a therapeutic maneuver, the net effect of monitoring a variable, which is not important in decision making, would be the sum total of the complications of the resulting therapy plus any direct complications from the mode of monitoring itself. Included in this negative effect would be the consequences of errors in the monitored data. The panel recommends encouraging research directed at detecting the outcome gain to be derived from the variables commonly monitored in ICUs. Similarly, the efficacy of specific interventions requires careful evaluation (see below). These two types of study (efficacy of monitoring and interventions) should include a careful assessment of the balance between gain and outcome, and iatrogenic complications.

For many of the disease states presently resulting in ICU admission the benefit is obvious (e.g., ventilation for apnea secondary to temporary neuromuscular paralysis). In such cases, the panel considers it inappropriate to conduct efficacy studies in the light of accumulated positive experience. The role of specific ICU protocols in influencing outcome is, for many diseases, not clear. There are wide variations among institutions regarding the interventions used for patients with the same disease. It is recommended that a series of protocol studies be carried out to determine optimal interventions for specific diagnoses. The term "protocol study" denotes a research plan where the study population, severity of disease, treatment intervention, and the objective measures of benefit are clearly stated. Ideally, such studies would include random allocation to treatment and control groups. Randomized studies may be difficult to carry out within a single unit or institution for many diagnoses because of the ethics and logistics of patient consent and the need to act quickly. Where this is the case, one may carry out a randomized study by enrolling more than one unit or institution to participate by randomizing units or institutions—not patients. Units or institutions would be randomized to a single treatment policy. They would treat a specified number of patients as dictated by the randomization allocation. After treating a specified number, a unit or institution would switch to the other treatment policy (in the case of studying two treatments). In this study plan, half the units or institutions would be first randomized to each treatment program and then crossed over. Adoption of such multicenter study plans will allow randomized prospective trials to be carried out which may lead to finding optimal intervention programs in intensive care units.

Human Resource Research

The complexity and intensity of care in the ICU requires the accumulation of information related to issues such as (a) the relationship between training levels and distribution of the various categories of staff, and patient care outcome, (b) consideration of factors leading to conflict and stress in staff, and (c) an evaluation of the efficacy of orientation and continuing education programs in the ICU.

Disease Entity Research

Numerous areas for research related to the various disease entities which result in ICU admission merit high priority. Among the more common causes of death are head injuries, sepsis, and multiple organ failure. While research in each of these areas has wider application than CCM, the panel recognizes that the teaching hospital ICU lends itself well to such clinical research. This should be encouraged as should more basic research at the level of mechanisms of the pathophysiology of brain damage following head injury, factors contributing to serious infections, and the mechanisms that lead to the adult respiratory distress syndrome.

In carrying out research in the ICU, certain difficulties must be recognized. In relation to natural history characterization, the existence of multiple subsets of any disease group and the very nonstandard way in which data are collected in the clinical setting pose a special problem. The relatively small number of patients in any one ICU and the multiple subsets suggest multicenter studies. The current nonstandard approach to data acquisition should be replaced with a uniform planned program of data collection which could be adopted by all ICUs. A minimum data set with common definitions would enable individual ICUs to evaluate the impact of their care over time and allow inter-ICU comparisons.

In conducting clinical studies in the ICU setting, special problems arise in obtaining informed consent. The unique dependency of the patient, the concern of the family, and the implications of the interventions under study all complicate an unemotional consideration of risks and benefits. This problem is compounded when the patient is unresponsive, and the net effect is to create a substantial difficulty in conducting research in this area. However, many of the questions to be addressed are of great import, both because of the enormous costs involved and the life-threatening nature of the factors requiring study.

Consensus Development Panel

Stephen M. Ayres, M.D. (Panel Chairman); Stephen C. Achuff, M.D.; Hon. Christopher J. Armstrong, Justice; Donna Lee Bertram, R.N., B.S.N.; Roger C. Bone, M.D.; Joseph M. Civetta, M.D., F.A.C.S.; H. Barrie Fairley, M.D.; Frank H. Gafford IV, M.D.; David Ross Garr, M.D.; Ake Grenvik, M.D., Ph.D.; Thomas E. Macnamara; Albert G. Mulley, M.D.; Thomas G. Rainey, M.D.; Norma J. Shoemaker, R.N., M.N.; W. Vickery Stoughton; Marvin Zelen, Ph.D.

Chapter 31

Pain Management and Physician Education

In May, the Annual Meeting of the American Society of Clinical Oncology (ASCO) released the results of a survey of 3,200 oncologists on end-of-life care for cancer patients. Among the survey's major findings were serious gaps in end-of-life care—including inadequate physician education, access to palliative services, and depression management.

According to Dr. Ezekiel Emanuel, who led the survey, it is especially significant because it is the first study of its kind to comprehensively examine specialty physicians who have a duty to the dying. Comparisons with international oncologists also revealed useful information. The 158-question survey of American, British, and Canadian oncologists was conducted by the Center for Survey Research at the University of Massachusetts.

Even more troubling is the analysis of questions that focuses on provider practices, which reveals that one-quarter of those surveyed do not provide optimal pain management.

Emanuel also notes that the survey covered a broad range of end-of-life topics, rather than any single issue. For instance, the survey looked at oncologists' knowledge of pain management and their views

From "American Society of Oncologists Releases Steps to Improve Care," by Charlotte Eichna, in *ABCD Exchange,* July 1998 [Online]. Available: http://www.abcd-caring.com/jul98.htm. © 1998 by Americans for Better Care of the Dying (ABCD), 2175 K St. NW, Ste. 820, Washington, DC 20037. For complete contact information, please refer to Chapter 60, "Resources." Reprinted with permission.

on physician-assisted suicide. Expanding pain management techniques might improve overall end-of-life care and thus decrease the demand for physician-assisted suicide.

ASCO hopes to help its members overcome many of the problems the survey identified. The May issue of *The Journal of Clinical Oncology* features the group's statement on how to overcome problems in end-of-life care by focusing on three primary areas: removing economic barriers that prevent patients from getting good care; improving physician education; and expanding research on the physical, psychological, and socioeconomic issues that surround end-of-life.

Kathleen Foley, M.D., director of the Project on Death in America and co-chief of the Pain Service and Palliative Care Service at Memorial Sloan-Kettering Cancer Center, was a member of the ASCO task force which developed the statement. She describes it as the policy agenda that ASCO will pursue to improve end-of-life care. Foley says, "It focuses on the need to address the complexity of the issue."

Foley notes that the survey also found that up to 25 percent of oncologists do not "like taking care of dying patients. Their attitudes about hospice and palliative care coupled with their lack of knowledge prevent them from providing high quality care."

The survey found many other reasons for the lack of good end-of-life care for oncology patients. Oncologists surveyed report that economic barriers are a primary problem for patients to access good care. More than half of American oncologists report trouble obtaining palliative care consultations for the terminally ill (10 times the rate in Britain or Canada). Insurance shortcomings for unskilled home care services seem to be the culprits: 40 percent of oncologists find it the most common obstacle in accessing care, and 31 percent characterize it as a frequent problem.

According to ASCO, steps to remove these barriers include reforming health care policy, improving insurance reimbursement policies, and reducing co-payments for end-of-life care, especially for pain management.

Inadequate physician education, including problems with provider attitudes about dying, doctor-patient communication, and the persistence of futile care, all preclude quality end-of-life care for cancer patients. Despite some innovations in medical school curricula, formal courses and clinical rotations that teach doctors and oncologists about end-of-life care are not widely available.

Yet some problems are not simply about the dearth of knowledge — some point to providers who do not recognize shortcomings in their own practices. For instance, although almost all (95 percent) say they are competent in pain management, more than half report that 20 percent of their patients still die in pain.

Even more troubling is the analysis of questions that focus on provider practices, which reveals that one-quarter of those surveyed do not provide optimal pain management. Oncologists also tend to pursue chemotherapy beyond its usefulness, either because it is hard to tell patients that a cure is not likely, or because such treatment permits new anti-cancer agents to be tested within an academic setting.

ASCO's recommendations for these problems include expanded training programs and formal curricula in symptom management, futility guidelines, palliative care, effective communication with patients, and improved leadership skills to manage end-of-life teams. The survey found that oncologists may learn best by observing role models of good end-of-life care.

Physical, psychological, and socioeconomic issues present other areas for improvement. Dealing with depression is particularly problematic: half of those surveyed do not feel competent in managing a dying patient's depression, leaving about 40 percent of dying patients depressed.

ASCO recommends increasing research into these physical, psychological, and socioeconomic issues as a way to dramatically improve end-of-life care. The survey's authors cited the areas of mental health, spirituality, communication, caregiving, and bereavement as areas in need of special attention.

The survey described changes in oncologists' attitudes about physician-assisted suicide: Currently, about one-fifth of those surveyed support physician-assisted suicide for patients experiencing severe, constant pain—a drastic drop from the previous 45 percent who had supported the practice in 1994 and 1995. Moreover, only 6.5 percent supported physician-assisted suicide, compared with more than 22 percent in 1994-95. Survey respondents point to inadequate pain control or failure to treat depression as the reason patients ask for aid in dying.

Expert, comprehensive end-of-life care at home or in a home-like environment is probably the most effective general solution to the problems facing oncologists in end-of-life care. Expanding and supporting hospice programs, which are underused because of late referrals and poor coordination between oncologists and hospice, may be one way to achieve this goal. Physicians must be more open to hospice, says ASCO, and recognize the appropriate time for palliative care, and be willing to share control of a patient's treatment.

325

ASCO's comprehensive statement of the problems besetting end-of-life care in conjunction with their plan of action renders improvement an attainable goal—especially when most can agree that death should be a dignified, meaningful process. "Most people when nearing death want empathetic care that preserves their dignity," says Robert J. Mayer, M.D., ASCO's president. "It is oncologists' professional responsibility to care for patients from diagnosis throughout the course of illness, including the last phase of life. Better physician education, greatly expanded research on end-of-life care, and relief from the economic burden of caring for the terminally ill must be aggressively addressed."

Task Force member Foley says she is hopeful that "this first step in articulating a need will translate into real change in education and care."

—by Charlotte Eichna

Charlotte Eichna is an undergraduate at Brown University majoring in biomedical ethics and history. She is a summer intern for the Center to Improve Care of the Dying and ABCD and is a hospice volunteer.

Chapter 32

Patient Participation in Medical Treatment

The right of patients and their surrogates to participate in medical decisions is now firmly established in law and ethics. What is currently being debated is how far this right of participation extends. The controversy arises from several recent court cases in which surrogates have demanded treatments physicians have judged medically futile. As a result, several new questions are at issue: Are there limits to the patient's right of participation? Are there conditions under which physicians may be ethically obliged to refuse to provide, or even to offer, specific treatments? Who defines treatment futility and by what criteria?

The right of participation was first asserted as a patient's right to refuse even life-sustaining treatments.[1,2] Fifteen years ago in the *Quinlan* case,[3] this was extended to include the right of surrogates of incompetent patients to refuse life-support measures even if a physician judged them medically and ethically appropriate. This extension was confirmed by the U.S. Supreme Court in the *Cruzan* case.[4] In 1983, the President's Commission further extended the range of participation when it recommended consent to "do not resuscitate" orders.[5] As a result of those developments, the negative right of refusal has come to be interpreted as a positive right to be offered and provided not only cardiopulmonary resuscitation, but life-support and other specific treatments.

From "Ethics," by Edmund D. Pellegrino, M.D., in the *Journal of the American Medical Association,* Vol. 270, No. 2, pp. 202-3, July 14, 1993. © 1993 by the American Medical Association, 515 N. State St., Chicago, IL 60610. Reprinted with permission.

One well-known example involves the case of an 87-year-old woman in a persistent vegetative state.[6] Several cases have involved infants or minors who were terminally ill (e.g., Baby L in 1990 and Baby Rena in 1991). In each case, for religious or other reasons, the surrogates demanded treatments they deemed beneficial, although their physicians had opposed those treatments on the ground of futility. In these cases, U.S. judicial opinions focused on who should make the decision, generally favoring the surrogates. They did not address the ethical question of the right to demand treatment. A British court *(In Re J* British Court of Appeal, June 3,1992; Lord Donaldson, Master of the Rolls), however, specifically upheld the right of physicians to refuse treatments they adjudged inappropriate.

Before the era of patient participation, physicians felt ethically justified in unilaterally withholding treatments they judged "futile." They could invoke the Hippocratic teaching in "on the Art," i.e., that the patient "overmastered" by the disease should not seek treatment, nor should the physician provide it. With the emergence of patient autonomy and informed consent, this tradition has become problematic for many physicians and ethicists.

At one end of the spectrum, the principles of autonomy and beneficence are interpreted to imply an obligation to offer and provide treatments that physicians adjudge useless. It is argued that to refuse to do so is to return to paternalism or to act maleficently, since only patients or surrogates can judge what is "beneficial."[7,8] At the least, physicians must not make unilateral decisions about life-support systems.[9]

At the other end of the spectrum, it is argued that there is no fundamental right to demand a specific treatment. It is the physician's obligation to determine what is in the patient's interests. Because physicians are qualified to make futility judgments, they have a duty not to offer or provide what is ineffective.[10-12] Some authors reaffirm the physician's traditional ethical obligations, but also require full consideration of the patient's goals in therapy.[13] Others would restrict delivery of futile treatment to very limited circumstances (e.g., to allow time for a family to assimilate a hopeless prognosis).

Beneath these differences in interpretation of what patient participation means in daily decision making there is an even sharper debate about the whole concept of futility. On the one side are those who argue that the moral weight of patient values is such that the traditional idea of medical futility as an objective construct is totally vitiated. From this view, the impossibility of disentangling the physician's values from his or her judgment of futility renders that judgment so ambiguous that it should be totally abandoned.[14] For some, the debate itself is fatuous and detrimental to good decision making.[15] A more moderate view acknowledges the primacy of the surrogate's or patient's wish to define the goals and benefits of therapy. The concept of futility is retained, but only for obvious situations like total brain death or permanent vegetative state.[16]

Opposing those views is the belief that the traditional idea of futility should be retained but refined by explicit criteria. One proposal suggests that a treatment should be considered futile if it has been ineffective in the last 100 cases, does not restore consciousness, or does not remove the need for intensive care.[17] The availability of studies of effectiveness of treatments like cardiopulmonary resuscitation strengthen these suggestions.[18,19] However, the potential shortcomings of objective criteria cannot be ignored (i.e., errors of diagnosis, prognosis, and medical information, or the problem of applying statistics to individual cases). Algorithms and models that predict outcomes (such as the APACHE scale) are helpful to attempt to objectify prognosis, but they, too, unavoidably include value judgments and thereby lose some of their objectivity.[20]

To mitigate the influence of value judgments, to protect patient autonomy, and to avoid the potential abuses of unilateral judgments, some have proposed that the criteria for futility be institutionalized in hospital policy of ethics committees. There are, however, objections to institutionalization: standards could vary between institutions or committees and the very fact a policy is needed might imply a patient's right to demand treatment.

The futility debate underscores a growing ethical conflict between the autonomy of the physician and of the patient. While the focus to date has been largely on terminal care and specific treatments like cardiopulmonary resuscitation, ventilators, and intubation, there are many other situations in which patients and society may request treatment that is judged medically inappropriate. This issue must be confronted as we enter more closely into managed health care systems in which cost containment, allocation decisions, and societal benefit are reshaping the fiduciary relationship of physician and patient. While this is happening, professional bodies continue to affirm the right of physicians to withhold medically inappropriate treatments (e.g., the Hastings Center's *Guidelines on the Termination of Life-Sustaining Treatment and the Treatment of the Dying;* the Society for Critical Care Medicine's Task Force on Ethics' *Consensus Report on the Ethics of Foregoing Life-Sustaining Treatments in the Critically Ill;* the American Thoracic Society's *Guidelines on Withholding and*

Withdrawing Life-Sustaining Therapy; and the President's Commission for the Study of Ethical Problems in Medicine and Biomedical and Behavioral Research's *Report of the Ethical and Legal Implications of Informed Consent in Patient-Practitioner Relationships).* Is the time approaching when physicians who follow their conscience might feel morally compelled to refuse to follow a policy they judge to be unethical? Or should the concept of medical discretionary latitude be severely limited?

The debate about medical futility is far from over. It has been and continues to be useful, however, because it exposes the need for carefully weighing the limits of both physician and patient autonomy, the explicit meaning of "participation," and the relative reliability and moral weight of "objective" medical and "subjective" value determinations. Underlying these issues are deeper philosophical questions about the nature of medical knowledge, the relationship between fact and value, and the moral status of the physician's conscience in a pluralistic and democratic society like ours, which so highly prizes individual autonomy. Debates about medical futility force confrontation with problems that would be disposed of as "abstract" were they not so important for some of the most urgent decisions physicians must make daily.

Notes

1. *Union Pacific Railroad v Botsford,* 141 US 250 (1891).

2. *Schoendorf v Society of New York Hospitals,* 105 NE 92, 93 (NY 1914).

3. In *re Quinlan* 70 NJ 10, 355, A2d 647 (1976).

4. *Cruzan v Director Mo Department of Health,* 497 US 110 S Ct 2841 (1990).

5. President's Commission for the Study of Ethical Problems in Medicine and Biomedical and Behavioral Research. 1983. *Deciding to Forego Life-Sustaining Treatment: Report of the Ethical, Medical, and Legal Issues in Treatment Decisions.* Washington, D.C.: U.S. Government Printing Office:241.

6. In *re Wanglie* No. PX-91-253, (4th JD) Hennepin County, Minn: July 1991.

7. Angell, M. 1991. The case of Helga Wanglie: a new kind of 'right to die' case. *N Engl J Med* 325:511-2.

8. Ackerman, F. 1991. The significance of a wish. *Hastings Cent Rep* 21:27-9.

9. Capron, A. M. 1991. In re Helga Wanglie. *Hastings Cent Rep* 21:26-8.

10. Stell, L. K. 1992. Stopping treatment on grounds of futility: a role for institutional policy. *St Louis Univ Public Law Rev* 11:481-97.

11. Tomlinson, T., and H. Brady. 1990. Futility and the ethics of resuscitation. *JAMA* 264:1276-80.

12. Jecker, N. S., and L. J. Schneiderman. 1993. The duty not to treat. *Camb Q Health Care Ethics* 2:151-9.

13. Lantos, J. D, P. A. Singer, R. M. Walker, et al. 1989. The illusion of futility in clinical practice. *Am J Med* 87:81-4.

14. Truog, R. D., A. S. Brett, and J. Frader. 1992. The problem with futility. *N EngI J Med* 326:1560-4.

15. Paris, J. J. 1993. Pipes, colanders and leaky baskets: reflections on the futility debate. *Camb Q Health Care Ethics* 2:147-9.

16. Youngner, S. J. 1988. Who defines futility? *JAMA* 260:2094-5.

17. Jecker, N. S., and L. J. Schneiderman. 1993. The duty not to treat. *Camb Q Health Care Ethics* 2:151-9.

18. Gray, W., R. J. Capone, and A. S. Most. 1991. Unsuccessful emergency room resuscitation: are continued efforts in the emergency room justified? *N Engl J Med* 325:1393-5.

19. Faber-Langendoen, K. 1991. Resuscitation of patients with metastatic cancer: is transient benefit still futile? *Arch Intern Med* 151:235-9.

20. Knaus, W. 1993. Ethical implications of risk stratification in the acute care setting. *Camb Q Health Care Ethics* 2:147-9.

Chapter 33

Assisted Suicide and Medical Illness

Dr. Herbert Hendin, medical director of the American Foundation for Suicide Prevention and Professor of Psychiatry at New York Medical College, delivered a compelling and learned presentation to PCC [Physicians for Compassionate Care] members and friends titled "Assisted Suicide and Medical Illness with Reference to the New Oregon Law."

In his opening remarks, Dr. Hendin said: "People assume that seriously or terminally ill people who wish to end their lives are different from those who are otherwise suicidal . . . such people are not significantly different from people who meet other crises with the desire to end the crisis by ending their lives." Hendin went on to say that "frightened patients are likely to listen to doctors who suggest assisted suicide."

Doctor Hendin further demonstrated that when the seriously ill patient's fear and untreated physical symptoms are effectively addressed in treatment, the desire for assisted suicide disappears. On the other hand, "Ignorance of how to care for the complex issues of severely ill patients is the most likely rationalization for a doctor to comply with assisted suicides," Hendin contended. In a series of case presentations, Dr. Hendin found that, "Doctors felt free to ignore

From "Assisted Suicide and Medical Illness: Herbert Hendin at PCC Spring Lecture," edited by Catherine Hamilton, in *PCC News*, Vol. 1, No. 2, pp. 1-2, May 1998. Produced by Physicians for Compassionate Care, P. O. Box 6042, Portland, OR 97228. For complete contact information, please refer to Chapter 60, "Resources." Reprinted with permission.

patient autonomy when they knew how to help the patient." However, "Patient autonomy was in essence a rationale for assisted suicide when doctors felt helpless and did not know what to do." According to Hendin, the danger in Oregon is in the fact that: "Under the Oregon law . . . They (the doctors) are not required to inquire into the source of the desperation that underlies such a request or to be knowledgeable about the alternatives that may relieve it."

When Dr. Hendin was asked by a member of the audience what doctors in Oregon should do with a patient who is requesting assisted suicide, he said: "I don't think it would be difficult to help a suicidal, severely ill patient get over suicidal desires, even if it is the law. It wouldn't be any different than helping any other patient who was suicidal."

The cultural effects of assisted suicide leading to complacency and stigmatization of a particular group within a population is addressed in Dr. Hendin's new book, *Seduced by Death,* but he added that the dangerous results of accepting assisted suicide is a medical profession and a general population that has no conceptualization of any other response to the elderly or seriously ill, except assistance in suicide.

In conclusion, Hendin said that Oregon doctors should improve the quality of care at the end of life. "Knowledge of how to minister to the physical and psychological needs of terminally ill people is the most promising development in medicine. Our challenge is to bring that knowledge and that care to all patients who are terminally ill."

Doctor Hendin is one of the world's leading experts in the study of suicide. He helped start the American Society of Suicide Prevention at a time when he had little interest in the subject of assisted suicide. As the Dutch experience unfolded, however Hendin visited Holland with no particular position on what public policy in the area of assisted suicide and euthanasia should be. After four trips to the Netherlands and extensive interviews and research, each trip lasting up to six weeks, he became increasingly convinced of the dangers of assisted suicide.

Physicians for Compassionate Care is a nonprofit educational foundation that promotes the compassionate, ethical care of severely ill patients without sanctioning or assisting suicide, affirms an ethic that all human life is inherently valuable, and holds that the physician's roles are to heal illness, alleviate suffering, and provide comfort care to the sick and dying.

Chapter 34

Improving Palliative Care as a Preventative Measure against Suicide

Calls to legalize physician assisted suicide point to public concern, supported by several studies, that the current health care system does not adequately relieve suffering for people with certain health care problems. People suffering from terminal or chronic illnesses or from disabilities are considered especially vulnerable to suicide because their need or desire for palliative or comfort care may not be adequately met in a health system that focuses on curative care. Palliative care encompasses a range of approaches to manage the physical, psychological, social, and spiritual suffering that may accompany health conditions that are not responsive to curative treatments. Its goal is to improve the quality of life for patients and their families by dealing with issues such as depression and pain and symptom management.

Concerned about the rates of suicide among persons whose health problems are not responsive to curative treatment, the Congress authorized funding to support the research of palliative care issues by passing the Assisted Suicide Funding Restriction Act of 1997, which became law on April 30, 1997. Section 12 of the act amended section 781 of the Public Health Service Act by adding topics related to

Excerpted from the report to Congressional Requesters, *Suicide Prevention: Efforts to Increase Research and Education in Palliative Care.* Produced by the United States General Accounting Office (USGAO), Health, Education, and Human Services Division (publication no. GAO/HEHS-98-128), April 1998. For complete contact information, please refer to Chapter 60, "Resources."

palliative care and suicide prevention to the list of topics that the Department of Health and Human Services (HHS) can support under the Health Professional Education Research Program. Under section 781, HHS can provide funds to public and nonprofit entities for research on a variety of health profession issues. The types of topics authorized by the Assisted Suicide Funding Restriction Act include those for educating and training health care providers in palliative care, advancing the biomedical knowledge of pain management, improving access to hospice programs, and assessing the quality of palliative care in different health care systems.

The act requires GAO to report by April 30, 1998, on the extent to which these section 781 projects have furthered the knowledge and practice of palliative care, particularly with regard to the curricula offered and used in medical schools. Our preliminary work showed that no fiscal year 1998 funding for section 781 projects would be awarded by our reporting date. For this reason, in consultation with authorizing committee staff, we focused our effort on determining (1) the extent to which the physician education and training process currently teaches and tests student competency in palliative care issues, (2) HHS' plans for funding palliative care projects under section 781, and (3) other federal and private palliative care research and education initiatives.

Our analysis of current educational efforts in palliative care is based on information obtained from a survey we conducted of all U.S. medical schools, surveys conducted by others on U.S. residency programs, and discussions with persons involved in the medical education and training process. Our discussion of HHS' plans for funding future palliative care projects under section 781 is based on information provided by HHS officials and HHS budgetary documents. Our information on other palliative care initiatives was obtained from various HHS entities, private foundations, nonprofit organizations, and professional associations. We conducted our work from November 1997 through March 1998 in accordance with generally accepted government auditing standards.

Background

Palliative care is an important and emerging issue for health care providers, educators, and the general public. As medical advances increase life expectancy, more and more people suffer from chronic and progressively disabling diseases that require treatment for depression and assistance with pain and symptom management. Some recent studies have pointed to significant problems within the health care system that preclude the achievement of the best possible quality of life for patients and their families. Areas identified for improvement include education and training for health care providers, improved pain and symptom management, and access to appropriate and quality health care services.

The Assisted Suicide Funding Restriction Act of 1997 contains a provision designed to focus federal funding on research, training, and demonstration projects that would address these specific problem areas. The act authorizes funding in a number of palliative care topics (see table 34.1.) and directs the Secretary of HHS to emphasize palliative medicine among its research and funding priorities under section 781. Section 781 is within title VII of the Public Health Service Act, which authorizes numerous programs for health professions education and training. Section 781 was first funded in 1993 to conduct health professions education research in four broad topic areas related to (1) educational indebtedness, (2) effect of programs for minority and disadvantaged individuals, (3) extent of investigations and disciplinary actions by state licensing authorities, and (4) primary care. The Bureau of Health Professions within the Health Resources and Services Administration (HRSA) is the HHS agency responsible for administering grants funded under section 781 of title VII.

Extent of Palliative Care in Medical Education Varies Considerably

The extent of palliative care instruction varies considerably across and within the three major phases of the physician education and training process. The first phase is undergraduate medical education—or medical school—where students typically receive 2 years of classroom, or didactic, instruction followed by 2 years of clinical training. The United States has 144 accredited medical schools. The second phase is graduate medical education—or residency training—where residents receive 3 to 8 years of clinical training in a medical specialty. The United States has over 7,700 accredited residency programs. The third phase is continuing medical education, which provides physicians who are already practicing medicine with the education and training necessary to maintain or learn new skills. Continuing medical education courses are provided primarily by medical schools and state medical societies, but such courses are also provided by medical associations and consultants. Throughout these three phases, a variety of formal accreditation and certification processes are used to test student competency and to judge the quality of instruction and training.

Table 34.1. Palliative Care Topics Added to Section 781 of the Public Health Service Act

General topic	Specific provision
Research	Assess the quality of care received by patients with disabilities or terminal or chronic illness by measuring and reporting specific outcomes.
	Compare coordinated health care (which may include coordinated rehabilitation services, symptom control, psychological support, and community based support services) to traditional health care delivery systems.
	Advance biomedical knowledge of pain management.
Training	Train health care practitioners in pain management, depression identification and treatment, and issues related to palliative care and suicide prevention.
	Train the faculty of health professions schools in pain management, depression identification and treatment, and issues related to palliative care and suicide prevention.
	Develop and implement curricula regarding disability issues, including living with disabilities, living with chronic or terminal illness, attendant and personal care, assistive technology, and social support services.
Demonstration projects	Reduce restrictions on access to hospice programs.
	Fund home health care services, community living arrangements, and attendant care services.

Extent of Palliative Care Education at Medical Schools Is Mixed

Our review at medical schools showed mixed amounts of attention given to palliative care issues. Accrediting organizations have generally steered away from standards requiring instruction in topics as specific as pain management, preferring to leave such matters to the discretion of the faculty at each school. To determine the extent to which the schools addressed these topics, we surveyed all U.S. medical schools on seven palliative care topics.

For each of the seven palliative care topics we asked about, at least half of the 125 U.S. medical schools that responded to our survey said they had some degree of required instruction. (See Fig. 34.1.) Instruction in palliative care for chronic illness was required by the fewest number of schools (56 percent). For the remaining topics, the percentage of schools requiring the topic was higher; for example, over three-quarters required instruction in the topic of pain management for the terminally or chronically ill, and 94 percent required instruction in depression identification and treatment. Our survey responses showed that some schools have added these topics fairly recently. For example, 24 percent of schools reported adding pain management as a required subject within the last 3 years.

Many schools reported a need to change palliative care instruction, particularly in the area of clinical training. Overall, 30 percent of schools reported a need to change their classroom curriculum in palliative care, and close to 50 percent reported wanting to provide students with more hands-on training experience in diagnosing and treating patients with pain due to chronic or terminal illness.

Evaluation processes vary in the extent to which they measure students' knowledge of palliative care issues. (See Fig. 34.2.) The percentage of medical schools that reported testing competency in the topics we surveyed ranged from 36 percent for interdisciplinary health care for end of life to 72 percent for identifying and treating depression.

Many medical schools also rely heavily on national examinations— the U.S. Medical Licensing Examination or the National Board of Osteopathic Medical Examiners' exam—to evaluate student knowledge. A study is currently under way to examine the degree to which the U.S. Medical Licensing Examination tests student knowledge in end-of-life care issues and to develop a method to evaluate student performance on these test questions in the future.

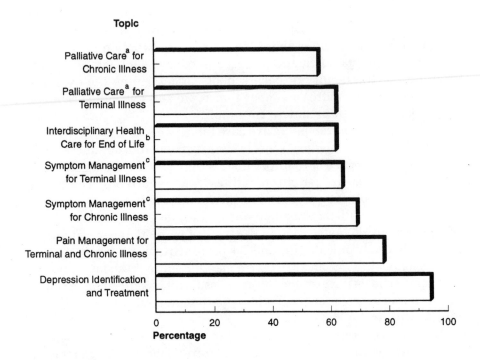

Figure 34.1. *Percentage of Medical Schools Requiring Instruction in Palliative Care Topics*

[a]*Palliative care encompasses many aspects of noncurative care, including the other topics in our survey. To capture the range of possible instruction, our survey included this broad topic as well as the more specific topics.*

[b]*Interdisciplinary health care for end of life is a multidiscipline team approach that incorporates a range of specialists and types of caregivers to provide comprehensive and coordinated care at the end of life.*

[c]*Symptom management is the treatment of patients' emotional and physical symptoms other than pain, such as confusion, fatigue, nausea, shortness of breath, loss of appetite, and muscle wasting.*

Topic

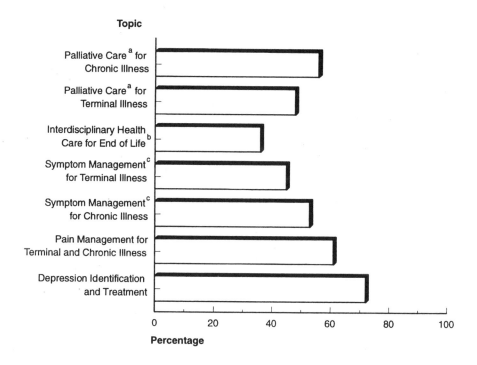

Figure 34.2. *Percentage of Medical Schools Testing Competency in Palliative Care Topics*

[a]*Palliative care encompasses many aspects of noncurative care, including the other topics in our survey. To capture the range of possible instruction, our survey included this broad topic as well as the more specific topics.*

[b]*Interdisciplinary health care for end of life is a multidiscipline team approach that incorporates a range of specialists and types of caregivers to provide comprehensive and coordinated care at the end of life.*

[c]*Symptom management is the treatment of patients' emotional and physical symptoms other than pain, such as confusion, fatigue, nausea, shortness of breath, loss of appetite, and muscle wasting.*

Palliative Care Education in Residency Programs Varied

Our review also indicated that attention to palliative care issues in residency programs varied as well. Accrediting bodies at the graduate level generally require some specific areas of instruction, although, as in medical schools, the primary responsibility for curriculum and training content is assumed by the program director and faculty. Required topics of instruction, such as domestic violence, vary by specialty, and few specialties have requirements including specific palliative care topics. Because of the large number of accredited residency programs in the United States, we did not administer a survey similar to the one we developed for medical schools. We relied on existing surveys done by professional associations that asked residency programs to report whether the subjects of end-of-life care and suicide were included in their training programs.

The American Medical Association's (AMA) 1996 survey showed that nearly half of the nation's 7,787 residency programs include instruction in end-of-life care and over a third teach issues related to suicide. While historical data on the subject of suicide prevention are not available, AMA's data show greater numbers of residency programs now offer instruction in end- of-life care than in the past. In 1996, nearly 50 percent of residency programs taught end-of-life care, compared with 38 percent in 1994.

To some extent, the percentage of residency programs that taught palliative care subjects corresponded to the degree to which these skills might be needed in the specialty area covered by the program. For example, 93 percent of family practice residency programs in the subspecialty of geriatrics reported teaching end-of-life care, while only 10 percent of pathology residency programs in the subspecialty of pediatric pathology reported teaching the subject. However, the percentage of programs that reported teaching end-of-life care was surprising for some specialties for which the need for physicians skilled in end-of-life care seems more evident. For example, nearly half of internal medicine residency programs in the subspecialty of oncology reported not teaching end-of-life care, although physicians treating patients with cancer often deal with terminal patients. (See Table 34.3. for a detailed summary of AMA's 1996 residency program survey results.)

The knowledge and skill of resident physicians is evaluated by each residency program's internal evaluations and national examinations. These examinations include the U.S. Medical Licensing Examination as well as examinations some physicians take to become certified in a medical specialty. The extent to which board examinations include questions related to palliative care has not been quantified, and student performance on palliative care questions that may be included on the exams has not been evaluated.

Few Continuing Medical Education Programs Are Dedicated to Palliative Care

The availability of continuing medical education courses that focus on palliative care issues for terminally or chronically ill people appears limited. Many states and medical associations require physicians to continue their medical education to maintain their medical license or membership benefits, but they generally do not require courses on specific topics such as palliative care. Because of the number and variety of continuing medical education providers, information on the existence of continuing medical education courses dedicated to palliative care issues was not readily available. However, we queried the AMA's database of over 2,000 accredited continuing medical education activities and found that few specifically addressed palliative care. In addition, an official with the American Osteopathic Association said there are few continuing medical education courses related to palliative care for doctors of osteopathy. An example of a course that specifically addresses palliative care issues is a self-study program developed by the American Academy of Hospice and Palliative Medicine, which covers a variety of palliative care topics. Recognizing a need for more courses in this area, private efforts are under way to develop more conferences on end-of-life care issues as well as promote those that already exist.

Plans to Use Section 781 for Palliative Care Projects Are Limited

The fiscal year 1998 conference committee report on HHS appropriations specifies $452,000 for section 781. Officials in HRSA plan to use $150,000 of this amount for seven medical education projects, including one project on palliative care. All seven projects will be conducted by one medical education research center. HRSA plans to provide the funds for the seven projects in May 1998. Because budgets are not maintained separately for each project, HRSA and medical education research center officials were not able to specify the amount of funding dedicated for the palliative care project. The project will assess current medical school courses on death and dying to determine if they meet recommended methods for teaching of end-of-life care.

The remaining $302,000 will be used to support projects focused on increasing the knowledge about the needs and resources of the nation's health professions. Information obtained through these projects will be used to assess the effectiveness of current workforce programs. HRSA officials said they consider this research as higher in priority. In addition, the officials said that due to the importance of health workforce research, future funding of palliative care projects in medical education is uncertain. HRSA did not include palliative care research for medical education in its fiscal year 1999 budget justification.

HRSA officials do not plan to fund any of the other types of palliative care topics authorized under the Assisted Suicide Funding Restriction Act. They said these other initiatives, such as demonstration projects to reduce restrictions on access to hospice programs, are not related to the traditional focus of title VII to support health professions education and training. Projects of these types are generally administered by HHS agencies other than HRSA. For example, the act authorizes research funding under section 781 for advancing the biomedical knowledge of pain management, which has been primarily the domain of the National Institutes of Health (NIH). The act also authorizes research under section 781 for using specific outcome measures to assess the quality of care for patients with disabilities or terminal or chronic illness; measuring outcomes and quality of care is an area of expertise for HHS' Agency for Health Care Policy and Research (AHCPR).

Other Federal and Private Palliative Care Initiatives outside Section 781 Are More Substantial

Several HHS agencies fund projects related to palliative care under their own program authority. Some of these projects directly address the types of research, training, and demonstration projects authorized in the Assisted Suicide Funding Restriction Act, including the following:

- Research authorized by the act includes projects to advance biomedical knowledge of pain management and assess the quality of care for patients with terminal illness by measuring and reporting specific outcomes. NIH—the federal government's primary focal point for biomedical research—estimates that in fiscal year 1997, it spent over $82 million on various types of pain management research. NIH also established a pain research consortium to enhance and coordinate pain research across the various components of NIH. NIH's National Institute of Mental Health has also begun suicide prevention research projects. HHS' Assistant Secretary for Planning and Evaluation is providing $174,000 to evaluate the quality of hospice care in nursing homes—a topic directly related to this provision.

- Training authorized by the act includes projects to teach physicians about palliative care issues. HRSA's HIV/AIDS Bureau is in the process of completing an evaluation of a Canadian instruction module on palliative care and plans to make recommendations on how the module should be modified for use in the United States. AHCPR, which funds projects to improve the effectiveness of health care services, issued guidance in 1994 on management of cancer pain that included discussions and recommendations on palliative therapies used to relieve or ease pain.

- Demonstrations authorized by the act include projects to fund home health care services, community living arrangements, and attendant care services. The Health Care Financing Administration, which is responsible for administering Medicare and Medicaid, has supported these types of demonstration projects. For example, states can obtain waivers to use Medicaid funds for home health care services, community living arrangements, and attendant care services, which are not normally covered by Medicaid but that are considered necessary to care for and improve the quality of life for medically fragile populations.

Other federal projects do not have an explicit objective related to palliative care and suicide prevention but provide opportunity for benefit in this area. For example, AHCPR has many research initiatives that could address improving palliative care for patient populations most prone to suicide. AHCPR and the American Association of Health Plans will provide $7 million over 3 years to assess the quality of care for patients with chronic diseases under varying features of managed care organizations. In addition, AHCPR has initiatives to develop and improve quality of care measures for health care providers and health service delivery, which could include outcomes for palliative care in the future. AHCPR's Medical Treatment Effectiveness Program—which has traditionally focused on identifying and promoting the most effective treatments to prevent, diagnose, or treat diseases such as cancer, AIDS, or cardiovascular disease—could also

345

incorporate palliative care for these and other terminal or chronic illnesses in future research projects.

Private foundations, nonprofit organizations, and professional associations have recognized palliative care as an emerging and important area of medicine and research. As a result, a variety of private initiatives are under way that cover many of the areas of research, training, and demonstration projects described in the act. The two most comprehensive initiatives we identified are Last Acts, funded by the Robert Wood Johnson Foundation, and Project on Death in

Table 34.2a. Selected Private Initiatives in Palliative Care (continued on next page)

Type of project	Project description
Research	Dartmouth College is conducting a study to learn more about the dying experience of seriously ill adults and will develop descriptions of "good" and "bad" dying experiences.
	The University of California, San Diego, is conducting a study to measure the effects of managed care on the type and volume of care delivered to terminally ill Medicare beneficiaries. The study will compare the treatment received in fee-for-service and managed care settings.
	The Center for Ethics in Health Care Research on End-of-Life Care at Oregon Health Sciences University is comparing end-of-life care provided in acute care hospitals, nursing homes, and home hospice.
Training	The AMA and the Robert Wood Johnson Foundation are sponsoring a 2-year, $1.4 million project to educate practicing physicians on the essential clinical competencies in end-of-life care.
	The American Academy of Hospice and Palliative Medicine has developed a six-part self-study program for practicing physicians. The six training modules provide education on

America, sponsored by the Open Society, a foundation created by philanthropist George Soros.

- Last Acts aims to raise awareness of the need to improve the care of persons who are dying, improve communication and decisionmaking related to end-of-life care, and change the way health care and health care institutions approach care for dying people. Last Acts has task forces and committees to pursue a variety of issues, including improving provider education on

Table 34.2b. Selected Private Initiatives in Palliative Care (continued from previous page)

Type of project	Project description
Training (continued)	such topics as alleviating psychological and spiritual pain in the terminally ill.
	The American Board of Hospice and Palliative Medicine's certification exam for hospice and palliative medicine tests physicians' palliative care knowledge and skills.
Demonstration projects	MediCaring, a project being developed by the Center to Improve Care of the Dying at The George Washington University, is designed to extend the concept of "hospice" to include a broader population of terminally ill individuals than those currently benefiting from the Medicare hospice program.
	Promoting Excellence in End-of-Life Care is a $12 million Robert Wood Johnson Foundation initiative to conduct a variety of demonstration projects aimed at fostering long-term changes in care for the dying.
	The Hospital Palliative Care Initiative, a multiyear, $1.1 million project conducted by the United Hospital Fund of New York, is aimed at promoting new hospital-based palliative care services in New York City hospitals. Projects have been funded in five hospitals.

palliative care and developing outcomes and evaluation tools for palliative care.

• Project on Death in America is a $30 million campaign to transform the culture of dying by supporting projects and fostering change in the provision of end-of-life care, public and professional education, and public policy. It conducts its own projects and provides grants to other individuals and institutions. Its major project is a $7 million faculty scholars program for innovative clinical care, research, and educational programs to improve the care of the dying.

Private entities also provide funding for a variety of other projects in palliative care—some with a specific focus in physician education or improving access and quality to palliative care. (See Table 34.2.).

Table 34.3a. U.S. Residency Programs Teaching End-of-Life Care and Suicide Prevention. The AMA surveyed 7,787 residency programs in the United States in 1996. We obtained data on the number of programs that included end-of-life care and suicide prevention topics. (Continued in Table 34.3b)

Specialty/subspecialty[a]	Number of resident physicians	Number of programs	Percent teaching end-of-life care	Percent teaching suicide prevention
Allergy and immunology	214	80	40%	26%
Clinical and laboratory immunology	15	15	40	20
Anesthesiology	3,998	150	43	33
Critical care medicine	87	54	69	39
Pain management	238	93	53	37
Colon and rectal surgery	49	31	39	42
Dermatology	851	101	35	34
Dermatopathology	54	41	27	24
Emergency medicine	3,034	116	77	53
Family practice	10,049	474	89	58
Geriatric medicine	22	14	93	29
Sports medicine	33	27	22	26
Internal medicine	21,298	417	88	44
Cardiovascular disease	2,244	202	48	25
Clinical cardiac electrophysiology	65	68	12	12
Critical care medicine	154	56	71	25
Endocrinology, diabetes, and metabolism	378	136	35	22
Gastroenterology	917	176	41	24
Geriatric medicine	220	89	82	26
Hematology	163	49	45	24
Hematology and oncology	628	99	64	30
Infectious disease	548	143	39	19
Nephrology	609	137	47	24
Oncology	277	59	53	29
Pulmonary disease	257	69	74	30
Pulmonary disease and critical care medicine	702	98	62	20
Rheumatology	266	114	39	22
Sports medicine	4	1	0	100
Medical genetics	39	18	17	22
Neurological surgery	854	99	41	30
Neurology	1,449	122	44	38

(continued)

Table 34.3b. U.S. Residency Programs Teaching End-of-Life Care and Suicide Prevention. The AMA surveyed 7,787 residency programs in the United States in 1996. We obtained data on the number of programs that included end-of-life care and suicide prevention topics. (Continued in Table 34.3c)

Specialty/subspecialty[a]	Number of resident physicians	Number of programs	Percent teaching end-of-life care	Percent teaching suicide prevention
Child neurology	150	75	32	28
Clinical neurophysiology	105	49	0	0
Nuclear medicine	151	82	21	28
Obstetrics and gynecology	4,941	267	68	36
Ophthalmology	1,532	135	33	25
Orthopedic surgery	2,790	157	43	31
Adult reconstructive orthopedics	14	12	25	25
Foot and ankle orthopedics	1	1	0	0
Hand surgery	87	53	30	19
Musculoskeletal oncology	4	8	38	25
Orthopedic sports medicine	86	58	24	17
Orthopedic surgery of the spine	19	15	20	33
Orthopedic trauma	9	5	60	60
Pediatric orthopedics	23	28	14	21
Otolaryngology	1,197	105	39	38
Pathology—anatomic and clinical	2,675	180	23	28
Blood banking and transfusion medicine	40	47	19	28
Chemical pathology	4	7	14	14
Cytopathology	74	68	21	26
Forensic pathology	47	39	15	28
Hematology	51	54	13	17
Immunopathology	6	9	11	0
Medical microbiology	5	9	33	33
Neuropathology	37	47	13	28
Pediatric pathology	12	20	10	25
Selective pathology	46	9	0	22
Pediatrics	7,618	216	61	39
Neonatal and perinatal medicine	404	101	50	15
Pediatric cardiology	233	48	40	23
Pediatric critical care medicine	251	63	75	24
Pediatric endocrinology	113	63	25	24
Pediatric gastroenterology	113	49	20	18
Pediatric hematology and oncology	252	65	35	23
Pediatric nephrology	74	46	43	24
Pediatric pulmonology	90	44	52	16
Physical medicine and rehabilitation	1,151	81	49	37

(continued)

Table 34.3c. U.S. Residency Programs Teaching End-of-Life Care and Suicide Prevention. The AMA surveyed 7,787 residency programs in the United States in 1996. We obtained data on the number of programs that included end-of-life care and suicide prevention topics. (Continued in Table 34.3d)

Specialty/subspecialty[a]	Number of resident physicians	Number of programs	Percent teaching end-of-life care	Percent teaching suicide prevention
Plastic surgery	464	99	41	25
Hand surgery	17	18	28	17
Preventive medicine	381	89	21	25
Psychiatry	4,743	198	56	59
Addiction psychiatry	16	12	25	42
Child and adolescent psychiatry	677	118	31	58
Geriatric psychiatry	82	44	68	41
Radiation oncology	493	82	38	34
Radiology—diagnostic	3,991	204	32	38
Neuroradiology	189	87	33	38
Nuclear radiology	34	33	21	24
Pediatric radiology	63	48	25	21
Vascular and interventional radiology	148	70	24	27
Surgery—general	7,921	267	61	39
Hand surgery	24	2	50	50
Pediatric surgery	48	32	22	31
Surgical critical care	86	52	75	33
Vascular surgery	131	78	46	40
Thoracic surgery	334	92	38	34
Urology	1,098	121	50	36
Pediatric urology	10	10	20	40
Transitional year	1,334	155	69	36
Internal medicine and emergency medicine	65	9	78	67
Internal medicine and family practice	16	2	50	50
Internal medicine and neurology	16	12	42	17
Internal medicine and pediatrics	1,300	98	76	42
Internal medicine, physical medicine, and rehabilitation	51	13	69	46
Internal medicine and preventive medicine	3	3	33	33
Internal medicine and psychiatry	78	21	67	67
Neurology, diagnostic radiology, and neuroradiology	0	4	0	0
Neurology, physical medicine, and rehabilitation	4	3	0	0
Pediatrics and emergency medicine	23	4	75	75
Pediatrics and physical medicine and rehabilitation	45	18	50	22
Pediatrics and child and adolescent psychiatry	54	10	50	50

(continued)

351

Table 34.3d. U.S. Residency Programs Teaching End-of-Life Care and Suicide Prevention. The AMA surveyed 7,787 residency programs in the United States in 1996. We obtained data on the number of programs that included end-of-life care and suicide prevention topics.

Specialty/subspecialty[a]	Number of resident physicians	Number of programs	Percent teaching end-of-life care	Percent teaching suicide prevention
Psychiatry and family practice	7	10	40	40
Psychiatry and neurology	9	6	50	50
Total	**98,076**	**7,787**	**n/a**	**n/a**

Note: Data for specialties do not include numbers and percents for subspecialties. While subspecialties fall under specific specialties, separate residency programs exist at both the specialty and subspecialty level.

[a]Subspecialties are indented.

Source: Data are extracted from the AMA's annual survey of (1) U.S. graduate medical education programs accredited by the Accreditation Council for Graduate Medical Education and (2) combined specialty programs as of December 31, 1996. Further information on the AMA's 1996 survey is published in the Journal of the American Medical Association, *Vol. 278, No. 9 (Sept. 3, 1997).*

Chapter 35

Alzheimer's Disease

Alzheimer's disease, the most common cause of dementia among older persons, is evidenced by a progressive, irreversible decline in mental functioning. As the disease progresses, individuals with Alzheimer's experience a loss of memory and gradually lose their capacity to reason, communicate, and carry out the simple tasks of daily life. Alzheimer's disease is devastating to individuals who have the disease and seriously disrupts the lives of those who care for them. Estimates of the annual cost of Alzheimer's disease in the United States run from $80 to $100 billion a year which makes this disease a major public health concern.

The National Institute on Aging (NIA) estimates that approximately 4 million persons (approximately 10.9 percent of the population over age 65) have Alzheimer's disease. Diagnosis is usually determined through a patient's medical history and a physician's examination of the individual's cognitive functioning. Physical examination, laboratory and neuropsychological testing are particularly useful in determining whether the individual may have some other illness which may be treatable or even cured. There is no single test to diagnose Alzheimer's accurately. Absolute confirmation of the diagnosis is only possible after death through an autopsy of the brain tissue.

From "Alzheimer's Disease," [Online] November 9, 1998. Available: http://www.aoa.dhhs.gov/factsheets/alz.html. Produced by the U.S. Department of Health and Human Services' Administration on Aging (AoA). For complete contact information, please refer to Chapter 60, "Resources."

Alzheimer's generally develops over an extended period of time with the duration of noticeable symptoms spanning four to eight years, and, in some instances, this illness may extend as long as 20 years or more. The disease usually begins between ages 40 and 90, with the greatest incidence occurring after age 65. The cause of death is usually pneumonia or other health problems which may or may not be associated with the decline in functioning.

In the past 20 years, research has unveiled new hope for the prevention and treatment of this disease. Even though scientists are making progress in understanding how this disease affects human beings, they are still unable to determine its cause. Two risk factors have been identified. One risk factor is advancing age with the risk doubling for each decade after age 65. The other known risk factor is having genetically-linked family members who have this disease. New research findings suggest that other factors, or some unknown combination of factors, may contribute to, or increase the potential for, developing Alzheimer's disease.

There are no known treatments or medications which cure this disease; however, clinical studies indicate a potential for delaying its onset or improving the functional ability of persons with it. Nevertheless, these clinical studies are ongoing and sometimes seem to be contradictory in their findings. The long-range goal is to prevent the disease altogether.

Research is creating some promising new approaches for working with persons who have Alzheimer's and their caregivers. Experience has taught families and caregivers new behavioral approaches that encourage greater independence and reduce disturbing behavior. Agitation, anger, frustration, and depression are the most common behavioral symptoms experienced by individuals with this disease.

In addition to the problems encountered by persons suffering from Alzheimer's, caregivers also are affected in meeting the many challenges of day-to-day needs. As the disease progresses, the caregiving "burden" severely impacts on both the mental and physical health of the caregiver.

Caregivers experience stress, fatigue, depression, insomnia, and other physical symptoms which may lead to more complicated health problems. The caregiver "burden" is significantly reduced through emotional support, training in how to provide home care, individual counseling and various in-home and community services, particularly respite care. Respite care is a welcome "time-out" for the caregiver. It may be in the form of in-home caregiving relief, adult day care, or temporary, short-term institutional care.

As the disease progresses, the person with Alzheimer's becomes increasingly dependent on others for basic needs. With the increasing demands of care, changing family situations, and progression of the disease, most caregivers feel the need for assistance from others. These needs may vary considerably based upon the family circumstances and physical environment.

In some instances, caregivers and families may only need information, or may benefit from training in how to provide care, and may find community support groups very helpful. Others may need in-home assistance, home-delivered meals, and/or respite or day care. Ultimately, many reach the point at which care in the home is no longer an option and some type of institutional care is the only alternative.

Finding Assistance

The type of assistance available varies considerably from community to community. Eligibility criteria for different programs vary also. Locating the "right" services requires persistence and, oftentimes, several telephone calls and conversations with different agencies. Sources of assistance include the Administration on Aging (AoA) and its nationwide network of 57 state and territorial units on aging, 655 Area Agencies on Aging (AAAs), 221 tribal organizations, and some 27,000 service providers who work to provide a range of supportive in-home and community-based services for older persons and their caregivers. These services range from transportation and home-delivered meals programs to homemaker-home health aide services and adult day care programs.

State and Area Agencies on Aging are responsible for helping people access services, coordinating available community services, and supporting gap-filling services. The AAA serving your area should be in the government section of your telephone directory under "aging services" or "elder services."

If you are unable to find your AAA or need information about AAAs in other parts of the country, you may call the Eldercare Locator. The Eldercare Locator is a nationwide toll-free telephone service, funded by the AoA, designed to help older persons and their caregivers locate local available resources. The hotline, 1-800-677-1116, is available from 9:00 a.m. to 8:00 p.m. EST. It is helpful for callers to provide the address and zip code of the older person who needs assistance. The Locator will help you contact the AAA serving that area.

The AoA and the Health Resources and Services Administration are working collaboratively on 15 Alzheimer's Disease Demonstration Grants awarded to individual states.

These projects carry out diverse activities and have used creative approaches to leverage community resources to expand services to families with Alzheimer's disease. The major services offered through the projects are caregiver support, training and assistance, respite care, care management, public education, and information dissemination. Recently, greater emphasis has been placed on working closely with health care providers for early diagnosis and improved care planning. The grantees have been especially successful in their outreach efforts to rural, low-income and minority individuals.

Resources

The National Institute on Aging is the lead federal agency for Alzheimer's research within the National Institutes of Health. NIA funds Alzheimer's Research Centers to study new methods of diagnosing and treating Alzheimer's disease.

NIA's Alzheimer's Disease Education and Referral Center, 1-800-438-4380, serves as a clearinghouse for public information about Alzheimer's disease, and offers free publications.

The Alzheimer's Association is a national voluntary organization that works to combat this disease, funds research, and contributes to public policy decisions related to this disease:

- The Association sponsors public education programs and offers supportive services to persons with Alzheimer's disease and their caregivers.

- A 24-hour toll-free hotline, 1-800-272-3900, provides information and links families to local Alzheimer's Association Chapters.

Chapter 36

The Burden of the Elderly Caregiver

Introduction

Families are the primary source of long-term care for sick and frail elders[1-4]. In the United States, as much as 80 percent of caregiving for the elderly is accomplished by a family member[1]. It has been reported that spouses provide 60 to 80 percent of home care for the elderly[5].

Evidence suggests that caregivers who have a closer blood or role relationship to the care recipient are more likely to experience higher levels of stress or strain than caregivers who are less closely related to the care recipient[4]. Most of the caregiving for the elderly is provided by their co-resident spouses who are at greatest risk of experiencing emotional difficulties with the stresses resulting from the caregiver role. Co-resident spouses tend to be the most vulnerable to increased stress, possibly due to intense emotional involvement with the patient on a consistent, daily basis[6].

Recent research has demonstrated that co-resident caregivers of HIV patients report more burden than those who are not co-resident[7]. In a recent study of adult child caregivers, caregiver burden was

Excerpted from "Traumatic Grief, Depression and Caregiving in Elderly Spouses of the Terminally Ill," by Laurel C. Beery, B.S., Holly G. Prigerson, Ph.D., Andrew J. Bierhals, M.P.H., Lisa M. Santucci, M.P.A., Jason T. Newsom, Ph.D., Paul J. Maciejewski, Ph.D., Stephen R. Rapp, Ph.D., Amy Fasiczka, B.A., and Charles F. Reynolds III, M.D., in *Omega: Journal of Death and Dying*, Vol. 35, No. 3, pp. 261-79, 1997. © 1997 by Baywood Publishing Co., Inc., 26 Austin Ave., Amityville, NY 11701. Reprinted with permission.

shown to account for 15 percent of the variance in caregiver depression[8]. Given that most elderly caregivers live with the spouse in need of care and that caregiver burden has been found to predict depression in adult child caregivers, we wish to examine the effects of caregiver burden on the mental health (i.e., depression, traumatic grief) of elderly spousal caregivers.

One would expect that spouses who are unable to perform such tasks as feeding, dressing, bathing, and transferring themselves (i.e., have significantly impaired Activities of Daily Living (ADLs)) will require more continuous, physically demanding, and possibly more demeaning, care than spouses who are unable to perform such tasks as shopping, cooking, and driving (Instrument Activities of Daily Living (IADLs)). Mangone found that the care recipient's extent of dependence in ADLs, primarily incontinence, bathing and feeding, revealed the highest correlation with caregiver burden[9]. A study by Schulz, et al., examining immediate family members who were primarily caregivers for spinal cord injured patients determined that the extent of the disability of the patient, as measured by level of dependence in ADLs or amount of time spent assisting the patient each day, was primarily responsible for creating perceived burden in the caregiver[10]. Motenko[11] reported that female in-home caregivers were more frustrated with patients who were more dependent with respect to their ability to perform ADLs. Despite these findings which indicate a connection between ADL tasks performed by the caregiver and a sense of burden, Tennstedt, Cafferata, and Sullivan[12] found *no* relationship between likelihood of depressive symptoms and caregiving tasks in 415 caregivers (>50 year old) of frail elders (>70 year old). Assuming caregiver burden is associated with depression and that ADLs are associated with burden, we would expect that IADL and ADL tasks performed by the caregiver to influence the caregiver's mental health (i.e., depression and traumatic grief).

There are two hypotheses which might explain the effects of the duration of caregiving on caregiver depression. One might assume that the longer the caregiver is performing the tasks, the more these tasks become their whole life to the point that they no longer do things for themselves. Thus, constraints imposed by caregiving might be expected to result in higher levels of depression. However, we have found among the late-life spousally bereaved that highly structured daily routines have proven protective against depression[13,14]. Therefore, an alternative explanation might be that the longer the caregiver is performing the tasks, the more routine these tasks become leading to lower levels of depression. Consistent with this latter explanation,

Hannappel, et al., found among caregivers of dementia patients that caregiving duration was positively associated with lower levels of depressive symptoms[15]. Thus, despite uncertainty of the direction of the relationship, we nonetheless expect to find a significant relationship between the duration of the caregiving and depression and/or traumatic grief.

The changes in roles between husband and wife that occur when one spouse becomes the caregiver of the other may be extremely difficult for both partners to accept. The change in role relationships and time commitment that result from becoming a caregiver for one's terminally ill spouse often result in occupational, financial, social, and emotional sacrifices which may further predispose the caregiver to a heightened sense of burden and depression[16]. Frequently, the demands of caregiving take precedence over other relationships, and occupational and recreational activities of the caregiver, possibly contributing to a heightened sense of loneliness or isolation[15]. Reduced personal time, having fewer social activities, role strain, disrupted household routines, and the caregiver's own deteriorating health have been shown to aggravate the stresses of caregiving[17,18]. According to a report by the Select Committee on Aging[3], caregiving often is associated with a constrained social life, infringement of privacy, and sleep deprivation. As a result of these sacrifices associated with caregiving, when compared with the general population, caregivers were three times more likely to be depressed, two to three times more likely to take psychotropic drugs (e.g., tranquilizers), and 12 percent more likely to use alcohol as away to cope with stress[3]. In consideration of the major life changes in their own lifestyles and habits that the spouses face as primary caregivers, we would expect a greater change in role function of the caregiver to predict higher traumatic grief and depression.

While most studies concentrate on caregiver burden, it has been shown in a few studies that caregiving is also rewarding. The Select Committee on Aging[3] revealed that 75 percent of caregivers find some aspect of caregiving satisfying in that it makes them feel useful. In a study of primary caregivers of stroke victims Schulz, et al.,[10] found that caregiving may actually be satisfying by providing company for the caregivers and improving the relationship between the caregiver and care recipient. We expect to see an inverse relationship between caregiver gratification and traumatic grief and depression.

Our previous reports have shown traumatic (formerly "complicated") grief to predict long-term global functional impairments, sleep disturbances, and heightened levels of depression[13,19,20]. We have identified the

presence of traumatic grief symptomatology up to six months following the loss of a spouse as a predictor for cancer, heart trouble, high
blood pressure, suicidal ideation, and changes in eating habits in 150
spouses of terminally ill[19]. We have recently replicated the distinct-
ness of traumatic grief from the symptoms of bereavement-related
depression and anxiety in a community-based sample[20], and in a pre-
loss, caregiving sample (unpublished data). Traumatic grief pre-loss
appears to be a trait-like tendency to be devastated by a significant
loss, whether that loss is the loss of a "healthy" spouse to illness or
the death of the loved one[21,22]. To our knowledge, no studies have explored
the influence of caregiving responsibilities on the caregiver's level of traumatic grief. We would expect that caregiving responsibilities such as
burden, role function, and activities of daily living would significantly
influence the spouse's level of traumatic grief prior to the loss.

Methods

Sample

Subjects were recruited for a prospective longitudinal study in
which spousal caregivers of terminally ill patients were interviewed
pre- and post-spousal death. The study was designed to investigate
the long-term effects of specific psychosocial factors (e.g., marital
quality, mastery events, lifestyle regularity) on bereavement-related
depression. Subjects recruited into the study were spouses of the terminally ill, aged fifty or above, residing in the Pittsburgh area. Study
participants were interviewed prior to the spouse's death while they
were caring for their spouse, and following the spouse's death at three,
six, and thirteen months post-loss. Semi-structured interviews were
conducted either in the participant's home, or at the University of
Pittsburgh. The Hamilton Rating Scale for Depression (HRSD)[23], a
clinician-rater scale to evaluate the respondent's level of depressive
symptomatology, was administered during the interview. Following
the interview, the respondent was asked to fill out several self-report
scales including the Inventory of Traumatic Grief (ITG Pre-loss version: Prigerson, et al., 1995, unpublished instrument), Caregiver Difficulties Questionnaire (CDQ: Schulz, et al., 1995) and a demographic
questionnaire. Respondents returned the packet of self-report questionnaires to us by mail. Seventy individuals participated in the initial interview, and sixty (86%) of them agreed to continue to
participate in the study. There was no significant difference between
those subjects who continued beyond baseline and those who did not

with respect to age, gender, race, religion, educational attainment, income, aspects of giving (role change, burden, gratification), or mental health measures (depression and traumatic grief).

The total baseline sample used in the present analyses contained twenty-two (31%) men and forty-eight (69%) women with a mean age of sixty-eight *(SD* = 8.9).The initial sample contained thirty-four (49%) Protestant, twenty-three (33%) Catholic, four (6%) Jewish, seven (10%) "Other," and two (3%) specified no religious affiliation. The sample consisted of sixty (86%) Caucasians, seven (10%) African Americans, two (3%) Native Americans, and one (1%) "Other." Sixty-two (88%) of the participants' spouses were being cared for at the respondent's home, with eight (11%) in a nursing home and one (1%) in the hospital. No statistically significant differences were detected between subjects whose spouses were at home and those who were not with respect to age, gender, race, religion, educational attainment, income, aspects of caregiving (role change, burden, gratification), or mental health measures (depression and traumatic grief). Twenty-four (34%) of the spouses receiving care were suffering from cancer, fourteen (20%) from Alzheimer's disease, fifteen (21%) from a stroke (or multiple strokes), five (7%) from heart-related problems, and twelve (18%) from "other" serious illness.

Measures

Depression. The interviewer-administered seventeen-item Hamilton Rating Scale for Depression, a scale with proven internal consistency and reliability, was used to assess the respondent's level of depression[23].

Traumatic Grief. The Inventory of Traumatic Grief, pre-loss version (ITG Pre-loss, Prigerson, et al., 1995 — unpublished instrument) contains nineteen items used to assess traumatic grief related to a spouse's critical illness (i.e., before death). These nineteen items correspond to the Inventory of Complicated Grief (ICG)[24], a self-report scale that measures the more pathologic symptoms of grief (i.e., symptoms of traumatic and separation distress) after the death of the spouse. Respondents reported no difficulty answering the questions posed by them in the ITG, which suggests the scale's face validity. Cronbach's alpha for the ITG scale in this sample was 0.92. The Pearson correlation coefficient between traumatic grief (pre-loss) and depression (ITG and HRSD: $r = 0.30$; $p = 0.02$) provided a measure of the scale's concurrent validity.

Caregiving Difficulties. Caregiver burden, caregiver change in role function, and activities of daily living (IADL and ADL) performed for the dying spouse were measured by subsections of the Caregiver Difficulties Questionnaire (CDQ: Schulz, et al., 1995). The caregiver burden subsection contained ten items that assess the emotional burden placed on individuals who are caring for their terminally ill spouse. A Cronbach's alpha of 0.94 suggested high internal consistency among the caregiver burden items. The subsection which measured caregiver change in role function contained eleven items which measured how much activity restriction was placed on the caregiver while caring for their ill spouse. In this sample, this subsection had high internal consistency (Cronbach's alpha 0.93). in order to assess activities of daily living (ADL) and instrumental activities of daily living (IADL), a subsection was used which contained sixteen (7 ADL, 9 IADL) activities which the caregiver might perform for the spouse. Caregivers indicated if they assisted with each of these activities ("yes" = 1, "no" = 0). All of the positive responses for each of the activities were added to obtain the ADL and IADL summary scores.

We measured caregiver gratification by extracting the last five items of the forty-four item Caregiver's Sentiments scale (Prigerson, et al., 1995—unpublished instrument). This scale was used to determine the amount of satisfaction the subject derived from caring for their terminally ill spouse. A Cronbach's alpha of 0.89 indicated that the caregiver gratification subscale had adequate reliability.

The measures to assess the duration of caregiving and time spent caring per week were obtained from the semi-structured interview and the CDQ respectively. In the demographics section of the interview, the caregiver was asked several questions about the illness of the spouse including the date of diagnosis. The duration of time caregiving was measured by subtracting the date of diagnosis from the date of the initial interview. In the occasion that the caregiver could only remember a year, or perhaps a month, the middle of the year (e.g., 6/15/XX) or month (X/15/XX) was used as the date of diagnosis. The CDQ includes a question, "How many hours a week do you spend helping your spouse or doing things for your spouse?" The responses range from zero to over forty hours (0 to 5, 6 to 10, 11 to 20, 21 to 40, and over 40).

Analyses

Pearson correlation coefficients were used to examine the relationships between all of the variables used in subsequent analyses. Correlations between the specific changes in role function variables and the mental health outcomes were also estimated. These analyses were used to identify measures to include as potential control variables in the regression models (described below) and to test for potential problems of multicollinearity.

First, we sought to examine the effects of *actual caregiving activities* and the amount of time required by caregiving tasks on mental health outcomes. Given that IADLs performed was a significant correlate of depression in the bivariate analyses, we regressed depressive symptoms on IADLs controlling for the time spent caring per week. The time spent caregiving weekly was entered into the model in order to obtain a general intensity of the IADL tasks.

The relationship between the *aspects of caregiving* (e.g., caregiver burden, caregiver change in role function, time since diagnosis, and weekly time spent caring), depression, and traumatic grief were determined by use of the multiple regression procedure. The mental health outcomes (i.e., depression and traumatic grief) were regressed on caregiver burden, and caregiver change in role function in separate models controlling for duration of caring (time since diagnosis).

Mental health outcomes (i.e., levels of depression and traumatic grief) were each regressed on individual changes in role function controlling for duration of caregiving. Those role function variables which had significant effects on the mental health outcomes were entered into a stepwise regression model. In stepwise regression, all variables which are not significant at $p < 0.15$ are removed from the model, allowing for the inspection of the role function variables which account for most of the variance in depression. In other words, stepwise regression models were used to determine the specific *types* of role change which explained the greatest amount of variance in the mental health outcomes.

Results

Bivariate correlations among all the primary variables entered into the analyses are found in Table 36.1. Depression was significantly associated with IADL ($r = -0.31, p < 0.05$), caregiver burden ($r = 0.31, p < 0.05$), and caregiver change in role function ($r = 0.34, p < 0.01$). Traumatic grief was not associated with any of these measures. As expected, traumatic grief and depression were significantly associated with one another, but not very closely ($r = 0.30, p < 0.05$). There were no significant associations between the ADL tasks performed for the spouse, caregiver gratification, duration of caregiving, and time spent caregiving each week with either of the mental health outcomes.

Table 36.1. Zero-Order Correlations among Analyzed Variables (N = 70)

Variable	1	2	3	4	5	6	7	8	9
1. Gratification	—	-0.23	0.09	0.01	-0.08	0.21	-0.06	0.17	-0.18
2. ADL		—	0.62****	0.00	0.07	-0.02	0.32*	0.12	-0.14
3. IADL			—	-0.10	-0.16	0.07	0.01	-0.08	-0.31*
4. Burden				—	0.70****	0.31*	0.40***	0.21	0.31*
5. Role function					—	0.15	0.52****	0.01	0.34**
6. Duration						—	0.09	-0.06	-0.08
7. Time							—	0.17	-0.09
8. Traumatic grief								—	0.30*
9. Depression									—

*p < 0.05
**p < 0.01
***p < 0.005
****p < 0.0001

There existed a significant correlation between the IADL and depression. When depression was regressed on the IADLs performed for the spouse, controlling for duration and weekly time spent caregiving (i.e., intensity of IADLs), fewer IADLs predicted higher levels of depression (beta = -0.54, $p < 0.05$).

The results of the regressions with depression and traumatic grief are summarized in Table 36.2. Change in caregiver role function, when entered in the model controlling for duration of caregiving, significantly predicted severity of depression (beta = 0.10, $p = 0.007$), but did not predict severity of traumatic grief. Caregiver burden, when entered into a model with duration of caregiving, significantly predicted severity of both depression (beta = 0.14, $p = 0.006$) and traumatic grief (beta = 0.36, $p = 0.02$). When all of these variables (caregiver burden, role function, and duration) were regressed with the mental health outcomes, caregiver burden remained a significant predictor of traumatic grief (beta = 0.49, $p = 0.01$). In the final (full) model it is important to note that the significant correlation between caregiver burden and caregiver role function, may make these estimates unstable.

Table 36.3. summarizes the regressions of the effects of the individual change in role function variables on the mental health outcomes, controlling for duration of caregiving. None of the regressions of the effects of the role function variables on traumatic grief were significant. Changes in caring for self (beta = 0.66, $p = 0.02$), eating habits (beta = 0.77, $p = 0.007$), household chores (beta = 0.96, $p = 0.01$), working on hobbies (beta = 0.85, $p = 0.008$), sports and recreation (beta = 1 .00, $p = 0.0006$), and going to work (beta = 0.61, $p = 0.02$) were shown to significantly influence the caregiver's level of depression.

In stepwise regressions of the significant change in role function variables (caring for self, caring for others, household chores, working on hobbies, sports and recreation, and going to work) on traumatic grief and depression, we found none of the role change variables was significantly associated with traumatic grief. In the stepwise models predicting depression levels, only the change in the caregiver's amount of time available for sports and recreational activities was retained. The change in sports and recreation variable accounted for 16 percent of the variance in the level of depressive symptomatology (beta = 0.91, $p = 0.002$).

Table 36.2. Regression of Depression and Traumatic Grief on Caregiver Burden, Change in Role Function, and Duration of Caregiving[a]

Variables	Depression			Traumatic Grief		
	Model 1 Beta (SE)	Model 2 Beta (SE)	Model 3 Beta (SE)	Model 1 Beta (SE)	Model 2 Beta (SE)	Model 3 Beta (SE)
Caregiver burden	—	0.14** (0.05)	0.09 (0.06)	—	0.36* (0.15)	0.49** (0.19)
Change in role function	0.10** (0.04)	—	0.06 (0.05)	0.03 (0.12)	—	-0.17 (0.14)
Duration of caregiving	-0.11 (0.11)	-0.16 (0.11)	-0.15 (0.11)	-0.52 (0.38)	-0.85* (0.39)	-0.88* (0.39)
R^2	0.13*	0.13*	0.16*	0.03	0.12*	0.14*
N	59	59	59	56	56	56

[a]Time since spouse's diagnosis
*$p < 0.10$
**$p < 0.05$
***$p < 0.01$
****$p < 0.005$

Table 36.3. Regression Coefficients for the Effects of Individual Role Function Variables on Mental Health Outcomes

	Dependent Variable							
	Traumatic Grief				Depression			
			Model				Model	
Independent Variable	Beta	SE	R^2	p-Value	Beta	SE	R^2	p-Value[a]
Caring for self	0.29	0.90	0.03	0.75	0.66*	0.28	0.09	**0.06**
Caring for others	-0.36	0.82	0.03	0.38	0.13	0.26	0.01	0.77
Eating habits	0.06	0.89	0.03	0.42	0.77***	0.27	0.12	**0.02**
Sleeping habits	-0.26	1.06	0.03	0.41	0.44	0.34	0.03	0.38
Household chores	1.78	1.17	0.07	0.13	0.96*	0.37	0.11	**0.04**
Going shopping for self	0.37	0.17	0.03	0.40	0.36	0.38	0.02	0.54
Visiting friends	0.04	1.07	0.03	0.42	0.67*	0.34	0.07	0.13
Working on hobbies	0.66	0.99	0.04	0.34	0.85**	0.31	0.04	0.34
Sports and recreation	0.09	0.94	0.03	0.42	1.00***	0.28	0.19	**0.002**
Going to work	0.64	0.86	0.04	0.32	0.61*	0.27	0.09	**0.07**
Maintaining friendships	-0.61	0.35	0.06	0.19	0.61	0.35	0.06	0.19

Notes: [a]Bold denotes significance or marginal significance for the full model. Each independent variable was regressed with each dependent variable in separate models, each controlling for duration of caregiving.
*$p < 0.05$; **$p < 0.01$; ***$p < 0.005$; ****$p < 0.0001$

Discussion

In this sample of spousal caregivers of the terminally ill, we identified certain aspects of caregiving to have important influences on the caregiver's level of both depression and pre-loss traumatic grief. In our examination the effects of caregiver burden on the mental health (i.e., depression, traumatic grief) of elderly spousal caregivers, we found that caregiver burden was a significant predictor of both traumatic grief and depression. Previous findings have shown that the burden of caregiving is a significant predictor of depression[12,25,26]. In fact, Bodnar and Kiecolt-Glaser found that both non-bereaved and bereaved caregivers were more likely than controls to meet criteria for syndromal depression and anxiety at the first and fourth years of a four-year longitudinal study of caregivers[26]. Additionally, caregivers who ruminated more about caregiving after bereavement reported higher levels of depression. We found caregiver burden to be a significant predictor of traumatic grief. Given the long-lasting effects of the burden of caregiving on the mental health of the caregiver suggests that caregiver burden may be an important target for future intervention.

We expected that IADL and ADL tasks performed by the caregiver to influence the caregiver's mental health. In the bivariate correlations, we found no significant associations between ADLs performed and either traumatic grief or depression. Tennstedt, et al.,[12] found that it was not the number of ADLs and the hours per week of care, but the negative impact of these caregiving activities which led to depressive symptoms in caregivers for elderly. Consistent with Tennstedt[12], we found no association between ADLs performed and depression, but there did exist a significant association between caregiver burden and depression. Thus, unlike caregiver burden (an attitudinal subjective response to caregiving), the actual activities performed (objective behavioral demands of caregiving) did not appear to influence these mental health measures among our sample of caregivers.

Interestingly, we found that IADL assistance provided by the caregiver was significantly negatively associated with caregiver depression. That is, the fewer IADL tasks with which the caregiver assisted, the greater the severity of the caregiver's depressive symptoms. Fewer IADLs may have been found to be associated with higher levels of depressive symptoms because caregiving activities may become routine, providing a sense of structure and purpose for the caregiver. As we have found among the late life spousally bereaved, highly structured daily routines have proven protective against depression[13,14]. If the spouse had performed more IADLs, he or she may have been protected against depression because caregiving provides a needed measure of lifestyle regularity, which may confer its own benefits of greater predictability and a sense of order in a situation that appears to be beyond anyone's control.

We sought to find a relationship between the duration of the caregiving and depression and/or traumatic grief. We found no significant associations between the time spent caregiving weekly and the duration of caregiving with the mental health outcomes, although duration was significantly associated with caregiver burden.

We expected a greater change in role function of the caregiver to predict higher traumatic grief and/or depression. Change in role function of the caregiver was not associated with traumatic grief, but was a predictor for depression. Upon closer inspection of the individual role function changes of the caregiver, we found that change in restriction in the caregiver's sports and recreational activities was the most significant predictor of depression levels among our sample of caregivers. It appears that it is not the time spent or the duration of caregiving, but rather the implications that this has on time for the caregiver to engage in activities that are personally fulfilling and enjoyable which may be a trigger for depression among spousal caregivers.

We expected to see inverse associations of caregiver gratification with traumatic grief and depression. We found no significant associations between caregiver gratification and either of these mental health problems. The literature suggests that caregiving can also be rewarding. It would be expected that if the caregiver is satisfied with the work involved in caring for the spouse, there is *not* going to be any adverse reaction to the caregiving role resulting in depression or traumatic grief. It was interesting, though, that *no* significant associations existed between depression and caregiver gratification. Apparently caregiver gratification in this sample did not influence the caregiver's level of depression or traumatic grief. These results should be interpreted with caution, however, given that caregiver gratification was measured with a five-item scale which has not been validated in other studies.

We hypothesized that aspects of caregiving such as burden, role function, and activities of daily living performed for the spouse would influence the spouse's level of traumatic grief prior to the loss. To our knowledge, we are the first to investigate traumatic grief in a preloss, caregiving sample. We have found an association with caregiver burden and traumatic grief, but duration of caregiving was significantly negatively associated with traumatic grief. Therefore, a shorter duration of caregiving predicted a higher traumatic grief score, suggesting that traumatic grief in caregivers is most intense shortly after the diagnosis of the spouse's terminal condition. This is consistent with the notion of traumatic grief representing features highly suggestive of a Post-Traumatic Stress Disorder reaction. That is, the spouse is more initially traumatized by the impending loss and may tend to adapt to the impending loss over time, resulting in diminishing level of traumatic grief symptomatology.

Conclusion

In this report, we examined possible factors associated with depression and traumatic grief among caregivers of terminally ill spouses. We found caregiver burden to be associated with both traumatic grief and depression. Changes in role function of the caregiver, specifically in time available for sports and recreation, and fewer IADL tasks performed for the spouse, were significantly associated with the severity of caregiver depression. Among the spouses participating in this study, it appears that depressive symptomatology was related to the extent to which caregiving resulted in a restriction of activities that contributed to feelings of personal fulfillment (e.g., recreational activities). IADLs performed for the spouse may provide the caregiver regularity/activity which has been shown to work as a buffer against depression in bereaved widows and widowers[14].

Future research might benefit from use of a more comprehensive and validated measure of caregiver gratification than was available to us in this study. Given recent studies which suggest the persistence of traumatic grief over time[21,27,7,28] and the substantial physical and mental health morbidity associated with traumatic grief[19], future research should attempt to identify other risk factors aside from caregiver burden which may result in syndromal levels of traumatic grief either before or after a loss. Finally, because the results of this study were obtained from a sample of spouses who provided care to individuals suffering from a wide range of terminal illnesses, and the small number of caregivers for specific terminal conditions, we would recommend that future studies test these results in a more homogeneous population (e.g., Alzheimer's disease, lung cancer).

References

1. E. Brody, Parent Care as a Normative Family Stress, _The Gerontologist, 25,_ pp. 19-29, 1985.

2. E. Shanas, The Family as Social Support Systems in Old Age, *The Gerontologist,* 19, pp. 169-174, 1979.

3. Subcommittee on Human Services, Select Committee on Aging, House of Representatives, *Exploding the Myths: Caregiving in America,* 100th Congress, 1st Session, Comm. Pub. No. 99-611, 1987.

4. L. K. George and L. P. Gwyther, Caregiver Well-Being: A Multidimensional Examination of Family Caregivers of Demented Adults, *The Gerontologist,* 26, pp. 253-259, 1986.

5. M. Horowitz, U.S. Department of Health and Human Services, Perceived Control and Adaptation in Elder Caregivers: Development of an Explanatory Model, *International Journal of Aging and Human Development,* 36:3, pp. 219-237, 1993.

6. L. W. Morris, R. G. Morris, and P. G. Britton, The Relationship between Marital Intimacy, Perceived Strain and Depression in Spouse Caregivers of Dementia Sufferers, *British Journal of Medical Psychology,* 61, pp. 231-236, 1988.

7. K. I. Pakenham, M. R. Dadds, and D. J. Terry, Carers' Burden and Adjustment to HIV, *AIDS-Care,* 7:2, pp. 189-203, 1995.

8. D. A. Chiriboga, P. G. Weiler, and K. Nielsen, The Stress of Caregivers, in *Aging and Caregiving: Theory, Research, and Policy,* D. E. Biegel and A. Blum (eds.), Sage Publications, Newbury Park, California, pp. 121-138, 1990.

9. C. A. Mangone, P. D. Sanguinette, P D. Baumann, et al., Influence of Feelings of Burden on the Caregiver's Perception of the Patient's Functional Status, *Dementia,* 4, pp. 287-293, 1993.

10. R. Schulz, C. A. Tompkins, and M. T. Rau, A Longitudinal Study of the Psychosocial Impact of Stroke on Primary Support Persons, *Psychology and Aging,* 3:2, pp. 31-141, 1988.

11. A. K. Motenko, The Frustrations, Gratifications, and Well-Being of Dementia Caregivers, *The Gerontologist,* 29:2, pp. 166-172, 1989.

12. S. Tennstedt, G. L. Cafferata, and L. Sullivan, Depression among Caregivers of Impaired Elders, *Journal of Aging and Health,* 4:1, pp. 58-76, 1992.

13. H. G. Prigerson, C. F. Reynolds III, E. Frank, D. J. Kupfer, C. J. George, and P. R. Houck, Stressful Life Events, Social Rhythms, and Depressive Symptoms among the Elderly: An Examination of Hypothesized Causal Linkages, *Psychiatry Research,* 51, pp. 33-49, 1994.

14. H. G. Prigerson, T. H. Monk, C. F. Reynolds, A. Begley, P. R. Houck, A. J. Bierhals, and D. J. Kupfer, Lifestyle Regularity and Activity Level as Protective Factors against Bereavement-Related Depression in Late-Life, *Depression,* 3, pp. 297-302, 1995/1996.

15. M. Hannappel, R. J. Calsyn, and G. Allen, Does Social Support Alleviate the Depression of Caregivers of Dementia Patients? *Journal of Gerontological Social Work,* 20:1-2, pp. 35-51, 1993.

16. T. Sommers and L. Shields, *Women Take Care: The Consequences of Caregiving in Today's Society,* Triad Publishing, Gainesville, Florida, 1987.

17. L. S. Noelker and R. W. Wallace, The Organization of Family Care for Impaired Elderly, *Journal of Family Issues,* 6, pp. 23-44, 1985.

18. C. L. Johnson and D. S. Catalano, A Longitudinal Study of Family Supports to Impaired Elderly, *The Gerontologist,* 23, pp. 612-618, 1983.

19. H. G. Prigerson, A. J. Bierhals, S. V. Kasl, C. F. Reynolds, M. K. Shear, N. Day, L. C. Beery, J. T. Newsom, and S. Jacobs, Traumatic Grief as a Risk Factor for Mental and Physical Morbidity, *American Journal of Psychiatry,* 154:5, pp. 616-623, 1996.

20. H. G. Prigerson, A. J. Bierhals, S. V. Kasl, C. F Reynolds III, M. K. Shear, J. T. Newsom, and S. Jacobs, Complicated Grief as a Distinct Disorder from Bereavement-Related Depression and Anxiety: A Replication Study, *American Journal of Psychiatry,* 153:11, pp. 1484-1486, November 1996.

21. H. G. Prigerson, M. K. Shear, A. J. Bierhals, P. A. Pilkonis, L. Wolfson, L. Ehrenpreis, and C. F. Reynolds III, Case Histories of Complicated Grief, *Omega Issue on Kinship Bereavement,* 35:1, pp. 9-24, 1997.

22. H. G. Prigerson, M. K. Shear, E. Frank, L. C. Beery, R. Silberman, J. Prigerson, and C. F. Reynolds III, Traumatic Grief: A Case of Loss-Induced Trauma, *American Journal of Psychiatry*, 154:7, pp. 1003-1009.

23. M. Hamilton, A Rating Scale for Depression, *Journal of Neurology, Neurosurgery, and Psychiatry*, 23, pp. 56-62, 1960.

24. H. G. Prigerson, P. K. Maciejewski, C. F. Reynolds III, A. J. Bierhals, J. T. Newsom, E. Frank, M. D. Miller, J. Doman, and A. Fasiczka, The Inventory of Complicated Grief: A Scale to Measure Certain Maladaptive Symptoms of Loss, *Psychiatry Research*, 59, pp. 65-79, 1995.

25. R. Schulz, C. A. Tompkins, D. Wood, and S. Decker, The Social Psychology of Caregiving: Physical and Psychological Costs of Providing Support to the Disabled, *Journal of Applied Social Psychology*, 17:4, pp. 401-428, 1987.

26. J. C. Bodnar and J. K. Kiecolt-Glaser, Caregiver Depression after Bereavement: Chronic Stress Isn't Over When It's Over, *Psychology and Aging*, 9:3, pp. 372-380, 1994.

27. H. G. Prigerson, E. Frank, S. V. Kasl, C. F. Reynolds III, B. Anderson, G. S. Zubenko, P. R. Houck, C. J. George, and D. J. Kupfer, Complicated Grief and Bereavement-Related Depression as Distinct Disorders: Preliminary Empirical Validation in Elderly Bereaved Spouses, *American Journal of Psychiatry*, 152:1, pp. 22-30, 1995.

28. A. J. Bierhals, H. G. Prigerson, A. Fasiczka, E. Frank, M. D. Miller, and C. F. Reynolds III, Gender Differences in Complicated Grief among the Elderly, *Omega*, 32:4, pp. 303-317, 1995-96.

— by Laurel C. Beery, B.S., Holly G. Prigerson, Ph.D.,
Andrew J. Bierhals, M.P.H., Lisa M. Santucci, M.P.A.,
Jason T. Newsom, Ph.D., Paul J. Maciejewski, Ph.D.,
Stephen R. Rapp, Ph.D., Amy Fasiczka, B.A.,
and Charles F. Reynolds III, M.D.

Direct reprint requests to Laurel C. Beery, B.S., Department of Psychiatry, University of Pittsburgh School of Medicine, Western Psychiatric Institute and Clinic, 745 Bellefield Towers, 3811 O'Hara Street, Pittsburgh, PA 15213.

Chapter 37

Assisting the Family Caregiver

The FRIENDS of the [National Institute of Nursing Research] (NINR) held the first in a series of three breakfast briefings this year on March 16, 1998. The topic was End-of-Life Care. FRIENDS, an independent, nonprofit membership organization, supports the NINR by promoting public awareness of the role of nursing research in advancing health care practice in the United States. Those attending the briefing included Congressional staff, nurse researchers and administrators, and members of public and private organizations having a special interest in the topic.

Colleen Conway-Welch, PhD, RN, FAAN, President of FRIENDS and Dean of Vanderbilt University School of Nursing, provided welcoming remarks and thanked the Congressional sponsors, Senator Ron Wyden (D-OR) and Representative Elizabeth Furse (D-OR). She also recognized Dick Thompson, Vice President of Government Affairs of Bristol-Myers Squibb, which hosted the breakfast.

Patricia A. Grady, PhD, RN, FAAN, Director of the [NINR], opened the scientific discussion by providing background information about

From "Summary of the Capitol Hill Breakfast Briefing on End-of-Life Care," [Online] March 16, 1998. Available: http://www.nih.gov/ninr/ eolbriefing.htm. Produced by the National Institute of Health's National Institute of Nursing Research (NINR). And from "Fact Sheet: National Family Caregiver Support Program," [Online] January 1999. Available: http:// www.aoa.dhhs.gov/pr/carefct.html. Produced by the Department of Health and Human Services' Administration on Aging (AoA). For complete contact information, please refer to Chapter 60, "Resources."

NINR's involvement in end-of-life issues. NINR's research portfolio over the past 10 years has included issues related to end-of-life, such as decisionmaking and managing symptoms, including pain. The Institute is therefore well- grounded to go forward with these lines of scientific inquiry and has been designated by the NIH as the lead Institute in the area of palliative care research.

In the Fall of 1997, NINR convened a multidisciplinary workshop on end-of-life issues that identified four major areas in need of research: pain, dyspnea (difficulty breathing), cognitive disturbances, and cachexia (weight loss and wasting). A program announcement was issued in December to stimulate research in these areas. Other NIH Institutes joining NINR in issuing the program announcement were the National Cancer Institute, the National Institute of Allergy and Infectious Diseases, the National Institute of Mental Health and the Office of Alternative Medicine.

The Research

End of Life Care at Home: The Living Room as the Intensive Care Unit. Marcia Grant, RN, DNSc, FAAN, Director and Research Scientist, Department of Nursing, Research and Education, City of Hope National Medical Center, Duarte, California

Dr. Grant stated that as a result of improved health care, the nation's people are living longer lives but are also dying more slowly. More than 2 million Americans will die in 1998, most from chronic illness that they have endured for a long period of time. More than 70% of deaths occur in those over 65 years of age. There has been a shift from patient care in the hospital to family care in the home, which presents a special challenge for health care professionals as they adjust their focus on providing support for these caregivers.

A 1997 Institute of Medicine report, *Approaching Death: Improving Care at the End of Life,* stated that people fear they will be technologically overtreated, leading to a protracted death. They also fear abandonment and untreated physical distress. There are gaps in knowledge as to how to best treat patients at the end of life and how to meet caregiver needs.

Recent surveys indicate family caregiver time spent in hands-on care can range from none to 15 hours a day. The average is 4 1/2 hours. More than 20% of patients need 10 hours of care a day. To illustrate her point that caregiving is "not just chicken soup and fluffing pillows—

it's heavy duty," Dr. Grant provided an example of an end-stage patient with stomach cancer living at home. She had earlier experienced surgery, radiation, and chemotherapy. Her family caregivers were her husband and her daughter, who had recently given birth. The home became an intensive care unit (ICU), with family members managing pumps, feeding her by a tube that sometimes leaked, and dispensing medications. They had to deal with wound care, incontinence, drug dementia, and her pain, which was particularly difficult. There were psychological problems for both the patient and the caregivers.

Clearly more resources need to be devoted to assisting family caregivers. Dr. Grant indicated that key areas for research include:

- Better pain management
- Strategies for families that care for relatives in a home setting
- Better transition from health care setting to home setting
- Effective ways to educate the public and the medical community about end-of-life issues

Patient and Family Perspectives on End-of-Life Care. Virginia Tilden, RN, DNSc, FAAN, Professor and Associate Dean, School of Nursing; Associate Director, Center for Ethics in Health Care, Oregon Health Sciences University, Portland

In providing background on the issues of end-of-life care, Dr. Tilden stated that technology can extend life far beyond the quality of life point. The majority of patients end up in the intensive care unit, often in pain, unable to communicate with loved ones. Most people do not want treatment if it is futile, but this can be difficult to judge. Many patients receive aggressive care at the end of their lives for several reasons—uncertainty about the prospects of death and when it might occur (no one wants to make a mistake), and a built-in unwillingness to give up on the part of the medical staff.

Internists are treatment-oriented, not comfort-oriented. This can be expensive and denies the principle that patients are qualified to decide about their care. Aggressive medical treatments at the end of life are estimated to be many thousands of dollars more per patient than the costs of palliative care. For example, the cost of two days of hospital ICU care is roughly equivalent to that of 30 days of hospice care. A 1994 study of dying in the ICU found that 5% of patients that died used 22% of the ICU resources. When staff knew the patient's wishes about treatment, however, an average of $14,000 was saved per patient.

Dr. Tilden described her joint (nursing/medicine) research project that began in 1990 and explores what patients and families want and expect in end-of-life care. Some of her findings are as follows:

- Families whose loved ones are dying in hospitals are willing to stop aggressive treatments if they understand the condition is terminal and they are convinced their loved one will receive high quality comfort-care.

- Families report that dying loved ones in the last week of life have much more pain and other physical distress, e.g., nausea, shortness of breath, than physicians and nurses think they have.

- In the present health care environment in which patients are discharged quickly from one setting to another, discontinuity and lapses in health services are very distressing to patients and families.

- Americans with inadequate health insurance lack access to good palliative care during dying. They are much more likely to arrive at emergency rooms in acute distress and require expensive hospitalization for symptoms that could have been managed by hospice or home-health nurses.

- A simple, bright pink form in the front of nursing home residents' medical records can prevent unwanted transfer to the hospital when a resident is dying and prefers to stay in the nursing home.

- For families whose loved ones died in a hospital, certain physician and nurse behaviors—such as viewing death as a medical failure—greatly increases the family's grief and distress.

Dr. Tilden concluded her remarks by stating that affordable, high quality, low-tech home care, with the guidance of a nurse practitioner to effectively manage the symptoms of dying, such as pain, is the best alternative to a pain-filled, lengthy and expensive dying process or to assisted suicide.

Challenges

Supportive care and symptom management during the final weeks and months of a patient's life have received little attention, but it is becoming increasingly clear that distressing symptoms considered inevitable at the end of life can be eased and that a patient's quality of life, sense of control, and dignity can be maintained. Various issues remain to be resolved through   multidisciplinary research:

- The increased aging of the population necessitates a strong focus on how the health care system manages end-of-life care. More needs to be known about the proper course of treatment during the dying phase.

- Despite the availability of painkillers, such as opioids, for terminally ill patients, reports indicate that pain is still inadequately treated. For example, a recent Institute of Medicine study found that 40 to 80% of patients with cancer, AIDS, and other diseases report inadequately treated pain. Concern about patient addiction to drugs has been largely unfounded.

- There is a need for improved assessment tools to help health care professionals properly evaluate symptoms at the end of life so that proper treatment may be prescribed. While pain is a major symptom, other symptoms include breathing difficulties, cognitive disturbances, wasting and weakness, nausea, fatigue, and depression. These symptoms often occur in combination and compound the suffering of dying patients and their caregivers.

- Patients' comfort needs and their wishes for end-of-life care must be respected. Research has found discrepancies between patient desires and the treatment they receive at the end of life. A recent NIH investigation, "Study to Understand Prognoses and Preferences for Outcomes and Risks of Treatments" (SUPPORT), found that:

  1. Forty percent of the patients were treated aggressively in ICUs

  2. Pain was commonly experienced by these patients

  3. Almost half of the physicians did not know that their patients preferred not to be resuscitated

- Family caregivers' needs must be addressed. They must become skilled in dispensing opiates, determining the changing food preferences of a dying person, and responding to changes in functioning and types of care required. They must also be helped to cope with stress and maintain their own health.

Budget Proposal for FY 2000 Budget Announced by President Clinton on January 4, 1999

The National Family Caregiver Support Program, one of four long-term care initiatives proposed by President Clinton on January 4, 1999, will help families sustain their efforts to care for an older relative who has a chronic illness or disability. The program, to be administered by the Administration on Aging of the Department of Health and Human Services will establish a multifaceted support system in each state for family caregivers. Through federal funding allocated to states on a population based formula, all states, working in partnership with area agencies on aging, community-service providers and consumer organizations, will be expected to put in place five basic program components:

- Information about resources that will help families in their caregiver roles;

- Assistance to families in locating services from a variety of private and voluntary agencies;

- Caregiver counseling, training, and peer support to help them better cope with the emotional and physical stress of dealing with the disabling effects of a family member's chronic condition;

- Respite care provided in a home, an adult day care center, or over a weekend in a nursing home or a residential setting such as an assisted living facility; and

- Limited supplemental services to fill a service gap that cannot be filled in any other manner.

Funding for the National Family Caregiver Support Program will primarily be allocated to states by formula to support the above program components. States would contract with area agencies on aging who would contract with provider agencies for services. In addition, the program will support the following functions:

- Competitive innovation grants to develop new approaches to specialized caregiving issues and developing emergency caregiving back-up systems. The results of such demonstrations and applied research will be translated into practice through incorporation into the ongoing operation of the state programs, thus providing a stimulus for continuous program innovation aimed at generating best practices which can most effectively support caregivers of persons living at home, in the community or on tribal reservations.

• Collaborative national activities to support program evaluation, training, technical assistance, research and public education efforts

[The Administration on Aging] (AoA) has drafted legislative language to amend Title III of the Older Americans Act (OAA) to establish the National Family Caregiver Support Program. This language refocuses an existing state formula grant program to establish a system of family supports targeted primarily to those caring for an older relative who has limitations in 2 or more activities of daily living. States would:

• target funds to families in the greatest social and/or economic need;

• establish sliding fee scales that will determine the amount of cost sharing expected of recipients based upon income. Low income persons would be exempt from cost sharing.

For further information about this initiative, contact: Moya Benoit Thompson, (202)401-4541.

Chapter 38

Quality Care and the Cost of Dying

For more than a decade, health policy analysts have noted—and some have decried—the high cost of dying.[1-7] With the acceleration of pressures on health care costs and calls for reform, considerably more attention has been focused on proposals to control costs at the end of life.[8] One proposal would require persons enrolling in a health care—plan to complete an advance directive.[9,10] Others would require hospitals to establish guidelines to identify and reduce futile care.[11-13] Similar ideas have been expressed by members of President Bill Clinton's Health Care Task Force and by Joycelyn Elders, the surgeon general.[14]

Advance directives and hospice care were developed to ensure patients' autonomy and to provide high-quality care at the end of life. Compassion and dignity are sufficient justification for their use. Nevertheless, the persistent interest in saving money at the end of life through the use of advance directives and hospice care makes it imperative to assess how much money might realistically be saved.

Cost at the End of Life and the Reasons for Cost Control

Expenditures at the end of life seem disproportionately large. Although the precise numbers vary, studies consistently demonstrate that 27 to 30 percent of Medicare payments each year are for the 5 to 6 percent of Medicare beneficiaries who die in that year.[15-17] The latest available figures indicate that in 1988, the mean Medicare payment for the last year of life of a beneficiary who died was $13,316, as compared with $1,924 for all Medicare beneficiaries (a ratio of 6.9:1).[15] Payments for dying patients increase exponentially as death approaches, and payments during the last month of life constitute 40 percent of payments during the last year of life.[15] Identical trends and ratios have been found since the early 1960s.[6, 15-17]

Many people believe that these expenditures are for the care of patients known in advance to be dying. The time of death is usually unpredictable, however, except perhaps when the patient has advanced cancer. There is no method to predict months or weeks in advance who will live and who will die. Consequently, it is difficult to know in advance what costs are for care at the end of life and what costs are for saving a life.[6,7] Only in retrospect, after a patient's death, can we identify the last year or month of life. Nevertheless, to many people, reducing expenditures at the end of life seems an easy and readily justifiable way of cutting wasteful spending and freeing resources to ensure universal access to health care.[9-11,18] General rules intended to curtail the use of unnecessary medical service have been shown to reduce both effective and wasteful services.[19] Consequently, there is some reluctance to limit interventions for relatively healthy people. Many believe, however, that interventions for patients whose death is imminent are inherently wasteful, since they neither cure nor ameliorate disease or disability.

Advance directives and hospice care have been proposed as methods of reducing medical costs at the end of life; both can transform "good ethics [into] good health economics."[9] In survey after survey, Americans indicate that they do not want to be kept alive if their disease is irreversible. If doctors would stop using high-technology interventions at the end of life, the argument goes, then we could simultaneously respect patients' autonomy and save tens of billions of dollars.[8-11,14] When we link ethics and economics to prevent futile care, it is claimed, "everyone wins—the patient, the family, and society as a whole."[11]

Despite the allure of these arguments, we are skeptical. Before making major changes in policy regarding the care of dying patients and formulating budget projections on the basis of cost savings of billions of dollars, we should review the economics of care at the end of life. The cost savings that could be achieved through the wider use of advance directives, hospice care, and curtailment of futile care have not been well studied. The available data suggest, however, that such savings would be less than many have imagined.

Advance Directives for Health Care and Cost Savings

One study evaluating the effect of advance directives on costs randomly assigned outpatients to either a physician-initiated discussion of advance directives and encouragement to use them or no intervention. There was no difference in medical costs or other variables between the groups: as the authors stated, "executing the California Durable Power of Attorney for Health Care and having a summary copy placed in the patient's medical record had no significant positive or negative effect on a patient's well-being, health status, medical treatments, or medical treatment charges."[20] Although this study involved small numbers of patients at only two hospitals and measured charges rather than actual costs, similar preliminary results were reported in another study involving 854 patients who died at five medical centers.[21] Executing an advance directive did not significantly affect the cost of patients' terminal hospitalizations. The average hospital bill for those without an advance directive was $56,300, as compared with $61,589 for those with a living will and $58,346 for those with a durable power of attorney.[21] Additional studies are certainly needed, but these reports suggest that the wider use of advanced directives is unlikely to produce dramatic cost savings.

Hospice Care and Cost Savings

Hospice patients refuse life-sustaining interventions, favor palliative care, and are often treated at home; they serve as another source of information on the magnitude of the potential savings from the reduced use of high-technology interventions at the end of life. A series of studies comparing hospice care and traditional care of terminally ill patients estimated that in the last month of life, home hospice care saves between 31 and 64 percent of medical care costs. [22-27] The difference is accounted for mostly by the reduced use of hospital services. Consequently, the savings for hospital-based hospice care are lower. However, the longer patients receive hospice care, the smaller the savings. As the National Hospice Study reported, for hospice patients "the longer the stay in hospice, the more likely [it was that] costs incurred exceeded those of conventional care patients in the last year of life; the economies associated with hospice occur primarily in the last weeks of life."[28] During the last six months of life, the mean medical costs for patients receiving hospice care at home are 27 percent less than for conventional care, and the savings with hospital-based hospice care are less than 15 percent. [22,24,26]

These studies may systematically overstate the savings associated with hospice care. Most have not been randomized and may have incorporated a selection bias, since hospice patients by definition want less aggressive care. The one randomized study of hospice care found no cost savings for long-term hospice patients.[23] Patients receiving care in a hospice also tend to be from higher socioeconomic groups and to have informal support structures that enable them to obtain additional services, such as personal attendants not covered by Medicare, that are invisible in most cost estimates.[29] As rates of hospitalization decline, so, too, may the savings from hospice care.[22] Finally, an overwhelming majority of hospice patients have cancer, a fact that limits the generalizability of these data.[28]

Futile Care and Cost Savings

A related proposal to save money at the end of life is to reduce "futile care."[10,11] What constitutes futile care is controversial,[30-33] but the paradigmatic case is cardiopulmonary resuscitation for patients dying of cancer.[30-34] Unfortunately, there have been no studies of the financial consequences of eliminating resuscitation for patients with cancer. In a study of the cost of care for all patients with do-not-resuscitate (DNR) orders at a tertiary care hospital, almost 25 percent of whom had cancer, it was found that among patients who died, medical care for those with DNR orders cost about the same as for those without DNR orders: a mean of $62,594 for 616 patients with DNR orders as compared with $57,334 For 219 patients without DNR orders.[35]

Advocates of cost cutting have suggested extending the concept of futility to curtail marginally beneficial care.[10,11] Chemotherapy for unresectable non-small-cell lung cancer is an example of marginal if not entirely futile therapy; it does not systematically enhance longevity, improve the quality of life, or palliate pain.[36,37] A randomized trial in Canada, comparing chemotherapy with high-quality supportive care for patients with non-small-cell lung cancer, found that the average cost of the supportive care was $8,595 (in 1984 Canadian dollars), whereas one chemotherapy regimen cost less ($7,645) and another regimen cost more ($12,232).[38] Some aspects of this study are controversial, and some costs were approximated because they were "not routinely identified in the Canadian health care system."[38,39]

Nevertheless, the authors concluded that even if chemotherapy is expensive, "a policy of supportive care for patients with advanced non-small-cell lung cancer was associated with substantial costs."[38]

Can We Save Any Money on Care at the End of Life?

Can we realize any savings by the more frequent use of advance directives, hospice care, and less aggressive care at the end of life? We can estimate the proportion of health costs that might be saved in a best-case scenario—that is, if every American who died had executed an advance directive, refused aggressive care at the end of life, and elected to receive hospice care at home. The only reliable cost data for the last year of life are Medicare costs for patients 65 years of age or older; there are no reliable data on the total costs of health care for patients either over or under 65 who die. Consequently, many approximations are necessary in calculating the savings that can be realized.

In 1988, the mean annual cost per Medicare beneficiary who died during that year was $13,316.[15] Medicare primarily pays for acute care, however, and accounts for only 45 percent of total health care costs for those 65 years old or older; the bulk of the excluded costs are for nursing home care.[40] The simplest way to estimate the additional health care costs for Medicare beneficiaries who die is to assume they use the same fraction of these other services that they do of services covered by Medicare. This means that patients 65 or older who die in a given year account for 27 percent of total health care expenditures— Medicare costs, nursing home costs, and the costs of other services for all patients 65 or older. Thus, we estimate that patients 65 years old or older who died in 1988 spent $29,295 for all their health care services, of which $13,316 was covered by Medicare.

How should we estimate costs during the last year of life for patients less than 65 years of age? Although costs for younger patients who die of cancer and the acquired immunodeficiency syndrome (AIDS) are probably substantially higher than costs for dying Medicare patients,[41] the costs for those who die of accidents, suicide, and homicide are probably less. Scitovsky showed that among a group of California patients who died, the mean total medical costs for the last year of life were about the same for those under 65 years of age as for those 65 to 79 years of age.[42] In 1988, the mean Medicare cost for 65-to-79-year-old patients who died was $15,346 (Lubitz J: personal communication). Assuming that this is 45 percent of total health care expenditures, we can estimate that the mean annual medical cost for patients under 65 who died in 1988 was $34,102.

Table 38.1. Estimated Savings from Greater Use of Advance Care
Directives, Hospice Care, and Less Aggressive Interventions.*

Variable	Total (Age < 65 Yr)	Total (Age ≥ 65 Yr)	Medicare
No. of patients who died in 1988	0.68 million	1.49 million	1.49 million
Average cost of health care in the last year of life per dying patient	$34,102[†]	$29.295[‡]	$13,316
Savings from the use of advance directives, hospice care, and less aggressive interventions by all patients[§]			
—Savings per patient	$9,208	$7,910	$3,595
—Total dollar savings	$6.3 billion	$11.8 billion	$5.4 billion

Variable	Total	Medicare
1988 U.S. health care spending	$546 billion	$88.5 billion
Savings in health care spending (%)	3.3	6.1[¶]

Notes: *Expenditures are shown is 1988 U.S. dollars.

[†]Extrapolated from the estimated $15,346 in Medicare health care expenditures for patients 65 to 79 years old during their last year of life, which constitutes 45 percent of the total health care costs of these patients.[15]

[‡]Includes $13,316 for Medicare costs and $15,979 for health care costs not covered by Medicare for these dying patients in 1988.[15,40]

[§]Savings were calculated as 27 percent of the average cost of health care in the last year of life.

[¶]Percentage shown is of the entire Medicare budget, not of Medicare payments for patients over 65 ($73 billion in 1988).[15]

We know that 2.17 million Americans died in 1988, of whom 1.49 million were Medicare beneficiaries. Using the hospice data, and assuming that the maximum we might save in health care costs during the last year of life by reducing interventions is 27 percent,[22,24,26] we can calculate how much could be saved if each of the 2.17 million Americans who died executed an advance directive, chose hospice care, and refused aggressive, in-hospital interventions at the end of life. As Table 38.1. shows, the total savings in health care expenditures would have been $18.1 billion in 1988, or 3.3 percent of all health care spending. In 1988, the savings in Medicare costs would have been $5.4 billion, or 6.1 percent of expenditures.[43] Since the percentage of health dollars spent on patients who died has been constant over 30 years, the savings as a percentage of total national health care costs and Medicare spending is unlikely to change over time.[6,15,44]

This calculation relies on best-case assumptions that err on the side of overestimating savings. We have extrapolated the savings for patients who receive hospice care to the use of advance directives and to the reduced use of futile interventions. Yet not everyone would refuse life-sustaining interventions in their advance directives, and futile interventions are hard to define, let alone stop. Moreover, achieving savings of any considerable magnitude depends on decreasing the numbers of days spent in the hospital, yet over the past decade there has already been a significant decline in both the number of hospital days for all patients and the proportion of costs for patients who die that are allocated to hospital care.[15] Furthermore, curtailing care at the end of life is likely to affect acute care and thus Medicare costs, but unlikely to decrease nursing home and other outpatient costs; indeed, it may even increase such costs. (Excluding nursing home costs would reduce the total savings from $18.1 billion to $15.9 billion, or 2.9 percent of total health care spending.)

Reducing health care expenditures by 3.3 percent cannot be dismissed lightly. Yet even with the most generous assumptions possible, the savings will be less than the scores of billions of dollars predicted by many commentators and the savings estimated from cutting administrative waste.[8-11,14,45]

Why Is There Not Much Money to Be Saved at the End of Life?

Why, despite the high cost of dying documented for Medicare beneficiaries, is there not likely to be much in the way of cost savings from the use of advance directives, hospice care, and fewer high-technology interventions? One explanation is that the Medicare data produce a distorted image of the cost of dying. Commentators extrapolate the data for Medicare patients who die to the entire population.[8,10,11,14] Using 1990 expenditures, for example, Singer and Lowy calculate that "the care of patients who died" cost $184 billion (27 percent of the $661 billion spent on health care in 1990).[8] They suggest that $55 billion to $109 billion might be saved "from a policy of asking all patients about their wishes regarding life-sustaining treatment and incorporating those wishes into advance directives."

Although Medicare data on mortality and expenditures may be the only reliable figures available, they cannot be extrapolated without adjustment to the whole health care system. Less than 1 percent of the total American population dies each year, yet 5 to 6 percent of Medicare beneficiaries die. Five percent of Medicare patients may account for 27 percent of Medicare payments, but it is improbable that the less than 1 percent of the American population who die account for 27 percent of the total national spending on health care. We estimate that the 2.17 million Americans who die annually account for about 10 to 12 percent of health care expenditures.

It may be difficult to reduce substantially the percentage of health care expenditures spent on patients who die because humane care at the end of life is labor-intensive and therefore expensive. Even when patients refuse life-sustaining interventions, they do not necessarily require less medical care, just a different kind of care. High-quality palliative care—providing pain medications, helping in the activities of daily living, using radiation therapy for pain relief, and so on— requires skilled, and costly, personnel. Thus, even low-technology health care that is administered outside hospitals to terminally ill patients is not cheap.

Another explanation is related to the unpredictability of death. Since there are no reliable ways to identify the patients who will die,[6,44,46] it is not possible to say accurately months, weeks, or even days before death which patients will benefit from intensive interventions and which ones will receive "wasted" care. Retrospective cost studies will inflate costs at the end of life as compared with costs for patients known in advance to be dying because they include many patients receiving expensive care who are not expected to die yet do die. This clinical uncertainty also means that resources are initially expended until a patient's prognosis becomes clearer and physicians, patients, and the family are sure about either forging ahead with aggressive treatment or withdrawing it. This process is both ethically correct and what most Americans seem to desire.[47] Advance directives are unlikely to reduce this type of care, since physicians, patients, and family members are hesitant to discontinue therapy when there is a real chance of survival.

In addition, medical practice has changed over the past decade. For the vast majority of patients who die, DNR orders are already in place and other interventions are terminated. For instance, at Memorial Sloan-Kettering Cancer Center, 85 percent of patients with cancer who have cardiac arrest have DNR orders[48]; other institutions have reported rates of DNR orders among patients with cancer that are as high as 97 percent.[35] Currently, in tertiary care hospitals, between 60 and 80 percent of dying patients have DNR orders.[49-51] Admittedly, the decision to give a DNR order or withdraw life-sustaining treatment is usually made late in the course of a patient's illness. Nevertheless, given the steep rise in costs as death approaches, reducing care in these final days of life should yield the most savings.[15,35] As the data on hospice care demonstrate, there may be additional—but smaller— cost savings if the decision to stop treatment is pushed back several weeks.[22,24,26,28]

Finally, the increased use of living wills and health care proxy forms may not necessarily curtail the use of life-sustaining treatment. We have no empirical evidence that patients are getting substantially more treatment than they or their families want. Although there have been a few well-publicized cases in which physicians have treated patients against their wishes, these are probably unrepresentative.[52] Studies consistently show that physicians are more willing than patients and family members to withhold or withdraw life-sustaining treatments.[53,54] A large minority of people consistently want treatment even after they become incompetent or have a low chance of survival. For instance, about 20 percent of patients want life-sustaining therapy even if they are in a persistent vegetative state.[47] Similarly, about half of patients with AIDS want aggressive life-sustaining treatment, including admission to an intensive care unit and cardiopulmonary resuscitation, in circumstances in which they have a relatively poor chance of survival.[55,56] Thus, patients who complete advance directives may request more life-sustaining treatment than they currently receive, precluding any cost savings. In addition, studies demonstrate that family members are consistently more hesitant to withhold or withdraw life-sustaining treatment than the patients themselves.[53,54,57,58] Thus, if patients are encouraged to select proxy decision makers by executing durable powers of attorney, the cost savings may be minimal.

Conclusions

None of the individual studies of cost savings at the end of life associated with advance directives, hospice care, or the elimination of futile care are definitive. Yet they all point in the same direction: cost savings due to changes in practice at the end of life are not likely to be substantial. The amount that might be saved by reducing the use of aggressive life-sustaining interventions for dying patients is at most 3.3 percent of total national health care expenditures. In 1993, with $900 billion going to health care, this savings would amount to $29.7 billion. It is important to note that achieving such savings would not restrain the rate of growth in health care spending over time.[59] Instead, this amount represents a fraction of the increase due to inflation in health care costs and less than the $50 billion to $90 billion needed to cover the uninsured population.

The unlikeliness of substantial savings in health care costs does not mean, however, that there are no good reasons to use advance directives, fund hospice care, and employ less aggressive life-sustaining treatments for dying patients. Respecting patients' wishes, reducing pain and suffering, and providing compassionate and dignified care at the end of life have overwhelming merit. But the hope of cutting the amount of money spent on life-sustaining interventions for the dying in order to reduce overall health care costs is probably vain. Our alternatives for achieving substantial savings seem limited to major changes in the financing and delivery of health care, difficult choices in the allocation of services, or both. Whatever we choose, we must stop deluding ourselves that advance directives and less aggressive care at the end of life will solve the financial problems of our health care system.

References

1. Leaf A. Medicine and the aged. N Engl J Med 1977;297:887-90.

2. Turnbull AD, Carlon G, Baron R, Sichel W, Young C, Howland W. The inverse relationship between cost and survival in the critically ill cancer patient. Crit Care Med 1979;7:20-3.

3. Ginzberg E. The high costs of dying. Inquiry 1980;17:293-5.

4. Schroeder SA, Showstack JA, Schwartz J. Survival of adult high-cost patients: report of a follow-up study from nine acute-care hospitals. JAMA 1981;245:1446-9.

5. Bayer R, Callahan O, Fletcher J, et al. The care of the terminally ill: mortality and economics. N Engl J Med 1983;309:1490-4.

6. Scitovsky AA. "The high cost of dying": what do the data show? Milbank Mem Fund Q Health Soc 1984;62:591-608.

7. Scitovsky AA, Capron AM. Medical care at the end of life: the interaction of economics and ethics. Annu Rev Public Health 1986;7:59-75.

8. Singer PA, Lowy FH. Rationing, patient preferences and cost of care at the end of life. Arch Intern Med 1992;152:478-80.

9. d'Oronzio JC. Good ethics, good health economics. New York Times. June 8, 1993:A25.

10. Fries JF, Koop CE, Beadle CE, et al. Reducing health care costs by reducing the need and demand for medical services. N Engl J Med 1993;329:321-5.

11. Lundberg GD. American health care system management objectives: the aura of inevitability becomes incarnate. JAMA 1993;269:2554-5.

12. Schneiderman LJ, Jecker N. Futility in practice. Arch Intern Med 1993;153:437-41.

13. Murphy DJ, Finucane TE. New do-not-resuscitate policies: a first step in cost control. Arch Intern Med 1993;153:1641-8.

14. Godec MS. Your final 30 days—free. Washington Post. May 2, 1993:C3.

15. Lubitz JD, Riley GF. Trends in Medicare payments in the last year of life. N Engl J Med 1993;328:1092-6.

16. Lubitz J, Prihoda R. The use and costs of Medicare services in the last 2 years of life. Health Care Financ Rev 1984;5(3):117-31.

17. McCall N. Utilization and costs of Medicare services by beneficiaries in their last year of life. Med Care 1984;22:329-42.

18. Siu AL, Brook RH. Allocating health care resources: how can we ensure access to essential cure? In: Ginzberg E, ed. Medicine and society: clinical decisions and societal values. Boulder, Colo.: Westview Press, 1987:20-33.

19. Siu AL, Sonnenberg FA, Manning WG, et al. Inappropriate use of hospitals in a randomized trial of health insurance plans. N Engl J Med 1986;315:1259-66.

20. Schneiderman LJ, Kronick R, Kaplan RM, Anderson JP, Langer RD. Effects of offering advance directives on medical treatments and costs. Ann Intern Med 1992;117:599-606.

21. Teno J, Lynn J, Phillips R, et al. Do advance directives save resources? Clin Res 1993;41:551A. abstract.

22. Kidder D. The effects of hospice coverage on Medicare expenditures. Health Serv Res 1992;27:195-217.

23. Kane RL, Wales J, Bernstein L, Leibowitz A, Kaplan S. A randomised controlled trial of hospice care. Lancet 1984;1:890-4.

24. Spector WD, Mor V. Utilization and charges for terminal cancer patients in Rhode Island. Inquiry 1984;21:328-37.

25. Hannan EL, O'Donnell JF. An evaluation of hospices in the New York State Hospice Demonstration Program. Inquiry 1984;21:338-48.

26. Mor V, Kidder D. Cost savings in hospice: final results of the National Hospice Study. Health Serv Res 1985;20:407-22.

27. Brooks CH, Smyth-Staruch K. Hospice home care cost savings to third-party insurers. Med Care 1984;22:691-703.

28. Greer DS, Mor V. An overview of National Hospice Study findings. J Chronic Dis 1986;39:5-7.

29. Moinpour CM, Polissar L. Factors affecting place of death of hospice and non-hospice cancer patients. Am J Public Health 1989;79:1549-51.

30. Schneiderman LJ, Jecker NS. Jonsen AR. Medical futility: its meaning and ethical implications. Ann Intern Med 1990;112:949-54.

31. Tomlinson T, Brody H. Futility and the ethics of resuscitation. 1990;264:1276-80.

32. Lantos JD, Singer PA, Walker RM, et al. The illusion of futility in clinical practice. Am J Med 1989;87:81-4.

33. Loewy EH, Carlson RA. Futility and its wider implications: a concept in need of further examination. Arch Intern Med 1993;153:429-31.

34. Blackhall LJ. Must we always use CPR? N Engl J Med 1987;317:1281-5.

35. Maksoud A, Jahnigen DW, Skibinski CI. Do not resuscitate orders and the cost of death. Arch Intern Med 1993;153:1249-53.

36. Ihde DC. Chemotherapy of lung cancer. N Engl J Med 1992;327:1434-41.

37. Ruckdeschel JC. Is chemotherapy for metastatic non-small cell lung cancer "worth it"? J Clin Oncol 1990;8:1293-6.

38. Jaakkimainen L, Goodwin PJ, Pater J, Warde P, Murray N, Rapp E. Counting the costs of chemotherapy in a National Cancer Institute of Canada randomized trial in nonsmall-cell lung cancer. J Clin Oncol 1990;8:1301-9.

39. Rapp E, Pater JL, Willan A, et al. Chemotherapy can prolong survival in patients with advanced non-small-cell lung cancer—report of a Canadian multicenter randomized trial. J Clin Oncol 1988;6:633-41.

40. Waldo DR. Sonnefeld ST, McKusick DR, Arnett RH III. Health expenditures by age group, 1977 and 1987. Health Care Financ Rev 1989;10(4):111-20.

41. Riley G, Lubitz J, Prihoda R, Rabey E. The use and costs of Medicare services by cause of death. Inquiry 1987;24:233-44.

42. Scitovsky AA. Medical care in the last twelve months of life: the relation between age, functional status, and medical care expenditures. Milbank Q 1988;66:640-60.

43. Levit KR, Lazenby HC, Cowan CA, Letsch SW. National health expenditures, 1990. Health Care Financ Rev 1991;13(1):29-54.

44. Newhouse JP. An iconoclastic view of health cost containment. Health Aff (Millwood) 1993;12:Suppl:152-71.

45. Woolhandler S, Himmelstein DU. The deteriorating administrative efficiency of the U.S. health care system. N Engl J Med 1991;324:1253-8.

46. Schapira DV, Studnicki J, Bradham DD, Wolff P, Jarrett A. Intensive care, survival, and expense of treating critically ill cancer patients. JAMA 1993;269:783-6.

47. Emanuel LL, Barry MJ, Stoeckle JD, Ettelson LM, Emanuel EJ. Advance directives for medical care—a case for greater use. N Engl J Med 1991;324:889-95.

48. Vitelli CE, Cooper K, Rogatko A, Brennan MF. Cardiopulmonary resuscitation and the patient with cancer. J Clin Oncol 1991;9:111-5.

49. Gleeson K, Wise S. The do-not-resuscitate order: still too little too late. Arch Intern Med 1990;150:1057-60.

50. Smedira NG, Evans BH, Grais LS, et al. Withholding and withdrawal of life support from the critically ill. N Engl J Med 1990;322:309-15.

51. Bedell SE, Pelle D, Maher PL, Cleary PD. Do-not-resuscitate orders for critically ill patients in the hospital: how are they used and what is the impact? JAMA 1986;256:233-7.

52. Emanuel EI. Who won't pull the plug? Washington Post. January 2, 1994:C3.

53. Seckler AB, Meier DE, Mulvihill M, Cammer Paris BE. Substituted judgment: how accurate are proxy predictions? Ann Intern Med 1991;115:92-8.

54. Uhlmann RF, Pearlman RA, Cain KC. Physicians' and spouses' predictions of elderly patients' resuscitation preferences. J Gerontol 1988;43(5):M115-M121.

55. Steinbrook R, Lo B, Moulton J, Saika G, Hollander H, Volberding PA. Preferences of homosexual men with AIDS for life-sustaining treatment. N Engl J Med 1986;314:457-60.

56. Haas JS, Weissman JS, Cleary PD, et al. Discussion of preferences for life-sustaining care by persons with AIDS: predictors of failure in patient-physician communication. Arch Intern Med 1993;153:1241-8.

57. Emanuel EJ, Emanuel LL. Proxy decision making for incompetent patients: an ethical and empirical analysis. JAMA 1992;267:2067-71.

58. Steiber SR. Right to die: public balks at deciding for others. Hospitals 1987;61:72.

59. Schwartz WB. The inevitable failure of current cost-containment strategies: why they can provide only temporary relief. JAMA 1987;257:220-4.

— by Ezekiel J. Emanuel, M.D., Ph.D.,
and Linda L. Emanuel, M.D., Ph.D.

From the Division of Cancer Epidemiology and Control, Dana-Farber Cancer Institute (E.J.E.), and the Division of Medical Ethics, Harvard Medical School (E.J.E., L.L.E.), both in Boston. Address reprint requests to Dr. E. Emanuel at the Division of Cancer Epidemiology and Control, Dana-Farber Cancer Institute, 44 Binney St., Boston, MA 02115.

Chapter 39

Problems in Hospice Eligibility

Most people who die in hospice are cancer patients. To better understand which seriously ill hospitalized patients use hospice, researchers at The Center to Improve Care of the Dying (CICD) analyzed the data in the Study to Understand Preferences and Prognoses for Outcomes and Risks of Treatments (SUPPORT).

Analysis revealed that the type of disease had the greatest influence on whether patients enrolled in hospice. Those with diseases such as congestive heart failure and emphysema are far less likely to be enrolled in hospice than are those with lung or colon cancer. Patients with lung cancer are 24 times more likely to be enrolled in hospice upon discharge than are CHF patients. Colon cancer patients are 18 times more likely to be enrolled upon discharge. Only about 10 percent (469) of all of those who died used hospice care directly after hospitalization. The type of illness was the greatest influence on hospice enrollment, even after adjusting for other variables, including the effects of insurance status, DNR preferences, functional status, disease severity, hospital of enrollment, and demographics.

From "Many Dying Patients Are Not Eligible for Hospice Benefits: SUPPORT Data Analysis Highlights Problems in Eligibility Rules," by Zhenshao Zhong, in *ABCD Exchange,* July 1998 [Online]. Available: http://www.abcd-caring.com/jul98.htm. © 1998 by Americans for Better Care of the Dying (ABCD), 2175 K St. NW, Ste. 820, Washington, DC 20037. For complete contact information, please refer to Chapter 60, "Resources." Reprinted with permission.

Among those least likely to be transferred to hospice upon discharge were acutely ill elderly patients, and patients with:

- congestive heart failure (CHF),
- chronic pulmonary obstructive disease (emphysema or COPD),
- acute respiratory failure (ARF), or
- multiple system organ failure with sepsis (MOSF).

Why was it so much easier for cancer patients to be admitted to a hospice than CHF patients? In part because the hospice structure is best suited to [the] way most cancer patients die. Most cancer patients function fairly well for a time after diagnosis, then enter a recognizable phase of deterioration and die within a predictable and relatively short time period. This pattern matches federal guidelines, under which hospice is available to people whose physicians certify that they have "a life expectancy of less than six months."

Prognosis is more difficult to estimate for CHF patients because their survival time is so unpredictable. CHF patients usually reach a point where it is clear that there is no cure and that they will eventually die. However, CHF patients usually have a slow decline in function, punctuated by periodic life-threatening crises. Even one week before death, the median 6-month survival prognoses for patients in SUPPORT is about 65 percent.

Recently, hospice providers have been interested in serving more patients who have non-malignant diseases. However, the different courses of disease affect which patients can be enrolled in hospice. The National Hospice Organization (NHO) has developed the Medical Guidelines for Determining Prognosis in Selected Non-cancer Diseases. These guidelines aim to identify patients with non-malignant diseases whose 6-month prognoses are likely to meet the federal guidelines.

In another recent study, CICD applied various criteria, including those proposed by the NHO for enrolling CHF patients, to the 1,312 CHF patients who survived of the enrollment hospitalization in SUPPORT. Results showed that the recommended criteria for enrolling CHF patients in hospice greatly reduced the potential number of people who could enroll, without identifying a group which actually died much earlier.

Strategies that effectively identify patients with short prognoses yield such small cohorts that most patients dying of CHF will never be eligible for hospice. To make hospice-type services more available to patients with diseases other than cancer, changes will have to go beyond the current guidelines. One way to do this is being proposed through MediCaring, a demonstration project spearheaded by Americans for Better Care of the Dying. MediCaring is a new way to structure, finance, and deliver end-of-life services so that patients with diseases such as CHF and emphysema can receive comprehensive and continuous end-of-life care. The national demonstration project is scheduled to begin in October.

For more information, contact Zhenshao Zhong at (202) 467-2222 or e-mail ihozxz@gwumc.edu.

—by Zhenshao Zhong

Zhenshao Zhong, a research associate at the Center to Improve Care of the Dying, is a Ph.D. candidate in statistics at the University of Maryland at College Park. He has a master's degree from the University of Southern Mississippi. He has given several presentations at many professional conferences.

Chapter 40

Expanding the Hospice Time Frame

Los Angeles internist Robert A. Blackman remembers the weekend as one of the worst of his life. On a Friday he had to tell his patient, a woman in her late 40s, that she would not recover from her fast-spreading cancer. After trying to soften the blow, he walked out of the exam room to order tests. From behind the door, he heard a sound—half moan, half stifled scream—that cut through him. Here was a woman trying to come to grips with her impending death, and he felt powerless to help. At the same time, his 235-physician multispecialty group—HealthCare Partners Medical Group—had no program available to offer support.

Blackman re-entered the room and tried his best to soothe the woman. They cried together. Eventually she calmed down and left the office, but Blackman felt "like a basket case" all weekend.

That's when Blackman got the idea for Options—a program that provides coordinated care for patients who are not expected to live more than two years. It's considered "pre-hospice" because traditional hospice is open only to people with an even grimmer prognosis: six months. And unlike hospice, which offers palliative care only, Options allows patients to continue aggressive treatment if they wish. The traditional social support services of hospice, including pastoral counseling

Excerpted from "Expanding the Hospice Time Frame," by Deborah Grandinetti., in *Medical Economics,* Vol. 74, No. 17, pp. 65-8, August 25, 1997. © 1997 by Medical Economics Publishing, 2 Northfield Plaza, Winnetka, IL 60093. Reprinted with permission.

or visits with a social worker or psychologist, are available to Options patients, regardless of their course of treatment.

About 15 percent of Options patients want to fight for their lives, using modern medicine's entire arsenal. Others elect "everything but chemotherapy." Some 60 percent choose noncurative treatment; approximately one-third of this group have signed DNR [Do Not Resuscitate] orders.

Since so many Options patients request palliative rather than heroic care, the cost savings for Blackman's capitated, physician-owned group are presumed to be considerable. He can't quantify the amount, however, because it's difficult to account for money not spent on ER visits, ambulance service, diagnostic technology, or hospital stays.

A Glaring Patient Need That Was Going Unmet

Saving money wasn't the original impetus for Options, Blackman is quick to point out. He says he was simply trying to address needs that go unmet when patients walk out of their doctor's office knowing they've got a terminal illness. "Life will never be the same for the patient or his family," says Blackman. "Once you've broken the news, the patient has the sword of Damocles hanging over him. Traditionally, we in medicine have waited until things reached crisis proportions, when death was just around the corner, to provide patients with psychosocial and spiritual support."

Although hospice also addresses terminal patients' emotional needs and the inevitable family crises, Blackman says that the dying need more than six months to wrap up financial affairs and say good-bye to loved ones.

HealthCare Partners is able to accommodate 150 to 200 new Options patients a year, and some 800 have availed themselves of the unique blend of services so far. Virtually every primary care physician in the group's various regional offices has referred a patient to the program.

Annie Holman, an 85-year-old East Los Angeles woman who elected to fight her vaginal cancer with surgery and radiation treatment, found Options a blessing. Weekly visits from a home care nurse allowed her to convalesce in familiar surroundings—the home she had shared with her husband for five decades, until his death. These days, Holman is doing so well that her home care nurse has cut back to two visits a month. Holman says her doctors consider her cured. Now she's just dealing with age-related medical complaints.

"Everyone involved couldn't be nicer," says Holman. "I know I'm in good hands."

The Key: Customizing Care to What the Patient Wants

Enrollment in Options begins with the primary care physician. Although candidates can be identified during a hospitalization, a visit to the urgent care center, or a home health checkup by a nurse or social worker, only the primary care physician can make the referral.

Next, a medical social worker does a psychosocial needs assessment, and provides counseling to help the family bear up under the bad news. It's not unusual to encounter some resistance at this stage, says Mary Bonilla, HealthCare Partners' bilingual social worker. Patients and families sometimes fear that Options is an effort to give up on them because their care is too expensive. That attitude stems from a general distrust of managed care, as well as misunderstandings about the purposes of programs for the terminally ill. Bonilla makes sure that patients know they can choose continued aggressive treatment or palliative care—and that they can change their minds at any time. She also explains the range of services available through Options.

"We try to get as much information as possible about the patient, his home environment, and his support system," says Bonilla. "Then we figure out what we can offer—whether it's home care, behavioral health services, or placement in a nursing facility if the patient can no longer be managed at home." (About 20 percent of Options patients require this last alternative.) The medical social worker also functions as a patient advocate, sometimes making a case for services that the physician or administrators are reluctant to provide.

Home care, for instance, is offered infrequently because it's so expensive. But the group might send a physician's assistant to the home of a bed-bound patient to spare him the ambulance ride to the doctor's office, and to see how the family is holding up. "A lot of times I do more to treat caretakers than patients," says PA Joe Geare. "I ask how they're doing, and check on medications and blood pressure."

The Options team tries to provide patients with extra measures of comfort. Recently, for example, staff members made phone calls on behalf of a woman whose final wish was to see a nephew stationed overseas. Similarly, Options helped an AIDS patient coordinate a trip to his birthplace in Mexico without interrupting his treatment regimen. "He returned much stronger," says internist Mohinderjit Neelam, who oversees Options in the Montebello clinic of HealthCare Partners.

Custom Care Can Mean No Medical Treatment at All

The medical care that isn't given to Options patients is as important as the care that is. Geare remembers a patient in the pre-Options days who made it clear he wanted to die at home after one last visit with a brother in Russia. The brother came, and the patient's body began to shut down. But someone at the bedside panicked—Geare thinks it was the home health nurse—and called 911. The patient was rushed to the ER, where he was "saved." He spent a week in the intensive care unit before being placed in a nursing home.

"Two or three months passed before he was able to go home and die, which is what he wanted to do in the first place," says Geare. "He had severe rheumatoid arthritis, and when he was brought to the ER, they broke his ribs and stuck tubes in him—all the things you don't want done to you. Nobody had spoken with the family about signing a DNR order. With Options, that discussion is more likely to occur."

The cancer patient who inspired Options met much the same fate. "In the three or four months it took me to put this program together, she was gone," says Blackman. "And her scenario was so painfully typical. She cycled through the intensive care unit a couple of times, had liver failure and respiratory failure, and was intubated. By the end, she just wanted to be left alone."

The woman died in the hospital ICU, with her family in the waiting room—away from her bedside. "It was the worst possible situation for everyone," says Blackman. "It just cemented my desire to change things. I knew we had to play by a different set of rules and provide patients and their families with choices much earlier on."

It Takes Teamwork to Get Everything Done

Blackman's colleagues agreed that changes in treating dying patients were overdue; he encountered no resistance when he presented his idea for Options to his group. Physicians and staff formed a committee to make sure all the components of the program would mesh.

The committee decided to give Options team members wide autonomy, so they could customize services to dying patients without having to wade through a bureaucracy. "Every team member can call for more services one level below himself; the social worker, for example, can arrange for homemaking assistance," says Blackman. "This doesn't have to be cleared with me or the patient's primary care physician, but it does have to be reported at the next meeting."

The multidisciplinary team includes the attending physician (either a primary care doctor, specialist, or hospital-based physician), nurses, behavioral health specialists, an urgent care center representative to ensure that unwanted emergency care is not administered if someone calls 911, a managed care representative, a medical social worker, a medical records department representative to make sure all care is being properly charted, and someone from homemaker services.

Team members meet to discuss cases every four weeks. Doctors have found the input from the home health nurses and social workers especially valuable, internist Neelam says, because patients aren't always able to express themselves to physicians during 15-minute office visits.

Neelam cites a situation in which a cancer patient was afraid he'd insult his specialist if he sought a second opinion. Fortunately, the patient told the Options nurse, whom he had come to know during home visits. When the nurse relayed the information to Neelam, who supervises the program, the discussion ultimately led to the patient being referred to a well-known tertiary care center for a second opinion.

The team approach also relieves the physician of having to meet all of the terminal patient's needs single-handedly. According to Neelam, doctors previously referred patients to a social worker or psychiatrist in the hope that emotional needs would be attended to, but most patients didn't go.

"I like knowing that we're taking care of the total patient," says Neelam. "Sometimes, we're the only ones there for the patient during this time. Patients will get dressed up just to see us. It's an event in their lives."

That's not to say that the Options staff is always greeted with gratitude and open arms. "This can be hard," Neelam admits. "Patients go through all those stages: anger, denial, and so forth. Sometimes they'll get angry at us, but we still have to be there for them. There are times when they'll close the door on us, and then call later to ask where we've been." The behavioral health specialists who counsel dying patients and their families are also available to the Options staff to listen and provide coping strategies.

The Options venture may be too extensive for smaller groups to duplicate, but even a pared-down program can improve quality of life for patients who cannot be cured of their illness, says Blackman. "The important thing is to provide them with choice and a sense of control. Find out what they want and don't want. Then provide some form of psychosocial support. I'm sure most primary care groups have some kind of home nursing service and behavioral health care, whether it's in-house or a carve-out.

"Patients with support predictably do much better. I've seen them strengthen their will to live once they've regained some measure of control over their life and their disease."

—by Deborah Grandinetti

Chapter 41

The MediCaring Project

Supporters of an innovative project intended to provide comprehensive treatment and services for chronically ill patients near the
end of life are looking for clinical sites to demonstrate and evaluate
the costs and efficacy of the program.

The Center to Improve Care of the Dying at George Washington
University Medical Center and Americans for Better Care of the Dying (ABCD), both in Washington, DC, are in the process of recruiting
10 to 18 hospices, large group practices, or other health care provider
sites around the country that are willing and able to participate in
the MediCaring National Demonstration and Evaluation Project.
Each site that participates in the 3-year project will have to enroll
annually at least 100 patients with advanced congestive heart failure (CHF) or chronic obstructive pulmonary disease (COPD)—patients for whom hospice services are not generally available, said
Joanne Lynn, M.D., director of the Center to Improve Care of the
Dying and founding president of ABCD, and Anne M. Wilkinson,
Ph.D., associate research professor of health care science and medicine at George Washington University Medical Center.

Speaking at the Innovators in End-of-Life Care National Conference, in Crystal City, Va., Lynn and Wilkinson described MediCaring

From "MediCaring Project to Demonstrate, Evaluate Innovative End-of-
Life Program for Chronically Ill," by Andrew A. Skolnick, in the *Journal of the
American Medical Association,* Vol. 279, No. 19, pp.1511-2, May 20, 1998. ©
1995-1998 by American Medical Association, 515 N. State St., Chicago, IL
60610. All rights reserved. Reprinted with permission.

as an innovative program for providing coordinated and comprehensive care—including early intervention to prevent disease complications, and palliative, life-prolonging, and supportive services that are tailored to the needs of patients with a terminal chronic illness, such as CHF, COPD, stroke, or dementia.

"The dying have different care needs than those who are sick but stable or likely to improve," Lynn said. "Good care of the dying calls for interdisciplinary teams that provide continuity of integrated services across a variety of health care settings. This will require changes in the orientation and culture of providers and public alike."

MediCaring would prioritize services differently than is done now in conventional health care settings or hospices, she said. Each patient would have an advanced practice nurse or a physician or both to provide primary care. Services would include, but not be limited to, coordinated and comprehensive health care, appropriate emergency medical care, medical equipment and supplies, access to 24-hour "urgent" care advice from a nurse authorized to manage the patient's care via telephone, rehabilitation and environmental adaptation services, and inpatient respite care.

"To replace 'rescue' care that may no longer serve the patient or reflect responsible stewardship of resources within the health care system, creative combinations of 'aggressive' and 'supportive' care services would be available either at the patient's home or in an institutional setting," Wilkinson said. "However, unlike usual hospice practice, no treatment, such as cardiopulmonary resuscitation or intensive care, will be barred. Patients would not have to explicitly give up access to life-sustaining measures."

Facing a Fragmented System

According to Lynn and Wilkinson, a largely unanticipated result of advances in health and medicine has been the emergence of chronic diseases as the major pathway to death. A study of 1993 Medicare claims found that more than 80% of all decedents had at least 1 of 5 kinds of illnesses in the year prior to death: CHF, COPD, stroke, dementia, or cancer. The U.S. health care system historically has focused on the treatment of acute diseases and accidents and on rescue care, with cure as the goal. This type of care is not matched with the needs of people who face a prolonged course of increasing disability and eventual death from chronic illness.

Medicare beneficiaries living with advanced and progressive chronic illnesses now face a disorganized health care system, in which "health care services are fragmented, both by payer and by provider, leading to inefficiencies in service delivery and cost-increasing incentives to overtreat patients," Lynn said. "Dying today too often entails unnecessary pain and suffering, invasive and burdensome medical interventions, and financial ruin for many patients and families."

Most health care in the United States is organized by site of care (i.e., hospital or nursing home), by disease, or by intervention (i.e., cardiothoracic surgery or radiology). Medical records generated in 1 setting are often unavailable in another. End-of-life care often falls to physician specialists such as oncologists or cardiologists who traditionally focus on rescue; multidisciplinary teams who focus on nursing and social issues would provide more effective and appropriate supportive care. The MediCaring Project will attempt to resolve many of these problems.

Hospice and Cancer Model

"Many of our end-of-life care concepts are founded on the cancer model, which does not fit the majority of dying patients well," said Lynn. "Most patients with solid tissue cancers have a long period of functional stability despite progressive illness, followed by a relatively brief and predictable course of decline that usually lasts less than 6 weeks. If the patient is referred to a hospice, it usually is during the patient's terminal or 'failing' phase."

In contrast to the cancer model, chronic diseases such as CHF are marked by a declining course that is resistant to accurate prognosis and, most often, has no identifiable failing phase. Even when patients are severely disabled by these diseases, there usually are no clear physiological events that can lead a doctor to label the patient as "dying." Because death from CHF occurs mostly from unpredictable heart attacks, strokes, arrhythmias, or infections, the patient's death is generally seen as "sudden." Following social conventions, both physicians and patients avoid describing such patients as "dying" until they are unambiguously close to death, Lynn said.

The only programs now established for specialized end-of-life care are hospices. "Hospice has set the standard for good end-of-life care through the use of interdisciplinary teams that coordinate care and manage costs; a focus on patient and family as the unit of care; and reliable and effective service delivery," she said. "The program has enjoyed widespread approval."

About 80% of patients receiving hospice care in the United States do so under the Medicare hospice benefit. By electing hospice, through either Medicare or private insurance, patients agree to forgo "life-prolonging" interventions and, instead, receive comprehensive medical and support services not otherwise available under Medicare or their insurance.

However, the problems for patients who are nearing the end of life with an array of chronic illnesses cannot be addressed by the Medicare hospice benefit as it is now structured. Medicare restricts hospice benefits to people who have a terminal illness with a life expectancy of 6 months or less. "The relatively predictable, brief final course of cancer is well suited to the prognostic limit and hospice model of care," Lynn said. "However, individuals dying with diseases other than cancer generally do not have access to hospice care, mostly because their illnesses do not have clinically evident phases of overt decline at the end of life."

In addition, the requirement that 80% of the days of care be days at home often makes hospice care unavailable for those without family or others who can assist them with medications, hygiene, nutrition, and other services. Thus, hospice ends up serving only a small portion of the people who need end-of-life care. In 1994, hospices provided services to 340,000 dying patients, about 15% of total deaths in the United States, Lynn said.

Moreover, hospices serve patients for only a short time. Large hospice providers report that they now have median lengths of stay of less than 2 weeks. A study of Medicare hospice patients published in 1996 showed that median survival was only 36 days; nearly 16% died within 7 days of enrollment, 28% died within 14 days, and only 15% who enrolled in a hospice were alive for 6 months or longer, she said.

Likely to Reduce Costs

"The MediCaring National Demonstration Project will test the hypotheses that many people with a serious, eventually fatal illness would opt out of invasive, high-tech treatments that hold little promise of success if more appropriate, home-based supportive care were readily available, and that the care delivered through MediCaring would be better and less costly," Wilkinson said. The potential cost reductions from MediCaring would arise mainly from the reduction in acute care interventions made possible by aggressive preemptive community-based care and by honoring the treatment decisions of patients and families.

Patients eligible for MediCaring would have advanced, life-limiting illnesses such as CHF, COPD, stroke, or dementia. Unlike a hospice, eligibility for MediCaring would be based on disease severity using threshold measures that are specific to the chronic disease category, such as 2 hospitalizations within the past year for CHF, COPD, or both; COPD requiring continuous oxygen (PO2 <55 mm Hg at rest), or CHF with ejection fraction less than 0.30. "Because the program would not bar access to any particular treatment, it therefore would not take on the 'toxicity' of the hospice label, which many people resist, in part, because it is perceived as a harsh turning away from treatment and as a marker for imminent death," she said.

According to Wilkinson, phase I of the demonstration and evaluation project is expected to begin in June, with 6 to 8 sites that already have palliative care programs and are able to work within their existing payment systems. The U.S. Department of Veterans Affairs has been very active in the project's development and is likely to participate. Data from this first phase would be used to evaluate the efficacy and cost of the program in hopes of obtaining a decision from the Health Care Finance Administration (HCFA) to help pay for the care of patients who enroll at additional demonstration and evaluation sites.

All sites taking part in the project will use a uniform data collection process and a rigorous research design that will include standard instruments for measuring disease severity, treatment utilization, demographics, quality of life, satisfaction with services, and the meaningfulness of the dying experience for the families of patients. If the study shows the program is cost-effective, the data will be used to negotiate with HCFA to develop a capitation rate and/or payment scheme for approved MediCaring programs, Wilkinson said.

—by Andrew A. Skolnick

Chapter 42

Nursing Homes and Palliative Care

During the 1980s nursing homes emerged as a dominant site of death for the elderly. Prior to this time hospitals had been the dominant site of death for the elderly. Medicare's prospective payment system (PPS) may have augmented this change (Merrill and Mor, 1993). The PPS encouraged cost savings in the delivery of health care. Since deaths in the hospital setting consume greater quantities of resources than those in the nursing home (McMillan, Mentnech, Lubitz, McBean, and Russell, 1990; Mor, Banaszak-Holl, and Zinn, 1996) this may have influenced this shift in the site of death. In the context of the nursing home, however, this may precipitate more innovative approaches to death and dying in this setting.

A recent study by Brannon, Castle, Callaway, and Zinn (1995) determined that nursing homes are actively involved in many innovative activities, but these innovations have not been well studied. Likewise, few innovations in the process of death and dying have been investigated. This study examines innovative approaches to death and dying in the nursing home setting. Specifically, hospice care and pain management programs are examined.

Hospice care in nursing homes is an emergent trend, for example, the number of special care hospice units in nursing homes increased by 100 percent from 1992 to 1995. Providing hospice care to termi-

Excerpted from "Innovations in Dying in the Nursing Home: The Impact of Market Characteristics," by Nicholas G. Castle, Ph.D., in *Omega: Journal of Death and Dying,* Vol. 36, No. 3, pp. 227-40, 1997-98. © 1998 by Baywood Publishing Co., Inc., 26 Austin Ave., Amityville, NY 11701. Reprinted with permission.

415

nally-ill nursing home residents may positively affect these residents as well as the organizations that serve them. For example, improvements in psychosocial symptoms for nursing home residents can be attained using the hospice philosophy. Information can be shared among hospice workers and nursing home staff, perhaps providing for more complete assessment and care planning and ultimately resulting in more continuity and improved care.

Pain is a common complaint in the elderly. As many as 51 percent of the elderly suffer from pain daily, and 34 percent describe their pain as continuous (Ferrell, Ferrell, and Osterweil, 1990). Many nursing home residents also suffer from pain, especially the terminally ill (Elliot and Elliot, 1992). However, as Ferrell, Ferrell, and Osterweil (1990, p. 412) describe "strategies for pain management in the long-term care setting appear to be limited in scope and application" although this may be changing. As with hospice special care units, our data show pain management programs to be an emergent trend in nursing homes. These programs doubled from 1992 to 1996.

In view of the changes in the site of death of the elderly, the emergence of hospice care and pain management programs in nursing homes are trends that are likely to continue. However, they are trends about which we have virtually no information. As a first step in examining these phenomena we provide a descriptive analysis of nursing homes that provide hospice care or pain management programs and an analysis of the impact of market characteristics as determinants of nursing homes providing pain management programs or hospice care.

Hypotheses

The majority of persons in nursing homes are Medicaid recipients. Medicaid recipients provide a low level of funding to nursing homes and as a consequence it may be difficult for facilities to provide adequate services (Kim, 1990; Wagner, 1987; Wagner, 1988). The effect of Medicaid census is also modified by the Medicaid reimbursement policies of the state. States have some degree of flexibility in establishing nursing home payments (Buchanan, Madel, and Persons, 1991). Facilities operating under retrospective reimbursement are reimbursed for actual costs incurred, whereas prospective payment is more likely to pay a flat rate. Most other payment methodologies range between these two methodologies in stringency (Cohen and Dubay, 1990). As Banaszak-Holl, Zinn, and Mor (1996, p. 103) state "compared to retrospective reimbursement, payment of a flat rate makes it more difficult to anticipate coverage for the costs of care." Therefore, facilities operating under prospective reimbursement may be less able to innovate because of these low reimbursement levels.

Hypothesis 1: Nursing homes operating in markets with prospective Medicaid reimbursement are less likely to provide hospice care or pain management programs.

Many states have focused on containing the supply of nursing home beds as a strategy aimed at controlling their Medicaid costs. Common methods of constricting the bed supply are through Certificate of Need (CON) legislation and new construction moratoria. In addition, CON legislation and new construction limitations may be a barrier to entry into the long-term care market (Banaszak-Holl, Zinn, and Mor, 1996). This may increase the demand for nursing home services and facilities may be less inclined to innovate because a greater proportion of residents with medical need for nursing home care exist. Therefore, we hypothesize:

Hypothesis 2: Nursing homes operating in markets with CON legislation or new construction moratoria are less likely to provide hospice care or pain management programs.

Markets can vary in their degree of competitiveness. Pfeffer and Salancik (1978) believe that in more competitive markets organizations share a limited pool of resources. The degree of market competitiveness could affect nursing home care. For example, competition may promote more innovative use of resources. Therefore, a measure of competition from other nursing homes (the Herfindahl index) is included in this analysis, and we propose:

Hypothesis 3: Nursing homes operating in competitive markets are more likely to provide hospice care or pain management programs.

Nursing homes also compete with other providers. For example, hospitals also provide a variety of long-term care services to the elderly, both on an inpatient and outpatient basis. Thus, following hypothesis 3, we propose:

Hypothesis 4: Nursing homes operating in markets with hospital sponsored outpatient long-term care services are more likely to provide hospice care or pain management programs.

Hypothesis 5: Nursing homes operating in markets with hospital inpatient long-term care services are more likely to provide hospice care or pain management programs.

The abundance of resources available to organizations can vary. In some markets resources are relatively abundant. These are generally referred to as munificent environments (Staw and Szwajkowski, 1975). In munificent environments nursing homes may have the resources available to innovate. Resources of importance to nursing homes are likely to be the number of elderly in the area, average income, and the number of hospitals in the area.

Hypothesis 6: Nursing homes operating in markets with many elderly are more likely to provide hospice care or pain management programs.

Hypothesis 7: Nursing homes operating in markets with higher incomes are more likely to provide hospice care or pain management programs.

Hypothesis 8: Nursing homes operating in markets with many hospital beds are more likely to provide hospice care or pain management programs.

Finally, managed care plans are increasingly forging links with long-term care providers. This market development is not well researched. Some authors believe that managed care beneficiaries with specific conditions, such as AIDS, are likely to be cared for in these less costly long-term care alternatives (Banaszak-Holl, Zinn, and Mor, 1996; Mason, 1992). This may increase the propensity of nursing homes to innovate. Therefore, we propose:

Hypothesis 9: Nursing homes operating in markets with greater HMO penetration are more likely to provide hospice care or pain management programs.

Data and Methods

Data

The data used in this investigation come from two sources, the 1996 Medicare/Medicaid Automated Certification Survey (MMACS) and the

1996 Area Resource File (ARF). The MMACS contains facility and aggregated resident data routinely collected through the nursing home certification process. The MMACS is conducted by state licensure and certification agencies. MMACS files include data relevant to this study. This includes the number of nursing personnel, by job category and full-time equivalent (FTE) status, and the number of residents, by payer category. Other general facility characteristics included in the MMACS include facility ownership, number of beds, and the average census. Approximately 18,000 nursing home facilities of the 21,000 in the United States are included in this survey. Those nursing homes that do not seek either Medicare or Medicaid certification and are not included in the MMACs, however, these facilities have "a relatively minor market presence" (Zinn, 1993, p. 723) and are thus unlikely to have a significant impact on this study.

We also use the 1996 ARF (Area Resource File). This is a publicly available data set summarizing a large array of census, health, and social resource information for all counties in the contiguous United States (Stambler, 1988). This data is compiled from a number of data sources, including the American Hospital Association (AHA) annual hospital survey, the U.S. Census of Population and Housing, the Centers for Disease Control (CDC), and the National Center for Health Statistics (NCHS). These data are at the county level and are commonly used in health services research (e.g., Banaszak-Holl, Zinn, and Mor, 1996; Nyman, 1989). We use the ARF to measure market characteristics such as the level of competition in the county in which the nursing home is located, number of hospital beds, HMO membership, and average income.

Although some criticism of using county level data has been provided by Luft, Robinson, Garnick, Hughes, McPhee, and Hunt (1986), others found some utility in this approach (Banaszak-Holl, Zinn, and Mor, 1996; Garnick, Luft, Robinson, Maerki, and McPhee, 1987). Banaszak-Holl, Zinn, and Mor (1996, p. 106) believe that at the county level patterns of funding and patient origin are "reasonably approximate" to the long-term care market.

Analytic Approach

The MMACS and the ARF data are used to examine the effect of nine market factors on the prevalence of hospice care and pain management programs in 14,646 nursing homes. This excludes hospital based facilities, or facilities that are part of a retirement center, because they tend to be unrepresentative of other nursing homes in terms of both staff and clients (Burns and Taube, 1984). We assume that the prevalence of hospice care and pain management programs can be estimated as a multivariate logistic regression function of organizational and market factors. The general logistic regression models can be represented by the equations:

logit (hospice care) = f (market variables + organizational variables)

logit (pain management programs) =
f (market variables + organizational variables)

Operationalization of Variables

The dependent variables, hospice care and pain management programs, are included in the MMACS data and were coded as dummy (0, 1) variables for the logistic regression analyses. The market factors are Medicaid reimbursement methodology (Hypothesis 1), CON and building moratoria (Hypothesis 2), Herfindahl index (Hypothesis 3), competition from hospital-based outpatient services (Hypothesis 4) competition from hospital-based inpatient services (Hypothesis 5), number of elderly (Hypothesis 6), average income (Hypothesis 7), number of hospital beds (Hypothesis 8), and HMO penetration (Hypothesis 9).

Table 42.1. shows how the variables are operationalized in these analyses, and where applicable the coding for the multivariate logistic regression models are included. The operational definitions of most of these are obvious, therefore we only elaborate upon the Herfindahl index variable. The Herfindahl index is a measure of how competitive a market is in which the facility is located. In this analysis the county was considered to be the market. The Herfindahl index is constructed by combining the squared market shares of all facilities in the county, and determining each facility's percentage share of beds in the county. The index ranges from 0 to 1, with higher values indicating a greater market share in the county (White and Chirikos, 1988).

We know very little regarding the relationship between organizational variables and hospice care and pain management programs. Thus, which organizational factors to include in the analysis as controls was unclear. We include variables that are significant in examinations of the provision of other health services in nursing homes, including occupancy rate (Morris, Fries, Mehr, et al., 1994; Mor, Banaszak-Holl, and Zinn, 1996), ownership (Banaszak-Holl, Zinn, and Mor, 1996; Morris, Fries, Mehr, et al., 1994; Mor, Intrator, Fries, et al.,

Table 42.1a. Operational Definition of Variables (continued in Table 42.1b)

Variable	Data Source[a]	Operational Definition
Dependent variables		
Hospice care	MMACS	Facility with residents receiving hospice care (1)[b] or not (1)
Pain management programs	MMACS	Facility with residents receiving pain management (1) or not (0)
Facility characteristics		
Activities of Daily Living (ADLs)	MMACS	A facility score (0 to 1) based on six items from the MMACS including transfer, locomotion, dressing, eating, toilet use, bathing, and bladder continence. Increasing score indicates greater average impairment.
Nurse staffing ratios	MMACS	(a) FTE RNs/resident, (b)FTE LPNs/resident, and (c) FTE nurse aides/resident
Ownership	MMACS	For-profit (1) or not-for-profit (0)
Medicaid census	MMACS	Average Medicaid occupancy rate
Occupancy rate	MMACS	Average overall occupancy rate
Size	MMACS	Number of beds
Chain	MMACS	Member of a nursing home chain (1), or not (0)
Special care units	MMACS	Include units for: AIDS, dialysis, disabled children, head trauma, Huntington's, ventilators, Alzheimer's and special rehabilitation (1), or none of these (0)
Specialists	MMACS	FTE specialists (Occupational Therapy, Physical Therapy, and Speech Pathology)/resident

Table 42.1b. Operational Definition of Variables (continued from Table 42.1a)

Variable	Data Source[a]	Operational Definition
Market characteristics		
Market competition	ARF	(a) Herfindahl index: each facility's percentage share of beds in the county/sum of the squared market shares of all facilities in the county (0 to 1) (see White and Chirikos, 1988); (b) Number of hospital-based long-term care outpatient services; (c) Number of hospital-based long-term care in-patient services
Environmental munificence	ARF	(a) Number of elderly in the county; (b) average income in the county; and (c) number of hospital beds per 1,000 persons in the county
CON/Moratoria	§	If the state has either a CON law or a moratorium on the building of new nursing home beds (1), or not (0)
Medicaid reimbursement policy	§	Retrospective (1) or flat rate (0)

Notes: [a]MMACS = Medicare/Medicaid Automated Certification Survey; ARF = Area Resource File

[b]Coding used for logistic regression analyses shown in parentheses.

§Taken from Harrington, DuNah, and Curtis (1994).

in press; Zinn, Aaronson, and Rosko, 1993; Davis, 1991), chain membership (Davis, 1991), staffing levels including FTE LPNs, RNs, nurse aides, and specialist providers (Linn, Gurel, and Linn, 1977; Rudman, Slater, Richardson, and Mattson, 1993), special care units (Morris, Fries, Mehr, et al., 1994; Sloan, Linderman, Phillips, Moritz, and Koch, 1995), and Medicaid census (Morris, Fries, Mehr, et al., 1994;

Mor, Intrator, Fries, et al., in press). We also include activities of daily living (ADLs) as a facility level control for case-mix (Banaszak-Holl, Zinn, and Mor, 1996).

Methods

Thirty-three percent of facilities had a pain management program and 16 percent reported caring for hospice residents. The average number of FTE RNs, LPNs, and nurse aides per resident were 0.12, 0.17, and 0.41, respectively. The average number of FTE specialists per resident was 0.06. As for the facility characteristics most of the nursing homes were for-profit (73%), and the average size was 112 beds. The average occupancy rate was 86 percent and the average Medicaid census was 66 percent. Nineteen percent of facilities had special care units. With regard to market characteristics, 85 percent of facilities were in areas with CON or moratoria on the expansion of services, while 29 percent were in areas with prospective Medicaid reimbursement. The average Herfindahl index was 0.18. Table 42.2. presents these descriptive statistics.

Odds ratios and confidence intervals are presented for the two multivariate logistic regression models in Table 42.3. Thirteen variables are significant for pain management programs, five of these are market variables. The proportion of pain management programs are significantly lower if facilities are located in areas with CON/Moratorium (Hypothesis 2), have a higher Herfindahl index (Hypothesis 3), and hospital-based outpatient services (Hypothesis 4). The proportion of pain management programs [is] significantly higher if facilities are located in areas with prospective Medicaid reimbursement (Hypothesis 1) and hospital-based inpatient services (Hypothesis 5). These later two effects are in the opposite directions to those hypothesized. Eight facility level control variables are also significant for the provision of pain management programs.

Five market variables are significant for the provision of hospice care. The provision of hospice care is significantly lower if facilities are located in areas with a high Herfindahl index (Hypothesis 3), prospective Medicaid reimbursement (Hypothesis 1), and hospital-based inpatient services (Hypothesis 5). The likelihood that hospice care will be provided is significantly higher if facilities are located in areas with hospital-based outpatient services (Hypothesis 4) and greater numbers of elderly (Hypothesis 6). The effects for hospital-based outpatient services are in the opposite direction to that hypothesized. Eight control variables are also significant for the provision of hospice care.

Table 42.2. Descriptive Statistics *(N=* 14,646 facilities)

Variables	Mean (or %)	Standard Deviation
Dependent variables		
Pain management program	33%	—
Hospice care	16%	—
Market characteristics		
CON/Moratorium	0.85	—
Herfindahl index	0.18	0.24
Prospective Medicaid reimbursement	29%	—
Number of hospital beds/1,000 population	0.38	0.23
HMO membership/1,000 population	0.11	0.29
Hospital-based inpatient services	6.66	13.37
Hospital-based outpatient services	9.51	19.11
Number of elderly/county	76,209	155,642
Average income ($)/county	16,695	4,180
Facility characteristics		
FTE RNs/resident	0.12	0.51
FTE LPNs/resident	0.17	0.62
FTE nurse aides/resident	0.41	0.35
FTE specialists/resident	0.06	0.89
Bed size	112	65
For-profit	73%	—
Chain membership	53%	—
Average occupancy	86%	17%
Percent Medicaid	66%	23%
Special care units	19%	—
Activities of Daily Living	0.53	0.26

Table 42.3. Multivariate Logistic Regression Odds Ratio *(N =* 14,646 facilities)

| Independent Variables | Odds Ratios (95% Confidence Interval) | |
	Pain Management	Hospice Care
Market characteristics		
CON/Moratorium	0.84 (0.76-0.93)**	1.08 (0.88-1.14)
Herfindahl index	0.77 (0.58-1.00)*	0.55 (0.36-0.85)**
Prospective reimbursement	1.14 (1.04-1.25)**	0.82 (0.72-0.92)***
Number of hospital beds	1.04 (0.87-1.23)	0.93 (0.73-1.18)
HMO membership	0.99 (0.99-1.01)	0.99 (0.99-1.001)
Hospital-based inpatient services	1.02 (1.01-1.03)*	0.97 (0.95-0.98)***
Hospital-based outpatient services	0.99 (0.97-0.99)*	1.03 (1.02-1.04)***
Number of elderly	0.96 (0.90-1.02)	1.06 (0.97-1.14)
Average income	1.12 (0.88-1.42)	1.30 (0.96-1.75)*
Facility characteristics		
FTE RNs/resident	1.01 (0.92-1.12)	1.03 (0.93-1.14)
FTE LPNs/resident	0.81 (0.67-0.96)**	0.84 (0.66-1.05)
FTE nurse aides/resident	0.98 (0.91-1.05)	0.94 (0.84-1.05)
FTE specialists/resident	1.14 (1.05-1.23)**	1.001 (1.001-1.008)*
Bed size	1.42 (1.29-1.55)***	1.70 (1.52-1.91)***
For-profit	0.91 (0.83-0.99)**	1.28 (1.13-1.45)***
Chain membership	1.00 (0.92-1.01)	1.32 (1.18-1.47)***
Average occupancy	2.75 (2.08-3.63)***	1.94 (1.36-2.75)***
Percent Medicaid	0.58 (0.48-0.71)***	0.47 (0.36-0.59)***
Special care units	1.14 (1.05-1.23)**	1.19 (1.08-1.30)***
ADLs	2.34 (1.76-3.31)***	3.21 (1.98-4.26)***

Notes: *significant at $p < .05$
**significant at $p < .01$
***significant at $p < .001$

Discussion

Studying pain management programs and hospice care in nursing homes is important for the dying elderly. Both of these innovations substantially help elderly nursing home residents in the processes of death and dying. For example, elderly persons with cancer are common in nursing homes. Approximately 25 percent of these residents report excruciating pain. Clearly, pain management programs or hospice care have a place in the nursing home setting. Moreover, nursing homes are admitting greater numbers of subacute residents than in the past, which includes those that are terminally ill, further necessitating programs such as pain management and hospice care. However, nursing homes have less resources than other settings such as hospitals, and programs such as pain management and hospice care are not always available to residents.

This analysis examines the impact of market characteristics on the provision of these services. Admittedly, market characteristics are one of several factors that could influence the provision of pain management and hospice care. Other important factors include influential physicians and nursing home administration. These are no less important and should also be examined, although, market characteristics are an important area of research. Studies that examine physicians or nursing home administration, although useful, provide few guidelines for regulators concerned about the provision of these services, whereas, factors such as CON and prospective reimbursement are under legislative purview.

Two analyses are provided, each showing the effect of nine market factors on the provision of pain management programs and hospice care. The results are instructive in that five of the nine hypotheses are supported for the provision of pain management programs and five of the nine hypotheses are supported for the provision of hospice care. This provides strong evidence that nursing homes are sensitive to their market environment. Government regulations (Hypothesis 2), competition from other providers (Hypotheses 3, 5, and 6), and the overall munificence of the market (Hypotheses 6) all influence the prevalence of these two innovations in death and dying.

Two results for the provision of pain management programs were significant in a direction contrary to that which was hypothesized. We hypothesized that facilities in areas with prospective Medicaid reimbursement would be less likely to provide pain management programs (Hypothesis 1) because this form of reimbursement is more stringent than other Medicaid reimbursement methodologies. We found facilities in areas with prospective Medicaid reimbursement were more likely to provide pain management programs. It was also hypothesized that facilities in areas with hospital-based inpatient services would be less likely to provide pain management programs (Hypothesis 5). When we examine the provision of hospice care these effects were in the expected directions, but the effect for pain management programs was in the opposite direction to that hypothesized.

The result for hospice care was significant in a direction contrary to that proposed in Hypothesis 4. We proposed that facilities in areas with hospital-based outpatient services would be less likely to provide hospice care. We found facilities in areas with hospital-based outpatient services were more likely to provide hospice care. Although, the effect for pain management programs was in the expected direction.

Kimberly and Evanisko (1981) have advocated examining several innovations to produce a consistent picture of factors influencing their use. Similarly, Flood and Scott (1987) have shown that a narrow focus on single outcome measures [is] misleading, and may lead to erroneous, or incomplete conclusions. By including two innovations our approach might not capture the overall picture of nursing home innovations in death and dying. This may account for these contrary findings. However, one limitation of the data used in this study is that no other innovations related to death and dying are included in the data.

We also only include one case-mix variable, ADLs. However, in retrospect a single clinical measure is unlikely to be a sensitive measure of facility case-mix. This highlights a further limitation of this study in that only aggregate measures of resident level data are available. Therefore, when several case-mix variables are introduced, such as ADLs and incontinence, one cannot determine whether these aggregate measures account for the same residents and therefore overspecify the model. Thus, we choose to include one case-mix variable. More precise analyses require resident level data, such as that found in the Minimum Data Set (MDS).

In conclusion, our findings suggest that the provision of pain management programs and hospice care are becoming prevalent in nursing home settings. Our analysis also indicates that nursing homes are quite sensitive to their market environment and policy changes could encourage further increases in these service innovations in death and dying.

References

Banaszak-Holl, J., Zinn, J. S., and Mor, V. (1996). The impact of market and organizational characteristics on nursing home service innovation: A resource dependency perspective. *Health Services Research,* 31(1), 97-117.

Brannon, D., Castle, N. G., Callaway, A., and Zinn, J. (1995). Innovations in the nursing home industry: Results of a Delphi study. *Nursing Home Economics,* March, 8-12.

Buchanan, R. J., Madel, R. P., and Persons, D. (1991). Medicaid payment policies for nursing home care: A national survey. *Health Care Financing Review,* 13, 55-71.

Burns, B. J., and Kamerow, D. B. (1988). Psychotropic drug prescriptions for nursing home residents. *Journal of Family Practice,* 26, 155-160.

Burns, B. J., and Taube, C. A. (1984). Mental health services in general medical care and in nursing homes. In: B. Fogel, A. Furino, and G. Gottlieb (Eds.), *Mental health policy for older Americans: Protecting minds at risk* (pp. 63-84). Washington, DC: American Psychiatric Press, Inc.

Cohen, J. W., and Dubay, L. C. (1990). The effects of reimbursement methods and ownership on nursing home costs, case mix and staffing. *Inquiry,* 27, 183-200.

Davis, M. A. (1991). On nursing home quality: A review and analysis. *Medical Care Review,* 48, 129-166.

Elliot, T. E., and Elliot, B. A. (1992). Physician attitudes and beliefs about use of morphine for cancer pain. *Journal of Pain and Symptom Management,* 7, 141-148.

Ferrell, B. A., Ferrell, B. R., and Osterweil, D. (1990). Pain in the nursing home. *Journal of the American Geriatrics Society* 38, 409-414.

Flood, A. B., and Scott, W. R. (1987). *Hospital structure and performance.* Baltimore, MD: Johns Hopkins University Press.

Garnick, D., Luft, H., Robinson, J., Maerki, S., and McPhee, S. (1987). Appropriate measures of hospital market areas. *Health Services Research,* 22, 69-90.

Harrington, C., DuNah, R., and Curtis, M. (1994). *Trends in state regulation of the supply of long term care services; Will health reform increase regulation?* San Francisco, Institute for Health and Aging, University of Califomia (unpublished manuscript).

Kim, H. (1990). Long-term care chains retrench to stem losses. *Modern Healthcare, 20,* 66-74.

Kimberly, J. R., and Evanisko, M. J. (1981). Organizational innovation: The influence of individual, organizational, and contextual factors on hospital adoption of technological and administrative innovations. *Academy of Management Journal, 24,* 689-713.

Linn, M., Gurel, L., and Linn, B. (1977). Patient outcomes as a measure of quality of nursing home care. *American Journal of Public Health, 67,* 337-344.

Luft, H., Robinson, J., Garnick, D., Hughes, R., McPhee, S., and Hunt, S. (1986). Hospital behavior in a local market context. *Medical Care Review, 43,* 217-251.

Mason, K. (1992). Caring for people with AIDS. *Provider, 18,* 30-44.

McMillan, A., Mentnech, R., Lubitz, J., McBean, A. M., and Russell, D. (1990). Trends and patterns in place of death for Medicine enrollees. *Health Care Financing Review, 12,* 1-7.

Merrill, D. M., and Mor, V. (1993). Pathways to hospital death among the oldest old. *Journal of Aging and Health, 5,* 516-535.

Mor, V., Intrator, O., Fries, B. E., Phillips, C., Teno, J., Hiris, J., and Hawes, C. (in press). Changes in hospitalization associated with introducing the resident assessment instrument. *Journal of the American Geriatric Society.*

Mor, V., Banaszak-Holl, J., and Zinn, J. S. (1996). The trend towards specialization in nursing care facilities. *Generations,* Winter, 24-29.

Morris, J. N., Fries, B. E., Mehr, D. R., Hawes, C., Phillips, C., Mor, V., and Lipsitz, L. A. (1994). MDS Cognitive Performance Scale. *Journal of Gerontology: Medical Sciences, 49*(4), M174-M182.

Nyman, J. (1989). Analysis of nursing home use and bed supply in Wisconsin 1983. *Health Services Research, 24,* 511-538.

Pfeffer, J., and Salancik, G. R. (1978). *The external control of organizations: A resource dependence perspective.* New York: Harper and Row.

Rudman, D., Slater, E. J., Richardson, T. J., and Mattson, D. E. (1993). The occurrence of pressure ulcers in three nursing homes. *Journal of General Internal Medicine*, 8, 653-658.

Sloane, P. D., Linderman, D. A., Phillips, C., Moritz, D. J., and Koch, G. (1995). Evaluating Alzheimer's special care units: Reviewing the evidence and identifying potential sources of study bias. *The Gerontologist*, 35, 103-111.

Stambler, H. (1988). The area resource file: A brief look. *Public Health Reports*, 103, 184-188.

Staw, B. M., and Szwajkowski, E. W. (1975). The scarcity-munificence component of organizational environments and the commission of illegal acts. *Administrative Science Quarterly*, 20, 345-354.

Wagner, L. (1987). Flat earnings spur nursing home chains to bolster balance sheets. *Modern Healthcare*, 17, 146-147.

Wagner, L. (1988). Nursing home giants pull back, smaller chains advance as industry profits plunge. *Modern Healthcare*, 18, 40-54.

White, S. L., and Chirikos, T. N. (1988). Measuring hospital competition. *Medical Care*, 26(3), 256-262.

Zinn, J. S., Aaronson, W. E., and Rosko, M. D. (1993). Variations in the outcomes of care provided in Pennsylvania nursing homes: Facility and environmental correlates. *Medical Care*, 31(6), 475-487.

Zinn, J. S. (1993). The influence of nurse wage differentials on nursing home staffing and resident care decisions. *The Gerontologist*, 33(6), 721-729.

— by Nicholas G. Castle, Ph.D.,
Brown University, Providence, Rhode Island

Supported in part by the Agency for Health Care Policy and Research (AHCPR) Institutional National Research Award (#HS 00011) and the Health Care Financing Administration (HCFA) Changing Nursing Homes Grant (#17C 90428). Direct reprint requests to Nicholas G. Castle, Ph.D., Director: Health Outcomes Research, AtlantiCare Health Systems, 6725 Delilah Road, Egg Harbor Township, NJ 08234.

Chapter 43

A Holistic Approach to
Care of the Dying

Twenty years ago, Illich complained that the medicalization of
health care in Western societies was also usurping individuals' right
to control their own dying:

> Like all other major rituals of industrial society, medicine in
> practice takes the form of a game. The chief function of the phy-
> sician becomes that of an umpire. He is the agent or representa-
> tive of the social body, with the duty to make sure that everyone
> plays the game according to the rules. The rules, of course, for-
> bid leaving the game and dying in any fashion that has not been
> specified by the umpire. Death no longer occurs except as the
> self-fulfilling prophecy of the medicine man (Illich, 1976, p. 205).

Illich was concerned that attempts by legal and ethical scholars
to draw moral boundaries to prevent various forms of hastening death
were ignoring the phenomenon of medicalization. He contended that
the medical termination of life was not a burning issue before the
medicalization of terminal care contributed to the extension of life
beyond natural bounds.

Some still share Illich's concern, if not his call for demedicalization
of society, and have raised other concerns regarding medicine's role

Excerpted from "The Medicalization of Dying: A Positive Turn on a New
Path," by R. J. Connelly, Ph.D., in *Omega: Journal of Death and Dying,* Vol.
36, No. 4, pp. 331-41, 1997-98. © 1998 by Baywood Publishing Co., Inc., 26
Austin Ave., Amityville, NY 11701. Reprinted with permission.

in death and dying. Recent developments, however, suggest that medicalization of dying has the potential for dramatically improving patient care, rather than curing, in the last stages of living.

The first section of this [chapter] briefly describes the origin and evolution of the new dying-well path of medicine that is grounded in holistic values. The next section shows why physician-assisted suicide (PAS) is demanding access to this path. The focus is on the Timothy Quill challenge. The remaining sections examine from a holistic perspective various criticisms of PAS, and suggest further research necessary to establish consistency and clarify ethical implications of using the dying-well path in medicine.

Medicalization—Two Paths

Until recently, medicine seemed to be obsessed with the new technology for saving lives that emerged after WWII. The goal of prolonging life, or equivalently, fighting against death, defined the main path of medicine. Whenever medicine could battle no more, dying patients in effect were left by the wayside with a minimum of comfort care and pain medication. It was clear to patients that saving their lives with technology was a higher priority than helping them die well without it. Nevertheless, medicine maintained control over the dying process and three-quarters of the population ended up dying in hospitals and long-term facilities under physician care.

Today, medicine seems to be moving toward a more balanced view of its role in death and dying. There are signs that medicine is becoming more holistic, that it has begun to take advantage of a new path, although a decidedly smaller side path, in the direction of helping patients die well.

The newer holistic path was first staked out in the mid-70s. Society and medicine began to realize that limits were necessary to check the unfettered technical progress in saving lives. The 1976 California Natural Death Act cited the problems related to medical technology that made it possible to "artificially prolong human living beyond natural limits" but also occasioned unnecessary pain, suffering, and loss of patient dignity. In response, natural death laws reinforced patient rights, while trying to maintain medicine's overall control of the dying process. Patients can forgo life-saving medical treatment, but only if physicians are the ones to determine: 1) that there is a terminal condition which is irreversible and further treatment would offer no further benefit, 2) what counts as life-saving treatment that can be removed, since most laws do not provide a list of possible treatments that are permitted, and 3) that the patient is competent. Physicians also control the use of drugs and other palliative means for relieving pain and discomfort. And the physician, of course, will be there to disconnect the machines that are to be discontinued, to pronounce death when it occurs, and then harvest organs if possible.

Nevertheless, with natural death legislation, medicalization has taken on a more positive meaning than Illich envisioned. These laws have stimulated medicine to be more responsive to the holistic needs of the dying patient. Death is being viewed more as a personal and moral, not just a clinical, event. Consequently, patients, not physicians, have primary responsibility for deciding when to refuse life-sustaining treatments. Death also is being seen as a natural part of the life cycle, not an aberration or unnatural event. Physicians seem more open to forgoing treatment when they can see beyond their own agency and acknowledge that the cause of death can be attributed to the underlying disease or condition when allowed to run its natural course. And the double effect doctrine, rather than an absolutist stance that never risks causing death, has been commonly accepted among physicians as a method of justification for relieving pain even if the means used to do so hastens death. In sum, medicine is becoming more sensitive to the total life context in which death occurs. The patient's right to say no to life-saving treatment is generally recognized and physicians are better at assuming a partnership, rather than a paternalistic, role in such decisions.

The hospice movement has contributed to clearing this new path in medicine. Hospice has evolved somewhat independently of medicine but currently remains a satellite enterprise attached to medicine. The physician by law must be the care team leader even though the philosophy of care is more collaborative than the traditional hierarchical model of health care. Hospice explicitly advocates a holistic philosophy that views the dying process, like all of life, as involving significant challenges to growth in all dimensions of mind, body, spirit, and relations with others. For example, hospice stresses that the family should be an integral part of end-of-life decisions. This is a new (or perhaps old) perspective when compared with natural death laws which focus almost exclusively on individual patient autonomy.

The hospice movement also has nudged medicine to become more self-conscious and sophisticated in using drugs for pain control. Pain does not always occur in terminal cases, but when it does it can be personally devastating. There is also increased awareness in medicine of the distinction between pain and suffering. As Cassel articulated this difference over ten years ago, pain refers to a person's perception that a breakdown is occurring in the body. And suffering refers to a "state of severe distress associated with events that threaten the intactness of the person" (Cassel, 1982, p. 640).

Medicine seems to accept this distinction in acknowledging that physicians "have an obligation to relieve pain and suffering and to promote the dignity and autonomy of dying patients in their care" (AMA, 1996, p. 40). Hospice would say that the goal of administering pain medication is to provide as much relief from suffering as possible so that patients can be restored to relative wholeness and handle effectively whatever challenges come with their dying.

Responding to the needs of the whole person also seems to be the spirit behind the AMA statements opposing euthanasia and assisted suicide.

Instead of engaging in euthanasia [or participating in assisted suicide], physicians must aggressively respond to the needs of patients at the end of life. Patients should not be abandoned once it is determined that cure is impossible. Patients near the end of life must continue to receive emotional support, comfort care, adequate pain control, respect for patient autonomy, and good communication (AMA, 1996, pp. 55-56).

In theory, this reinforces the idea that a second path is emerging in medicine today. On the traditional life-saving path, aggressive treatment is directed primarily at curing the patient's underlying disease. The goal is to prolong life, and compassionate care is subordinate to this goal. After successful treatment, patients are expected to return to their normal world and the pursuit of well-being as they envision it. On the newer dying-well path, aggressive efforts in compassionate care are to be directed more immediately at the quality of life, holistic needs of the person. There seems to be a growing sense of responsibility in medicine for helping persons experience well-being in the here and now of their dying, whether in the hospital or at home.

The threat of legalized PAS has stimulated much needed action along this path. Passage of the Oregon legislation occasioned the establishment of numerous pain control and comfort-care programs around the state (Lee and Tolle, 1996). The Oregon Health Science Center increased instruction about end-of-life care to medical students. And physicians are referring more patients to hospice. At the national level, in the last two years the AMA House of Delegates has approved recommendations, for example, that should lead to more research on improving care for the dying, education of providers, especially about pain control, and clarification of the meaning of "futile care."

434

Physician-Assisted Suicide (PAS)

In the United States there is general consensus, after twenty years of heated debate, that physician assistance in forgoing life-saving treatment is appropriate when the patient is voluntary, competent, and the condition is terminal and irreversible. The debate is just heating up over issues surrounding PAS. There seems to be strong public and medical support for this practice as the Oregon vote and various opinion polls indicate. Some of the arguments in favor of PAS are consistent with the holistic objectives of the dying-well path, even though current AMA policy and virtually all professional health care organizations, including the National Hospice Organization, prohibit PAS.

Timothy Quill's recent articles and book challenge AMA policy and are an example of a cautious attempt to encourage medicine further along the dying-well path. He describes the experience of supplying his patient Diane with sufficient drugs to relieve pain but also hasten death. That experience encouraged him to develop seven Potential Clinical Criteria for PAS. "Clinical" underlines his intent to place PAS clearly within the scope and control of medicine and the physician role. In the past, when physicians assisted their patients, it was more of a question of personal conscience and moral decision making that fell outside the professional role.

Quill's criteria, like those in the recent Oregon legislation, respect choice and view the physician as a facilitator. Patients may choose to hasten death, but physicians must be present at critical moments to oversee medically related aspects of the process: 1) to provide information on medical prognosis and options, 2) to determine patient competency from the vantage point of a meaningful doctor/patient relationship, 3) to be sure that requests for assistance are repeated and are not the result of inadequate comfort care, 4) to determine with another physician that the condition is incurable, and 5) to determine that the condition is associated with "severe, unrelenting, intolerable suffering" (Quill, 1993, p. 162). This last criterion seems to set a standard that would apply to very few patients. But Quill implies that the degree of suffering is a matter of patient subjective evaluation. At the time that Diane was ready to take her life, Quill (1993, pp. 169-170) notes that

> her suffering had become intolerable to her. Not only was acute medical treatment unacceptable, but at the end, traditional comfort care measures offered little of value to Diane. In her eyes, since death was inevitable, why subject herself to the

435

humiliation of total physical and emotional dependence on others for her last moments.

Quill is vague about the physician's responsibility for assessing the degree of suffering on more objective grounds. Nor is it clear to what extent he communicated with the family or thought they should be involved in the decision-making process.

What is clear is that Quill intends to position himself further on down the same path medicine and society began traveling with natural death legislation. On this path, medicine tries to assure that when bodies can no longer be cured, persons still can die with dignity. At this point, the holistic dimensions that define quality of life as determined by the patient, and hopefully family, become more significant than the goal of prolonging life. And the physician has the role of a facilitator who brings the expertise and techniques of medicine to bear on helping persons die well.

Healing as the Goal of Medicine

Examination from a holistic point of view of some of the arguments against PAS may suggest needed research for clarifying medical options on the dying-well path.

Some opponents of PAS have argued that medicalization of the practice of assisted suicide contradicts the traditional goal of medicine to heal and do no harm. This criticism fails to make a crucial distinction between the two paths adopted by medicine, one to cure disease and one to help the dying. We should not automatically assume that the logic of one can be used to critique the other, or that one path is reducible to the other. The saving-life path tends to rely more on the traditional biomedical model and its emphasis on physical health. For example, in an emergency situation actions are immediately taken to repair the body and, because of the urgency of the situation, very little attention is paid to more holistic concerns. On the other hand, in ordinary life situations, as when persons elect the dying-well path, holistic interests may gain prominence so that quantity of life is a secondary issue. For example, many behaviors that provide satisfaction in daily life, like smoking, may in fact shorten life.

But even though the objectives of the two paths are different, the overall goal of healing as broadly construed is comprehensive enough to include both. An older Anglo Saxon meaning for "heal" is to make or become whole. If we can interpret wholeness to mean a balance and integration of body, mind, spirit, and relations with others, then healing would be the restoration or better integration of wholeness. Curing disease is one form of such healing, and compassionate care of the dying is another. The paths represent complementary approaches, not necessarily irreconcilable differences in philosophical assumptions about the goals of medicine. But more needs to be done in developing a model of complementarity that emphasizes the broad goal of healing for medicine and reflects a more holistic approach.

Determination of Quality of Life

Callahan has long criticized a broader definition of healing as not within the competence of medicine.

It is not medicine's place to determine when lives are not worth living or when the burden of life is too great to be borne. Doctors have no conceivable way of evaluating such claims on the part of patients, and they should have no right to act in response to them (Callahan, 1992, p. 55).

Callahan is surely right in asserting that physicians on their own cannot make quality of life decisions for their patients. This, however, is not a dilemma specific to the dying stage, as Veatch shows in his article on the inadequacy of the general concept of informed consent in health care (Veatch, 1995). Only patients can adequately assess what treatments mesh with their best interests.

Does it necessarily follow that physicians should not assist in suicide? Callahan makes it sound like physician action without full knowledge of patient quality of life is a brand new challenge. Historically speaking, of course, physicians have always made quality of life determinations, in all kinds of situations including life-threatening ones, and assumed a right to act in both starting and stopping treatments, and in some cases to assist in suicide or even administer euthanasia.

More recently, patients have begun to reclaim their rights to make such decisions but also to enlist cooperation from physicians. Today the focus is on assisted suicide.

What is the basis for saying that a physician has the right to participate in suicide? Western medicine in the twentieth century has played a unique role in the dying process and this may entail unique responsibility. As Illich argued, physicians have contributed directly to the medical dilemma that patients find themselves in and from which they now seek release. Physicians must accept major responsibility for the development and wide-spread use of aggressive technology at the end of life. Further, medical science is the source of research and development for all potentially lethal drugs, and physicians are the gatekeepers who decide who has legal access to them. In the clinical setting, physicians are uniquely situated to help patients who choose to hasten death. Physicians know about the medical condition of their patients, their decision-making capacity, degree of suffering, effective and humane methods of dying, and how to determine when death has occurred (Cranford, 1996). And they have legal access to lethal drugs.

Other options for taking your own life without the aid of a physician are limited: find a Kevorkian, or ask family and friends with plastic bags and other questionable and often violent means, or do-it-yourself by using whatever happens to be in the medicine cabinet. If people knew how to produce reliable, painless hemlock on their own, they might not need to request physician help.

As things stand now, medicine seems to bear some responsibility for using its special knowledge and experience to assure efficient and humane dying including suicide. This form of assistance is logically closer to assistance in forgoing treatment than it is to euthanasia or directly killing patients. But the line is a fine one.

In any case, it seems that we are rapidly approaching the point of having to decide as a society, not whether, but how to accommodate and regulate PAS. Short of regulation we can look forward to more mishandled and degrading suicide attempts as individuals try to take matters into their own hands (Morain, 1994). Kevorkian's machines do seem humane and reliable, even though it appears that his actions so far fall short of satisfying criteria like Quill's. The pragmatic public policy response is to develop clear criteria that include medical supervision in medical institutions and with adequate safeguards that minimize abuse.

Quick Fix?

Regulating PAS does represent further medicalization of dying, a step beyond forgoing treatment, but it need not imply the "quick fix" mentality that Kass decries.

> Having adopted a largely technical approach to healing, having medicalized so much of the end of life, doctors are being asked . . . to provide a final technical solution for the evil of human finitude and for their own technical failure: If you cannot cure me, kill me (Kass, 1989, p. 35).

This criticism may carry more weight against euthanasia as mercy killing than PAS. There is growing evidence that medicine, having adopted more of a holistic approach, is beginning to seriously explore the middle ground of care between cure and the direct killing of patients as in the Netherlands. Medicine is seeking better ways to identify and then address factors that can lead to requests for hastening death. These factors include: clinical depression, inadequate pain control or social support, concerns about being a burden, feelings of hopelessness, fear of abandonment, or loss of self-esteem.

But, at the same time, medicine must become more sensitive to the possibility of rational suicide based on holistic criteria in a pluralistic society. Moral pluralism means that some competent patients will decide on suicide. Their perceptions of quality of life, the balance of physical, mental, emotional, spiritual, and relational components, may lead them to judge that enough is enough and desire to hasten death. Learning to respect such decisions and then facilitating patient action, by the willing physician, seems consistent with the dying-well path.

In this sense, it seems we could use more of a quick fix for the dying. Physicians and patients should initiate at an earlier stage discussions about the option of shifting to the dying-well path of care, whether or not that includes PAS. The art of medicine is knowing when and how to help patients make their decision earlier rather than later, as happens all too often now. More research is necessary to identify the obstructions to earlier dialogue about options at the end of life.

Hope

The role of hope in particular deserves more consideration. What are the dynamics of hope and how can we better understand what happens when the shift occurs from hope for a cure to hope for compassionate care and satisfaction of other holistic needs of the patient? Thus far, most of the research has concentrated on hope for a cure. How do religious beliefs, cultural values, the presence of family and others, and the institution of medicine influence this shift or inhibit it?

We also need to dispel the illusion that health care providers either give or take away hope. This mistakes hope for a commodity to be dispensed or withheld. Providers can communicate information about the possibility of recovery and other options. But patients must respond with a hopeful attitude toward recovery or decide what is worth hoping for. It seems better to view hope as a matter of patient responsibility rather than a benefit bestowed by medicine. That is not to say that medicine cannot have a strong influence on the quality and directionality of hope. How it does so deserves more investigation. We also need to know more about current attitudes and beliefs of physicians and other providers as regards hope.

The Meaning of Death

We also should take a fresh look at what is meant by death, the causes of death, and the timing of death. If we look at dying as a holistic process, then biological factors obviously are relevant. But in a holistic context, the biological is integrally connected with mental, emotional, spiritual, and relational factors. How can we separate quantity and quality of life issues? For example, it would seem that the timing and circumstances of dying are always a matter of control and responsibility, not just in refusing treatment or committing suicide. The process of dying is prolonged/hastened by our whole history, by everything we are and do and allow others to do to us, and not just at the end of life. To identify the underlying disease as the cause of death is to focus on the tip of the iceberg and underestimate all the other factors and decisions that can influence death. "Underlying disease" is the biomedical language of the saving-life path. How relevant is it when patients are on the holistic dying-well path at the end of life? We seem to need new concepts and language to better reflect a holistic way of understanding death and dying.

Intentionality

Intentionality as it has been discussed with the doctrine of double effect also deserves more analysis from a holistic perspective. The traditional reading, that physician intent must be to relieve pain but not cause death, is stated in the physicalistic and biomedical terms of the saving-life path of medicine. But, as noted above, medicine now seems to recognize that the dying-well path assumes an interconnection between pain and suffering. And suffering indicates that more must be addressed than just physical symptoms. From a holistic perspective, it would seem that use of pain medication, for example, has the overall goal of providing patients the comfort and clarity of mind necessary to attend to whatever wholeness or well being means to them. The guideline of not directly intending physical death may not do justice to the complexity of end-of-life decisions that a holistic approach takes for granted.

440

How do we evaluate alternative holistic expressions of intent? Could we say that pain medication is intended to support that degree of wholeness that the patient desires at the end of life? Or, could we combine the latter with the intent of bringing about peaceful unconsciousness that precedes death? More needs to be done in developing holistic theories of intentionality that fit better with dying well than familiar consequential and deontological formulations. Perhaps casuistry or narrative ethics hold some promise here.

Drugs

A holistic perspective also challenges us to evaluate our accepted ideas about the nature of drugs. According to the biomedical model, drugs as "magic bullets" are chemical substances aimed at combating specific problems in the body. But medicine already acknowledges, if somewhat reluctantly, a more holistic view of drugs as complex, multi-dimensional phenomena created by many factors operating in the patient and the total healing environment. Studies of the placebo response, the emergence of psychoneuroimmunology, and alternative medicine, all attest to the complex and potent holistic dimensions of drug use. This should stimulate us to be open to other ways of thinking about and using drugs in the care of the dying, including PAS.

It could be argued that even in the case of assisted suicide, drugs may produce many positive, holistic effects and serve many ends besides those of relieving physical pain and causing physical death. For example, providing drugs can be a sign of respect for patients and their decisions about dying. It also reinforces the perception that physicians are not abandoning patients in their time of greatest need. Having drugs in hand can reassure patients and family/friends that if patients follow through with suicide, then it will be efficient and successful because of the physician's directions on how much drugs to use and the physician's presence if further [counsel] or intervention is necessary. Not having to worry about the technical means to hasten death frees patients to concentrate on last minute wholeness adjustments to body, mind, spirit, and relations with others. In fact, the positive effects of providing drugs may lessen anxieties and fears to the extent that patients subsequently decide not to take the drugs, and then die naturally. This phenomenon has been reported by a number of physicians who have supplied drugs for their patients (Morain, 1994; Back, Wallace, Starks, and Pearman, 1996). But even if patients do take the drugs, does that fact morally negate the positive effects just discussed? Could we conclude overall that the act of providing drugs can stimulate a multifaceted placebo response in patients that contributes positively to their experience of wholeness in dying? More anecdotal evidence needs to be compiled to validate the latter conclusion.

Conclusion

This article has argued that medicalization of dying is a positive development to the extent that medicine has begun to adopt a more holistic approach to dying. Further study is warranted to explore the connection between the two paths of medicine, and the possible impact of holistic thinking on the biomedical model. We also need to clarify and explore the ethical implications of commitment to the dying-well path, including the most pressing issue of PAS.

Perhaps the best answer to Illich's call for radical demedicalization of society is to show that the two existing paths of medicine, saving life and dying well, can converge so that holistic values are present at every level of encounter between patients and physicians and other health care providers. Then, those who are severely ill will not have to wait until the bitter end to be shunted over to the path of dying well. Dying will be seen as a natural event in the life process, not the enemy of medicine. And "aggressive" care of the dying, even that which hastens death, will be a more common expectation, not the means of last resort when aggressive curing fails.

References

American Medical Association (1996). *Code of medical ethics: Current opinions with annotations.* Chicago, AMA.

Back, A. L., Wallace, J. I., Starks, H. E., and Pearman, R. A. (1996). Physician-assisted suicide and euthanasia in Washington. *Journal of the American Medical Association, 275,* 919-925.

Callahan, D. (1992). When self-determination runs amok. *Hastings Center Report, 22,* 52-55.

Cassel, E. (1982). The nature of suffering and the goals of medicine. *New England Journal of Medicine, 306,* 639-645.

Cranford, R. E. (1996). The physician's role in killing and the intentional withdrawal of treatment. In T. L. Beauchamp (Ed.), *Intending death.* Upper Saddle River, NJ: Prentice Hall.

Illich, I. (1976). *Medical nemesis.* New York: Pantheon Books.

Kass, L. (1989). Neither for love nor money: Why doctors must not kill. *Public Interest, 94,* 25-46.

Lee, M. A., and Tolle, S. W. (1996). Oregon's assisted suicide vote: The silver lining. *Annals of Internal Medicine, 124,* 267-269.

Morain, C. (1994). Out of the closet on the right to die. *American Medical News, 37 (Dec 12),* 13-15.

Quill, T. (1993). *Death and dignity.* New York: W. W. Norton.

Veatch, R. (1995). Abandoning informed consent. *Hastings Center Report, 25,* 5-12.

— by R. J. Connelly, Ph.D.,
University of the Incarnate Word, Texas

Direct reprint requests to R. J. Connelly, 4301 Broadway, San Antonio, TX 78209.

Part Five

Approaching Death

Chapter 44

Alleviating Common Physical Discomforts as Death Approaches

Executive Summary

Patients at the end of life experience many of the same symptoms and syndromes, regardless of their underlying medical condition. Pain is the most obvious example, but others are difficult breathing (dyspnea), transient episodes of confusion and loss of concentration (cognitive disturbances and delirium), loss of appetite and muscle wasting (cachexia), as well as nausea, fatigue, and depression. Taken together, these and other symptoms add significantly to the suffering of patients and their families, and to the costs and burden of their medical care. Yet in many cases the symptoms could be treated or prevented.

Pain, for example, is a multibillion-dollar public health problem in the United States. Over half of all cancer patients experience pain related to their disease or its treatment. Similarly, half of all cancer patients and 70 percent of all hospice patients experience shortness of breath in the last weeks of life. Yet dyspnea remains under-diagnosed and under-treated. Forty percent of all patients experience cognitive disturbances during the final days of life, and high numbers of terminally ill patients experience cachexia regardless of their primary disease. Significantly, these symptoms occur not in isolation but in clusters, with most patients experiencing combinations of symptoms

Excerpted from "Symptoms in Terminal Illness: A Research Workshop," [Online] September 22-23, 1997. Available: http://www.nih.gov/ninr/end-of-life.htm. Produced by the National Institutes of Health. For complete contact information, please refer to Chapter 60, "Resources."

that vary greatly in their prevalence and severity, as well as in the suffering they cause.

Basic research has improved our understanding of the underlying mechanisms of symptoms that are commonly experienced at the end of life, particularly with respect to pain. Clinical research has in some cases translated this knowledge into new drugs and other interventions that can effectively relieve or prevent these symptoms, even where the underlying disease cannot be cured. At present, however, there remain a number of important gaps in knowledge.

Clinical care would benefit from an integrative, multidisciplinary research initiative that brings basic and clinical researchers together to address the *constellation* of symptoms at the end of life. The following areas should receive priority:

- Epidemiology. There is a need for better data on the incidence and combinations of symptoms that are experienced at the end of life in specific populations. Epidemiological data will demonstrate the magnitude and costs of the problem, as well as suggest specific topics for basic and clinical research.

- Basic research. Additional research is needed on the mechanisms and interactions of these symptoms, including biochemical, neuronal, endocrine, and immune approaches. The possibility of common factors, mechanisms and pathways across different symptoms should be examined. There is also a need for research on the mechanism of action of successful therapies, with particular attention to the role of opioid receptors. This research could lead to therapies that are better targeted, more selective in their action, and thus produce fewer side effects.

- Clinical research. Because these symptoms have multiple determinants, and occur in clusters, successful interventions will also be multifactorial, including behavioral as well as pharmacological approaches. Combination therapies and off-label drugs should be explored. Researchers should be alert to differences in outcome based on age, gender, and underlying disease. Interventions to mobilize psychosocial and spiritual resources may be of help mediating the perception and interpretation of symptoms. The goal of research should be to test a wide range of interventions that could be successfully implemented in the home or hospice, as well as in the hospital.

- Methodology. Researchers will need better tests for diagnosing and assessing the level of severity of these symptoms, as well as for monitoring the effectiveness of interventions. Standardized terminology and definitions of symptoms should be established. Particular attention should be paid to validating subjective and nonverbal measures. Better data and tools are also needed for evaluating outcomes, in order to determine costs and strengthen accountability for the quality of care at the end of life. It is important to develop and use measures which reflect the subjective experience of the effects of symptoms on quality of life.

Research is also needed on the ethical issues that may be barriers to research at the end of life, including the needs and protection of vulnerable populations, especially the role of privacy during this important phase of life. Attention must be paid to community and individual preferences about the relative value of symptom management at different points in the dying trajectory, and to the development of comprehensive strategies for the early detection and treatment of the full range of symptoms at the end of life—an approach that will reduce costs as well as burdens, while preserving the patient's dignity and quality of life.

Background

There is widespread dissatisfaction in the United States with care at the end of life. A recent investigation, the "Study to Understand Prognoses and Preferences for Outcomes and Risks of Treatments" (SUPPORT) documented many problems with the delivery of palliative care in the U.S. and has received considerable attention and response in the medical literature. Broad public interest in and support for physician-assisted suicide is widely viewed as a proxy for public dissatisfaction with the medical profession's concern for and treatment of the terminally ill.

There has been substantial professional response to these concerns. The Institute of Medicine conducted an important study "Approaching Death: Improving Care at the End of Life". Many of the major medical professional organizations now have initiatives to improve health care provider education, quality of care of the terminally ill, and public perceptions of their profession's concern for palliative care. Several major foundations have established multi-million-dollar initiatives in various aspects of palliative care. The Robert Wood Johnson Foundation is establishing a national program to fund demonstration projects in palliative care. Palliative care is the focus of its most recent annual report, and the foundation is convening a nationwide videoconference ". . . on the current state of dying in America, and how we can achieve a better death for loved ones and ourselves." The Soros Foundation has established the Project on Death in America, which, among other things, funds research, demonstration projects, and training fellowships. The Commonwealth Fund and the Milbank Memorial Fund also have end-of-life or palliative care initiatives.

The end of life is finally being recognized as an important phase of life, one in which individuals have the right to expect quality of life and the opportunity to address key personal issues. Yet as Dr. Robert Dunlop, the head of St. Christopher's Hospice in England, noted in a recent interview, it is only "when pain and symptoms like breathlessness and nausea are controlled, [that] patients can move on to focus on more important, emotional issues—on anxieties about death, and on decisions about relationships, medical care, and finances that might have been put off." Good symptom control is an essential component of quality care at the end of life.

In the recommendations made at the conclusion of its study, the Institute of Medicine recognized the need for action on the part of clinicians, educators, researchers, policy makers, and the public. Specifically, the nation's research establishment was encouraged to strengthen the knowledge base of end-of-life care, to advance basic and clinical research on the physiological mechanisms and treatments of symptoms common during the end of life.

The Research Workshop "Symptoms in Terminal Illness" was convened by the National Institutes of Health (NIH) to accomplish three principal goals: (1) to summarize the current state of knowledge concerning the most common symptoms associated with terminal illness; (2) to identify important needs and opportunities for research that would be appropriate for NIH funding; and (3) to initiate a process for enhancing interdisciplinary collaboration and interagency collaboration in research in palliative care.

The workshop was organized into four topic sessions that focused on specific symptom areas: pain, dyspnea, cognitive disturbances, and cachexia/wasting. During each session, presenters addressed these symptoms from three perspectives: clinical (prevalence and current treatment strategies), basic (pathophysiology), and methods (measurement and experimental design). Following these presentations, the participants broke out into four working groups to identify priorities, and reconvened to present their recommendations to the entire group. This document summarizes those presentations and recommendations, with a particular focus on the compelling research opportunities.

Overviews

Issues from a Clinician's Perspective, Dr. Ira Byock

Palliative care takes place in a context where, by definition, cure is no longer possible and disease modification provides diminishing returns. In such a context, there is a need for new research markers—especially subjective measures of outcome such as physical comfort and "quality of life"—that are relevant to the lived experience of patients and their families. That experience is not limited to the absence of pain, or functional status, but can also include such spiritual states as peacefulness or sense of life completion.

There are certain symptoms and physiological problems that demand scientific attention. Pain is foremost among them, and with it the attendant problem of blocking nociception without causing psychological or gastrointestinal side effects. Other symptoms that deserve priority attention are dyspnea, delirium, and cachexia—symptoms that are addressed below. Several new medications may be worthy of study, but there is also a need to study combinations of medications, a research area that is ignored, leaving clinicians to rely on anecdotal evidence on the efficacy and compatibility of medications in combination. In addition, there is a need for research on preventing and/or treating the side effects of those interventions (e.g., nausea and constipation), and for controlled trials of alternative routes of medication (e.g., transdermal and inhaled) that might increase efficacy or reduce side effects.

Finally, many patients experience suffering that is not primarily physical in etiology. Consequently, there is a need for better screening tools for depression, better psychiatric and counseling approaches, and better pharmaceutical and nonpharmaceutical treatments for depression and other psychological symptoms in the context of progressive, incurable disease.

In response to questions, Dr. Byock suggested that the greatest need was for assessment tools for evaluating terminally ill patients. Other participants suggested that there should be broader use of the analgesics that are already available, and to concentrate on common characteristics of pain across various diseases. Participants acknowledged the difficulties associated with identifying the "transition point" at which disease becomes terminal. Several participants recommended

451

greater attention to the *setting* of terminal care, which is more likely to be outpatient and even in the home.

Symptoms Commonly Experienced in Terminal Illness, Dr. Russell Portenoy

Researchers are continuously challenged by the complexity of symptoms in advanced disease. Survey research has shown that patients with advanced disease experience multiple symptoms, some of them more severe or distressing than others. In most cases these include both physical symptoms—fatigue and pain—and psychological distress.

One study found that pain was the most *prevalent* symptom among advanced cancer patients (89 percent of respondents), followed by weakness, anorexia, dyspnea, constipation, early satiety, fatigue, and dry mouth, all experienced by over 40 percent of patients. When patients were asked to rate the *severity* of their symptoms, 87 percent of those who experienced pain rated their symptoms as moderate to severe. Another study, however, found that other symptoms were more *distressing* to terminal patients than pain, including dyspnea, asthenia, dry mouth, anorexia, depression, and insomnia.

More recent research using the Memorial Symptom Assessment Scale (MSAS) has found that fatigue is the most prevalent of 32 symptoms in adult cancer patients, but that three of the five most prevalent symptoms are inherently psychological: worrying, feeling sad, and feeling nervous. Most patients experienced multiple symptoms, an average of 13.7 symptoms per inpatient and 8.9 per outpatient among 240 cancer patients, and 17.5 among 450 ambulatory AIDS patients. Analysis has also shown that the average number of symptoms per patient is highly associated with impairment and quality of life.

Symptoms are also multidimensional, varying not only in frequency, intensity, and distress, but also in *desire for treatment*. For this reason, multidimensional analysis yields more information, for example, by revealing comorbidities among symptoms. It also reveals interactions among symptoms, pointing to the possibility of symptom complexes that might affect the results of clinical studies. For example, there appear to be statistically significant relationships between pain and nausea, and between pain and dyspnea, but not between nausea and dyspnea. Symptoms are also dynamic, changing over time, and they appear to have a relation to survival. Symptoms of physical distress, in particular, are an independent predictor of survival time in cancer patients.

452

These findings point to several issues. First, symptoms need to be examined over time within the context of the underlying disease. Multiple related variables must be considered, including the consumption of analgesics, adjuvant analgesics used in conjunction with treatment protocols, and pharmacokinetic variability among patients. Secondly, attention must be paid to methods issues. Further evaluation of the reliability, validity, and utility of research instruments is needed for a better understanding of the role of interviewer, instruction, and respondent bias. Improvements are needed in methods of analysis to address missing data.

Finally, there is a need to investigate the impact of practice change and systems change. There needs to be research to test whether systematic attention to various symptoms makes a difference in patient outcomes. Obviously, however, the ultimate goal would be the development of evidence-based decision-making tools for evaluating and treating patients with specific constellations of symptoms.

Pain

Of the four symptoms addressed at the workshop, pain has been the most studied by basic researchers, clinicians, and health services investigators. As a result, it may offer some lessons— positive and negative—for other symptoms.

Clinical Perspective, Dr. Richard Payne

Pain is a multibillion-dollar public health problem and the number-one reason for patients to see a health care provider, accounting for 42 million patient visits per year. Surveys show that 55 percent of cancer patients experience disease- or treatment-related pain. Yet despite evidence of the effectiveness of the "analgesic ladder" promulgated by the World Health Organization (WHO), studies also show that pain is undertreated in as many as 46 percent of patients, based on comparison of reported severity with the potency of the prescribed analgesic. From the clinical perspective, this raises four major research issues: (1) assessment, (2) therapies, (3) medical decision making, and (4) health policy.

Inadequate assessment is probably the principal barrier to the effective treatment of pain in both hospital and outpatient settings. The challenge for research, therefore, is to develop better tools for evaluating and managing patients with pain. This is particularly true for patients in the home, perhaps using computer- or telephone-based

453

interactive systems. There is also a need to validate behaviorally based assessment tools in nonverbal children, cognitively impaired patients, and culturally diverse populations.

Neuropathic pain remains a particularly difficult challenge for clinical assessment and treatment. Studies have shown that 70 percent of patients do not get effective relief from opioids alone for peripheral neuropathy. There is a need for research on microneurography and pharmaceutical probes, correlating results with patient self-reports.

The complexity and variability of pain as a symptom points to the need for more selective and individualized therapies. Despite the impressive statistical validation of the WHO analgesic ladder, there are still some patients for whom available therapies are not enough. Better therapies are needed for these patients, including pharmacotherapies that are better targeted and more specific in their action. In some cases this will mean targeting specific pain receptors in order to improve efficacy or reduce side effects; in others it will mean combinations of analgesics, possibly in conjunction with antagonists for neurotransmitters that are implicated in inflammatory and central sensitization. These improvements require a better understanding of the mechanisms of drug action.

Large-scale clinical trials are currently underway that will evaluate pain-management protocols as part of a cancer-treatment protocol. These and other studies, which would be appropriate for NIH funding, should be effective in moving more effective practices from pain-management specialists into mainstream medical practice. The end point of this research is to transform the selection of interventions into new standards of practice for the treatment of pain. Further research will be needed on the influence of patient preferences, practitioner biases, and the influence of the health care system on the implementation of these standards.

Finally, there is a need for health policy research that will facilitate the transfer of clinical trial findings into general practice. This will include both outcomes research and cost-effectiveness research. But it must also include outreach efforts to encourage the implementation of evidence-based guidelines by physicians, for many of whom the issue of effective pain management is not yet a high priority.

Basic Perspective, Dr. Donald Price

Pain is an ideal model for examining the relationship between nociception, cognition, and emotion. The nociceptive input itself is perhaps the least measurable aspect of the process. This sensation, accompanied by arousal, leads to cognitive appraisal—awareness of pain as pain— and an initial affective response. This stage 1 affect is largely one of intrusion—at least initially, pain is an annoyance, an unpleasantness, an immediate distress.

Over time, however, as the symptom continues and the patient ruminates on it, there is a growing awareness of pain as a disruption to normal life and routines, a possible threat to future happiness and even to life itself. This stage 2 affect corresponds to suffering, in its usual sense, and gives rise to depression, frustration, anxiety, anger, and even fear. Both stage 1 and stage 2 affect can be expressed in words or behaviors.

This model has both physical and psychological dimensions. Typically, however, neurobiologists treat pain as a physical stimulus-response process in the peripheral neurons that leads to verbal and behavioral expression by the patient. Working essentially as neurophysicists, they have successfully developed a neurobiology and psychophysics capable of explaining the sensory processing of pain, including (most recently) neuropathic pain.

But pain also and more importantly leads to unpleasant emotions, and there is thus a need for the parallel investigation of the hedonic or emotional processing of pain. Experiments with normal volunteers as well as patients have shown that there are consistent and significant differences between the *intensity* of the stimulus and its *unpleasantness*. In some kinds of clinical pain, such as labor pain, the emotional response—the meaning of the pain—can moderate and even outweigh the immediate physical sensation. Researchers have also been able to use hypnotic suggestion to manipulate the perceived unpleasantness of a controlled stimulus, such as electrical shock or heat pulse. These results confirm that there is a psychological component in the processing of pain.

Using positron emission tomography (PET) scans, researchers have been able to identify the brain structures that are involved in the physical and emotional processing of pain stimuli. While both areas are activated during pain, the S-I and S-II somatosensory cortex shows no difference in response to high and low unpleasantness. The anterior cingulate cortex, on the other hand, shows significantly greater activity during high-unpleasantness stimulus. These areas of the brain have not been extensively investigated by sensory biologists, although they are known to be active in gustatory processing.

Psychological testing has also revealed that patients who score high for neuroticism, variously measured, showed no difference in their response to the immediate unpleasantness of experimental or clinical pain. However, neurotic patients did demonstrate much higher levels of depression and frustration in response to chronic pain. This suggests that personality profile can also be a powerful influence on stage 2 affect. These findings point to the need for psychological research on the relationship between pain and suffering, and for the development of a "psychology of suffering," just as there are the beginnings of a pharmacology of suffering.

Methods Perspective, Dr. Charles Cleeland

Three fundamental assumptions drive the workshop's focus on pain: that too many patients experience the symptoms of pain; that most of these symptoms can be effectively treated; and that resources (federal and other) should be committed to finding those treatments. From the policy perspective, however, the assumptions are somewhat different: that reducing needless pain would be of value; that there would be the will to do so if we knew the way to do so; and that research can show us the way.

There are two methodologies for pursuing this research. The first is descriptive research, and considerable progress has been made in this avenue. That is, past research has established that pain is poorly managed, that it can be better managed, and that certain predictable groups are at risk for poor pain management, namely women, minorities, and the underserved. Research has also established that most health care professionals are not adequately trained in pain management, and the costs of pain, in dollars and in quality of life, are very high. It is even possible to characterize the levels of pain that patients experience, and to make comparisons across institutions, regions, and nations in terms of pain management.

The questions that remain to be answered have to do with what kind of interventions are needed to change this situation. Institutionally, for example, what is the relative value of pain control to the general community, how can you make it a treatment priority, and what can be done to make poor pain control just as much of an embarrassment for the hospital as poor infection control would be? How do patients and their families negotiate for better pain relief? And what policy or economic interventions would make a difference in the performance of hospitals and physicians?

A number of recent and ongoing studies are designed to answer these questions. Several randomized clinical studies are being sponsored by NCI-funded cancer cooperative groups. These studies are designed to assess motivational and skill changes among patients (e.g., how to report pain), to improve the assessment skills and knowledge base of health care professionals (e.g., personnel exchanges), or to provide new models and protocols for medical practice (making something happen when pain reaches a certain level). The results have been promising, but to date most of these studies have been small and inconclusive and need to be repeated.

In the discussion that followed, there appeared to be general agreement that pain, and especially cancer pain, is an area in which it is important to move beyond descriptive research to intervention studies. At the same time, pain paves the way for other symptoms: research on fatigue, in particular, has advanced rapidly in part because of the methodological advances made by pain researchers. Consequently, efforts to advance pain research will also help to advance knowledge in other symptom areas. This also points to the need for collaboration and cross-fertilization across medical specialties.

Dyspnea

Clinical Perspective, Dr. Deborah Dudgeon

Dyspnea, an uncomfortable awareness of breathing, is another common symptom at the end of life. Yet it often goes unrecognized and is difficult to treat. Breathlessness is virtually synonymous with end-stage chronic obstructive lung (COPD) and heart disease. One study found that 50 percent of general cancer patients complain of shortness of breath, with 20 percent rating the symptom as moderate to severe. Other studies show that 60 percent of lung cancer patients report shortness of breath at diagnosis, rising to 90 percent just prior to death, and that 70 percent of hospice patients experience shortness of breath in the last 6 weeks of life. Dyspnea causes patients to limit their activities, leading to social isolation and decreased quality of life.

Optimal treatment of dyspnea is to treat reversible causes; when this is no longer possible, both pharmacological and nonpharmacological methods are used to relieve symptoms, with limited success. Current treatment strategies are often ineffective or cause limiting side effects. Clinicians often develop and disseminate new treatment strategies without benefit of data from basic or clinical research. More research is needed to develop more effective treatments.

Opioids have been used since the nineteenth century, and several studies have demonstrated their benefit for control of dyspnea. Other studies have been negative, and several have produced negative side effects (sedation). Nebulized opioids might reduce side effects by limiting the dosage needed, but four randomized controlled trials did not find that nebulized opiates relieved breathlessness. A problem in all of these studies was that many patients died before the end of the trial. It may be that treatment is being started too late, just as it formerly was with pain, but this question has not been addressed in research.

Combination therapy using morphine with chloropromazine and morphine with promethazine were effective, but morphine with prochloroperazine was not an effective combination. Chloropromazine and promethazine alone were also effective in reducing symptoms in healthy subjects and COPD patients, but promethazine was not. These medications warrant further research.

Clinical trials of anxiolytics to treat dyspnea have also been variable. There have been both positive and negative studies of diazepam and alprazolam. Clorazepate was not found to be effective, and buspirome (a nonbenzodiazepine anxiolytic) improved exercise tolerance but had no effect on pulmonary function or arterial blood gases in patients with COPD. Indomethacin and bupivacaine reduced exercise-induced breathlessness in normal volunteers but did not benefit patients with lung disease. Inhaled lidocaine and dextromethorphan failed to relieve dyspnea in patients with cancer and COPD, respectively. None of these medications can be recommended for the treatment of dyspnea at this time.

Nonpharmacological interventions have been used with both COPD and cancer patients. Acupuncture significantly reduced breathlessness in cancer patients. Exercise reconditioning and rehabilitation techniques are effective in lung disease. Other widely used techniques include pursed-lip breathing, diaphragm training, meditation and relaxation training, biofeedback, and psychotherapy. These approaches have not been studied systematically, and their long-term efficacy has been questioned.

Basic Perspective, Dr. Denis O'Donnell

Basic research has increased our knowledge of the factors that give rise to dyspnea in advanced lung disease. The pathophysiological mechanisms include increased ventilation, increased intrinsic mechanical loading, weakness of the inspiratory muscles, or a combination of the above. The neurophysiological corollaries of these mechanisms are (1) an increase in the central respiratory drive from the respiratory controller and (2) a disparity between the inspiratory effort and the mechanical response achieved. It is the patient's awareness of this disparity— especially difficult and unrewarded inspiration—that gives rise to the distress that defines dyspnea.

Physiological factors that can lead to increased ventilatory demand include increased wasted ventilation, hypoxemia, and excessive metabolic acidosis during exercise. Mechanical impairment and psychogenic factors such as anxiety can also be involved. Consequently, dyspnea can be reduced by interventions that reduce central respiratory drive (e.g., oxygen, opiates), improve the effectiveness of CO_2 elimination (e.g., altering breathing pattern), or reduce metabolic load (e.g., exercise training, oxygen).

In COPD, the most obvious mechanical defect is airway obstruction, and dyspnea is shown to improve after interventions that reduce air trapping and hyperinflation. Examples include bronchodilators, lung volume reduction surgery, and continuous positive airway pressure therapy. Many other terminal diseases also have as their final common pathway a restrictive ventilatory deficit, including pulmonary fibrosis, chest wall restriction, cardiogenic and noncardiogenic pulmonary edema, lung resection, lymphangitis, and pleural effusions. In these diseases, as in COPD, patients have a diminished inspiratory capacity and experience a disparity between respiratory effort and thoracic displacement during exercise. Consequently, qualitative descriptions of the symptom are remarkably similar in severe obstructive and restrictive pulmonary disease.

In response to questions from other participants, Dr. O'Donnell reported that there is at present no animal model of dyspnea. Dyspnea researchers are far behind pain researchers in investigating the role of opioid receptors in treatment of dyspnea, but this avenue has considerable promise. There has been little neurochemical research, and only a few PET studies. Consequently, the neural pathways have not been defined. The role of the vagus nerve has been studied, but it does not seem to be central to the experience of dyspnea.

Methods Perspective, Dr. Audrey Gift

Dyspnea is difficult to measure because it involves several qualitatively distinct sensations and manifests itself differently in different patients. In addition, measurement is contextual, varying with age, condition, and psychological state, as well as underlying disease. Nevertheless, several scales have been validated for measuring the symptoms of the dyspnea.

- The Fletcher Scale, which dates from the 1950s, measures the amount of work that is required before the patient experiences shortness of breath. It has five levels. Several modifications have been developed in subsequent years.

- Two scales were developed in rehabilitation medicine. The Baseline Dyspnea Index measures the degree of impairment as well as the amount of effort required for a standard task. The Transitional Dyspnea Index measures how much the baseline has changed as a result of either disease or rehabilitation. Both scales are marked by the rater rather than by the subject, and neither scale is particularly useful in critical care or terminal care settings, where results are subject to many confounding variables.

- Two additional scales are somewhat more useful for measuring the symptom itself. One is the Borg Scale, which measures symptoms directly by using a scale from 0 to 10 and a series of descriptive words ("strong," "very strong") to gauge perceived exertion. These words can be vague, but the scale has been validated in rehabilitation settings. The other is the Vertical Visual Analogue Scale (VVAS), which uses a 100 mm line rather than words. It is used to measure how much breathlessness the patient experiences before, during, and following exercise. There is a high correlation between the Borg and VVAS findings.

- Researchers have also validated a Numeric Rating Scale that rates dyspnea symptoms from 1 to 10. Results are reliable and valid in the home and in the clinic. However, they found that the severity of dyspnea *now* (measured while at rest) does not correlate with reported severity in the past week.

One complication for verbal measures of dyspnea is its multiple dimensions—not only intensity or severity, but also frequency, distress, and quality, each of which can generate many different descriptors. Indeed, 19 different descriptors have been used to measure quality alone. The descriptors most frequently used by COPD patients are "My breathing requires effort" and "I feel out of breath." Dyspnea also occurs with other symptoms, such as nervousness and fatigue, and it was the number of those symptoms, rather than the degree of distress, that proved to be the best predictor of dyspnea. These measures have not been widely tested in terminal illness, however, and there would be special problems with children and other vulnerable populations.

In response to questions, Drs. O'Donnell and Gift added that the nature of the underlying medical condition might contribute additional complications, as might the emotional impact of terminal illness itself, which also makes it problematic to administer exercise tests. The distress of dyspnea does not appear to sensitize the patient to further symptoms, as in the case of pain; indeed, conditioning can reduce severity, which may point to future interventions. Dyspnea may covary with cachexia and muscle wasting. There has been no research on the connection between dyspnea and agonal breathing. Many of these methodological questions are similar to those faced in pain research, and indeed dyspnea researchers are closely watching the progress of pain research.

Cognitive Disturbances

Clinical Perspective, Dr. Jane Ingham

Delirium is a transient organic brain syndrome characterized by the acute onset of disordered attention and cognition and accompanied by perceptual disturbances and various behavioral manifestations including confusion and restlessness. Surveys have suggested that symptoms of delirium and other cognitive disturbances are prevalent towards the end of life. A large survey of 16,000 decedents in the United States found that 40% had evidence of cognitive disturbance in the last year of life. Other studies have suggested that cognition may be impaired and delirium present in as many as 85% of patients in certain sub-populations in the last days of life.

There are numerous possible etiological factors that may contribute to impaired cognition and delirium towards the end of life and, therefore, to the distress and the numerous symptoms which accompany these conditions. Such factors include medications, sepsis and metabolic disturbances. Many of these factors can be addressed and the syndrome and symptoms successfully treated.

Assessment of delirium and impaired cognition is challenging. The disturbance to perception and cognition itself complicates assessment, diagnosis, and the selection of appropriate interventions. The use of imprecise terminology is common. Tools sensitive to variation in severity are in need of further development as are methods for quantifying distress associated with delirium for both the patient and the family. There is a need to refine instruments for clinical use in diagnosis and, particularly, in monitoring the effect of treatments.

Clinical concerns in need of focused attention include the evidence that delirium is both under-recognized and under-treated. Further research is also needed on the role of patient and family counseling, optimal nursing interventions, optimal pharmacological strategies, and the effects of various treatment combinations. Further, there are few prognostic guidelines that define the likelihood or predictability of recovery for those experiencing delirium towards the end of life. Other research priorities include the need for testing therapies that treat the entire syndrome as well as specific symptoms; educational initiatives that may change the attitudes, knowledge, and skills of healthcare professionals; instruments for diagnosis and monitoring; treatment strategies and guidelines; and tools for measuring quality and outcomes of care.

Basic Perspective, Dr. Paula Trzepacz

From a basic perspective, the study of delirium is complicated by its numerous etiologies, which have different biochemical impacts on many different parts of the brain. There are gaps in our knowledge of the pathophysiology of some of these manifestations. However, the syndrome of delirium appears to have certain common pathways—neurotransmitter dysfunctions in certain cortical and subcortical parts of the brain—regardless of etiology.

Several studies have found that stroke-related lesions in certain areas of the brain—particularly the right frontal and temporal regions—are also associated with delirium. This is supported by PET studies. Many of the symptoms that make up the syndrome have also been associated with specific neuroanatomical regions and/or neurochemical systems. Examples include sleep disturbances, delusional thinking, and short-term memory loss, each of which has well-established links with particular regions or neurotransmitters.

These findings are the basis for several theories about the role of neurotransmitters in delirium. The two best-known theories center on deficiencies in acetylcholine and excesses of dopamine; others involve norepinephrine, serotonin, GABA, glutamate, histamine, glycine, somatostatin, and opiates. Certain cholinergic regions that are implicated in Alzheimer syndrome are also suspected of playing a role in delirium. Studies in rats confirm a correlation between acetylcholine levels and cognitive disturbances.

The common pathway for these systems appears to be the interconnections among the thalamus, prefrontal cortex, and basal ganglia. The thalamus in particular is an important gating and filtering area for information entering the brain. Further studies will be needed to determine the precise operation of these complex, overlapping systems.

Some drugs used to treat pain, especially the opiates, have unfortunate side effects of increasing delirium in part through their anticholinergicity. For example, meperidine and fentanyl have nor-metabolites that are very anticholinergic and delirogenic. Thus, comforting the patient's pain might impair their cognition and quality of life via higher brain function deficits. Many drugs are deliriogenic, especially if the blood-brain barrier is more penetrable than usual, for example, in renal failure.

Additionally, the presence of other symptoms may contribute to the development of delirium. Poor perfusion associated with dyspnea cause hypoxemia that exacerbates delirium. Hepatic insufficiency might mean hypoalbuminemia or impaired drug metabolism which has the effect of raising serum levels of drugs above what we might anticipate from particular doses or from total serum drug level assays. It is the free (unbound) drug levels that impact tissues, including the brain, and can cause delirium. Cachexia also affects cognition through vitamin deficiency (vitamins are cofactors in the brain's enzymatic reactions) and hypoalbuminemia. The brain does not store any energy—it relies on blood to carry glucose, oxygen, choline from the diet to make acetylcholine) to it and it will malfunction with inadequate supplies. The brain will suffer permanent damage if oxygen and glucose supplies cease for more than several minutes.

Methods Perspective, Dr. James Levenson

Delirium is little studied in part because it is so difficult to study. Diagnosis is complicated by the multidimensional nature of the symptoms (perception, cognition, behavior, etc.), and there has been little research on the intercorrelations among these dimensions and severity of condition. In addition, delirium has multiple etiologies, changes rapidly, and is difficult to distinguish from dementia. As a result, there is no "gold standard" for diagnosis.

Measurement of the severity of delirium also presents problems. The symptoms vary considerably in their quantifiability and reliability, and many are confounded by underlying medical illness and by medications. Delirium also interferes with comprehension; critically ill patients often cannot respond to questions, making it impossible to assess the reliability of tests. Cognition, the most frequently measured symptom, can be confounded not only by dementia but also by nausea, pain, and pain medications. Currently available instruments require that patients be able to talk, or must be administered by an experienced clinician, or take so long to administer that they can't be repeated.

There are additional problems with consent. Because delirium prevents informed consent, it eliminates the very patients that are most in need of treatment. It also introduces selection bias, excluding the sickest patients and those unable to respond. Solutions are to use a family member for proxy consent, or a durable power-of-attorney, or assent rather than consent. However, there is no legal or regulatory basis for these measures. The National Bioethics Advisory Commission may turn its attention to this area in the near future.

In response to questions, the panelists reported that awareness of the problems of delirium is higher in cancer and AIDS patients than in other terminally ill populations. Early detection and assessment are likely to improve outcomes. Close monitoring in addition to a high level of clinical awareness and skill is needed to detect and treat this problem in the last days of life. Instrument development is needed. The ideal instrument would assess the many dimensions of delirium and optimally assist in guiding treatment. Studies are needed to elucidate the correlates of distress in this condition, including the behavioral correlates. There is also a need for studies of best practice. In too many cases delirium is under-evaluated, under-diagnosed, and under-treated. Further studies of basic mechanisms and pharmacological treatment strategies are needed. The roles of various medications, hydration, and other interventions in preventing or reducing prevalence and distress associated with delirium remain uncertain.

Cachexia or Wasting

Clinical Perspective, Dr. Neil MacDonald

Cachexia or wasting is another obvious and disturbing symptom at the end of life, and another symptom that—despite its costs and the distress that it causes to both patients and their families—nevertheless receives relatively little attention. While its pathophysiology remains to be fully elucidated, sufficient information is available to design studies that link the laboratory and the bedside. The McMaster Loop provides a framework for assessing the feasibility and importance of such initiatives. Success could be measured in terms of both alleviating suffering and reducing health care costs.

Like pain, cachexia is a symptom that can kill, and it is a major contributor to the death of cancer patients. However, weight loss varies considerably in different forms of cancer: breast cancer causes little weight loss, while lung cancer causes profound weight loss. Clinicians previously believed that cancer increased metabolic demand, stole protein, and produced toxins that suppressed appetite, resulting in malnutrition. Recent research has shown that this view is wrong—cancer may raise resting metabolic rate, but improved nutrition does not relieve symptoms that include not only anorexia but also chronic nausea, early satiety, and changes in taste that make even favorite foods unpalatable.

The emerging view is that cachexia is a result of the combined action of tumor products (in cancer) and host immune factors, particularly cytokines, that lead to poor appetite, muscle wasting, and altered metabolism. By identifying potential causative agents, this model suggests several targets for therapeutic interventions. A particular goal would be to identify agents that can increase protein synthesis and decrease proteolysis.

Gemcitabine, a chemotherapeutic drug, has been shown to have measurable clinical benefit in treating cachexia. This suggests that oncologists should take a broader look at agents that, while they might not kill the tumor, might modify the host immune response with benefits in terms of pain as well as cachexia. Corticosteroids interfere with cytokine production and give temporary relief from anorexia, but not from cachexia. Progestin improves appetite and may best be combined with exercise. CNS agents, androgen, and growth factors are being tested but are unproven. It may also be possible to modify diet, but this approach has failed thus far.

From the clinical perspective, the greatest research needs are for a clearer classification and definition of symptoms; a better understanding of the underlying mechanisms of cachexia; investigation of gender differences in pathophysiology and therapy (females lose less weight and survive longer); and trials of both single-agent and combination therapies.

Basic Perspective, Dr. Carlos Plata-Salaman

Cachexia occurs not only in cancer but in AIDS, chronic bacterial and parasitic diseases, rheumatoid arthritis, and chronic diseases of the bowel, liver, lungs, and heart. The same cytokines appear to increase in all of these diseases. Among the cytokines proposed to participated in the development and progression of cachexia are interleukin-1 (IL-1), IL-6, interferon-gamma, tumor necrosis factor-alpha, and brain-derived neurotrophic factor. The involvement of theses cytokines has been confirmed in animal models, and evidence suggests their predominant mode of action is paracrine: that is, not

465

through increased levels in circulation but rather through local synthesis of cytokines in an organ (e.g., brain, liver).

Cachexia is also associated with metabolic alterations including hypertriglyceridemia, lipolysis, and accelerated protein turnover, resulting in the loss of fat mass and body protein. Evidence points to a dysregulation of metabolic processes that produces a negative energy balance. Three other pathophysiological mechanisms in cachexia need further study:

1. Analysis of changes in the interface between the periphery and the brain;

2. Characterizations of the interactions among cytokines (e.g., interleukins, tumor necrosis factors, interferons, growth factors, leptin), peptide/neuropeptides (e.g., neuropeptide Y, endogenous opioids, CRH), and neurotransmitters (e.g., serotonin, catecholamines); and

3. Analysis of neuronal mechanisms at the molecular level under cachexic conditions.

Many of the proposed interventions for cachexia—nutritional manipulations, inhibitors of cytokine action, steroids, hormones, cannabinoids, thalidomide, etc.—have immunosuppressive and/or other adverse effects, and most have had inconsistent results. Novel nutritional manipulations, megestrol acetate derivatives, Y receptor agonists, amino acid manipulations, myostatin inhibitors, uncoupling protein modifiers, and antisense strategies could provide new leads.

Methods Perspective, Dr. Jamie Von Roenn

Methodological issues in cachexia research include questions of ethics, design, and measurement. Ethical issues inform and often subsume other questions, for example the goals and timing of intervention and even the definition of the patient population. In cachexia as in other symptoms at the end of life, the nature of the syndrome suggests that it would be better to intervene earlier rather than later, for the sake of the patient as well as the effectiveness of the intervention. Average time on study for published studies has been about 2 months.

For ambulatory patients, the primary measurement issue is not to correlate outcomes with changes in body weight, but rather with changes in lean body mass as reflected in changes in performance. Patients at the end of life pose special ethical problems, however, requiring a less aggressive or intrusive approach. At the end of life, for example, performance status may be irrelevant, and a more appropriate end point may be improvement in appetite. Past research has shown that there is a large placebo effect from attention to appetite. In terminal patients, stabilization or decreased rate of weight loss might be better measures than caloric intake or weight gain.

It might be best to design interventions that are as broadly applicable as possible, since current stratification and eligibility standards have created barriers to research. Studies should also rely on simpler laboratory techniques such as measuring changes in body composition using bioelectric impedance analysis (an inexpensive, ten-minute test that is statistically correlated with body composition), rather than whole-body calcium and other sophisticated, time-consuming tests. Studies should also include nonpharmacological interventions such as exercise, which has been shown to be effective in frail elderly patients and could certainly be tried in terminal patients.

In summary, efforts are needed to educate patients and health care providers about the importance of addressing cachexia early on. Research should probably target early-stage patients, as well, in hopes of learning lessons that can be applied in more seriously debilitated patients. Small, intensive studies should be able to clarify the most useful endpoints and measurement tools. Interventions to be investigated should include exercise, combination therapies, and even steroids, the latter being in wide use among male AIDS patients. There is also a need to describe the correlations among these endpoints, but the overriding need is to integrate this kind of palliative care into the patient's medical care at a much earlier stage.

In response to questions, Dr. MacDonald, Plata-Salaman, and Von Roenn reiterated that the time for nutritional interventions was early onset, when weight loss is first noticed, rather than at the end of life, although such studies might reveal treatments that would be useful at later stages. Cathexic patients do develop food aversions, but these can be circumvented to provide proper micronutrition. "Alternative" therapies (e.g., omega-3 fatty acids, DHEA, and androgens) are widely available in health food stores, but despite their apparent usefulness they haven't been examined by mainstream science, and the "alternative" label may be a barrier to the study and broader use of potentially effective agents.

467

Common Research Issues, Dr. Joanne Lynn

A number of common research issues emerged in these four symptom areas, issues that may have more to do with conducting research at the end of life than with any particular symptom or disease. Many of these issues were methodological, but other equally difficult questions had to do with the ethics and even the purpose of conducting research at the end of life.

One of the most difficult methodological issues was that these symptoms tend to occur in clusters, and we have little knowledge of the interactions among the symptoms or between symptoms and lifespan. Another is the lack of a "gold standard" for measuring these symptoms with accuracy or even conceptual clarity. An even more troublesome issue is the problem of missing and inadequate data: when patients die in the middle of a study, or are unable to respond to investigators' questions, statistical analysis becomes very difficult and the findings have far less power and clarity.

There is also a problem with generalizability, given the selection bias in most studies (which prefer the youngest patients and simplest conditions) and the ambiguity of the inception cohort (what exactly is a "dying patient"?). Better models of prognosis may be needed to establish meaningful inception thresholds for these studies. The lack of animal models is a difficult technical problem in most symptom areas, but an even more serious conceptual problem is the unfamiliarity of the domains being measured (e.g., life closure) and the difficulty in determining the clinical, statistical, and policy significance of the findings. From a health services perspective, for example, what's needed are composite measures and nonrandom comparisons; paradoxically, however, every composite measure of pain and suffering could be improved simply by shortening the life of each suffering patient by three months.

Ethical issues can represent a serious barrier to even the best research. Some dying patients are incompetent, others marginalized or vulnerable or poor. Current regulations, strictly interpreted, would forbid the use of incompetent subjects in research, even if it clearly benefits them, if there is more than a trivial level of risk. By the same token, there is an ethical question about the decency or propriety of intruding on patients at a particularly important time in their lives. Finally, there will inevitably be some drugs that are proven effective in relieving specific symptoms—pain, cachexia, etc.—that also shorten lifespan. Society has yet to decide how to proceed when desirable ends are in conflict.

This leads to a final set of common issues dealing with the goal of research—is it to understand the mechanisms involved in these syndromes, to develop products to alleviate the symptoms, to enable practitioners to serve individual patients, or to guide reform by responding to perceived failures in the public health system? These choices beg the larger question of what the end of life should be like, what is meant by a "good death," and what tasks are to be accomplished at the end of life. These questions have larger family and social ramifications, and at present there is no focus of communications among the many professional groups who all have a partial, but not central, interest in these questions.

Recommendations

Following the presentations on these four symptom areas, the workshop broke into subgroups in which participants attempted to determine priorities and make recommendations on each of the four symptom areas. The following preamble for these recommendations reflected the consensus of the entire workshop:

> To adequately address symptom control in the terminally ill, an important first step is to invest resources in the development of new methodologies for assessing symptoms and evaluating treatments. These tools will allow us to elucidate the extent of the problem and to set national priorities to improve quality of life for those facing life-limiting illness.

Pain

1. *Epidemiology.* There is still a great need for epidemiological data on the incidence and types of pain at the end of life. Research in this area will provide direction for researchers regarding what specific topics should be tackled next.

2. *Treatment.* There is a clear need to discover new drugs for the treatment of pain, including analgesic combinations. Neuropathic pain, because of its incidence and burden, should be a particular priority. There should also be studies of the relationship between disease, pain, and suffering at the end of life, which would also include psychosocial mediators. Clinical Trials Groups should be developed to study promising interventions.

3. *Measurement.* Methods should be developed for collecting valid data on pain in the home, in nursing homes, etc., possibly using telephones or computer technology. Measurement of other outcomes of subjective experience, such as the suffering caused by pain, should also be developed and utilized.

Dyspnea

1. *Epidemiology.* What are the incidence and impact of dyspnea in different populations? There is some information about dyspnea in cancer and COPD patients, but almost none in cardiac disease, and other terminal conditions.

2. *Mechanisms.* Relatively little is known about the various determinants of dyspnea, including respiratory muscle strength, exercise capacity, respiratory controller, gas exchange, and psychosocial factors. Neurobiological models, like those developed for pain, will be useful, but the overall approach must be integrative. The determinants are almost certainly multifactorial, necessitating multidisciplinary strategies.

3. *Measurement.* Research is needed to refine available instruments and develop new ones for measuring both the causes of symptoms and the effects of treatment. There is at present no standardized approach for assessing the degree of dyspnea in a given disease (e.g., chronic vs. acute, COPD vs. cancer). The goal would be to formulate guidelines for optimal assessment, which would point to optimal treatment.

4. *Treatment.* A number of potential treatments are available, but there is little information on their relative effectiveness. Particular attention should be given to the choice and timing of anxiolytics, phenothiazines, oxygen, opiates, and exercise. Attention should also be given to the timing and management of terminal weaning (removal of ventilation), including the role of families.

The collaborative and integrative nature of this research is well suited to sponsorship and funding by NIH. It would be useful, for example, for the various NIH Institutes to sponsor a series of joint workshops that would characterize clinical experience and impact of therapies on dyspnea in diseases other than lung cancer.

Cognitive Disturbances

There is a considerable amount of epidemiological data on delirium already, and while it might be useful to gather additional information on specific patient populations, this symptom is known to be under-recognized and under-treated. Consequently, the research priorities in this symptom area are as follows:

1. *Measurement.* Research is needed to enhance the recognition of delirium in different treatment settings (homes, hospices, hospitals), including common diagnostic criteria and terminology. Also needed are better instruments to describe and rate the severity and course of episodes of delirium. This research will lead to a better understanding of the phenomenology of delirium—its signs, patterns, and subtypes—which in turn should produce benefits in terms of newer, more sensitive, and more effective treatments.

2. *Treatment.* Two aspects of treatment research deserve simultaneous attention. First, there should be randomized, placebo-controlled trials to systematically assess the efficacy of currently available therapies, as well as emerging approaches, including both pharmacological and nonpharmacological strategies. Second, there should be research on the relation between the mechanism of action of these therapies and the underlying pathophysiology of delirium. In both cases, studies should include both random populations and populations with delirium of homogeneous etiology.

3. *Epidemiology.* Finally, there is a need for additional research on the interactions of delirium between delirium and other symptoms at the end of life.

A concurrent policy issue that must also receive priority attention is the need for guidelines for research in patients who are incapable of giving informed consent because of serious medical illness.

Cachexia

1. *Epidemiology.* High priority should go to epidemiological studies of anorexia-cachexia, in order to establish the magnitude of the problem, its impact on the patient and family, and its costs to society. However, it is important that cachexia not be

studied in isolation from other symptoms. If the ultimate goal of cachexia research is prevention and early intervention, then it would be useful to conduct studies that examine the epidemiology of several related symptoms—e.g., pain, dyspnea, delirium—at an earlier stage in their development.

2. *Mechanisms.* Basic and clinical research on cachexia should be done in parallel. Basic research should emphasize the interactions among multiple underlying pathophysiological mechanisms, both central and peripheral, including biochemical, neuronal, metabolic, endocrine, and immunological. Research is also needed on the varying clinical manifestations of these mechanisms, both neuropsychiatric and gastrointestinal. This calls for a multidisciplinary approach.

3. *Treatment.* Similarly, since it is unlikely that any single therapeutic intervention will be successful, clinical research should emphasize multiple combination therapies that include nutritional, pharmacological, and nonpharmacological components. Combination therapies should be evaluated for their effects on other symptoms such as pain, dyspnea, and delirium. Particular attention should also be paid to differences in outcome based on age, gender, and underlying disease. In considering drug trials, NIH should concentrate on studies that would not otherwise be funded by drug companies.

Given the wide range of mechanisms and therapeutic strategies in cachexia, it would be useful to convene a preliminary, integrative workshop that would include both basic and clinical researchers.

Cross Cutting Recommendations

Methods issues that need to be addressed in all four symptom areas include the following:

- Statistical handling of missing data

- Proxy reporting for subjective symptoms

- Outcome measures that indicate quality care

- Ethics issues are also important. What are the barriers to research at the end of life, including the needs and expectations of vulnerable populations? What are community and individual preferences with respect to symptom management of dying persons?

- Economics questions include the direct and indirect costs and burdens of symptoms.

List of Participants

Dr. Ira Byock
Associate Medical Director
Partners Hospice
341 University Ave.
Missoula, MT 59801

Dr. Charles S. Cleeland
Director, Pain Research Group
M. D. Anderson Cancer Center
University of Texas
1100 Holcombe Blvd., Box 221
Houston, TX 77030

Dr. Deborah Dudgeon
Dir. of Palliative Care Medicine
Queen's University
Rm. 2025, Etherington Hall
Stuart St.
Kingston, ON, Canada K7L 3N6

Dr. Betty R. Ferrell
Associate Research Scientist
City of Hope Natl. Medical Cntr.
Dept. of Nursing Research
1500 E. Duarte Rd.
Duarte, CA 91010

Dr. Marilyn J. Field, Deputy Dir.
Health Care Services
Institute of Medicine
National Academy of Sciences
2102 Constitution Ave.
Washington, DC 20418

Dr. Kathleen Foley
Dept. of Neurology
Memorial Sloan Kettering Cancer
  Center
1275 York Ave.
New York, NY 10021

Dr. Audrey Gift
Associate Professor, School of
  Nursing
University of Pennsylvania
420 Guardian Dr.
Philadelphia, PA 19104-6096

Dr. Jane Ingham
Director, Palliative Care Program
Georgetown Univ. Medical Center
3800 Reservoir Rd. NW
Washington, DC 20007-2197

Dr. James L. Levenson
Professor of Psychiatry
Virginia Commonwealth Univ.
Box 980268
Richmond, VA 23298

Dr. Joanne Lynn
Director, The Center to Improve
  Care of the Dying
The George Washington University Medical Center
1001 22nd St. NW, Ste. 820
Washington, DC 20037

473

Dr. Neil MacDonald, Director,
Cancer Bioethics Program
Clinical Research Institute of
   Montreal
110 Pine Ave. W.
Montreal, PQ, Canada H2W 1R7

Dr. Denis E. O'Donnell
Dept. of Medicine
Kingston Hospital
Richardson House
102 Stuart St.
Kingston, ON, Canada K7L 3N6

Dr. Richard Payne
Professor and Chief of Pain Man-
   agement
M. D. Anderson Cancer Center
Dept. of Neuro-Oncology, Box 8
1515 Holcombe Blvd.
Houston, TX 77030

Dr. Carlos R. Plata-Salaman
Professor of Neuroscience
University of Delaware
School of Life and Health Sci-
   ences
Newark, DE 19716

Dr. Russell Portenoy
Chairman, Dept. of Pain Medi-
   cine and Palliative Care
Beth Israel Medical Center
First Ave. at 16th St.
New York, NY 10003

Dr. Donald Price
Professor of Anesthesiology
Medical College of Virginia
Box 980337
Richmond, VA 23298

Dr. Christopher Squier
Professor, The University of Iowa
Dows Institute for Dental Re-
   search
N419DSB
Iowa City, IA 52242-1010

Dr. Paula T. Trzepacz
Professor of Psychiatry and Neu-
   rology
University of Mississippi Medical
   Center
2500 N. State St.
Jackson, MS 39216

Dr. Lynn Underwood
Program Director
Fetzer Institute
9292 W. KI Ave.
Kalamazoo, Michigan 49009-9398

Dr. Jamie Von Roenn
Associate Professor of Medicine
Northwestern University
Division of Hematology/Oncology
250 E. Superior St.
Chicago, IL 60611

Chapter 45

The Dying Process

When a person enters the final stage of the dying process, two different dynamics are at work which are closely interrelated and interdependent. On the physical plane, the body begins the final process of shutting down, which will end when all the physical systems cease to function. Usually this is an orderly and undramatic progressive series of physical changes which are not medical emergencies requiring invasive interventions. These physical changes are a normal, natural way in which the body prepares itself to stop, and the most appropriate kinds of responses are comfort enhancing measures.

The other dynamic of the dying process at work is on the emotional-spiritual-mental plane, and is a different kind of process. The spirit of the dying person begins the final process of release from the body, its immediate environment, and all attachments. This release also tends to follow its own priorities, which may include the resolution of whatever is unfinished of a practical nature and reception of permission to "let go" from family members. These events are the normal, natural way in which the spirit prepares to move from this existence into the next dimension of life. The most appropriate kinds of responses to the emotional-spiritual-mental changes are those which support and encourage this release and transition.

Excerpted from "Preparing for Approaching Death," [Online]. Available: http://hospice-cares.com/signs.html. © 1996 by North Central Florida Hospice, Inc., 4200 NW 90th Blvd., Gainesville, FL 32606. For complete contact information, please refer to Chapter 60, "Resources." Reprinted with permission.

When a person's body is ready and wanting to stop, but the person is still unresolved or unreconciled over some important issue or with some significant relationship, he or she may tend to linger in order to finish whatever needs finishing even though he or she may be uncomfortable or debilitated. On the other hand, when a person is emotionally-spiritually-mentally resolved and ready for this release, but his or her body has not completed its final physical shut-down, the person will continue to live until that shut-down process ceases.

The experience we call death occurs when the body completes its natural process of shutting down, and when the spirit completes its natural process of reconciling and finishing. These two processes need to happen in a way appropriate and unique to the values, beliefs, and lifestyle of the dying person.

Therefore, as you seek to prepare yourself as this event approaches, the members of your Hospice care team want you to know what to expect and how to respond in ways that will help your loved one accomplish this transition with support, understanding, and ease. This is the great gift of love you have to offer your loved one as this moment approaches.

The emotional-spiritual-mental and physical signs and symptoms of impending death which follow are offered to help you understand the natural kinds of things which may happen and how you can respond appropriately. Not all these signs and symptoms will occur with every person, nor will they occur in this particular sequence. Each person is unique and needs to do things in his or her own way. This is not the time to try to change your loved one, but the time to give full acceptance, support, and comfort.

The following signs and symptoms described are indicative of how the body prepares itself for the final stage of life.

Coolness

The person's hands and arms, feet and then legs may be increasingly cool to the touch, and at the same time the color of the skin may change. This a normal indication that the circulation of blood is decreasing to the body's extremities and being reserved for the most vital organs. Keep the person warm with a blanket, but do not use one that is electric.

Sleeping

The person may spend an increasing amount of time sleeping, and appear to be uncommunicative or unresponsive and at times be difficult to rouse. This normal change is due in part to changes in the metabolism of the body. Sit with your loved one, hold his or her hand, but do not shake it or speak loudly. Speak softly and naturally. Plan to spend time with your loved one during those times when he or she seems most alert or awake. Do not talk about the person in the person's presence. Speak to him or her directly as you normally would, even though there may be no response. Never assume the person cannot hear; hearing is the last of the senses to be lost.

Disorientation

The person may seem to be confused about the time, place, and identity of people surrounding him or her including close and familiar people. This is also due in part to the metabolism changes. Identify yourself by name before you speak rather than to ask the person to guess who you are. Speak softly, clearly, and truthfully when you need to communicate something important for the patient's comfort, such as, It is time to take your medication, and explain the reason for the communication, such as, so you won't begin to hurt. Do not use this method to try to manipulate the patient to meet your needs.

Incontinence

The person may lose control of urine and/or bowel matter as the muscles in that area begin to relax. Discuss with your Hospice nurse what can be done to protect the bed and keep your loved one clean and comfortable.

Congestion

The person may have gurgling sounds coming from his or her chest as though marbles were rolling round inside. These sounds may become very loud. This normal change is due to the decrease of fluid intake and an inability to cough up normal secretions. Suctioning usually only increases the secretions and causes sharp discomfort. Gently turn the person's head to the side and allow gravity to drain the secretions. You may also gently wipe the mouth with a moist cloth. The sound of the congestion does not indicate the onset of severe or new pain.

Restlessness

The person may make restless and repetitive motions such as pulling at bed linen or clothing. This often happens and is due in part to the decrease in oxygen circulation to the brain and to metabolism changes. Do not interfere with or try to restrain such motions. To have a calming effect, speak in a quiet, natural way, lightly massage the forehead, read to the person, or play some soothing music.

Urine Decrease

The person's urine output normally decreases and may become tea-colored referred to as concentrated urine. This is due to the decreased fluid intake as well as decrease in circulation through the kidneys. Consult with your Hospice nurse to determine whether there may be a need to insert or irrigate a catheter.

Fluid and Food Decrease

The person may have a decrease in appetite and thirst, wanting little or no food or fluid. The body will naturally begin to conserve energy which is expended on these tasks. Do not try to force food or drink into the person, or try to use guilt to manipulate them into eating or drinking something. To do this only makes the person much more uncomfortable. Small chips of ice, frozen Gatorade or juice may be refreshing in the mouth. If the person is able to swallow, fluids may be given in small amounts by syringe (ask the Hospice nurse for guidance). Glycerine swabs may help keep the mouth and lips moist and comfortable. A cool, moist washcloth on the forehead may also increase physical comfort.

Breathing Pattern Change

The person's regular breathing pattern may change with the onset of a different breathing pace. A particular pattern consists of breathing irregularly, i.e., shallow breaths with periods of no breathing of 5 to 30 seconds and up to a full minute. This is called Cheyne-Stokes breathing. The person may also experience periods of rapid shallow pant-like breathing. These patterns are very common and indicate decrease in circulation in the internal organs. Elevating the head, and/or turning the person onto his or her side may bring comfort. Hold your loved one's hand. Speak gently.

Normal Emotional, Spiritual, and Mental Signs and Symptoms with Appropriate Responses

Withdrawal

The person may seem unresponsive, withdrawn, or in a comatose-like state. This indicates preparation for release, a detaching from surroundings and relationships, and a beginning of letting go. Since hearing remains all the way to the end, speak to your loved one in your normal tone of voice, identifying yourself by name when you speak, hold his or her hand, and say whatever you need to say that will help the person let go.

Vision-Like Experiences

The person may speak or claim to have spoken to persons who have already died, or to see or have seen places not presently accessible or visible to you. This does not indicate an hallucination or a drug reaction. The person is beginning to detach from this life and is being prepared for the transition so it will not be frightening. Do not contradict, explain away, belittle, or argue about what the person claims to have seen or heard. Just because you cannot see or hear it does not mean it is not real to your loved one. Affirm his or her experience. They are normal and common. If they frighten your loved one, explain that they are normal occurrences.

Restlessness

The person may perform repetitive and restless tasks. This may in part indicate that something still unresolved or unfinished is disturbing him or her, and prevents him or her from letting go. Your Hospice team members will assist you in identifying what may be happening, and help you find ways to help the person find release from the tension or fear. Other things which may be helpful in calming the person are to recall a favorite place the person enjoyed, a favorite experience, read something comforting, play music, and give assurance that it is OK to let go.

Fluid and Food Decrease

When the person may want little or no fluid or food, this may indicate readiness for the final shut-down. Do not try to force food or fluid. You may help your loved one by giving permission to let go whenever he or she is ready. At the same time affirm the person's ongoing value to you and the good you will carry forward into your life that you received from him or her.

Decreased Socialization

The person may only want to be with a very few or even just one person. This is a sign of preparation for release and affirms from whom the support is most needed in order to make the appropriate transition. If you are not part of his inner circle at the end, it does not mean you are not loved or are unimportant. It means you have already fulfilled your task with your loved one, and it is the time for you to say Good-bye. If you are part of the final inner circle of support, the person needs your affirmation, support, and permission.

Unusual Communication

The person may make a seemingly out of character or non sequitur statement, gesture, or request. This indicates that he or she is ready to say Good-bye and is testing you to see if you are ready to let him or her go. Accept the moment as a beautiful gift when it is offered. Kiss, hug, hold, cry, and say whatever you most need to say.

Giving Permission

Giving permission to your loved one to let go, without making him or her guilty for leaving or trying to keep him or her with you to meet your own needs, can be difficult. A dying person will normally try to hold on, even though it brings prolonged discomfort, in order to be sure those who are going to be left behind will be all right. Therefore, your ability to release the dying person from this concern and give him or her assurance that it is all right to let go whenever he or she is ready is one of the greatest gifts you have to give your loved one at this time.

Saying Good-Bye

When the person is ready to die and you are able to let go, then is the time to say, Good-bye. Saying Good-bye is your final gift of love to your loved one, for it achieves closure and makes the final release possible. It may be helpful to lie in bed and hold the person, or to take his or her hand and then say everything you need to say.

It may be as simple as saying, I love you. It may include recounting favorite memories, places, and activities you shared. It may include saying, I'm sorry for whatever I contributed to any tension or difficulties in our relationship. It may also include saying, Thank you for...

Tears are a normal and natural part of saying, Good-bye. Tears do not need to be hidden from your loved one or apologized for. Tears express your love and help you to let go.

How Will You Know when Death Has Occurred?

Although you may be prepared for the death process, you may not be prepared for the actual death moment. It may be helpful for you and your family to think about and discuss what you would do if you were the one present at the death moment. The death of a hospice patient is not an emergency. Nothing must be done immediately.

The signs of death include such things as no breathing, no heartbeat, release of bowel and bladder, no response, eyelids slightly open, pupils enlarged, eyes fixed on a certain spot, no blinking, jaw relaxed and mouth sightly open.

A Hospice nurse will come to assist you if needed or desired. If not, phone support is available.

The body does not have to be moved until you are ready. If the family wants to assist in preparing the body by bathing or dressing, that may be done. Call the funeral home when you are ready to have the body moved, and identify the person as a Hospice patient. The police do not need to be called. The Hospice nurse will notify the physician.

Chapter 46

Pronouncement of Death

The physician who pronounces a patient dead will enter in the progress notes the following information as soon as possible:

- Time and date of death
- Pertinent comments on condition prior to death
- Clinical diagnosis
- Signature
- *Report of Death*

The first section of the *Report of Death (NIH-1082)* is to be completed by an Institute physician. The second section is to be completed by the pathologist. This form must be completed in all cases.

Notification of Family

The next of kin should be notified by the patient's physician, or, in his/her absence, by a physician representing the Institute concerned.

Excerpted from "Death of a Patient," in the Clinical Center *Medical Staff Handbook,* November 20, 1995 [Online]. Available: http://www.cc.nih.gov/ccc/aboutcc/msh/death.html. Produced by the National Institutes of Health (NIH). For complete contact information, please refer to Chapter 60, "Resources." Although the text in this chapter refers to procedures at the Clinical Center, readers may find similar procedures and policies in effect at other institutions.

Notification of Referring Physicians

The Admissions Office will notify the referring physician of the death by telegram.

Permission for Autopsy

(see also Medical Examiner's Case, below)

After the patient has been pronounced dead, physicians should request permission for autopsy. Consent obtained prior to death is invalid. Consent must be in writing and witnessed by the physician obtaining consent, or by telegram. Discussion with the family of the arrangements and permission for the autopsy should occur in the presence of the hospital administrator on call (496-3315, see below). SF-523, Authorization for Autopsy, should be completed. Telegrams should be addressed to the Admissions Office and sent Government Collect. Consent must be obtained from the person legally responsible under Maryland law, which prescribes the following order of responsibility:

1. Surviving spouse.

2. Surviving legally competent children. (If more than one child survives, the child accepting responsibility for burial is authorized to sign for the autopsy.)

3. Legally competent descendants of children of the deceased.

4. Father or mother of the deceased.

5. Legally competent brothers or sisters of the deceased. (Again, the person accepting responsibility for burial is authorized to sign the autopsy consent.)

6. Legally competent descendants of the brothers and sisters of the deceased.

7. Grandparents.

8. Friends or other interested parties who assume responsibility for burial.

Search for Next of Kin

When a patient dies at the Clinical Center, Maryland law requires that a reasonable search be made for the next of kin. Reasonable search is not clearly defined in the law but is interpreted by the medical examiner to have been carried out after completion of the following:

1. Attempt to locate the nearest of kin at the last available address.

2. Request the police to find the surviving next of kin at the last available address.

3. Request social service agencies to find the next of kin at the last available address. A 48-hour search is considered adequate.

Do not give a specific time that the body will be available for the undertaker. Refer the family to the Admissions Office which will discuss this with them and make the following arrangements:

1. Obtain administrative clearance for autopsy from the administrator on call.

2. Have the next of kin sign for disposition of the body (SF-523A and NIH-1286).

3. Release the patient's property.

4. Make arrangements with the undertaker, if the family so wishes.

5. Help the family with other problems that may occur.

Medical Examiner's Case

Under Maryland law, the term, "medical examiner's case," means any death that is the result, wholly or in part, of a casualty or accident, homicide, poisoning, suicide, criminal abortion, rape, therapeutic misadventure, drowning, any death of a suspicious or unusual nature, or any death of an apparently healthy person. Any person pronounced dead on arrival at the Clinical Center is a medical examiner case.

Any death that is directly associated with a diagnostic or therapeutic procedure is a possible medical examiner's case, whether or not it occurs in the operating room. This includes any death under induction of anesthesia and any death that occurs during, or as a result of, unusual complications from any operative or therapeutic procedure. It does not include indirect complications such as postoperative wound infection, pneumonia, renal or hepatic failure, etc., unless they result from an unusual complication or break in technique (retained sponge, for example). Because the medical examiner may order an autopsy in any case in which he/she has jurisdiction, permission for autopsy should not be requested in any potential medical examiner case until the medical examiner has been consulted.

After the medical examiner has been notified of a potential medical examiner case, he/she may either release the remains to NIH, in which case permission for autopsy should be requested, or he/she may retain jurisdiction. If the medical examiner retains jurisdiction, permission for autopsy should not be requested from the family. In medical examiner cases, the death certificate is either completed or countersigned by the medical examiner. If the medical examiner orders an autopsy, this decision must, of course, be carefully explained to the family.

If Clinical Center pathology staff believe a case should have been referred to the medical examiner, an autopsy will not be performed until the medical examiner has been contacted and permission to proceed has been obtained. Similarly, if in the course of an autopsy the findings indicate that a case should be referred to the medical examiner, the autopsy will be halted until the medical examiner has been contacted.

Radioactive Body

If a patient who has received a therapeutic dose of any radioisotope dies in the hospital within a 3-week period after that dose, the physician authorized to use the radioisotope and the radiation safety officer are to be notified immediately.

Deaths Occurring Away from the Clinical Center

Dead on Arrival: A patient pronounced dead on arrival at the Clinical Center is presumed by Maryland law to have died in Maryland regardless of any evidence to the contrary, and is a medical examiner case until the medical examiner releases the body. Follow instructions in the Death Packet for a medical examiner case.

If the medical examiner releases the body, the procedure is the same as if the patient died in the hospital.

When a patient is pronounced dead elsewhere and the Clinical Center is notified:

1. Contact the patient's NIH physician or an NIH investigator on the service to determine whether autopsy is desired.

2. Contact the chief, postmortem service, for permission to do an autopsy at NIH.

3. Contact the Admissions Office to inform them and to obtain assistance with the arrangements.

4. Obtain written or telegraphic consent from the legal next of kin for the autopsy to be done at NIH. (Do not insist the body be brought to NIH if the patient died at another hospital that wants to do the autopsy. An interested investigator can go there.)

5. Make certain that the completed death certificate will accompany the body.

6. Instruct the family to have the body brought to NIH by the undertaker (at NIH expense), or ask the Admissions Office to arrange transportation.

Completing Death Certificate

Usual Procedure: The Admissions Office will prepare the death certificate (Maryland 1625M) for signature by an NIH physician, usually after the autopsy has been completed. When the physician responsible for the patient's care is not available, the Institute OD or another physician on the service will be asked to sign.

Death certificates may be signed by any physician employed by the Federal Government if pronouncement of death occurred within the Federal installation to which this physician is assigned. It is proper for any patient care physician of the patient's Institute to sign the death certificate, even when the signing physician had no personal knowledge of the case.

Medical Examiner Cases: The death certificate (Maryland 1720M) will be completed by the medical examiner.

Organ Donation, Determination of Death

When a patient is a candidate for organ donation or when the fact of death needs to be determined, the patient's physician should request a consultation for this purpose with a neurologist who is board certified and a member of the senior Clinical Center staff, and who has not had primary responsibility for treatment of the patient.

487

The central focus of the definition of death is based upon brain functions. Before diagnosing brain death, the following conditions should be met:

1. Spontaneous respiratory function has ceased irreversibly.

2. A metabolic encephalopathy (including disturbances of fluid/electrolyte balance, hepatic or renal failure, endocrine disease, and drug intoxication) has been excluded.

3. Hypothermia (a temperature below 35 degrees centigrade) has been excluded.

4. Artificial ventilation is in progress because of previous inadequate respiration (not attributable to muscular weakness or neuromuscular agents).

5. A disorder has been diagnosed that is capable of causing irremediable brain damage.

Factors normally taken into consideration in determining the presence of brain death include:

1. Loss of pupillary reflexes.

2. Loss of corneal reflexes.

3. Loss of oculocephalic (doll's head) reflexes.

4. Loss of oculovestibular (caloric) reflexes.

5. Loss of responses to painful stimuli applied in cranial nerve territory.

6. Loss of responses to bronchial stimulation with a suction catheter.

7. Loss of ventilatory response to elevated blood carbon dioxide (arterial pCO_2 rising over 50 mm Hg from a background of normal blood gases).

8. Reproducibility of observations to exclude error and affirm the stability of the finding; the minimum interval between examinations will depend on the causal pathology and may be as long as 24 hours.

In patients with respiratory disease, it is essential to obtain the opinion of a pulmonary physician.

The CC's [Clinical Center] policy concerning the donation of organs and/or tissues by CC patients is designed in cooperation with the Washington Regional Transplant Consortium [WRTC] and the Lions Eye Bank of Maryland. These outside agencies assist the CC in evaluating potential organ and/or tissue donors and coordinating the retrieval of suitable organs or tissues for transplantation.

Many CC patients have diseases that exclude them from being organ or tissue donors; however, the criteria for cornea transplantation are less restrictive, and may include a larger population of CC patients. To ensure optimal use of these valuable and scarce resources, Institute and CC personnel should be aware of both the WRTC program and the Lions Eye Bank program. Discussion with patients and/or families about potential donation of organs, tissue, and/or corneas should, whenever possible, be conducted by the physician providing care for the patient. The patient's primary or attending physician may contact the WRTC at any time whenever a patient requests additional information, would like to be identified as a potential organ and/or tissue donor, or the physician believes that the patient may be an appropriate organ/tissue donor. When a patient consents to organ donation prior to death, documentation of this discussion should be recorded in the progress notes by the physician.

Chapter 47

Death Certification

Introduction

A death certificate is a permanent record of an individual's death. One purpose of the death certificate is to obtain a simple description of the sequence or process leading to death rather than a record describing all medical conditions present at death.

Causes of death on the death certificate represent a medical opinion that might vary among individual physicians. In signing the death certificate, the physician, medical examiner, or coroner certifies that, in his/her medical opinion, the individual died from the reported causes of death. The certifier's opinion and confidence in that opinion are based upon his/her training, knowledge of medicine, available medical history, symptoms, diagnostic tests, and available autopsy results for the decedent. Even if extensive information is available to the certifier, causes of death may be difficult to determine, so the certifier may indicate uncertainty by qualifying the causes on the death certificate.

Cause-of-death data is important for surveillance, research, design of public health and medical interventions, and funding decisions for research and development. While the death certificate is a legal

From "Possible Solutions to Common Problems in Death Certification," [Online] January 1997. Available: http://www.cdc.gov:80/nchswww/about/major/dvs/brief.htm. Produced by the CDC's National Center for Health Statistics (NCHS). For complete contact information, please refer to Chapter 60, "Resources."

document used for legal, family, and insurance purposes, it may not be the only record used, because, in some cases, the death certificate may only be admissible as proof of death. The following provides suggestions, largely from Hanzlick (1994), for handling situations where cause of death is difficult to certify.

Uncertainty

Often several acceptable ways of writing a cause-of-death statement exist. Optimally, a certifier will be able to provide a simple description of the process leading to death that is etiologically clear and to be confident that this is the correct sequence of causes. However, realistically, description of the process is sometimes difficult because the certifier is not certain.

In this case, the certifier should think through the causes about which he/she is confident and what possible etiologies could have resulted in these conditions. The certifier should select the causes that are suspected to have been involved and use words such as "probable" or "presumed" to indicate that the description provided is not completely certain. If the initiating condition reported on the death certificate could have arisen from a pre-existing condition but the certifier cannot determine the etiology, he/she should state that the etiology is unknown, undetermined, or unspecified, so it is clear that the certifier did not have enough information to provide even a qualified etiology.

The Elderly

When preparing a cause-of-death statement for an elderly decedent, the causes should present a clear and distinct etiological sequence, if possible. Causes of death on the death certificate should not include terms such as senescence, old age, infirmity, and advanced age because they have little value for public health or medical research. Age is recorded elsewhere on the death certificate. When malnutrition is involved, the certifier should consider if other medical conditions could have led to malnutrition.

When a number of conditions or multiple organ/system failure resulted in death, the physician, medical examiner, or coroner should choose a single sequence to describe the process leading to death and list the other conditions in Part II of the certification section. "Multiple system failure" could be included as an "other significant condition" but also specify the systems involved. In other instances, conditions listed in Part II of the death certificate may include causes that resulted from the underlying cause but did not fit into the sequence resulting in death.

If the certifier cannot determine a descriptive sequence of causes of death despite carefully considering all information available and circumstances of death did not warrant investigation by the medical examiner or coroner, death may be reported as "unspecified natural causes." If any potentially lethal medical conditions are known but cannot be cited as part of the sequence leading to death, they should be listed as other significant conditions.

Infant Deaths

Maternal conditions may have initiated or affected the sequence that resulted in an infant death. These maternal conditions should be reported in the cause-of-death statement in addition to the infant causes.

When Sudden Infant Death Syndrome (SIDS) is suspected, a complete investigation should be conducted, typically by a medical examiner. If the infant is under 1 year of age, no cause of death is determined after scene investigation, clinical history is reviewed, and a complete autopsy is performed, then the death can be reported as (SIDS). If the investigation is not complete, the death may be reported as presumed to be (SIDS).

Avoid Ambiguity

Most certifiers will find themselves, at some point, in the circumstance in which they are unable to provide a simple description of the process of death. In this situation, the certifier should try to provide a clear sequence, qualify the causes about which he/she is uncertain, and be able to explain the certification chosen.

When processes such as [those listed in Table 47.1] are reported, additional information about the etiology should be reported if possible.

If the certifier is unable to determine the etiology of a process such as those shown above, the process must be qualified as being of an unknown, undetermined, probable, presumed, or unspecified etiology so it is clear that a distinct etiology was not inadvertently or carelessly omitted.

The conditions and types of death [listed in Table 47.2] might seem to be specific but when the medical history is examined further may be found to be complications of an injury or poisoning (possibly occurring long ago).

Table 47.1a. Ambiguous Causes of Death (continued in Table 47.1b).

Cardiovascular

Acute myocardial infarction
Arrhythmia
Atrial fibrillation
Cardiac arrest
Cardiac dysrhythmia

Congestive heart failure
Cardiomyopathy
Dysrhythmia
Heart failure
Hypotension

Myocardial infarction
Shock
Ventricular fibrillation
Ventricular tachycardia

Central Nervous System

Altered mental status
Anoxic encephalopathy
Brain injury
Brain stem herniation
Cerebrovascular accident
Cerebral edema
Cerebellar tonsillar herniation

Dementia (when not otherwise specified)
Epidural hematoma
Increased intracranial pressure
Intracranial hemorrhage
Metabolic encephalopathy

Open (or closed) head injury
Seizures
Subdural hemotoma
Subarachnoid hemorrhage
Uncal herniation

Respiratory

Aspiration
Pleural effusions

Pneumonia
Pulmonary embolism

Pulmonary insufficiency
Pulmonary edema

Gastrointestinal

Biliary obstruction
Bowel obstruction
Cirrhosis

Diarrhea
End-stage liver disease
Gastrointestinal hemorrhage

Hepatic failure
Hepatorenal syndrome
Perforated gallbladder

Blood, Renal, Immune

Coagulopathy
Disseminated intravascular coagulopathy
End-stage renal disease

Hepatorenal syndrome
Immunosuppression
Pancytopenia
Renal failure

Thrombocytopenia
Urinary tract infection

Table 47.1b. Ambiguous Causes of Death (continued from Table 47.1a).

Not System-Oriented

Abdominal hemor-rhage	Decubiti	Multi-organ failure
Ascites	Dehydration	Necrotizing soft-tissue
Anoxia	Exsanguination	infection
Bacteremia	Failure to thrive	Peritonitis
Bedridden	Gangrene	Sepsis
Carcinogenesis	Hemothorax	Septic shock
Carcinomatosis	Hyperglycemia	Shock
Chronic bedridden state	Hyperkalemia	Volume depletion
	Hyponatremia	

Source: Hanzlick, pp. 106-7

Table 47.2. Possible Complications of Injury or Poisoning

Subdural hematoma	Pulmonary emboli	Hypothermia
Epidural hematoma	Thermal burns/chemi-cal burns	Hip fracture
Subarachnoid hemor-rhage	Sepsis	Seizure disorder
Fracture	Hyperthermia	Drug or alcohol over-dose/drug or alcohol abuse

Source: Hanzlick, p. 68

Is it possible that the underlying cause of death was the result of an injury or poisoning? If it might be, check with the medical examiner/coroner to find out if the death should be reported to him/her.

When indicating neoplasms as a cause of death indicate the following: 1) primary site or that the primary site is unknown, 2) benign or malignant, 3) cell type or that the cell type is unknown, 4) grade of a neoplasm, and 5) part or lobe of an organ affected. For example, a well-differentiated squamous cell carcinoma, lung, left upper lobe (Hanzlick p. 58).

Medical Examiner/Coroner

The medical examiner/coroner investigates deaths that are unexpected, unexplained, or if an injury or poisoning was involved. State laws often provide guidelines for when a medical examiner/coroner must be notified. In the case of deaths known or suspected to have resulted from injury or poisoning, report the death to the medical examiner/coroner as required by state law. The medical examiner/coroner will either complete the cause-of-death section of the death certificate or waive that responsibility. If the medical examiner/coroner does not accept the case, then the certifier will need to complete the cause-of-death section.

References and Sources

Hanzlick R, ed. 1994. *The Medical Cause of Death Manual*. Northfield, IL: College of American Pathologists.

National Center for Health Statistics. 1987. *Physicians' Handbook on Medical Certification of Death*. Hyattsville, MD: Public Health Service.

National Center for Health Statistics. 1989. *Report of the Workshop on Improving Cause-of-Death Statistics*. Hyattsville, MD: Public Health Service.

National Center for Health Statistics. 1991. *Report of the Second Workshop on Improving Cause-of-Death Statistics*. Hyattsville, MD: Public Health Service.

National Center for Health Statistics. 1996. *Technical Appendix. Vital Statistics of the United States, 1992, vol II, mortality, part A*. Washington: Public Health Service.

Part Six

Final Arrangements

Chapter 48

Federal Regulation of Funeral Goods and Services

Each year, Americans arrange more than 2 million funerals for family and friends. Because funerals can cost thousands of dollars, you should be aware of federal regulations that can help protect you from overpaying.

The Funeral Rule, enforced by the Federal Trade Commission, makes it easier for you to choose only those goods and services you want or need and to pay for only those you select. According to the Rule, you can find out the cost of individual items whether you shop by telephone or in person.

If you inquire about funeral arrangements in person, the funeral home must give you a written price list of available goods and services. Keep in mind that when you arrange for a funeral, you can buy a package of goods and services or individual items. If you want to buy a casket for example, the funeral provider must supply lists that describe the available selections and their prices.

Telephone Price Disclosures

You can shop by phone to compare prices among funeral providers. Getting price information over the phone may help you select a

Excerpted from "Funerals: A Consumer Guide," [Online] November 1996. Available: http://www.pueblo.gsa.gov/cic_text/misc/funeral/funeral.htm. And from "Caskets and Burial Vaults," [Online] November 1996. Available: http://www.ftc.gov/bcp/conline/pubs/services/caskets.htm. Produced by the Federal Trade Commission (FTC) Washington, DC 20580. For complete contact information, please refer to Chapter 60, "Resources."

funeral home and the arrangements you want. When you call a funeral provider to ask about terms, conditions, or prices of funeral goods and services, the funeral provider must give you prices and other information from the price lists to answer your questions reasonably.

General Price List

If you inquire in person about funeral arrangements, the funeral provider will give you a general price list that contains the cost of each funeral item and service offered. Use this information to help select the funeral provider and funeral items you want, need, and can afford.

The price list also must include information about embalming, caskets for cremation, and required purchases.

Embalming Information

The Funeral Rule requires funeral providers to give consumers information about embalming. Under the Rule, a funeral provider:

- may not falsely state that embalming is required by law.

- must disclose in writing that embalming is not required by law, except in certain special cases.

- may not charge a fee for unauthorized embalming unless embalming is required by state law.

- will disclose in writing that you usually have the right to choose a disposition—such as direct cremation or immediate burial—if you do not want embalming.

- will disclose to you in writing that certain funeral arrangements, such as a funeral with viewing, may make embalming a practical necessity and, so, a required purchase.

Cash Advance Sales

The Funeral Rule requires funeral providers to disclose in writing if they charge a fee for buying cash advance items—goods or services that funeral providers pay for on your behalf. Examples of cash advance items are flowers, obituary notices, pallbearers, and clergy honoraria. Some funeral providers charge you their cost for these items. Others add a service fee to their cost. The Funeral Rule requires funeral providers to tell you when a service fee is added to the price of cash advance items, or if there are refunds, discounts, or rebates from the supplier on any cash advance item.

Caskets for Cremation

Some consumers may want to select direct cremation—cremation of the deceased without a viewing or other ceremony where the body is present. If you choose a direct cremation, the funeral provider will offer an inexpensive alternative container or an unfinished wood box. An alternative container is a non-metal enclosure—pressboard, cardboard, or canvas—to hold the deceased.

Because any container you buy will be destroyed during the cremation, you may wish to use an alternative container or an unfinished wood box. These could lower the funeral cost because they are less expensive than traditional caskets.

Under the Funeral Rule, funeral directors who offer direct cremations:

- may not tell you that state or local law requires a casket for direct cremations;

- must disclose in writing your right to buy an unfinished wood box (a type of casket) or an alternative container for a direct cremation; and

- must make an unfinished wood box or alternative container available for direct cremation.

Required Purchases

You do not have to buy goods or services you don't want, or pay any fees as a condition to obtaining the products and services you do want, except one permitted fee for the services of the funeral director and staff, and the fees for the goods and services you select or state law requires. Under the Funeral Rule:

- you have the right to choose the funeral goods and services you want, with some exceptions.

- the funeral provider must disclose this right in writing on the general price list.

- the funeral provider must disclose the specific state law that requires you to purchase any particular item on your itemized statement of goods and services selected.

- the funeral provider may not refuse, or charge a fee, to handle a casket you bought elsewhere.

Statement of Funeral Goods and Services Selected

The funeral provider will give you an itemized statement of the total cost of the funeral goods and services you select. This statement also will disclose any legal, cemetery, or crematory requirements that require you to purchase any specific funeral goods or services.

The funeral provider must give you this statement after you select the funeral goods and services that you would like. The statement includes the prices of the individual items you are considering for purchase, as well as the total price, in one place. You can decide whether to add or subtract items. If the cost of cash advance items is not known at this time, the funeral provider must write down a "good faith estimate." The Rule does not require any specific form for this information. Funeral providers may include it in any document they give you at the end of your discussion about funeral arrangements.

Caskets and Burial Vaults

When a loved one dies, difficult and sometimes costly decisions about a funeral have to be made quickly, often under great emotional stress. Your emotional state may dictate decisions not in your best interests. You may want to consult with a disinterested person, perhaps a clergyman or an experienced friend, if you feel unable to objectively evaluate a funeral provider's products and services.

For example, sometimes manufacturers of caskets and burial vaults give to the funeral providers promotional materials that may appeal to the desire to protect the physical remains of the deceased. They may do this by making false or exaggerated claims about the durability of their products. They may make insupportable claims that their products are "waterproof" or impermeable to the elements. The Federal Trade Commission (FTC) has issued orders against some manufacturers, prohibiting them from making such false or deceptive durability claims.

This [section] discusses caskets and burial vaults, their use, and their protective claims. It also briefly discusses the option of funeral pre-planning, and lists organizations you may contact for further information.

Caskets

A casket, also called a coffin, is frequently the single most expensive funeral item you may have to buy if you are planning a traditional funeral.

Caskets vary widely in style and price and typically are sold for their visual appeal. They generally are made of metal or wood, although some are constructed of fiberglass or plastic. Most metal caskets are made from rolled steel in different gauges—the lower the gauge, the thicker the steel. Wooden caskets come in hardwood, softwood, and plywood.

The terms "gasketed," "protective," and "sealer" are frequently used to describe a metal casket. These terms mean that the casket has a rubber gasket or other features that delay the penetration of water and prevent rust. Some metal caskets come with a warranty for longevity. Protective features in caskets add to their cost.

Unlike metal caskets, wooden caskets generally are not gasketed and do not carry a warranty for longevity. However, manufacturers of both wooden and metal caskets usually warrant workmanship and materials.

Burial Vaults or Grave Liners

Often, cemeteries require a burial vault or a grave liner to enclose the casket in a grave. The casket is placed into either a vault or a liner to prevent the ground from caving in as the casket deteriorates. A grave liner, also called a "rough box," is made of reinforced concrete and lowered into the grave prior to burial. A burial vault is more substantial and expensive than a grave liner, is typically sold for its visual appeal, and is usually gasketed. Most vaults are constructed of steel-reinforced concrete and lined with other materials, including plastic. Like some caskets, the vault may be sold with a warranty of protective strength.

Preservative and Protective Claims

Under the FTC's Funeral Rule, funeral providers are prohibited from making claims that funeral goods, such as caskets or vaults, will keep out water, dirt, and other gravesite substances when that is not true. The Rule also prohibits funeral providers from telling you a particular funeral item or service can indefinitely preserve a body in the grave. Such claims are untrue.

Pre-Planning Funerals

Decisions about purchasing funeral goods and services are often made when people are grieving and under time constraints. For this reason, some people choose to prearrange a funeral. If you are considering prearranging a funeral for yourself or for a loved one, ask funeral directors about the different types of dispositions and ceremonies available. At the same time, scrutinize claims made by the manufacturers of such products as caskets and burial vaults.

The FTC's Funeral Rule requires funeral directors to itemize prices and provide consumers with price lists, and price information over the phone, which are essential for comparing costs.

If you are considering pre-paying for funeral goods and services, there are a number of issues to consider and questions to ask before pre-paying for funeral arrangements:

- Be sure you know what you are paying for. Are you buying only merchandise, such as a casket and vault, or are you purchasing funeral services as well?

- What happens to money you have pre-paid? Some states have different requirements concerning the handling of funds paid for pre-arranged funeral services.

- What happens to the interest income on money that is pre-paid and put into a trust account?

- Are you protected if the firm with which you are doing business should go out of business?

- Can you cancel the contract and get back any money you have pre-paid if you should change your mind about the pre-planned funeral?

- What if you should move to a different area or death occurs away from home? Some pre-paid funeral plans can be transferred, but often there is an added cost in doing so.

In addition, it is important to keep copies of any documents that you sign or that are given to you at the time pre-arrangements are made. It also is especially important to inform family members about such plans and arrangements and the whereabouts of these documents.

For More Information

Most states have a licensing board that regulates the funeral industry. You may contact the licensing board in your state for information or help.

If you want additional information about how to make funeral arrangements and the options available, you may want to contact interested business, professional, and consumer groups. Some of the largest include:

American Association of Retired Persons
AARP Fulfillment
601 E Street, N.W.
Washington, DC 20049

AARP is a nonprofit, nonpartisan organization dedicated to helping older Americans achieve lives of independence, dignity and purpose. AARP publishes *Pre-Paying for Your Funeral?* This publication is available free by writing to the address listed above.

Funeral and Memorial Societies of America
P.O. Box 10
Hinesburg, VT 05461
(800) 458-5563

FAMSA is a consumer organization that disseminates information about alternatives for funeral or non-funeral dispositions. It encourages advance planning and cost efficiency.

Cremation Association of North America
401 North Michigan Ave.
Chicago, IL 60611
(312) 644-6610

CANA is an association of crematories, cemeteries, and funeral homes that offer cremation. More than 750 members own and operate crematories and encourage the concept of memorialization.

International Order of the Golden Rule
P.O. Box 3586
Springfield, IL 62708
(217) 793-3322

OGR is an international association of independent funeral homes. Membership is by invitation only. Approximately 1,500 funeral homes are members of OGR.

Jewish Funeral Directors of America
Seaport Landing
150 Lynnway, Ste. 506
Lynn, MA 09102
(617) 477-9300

JFDA is a national trade association of funeral directors serving the Jewish community. It has approximately 200 members.

National Funeral Directors Association
11121 West Oklahoma Ave.
Milwaukee, WI 53227
(414) 541-2500
(800) 228-NFDA

NFDA is the largest educational and professional association of funeral directors. It has 14,000 members throughout the United States.

National Funeral Directors and Morticians Association
3951 Snapfinger Pkwy., Ste. 570
Decatur, GA 30035
(404) 286-6680
(800) 434-0958

NFDMA is a national association primarily of African-American funeral providers. It has 2,000 members.

National Selected Morticians
5 Revere Dr., Ste. 340
Northbrook, IL 60062-8009
(847) 559-9569

NSM is a national association of funeral firms in which membership is by invitation only and conditioned upon the commitment of each firm to comply with the association's Code of Good Funeral Practice. Consumers may request a variety of publications through NSM's affiliate, the Consumer Information Bureau, Inc.

Funeral Service Consumer Assistance Program
National Research and Information Center
2250 E. Devon Ave., Ste. 250
Des Plaines, IL 60018
(800) 662-7666

FSCAP is a program designed to help consumers and funeral directors resolve disagreements about funeral service contracts. FSCAP is a service of the National Research and Information Center, an independent, nonprofit organization that researches and provides consumer information on death, grief, and funeral service.

For Further Help

If you have a problem concerning funeral matters, first try to resolve it with your funeral director. If that doesn't work, contact your federal, state, local consumer protection agencies, or FSCAP. You also can file a complaint with the FTC by contacting the Consumer Response Center by phone: (202) FTC-HELP (382-4357); TDD: (202) 326-2502; by mail: Consumer Response Center, Federal Trade Commission, 600 Pennsylvania Ave., N.W., Washington DC 20580; or through the Internet, using the online complaint form. Although the Commission cannot resolve individual problems for consumers, it can act against a company if it sees a pattern of possible law violations.

Chapter 49

Funerals, Cremations, and Burials: A Consumer Guide

Basic Costs and Services of Funeral Director and Staff

Usually, each funeral home charges a basic comprehensive charge for a set standard of services. This will vary per location. These services include generally a conference with a responsible party to determine service desired; coordinating services of all involved (i.e., plans with cemetery, crematory and/or other parties involved in the final disposition of the deceased); retention and care of remains prior to the commencement of post death activities; [processing] death certificate, state permits, and other required authorizations and forms; basic overhead costs; fee added to anything you select unless you chose direct cremation/immediate burial; and forwarding or receiving remains and aftercare services.

Price: $1,110-$1,250

Special Services

Your passing may not occur at the site of your choosing. You may be away from home for example. When this happens, funeral homes make arrangements with each other to get you back to the place you have chosen for your ceremony. Below [are listed] the average services rendered and the average costs we have found for forwarding and receiving remains.

Forwarding Remains

The average package contains the removal of remains to the local funeral home, basic services of funeral director and staff, a proportionate share of overhead costs, the basic sheltering of remains, embalming, obtaining necessary permits and authorizations.

Extra charges not included with the base price [are for] a casket or alternative shipping container, the use of facilities for any visitation or ceremony, public or private, . . . transferring the remains to the airport or other destination, the charges of a common carrier, and anything not expressly stated as being provided. These vary depending on area. Check with your local funeral home.

Price: $825-$1,845

Receiving of Remains

Not much is different from receiving the remains versus sending the remains. The funeral home typically receives remains from another funeral home, offers the basic services of the funeral director and staff, charges you for a proportionate share of overhead costs, provides basic sheltering of the remains, obtains necessary permits and authorizations, and [provides] local transportation to the cemetery or crematory.

Not included in this charge is the use of facilities and staff for any visitation or ceremony, public or private, prior to final disposition. Nor does it include transferring the remains from the airport or other source, or the charges of a common carrier or anything not expressly stated as being provided. These are all extra based on the funeral home, state, and city.

Price: $550-$1,420

Embalming

Embalming is a chemical process which provides temporary preservation of the body for the purpose of ceremonial viewing. A person examined and licensed by the state they live in must complete this procedure. The price generally includes the use of preparation room and sanitary care.

Except in certain special cases, embalming is not required by law. Embalming may be necessary, however, if you select certain funeral arrangements, such as a funeral with viewing. If you do not want embalming, you usually have the right to choose an arrangement that does not require you to pay for it, such as direct cremation or immediate burial.

Price: $225-$450

Other Preparation of the Body

Dressing, casketing, and cosmetology: $150-$195
Sanitary care without embalming: $185
Restoration and other procedures: $65/hr.
Refrigeration per day: $45
Autopsied remains: $80
Washing and disinfecting deceased when not embalming: $50

Transportation

Below are some typical [transportation] services offered by funeral homes and the average price.

Most funeral homes charges reflect transportation within a certain radius (generally 30 miles). Outside of the local radius, additional charges per mile average $1.50 per mile.

Table 49.1. Transportation Services

Service	Price
Transfer of remains (from private home or hospital) to funeral home	$110-$225
Additional assistance charge for removal, per person, from private residence	$45-$50
Hearse to church (3 hours)	$150-$225
Delivery only—cemetery, crematory, or airport	$200
Funeral sedan (each)	$75
Office service car/flower car	$60
Clergy/lead car	$100
Limousine	$120

Funeral Goods

Below are some average prices for items you will need for your funeral ceremony.

Table 49.2. Funeral Goods

Burial Goods	Price
Caskets	$595-$16,000
Cremation caskets	$795-$2,700
Alternative containers	$125-$225
Outer burial containers	$575-$8,400
Urns	$125-$3,000

Other Goods	Price
Memorial prayer cards per 100	$40-$55
Acknowledgement cards per box of 25	$5-$8.50
Register books	$20-$115
Burial clothing, men's and women's	$90-$180
Crosses and crucifixes	$20-$40
Veteran's flag case	$125
Urn or casket engraving	$15-$50

Cash Advances

There are some items you may need to complete your funeral arrangements. As a service to you, the funeral home arranges these services for you and then passes the charges on to you. Generally, reimbursement is made prior to the funeral service. You can arrange these services without the assistance of the funeral home if you choose.

Services

A Viewing, Visitation, or Gathering

Many people prefer to have a viewing or wake for the deceased. Most funeral homes prepare the setting, arrange physical remains, position floral displays and mementos, and are ready to assist at any time during your stay.

Set-up fee: $75-$185
Fee per hour at funeral home or another location: $75-$90

Service at the Funeral Home

Funeral homes are more than happy to hold the service at their facility. Included in the charge is the convenience of having the staff coordinate the arrangements for the ceremony and be on the premises if you need anything.

Funeral home or other facility (3 hrs.): $185-$345
Additional charge per hour: $65
Staff overtime (services after 5 PM and all day Saturday): $150
Sunday and holidays: $300
Recorded service music at funeral home: $45

Graveside Service

Funeral homes can assist you with a [graveside] service by helping set up the processional, coordinate the arrangements for the service, prepare the setting where the service will occur, and accompany the remains to the cemetery or crematory.

Local (3 hrs.): $200
Additional charge per hour: $65

Table 49.3. Cash Advances

Services	Price
Cemetery charges (excluding price of lot)	$600-$700
Vault install	$30-$85
Crematory charges	$170-$350
Motorcycle escorts	$115 +
Obituary notice	$100/day
Clergy honorarium	$75-$150
Organist	$75-$150
Soloist	$60-$150
Copies of death certificate	$8 first, $2 ea. addtl.
Flowers	$15-$1,500 plus tax
Hairdresser/barber	Varies
Phone calls	Varies

Grave Sites

Prices vary depending on what site you choose at the cemetery, what part of the country you are living in (bigger the city, higher the cost), whether you choose multiple graves together, lawn crypts . . . , vaults . . . , what type of memorial marker is placed for the headstone, perpetual care, non-perpetual care, or whether the final resting place is a Mausoleum.

Remember, these are estimates. Please check your local areas for final cost.

Table 49.4. Grave Sites

Product	Price
Marker (granite)	Starts at $289 plus tax and installation
Marker (bronze)	Starts at $520 plus tax and installation

Burial Location	Price
2 lawn vaults and 2 markers	$7,600
2 lawn crypts (includes vault and marker for two)	$3,295-$3,795
2 regular average lots	$2,400-$3,650
Cremation garden	Starts at $2,400

Immediate Burial

Immediate burial DOES NOT include the use of facilities and staff for any public visitation prior to burial, any refrigeration of remains, the actual cost of the grave at the cemetery, or the cemetery's charges for opening and closing of the grave, any required other burial container or cash advances, or anything not expressly stated as being provided.

Price: $795-$1,533

Add a casket and minimum outer burial [container] and the price jumps to $2,508-$7,060.

Direct Cremation

Full Service

For the most splendid type of cremation service, a funeral home typically provides a comprehensive package that includes the basic services of funeral director and staff (including a share of overhead costs), the local transfer to the crematory and cremation of remains, the basic sheltering of remains prior to cremation, sanitary care, obtaining and helping with the necessary paperwork, composing of obituary notices, memorial folders, register books, and complete aftercare services.

IT DOES NOT include generally the use of facilities and staff for any public visitation prior to cremation, or anything not expressly stated as being provided. This of course will cost extra.

If you want to arrange a direct cremation, (no viewing, no anything) you can use an alternative container. Alternative containers encase the body and can be made of fiberboard or composite materials, with or without an outside covering (A nice way of saying a cardboard box).

Price: $1,305-$5,881

Direct cremation with container provided by purchaser: $1,305
Direct cremation with alternative container: $1,480
Direct cremation with a premium cremation casket: $3,900
Interment of remains following direct cremation: $75

Limited Service

For those people who are less interested in the top of the line cremation, there is the limited package that still covers all of the basics. The package generally covers the minimum services of funeral director and staff, share of overhead costs, the local transfer to crematory and cremation of remains, sanitary care, obtaining the necessary permits and authorizations, and the filing of the death certificate.

NO OTHER secretarial staff services are included in this package.

Price: $720-$895

Chapter 50

Financial Arrangements

The death of a spouse, parent, or loved one is a very difficult time. Yet even during this period of grief and emotional readjustments, important financial arrangements must be made. Some attention may have been focused on these items prior to a death. This [chapter] was developed to help you prepare for and handle the many details which must be attended to, whether or not any prior arrangements were made. We hope the following information will help to guide you through the many decisions that need to be made and actions that need to be taken in the first few months after death.

Collecting the Papers

The first step is to collect the necessary papers you will need to file for various benefits and to finalize the estate.

- *Copies of the death certificate* — You will need to give copies of the death certificate to many of the offices or agencies you contact. You can purchase certified copies of the death certificate through your funeral director or directly from the county Health Department. Each certificate will cost a few dollars. You may save money by using a photocopy when possible, but many

From "Final Details: A Helpful Guide for Survivors when Death Occurs." © 1998 by the American Association of Retired Persons (AARP), 601 E St. N. W., Washington, DC 20049. For complete contact information, please refer to Chapter 60, "Resources." Reprinted with permission.

companies will require a certified copy. You will want 10-12 copies initially, but you may need more later.

- *All insurance policies*—These documents may be stored in a safe deposit box or with the personal belongings of the deceased.

- *Social Security numbers*—of the deceased, the spouse, and any dependent children. The Social Security number for the deceased can be found on the death certificate.

- *Copy of a certificate of honorable (or other than dishonorable) discharge*—if the deceased was a veteran. Write the National Personnel Record Center, 9700 Page Ave., St. Louis, MO 63132, attention to the branch of service for which your spouse served, if you cannot find a copy of the discharge.

- *Marriage certificate*—if the spouse of the deceased will be applying for benefits. Copies are available at the Office of the County Clerk where the marriage license was issued.

- *Birth certificates*—for dependent children. Copies are available at either the state or county Public Health offices where the child was born.

- *Will*—The lawyer of the deceased may have the will, or it may be in a safe deposit box or with the personal belongings of the deceased.

- *A complete list of all property*—including real estate, stocks, bonds, savings accounts, and personal property of the deceased. Land titles, stocks, certificates, and other financial papers may be stored in a safe deposit box or other secure place.

Insurance Policies

The deceased may have had several types of insurance policies. These could include:

- life insurance
- mortgage or loan insurance
- accident insurance (if applicable)
- auto insurance (if applicable)
- credit card insurance
- various types of insurance provided by the deceased's employer.

The proceeds from a life insurance policy can generally be paid directly to the named beneficiary. These claims are usually processed quickly and can be an important source of money for the survivors. The survivor should file claims for insurance policies as soon as possible, especially if finances are a concern.

A decision regarding the type of payment plan you desire may need to be made. Your options might include taking the money in a lump-sum payment, or having the insurance company make fixed payments over a period of time. The decision depends on your financial situation. You may want smaller fixed payments in order to have a steady income and pay less tax on the money. Or you may want the full amount immediately to pay bills or to invest. You should consider consulting a lawyer or financial advisor about this decision before contacting the insurance company.

Social Security

The deceased is considered to be covered by Social Security if he/she paid in to Social Security for at least 40 quarters. Check with your local Social Security office or call 800-772-1213 to determine if the deceased was eligible. If the deceased was already receiving benefits, do not deposit any checks received after death. Check with Social Security. If the deceased was eligible, two types of benefits are possible.

- A death benefit of $255 (in 1999) toward burial expenses. The survivor can complete the necessary form at your local Social Security office, or the funeral director can be asked to complete the application and apply the payment directly to the funeral bill. This payment is made only to eligible spouses or to a child entitled to survivor's benefits.

- Survivor's benefits for a spouse or children.

- If the spouse is age 60 or older, he/she may be eligible for benefits. The amount of the benefit received prior to age 65 will be less than the benefit due at age 65 or over.

- Disabled surviving spouses age 50 or older will be eligible for benefits.

- The surviving spouse who is under 60 but who cares for dependent children under 16 or cares for disabled children may be eligible for benefits.

- The children of the deceased who are under the age 18 or are disabled may also be entitled to benefits.

When applying for Social Security benefits, you should have available birth and death certificates of the deceased, marriage certificate of the spouse, birth certificates of any dependent children, Social Security numbers, and copies of the deceased's most recent federal income tax return.

Veterans' Benefits

If the deceased was a veteran who received a discharge other than dishonorable, the survivors may be eligible to receive a lump-sum payment of $300 for burial expenses and an allowance of $150 toward a plot in a private cemetery; (Burial in a national cemetery is free to a veteran, his/her spouse, and dependent children.) Veterans are also eligible for a headstone or grave marker at no charge. The funeral director often can help survivors apply for these benefits, or you can contact the regional Department of Veterans' Affairs (VA) office.

The surviving spouse and dependent children of veterans receiving disability benefits may also be entitled to monthly payments. Check with the regional VA office.

Employee Benefits

If the deceased was employed at the time of death, the survivor should contact the employer regarding any benefits for the survivor. The employer may have provided life, health, or accident insurance. The deceased may be due a final paycheck for vacation or sick leave. If the death was work-related, there may be worker's compensation benefits.

The survivor should contact all past employers, including federal, state, or local government, to determine if the survivors of the deceased are entitled to any payments from a pension plan.

Also check with the employer to see if the deceased belonged to a union or professional organization. These groups may offer death benefits for their members.

If the deceased was already retired and received a pension, you should check with the employer to determine if survivors will continue to receive a pension payment and whether the payment will be reduced.

The Will

The will of the deceased will need to be located. Check with the lawyer, family, and friends of the deceased who might know where the will is kept. It may be stored in a safe deposit box, which is sealed at the time of death in some states. (See the section on safe deposit boxes).

If the deceased did not have a will, this is referred to as dying "intestate." In this case, the estate, including property and assets belonging to the deceased, will be disbursed according to state law. Laws vary from state to state, but generally the spouse receives a portion of the real property or a "life estate" (the right to use but not own it for the remainder of his/her life). In addition, the spouse is eligible for a share of the deceased's personal property (goods, money, investments, etc.), and the surviving children inherit the rest. Contact the Probate Court in your state for details. Neither the intestate distribution law nor the will affect property where the title is in the name of the deceased and another person who has a right of survivorship. This property automatically passes to the co-owner.

Probate

Probate is the process of paying the deceased's debts and distributing the estate to the rightful beneficiaries. This process begins with the court appointing someone to administer the estate. The will usually nominates the "executor." If there is no will, the court will appoint a "personal representative," usually a spouse or relative. This representative will need to pay a filing fee, inform interested parties, especially creditors, that the estate is being probated, make an inventory of assets, and dispose of the estate according to the will or state laws.

Depending on the size and complexity of the estate, legal assistance may be required.

The probate estate does not include property where the deceased and someone else are listed as owners. Proceeds from a life insurance policy or Individual Retirement Account (IRA) which are paid directly to a beneficiary are also not subject to probate.

Taxes

Federal Estate Taxes

Very few estates have to pay federal estate tax. In 1998, estate tax is only due on estates exceeding $625,000; in 1999 the amount will be $650,000. Contact your local Internal Revenue office for form 706. A federal estate tax return must be filed and taxes paid within nine months of the date of death.

State Estate Taxes

State laws vary, but generally any estate which pays a federal estate tax must also file a state estate tax. This amount is paid by the estate to the state where the deceased lived. For details, contact your state tax or revenue department. A telephone number and address are usually listed in the government section of your telephone directory.

State Inheritance Taxes

Again, state requirements vary. Some states charge no inheritance tax and others levy one percent or more. For more information, contact your state tax department.

Income Taxes

The federal and state income taxes of the deceased are due for the year of death. The taxes are due on the normal filing date of the following year, unless an extension is requested.

The spouse of the deceased may file jointly for the year of death. A spouse with dependent children may file jointly for two additional years. The IRS offers a booklet, publication #559, *Information for Survivors, Executors and Administrators,* which may be helpful. You can obtain this booklet by contacting your local IRS office. The phone number is listed under IRS in the government section of your directory.

Steps for Surviving Spouses

The death of a spouse may cause significant changes in the survivor's financial circumstances. Here are some steps that should be considered to determine whether you should modify your own financial affairs.

- *Insurance policies:* The survivor may need to consider whether the beneficiaries who have been named on your own life insurance policies need to be changed now that your spouse has died. You should also consider if you need the same amount of life insurance. You should also review your auto and home insurance policies for any necessary changes. If your medical insurance was provided by your spouse's employer, you and any dependent children can continue to receive coverage for up to 36 months, provided you pay the premiums. Contact the company issuing the policy for more information. Or, you may need to purchase your own medical insurance.

- *Auto:* The title of the car owned by your spouse may need to be changed. Contact your State Department of Motor Vehicles.

- *Safe deposit box:* In most states, if the box was rented in only the name of the deceased, it will require a court order to open the box. Only the will or any other materials pertaining to the death can be removed before the will has been probated.

- *Bank accounts, stocks, bonds:* If you, as a survivor, had a joint bank account with your spouse, it will automatically pass to you. You should check with the bank representative to change the title and signature card on the account. To change stocks or bond titles, check with your stockbroker. If the bank account was held only in the name of your spouse, those assets will have to go through probate.

- *Will:* Your will may have passed property to your spouse. If so, it should be updated. You may want to contact your attorney for assistance.

Credit Cards

Cancel any credit cards which were held exclusively in the name of the deceased. Any payments due on these credit cards should be paid by the estate.

In the case of a spouse, you may have credit cards in both names, or you may have used cards which listed only the name of the deceased. In this situation, you will want to try to make payments in order to keep you own good credit rating. You should notify the credit card companies that your spouse is deceased, and that the credit card should list your name only. Some people, particularly widows, may experience difficulties in getting a new card if they do not have their own credit rating. When applying for a card, be sure to inform the lender about credit cards you shared with your spouse, even if your name was not listed.

General Finances

Debts owed by the deceased will be the responsibility of the estate, and should be forwarded to the personal representative or executor who is settling the estate. However, debts which are jointly owed, particularly mortgage payments, and utility or phone bills should generally be paid by the survivor in order to keep a good credit rating.

An extra word of caution to widows and widowers: it is generally suggested that you do not immediately make permanent significant financial decisions, such as selling your home, moving or changing jobs. You will need some time to consider your situation before you can make these decisions responsibly. If at all possible, don't rush into a decision you might later regret.

Professional Assistance

You may need or desire the services of a professional, particularly a lawyer or a financial advisor. It may be easier initially to use the services of the lawyer who wrote the will for the deceased, or to work with the financial advisor of the deceased. Or you may wish to locate another professional with whom you feel more comfortable.

One good place to begin finding names of competent professionals is from friends or family members who have had successful dealings with the kind of advisors you are seeking. Professional organizations such as the local Bar Association may be able to provide referrals.

Support

Many programs across the country have been developed to provide support and assistance to the surviving spouse and children. For more information and to locate a widowed persons program near you, write to AARP Grief and Loss Programs, 601 E Street N.W., Washington, DC 20049, or http://www.aarp.org. A bibliography of books entitled *Bibliography On Grief and Loss* (D435), is also available from AARP Fulfillment.

This information was developed as a guide for what to do after a death in the family. It should not be considered all-inclusive, and other legal or professional advice may be necessary.

Chapter 51

How to Become an Organ and Tissue Donor

Transplantations save lives, but only if you help. All you need to do is say yes to organ and tissue donation on your donor card and/or driver's license and discuss your decision with your family.

Each day about 55 people receive an organ transplant, but another 10 people on the waiting list die because not enough organs are available.

Talk to your family members about organ and tissue donation so they know your wishes. Even if you've signed something, your family will be asked to give consent before donation can occur.

Be an organ and tissue donor. You could save or enhance the lives of more than 50 people!

Facts about Transplantation in The United States

The UNOS [United Network for Organ Sharing] national patient waiting list for organ transplant contains over 64,500 registrations. On January 13, 1999 there were:

- 42,365 registrations for a kidney transplant
- 12,130 registrations for a liver transplant

From "How to Become an Organ and Tissue Donor," [Online] 1999. Available: http://www.organandonor.gov/; and from "HHS Announces New Hospital Rules to Increase Organ Donation," [Online] June 17, 1998. Available: http://www.hcfa.gov/news/pr61798.htm. Produced by the U.S. Department of Health and Human Services (HHS). For complete contact information, please refer to Chapter 60, "Resources."

- 460 registrations for a pancreas transplant
- 121 registrations for a pancreas islet cell transplant
- 1,843 registrations for a kidney-pancreas transplant
- 99 registrations for an intestine transplant
- 4,158 registrations for a heart transplant
- 253 registrations for a heart-lung transplant
- 3,151 registrations for a lung transplant
- 64,580 TOTAL

Number of donors recovered in 1997*:

- 5,477 cadaveric
- 3,809 living
- 9,286 TOTAL

*Based on UNOS Scientific Registry data as of December 2, 1998. Double kidney, double lung and heart-lung transplants are counted as one transplant. NOTE: Data subject to change due to future data submission or correction.

Frequently Asked Questions

Who can become a donor?

All individuals can indicate their intent to donate. Medical suitability for donation is determined at the time of death.

Are there age limits for donors?

There are no age limitations on who can donate. The deciding factor on whether a person can donate is the person's physical condition, not the person's age. Newborns as well as senior citizens have been organ donors. Persons under 18 years of age must have parent's or guardian's consent.

How do I express my wishes to become an organ and tissue donor?

1. Indicate your intent to be an organ and tissue donor on your driver's license. Look here for driver's licensing information for your state.

2. Carry an organ donor card.

3. Most importantly, DISCUSS YOUR DECISION WITH FAMILY MEMBERS AND LOVED ONES.

If I sign a donor card, or indicate my donation preferences on my driver's license, will my wishes be carried out?

Even if you sign a donor card, it is ESSENTIAL THAT YOUR FAMILY KNOWS your wishes. Your family will be asked to sign a consent form in order for your donation to occur.

What organs and tissues can I donate?

*   Organs: heart, kidneys, pancreas, lungs, liver, and intestines
*   Tissue: cornea, skin, bone marrow, heart valves, and connective tissue

If I sign a donor card, will it affect the quality of medical care I receive at the hospital?

No! Every effort is made to save your life before donation is considered.

Will donation disfigure my body? Can there be an open casket funeral?

Donation does not disfigure the body and does not interfere with funeral plans, including open casket services.

Why should minorities be particularly concerned about organ donation?

Some diseases of the kidney, heart, lung, pancreas, and liver are found more frequently in racial and ethnic minority populations than in the general population. For example, African Americans, Asian and Pacific Islanders, and Hispanics are three times more likely to suffer from end-stage renal disease than Whites. Native Americans are four times more likely than Whites to suffer from diabetes. Some of the these diseases are best treated through transplantation; others can only be treated through transplantation.

Successful transplantation often is enhanced by the matching of organs between members of the same ethnic and racial group. For example, an African American patient is often less likely to reject a kidney if it is donated by an individual who is genetically similar.

Generally, people are genetically more similar to people of their race than to people of other races. A shortage of organs donated by minorities can contribute to death and longer waiting periods for transplants for minorities.

More Information on Minorities and Organ Donation and Transplantation

National Institutes of Allergy and Infectious Diseases of the National Institutes of Health: Minority Programs and Initiatives—Allergy, Immunology, and Transplantation: http://www.niaid.nih.gov/facts/mwhhp1.htm

Minority Organ Tissue Transplantation Education Program (MOTTEP): 202-865-4888

United Network for Organ Sharing (UNOS) Minority Affairs Committee: http://www.unos.org/About/Frame_About.asp?SubCat=Committees

New Method of Matching Donated Kidneys May Mean More Transplants for Minorities (UNOS Press Release): http://www.unos.org/Newsroom/archive_newsrelease_062597b.htm

Health Care Financing Administration's End Stage Renal Disease (ESRD) Program Management and Medicaid Information System provides downloadable information on approved providers of kidney dialysis and transplantation: http://www.hcfa.gov/stats/pub files.htm

National Institute of Diabetes and Digestive and Kidney Diseases of the National Institutes of Health provides patient information on kidney diseases: http://www.niddk.nih.gov

Office of Minority Health (OMH) within the Office of the Secretary: http://www.omhrc.gov

Are there any costs to my family for donation?

The donor's family does NOT pay for the cost of the organ donation. All costs related to donation of organs and tissues are paid by the recipient, usually through insurance or Medicare.

Can I sell my organs?

No! The National Organ Transplant Act (Public Law 98-507) makes it ILLEGAL to sell human organs and tissues. Violators are subject to fines and imprisonment. Among the reasons for this rule is the concern of Congress that buying and selling of organs might lead to inequitable access to donor organs with the wealthy having an unfair advantage.

How are organs distributed?

Patients are matched to organs based on a number of factors including blood and tissue typing, medical urgency, time on the waiting list, and geographical location.

How many people are currently waiting for each organ to become available so they can have a transplant?

[See the section above: Facts about Transplantation in the United States.]

Can I be an organ and tissue donor and also donate my body to medical science?

Total body donation is an option, but not if you choose to be an organ and tissue donor. If you wish to donate your entire body, you should directly contact the facility of your choice to make arrangements. Medical schools, research facilities, and other agencies need to study bodies to gain greater understanding of disease mechanisms in humans. This research is vital to saving and improving lives.

New Hospital Rules to Increase Organ Donation

HHS Secretary Donna E. Shalala today announced new regulations aimed at saving lives by substantially increasing organ donation in the United States.

Under the final rule, U.S. hospitals will be required to notify an organ procurement organization (OPO) of all deaths that occur in the hospital. The new requirement will ensure that OPOs have the opportunity to determine the suitability of every potential organ donor, thus increasing the opportunities to contact families and request organ donation. HHS estimates that the new provisions can increase donation by 20 percent over the next two years.

"Organ donation saves lives. But in too many cases today, we are missing opportunities to save people simply because families are never contacted and donation is never even considered as an option," Secretary Shalala said.

"I want our organ procurement organizations to do a better job of making more organs available to save more lives," she said. "The first step is to assure that OPOs are informed of all deaths in hospitals. Then they can determine in each case whether there is the potential for organ donation and, using appropriate discretion and sensitivity, approach the subject of donation with the families."

The regulation, affecting all 5,200 short-stay hospitals in the country, becomes a condition for participation in the Medicare program. The new final rule is the latest step in the National Organ and Tissue Donation Initiative, launched by Vice President Gore last December.

An estimated 12,000 to 15,000 deaths each year could result in organ donation. However, in 1997 only 5,475 deaths resulted in donation. One 1996 study indicated that, out of all deaths that could result in donation, families agreed to donation in 32 percent of cases, and families denied consent in 37 percent of cases. But in 27 percent of cases, representing some 3,000 to 4,000 deaths, either potential donors were not identified or no request was made to the family. (Another 5 percent ultimately proved medically unsuitable.)

At the same time, the number of Americans who die each year waiting for an organ transplant is about 4,000. "In the absence of the requirement we are making today, we have been missing thousands of opportunities for donation each year," Secretary Shalala said. "With better identification of potential donors, we can substantially reduce the number of deaths among those awaiting a transplant."

Under the rule, hospitals will refer 2.1 million hospital deaths annually to the nation's 63 OPOs or to a third party designated by the OPOs to handle the referrals. Hospitals also will work with the OPO to ensure that the family of every potential donor knows about its option to donate organs or tissues. Hospitals will also have agreements with at least one tissue bank and one eye bank to preserve and distribute tissues and eyes, as long as these agreements do not interfere with organ donation.

"By requiring hospitals to report all deaths and imminent deaths to OPOs, we hope to increase the supply of organs and thus reduce the number of people on waiting lists for organ transplants." said Nancy-Ann DeParle, administrator of the Health Care Financing Administration, the HHS agency that oversees Medicare. OPOs in states that have passed similar laws have seen an increase of up to 40 percent in organ donation.

Consent for organ donation is requested even in cases where the individual has signed an organ donor card. The card provides an indication of the individual's wish, but consent by survivors is still needed. "That's why it's so important to not only sign the organ donor card, but also to tell your family your wishes," Secretary Shalala said.

In working directly with families, hospitals and OPOs must demonstrate discretion and sensitivity with respect to the circumstances, views, and beliefs of the families of potential donors. To this end, hospitals must select an OPO representative, or others who have completed a training course offered or approved by the OPO. Hospitals also must work with OPOs and the eye and tissue banks to educate hospital staff on donation issues and review death records to make sure potential donors were identified correctly.

Chapter 52

Body Donation at Death

Among the methods that can be chosen for the final disposition of one's remains, body donation for educational and scientific purposes is one of the least frequently chosen. Nevertheless, several thousand individuals annually choose whole body donations as a method of making one's final contribution. Reasons individuals choose to donate their bodies upon death vary but generally include an act of altruism and gratitude to the medical profession, the desire to aid and expand medical science, the wish to minimize funeral ceremonies, and in a few cases, a vehicle for evading cost of a typical funeral (Iserson, 1994; Nagy, 1985; Richardson and Hurwitz, 1995).

Body donation is considered by many to be the ultimate donation an individual can make, and it is an invaluable gift to health and medical communities (Corr, Nabe, and Corr, 1977; Morgan, 1988). An estimated twelve to fifteen thousand donated bodies are required annually for teaching and research purposes within the 126 U.S. medical schools, allowing first-year medical students and other related professionals the experience of studying anatomy through dissection of the human body. Donated bodies also are used in other health programs such as dentistry, physical therapy, and podiatry. In addition, surgeons use donated bodies to develop new and better surgical techniques and to practice trauma procedures which must be performed

From: "The Ultimate Gift: Body Donation," by Daryll Billen, M.S., and Darrell Crase, Ph.D., in *Omega: Journal of Death and Dying*, Vol. 37, No. 1, pp. 75-83, 1998. © 1998 by Baywood Publishing Co., Inc., 26 Austin Ave., Amityville, NY 11701. Reprinted with permission.

on a human being so that, when the procedure is needed on a patient in critical condition, the physician is better prepared to execute the necessary lifesaving procedure. The donation of one's body is a gift which benefits humanity and saves lives.

The medical community receives bodies for purposes of enhancing medical education and research through several pathways of which donation is the most common. While medical schools can legally obtain the cadavers of indigent persons from state prisons and mental institutions, a small percentage is taken due to the required administrative "red tape" and the current availability of voluntary donations (Iverson, 1990). The purpose of this study was to examine the various policies and procedures of a non-random sample of medical schools regarding body donations for scientific purposes.

Methods

Data were collected by requesting information regarding the policies and procedures pertaining to body donation at eleven state funded and three privately funded university medical schools located throughout the United States. The institutions selected, while appearing to be geographically representative, do not constitute a random sample of 126 U.S. medical schools and thus results discussed here are not necessarily generalizable over the entire medical school community. Policies and procedures, however, of these fourteen medical schools relative to the acquisition and subsequent use of donated cadavers, appear to be consistent with those of other schools as discussed by Iserson (1994), Iverson (1990), and Wear (1987).

University sites were searched on the World Wide Web and requests for information regarding policies and procedures were made via surface or e-mail. Responses were primarily in the form of informational brochures and packets sent to prospective donors through the postal service. Additional information was received by e-mail in response to the requests made. Information was also obtained through several university Web pages on the Internet that contained information on their willed-body program. Also, the legal codes from several states were obtained through a legal documents database.

Results and Discussion

Policies and Procedures

The 126 medical schools throughout the United States generally follow and abide by guidelines promulgated by the Uniform Anatomical

Gift Act (UAGA) of 1968. By the early 1970s, all states plus the District of Columbia had adopted some form of the legislation. Among its six major provisions, perhaps the most relevant to the donor initiative stipulates that "persons 18 years or older may donate all or part of their body after death for transplantation or medical research or education" (Fulton and Metress, 1995, p. 449). Its several guidelines, as reviewed by Fulton and Metress, provide for the transfer of human tissue and organs as well as the donation of the body for the purpose of medical education and anatomical study.

Policies and procedures governing receipt and use of cadavers by medical schools vary from state to state as well as from school to school. For example, schools have differing policies as to how they process the request of a person who wishes to will his or her body to the school. Many schools inform donors that they must be residents of the state and/or live within a certain distance to the school in order to have the school accept the donation at the time of death. Most schools will pay for transporting the body to the school, however, the distance a school is willing to pay for transportation costs varies. These distances generally range from 30 to 250 miles (e.g., East Tennessee State University and the University of Texas). Other schools including Dartmouth College, the University of Kentucky, and the University of Michigan do not specify how much they are willing to pay; instead they give general guidelines regarding the transport of a body that is within the "area." If the individual's estate is willing to pay for the transportation in excess of what the school is willing to pay, then some schools will accept the body from greater distances. Among the schools included in this study, all would pay for body preparations, including embalming. The Virginia State Medical Examiner (for the medical schools in Virginia) and UCLA, however, require that embalming be performed by their staff. Schools such as East Tennessee State University, the Mayo Clinic, and Ohio University indicated that embalming could be done by any competent licensed embalmer, and one school sends instructions as to how the embalming should be performed.

Donations of a body by the next of kin are accepted by East Tennessee State University, Virginia Medical Examiner, the University of Kentucky, and the University of Tennessee. This allows the individual's next of kin to donate their family member's body without the prior consent of the individual being donated. However, few schools, including Dartmouth College and Vanderbilt University, accept body donations unless they have a donor card on file at the time of death. Vanderbilt University only accepts registration into its willed-body program during certain times of the year. Most schools will relinquish claim to the body if a family member objects to the donation after the individual has died. It was observed that schools with more restrictions regarding body donations tended to be private institutions, however the number of schools in this study is limited.

Limitations

A medical school may reject a body for many reasons. Therefore, coordinators of anatomical bequest programs suggest that the family have backup arrangements in case the body is not accepted. As an example, the University of Kentucky's medical school may reject potential donors for one or more of the following reasons:

- Individuals who have infections or contagious diseases.

- Individuals who have had recent surgery.

- Individuals who are obese.

- Individuals who die of trauma.

- Individuals whose bodies have been partially or completely autopsied.

- Individuals who have been organ donors (exceptions are individuals who have willed their corneas only to the University's Lions Eye Bank).

- Individuals who die outside the state.

- Individuals who die a long distance away and whose family refuses to pay transportation charges from the place of death to the university.

- Willing donors who die but have family members who object to the bequeathal of their loved one's body to the university.

Most schools have similar lists. Differences in this list and those of other schools include the amount a school is willing to spend transporting a body and the location of the death. Some schools (Dartmouth, University of Kentucky, UCLA, University of Tennessee, and Vanderbilt) do require that the death occur within the state. Most schools in this sample require that the death occur within a certain distance to the school, otherwise the body will be rejected unless the individual's estate assumes the cost of transportation of the body.

Schools advise the donor or the donor's family to consider making the donation to a local school when they live beyond the distance the preferred school is willing to pay for transport so there will not be any unnecessary expenses to the estate. For the international traveler, note that the law prohibits international shipping of bodies as anatomical specimens (Iserson, 1994).

Few medical schools accept bodies that have been autopsied, and the acceptance of these bodies is at the discretion of the school. Schools that may accept autopsied bodies include the University of Michigan, University of Tennessee, University of California, Irvine, and the University of Louisville. And as previously indicated, some schools follow guidelines that put limits on body weight. Upper age limits at the time of donation may also be an exclusionary factor (Iverson, 1990). Implicit here is the fact that medical schools and research units, in order to enhance educational and research efforts, need specimens that have not been severely damaged through disease or trauma. Apart from this, diseases and advancing age of donors are generally not factors in whole body donation. They are, of course, critical to tissue and organ donation.

Body Preparation

Preparation of the body must be done according to a school's guidelines, and some schools such as UCLA and the University of Virginia require that the body be prepared by their own staff. East Tennessee State University prefers certain mortuaries perform the embalming of their cadavers. The Mayo Clinic sends embalming instructions when a donor enrolls in their program so that the embalming can be done properly at a local mortuary. Such directives are necessary because body preservation for educational and research purposes may require more complex and extensive procedures than that required for the average funeral (Corr, Nabe, and Corr, 1997).

These preparation guidelines restrict the possibility of funerals with the body present. In fact, few schools permit a funeral with the body present due to the need for quick preparation of the body. With early attention to body preservation, however, some schools allow funerals to be conducted in the presence of the body. Perhaps it is important to note that there are final exit options donor families can exercise.

Body Disposition

The body is embalmed and then usually stored for two to six months before being used in order to allow the embalming chemicals to permeate all tissues. Schools complete use of the body typically within one to three years then dispose of the remains in an appropriate manner. As with donor families, there are options open to medical schools for the disposition of cadavers. Six schools (Dartmouth, University of Kentucky, University of Virginia, Ohio University, University of Tennessee, and Baylor University) adhere to a policy of mandatory cremation of the remains. Once cremated, school representatives then scatter the cremains at some appropriate site or arrange to bury them in a cemetery plot at little or no cost to next of kin. If arrangements are made in advance, some schools will return the cremains or ashes to the family for interment or disposal. The family, however, generally must incur the cost of transport and interment as indicated by five schools. The local funeral director can serve as intermediary and make appropriate arrangements. Iverson (1990) estimates that the number of families claiming bodies or cremains each year, which apparently is on the increase, varies so much that it is difficult to determine estimates.

Many schools have memorial services once a year to honor those who donated their bodies for use in gross anatomy and research laboratories and for helping those cope who encounter the emotional experiences of working intimately with the cadaver. Others hold services at the school's cemetery plot to which the family is invited to attend. These and similar memorial experiences at the end of dissection provide requisite closure experiences for both students and family (Wear, 1987, 1989). Still other medical schools, as reviewed by MacPherson (1990), such as the University of South Alabama, State Anatomy Board of Maryland, University of South Dakota, and Southwestern Medical School of Dallas will dispose of all enrolled donors whether or not their bodies are used. Some large cemeteries donate land space for burial as a memorial garden to the cremains of anatomical cadavers (MacPherson, 1990).

Supply

Many individuals desire to donate their body to a particular medical school. Individuals generally donate their body to their school of choice by contacting the school and filling out the required documentation, provided the individual fulfills the requirements of residence and/or death occurs in the proximity as mandated by the school. Requirements may vary widely with individual schools.

The number of cadavers required each year varies considerably with individual academic institutions and their medical operations.

Iserson (1994), in his review of body donation programs, identifies a few states/institutions and their required one-year supply of cadavers as follows: the state of Maryland (700-800), the state of Pennsylvania (500-600), University of California, San Francisco (300), and the University of Utah (49). An average size medical school such as the University of Tennessee receives approximately 100 donations per year. About forty of these are used in teaching; the other sixty are dispersed for research purposes and allied functions. The total number of cadavers required each year for medical education and research purposes is not readily available, though a safe estimate would put the number somewhere between twelve to fifteen thousand. In recent years, there has not been a shortage of body donations (Corr, Nabe, and Corr, 1997).

Some schools receive more anatomical cadavers than they need for teaching and research purposes. For example, the state of Texas, according to Murrell (1996), had approximately 4,000 body donations in 1994, far more than needed by the state's medical facilities. Such excess is generally managed by donating the bodies, with the permission of families, to medical facilities in other states which may be in need of them. It is against the law for a body to be sold, but the receiving school pays for all preparation and transportation costs averaging about $500 per cadaver depending on the distance it has to be transported.

According to Iserson's (1994) review, some schools allow individuals to donate their bodies for use in designated research studies. While autopsies and detailed analyses of body fluids, cells, and tissues are performed by pathologists and other medical specialists for purposes of determining causes of death, disease detection, and the extension of medical science, they are not performed on cadavers donated for use by medical students and other health care professionals. One institution (Dartmouth College) indicated in their promotional literature that, while it was not providing an autopsy report on the body, specific requests, like the weight of the heart or presence of cancer in lungs, could likely be accommodated. Families are not usually given scientific reports on findings when the use of the cadaver has been completed. Such a practice of extensive record keeping and reporting would undoubtedly add to the work load and increase administrative costs.

The Virginia State Medical Examiner indicated that the state anatomical board handled all body donations and that individuals interested in donating their bodies are required to go through the board, not the school. A similar practice exists in the state of Texas. The examiner's office also indicated that the remains or cremains could not be returned following use by the school.

Conclusion

Donating one's body at death for use in educating and training medical doctors and allied professionals and for scientific purposes supporting the biological and medical sciences represents an act of altruism. It is an acceptable, alternative form of body disposition in addition to ground or mausoleum interment and cremation. In pursuing this action, individuals should do some background investigating before deciding if they wish to donate their body to science and discuss it with their family and/or others within their support network. Once a decision has been made to donate, the individual then needs to decide on a specific school and acquire that school's descriptive materials and specific guidelines governing body donations. After reviewing the information the individual may decide that the school of interest will not accept his/her body due to restrictive policies, or a donation to that school will be troublesome for survivors. The individual may then wish to pursue another school whose location and/or policies are amenable to the donor.

An individual who does not have a preference should look for the closest school and complete the appropriate documents promulgated by that school. However, individuals should be aware of other options should the death occur away from their home locality. In this instance, the family may wish to donate the body to an alternative school in the locality where the death occurred so as to avoid transportation costs and the possibility that the original school may not accept the body if the death occurred outside of their range of acceptance. A committed individual also must be informed of the options regarding body donation if he or she moves to another location prior to death. And, prior to death, any individual can change his/her mind about donation and, if so, should inform the school in writing of such decision.

Body donation at death represents an indispensable program for the education of tomorrow's physicians, dentists, and other health care professionals according to University of Tennessee's body bequeathal literature. The ongoing donor program is also necessary in the promotion of biomedical research. By examining and studying the dead, medical knowledge and practical skills of living individuals can be expanded.

The overall satisfaction factor among the next of kin to the donor's dissection and use by medical schools appears to be largely unknown other than in a few isolated cases. One such example of closure has been initiated by the medical school of Wright State University (Nagy, 1985; Reece and Ziegler, 1990) as it has endeavored to connect students and donor families through a year-ending memorial ceremony sponsored by the university. The major focus of the ceremony is to assist families further in managing their grief, helping them to find meaning and hope in their lives. The school also initiates and maintains considerable communication with donor families during and following use of the body. Such concern and involvement promotes closure and increases the satisfaction factor among the next of kin.

Medical schools, in guaranteeing the continuation of donor programs, strive to maintain their reputation as institutions that insure the respectful treatment of human cadavers (Iverson, 1990). Various schools suggest that cadavers are treated respectfully by medical and dental students, though the dissecting process itself may minimize one's respect for a person's body leading to brief displays of levity tossed among medical students (Kass, 1985). Morgan (1988), however, reminds medical students that the donor is crucial in the development of themselves as dentists and physicians and that the cadaver was once a person, maybe even a dentist or a physician.

Participating medical schools/state anatomical programs:

- Baylor University
- Dartmouth College
- East Tennessee State University
- Mayo Clinic
- Ohio University
- University of California, Irvine
- University of California, Los Angeles
- University of Kentucky
- University of Louisville
- University of Michigan
- University of Texas, Houston
- University of Tennessee
- Vanderbilt University
- Virginia State Anatomical Board

References

Corr, C. A., Nabe, M., and Corr, D. M. (1997). *Death & dying: Life & living,* (2nd ed.). Pacific Grove, CA: Brooks/Cole.

Fulton, G. B., and Metress, E. K. (1995). *Perspectives on dying and death*. Boston: Jones and Bartlett.

Iserson, K. V. (1994). *Death to Dust: What happens to dead bodies?* Tucson, AZ: Glaen Press.

Iverson, B. A. (1990). Bodies for science. *Death Studies, 14,* 577-587.

Kass, L. R. (1985). Thinking about the body. *Hastings Center Report, 15,* 20-30.

MacPherson, P. (1990, February 9). Remembering the donation: Memorial service honors those who gave their bodies to science. *American Medical News,* p. 9.

Morgan, E. (1988). *Dealing creatively with death / A manual of death education and simple burial* (11th ed.). Burnsville, NC: Celo Press.

Murrell, L. R. (1996, August 25). Personal communication.

Nagy, F. (1985). Model for donated body programs. *Death Studies, 9,* 245-251.

Reece, R. D., and Ziegler, J. H. (1990). How a medical school (Wright State University) takes leave of human remains. *Death Studies, 14,* 589-600.

Richardson, R., and Hurwitz, B. (1995). Donors' attitudes towards body donation for dissection. *Lancet, 346,* 277-279.

Wear, D. (1987). Medical students' encounters with the cadaver: A poetic response. *Death Studies. 11,* 123-130.

Wear, D. (1989). Cadaver talk: Medical students' accounts of their year-long experience. *Death Studies. 13,* 379-391.

— by Daryll Billen, M.S., and Darrell Crase, Ph.D.

Direct reprint requests to Darrell Crase, Ph.D., The University of Memphis, Department of Human Movement Sciences and Education, Elma N. Roane Field House 204, Memphis, TN 38152.

Chapter 53

Ethical Issues in Organ Donation and Transplantation

Ethical issues have always been apparent in the transplantation process and are becoming more evident as the demand for organs increases. The basic question is how just and ethical are the new policies enacted to encourage organ donation, considering that they affect the total public and benefit the small percentage of patients who require transplantation? Pros and cons of several of these policies will be discussed as will several clinical situations that raise ethical questions.

Listen to any discussion concerning transplantation and there will be the essence of a debate of the rights of the people involved. Because transplantation involves both donation of organs and the identification of an appropriate recipient, ethical issues are factors for patients, families, health care providers, legislators, and the general public.

An open forum for debate regarding ethical issues in health care has been apparent in the 1990s. As the scrutiny of the health care system for quality and cost-effectiveness unfolds, discussion of ethical implications will magnify. Ethical issues have always been debated in organ transplantation because of the unique exchange that must occur. No other treatment so intimately involves the public. People must donate their organs or tissues to make the treatment possible.

From "Ethical Issues in Organ Donation and Transplantation: Are We Helping a Few at the Expense of Many?", by Judith A. DePalma and Ricard Townsend, in *Critical Care Nursing Quarterly,* Vol. 19, No. 1, pp. 1-9, May 1996. © 1996 by Aspen Publishers, Inc., 200 Orchard Ridge Dr., Gaithersburg, MD 20878. Reprinted with permission.

One Process—Two Phases

Health care providers who work with potential donors and potential recipients often view themselves in separate camps, at times in almost adversarial roles. Organ transplantation could be viewed as a single process, with two phases—donation and allocation. Because the two phases are separate but interdependent, an appropriate comparison might be a bicycle. The two wheels of the bicycle are separate and each must be sized correctly and inflated properly. However, it is the combination of the two wheels working in tandem that allows the bicycle to function. Any difficulty with one of the wheels will affect the balance and safety of the rider.

Ethically and legally some mandated separations must occur to protect the rights of the donor. For example, the health care providers who approach the potential donor or family cannot be members of the transplantation team. This separation prevents any perception of coercion by the transplant team for the donation of organs that would, in turn, advance the transplantation team's practice.

Because the two phases of transplantation are so interdependent, any action that is viewed as ethically questionable in one phase affects the success of the other phase. If health care providers would see more similarities and connectedness rather than differences in their purpose, the total transplantation process would be enhanced. For example, a trauma nurse who was well informed regarding the transplantation process, its benefits, and quality of life outcomes might be a strong advocate for organ donation. This nurse might offer a stronger case to the families for organ donation by providing realistic success stories. Answers to the family's questions might be enhanced with examples of actual patient experiences. On the other hand, nurses working on a transplantation unit might be better able to deal with the questions of the waiting recipient if they could appreciate what donor families experience. Nurses who have an understanding of the policies governing donation and actual clinical scenarios of families who hesitate to donate might more effectively help the recipients deal with their frustration and anger about the wait for the needed organs.

Imbalances in the Process

The concept of an imbalance has been chosen as the focus of this discussion because it is a familiar one to health care providers. Health care providers deal with imbalances in the clinical setting routinely.

For example, electrolyte imbalances, cardiac dysrhythmias, and nutritional imbalances are constantly assessed and treated. This concept of an imbalance will be applied to organ transplantation and more specifically to the ethical dilemmas that are apparent and frequent within transplantation practice. Imbalances can and do occur with the two-phase process of transplantation. These imbalances include lack of sufficient number of organs, ethical dilemmas in clinical situations, and policies that affect the entire public.

Too Few Organs Donated

The most widely publicized and overriding imbalance is the limited number of organs donated compared with the number of potential recipients. "The gap between those who need a transplant and the number of available organs is steadily increasing. On October 31, 1993, the waiting list for solid organ transplants in the United States contained over 32,000 registrations."[1] (p. 71) As of March, 1995, there were 39,082 patients on the national waiting list for organ transplantation. This number may be slightly greater than the actual number of patients because patients are permitted to be listed from more than one transplant center. From January through November 1994, 16,509 organ transplants were performed. According to the United Network For Organ Sharing (UNOS) Scientific Registry in Richmond, Virginia (unpublished report, 1995), 3,098 patients on the waiting list died before they could receive the needed organ during that same period. The point is frequently made that if all the organs from potential organ donors were donated, the needs of those awaiting transplantation would be met. Each year "at least 5,000 human organs deemed medically suitable for transplantation" are not donated.[2] (p. 1,572) The difficulty is in identifying why the organ donation does not occur. In attitude surveys conducted by the Gallup Organization in the early 1980s, people generally expressed a positive view of organ donation, but few actually had signed donor cards.[3] This is true for the lay public as well as health care providers.[4] Positive attitudes are not sufficient to produce an increase in organ donation.

Ethical Dilemmas

The ethical imbalance involves the rights of the general public versus the medical benefits to a special population. More broadly, is the need for this widespread legislation and policy based on anything other than lack of sufficient numbers of donated organs? The transplant community has many advocates who champion the needs and successes of transplantation, while the organ donor has few champions. Families who agree to donate actually must see the value of both donation of organs and treatment by transplantation. The family who refuses to donate is sometimes viewed by the transplant community as misled, misinformed, or uneducated because the logic of donation is so apparent to those who are waiting with potential recipients. There appears to be no place in the system for well-informed, pensive determinations by potential organ donors that they do not want to donate even though they understand that it may save a life.

Other questions that need to be addressed are why do people and families choose not to donate organs? Will organ donation increase if the public is guaranteed an opportunity to donate or a tangible offering? Are there more subtle approaches that can be used to increase donation?

More subtle approaches have been successful. An increase in consents from families for organ donation has been achieved by simple communication techniques used by health care workers who were extremely comfortable with the request process. Garrisons reported success simply by separating the discussion of possible organ donation from the initial discussion of brain death determination. Allowing time between the two discussions seemed to facilitate donation. Sanders, et al.[2] proposed a subcommittee of a hospital ethics committee to provide effective communicators from either the hospital staff or the local organ procurement organization (OPO) who would counsel the families regarding organ donation possibilities.

Public Policies

Another imbalance is widespread legislation and public policy implemented to increase the incidence of organ donation. This legislation benefits the relative few who need the treatment of transplantation, but it affects the total public.

The impetus for several of the broad, sweeping policies is the belief that organ donation can be facilitated by a mandated opportunity to donate, a tangible offering, or a simpler process to donate than not donate.

Mandated Opportunity

The required request state law is one piece of legislation that already exists, as recommended by the 1986 Task Force on Organ

Transplantation.[6] Each state's legislation differs, but the essence of all the legislation is that the following must occur in every acute care setting:

- The local OPO must be notified of potential donors.

- Families must be asked to donate organs.

- Statistics must be kept on the number of requests made and the number of organs procured.

The expected outcome of this legislation was that hospital personnel would identify potential donors and involve OPO representatives more frequently and in a more timely manner. Increased organ donation numbers would hopefully result because more families would be approached and given the opportunity to donate. However, significantly more organs have not been donated since this legislation was enacted. Many states have other legislation that attaches organ donation in some manner to drivers' registration to provide formal access to a large number of adult citizens. The willingness of citizens to donate organs is indicated on their driver's licenses. In some states, such as Colorado, it is mandatory to respond to the organ donation question to renew the registration.

Financial Incentive

Because altruistic donations are not keeping pace with the need for organs, several plans have been proposed for financial incentives to motivate organ donations. These incentives may be in the form of a lump sum offering,[7,8] assistance with funeral expenses, reduced estate taxes,[9] or free medical care. Two schools of thought exist concerning offering payment to families as a motivation to donate the organs of their dying family member. The following rationale would support financial incentives:

- The present system does not produce a sufficient number of organs.

- A tangible exchange might stimulate interest.

- The fairest system offers the family something in return for organs.

Those who oppose financial incentives believe that altruism should continue to be the only acceptable motivation for donation of either one's own organs or close of a family member who has been declared brain dead.[10] Those in opposition to financial incentives would challenge the total premise that such payments will serve as incentives or are appropriate incentives. The rationale for opposition to this plan would include the following assumptions:

- Autonomy is best served by an altruistic approach.

- The potential exists for coercion, especially with financially desperate families.

- Selling of organs eliminates the therapeutic effect for the family of voluntarily donating.

- Some financial incentives already exist. Such a course may lead to bartering about the price of organs.

The existing financial incentives are often not apparent to families. Once the family has agreed to an organ donation, the cost of the medical care beginning at that point is covered by the local OPO. However, families may only be informed about the financial aspect once the decision has been made to donate the organs or if the family expresses a concern regarding additional hospital costs. Because financial incentives are not always disclosed to families during the initial discussions about organ donation, it is difficult to correlate such incentives with the family's willingness to donate.

The essence of the financial incentive issue appears to be twofold: (1) In a global sense, is it ethically acceptable to connect financial incentives to donation of organs, and (2) in a more specific sense, is the connection of financial incentives with organ donation coercion of families at a time of personal loss and vulnerability?

It appears to be one thing to provide assistance with medical care incurred as a result of the preservation of the organs for transplant, but another to have the family appear to profit from donating a family member's body parts. Some may say that a death benefit payment would foster the belief that "society dealt fairly with the family in this matter,"[8] (p. 1,303) whereas others would view it as creating a market for organs.

Presumed Consent

Under presumed consent legislation, everyone may be considered a potential organ donor unless he or she carries a card that declares an objection to such donation or the family objects at a time when death and donation seems inevitable. Those who favor presumed consent see it as a means to make it easier to donate than to not donate, eliminate the need for health care providers to request donations from families, spare families from making the decision about donation at times of vulnerability, and achieve beneficence, although autonomy is sacrificed.[2]

The strong opposition to presumed consent legislation is based on the view that such legislation

- violates the principle of autonomy by denying patients and families participation in the decision,

- cannot guarantee informed consent because not all individuals may be aware of or understand the terms of the legislation and their rights in this matter, and

- does not promote beneficence.

Beneficence refers to the obligation to prolong life and relieve suffering whenever possible. "Because a donor's organs are not the physician's property, the provision of transplantable organs escapes the definitional bounds of medical beneficence. Transplantation is medical beneficence, but donation is not."[2] (p. 1,574)

Case Studies

Ethical dilemmas occur in all specialty areas. With transplantation, ethical dilemmas are both apparent and frequent. One view of an ethical dilemma can be that of an imbalance within a clinical situation. This imbalance exists because there are at least two actions that can be taken in any particular clinical situation. All parties involved may have their own clear view of the best action to take, and these views may be considerably different.

When there is difficulty coming to a consensus, ethics can provide a guideline for the appropriate actions and clarify which perspective should be considered. In other words, ethics aids in deciding who has the right to make the final decision and whose best interest is being served by that decision.

Several ethical dilemmas are discussed in this article using case studies that have occurred in practice. Each case is discussed from the point of view of what actions or questions are appropriate and what ethical principles are involved with the imbalance.

549

Case Study 1

A 24-year-old female pedestrian is struck by a car. She suffers a severe closed-head injury and is brain dead within 24 hours of admission. She has a valid, witnessed organ donor card and had verbally told her family and friends that she thought organ donation and transplantation were very worthwhile. As next of kin, her mother refuses to allow donation to occur. The regional OPO has never acted against a family's wishes, but legislation allows for the patient's wishes to prevail.

The following three actions may occur: (1) the patient's wishes can be complied with and the organs secured for donation, (2) the family's wishes can be complied with and the organs not secured for donation, or (3) the family members can be approached about changing their decision.

The primary question is: who has the right to donate the patient's organs? The principle of autonomy gives the person the right to self-determination. The patient completed the donor card while alive for use in just such a situation when she would not be capable of expressing her wishes. Another view may be that the patient's right of autonomy ends at death and that the surviving family has the right to make the final decisions.

Legally the patient's wishes can be followed because she had a valid donor card. However, in most clinical situations when the family's wishes are in opposition or are not clear, the organs will not be procured. The reasoning for this may include the fact that the family members survive the incident to live with their decision or to pursue legal action against the hospital. Health care providers are in an ethical and legal bind and generally err on the side of caution and the intent of the family. The danger of health care agencies not honoring valid predetermined decisions such as organ donation and advance directives is that a clear message is sent to the public that completing such legal documents is futile without family support. Ethically, one approach would be to talk with the family members to ascertain why they are refusing organ donation. Families may see the situation differently if they view it from the patient's perspective and with more realistic information about organ donation and the transplantation process. Sometimes this can be accomplished simply by the manner in which the family is approached. Both members of the trauma team and the ethics committee have been successful in having the family view the situation anew from the perspective of the patient. Sometimes it is as simple as taking the time to sit and talk with family members after they have had an opportunity to think about the situation and to come to the full realization that the patient will not recover.

It definitely helps to propose organ donation in a separate discussion from the one in which the family is notified of the brain death status of the patient. Linking the notification of brain death and the request for organ donation in the same conversation frames the organ request within a negative connotation. Families may have ideas about donation or transplantation that are not true. For example, they may think that donation is mutilating to the donor, is not allowed by their church, or will be more costly for them or their insurance payer. If family members can verbalize a reason, the health care provider can explain the aspect about which they have concern and tell them about similar family situations. This may help family members change their decision or at least think through their objection to donation.

Some approaches that appear most successful are those that are empathetic rather than sympathetic, calm rather than dramatic or rushed, and individualized rather than a rote presentation.

Case Study 2

A 50-year-old man commits suicide by shooting himself in the head. He is brain dead and the family consents to donation. He had little contact with his family recently, although they are aware that he may have been involved in homosexual relations. His blood test (Western blot) for human immunodeficiency virus (HIV) is negative, but the test has a window period. The cardiac transplant surgeons decide to use the heart but the renal transplant surgeons refuse the kidneys.

As in case 1, this case raises the question of who has the right to decide, but this time the decision involves the transplant recipient. In this case, the following three questions arise:

1. Does the organ recipient have the right to be included in the decision to accept or reject the potentially high-risk organ?

2. What are the implications of one team of surgeons rejecting the potentially high-risk organs while the other team accepted the organ?

3. What is true informed consent in the case of a high-risk organ?

This situation is more controversial than the first case because even some health care providers who strongly support patient autonomy rights regarding donation may not see that the patient has any right to enter into this particular decision. The decision whether to use a high-risk organ may be perceived as a purely medical one and therefore it should not be discussed with the patient. Those opposed to involving patients in this decision would express doubt that the provision of informed consent could ever be truly satisfied in such cases. The patient's physical need for the organ might be so great that he or she would not be able to objectively consider the risks.

The different decision made by the two surgical teams can be supported by the Public Health Service's (PHS) guidelines, which state that regardless of HIV antibody test results, organs from persons meeting any of the exclusionary behavior or history criteria should not be used unless the risk of not having the transplant is greater to the recipient than the risk of HIV transmission.[11] In such cases the recipient should be informed and sign a consent to use the high-risk organ. The heart was used because it was lifesaving; the kidneys were not used because they were viewed as only improving the recipient's lifestyle, not saving his or her life.

The behavior or history exclusionary criteria include persons who in the preceding 5 years have engaged in sex with same gender, used nonmedical injected drugs, received human-derived clotting factor concentrates for blood clotting disorders, engaged in sex when the exchange of money or drugs occurred, engaged in sex with someone who is drug user, engaged in sex with any person known or suspected to have HIV infection (1-year limitation), been exposed to known or suspected HIV-infected blood (12-month limitation), or resided at the time of donation in a correctional system.[12]

The other key issue in this case is the informed consent status of the recipient patient. The surgical team that accepted the organ for transplant had a clear responsibility, according to the PHS guidelines, to inform the organ recipient of possible HIV transmission even though the blood test was negative. How can the physician truly judge whether the patient is informed enough to be willing to take the risk? How can health care providers adequately convey the risk? More basically, does the recipient patient have the right to be part of the decision?

What about the potential organ recipients who were denied the kidneys because their teams of surgeons assessed the risk as too great when weighed with potential benefits? Should these patients be permitted to make a decision to accept the organs after being made totally aware of the risks?

The surgeons who rejected the kidneys weighed the risks and benefits and decided that the risks were too great for the particular patients. This might be seen as nonmaleficence, acting in ways to not cause needless harm or injury. Did they, however, harm the patients by not giving them an opportunity to accept or reject the organ? The patients may have seen the case of risks versus benefits as very different and may have accepted the kidney. In 1994, 1,375 patients died while waiting for kidney transplant (UNOS Scientific Registry, unpublished report, 1995). If an adequate number of organs were donated, practice would have the luxury of excluding all organs that carry even a minimal risk, and these questions of patient involvement with the decision would not be an issue.

Case Study 3

A cardiac transplant team has not performed any transplants recently because of a lack of recipients high on the transplant list. The cardiologist decides to place a patient on a dobutamine infusion. The patient does not clinically need the infusion but does need a transplant. Because of the perception that the dobutamine infusion means the patient requires support, he is moved up on the transplant priority list. An organ becomes available within a few days and he is transplanted. The transplant team and the patient are both happy with the outcome.

This case represents the numerous manipulations that are possible within the prioritizing system for organ allocation. The questions in this case concern the system of allocation of organs, which are a scarce resource. Three principles have been suggested for prioritization: (1) beneficence—giving help to those with the greatest need, with priority given to those who are the most ill or require more than one organ; (2) justice—all cases should be treated alike in that time on the waiting list would be considered but lifestyle or position in society would not[13]; and (3) public utility—social worth of the recipient, considering the quality and productivity of the life.[14]

UNOS has established criteria for the allocation of donated organs. The criteria differ according to the particular organ involved, but in general UNOS relies on medical criteria (beneficence) and justice. Likelihood of success, tissue and size match of the organ, medical urgency, waiting time, and geographical proximity are all elements within the criteria.[15]

Although criteria exist for the allocation of organs in actual practice, ability to pay, status in society, and compliant behavior do appear to influence who receives organs. Physicians may be influenced by their commitment to the case as a result of previous transplants or an unusual course of the underlying disease that has left the physician especially frustrated. As in case 3, physicians can manipulate the care of patients to increase their medical need or urgency for transplantation. Some physicians may rationalize this manipulation more easily for recipients who they feel are important to society. More study is needed of the decision-making processes of physicians, of both the referral physician and of the transplant team. This information would be helpful in assessing whether the established criteria are congruent with actual practice.

Patients can also manipulate the system. At present the system favors local potential recipients when donated organs become available. The more medically informed patients (often the patients of higher socioeconomic status) are able to take advantage of being on multiple local center waiting lists, placing them at an advantage for being matched with organs that become available in different geographical areas. This practice is especially advantageous in geographical areas with shorter waiting lists.

The Council on Ethical and Judicial Affairs of the American Medical Association has made several suggestions for revisions in the allocation system. A few of these include

- considering quality of life issues;

- considering amount of resources required for success;

- prohibiting geographical priorities, except when transport of the organ would endanger the success of the transplant; and

- prohibiting patients' names from being on multiple local waiting lists.[13]

Health Care Reform

Ethical dilemmas exist in the current practice of transplantation and will escalate with health care reform. The imbalance will be between basic health care for all and allocation of scarce resources. Health care reform is searching for a level of basic health care for all citizens that is fair and just. The majority of Americans may agree with the concept of basic health care for all, but the definition of basic health care is the stumbling block. One of the difficult decision-making points is the area of transplantation. Many plans exclude transplantation from the universal coverage because of the cost of transplantation, the relatively small number of patients benefiting from the treatment, or the experimental status of treatment. Presently only lung transplantation is considered experimental, but many plans for universal health care do not include any type of transplantation. If such plans are enacted, availability of organs will increase as a result of the decreased length of time that a patient will be eligible for health care once brain death is established. At the same time the number of patients who are eligible by their health care plan for transplantation will be decreased. Only patients who can afford to buy health care plans greater than the basic or universal coverage will have the option to receive transplantation. If such plans are enacted, there will be a definite imbalance, with poor people providing organs for a relatively smaller group of economically advantaged people who can afford to purchase supplemental health care programs.

Conclusion

Discussions of ethical issues regarding transplantation only lead to more questions. Many areas of disagreement must be further discussed and studied to provide credible data on which to base future policies regarding transplantation. The overriding question remains the balance of the rights and needs of the total society and those of the patients who are awaiting transplantation.

A few of the many areas of imbalances in transplantation that should be explored are the key factors that actually influence a family to agree to donate the organs of their family member, compared with the present and proposed public policy and legislation; the cost of the total transplantation process from time of permission for donation through posttransplantation, life-long care compared with the maintenance care of potential recipients; and the functional status and quality of life of recipients, before and after transplantation.

References

1. Edwards EB, Guo T, Breen TJ, Bowen GR, Daily OP. The UNOS OPTN waiting list from 1988 to 1993. In: Terasaki PI, Cecka JM, eds. Clinical Transplants. Los Angeles, Calif: UCLA Tissue Typing Laboratory; 1993.

2. Sanders LM, Devney P, Young E, Raffin TA. The organ donation committee: an ethically responsible approach to increasing the organ donation rate. Chest. 1992;102:1,572-7.

3. Gallup Organization, Inc. The U.S. Public's Attitudes toward Organ Transplant/Organ Donation. Survey conducted for the Dow Chemical Co. Princeton, NJ: Gallup Organization, Inc.; 1987.

4. Perkins KA. The shortage of cadaver donor organs for transplantation: can psychology help? Amer Psychol. 1987;42:236-52.

5. Garrison RN, Bentley FR, Raque GH, et al. There is an answer to the shortage of organ donors. Gyn Obstet. 1991;173:391-6.

6. Task Force on Organ Transplantation. Organ Transplantation: Issues and Recommendations. Washington, DC: U.S. Department of Health and Human Services; 1986.

7. Cohen LR. A market proposal for increasing the supply of cadaveric organs. Clin Transplant. 1991;5:467-74.

8. Peters TG. Life or death: the issue of payment in cadaveric organ donation. J Am Med Assoc. 1991;265(10):1,302-5.

9. Rapaport FT, Anaise D. Organ donation—1990. Transplant Proc. 1991;23(1):899-900.

10. McNatt G. Testimony: controversies in organ donation. ANNA J. 1992;19(4):341-3, 354.

11. Stoekle ML. Issues of transplantation: ethics of potential legislative changes. Dimens Crit Care Nurs. 1993;12(3):158-66.

12. Centers for Disease Control. Guidelines for preventing transmission of human immunodeficiency virus through transplantation of human tissue and organs. MMWR. 1994;43: 1-17.

13. Dickens BM. Ethics committees, organ transplantation and public policy. Law Med Health Care. 1992;20(4):300-6.

14. Halasz NA. Medicine and ethics: how to allocate transplantable organs. Transplantation. 1991;42(1):43-6.

15. Council on Ethical and Judicial Affairs, American Medical Association. Ethical considerations in the allocation of organs and other scarce medical resources among patients. Arch Intern Med. 1995;155:29-40.

— by Judith A. DePalma, M.S.N., R.N., Director of Nursing Research, and Ricard Townsend, M.D., Trauma Surgeon, Allegheny General Hospital, Pittsburgh, Pennsylvania.

Chapter 54

Regulations for Use of Body Tissues in Research

Once a physician has removed cells from a person's body, who owns them? Who decides who can use them and for what purposes? Is the person's control over his or her tissue severed along with the cells themselves?

In the late 1950s, pathologist Oscar Auerbach nailed down the link between smoking and lung cancer by examining tissue taken from the airways of several hundred people during autopsies. When he compared his observations with information gathered during interviews with relatives of the deceased, he discovered that lung cells reflect smoking habits: the more cigarettes, the greater the damage (*SN:* 8/19/61, p. 120). Surgeon General Luther L. Terry cited Auerbach's findings in his first report on the dangers of smoking, and many people credit that research with motivating the warnings that cigarette packages carry to this day. Auerbach's studies would raise concerns in the 1990s, however. The people whose tissue samples he examined never agreed to participate in the project. Furthermore, researchers these days can look for inherited as well as acquired bases of disease (*SN:* 11/5/94, p. 298; 12/17/94, p. 408).

Suppose a researcher found a correlation between the presence of a certain gene and lung cancer. Should he or she tell family members who may be at risk? Even if there's no way to prevent or cure the

From "The Tissue Issue: Losing Oneself to Science?", by Evelyn Strauss, in *Science News,* Vol. 152, No. 12, September 20, 1997, pp. 190-1. © 1997 by Science Service Inc., 1719 N St. NW, Washington, DC 20036. Reprinted with permission.

disease? And knowing that their health insurance companies or employers might misuse such information (*SN:* 10/26/96, p. 262)? What about people who might not want to contribute their tissue, even after death, to some kinds of research projects—such as searches for possible genetic roots of sexual orientation? "Because of the power of genetics, you can study these materials and find out secrets about a person and his or her relatives," says Arthur L. Caplan, director of the Center for Bioethics at the University of Pennsylvania in Philadelphia. "The old rules for taking tissues aren't cutting it anymore."

The issue comes down to how much control an individual should retain over the use of material from his or her body and the information derived from it. Researchers, ethicists, advocacy groups, legislators, and others are wending their way through the labyrinth of dilemmas surrounding appropriate research on tissue. Although most participants in the debate seem to agree on the goals—providing protection and respect for individuals while continuing to support research—recipes for success differ. Many ethicists and others proclaim that tighter control is essential to ensure personal privacy and autonomy, while many biomedical investigators envision their research mired in excessive cost and administrative burdens.

"The legal and ethical issues about the use of stored tissue are probably the most profound, complex, and troubling of any ethical issue we have in science today," says Lawrence O. Gostin, a professor of law at Georgetown University in Washington, D.C. "It pits two fundamental values against each other, and there's no easy resolution."

Federally funded research on tissue that can be linked to living persons is tightly regulated. The individuals must give specific consent for the research, or the investigation must meet certain criteria, such as imposing minimal risk upon the subjects. Decisions governing whether projects fulfill these conditions fall to groups called Institutional Review Boards (IRBs), which consist of scientists and other representatives of the local community.

Despite the regulations, plenty of room for controversy remains. Various IRBs interpret the guidelines differently, and people disagree about whether these groups should wield more or less power than they do now. Furthermore, because people who have died are not technically "human subjects," the rules don't apply to many stored samples, says J. Thomas Puglisi of the Office for Protection from Research Risks in Rockville, Md.—even though investigations on such materials may reveal information that could affect surviving relatives.

Policy makers have begun proposing, and in some cases passing, legislation aimed at protecting individuals. Many researchers say that some of the regulations would erect unnecessary barriers between themselves and the tissues they rely on for medical research. "People are in so much of a rush to legislate, they're writing things with language that's so sweeping, it has all kinds of unintended consequences," says David Korn, senior vice president for biomedical research at the Association of American Medical Colleges in Washington, D.C.

Several states have enacted legislation that deals specifically with the use of tissue in research. A 1995 Oregon law, amended last July, grants ownership of tissue, as well as the information derived from it, to the person from whom it was taken. In contrast, the California supreme court ruled that a man whose cells were used to make a valuable commercial product could not claim a share of the proceeds. The court did find that the doctors had violated the man's rights by not informing him of what they were doing with the tissue.

Senator Pete V. Domenici (R-N.M.) has introduced a bill aimed at tightening the rules about use of tissue in genetic research. Even trying to define words such as "genetic" presents problems, says Korn. "You can get genetic information by all different approaches—family history, a variety of lab tests, or directly looking at DNA."

The National Bioethics Advisory Commission (NBAC) will make recommendations regarding the use of human tissue in research in January 1998, says NBAC genetics subcommittee chairman Thomas H. Murray.

Human tissue enters the research domain by two main routes. In one, investigators ask volunteers to provide samples for a research project. In the other, pathologists collect and store material left over from medical procedures.

"Since microscopes began being used to study tissue samples, these tissues have provided the knowledge base on which our current understanding of medicine rests," says Korn.

Current regulations aim to inform patients about what will happen to their samples, at least if investigators use them in federally funded studies. Anyone undergoing a medical procedure must indicate that they understand the possible risks and benefits by signing a form. Many institutions incorporate into their consent forms a request for permission to use surplus tissue for research. These documents and the process of requesting such approval have come under close scrutiny in the last several years.

"The forms stink," says Caplan. "People don't read them because they're in language that's too difficult." The general language about research may be too imprecise to provide meaningful—and legally binding—permission, adds Gostin. People can't agree to a use if they don't know exactly what they're agreeing to, he continues.

Most forms do not reveal how researchers intend to handle the information they obtain in terms of confidentiality and privacy, says Robert F. Weir of the University of Iowa College of Medicine in Iowa City. Weir published a study on informed consent in the July-August and September-December 1995 issues of *Irb*.

How much information should potential tissue donors receive? Covering all of the possibilities may not be realistic. "At the time the tissue is being removed, there's no way to tell the patient what kind of technology may come up in the future," notes Korn.

Furthermore, many people—not just investigators—worry that too much information might overwhelm potential research subjects, thereby interfering with volunteer recruitment or education. "People get freaked out about a five-page consent form," says Iowa's Richard G. Lynch, head of the Federation of American Societies for Experimental Biology committee that's addressing ethical issues in biomedical research. "They say,'Leave me alone. Just tell me where to sign.'"

At the same time, more informative consent forms may strengthen research projects because "better-informed subjects will probably feel like they're really partners," says Mary Ann Wilson, consumer staff representative at the Alliance of Genetic Support Groups in Chevy Chase, Md. "They're more likely to continue in the project."

The National Action Plan on Breast Cancer (NAPBC) in Washington, D.C., has developed a prototype consent form in which participants make a few general choices. They indicate whether scientists may use their tissue for research on cancer. In a separate question, they can grant permission for use of the tissue in studies of other health problems. The form also asks people to specify whether they want to be invited to take part in future research.

"If it's a preventable disease, a lot of people want to know the results of sample testing," says Abbey S. Meyers, president of the National Organization for Rare Disorders in New Fairfield, Conn., "but most conditions are not treatable—like Alzheimer's, for example."

"When people give samples, they should be able to say,'Use this to save the world but leave me out of it,'" says Mary Jo Kahn of the Virginia Breast Cancer Foundation in Richmond. She points out that even being offered the choice of knowing can disturb people. "Someone can say,'I know something about you that you don't know; do you want to know it?' You're either going to freak out and wonder forever or just ask. "It's wonderful that we have the chance to develop good policy before there is widespread [genetic] testing and before we make a lot of mistakes," Kahn continues. "it just takes one *60 Minutes* show to make it so no one will sign a consent form."

Even if people develop wise guidelines, many dilemmas will remain. What should researchers do with the millions of tissue specimens currently stored in pathology labs around the country? Most of these samples are not accompanied by adequate consent forms because the tissues were collected long before people became as sensitive to the issues as they are today.

Researchers should either go back and get consent or start a new study, says George J. Annas, a medical ethicist at Boston University School of Public Health. Annas has drafted model federal legislation for the use of human tissue in research. "It's not right for you to know more about people than they do without their consent," he says.

The issue should be resolved on a case-by-case basis, argues Elizabeth J. Thomson, program director of clinical genetics research at the National Human Genome Research Institute in Bethesda, Md. "Researchers should ask,'Do I need to use archival tissue when I know that consent was less than adequate?'" she says. "If the sample's been there for 50 years, it's absurd to request permission," says Ellen W. Clayton, associate professor of law and pediatrics at Vanderbilt University Medical Center in Nashville. "But if it was last week and you know where the patient is, it would be pretty hard to argue not to ask."

Many scientists contend that demanding consent for every purpose would result in squandering a valuable resource. "Say I want to look at outcomes of different treatment regimens on people who have a particular mutation," says Mark E. Sobel, chief of the molecular pathology section of the National Cancer Institute in Bethesda, Md. "If I can't use old material and I want to look at outcomes, it'll be at least 5 years before I start getting information and another 5 until it's really useful."

Korn suggests setting up a system whereby scientists can tap into follow-up information. "I don't need to know who the patients are, but I need to know what happened to them."

In principle, confidentiality can be achieved if someone strips the samples of names and gives them numbers instead, retaining the key so researchers can obtain information later in order to interpret their findings. IRBs review proposals for such research and decide whether they meet the requirements for waiving consent. Among other criteria, the board requires that it must not be "practicable" to obtain informed consent. "That means almost impossible," says Puglisi. "It's more than just inconvenient." "Many of us would like to see a broader interpretation that would permit the review board to waive informed consent for coded samples more easily in some cases," says Sobel. Annas disagrees. "The IRB can grant exceptions, and that's a problem," he says. "They're the weak link in the current set of regulations."

Weak link or not, IRBs don't always get the chance to deliberate on research use of stored tissue, says Clayton. "It's really easy to pull up the medical records for everyone admitted to the hospital with condition X," she says. "Then you can go look at those people's tissues. It isn't allowed [without IRB approval], but it's as common as pig tracks."

Coded samples create a fundamental security problem: The person with the key can put everything together. "A lot of these problems have been solved in the banking industry," says Lynch. "I can go to the same ATM as you and get into my account but not yours. I think we should be preventing misuse, not preventing getting at information."

Federal regulations regarding informed consent do not apply to these so-called anonymized samples as long as they were stored before a study began and cannot be linked with the donor—a condition not easily met, says Puglisi. Such research comes at a cost, however: It can deprive participants of medical information that might someday benefit them.

Although participants in the debate over who should control tissue have made great strides in understanding and responding to each others' concerns over the last several years, many issues remain unresolved.

"The problem at the beginning was that people were at different tables, coming up with proposals to deal with the thing they were legitimately concerned about," says Lynch. "Since they didn't know about the other concerns, they created problems. Now we're all sitting at the same table."

Murray suggests that solutions won't necessarily require a strict trade-off between benefits for society and protection for individuals. "This isn't a zero-sum game," he says. "There may well be some creative responses that will maintain what we care about most with respect to both research and privacy."

—by Evelyn Strauss

Part Seven

Bereavement

Chapter 55

Loss, Grief, and Bereavement

Introduction

This [chapter] on loss, grief, and bereavement is adapted from the summary written for health professionals by cancer experts. This and other credible information about cancer treatment, screening, prevention, supportive care, and ongoing clinical trials, is available from the National Cancer Institute. The passage from the final stage of cancer to the death of a loved one is different for everyone. This summary describes loss, grief, and bereavement, the stages of grief, and methods for coping with grief. This summary also includes sections on children and grief.

Overview

People cope with the loss of a loved one in many ways. For some, the experience may lead to personal growth, even though it is a difficult and trying time. There is no right way of coping with death. The way a person grieves depends on the personality of that person and the relationship with the person who has died. How a person copes with grief is affected by the experience with cancer, the way the disease progressed, the person's cultural and religious background, coping

Excerpted from "Loss, Grief, and Bereavement," [Online] May 1999. Available: http//:cancernet.nci.nih.gov. Produced by NIH's National Cancer Institute (NCI). For complete contact information, please refer to Chapter 60, "Resources."

skills, mental history, support systems, and the person's social and financial status.

The terms bereavement, grief, and mourning are often used in place of each other, but they have different meanings. Bereavement is the state of having suffered a loss and experiencing many emotions and changes. The time spent in a period of bereavement depends on how attached the person was to the person who died, and how much time was spent anticipating the loss.

Grief is the normal process of reacting to the loss. Grief reactions may be felt in response to physical losses (for example, a death) or in response to symbolic or social losses (for example, divorce or loss of a job). Each type of loss means the person has had something taken away. As a family goes through a cancer illness, many losses are experienced, and each triggers its own grief reaction. Grief may be experienced as a mental, physical, social, or emotional reaction. Mental reactions can include anger, guilt, anxiety, sadness, and despair. Physical reactions can include sleeping problems, changes in appetite, physical problems, or illness. Social reactions can include feelings about taking care of others in the family, seeing family or friends, or returning to work. As with bereavement, grief processes depend on the relationship with the person who died, the situation surrounding the death, and the person's attachment to the person who died. Grief may be described as the presence of physical problems, constant thoughts of the person who died, guilt, hostility, and a change in the way one normally acts.

Mourning consists of the conscious, unconscious, and cultural reactions to loss. Mourning includes the process of incorporating the experience of loss into ongoing life. Mourning is also influenced by cultural customs, rituals, and society's rules for coping with loss.

"Grief work" includes the processes that a mourner needs to complete before resuming daily life. These processes include separating from the person who died, readjusting to a world without him or her, and forming new relationships. To separate from the person who died, a person must find another way to redirect the emotional energy that was given to the loved one. This does not mean the person was not loved or should be forgotten, but that the mourner needs to turn to others for emotional satisfaction. The mourner's roles, identity, and skills may need to change to readjust to living in a world without the person who died. The mourner must give other people or activities the emotional energy that was once given to the person who died in order to redirect emotional energy.

566

People who are grieving often feel extremely tired because the process of grieving usually requires physical and emotional energy. The grief they are feeling is not just for the person who died, but also for the unfulfilled wishes and plans for the relationship with the person. Death often reminds people of past losses or separations. Mourning may be described as having three phases, including the urge to bring back the person who died, disorganization and sadness, and reorganization.

Phases of a Life-Threatening Illness

Understanding how other people cope with a life-threatening illness may help the patient and his or her family prepare to cope with their own illness. A life-threatening illness may be described as having four phases, including the phase before the diagnosis, the acute phase, the chronic phase, and recovery or death.

The phase before the diagnosis of a life-threatening illness is the period of time just before the diagnosis when a person realizes that he or she may develop an illness. This phase is not usually a single moment, but extends throughout the period when the person has a physical examination, including various tests, and ends when the person is told of the diagnosis.

The acute phase occurs at the time of the diagnosis when a person is forced to understand the diagnosis and make decisions about his or her medical care.

The chronic phase is the period of time between the diagnosis and the result of treatment. It is the period of time when patients try to cope with the demands of life while also undergoing treatment and coping with the side effects of treatment. In the past, the period between a cancer diagnosis and death usually lasted only a few months, and this time was usually spent in the hospital. Today, people can live for years after being diagnosed with cancer.

In the recovery phase, people cope with the mental, social, physical, religious, and financial effects of cancer.

The final (terminal) phase of a life-threatening illness occurs when death is likely. The focus then changes from curing the illness or prolonging life, to providing comfort and relief from pain. Religious concerns are often the focus during this time.

End-Of-Life Decisions

Caring for a person with cancer starts after symptoms begin and the diagnosis is made and continues until the patient is in remission, is cured, or has died. End-of-life decisions should be made early after the diagnosis, before there is a need for them. These issues are not pleasant or easy to think about. They usually reflect a person's philosophical, moral, religious, or spiritual background. If a person has certain feelings about end-of-life issues, they should be made known so that they can be carried out. However, since these are sensitive issues, they are frequently not discussed by patients, families, or doctors. People often feel that there will be plenty of time to talk later about the issues. Many times, though, when the end-of-life decisions are necessary, the patient and family are not able to make the decisions, and the decisions are made by people who may not know the patient's wishes.

As a first step in making decisions for the end of life, patients should complete a Health Care Proxy (HCP) form. These forms are not the same in each state, but they have the same purpose. The HCP allows the patient to identify a person (called a proxy) to make medical decisions if the patient becomes unable to do so. The form may not need to be notarized, but it must be witnessed by two other people. In some states, the HCP is better than a living will because the patient does not have to say exactly which decisions need to be made, but that the proxy knows "what I would want."

A living will is similar to the HCP. It allows a person to state in more detail what his or her feelings are about medical care, nutrition, and other medical issues so that doctors and caregivers can carry out these wishes. Living wills are not available or legal in all states. Living wills usually require a lawyer and notarization to be complete in states where they are recognized.

Do Not Resuscitate (DNR) orders tell doctors and other health care givers that a patient does not want extreme measures to be taken to save his or her life. The patient will not be resuscitated if his or her heart stops or if he or she stops breathing. People who do not want extreme measures taken should talk with their doctor and other caregivers and complete forms as early as possible (for example, when they are admitted to the hospital) instead of waiting until they cannot make this decision. Although people with end-stage disease and their families are usually uncomfortable talking about these issues, doctors and nurses may gently and respectfully bring up the issues when the time is right.

Programs like hospice are now available that allow patients to die at home. Some states have DNR forms available for people wishing to die at home which protects them from being resuscitated. These advanced directive forms are signed by the patient's doctor and express the patient's wishes and intent not to be resuscitated. These issues are important to discuss wherever a patient is being cared for, whether at home, in the hospital, at hospice, in a nursing home, or elsewhere.

The Pathway to Death

People who are dying may move towards death over longer or shorter periods of time and in different ways. Different causes of death result in different paths toward death.

The pathway to death may be long and slow, sometimes lasting years, or it may be a rapid fall towards death (for example, after a car accident) when the chronic phase of the illness, if it exists at all, is short. The "peaks and valleys" pathway describes the patient who repeatedly gets better and then worse again (for example, a patient with AIDS or leukemia). Another pathway to death may be described as a long, slow period of failing health and then a period of stable health (for example, patients whose health gets worse and then stabilizes at a new, more limiting level). Patients on this pathway must readjust to losses in functioning ability.

Deaths from cancer often occur over a long period of time, and may involve long-term pain and suffering, and/or loss of control over one's body or mind. Deaths caused by cancer are likely to drain patients and families physically and emotionally because they occur over a long period of time.

Anticipatory Grief

Anticipatory grief is the normal mourning that occurs when a patient or family is expecting a death. Anticipatory grief has many of the same symptoms as those experienced after a death has occurred.

Anticipatory grief includes depression, extreme concern for the dying person, preparing for the death, and adjusting to changes caused by the death. Anticipatory grief gives the family more time to slowly get used to the reality of the loss. People are able to complete "unfinished business" with the dying person (for example, saying "good-bye," "I love you," or "I forgive you").

Anticipatory grief may not always occur. Anticipatory grief does not mean that before the death, a person feels the same kind of grief as the grief felt after a death. There is not a set amount of grief that a person will feel. The grief experienced before a death does not make the grief after the death last a shorter amount of time.

Grief that follows an unplanned death is different from anticipatory grief. Unplanned loss may overwhelm the coping abilities of a person, making normal functioning impossible. Mourners may not be able to realize the total impact of their loss. Even though the person recognizes that the loss occurred, he or she may not be able to accept the loss mentally and emotionally. Following an unexpected death, the mourner may feel that the world no longer has order and does not make sense.

Some people believe that anticipatory grief is rare. To accept a loved one's death while he or she is still alive may leave the mourner feeling that the dying patient has been abandoned. Expecting the loss often makes the attachment to the dying person stronger. Although anticipatory grief may help the family, the dying person may experience too much grief, causing the patient to become withdrawn.

Phases of Grief

The process of bereavement may be described as having four phases:

1. Shock and numbness: Family members find it difficult to believe the death; they feel stunned and numb.

2. Yearning and searching: Survivors experience separation anxiety and cannot accept the reality of the loss. They try to find and bring back the lost person and feel ongoing frustration and disappointment when this is not possible.

3. Disorganization and despair: Family members feel depressed and find it difficult to plan for the future. They are easily distracted and have difficulty concentrating and focusing.

4. Reorganization

Treatment

Grief counseling helps mourners with uncomplicated grief go through the phases of grief. Grief counseling can be provided by professionally trained people, or in self-help groups where bereaved people help other bereaved people. All of these services may be available in individual or group settings.

The goals of grief counseling include:

•   helping the bereaved to accept the loss by helping him or her to talk about the loss

- helping the bereaved to identify and express feelings related to the loss (for example, anger, guilt, anxiety, helplessness, and sadness)

- helping the bereaved to live without the person who died and to make decisions alone

- helping the bereaved to separate emotionally from the person who died and to begin new relationships

- providing support and time to focus on grieving at important times such as birthdays and anniversaries

- describing normal grieving and the differences in grieving among individuals

- providing continuous support

- helping the bereaved to understand his or her methods of coping

- identifying coping problems the bereaved may have and making recommendations for professional grief therapy

Grief therapy is used with people who have complicated grief reactions. The goal of grief therapy is to identify and solve problems the mourner may have in separating from the person who died. When separation difficulties occur, they may appear as physical or behavior problems, delayed or extreme mourning, conflicted or extended grief, or unexpected mourning (although this is seldom present with cancer deaths).

Grief therapy may be available as individual or group therapy. A contract is set up with the patient that establishes the time limit of the therapy, the fees, the goals, and the focus of the therapy.

In grief therapy, the mourner talks about the deceased and tries to recognize whether he or she is experiencing an expected amount of emotion about the death. Grief therapy may allow the mourner to see that anger, guilt, or other negative or uncomfortable feelings can exist at the same time as more positive feelings about the person who died.

Human beings tend to make strong bonds of affection or attachment with others. When these bonds are broken, as in death, a strong emotional reaction occurs. After a loss occurs, a person must accomplish certain tasks to complete the process of grief. These basic tasks of mourning include accepting that the loss happened, living with and feeling the physical and emotional pain of grief, adjusting to life without the loved one, and emotionally separating from the loved one and going on with life without him or her. It is important that these tasks are completed before mourning can end.

In grief therapy, six tasks may be used to help a mourner work through grief: 1) develop the ability to experience, express, and adjust to painful grief-related changes, 2) find effective ways to cope with painful changes, 3) establish a continuing relationship with the person who died, 4) stay healthy and keep functioning, 5) reestablish relationships and understand that others may have difficulty empathizing with the grief they experience, and 6) develop a healthy image of oneself and the world.

Complications in grief may come about due to uncompleted grief from earlier losses. The grief for these earlier losses must be managed in order to handle the current grief. Grief therapy includes dealing with the blockages to the mourning process, identifying unfinished business with the deceased, and identifying other losses that result from the death. The bereaved is helped to see that the loss is final and to picture life after the grief period.

Complicated Grief

Complicated grief reactions require more complex therapies than uncomplicated grief reactions. Adjustment disorders (especially depressed and anxious mood or disturbed emotions and behavior), major depression, substance abuse, and even post-traumatic stress disorder are some of the common problems of complicated bereavement. Complicated grief is identified by the extended length of time of the symptoms, the interference caused by the symptoms, or by the intensity of the symptoms (for example, intense suicidal thoughts or acts).

Complicated or unresolved grief may appear as a complete absence of grief and mourning, an ongoing inability to experience normal grief reactions, delayed grief, conflicted grief, or chronic grief. Factors that contribute to the chance that one may experience complicated grief include the suddenness of the death, the gender of the person in mourning, and the relationship to the deceased (for example, an intense, extremely close, or very contradictory relationship). Grief reactions that turn into major depression should be treated with both drug and psychological therapy. One who avoids any reminders of the person who died, who constantly thinks or dreams about the person who died, and who gets scared and panics easily at any reminders of the person who died may be suffering from post-traumatic stress disorder. Substance abuse may occur, frequently in an attempt to avoid painful feelings about the loss and symptoms (such as sleeplessness), and can also be treated with drugs and psychological therapy.

Culture and Response to Grief and Mourning

Grief felt for the loss of a loved one, the loss of a treasured possession, or a loss associated with an important life change, occurs across all ages and cultures. However, the role that cultural heritage plays in an individual's experience of grief and mourning is not well understood. Attitudes, beliefs, and practices regarding death must be described according to myths and mysteries surrounding death within different cultures.

Individual, personal experiences of grief are similar in different cultures. This is true even though different cultures have different mourning ceremonies, traditions, and behaviors to express grief. Helping families cope with the death of a loved one includes showing respect for the family's cultural heritage and encouraging them to decide how to honor the death. Important questions that should be asked of people who are dealing with the loss of a loved one include:

1. What are the cultural rituals for coping with dying, the deceased person's body, the final arrangements for the body, and honoring the death?

2. What are the family's beliefs about what happens after death?

3. What does the family feel is a normal expression of grief and the acceptance of the loss?

4. What does the family consider to be the roles of each family member in handling the death?

5. Are certain types of death less acceptable (for example, suicide), or are certain types of death especially hard to handle for that culture (for example, the death of a child)?

Death, grief, and mourning spare no one and are normal life events. All cultures have developed ways to cope with death. Interfering with these practices may interfere with the necessary grieving processes. Understanding different cultures' response to death can help physicians recognize the grieving process in patients of other cultures.

To Learn More

For more information, call the National Cancer Institute's Cancer Information Service at (800) 4-CANCER (800-422-6237); TTY at (800) 332-8615. The call is free and a trained information specialist is available to answer your questions.

There are many other places to get information about cancer treatment and services. Check the social service office at your hospital for local and national agencies that can help with finances, getting to and from treatment, care at home, and dealing with other problems.

Write to the National Cancer Institute at this address:

National Cancer Institute
Building 31, Room 10A24
9000 Rockville Pike
Bethesda, MD 20892

Chapter 56

Stages of Grief in Children

In the past, children were thought to be miniature adults and were expected to behave as adults. It is now understood that there are differences in the ways in which children and adults mourn.

Unlike adults, bereaved children do not experience continual and intense emotional and behavioral grief reactions. Children may seem to show grief only occasionally and briefly, but in reality a child's grief usually lasts longer than that of an adult. Mourning in children may need to be addressed again and again as the child gets older. As the surviving child grows, he or she will think about the loss repeatedly, especially during important times in his or her life, such as going to camp, graduating from school, getting married, or giving birth to his or her own children. This longer period of grief is due to the fact that the child's ability to experience intense emotions is limited.

A child's grief may be influenced by his or her age, personality, stage of development, earlier experiences with death, and his or her relationship with the deceased. The surroundings, cause of death, family members' ability to communicate with one another and to continue as a family after the death can also affect grief. The child's ongoing need for care, the child's opportunity to share his or her feelings and memories, the parent's ability to cope with stress, and the child's steady relationships with other adults are also other factors that may influence grief.

Excerpted from "Loss, Grief, and Bereavement," [Online] May 1999. Available: http//:cancernet.nci.nih.gov. Produced by NIH's National Cancer Institute (NCI). For complete contact information, please refer to Chapter 60, "Resources."

Children do not react to loss in the same ways as adults. Grieving children may not show their feelings as openly as adults. Grieving children may not withdraw and dwell on the person who died, but instead may throw themselves into activities (for example, they may be sad one minute and playful the next). Often families think the child "doesn't really understand" or has "gotten over" the death. Neither is true; children's minds protect them from what is too powerful for them to handle. Children's grieving periods are shortened because they can not think through their thoughts and feelings like adults. Also, children have trouble putting their feelings about grief into words. Instead, his or her behavior "speaks" for the child. Strong feelings of anger and fears of abandonment or death may show up in the behavior of grieving children. Children often play death games as a way of working out their feelings and anxieties. These games are familiar to the children and provide safe opportunities to express their feelings.

Children's Grief and Developmental Stages

Children at different stages of development have different understandings of death and the events near death.

Infants

Infants do not recognize death, but feelings of loss and separation are part of developing an awareness of death. Children who have been separated from their mother may be sluggish, quiet, unresponsive to a smile or a coo, undergo physical changes (for example, weight loss), be less active, and sleep less.

Age 2-3 Years

Children at this age often confuse death with sleep and may experience anxiety as early as age 3. They may stop talking and appear to feel overall distress.

Age 3-6 Years

At this age children see death as a kind of sleep; the person is alive, but only in a limited way. The child cannot fully separate death from life. Children may think that the person is still living, even though he or she might have been buried, and ask questions about the deceased (for example, how does the deceased eat, go to the toilet, breathe, or play?). Young children know that death occurs physically, but think it is temporary, reversible, and not final. The child's concept of death may involve magical thinking. For example, the child may think that his or her thoughts can cause another person to become sick or die. Grieving children under 5 may have trouble eating, sleeping, and controlling bladder and bowel functions.

Age 6-9 Years

Children at this age are commonly very curious about death, and may ask questions about what happens to one's body when it dies. Death is thought of as a person or spirit separate from the person who was alive, such as a skeleton, ghost, angel of death, or "bogey man." They may see death as final and frightening but as something that happens mostly to old people (and not to themselves). Grieving children can become afraid of school, have learning problems, develop antisocial or aggressive behaviors, become overly concerned about their own health (for example, developing symptoms of imaginary illness), or withdraw from others. Or, children this age can become too attached and clinging. Boys usually become more aggressive and destructive (for example, acting out in school), instead of openly showing their sadness. Children may feel abandoned by both their deceased parent and their surviving parent because the surviving parent is grieving and is unable to emotionally support the child.

Ages 9 and Older

By the time a child is 9 years old, death is known to be unavoidable and is not seen as a punishment. By the time a child is 12 years old, death is seen as final and something that happens to everyone.

In American society, many grieving adults withdraw and do not talk to others. Children, however, often talk to the people around them (even strangers) to see the reactions of others and to get clues for their own responses. Children may ask confusing questions. For example, a child may ask "I know grandpa died, but when will he come home?" This is a way of testing reality and making sure the story of the death has not changed.

Other Issues for Grieving Children

Children's grief expresses three issues: (1) Did I cause the death to happen? (2) Is it going to happen to me? (3) Who is going to take care of me?

Did I cause the death to happen?

Children often think that they have magical powers. If a mother says in irritation, "You'll be the death of me" and later dies, her child may wonder if he or she actually caused the mother's death. Also, when children argue, one may say (or think), "I wish you were dead." Should that child die, the surviving child may think that his or her thoughts actually caused the death.

Is it going to happen to me?

The death of another child may be especially hard for a child. If the child thinks that the death may have been prevented (by either a parent or a doctor) the child may think that he or she could also die.

Who is going to take care of me?

Since children depend on parents and other adults to take care of them, a grieving child may wonder who will care for him or her after the death of an important person.

Grieving Children: Treatment

A child's grieving process may be made easier by being open and honest with the child about death, using direct language, and incorporating the child into memorial ceremonies for the person who died.

Explanation of Death

Not talking about death (which indicates that the subject is off limits) does not help children learn to cope with loss. When discussing death with children, explanations should be simple and direct. Each child should be told the truth using as much detail as he or she is able to understand. The child's questions should be answered honestly and directly. Children need to be reassured about their own security (they often worry that they will also die, or that their surviving parent will go away). Children's questions should be answered, making sure that the child understands the answers.

Correct Language

A discussion about death should include the proper words, such as "cancer," "died," and "death." Substitute words or phrases (for example, "passed away," "he is sleeping," or "we lost him") should never be used because they can confuse children and lead to misunderstandings.

Planning Memorial Ceremonies

When a death occurs, children can and should be included in the planning and participation of memorial ceremonies. These events help children (and adults) remember loved ones. Children should not be forced to be involved in these ceremonies, but they should be encouraged to take part in those portions of the events with which they feel most comfortable. If the child wants to attend the funeral, wake, or memorial service, he or she should be given in advance a full explanation of what to expect. The surviving parent may be too involved in his or her own grief to give their child full attention, therefore, it may be helpful to have a familiar adult or family member care for the grieving child.

References and Resources for Grieving Children

There are many helpful books and videos that can be shared with grieving children.

Corr, C. A, and J. N. McNeil. *Adolescence and Death.* New York: Springer Publishing Company, 1986.

Corr, C. A., C. M. Nabe, and D. M. Corr. *Death and Dying, Life and Living.* 2nd ed., Pacific Grove: Brooks/Cole Publishing Company, 1997.

Doka, K. J., Ed. *Children Mourning, Mourning Children.* Washington, DC: Hospice Foundation of America, 1995.

Grollman, E. A. *Talking About Death: A Dialogue Between Parent and Child.* 3rd ed., Boston: Beacon Press, 1990.

Schaefer, D., and C. Lyons. *How Do We Tell the Children?: Helping Children Understand and Cope When Someone Dies.* New York: Newmarket Press, 1988.

Tiffault, B. W. *A Quilt for Elizabeth.* Omaha: Centering Corporation, 1992.

Viost, J. *The Tenth Good Thing about Barney.* New York: Atheneum, 1971.

Walker, A. *To Hell with Dying*. San Diego: Harcourt Brace Jovanovich, 1988.

Wass, H., and C. A. Corr. *Childhood and Death*. Washington, DC: Hemisphere Publishing Corporation, 1984.

Williams, M. *Velveteen Rabbit*. Garden City: Doubleday, 1922.

Wolfelt, A. *Helping Children Cope with Grief*. Muncie: Accelerated Development, 1983.

Worden, J. W. *Children and Grief: When a Parent Dies*. New York: The Guilford Press, 1996.

Chapter 57

Advice for Grieving Parents

Although the experience of losing a child is very painful, and difficult to deal with, here are some suggestions to parents who are undergoing one of life's most difficult experiences. Hope these are helpful to you:

1. Know that the paperwork for the hospital is very detailed and overwhelming at times. However, it is a necessity. Here are some of the things you may be asked to decide or consent to:

   - Autopsy consents—in some states, and for varying situations, this is REQUIRED—although your consent is asked for. In other situations, you may be asked for your consent for autopsy to determine various aspects of your child's death, in which your consent is voluntary. Although many parents find this detail upsetting, it is a necessary part of this painful process.

   - Funeral arrangements: sometimes called in medical terms, "disposal of remains". You will need to decide how you want your child's body handled. Do you wish the hospital to take care of the arrangements, or do you wish to have a religious ceremony/funeral for your child—all of these options must be dealt with by the parents, and the appropriate consents filled out.

- Birth/Death Certificates: if your child is born alive and then dies, even one minute later, birth and death certificates will have to be issued according to law. Do you want to name your child? If so, then that is your option, you can choose not to name your child also. Please be aware though, if you choose not to name your child, that the birth and death certificates will say: Baby boy or Baby girl, and the MOTHER'S last name.

Here are some other papers that may, or may not be asked for you to complete: insurance forms, hospital forms, consents to photograph (this allows the hospital to take pictures of your child), genetic counseling permissions, genetic testing consents, and other such forms.

2. You may be asked if you would like to hold your child. Although many parents fear this, especially when [their] child has birth defects—most parents find that spending even brief moments holding their child very comforting during the grief process and beyond.

3. Ask if mementoes of your child are available. Things such as the blankets used for the baby, baby bracelets, hats, footprints, etc., are usually taken, and kept for the parents. Even if you don't desire these objects at the present time, many times hospitals retain these items indefinitely in case you change your mind later.

4. It's OK to question your nurses and other staff members about their experiences in dealing with situations such as your particular one. If you feel uncomfortable with a health care provider, then please ask to have another provider assist you.

5. Ask to have unnecessary medical staff not be present in your room. Most hospitals are sensitive to this, and make every effort to reduce unnecessary staff coming and going out of your room.

6. Write down questions and concerns to ask later. Many times it is difficult to remember to ask every question you have at the "moment." Writing things down, especially in stressful times, makes it easier to remember later.

7. As much as possible, your religious and personal views will, and should, be taken into consideration. For children who are

born alive, but will die shortly after birth—last rites, for example, can be performed either by a hospital chaplain or a priest of your choosing. Other religious ceremonies can be arranged in similar instances.

8. There are many support groups available that deal with grief issues, some specifically deal with the loss of children. You may find it helpful to attend some of these groups to be with others who have suffered the same type of loss.

9. While losing a child is one of life's most difficult issues, and grieving is a natural part of losing a child—if you find that the days are not slowing getting better, or you feel that you are not "getting over" this loss, please discuss your feelings openly and honestly with your doctor, or health care provider. Also remember, that everyone grieves at his or her own pace, it's not up to OTHERS to tell you how you should grieve, or feel about such a loss.

Chapter 58

Hospice Bereavement Services

In Western culture, death is usually a taboo subject, and grieving is regarded as a private affair. These social inhibitions make bereavement more difficult to cope with, and add to the difficulties of individuals and groups who can't accept it.

Two years ago there was a strong feeling in our hospice that the bereavement service to families, friends, and partners needed to be developed. But it wasn't obvious what we could do to reach as many people as possible and to make it clear they were not forgotten.

The hospice serves a wide catchment area and we have many black and ethnic minority patients, including some refugees. We wanted to make sure our bereavement service would also meet their needs and those of their loved ones.

The hospice already had a bereavement programme which consisted of a condolence letter, a follow-up phone call two or three weeks after a death, and individual bereavement counselling with one of the social workers, if needed.

But we guessed that many people who seemed to cope well at the time of a death might, perhaps three months later, be having a difficult time. Where would they get the help and support they might need? Despite the fact that nurses always make it clear that people are welcome to return at any time, would they feel able to do this, or telephone the hospice to ask for help after a gap of a few months?

From "Tea and Sympathy," by Suzy Croft and Lesley Adshead, in *Community Care,* No. 1137, pp. 30-1, September 12-18, 1996. © 1996 by Reed Business Information Ltd. Reprinted with permission.

This gave us the idea of a bereavement tea—a group work and community development approach to offering support. We decided to organise an afternoon tea every four months, inviting those who had been bereaved for between three and six months. We felt it would be too painful for people who had been bereaved for less than this period. About 70 invitations went out.

Hospice volunteers laid on the first tea in June 1995. The idea of an afternoon tea may seem a simple one; this is not a structured bereavement group and we had no formal agenda. Now we have had six teas, we realise simple ideas are often best.

Before the first tea, we were worried how we would be able to find time to talk to everyone, particularly those who might be deeply upset. In fact, one young woman walked in, burst into tears, and cried throughout the whole afternoon. But we quickly found people were able to talk to each other and share their varied experiences.

An 80-year-old widow could be seen chatting to the male partner of a young man who died of AIDS. People were often anxious to find out what had happened to other patients and their families. Sometimes they were pleased to meet up with those with whom they had shared bedside vigils or a nervous cigarette. Many friends and families of black and other ethnic minority patients came.

We realised people often wanted to come back to the hospice but had not felt able to do so. Over and over we heard: "I've walked past the place many times, but never felt able to come through the door." One woman said: "I thought you would have forgotten me by now. It's so nice to be remembered."

Several people wanted to walk round the hospice and look into the room where the person they loved died. One woman bought flowers to put into what had been her mother's room. Her mother had died soon after she came in. "We weren't able to give her much here before she died so I wanted to bring these flowers," she said.

This reliving of memories seems important and people say how helpful it is to be able to describe all the details of a death again, to someone who won't be bored or embarrassed. The need to retell a story is a strong one. But many people we have met say how it's often not possible to do this with friends or people at work or other family members.

Many people need reassurance that there is nothing wrong with them if they still feel sad after a few months or even years. Unfortunately, people who haven't been bereaved often expect the rest of us to feel better after a couple of months. Feelings of despair can even be met with incredulity and irritation.

We have tried to create an open atmosphere where people can remember and give expression to the bad as well as the good. One widow, who thoroughly enjoyed her tea and ate a pile of cream cakes, was able to tell both of us of her relief her husband was dead.

She told us of all the restrictions he had placed on her throughout their married life. We felt because we did not express shock and disgust at what she said, she was able to tell us of her confused feelings. Others have also talked about ambivalent feelings. One woman's mother always told her off, even on the day she died, making her feel worthless and angry.

People raise other, often terrible, problems they have. They may have had cancer themselves, have lost other close friends and family, or have serious financial difficulties. One disabled man telephoned one of us after the tea and told us he was in danger of being evicted. His benefits were being underpaid, so one of us was able to point this out to the Department of Social Security and the threat of eviction was lifted. Another person told us that at the same time as his father was dying, a colleague at work was murdered.

The informal atmosphere of the teas is a good way to offer support to men who may have previously had difficulty in asking for help. Many people say the tea gave them the chance to come back and say thank you: "I feel so guilty I never said a proper thank you. I was too shocked at the time and it's been worrying me ever since."

Others have used it as an opportunity to tell us what they were less happy about: "I didn't feel my father should have been sent home with a nurse he didn't know. He wasn't properly prepared and he said: 'Who is this in my room?'."

There may be those for whom the teas are less attractive and this is a problem we may need to tackle. What stops people coming? A few have said that at the last minute they cannot face coming to the hospice again. Occasionally people leave the tea early and we wonder if this is because they feel overwhelmed.

Others have said they would like to come to another tea, but this is not possible because of the numbers involved. All we then have to offer, if people don't want individual or group counselling, is an annual service—not necessarily appropriate for those with no religious beliefs or of other faiths.

After six teas we've learned some lessons. An informal atmosphere is crucial. At first we panicked when guests arrived early. We worried the room wasn't set out and the tea on the table. But this doesn't matter and may even be an advantage. If it seems too formal people may feel they've come to be 'counselled'. One woman did say: "I won't come if I'm going to be psycho-analysed."

Also, good food is a must. It makes people feel cherished and important. "Oh, look at that spread. I hadn't expected I'd be so well looked after." Then there have to be plenty of helpers to pass the food around. People feel too embarrassed to help themselves and they need people who are prepared to chat and break the ice.

It also shouldn't be assumed people won't come because they live a long way away. One woman came on the overnight coach from Glasgow. Nor should it be assumed distant relatives are not just as sad as relatives living closer to the deceased. Others may think this and the tea may be their first chance to say how sad they feel and to have their grief publicly acknowledged.

It is important people can freely come in and go out of the room. We try to have a grief room available and encourage those who want to look round the hospice again. We have not found that this infringes patients' privacy. Interpreters should be present if necessary. If they are to be included in the bereavement tea, it is important to have someone there who can speak their language.

Nurses should be encouraged to drop in. Relatives, friends, and partners want to see the nurses who have offered them support at a difficult time. One woman cried throughout the first tea. On her way out, one of us rather anxiously asked her if she'd found the afternoon helpful. She said: "I am so pleased I came. It's helped me such a lot."

—by Suzy Croft and Lesley Adshead

Suzy Croft and Lesley Adshead are social workers at St. John's Hospice, London.

Part Eight

Additional Help and Information

Chapter 59

Glossary

This chapter includes definitions excerpted from "Alzheimer's Disease," November 9, 1998, by Administration on Aging (AoA); "Current Trends Autopsy Frequency—United States, 1980-1985," April 1, 1988, and "Possible Solutions to Common Problems in Death Certification," January 1997, by Centers for Disease Control and Prevention (CDC); "Advance Directives," July 7, 1998, by Health Care Financing Administration (HCFA); "Loss, Grief, and Bereavement," May 1999, by National Cancer Institute; "Births and Deaths: United States, 1996," in *Monthly Vital Statistics Report,*Vol. 46, No. 1, 1997, by the National Center for Health Statistics; "Symptoms in Terminal Illness: A Research Workshop," September 23, 1997, and "Death of a Patient," November 20, 1995, by National Institutes of Health (NIH); "How to Become an Organ and Tissue Donor," 1999, by the U.S. Department of Health and Human Services; "Final Details: A Helpful Guide for Survivors when Death Occurs," © 1998 by American Association of Retired Persons (AARP); "What Consumers Need to Know about Private Long-Term Care Insurance," by American Health Care Association (AHCA); "Ethical Issues in Organ Donation and Transplantation: Are We Helping a Few at the Expense of Many?", in *Critical Care Nursing Quarterly,* May 1996, © 1996 by Aspen Publishers, Inc.; "Funeral Planner," © 1997, 1998 by Death & Dying; "A Death in the Family," in *HUMAN LIFE News,* June 1998, © 1998 by HUMAN LIFE of Washington; "Ethics," in the *Journal of the American Medical Association,* July 14, 1993, © 1993 by the American Medical Association; "How to Choose a Home Care Provider," © 1996 by National Association for Home Care; "Opposing the Legalization of Euthanasia and Assisted Suicide," © 1997 by National Hospice Organization; "Preparing for Approaching Death," © 1996 by North Central Florida Hospice, Inc.; "The Nursing Home Information Site," © 1996,1997, 1998, 1999 by The Nursing Home Information Site; "Death and Dying: A Cross-Cultural Perspective," by Gottfried Oosterwal, Center for Intercultural Relations; and "Strokes and the South," in *American Demographics,* May 1998, © 1998 by Primedia Intertec.

A

accelerated death benefits: Some life insurance companies offer life insurance policies with a special feature that allows payment of the death benefit when the insured person is still alive. Such payment usually is limited to situations in which the individual is terminally ill. The benefits are available to cover the costs of long term care services.

activities of daily living (ADLs): assistance with bathing, toileting, transferring, eating, locomotion, and dressing).

adult day care services: Available in many communities, providing personal care, skilled care, and recreational services.

advance directive: Written document that tells your family, friends, and physician how to make your medical decisions when you can't make them for yourself. An advance directive can also designate someone else to make medical decisions for you. Usually, advance directives are in the form of a Living Will or a Durable Power of Attorney for Health Care.

allocation: The system of ensuring that organs and tissues are distributed fairly to patients who are in need.

Alzheimer's disease: The most common cause of dementia among older persons, evidenced by a progressive, irreversible decline in mental functioning. As the disease progresses, individuals with Alzheimer's experience a loss of memory and gradually lose their capacity to reason, communicate, and carry out the simple tasks of daily life.

assisted living facilities: Facilities that provide general supervision, housekeeping services, medical monitoring, and planned social, recreational, and spiritual activities for people who are still independent and ambulatory. Assisted living facilities do not provide medical care.

assisted suicide: The term "assisted suicide" is most commonly used to represent an act in which a patient is given the means and specific instructions to take his or her own life.

autopsy: Internal and external medical examination of a human corpse required by law in cases of traumatic, sudden, or unexpected deaths. Autopsies are performed by coroners or medical examiners, depending on the local medicolegal system.

B

bereavement: The state of having suffered a loss and experiencing many emotions and changes. The time spent in a period of bereavement depends on how attached the person was to the person who died, and how much time was spent anticipating the loss.

brain death: The central focus of the definition of death. Factors considered in determining brain death include loss of pupillary and corneal reflexes, loss of oculocephalic (doll's head) and oculovestibular (caloric) reflexes, loss of responses to painful stimuli applied in cranial nerve territory, loss of responses to bronchial stimulation with a suction catheter, loss of ventilatory response to elevated blood carbon dioxide (arterial $pCO2$ rising over 50 mm Hg from a background of normal blood gases), and reproducibility of observations to exclude error and affirm the stability of the finding; the minimum interval between examinations will depend on the causal pathology and may be as long as 24 hours.

C

cachexia: Loss of appetite and muscle wasting, a common symptom in terminal illness. The emerging view is that cachexia is the result of the combined action of tumor products (in cancer) and host immune factors.

cadaveric donors: Persons who donate their organs or tissue after they have been declared brain dead.

case management: A system in which one individual helps the insured person and his/her family determine necessary services, and the best setting for those services.

Cheyne-Stokes breathing: A particular pattern of breathing irregularly during the dying process, i.e., shallow breaths with periods of no breathing of 5 to 30 seconds and up to a full minute. The dying person may also experience periods of rapid, shallow pant-like breathing. These patterns are very common and indicate decrease in circulation in the internal organs.

593

cognitive impairment: A diminished mental capacity, such as difficulty with short-term memory.

cohort: Group of individuals having a statistical factor in common in a demographic study.

companions: As part of home care services, they provide companionship and comfort to individuals who, for medical and/or safety reasons, may not be left at home alone. Some companions may assist clients with household tasks, but most are limited to providing sitter services.

coroner/medical examiner: Has the legal authority to order autopsies for traumatic, sudden, or unexpected deaths.

cremation: The process of reducing a human corpse to ashes by burning.

crematory: A furnace for cremating.

curative treatment: Medical treatment that aims to cure, rather than comfort the terminally ill patient; judged to be inappropriate by a growing number of the medical community.

custodial care: Board, room, and other personal assistance services (including assistance with activities of daily living, taking medicine, and other similar personal needs), that do not include a health care component and may be provided by people without medical skills or training.

D

death certificate: A permanent record of an individual's death that gives a simple description of the sequence or process leading to death. The death certificate is a legal document used for legal, family, and insurance purposes.

delirium: Transient organic brain syndrome characterized by the acute onset of disordered attention and cognition and accompanied by perceptual disturbances and various behavioral manifestations including confusion and restlessness. It is a common symptom in terminal illness.

dementia: Progressive mental disorder that affects memory, judgment, and cognitive powers. One type of dementia is Alzheimer's disease.

dietitians: Provide counseling services to individuals who need professional dietary assessment and guidance to properly manage an illness or disability.

DNR (do not resuscitate): An advance directive that states that in the event of cardiac arrest, the patient does not wish cardiac resuscitation.

donor: Person who gives his organs or tissue to someone else.

DRG (diagnosis-related group): Created in the 1970s for use by reimbursement agencies such as Medicare, it is a system of classifying patients according to diagnosis, length of hospital stay, and therapy received. Hospitals are allotted a certain amount of money for each patient according to the DRG profile.

Durable Power of Attorney for Health Care: Signed, dated, and witnessed paper that authorizes someone else to make your medical decisions if you are unable to make them for yourself. This can include instructions about any treatment you want to avoid, for example, cardiac resuscitation.

dyspnea: Difficult breathing, or an uncomfortable awareness of breathing, a common symptom in terminal illness.

E

embalming: A chemical process which provides temporary preservation of the body for the purpose of ceremonial viewing. A person examined and licensed by the state they live in must complete this procedure. Except in certain circumstances, embalming is not required by law.

end-stage organ disease: A disease that leads, ultimately, to functional failure of an organ. Some examples are emphysema (lungs), cardiomyopathy (heart), and polycystic kidney disease (kidneys).

end-stage renal disease (ESRD): A very serious and life-threatening kidney disease that minorities suffer much more frequently than do

Whites. ESRD is treatable with dialysis, however, dialysis is costly and can result in a poor quality of life for the patient. The preferred treatment of ESRD is kidney transplantation.

euthanasia: An act which intentionally and directly causes a patient's death. This definition of euthanasia encompasses active euthanasia, voluntary euthanasia, aid-in-dying, and in some settings, physician-assisted suicide.

F

facility care services: Include skilled nursing care, speech, physical, or occupational therapy, facility health aides, or help from facility makers. Sometimes, family members or caregivers provide most of the care with the help of facility aides and skilled professionals.

futile medical treatment: Medical treatment which, because of the patient's terminal state, offers diminishing returns and, until recently, could be unilaterally withheld by the treating physician.

G

grief: The normal process of reacting to loss. As a family goes through a cancer illness, many losses are experienced, and each triggers its own grief reaction. Grief may be experienced as a mental, physical, social, or emotional reaction. Mental reactions can include anger, guilt, anxiety, sadness, and despair. Physical reactions can include sleeping problems, changes in appetite, physical problems, or illness.

H

home health aides (HCAs): Assist patients with activities of daily living such as getting in and out of bed, walking, bathing, toileting, and dressing. Some aides have received special training and are qualified to provide more complex services under the supervision of a nursing professional.

heart disease: The leading cause of death in the United States.

home care services: Health care services delivered at home to recovering, disabled, chronically, or terminally ill persons in need of medical, nursing, social, or therapeutic treatment and/or assistance with the essential activities of daily life.

home health agency: Home care provider that is a Medicare-certified agency, meeting federal minimum requirements for patient care and management and therefore can provide Medicare and Medicaid home health services. Individuals requiring skilled home care services usually receive their care from a home health agency. Due to regulatory requirements, services provided by these agencies are highly supervised and controlled. Some agencies deliver a variety of home care services through physicians, nurses, therapists, social workers, homemakers and HCAs, durable medical equipment and supply dealers, and volunteers. Other home health agencies limit their services to nursing and one or two other specialties.

homemaker and chore workers: As part of home health services, they perform light household duties such as laundry, meal preparation, general housekeeping, and shopping. Their services are directed at maintaining patient households rather than providing hands-on assistance with personal care.

hospice: Hospice care involves a core interdisciplinary team of skilled professionals and volunteers who provide comprehensive medical, psychological, and spiritual care for the terminally ill and support for patients' families. Hospice care also includes the provision of related medications, medical supplies, and equipment. It is based primarily in the home, enabling families to remain together. Trained hospice professionals are available 24 hours a day to assist the family in caring for the patient, ensure that the patient's wishes are honored, and keep the patient comfortable and free from pain. Most hospices are Medicare certified and licensed according to state requirements.

I

immunosuppressive drugs: Chemical agents that cause the human body not to produce antibodies that normally fight off foreign material in the body. The production of these antibodies needs to be suppressed in order to permit the acceptance of a donor organ by the recipient's body.

indemnity benefit: A flat payment made directly to the policyholder, rather than to the nursing facility or facility care agency for services rendered.

informed consent: This means that the patient and/or family member has a right to make decisions concerning health care once they are told by the physician, in understandable language, what the prognosis is, and what options are available.

infusion therapy services: Provide the delivery of drugs, equipment, and professional services for individuals receiving intravenous or nutritional therapies through specially placed tubes.

intermediate care facility (ICF): Facility that is required to provide 8 hours of nursing supervision per day. Because of their physical appearance, these facilities are often confused with the SNFs (skilled nursing facilities). Intermediate care, however, is less extensive than skilled nursing care and generally serves patients who are ambulatory and need less supervision and care. Licensed nurses are not always immediately available in an ICF. At a minimum, ICFs provide medical, intermittent nursing, dietary, pharmacy, and activity services.

intestate: If the deceased did not have a will, this is referred to as dying "intestate." In this case, the estate, including property and assets belonging to the deceased, will be disbursed according to state law.

ischemic strokes: Occur when constriction or obstruction in a blood vessel reduces blood supply to an organ. Ischemic strokes are far more common than massive strokes and have a lower fatality.

K

kaddish: In the Jewish religion, a prayer praising God, recited at the gravesite and during the first year of mourning.

L

life-sustaining treatments: Cardiopulmonary resuscitation, ventilation, intubation, and other life-saving treatments for the terminally ill.

living donors: Persons who donate a kidney, part of a lung, or part of a liver while they are still alive.

living will: Written document that generally states the kind of medical care you want (or do not want) in case you become unable to make your own decisions. It is called a living will because it takes effect while you are still living. While most states have their own living will forms, you might also be able to write a personal statement of your preferences for treatment.

long-term care: Four out of every ten people age 65 will use a nursing home at some point in their lives, and many others will require home care and related services as well.

M

malignant neoplasms: Cancerous tumors, one of the leading causes of death in the United States.

Medicaid: The federally supported, state operated and administered public assistance program that pays for health care services to low-income people, including elderly or disabled persons. Medicaid pays for long term nursing facility care and some limited facility health services.

Medicare: The federal program providing hospital and medical insurance for people aged 65 and older, some disabled persons, and those with end-stage renal disease. Medicare provides only very limited benefits for skilled care, and under specific conditions, for nursing facility and facility health care.

Medigap: Private insurance that supplements Medicare. While Medigap policies typically cover Medicare's deductibles and coinsurance amounts, they do not provide benefits for long term care. Like Medicare, Medigap policies primarily cover hospital and doctor bills.

mourning: Consists of the conscious, unconscious, and cultural reactions to loss. Mourning includes the process of incorporating the experience of loss into ongoing life. Mourning is also influenced by cultural customs, rituals, and society's rules for coping with loss.

N

Nirvana: In the Buddhist religion, Nirvana is final spiritual liberation, illumination, and peace.

nonforfeiture benefit: A policy feature that provides for some return on premiums paid or reduced benefits, even if the policyholder quits paying the premium after a minimum period of time. This feature makes the insurance purchase more of an investment than true insurance, and raises the basic policy price.

nursing facilities: The primary settings for people who require medical care daily or intermittently. You must have a physician specify needed services in a written treatment plan for admission to a nursing facility. Many nursing facility stays are short periods of recuperation from an acute medical episode such as a hip fracture or surgery.

O

occupational therapists (OTs): Help individuals who have physical, developmental, social, or emotional problems that prevent them from performing the general activities of daily living (ADLs). OTs instruct patients on using specialized rehabilitation techniques and equipment to improve their function in tasks such as eating, bathing, dressing, and basic household routines.

ombudsman: His mission is to protect the health, safety, welfare, and rights of the elderly in nursing homes. The local ombudsman can provide assistance with useful advice on finding a good nursing home, assisting with admissions, investigating complaints, quality of care issues, financial information, Medicaid eligibility, residents' rights, Social Security information, estate problems, and/or alternative care options.

organ procurement organizations (OPO): Organizations that coordinate activities relating to organ retrieval (procurement) in a designated area. OPO activities include: evaluating potential donors, discussing donation with surviving family members, arranging for the surgical removal and transport of donated organs, and educating the public about the need for donations.

out-of-pocket payments or costs: Costs borne without benefit of insurance, or payment required under insurance cost-sharing provisions.

P

pain management: Controlling pain in the terminally ill.

palliative care: Patient treatment that is aimed at pain relief and symptom control, rather than being curative, and is appropriate care for the terminally ill.

patient rights: The involvement of patients and their families in making decisions about medical treatment, as supported by medical ethics experts.

period of confinement: The time during which you receive care for a covered illness. The period ends when you have been discharged from care for a specified period of time, usually six months.

physical therapists (PTs): work to restore the mobility and strength of patients who are limited or disabled by physical injuries through the use of exercise, massage, and other methods. PTs often alleviate pain and restore injured muscles with specialized equipment. They also teach patients and caregivers special techniques for walking and transfer.

preexisting conditions: Medical conditions that existed, were diagnosed, or were under treatment before you took out a policy. Long-term care insurance policies may limit the benefits payable for such conditions.

probate: The process of paying the deceased's debts and distributing the estate to the rightful beneficiaries. This process begins with the court appointing someone to administer the estate. The will usually nominates the "executor." If there is no will, the court will appoint a "personal representative," usually a spouse or relative. This representative will need to pay a filing fee, inform interested parties, especially creditors, that the estate is being probated, make an inventory of assets, and dispose of the estate according to the will or state laws.

procurement: The process of retrieving organs and/or tissue from a donor.

prospective payment system (PPS): Instead of depending on after-the-fact reimbursement, PPS revolves around a preexisting classification and payment schedule for diseases and patient recuperation time.

Public Health Service (PHS): Offers guidelines on the acceptability of using certain human organs for safe transplantation.

Q

Qur'an: The sacred scripture of the Islamic religion.

R

registered nurses: (RNs) and licensed practical nurses (LPNs) provide skilled services that cannot be performed safely and effectively by nonprofessional personnel. Some of these services include injections and intravenous therapy, wound care, education on disease treatment and prevention, and patient assessments.

respite care: A "time-out" for the caregiver of a loved one who is terminally ill. Respite care may be in the form of in-home caregiving relief, adult day care, or temporary, short-term institutional care.

S

skilled nursing facility (SNF): Facility that is required to provide continuous (24-hour) nursing supervision by registered or licensed vocational nurses. Commonly referred to as "nursing homes" or "convalescent hospitals," these facilities normally care for the incapacitated person in need of long- or short-term care and assistance with many aspects of daily living (walking, bathing, dressing, eating). At a minimum, SNFs provide medical, nursing, dietary, pharmacy, and activity services.

social workers: Evaluate the social and emotional factors affecting ill and disabled individuals and provide counseling. They also help patients and their family members identify available community resources. Social workers often serve as case managers when patients' conditions are so complex that professionals need to assess medical and supportive needs and coordinate a variety of services.

speech language pathologists: Work to develop and restore the speech of individuals with communication disorders; usually these disorders are the result of traumas such as surgery or stroke. Speech therapists also help retrain patients in breathing, swallowing, and muscle control.

symptom management: The treatment of patients' emotional and physical symptoms other than pain, such as confusion, fatigue, nausea, shortness of breath, loss of appetite, and muscle wasting.

stroke: An injury to brain tissue resulting from a blocked or burst blood vessel.

T

Torah: The sacred scripture of the Jewish religion.

tPA (tissue plasminogen activator): Introduced in 1996, tPA was the first drug therapy for ischemic stroke, which increases the likelihood of complete or near-complete recovery in 30 to 50 percent of ischemic stroke patients.

transplant centers: Hospitals or medical centers that perform organ and/or tissue transplants.

transplantation: The transfer of cells, tissues, or organs from an area of the body to another or from one organism to another.

transplantation, allogeneic (allograft): Transplantation between genetically different members of the same species. Nearly all organ and bone marrow transplants are allografts. These may be between brothers and sisters, parents and children, or between donors and recipients who are not related to each other.

U

UNOS (United Network for Organ Sharing): Tracks a national patient waiting list for organ transplantation.

V

volunteers: Meet a variety of patient needs in home health care. The scope of a volunteer's services depends on his or her level of training and experience. Volunteer activities include, but are not limited to providing companionship, emotional support, and counseling and helping with personal care, paperwork, and transportation.

Chapter 60

Resources

For further assistance, this chapter lists in alphabetical order contact information for some of the government agencies, professional associations, and individual experts involved in the medical, ethical, and legal concerns associated with the issues of death and dying.

Government Agencies

The following list features some of the public sector agencies involved in providing information and statistical data in areas of concern for the aged, life expectancy and causes of death, long-term health care, improving care of the dying, and organ and tissue donation and transplantation.

Administration on Aging (AoA)
330 Independence Ave. SW
Washington, DC 20201
Phone: (800)677-1116; (202)619-7524
Fax: (202)260-1012
E-mail: aoainfo@aoa.gov
Website: http://www.aoa.gov

Agency for Health Care Policy and Research (AHCPR)
Office of Health Care Information
Executive Office Center,
Ste. 501
2101 E. Jefferson St.
Rockville, MD 20852
Phone: (301)594-1360
E-mail: info@ahcpr.gov
Website: http://www.ahcpr.gov

Centers for Disease Control and Prevention (CDC)

1600 Clifton Rd. NE
Atlanta, GA 30333
Phone: (404)639-3286; (800)311-3435
Fax: (404)639-7394
Website: http://www.cdc.gov

Department of Health and Human Services (HHS)

200 Independence Ave. SW
Washington, DC 20201
Phone: (202)619-0257
E-mail: hhsmail@os.dhhs.gov
Website: http://www.hhs.gov

Federal Trade Commission (FTC)

Consumer Response Center
600 Pennsylvania Ave. NW
Washington, DC 20580
Phone: (202)382-4357; TDD: (202)326-2502
Website: http://www.ftc.gov

Health Care Financing Administration (HCFA)

7500 Security Blvd.
Baltimore, MD 21244
Phone: (410)786-3000; Medicare Pubs: (800)633-4227
Website: http://www.hcfa.gov

National Cancer Institute (NCI)

Bldg. 31, Rm. 10A24
9000 Rockville Pike
Bethesda, MD 20892
Phone: (800)422-6237; TTY: (800)332-8615
Website: http://cancernet.nci.nih.gov

National Center for Health Statistics (NCHS)

6525 Belcrest Rd.
Hyattsville, MD 20782-2003
Phone: (301)436-8500
E-mail: nchsquery@cdc.gov
Website: http://www.cdc.gov/nchswww/default.htm

National Institute for Occupational Safety and Health (NIOSH)

200 Independence Ave. SW
Rm. 715H
Washington, DC 20201
Phone: (202)401-6995: (800)356-4674
E-mail: pubstaft@cdc.gov
Website: http://www.cdc.gov/niosh/homepage.html

National Institute of Neurological Disorders and Stroke (NINDS)

Office of Communications and Public Liaison
P.O. Box 5801
Bethesda, MD 20824
Phone: (800)352-9424
Website: http://www.ninds.nih.gov

National Institute of Nursing Research (NINR)

31 Center Dr., Rm. 5B10
MSC2178
Bethesda, MD 20892-2178
Phone: (301)496-0207
E-mail: info@ninr.nih.gov
Website: http://www.nih.gov/ninr

National Institutes of Health (NIH)
Bethesda, MD 20892
Phone: (301)496-4000
E-mail: NIHInfo@od.nih.gov
Website: http://www.nih.gov

Social Security Administration (SSA)
Office of Public Inquiries
6401 Security Blvd.
Rm. 4-C-5 Annex
Baltimore, MD 21235
Phone: (800)772-1213; TTY: (800)325-0778
Website: http://www.ssa.gov

U.S. General Accounting Office (USGAO)
Health, Education, and Human Services Division
441 G St. NW
Washington, DC 20543
Phone: (202)512-6000; TDD: (202)512-2537
Fax: (202)512-6061
E-mail: info@www.gao.gov
Website: http://www.gao.gov

Professional Associations

The following list includes some of the professional associations that contributed articles to (or were featured in) this book.

Attitudes toward Death and Dying

Center for Intercultural Relations
4534 Hillcrest Dr., P. O. Box 133
Berrien Springs, MI 49103
Phone: (616)471-1325
Fax: (616)473-1220

Project on Death in America
Open Society Institute
400 W. 59th St.
New York, NY 10019
E-mail: pdia@sorosny.org
Website: http://www.soros.org/death.html

Education in Life Issues

HUMAN LIFE of Washington
2725 152nd Ave. NE
Redmond, WA 98052
Phone: (425)882-4397
Fax: (425)881-1199
E-mail: letters@humanlife.net
Website: http://www.humanlife.net

Financial Arrangements

American Association of Retired Persons (AARP)
601 E St. NW
Washington, DC 20049
Phone: (800)424-3410
E-mail: member@aarp.org
Website: http://www.aarp.org

Home Care Providers

National Association for Home Care (NAHC)
228 Seventh St. SE
Washington, DC 20003
Phone: (202)547-7424
Fax: (202)547-3540
E-mail: webmaster@nahc.org
Website: http://www.nahc.org/home.html

Hospice Care

National Hospice Organization (NHO)
1901 N. Moore St., Ste. 901
Arlington, VA 22209-1714
Phone: (703)243-5900; (800)658-8898
Fax: (703)525-5762
E-mail: drsnho@cais.com
Website: http://www.nho.org

North Central Florida Hospice, Inc.
4200 N.W. 90th Blvd.
Gainesville, FL 32606-6290
Phone: (352)378-2121
Fax: (352)379-6290
E-mail: team@hospice-cares
Website: http://hospice-cares.com

Palliative Care for the Terminally Ill

Americans for Better Care of the Dying (ABCD)
2175 K St. NW, Ste. 820
Washington, DC 20037
Phone: (202)530-9864
Fax: (202)467-2271
E-mail: caring@erols.com
Website: http://www.abcd-caring.com

PCC News (Physicians for Compassionate Care)
P.O. Box 6042
Portland, OR 97228
Phone: (503)533-8154
Fax: (503)533-0429

Private Long-Term Care Insurance

American Health Care Association (AHCA)
1201 L St. NW
Washington, DC 20005
Phone: (202)842-4444
Fax: (202)842-3860
E-mail: jmartin@ahca.org
Website: http://www.ahca.org

Health Insurance Association of America
555 13th St. NW
Washington, DC 20004
Phone: (202)824-1600

United Seniors Health Cooperative
1331 H St. NW
Washington, DC 20005
Phone: (202)393-6222

Individual Contributors

The following list features some of the medical specialists who contributed articles to this book. They are classified by topic.

Body Donation

Darrell Crase, Ph.D.
The University of Memphis
Dept. of Human Movement Sciences and Education
Elma N. Roane Field House 204
Memphis, TN 38152

Coping with Life-Threatening Illness

Alice S. Demi, D.N.S., F.A.A.N.
School of Nursing
Box 4019
Georgia State University
Atlanta, GA 30302

Cost of End-Of-Life Care

Ezekiel J. Emanuel, M.D., Ph.D.
Division of Cancer Epidemiology and Control
Dana-Farber Cancer Institute
44 Binney St.
Boston, MA 02115

Elderly Spouses of the Terminally Ill

Laurel C. Beery, B.S.
Dept. of Psychiatry
University of Pittsburgh School of Medicine
Western Psychiatric Institute and Clinic
745 Bellefield Towers
3811 O'Hara St.
Pittsburgh, PA 15213

Innovations in Nursing Home Care

Nicholas G. Castle, Ph.D.
Director, Health Outcomes Research
AtlantiCare Health Systems
6725 Delilah Rd.
Egg Harbor Township, NJ 08234

Medicalization of Dying

R. J. Connelly, Ph.D.
University of the Incarnate Word
4301 Broadway
San Antonio, TX 78209

Internet Resources

Access America for Seniors
Website: http://www.seniors.gov

The Access America for Seniors Web site is designed to let seniors conduct business online easier and faster with federal agencies.

Consumer
Website: http://www.consumer.gov

The first Internet site with one-stop access to federal consumer information including information on health and health care quality.

Death & Dying, Where Life Surrounds Death
Website: http://www.death-dying.com

The site offers comprehensive information on funeral, cremation, and burial goods, services, and costs; advice for grieving parents; information on how children grieve, etc.

Department of Veterans Affairs
Website: http://www.va.gov

The Department of Veterans Affairs site provides information on VA programs, veterans' benefits, VA facilities worldwide, and VA medical automation software. This site services several major constituencies including the veteran and his/her dependents, Veterans Service Organizations, the military, the general public, and VA employees around the world.

Elderly Americans: Protecting Wishes and Assets
Website: http://www.options4seniors.com/page5.html

Online article by Gregory Bator, Attorney at Law, Bator & Berlin, P.C., about such issues as durable power of attorney, wills, probate, and trusts.

Growth House, Inc.
Website: http://www.growthhouse.org

Provides information and newsletter concerning the issues of death and dying including hospice care, pain management, bereavement, eldercare, Alzheimer's disease, etc.

Healthfinder
Website: http://www.healthfinder.gov

Healthfinder.gov helps consumers find reliable health information from many federal agencies, states, professional associations, non-profit organizations and universities. Healthfinder brings information to consumers to help them stay healthy, understand diagnosis, explore treatment options, find support, and generally become more informed about health and medical topics of interest to them.

Insure Kids Now
Website: http://www.insurekidsnow.gov

The Child Health Insurance Program (CHIP) is the largest single expansion of health insurance coverage for children in more than 30 years. Today, nearly 11 million American children—one in seven are uninsured. CHIP enables states to insure children from working families with incomes too high to qualify for Medicaid, but too little to afford private coverage.

Nursing Home Information Site
http://www.jeffdanger.com/Options.htm

Detailed information on how to select the right nursing home by Gary Hickerson, M.S.S.W.

Index

Index

Page numbers followed by 'n' indicate a footnote. Page numbers in *italics* indicate a table or illustration.

A

AARP *see* American Association of Retired Persons (AARP)

ABCD *see* Americans for Better Care of the Dying (ABCD)

accelerated death benefits, defined 592

Access America for Seniors, Internet web site 610

accidents, cause of death statistics *34–39*

see also motor vehicle accidents

ACSUS *see* AIDS Cost and Services Utilization Study (ACSUS)

activities of daily living (ADL)
defined 592
elderly caregivers 358, 362, 368
home care providers 254
long-term care facilities 22, 159–60
long-term care insurance 198
nursing homes 157

ADL *see* activities of daily living (ADL)

Adshead, Lesley 585n, 588

adult day care
long-term care insurance 196
services, defined 592

advance directives 283–90
defined 592
described 284
economic considerations 385

"Advance Directives" (HCFA) 283n

"Advance Report of Final Mortality Statistics, 1995" (Anderson et al.) 29n

AFDC *see* Aid to Families with Dependent Children (AFDC)

African Americans
death attitudes *94*
health facts 53
infant mortality 43, *47–48*
spirituality 128
stroke rates 58–59

age factor, workplace homicides 68

Aging, Administration on (AoA)
contact information 605
elderly health projections 143n
legislation 381

AHCA *see* Health Care Association, American (AHCA)

AHCPR *see* Health Care Policy and Research, Agency for (AHCPR)

O

Health Reference Series
COMPLETE CATALOG

AIDS Sourcebook, 1st Edition

Basic Information about AIDS and HIV Infection, Featuring Historical and Statistical Data, Current Research, Prevention, and Other Special Topics of Interest for Persons Living with AIDS, Along with Source Listings for Further Assistance

Edited by Karen Bellenir and Peter D. Dresser. 831 pages. 1995. 0-7808-0031-1. $78.

"One strength of this book is its practical emphasis. The intended audience is the lay reader . . . useful as an educational tool for health care providers who work with AIDS patients. Recommended for public libraries as well as hospital or academic libraries that collect consumer materials." — *Bulletin of the MLA, Jan '96*

"This is the most comprehensive volume of its kind on an important medical topic. Highly recommended for all libraries." — *Reference Book Review, '96*

"Very useful reference for all libraries." — *Choice, Oct '95*

"There is a wealth of information here that can provide much educational assistance. It is a must book for all libraries and should be on the desk of each and every congressional leader. Highly recommended." — *AIDS Book Review Journal, Aug '95*

"Recommended for most collections." — *Library Journal, Jul '95*

AIDS Sourcebook, 2nd Edition

Basic Consumer Health Information about Acquired Immune Deficiency Syndrome (AIDS) and Human Immunodeficiency Virus (HIV) Infection, Featuring Updated Statistical Data, Reports on Recent Research and Prevention Initiatives, and Other Special Topics of Interest for Persons Living with AIDS, Including New Antiretroviral Treatment Options, Strategies for Combating Opportunistic Infections, Information about Clinical Trials, and More; Along with a Glossary of Important Terms and Resource Listings for Further Help and Information

Edited by Karen Bellenir. 751 pages. 1999. 0-7808-0225-X. $78.

Allergies Sourcebook

Basic Information about Major Forms and Mechanisms of Common Allergic Reactions, Sensitivities, and Intolerances, Including Anaphylaxis, Asthma, Hives and Other Dermatologic Symptoms, Rhinitis, and Sinusitis, Along with Their Usual Triggers Like Animal Fur, Chemicals, Drugs, Dust, Foods, Insects, Latex, Pollen, and Poison Ivy, Oak, and Sumac; Plus Information on Prevention, Identification, and Treatment

Edited by Allan R. Cook. 611 pages. 1997. 0-7808-0036-2. $78.

Alternative Medicine Sourcebook

Basic Consumer Health Information about Alternatives to Conventional Medicine, Including Acupressure, Acupuncture, Aromatherapy, Ayurveda, Bioelectromagnetics, Environmental Medicine, Essence Therapy, Food and Nutrition Therapy, Herbal Therapy, Homeopathy, Imaging, Massage, Naturopathy, Reflexology, Relaxation and Meditation, Sound Therapy, Vitamin and Mineral Therapy, and Yoga, and More

Edited by Allan R. Cook. 737 pages. 1999. 0-7808-0200-4. $78.

Alzheimer's, Stroke & 29 Other Neurological Disorders Sourcebook, 1st Edition

Basic Information for the Layperson on 31 Diseases or Disorders Affecting the Brain and Nervous System, First Describing the Illness, Then Listing Symptoms, Diagnostic Methods, and Treatment Options, and Including Statistics on Incidences and Causes

Edited by Frank E. Bair. 579 pages. 1993. 1-55888-748-2. $78.

"Nontechnical reference book that provides reader-friendly information." — *Family Caregiver Alliance Update, Winter '96*

"Should be included in any library's patient education section." — *American Reference Books Annual, '94*

"Written in an approachable and accessible style. Recommended for patient education and consumer health collections in health science center and public libraries." — *Academic Library Book Review, Dec '93*

"It is very handy to have information on more than thirty neurological disorders under one cover, and there is no recent source like it." — *RQ, Fall '93*

Alzheimer's Disease Sourcebook, 2nd Edition

Basic Consumer Health Information about Alzheimer's Disease, Related Disorders, and Other Dementias, Including Multi-Infarct Dementia, AIDS-Related Dementia, Alcoholic Dementia, Huntington's Disease, Delirium, and Confusional States; Along with Reports Detailing Current Research Efforts in Prevention and Treatment, Long-Term Care Issues, and Listings of Sources for Additional Help and Information

Edited by Karen Bellenir. 524 pages. 1999. 0-7808-0223-3. $78.

Arthritis Sourcebook

Basic Consumer Health Information about Specific Forms of Arthritis and Related Disorders, Including Rheumatoid Arthritis, Osteoarthritis, Gout, Polymyalgia Rheumatica, Psoriatic Arthritis, Spondyloarthropathies, Juvenile Rheumatoid Arthritis, and Juvenile Ankylosing Spondylitis; Along with Information about Medical, Surgical, and Alternative Treatment Options, and Including Strategies for Coping with Pain, Fatigue, and Stress

Edited by Allan R. Cook. 550 pages. 1998. 0-7808-0201-2. $78.

"... accessible to the layperson."
— *Reference and Research Book News, Feb '99*

Back & Neck Disorders Sourcebook

Basic Information about Disorders and Injuries of the Spinal Cord and Vertebrae, Including Facts on Chiropractic Treatment, Surgical Interventions, Paralysis, and Rehabilitation, Along with Advice for Preventing Back Trouble

Edited by Karen Bellenir. 548 pages. 1997. 0-7808-0202-0. $78.

"The strength of this work is its basic, easy-to-read format. Recommended."
— *Reference and User Services Quarterly, Winter '97*

Blood & Circulatory Disorders Sourcebook

Basic Information about Blood and Its Components, Anemias, Leukemias, Bleeding Disorders, and Circulatory Disorders, Including Aplastic Anemia, Thalassemia, Sickle-Cell Disease, Hemochromatosis, Hemophilia, Von Willebrand Disease, and Vascular Diseases; Along with a Special Section on Blood Transfusions and Blood Supply Safety, a Glossary, and Source Listings for Further Help and Information

Edited by Karen Bellenir and Linda M. Shin. 554 pages. 1998. 0-7808-0203-9. $78.

"Recent and recommended reference source."
— *Booklist, Feb '99*

"An important reference sourcebook written in simple language for everyday, non-technical users. "
— *Reviewer's Bookwatch, Jan '99*

Brain Disorders Sourcebook

Basic Consumer Health Information about Strokes, Epilepsy, Amyotrophic Lateral Sclerosis (ALS/Lou Gehrig's Disease), Parkinson's Disease, Brain Tumors, Cerebral Palsy, Headache, Tourette Syndrome, and More; Along with Statistical Data, Treatment and

Rehabilitation Options, Coping Strategies, Reports on Current Research Initiatives, a Glossary, and Resource Listings for Additional Help and Information

Edited by Karen Bellenir. 481 pages. 1999. 0-7808-0229-2. $78.

Burns Sourcebook

Basic Consumer Health Information about Various Types of Burns and Scalds, Including Flame, Heat, Cold, Electrical, Chemical, and Sun Burns; Along with Information on Short-Term and Long-Term Treatments, Tissue Reconstruction, Plastic Surgery, Prevention Suggestions, and First Aid

Edited by Allan R. Cook. 604 pages. 1999. 0-7808-0204-7. $78.

Cancer Sourcebook, 1st Edition

Basic Information on Cancer Types, Symptoms, Diagnostic Methods, and Treatments, Including Statistics on Cancer Occurrences Worldwide and the Risks Associated with Known Carcinogens and Activities

Edited by Frank E. Bair. 932 pages. 1990. 1-55888-888-8. $78.

"Written in nontechnical language. Useful for patients, their families, medical professionals, and librarians."
— *Guide to Reference Books, '96*

"Designed with the non-medical professional in mind. Libraries and medical facilities interested in patient education should certainly consider adding the Cancer Sourcebook to their holdings. This compact collection of reliable information ... is an invaluable tool for helping patients and patients' families and friends to take the first steps in coping with the many difficulties of cancer."
— *Medical Reference Services Quarterly, Winter '91*

"Specifically created for the nontechnical reader ... an important resource for the general reader trying to understand the complexities of cancer."
— *American Reference Books Annual, '91*

"This publication's nontechnical nature and very comprehensive format make it useful for both the general public and undergraduate students."
— *Choice, Oct '90*

New Cancer Sourcebook, 2nd Edition

Basic Information about Major Forms and Stages of Cancer, Featuring Facts about Primary and Secondary Tumors of the Respiratory, Nervous, Lymphatic, Circulatory, Skeletal, and Gastrointestinal Systems, and Specific Organs; Statistical and Demographic Data; Treatment Options; and Strategies for Coping

Edited by Allan R. Cook. 1,313 pages. 1996. 0-7808-0041-9. $78.

"This book is an excellent resource for patients with newly diagnosed cancer and their families. The dialogue is simple, direct, and comprehensive. Highly recommended for patients and families to aid in their understanding of cancer and its treatment."
— *Booklist Health Sciences Supplement, Oct '97*

"The amount of factual and useful information is extensive. The writing is very clear, geared to general readers. Recommended for all levels."
— *Choice, Jan '97*

Cancer Sourcebook, 3rd Edition

Basic Consumer Health Information about Major Forms and Stages of Cancer, Featuring Facts about Primary and Secondary Tumors of the Respiratory, Nervous, Lymphatic, Circulatory, Skeletal, and Gastrointestinal Systems, and Specific Organs; Along with Statistical and Demographic Data, Treatment Options, Strategies for Coping, a Glossary, and a Directory of Sources for Additional Help and Information

Edited by Edward J. Prucha. 1,100 pages. 1999. 0-7808-0227-6. $78.

Cancer Sourcebook for Women, 1st Edition

Basic Information about Specific Forms of Cancer That Affect Women, Featuring Facts about Breast Cancer, Cervical Cancer, Ovarian Cancer, Cancer of the Uterus and Uterine Sarcoma, Cancer of the Vagina, and Cancer of the Vulva; Statistical and Demographic Data; Treatments, Self-Help Management Suggestions, and Current Research Initiatives

Edited by Allan R. Cook and Peter D. Dresser. 524 pages. 1996. 0-7808-0076-1. $78.

". . . written in easily understandable, non-technical language. Recommended for public libraries or hospital and academic libraries that collect patient education or consumer health materials."
— *Medical Reference Services Quarterly, Spring '97*

"Would be of value in a consumer health library. . . . written with the health care consumer in mind. Medical jargon is at a minimum, and medical terms are explained in clear, understandable sentences."
— *Bulletin of the MLA, Oct '96*

"The availability under one cover of all these pertinent publications, grouped under cohesive headings, makes this certainly a most useful sourcebook."
— *Choice, Jun '96*

"Presents a comprehensive knowledge base for general readers. Men and women both benefit from the gold mine of information nestled between the two covers of this book. Recommended."
— *Academic Library Book Review, Summer '96*

"This timely book is highly recommended for consumer health and patient education collections in all libraries."
— *Library Journal, Apr '96*

Cancer Sourcebook for Women, 2nd Edition

Basic Consumer Health Information about Specific Forms of Cancer That Affect Women, Including Cervical Cancer, Ovarian Cancer, Endometrial Cancer, Uterine Sarcoma, Vaginal Cancer, Vulvar Cancer, and Gestational Trophoblastic Tumor; and Featuring Statistical Information, Facts about Tests and Treatments, a Glossary of Cancer Terms, and an Extensive List of Additional Resources

Edited by Edward J. Prucha. 600 pages. 1999. 0-7808-0226-8. $78.

Cardiovascular Diseases & Disorders Sourcebook, 1st Edition

Basic Information about Cardiovascular Diseases and Disorders, Featuring Facts about the Cardiovascular System, Demographic and Statistical Data, Descriptions of Pharmacological and Surgical Interventions, Lifestyle Modifications, and a Special Section Focusing on Heart Disorders in Children

Edited by Karen Bellenir and Peter D. Dresser. 683 pages. 1995. 0-7808-0032-X. $78.

". . . comprehensive format provides an extensive overview on this subject."
— *Choice, Jun '96*

". . . an easily understood, complete, up-to-date resource. This well executed public health tool will make valuable information available to those that need it most, patients and their families. The typeface, sturdy non-reflective paper, and library binding add a feel of quality found wanting in other publications. Highly recommended for academic and general libraries. "
— *Academic Library Book Review, Summer '96*

Communication Disorders Sourcebook

Basic Information about Deafness and Hearing Loss, Speech and Language Disorders, Voice Disorders, Balance and Vestibular Disorders, and Disorders of Smell, Taste, and Touch

Edited by Linda M. Ross. 533 pages. 1996. 0-7808-0077-X. $78.

"This is skillfully edited and is a welcome resource for the layperson. It should be found in every public and medical library."
— *Booklist Health Sciences Supplement, Oct '97*

Congenital Disorders Sourcebook

Basic Information about Disorders Acquired during Gestation, Including Spina Bifida, Hydrocephalus, Cerebral Palsy, Heart Defects, Craniofacial Abnormalities, Fetal Alcohol Syndrome, and More, Along with Current Treatment Options and Statistical Data

Edited by Karen Bellenir. 607 pages. 1997. 0-7808-0205-5. $78.

"Recent and recommended reference source."
— *Booklist, Oct '97*

Consumer Issues in Health Care Sourcebook

Basic Information about Health Care Fundamentals and Related Consumer Issues, Including Exams and Screening Tests, Physician Specialties, Choosing a Doctor, Using Prescription and Over-the-Counter Medications Safely, Avoiding Health Scams, Managing Common Health Risks in the Home, Care Options for Chronically or Terminally Ill Patients, and a List of Resources for Obtaining Help and Further Information

Edited by Karen Bellenir. 618 pages. 1998. 0-7808-0221-7. $78.

"The editor has researched the literature from government agencies and others, saving readers the time and effort of having to do the research themselves. Recommended for public libraries."
— *Reference and Users Services Quarterly, Spring '99*

"Recent and recommended reference source."
— *Booklist, Dec '98*

Contagious & Non-Contagious Infectious Diseases Sourcebook

Basic Information about Contagious Diseases like Measles, Polio, Hepatitis B, and Infectious Mononucleosis, and Non-Contagious Infectious Diseases like Tetanus and Toxic Shock Syndrome, and Diseases Occurring as Secondary Infections Such as Shingles and Reye Syndrome, Along with Vaccination, Prevention, and Treatment Information, and a Section Describing Emerging Infectious Disease Threats

Edited by Karen Bellenir and Peter D. Dresser. 566 pages. 1996. 0-7808-0075-3. $78.

Death & Dying Sourcebook

Basic Consumer Health Information for the Layperson about End-of-Life Care and Related Ethical and Legal Issues, Including Chief Causes of Death, Autopsies, Pain Management for the Terminally Ill, Life Support Systems, Insurance, Euthanasia, Assisted Suicide, Hospice Programs, Living Wills, Funeral Planning, Counseling, Mourning, Organ Donation, and Physician Training; Along with Statistical Data, a Glossary, and Listings of Sources for Further Help and Information

Edited by Annemarie S. Muth. 641 pages. 1999. 0-7808-0230-6. $78.

Diabetes Sourcebook, 1st Edition

Basic Information about Insulin-Dependent and Noninsulin-Dependent Diabetes Mellitus, Gestational Diabetes, and Diabetic Complications, Symptoms, Treatment, and Research Results, Including Statistics on Prevalence, Morbidity, and Mortality, Along with Source Listings for Further Help and Information

Edited by Karen Bellenir and Peter D. Dresser. 827 pages. 1994. 1-55888-751-2. $78.

"... very informative and understandable for the layperson without being simplistic. It provides a comprehensive overview for laypersons who want a general understanding of the disease or who want to focus on various aspects of the disease." — *Bulletin of the MLA, Jan '96*

Diabetes Sourcebook, 2nd Edition

Basic Consumer Health Information about Type 1 Diabetes (Insulin-Dependent or Juvenile-Onset Diabetes), Type 2 (Noninsulin-Dependent or Adult-Onset Diabetes), Gestational Diabetes, and Related Disorders, Including Diabetes Prevalence Data, Management Issues, the Role of Diet and Exercise in Controlling Diabetes, Insulin and Other Diabetes Medicines, and Complications of Diabetes Such as Eye Diseases, Periodontal Disease, Amputation, and End-Stage Renal Disease; Along with Reports on Current Research Initiatives, a Glossary, and Resource Listings for Further Help and Information

Edited by Karen Bellenir. 688 pages. 1998. 0-7808-0224-1. $78.

"Recent and recommended reference source."
— *Booklist, Feb '99*

Diet & Nutrition Sourcebook, 1st Edition

Basic Information about Nutrition, Including the Dietary Guidelines for Americans, the Food Guide Pyramid, and Their Applications in Daily Diet, Nutritional Advice for Specific Age Groups, Current Nutritional Issues and Controversies, the New Food Label and How to Use It to Promote Healthy Eating, and Recent Developments in Nutritional Research

Edited by Dan R. Harris. 662 pages. 1996. 0-7808-0084-2. $78.

"Useful reference as a food and nutrition sourcebook for the general consumer."
— *Booklist Health Sciences Supplement, Oct '97*

"Recommended for public libraries and medical libraries that receive general information requests on nutrition. It is readable and will appeal to those interested in learning more about healthy dietary practices."
— *Medical Reference Services Quarterly, Fall '97*

Diet & Nutrition Sourcebook, 2nd Edition

Basic Consumer Health Information about Dietary Guidelines, Recommended Daily Intake Values, Vitamins, Minerals, Fiber, Fat, Weight Control, Dietary Supplements, and Food Additives; Along with Special Sections on Nutrition Needs throughout Life and Nutrition for People with Such Specific Medical Concerns as Allergies, High Blood Cholesterol, Hypertension, Diabetes, Celiac Disease, Seizure Disorders, Phenylketonuria (PKU), Cancer, and Eating Disorders, and Including Reports on Current Nutrition Research and Source Listings for Additional Help and Information

Edited by Karen Bellenir. 650 pages. 1999. 0-7808-0228-4. $78.

Digestive Diseases & Disorders Sourcebook

Basic Consumer Health Information about Diseases and Disorders that Impact the Upper and Lower Digestive System, Including Celiac Disease, Constipation, Crohn's Disease, Cyclic Vomiting Syndrome, Diarrhea, Diverticulosis and Diverticulitis, Gallstones, Heartburn, Hemorrhoids, Hernias, Indigestion (Dyspepsia), Irritable Bowel Syndrome, Lactose Intolerance, Ulcers, and More; Along with Information about Medications and Other Treatments, Tips for Maintaining a Healthy Digestive Tract, a Glossary, and Directory of Digestive Diseases Organizations

Edited by Karen Bellenir. 325 pages. 1999. 0-7808-0327-2. $48.

Disabilities Sourcebook

Basic Consumer Health Information about Physical and Psychiatric Disabilities, Including Descriptions of Major Causes of Disability, Assistive and Adaptive Aids, Workplace Issues, and Accessibility Concerns; Along with Information about the Americans with Disabilities Act, a Glossary, and Resources for Additional Help and Information

Edited by Dawn D. Matthews. 600 pages. 1999. 0-7808-0389-2. $78.

Domestic Violence & Child Abuse Sourcebook

Basic Information about Spousal/Partner, Child, and Elder Physical, Emotional, and Sexual Abuse, Teen Dating Violence, and Stalking, Including Information about Hotlines, Safe Houses, Safety Plans, and Other Resources for Support and Assistance, Community Initiatives, and Reports on Current Directions in Research and Treatment; Along with a Glossary, Sources for Further Reading, and Governmental and Non-Governmental Organizations Contact Information

Edited by Helene Henderson. 600 pages. 1999. 0-7808-0235-7. $78.

Ear, Nose & Throat Disorders Sourcebook

Basic Information about Disorders of the Ears, Nose, Sinus Cavities, Pharynx, and Larynx, Including Ear Infections, Tinnitus, Vestibular Disorders, Allergic and Non-Allergic Rhinitis, Sore Throats, Tonsillitis, and Cancers That Affect the Ears, Nose, Sinuses, and Throat, Along with Reports on Current Research Initiatives, a Glossary of Related Medical Terms, and a Directory of Sources for Further Help and Information

Edited by Karen Bellenir and Linda M. Shin. 576 pages. 1998. 0-7808-0206-3. $78.

"Overall, this sourcebook is helpful for the consumer seeking information on ENT issues. It is recommended for public libraries."
— *American Reference Books Annual, '99*

"Recent and recommended reference source."
— *Booklist, Dec '98*

Endocrine & Metabolic Disorders Sourcebook

Basic Information for the Layperson about Pancreatic and Insulin Related Disorders Such as Pancreatitis, Diabetes, and Hypoglycemia; Adrenal Gland Disorders Such as Cushing's Syndrome, Addison's Disease, and Congenital Adrenal Hyperplasia; Pituitary Gland Disorders Such as Growth Hormone Deficiency, Acromegaly, and Pituitary Tumors; Thyroid Disorders Such as Hypothyroidism, Graves' Disease, Hashimoto's Disease, and Goiter; Hyperparathyroidism; and Other Diseases and Syndromes of Hormone Imbalance or Metabolic Dysfunction, Along with Reports on Current Research Initiatives

Edited by Linda M. Shin. 574 pages. 1998. 0-7808-0207-1. $78.

"Recent and recommended reference source."
— *Booklist, Dec '98*

Environmentally Induced Disorders Sourcebook

Basic Information about Diseases and Syndromes Linked to Exposure to Pollutants and Other Substances in Outdoor and Indoor Environments Such as Lead, Asbestos, Formaldehyde, Mercury, Emissions, Noise, and More

Edited by Allan R. Cook. 620 pages. 1997. 0-7808-0083-4. $78.

"Recent and recommended reference source."
— *Booklist, Sept '98*

"This book will be a useful addition to anyone's library."
— *Choice Health Sciences Supplement, May '98*

". . . a good survey of numerous environmentally induced physical disorders . . . a useful addition to anyone's library."
— *Doody's Health Science Book Reviews, Jan '98*

". . . provide[s] introductory information from the best authorities around. Since this volume covers topics that potentially affect everyone, it will surely be one of the most frequently consulted volumes in the *Health Reference Series.*"   — *Rettig on Reference, Nov '97*

Ethical Issues in Medicine Sourcebook

Basic Information about Controversial Treatment Issues, Genetic Research, Reproductive Technologies, and End-of-Life Decisions, Including Topics Such as Cloning, Abortion, Fertility Management, Organ Transplantation, Health Care Rationing, Advance Directives, Living Wills, Physician-Assisted Suicide, Euthanasia, and More; Along with a Glossary and Resources for Additional Information

Edited by Helene Henderson. 600 pages. 1999. 0-7808-0237-3. $78.

Fitness & Exercise Sourcebook

Basic Information on Fitness and Exercise, Including Fitness Activities for Specific Age Groups, Exercise for People with Specific Medical Conditions, How to Begin a Fitness Program in Running, Walking, Swimming, Cycling, and Other Athletic Activities, and Recent Research in Fitness and Exercise

Edited by Dan R. Harris. 663 pages. 1996. 0-7808-0186-5. $78.

"A good resource for general readers."
— *Choice, Nov '97*

"The perennial popularity of the topic . . . make this an appealing selection for public libraries."
— *Rettig on Reference, Jun/Jul '97*

Food & Animal Borne Diseases Sourcebook

Basic Information about Diseases That Can Be Spread to Humans through the Ingestion of Contaminated Food or Water or by Contact with Infected Animals and Insects, Such as Botulism, E. Coli, Hepatitis A, Trichinosis, Lyme Disease, and Rabies, Along with Information Regarding Prevention and Treatment Methods, and a Special Section for International Travelers Describing Diseases Such as Cholera, Malaria, Travelers' Diarrhea, and Yellow Fever, and Offering Recommendations for Avoiding Illness

Edited by Karen Bellenir and Peter D. Dresser. 535 pages. 1995. 0-7808-0033-8. $78.

"Targeting general readers and providing them with a single, comprehensive source of information on selected topics, this book continues, with the excellent caliber of its predecessors, to catalog topical information on health matters of general interest. Readable and thorough, this valuable resource is highly recommended for all libraries."
— *Academic Library Book Review, Summer '96*

"A comprehensive collection of authoritative information."   — *Emergency Medical Services, Oct '95*

Food Safety Sourcebook

Basic Consumer Health Information about the Safe Handling of Meat, Poultry, Seafood, Eggs, Fruit Juices, and Other Food Items, and Facts about Pesticides, Drinking Water, Food Safety Overseas, and the Onset, Duration, and Symptoms of Foodborne Illnesses, Including Types of Pathogenic Bacteria, Parasitic Protozoa, Worms, Viruses, and Natural Toxins; Along with the Role of the Consumer, the Food Handler, and the Government in Food Safety; a Glossary, and Resources for Additional Help and Information

Edited by Dawn D. Matthews. 339 pages. 1999. 0-7808-0326-4. $48.

Forensic Medicine Sourcebook

Basic Consumer Information for the Layperson about Forensic Medicine, Including Crime Scene Investigation, Evidence Collection and Analysis, Expert Testimony, Computer-Aided Criminal Identification, Digital Imaging in the Courtroom, DNA Profiling, Accident Reconstruction, Autopsies, Ballistics, Drugs and Explosives Detection, Latent Fingerprints, Product Tampering, and Questioned Document Examination; Along with Statistical Data, a Glossary of Forensics Terminology, and Listings of Sources for Further Help and Information

Edited by Annemarie S. Muth. 574 pages. 1999. 0-7808-0232-2. $78.

Gastrointestinal Diseases & Disorders Sourcebook

Basic Information about Gastroesophageal Reflux Disease (Heartburn), Ulcers, Diverticulosis, Irritable Bowel Syndrome, Crohn's Disease, Ulcerative Colitis, Diarrhea, Constipation, Lactose Intolerance, Hemorrhoids, Hepatitis, Cirrhosis, and Other Digestive Problems, Featuring Statistics, Descriptions of Symptoms, and Current Treatment Methods of Interest for Persons Living with Upper and Lower Gastrointestinal Maladies

Edited by Linda M. Ross. 413 pages. 1996. 0-7808-0078-8. $78.

". . . very readable form. The successful editorial work that brought this material together into a useful and understandable reference makes accessible to all readers information that can help them more effectively understand and obtain help for digestive tract problems." — *Choice, Feb '97*

Genetic Disorders Sourcebook

Basic Information about Heritable Diseases and Disorders Such as Down Syndrome, PKU, Hemophilia, Von Willebrand Disease, Gaucher Disease, Tay-Sachs Disease, and Sickle-Cell Disease, Along with Information about Genetic Screening, Gene Therapy, Home Care, and Including Source Listings for Further Help and Information on More Than 300 Disorders

Edited by Karen Bellenir. 642 pages. 1996. 0-7808-0034-6. $78.

"Provides essential medical information to both the general public and those diagnosed with a serious or fatal genetic disease or disorder." — *Choice, Jan '97*

"Geared toward the lay public. It would be well placed in all public libraries and in those hospital and medical libraries in which access to genetic references is limited." — *Doody's Health Sciences Book Review, Oct '96*

Head Trauma Sourcebook

Basic Information for the Layperson about Open-Head and Closed-Head Injuries, Treatment Advances, Recovery, and Rehabilitation, Along with Reports on Current Research Initiatives

Edited by Karen Bellenir. 414 pages. 1997. 0-7808-0208-X. $78.

Health Insurance Sourcebook

Basic Information about Managed Care Organizations, Traditional Fee-for-Service Insurance, Insurance Portability and Pre-Existing Conditions Clauses, Medicare, Medicaid, Social Security, and Military Health Care, Along with Information about Insurance Fraud

Edited by Wendy Wilcox. 530 pages. 1997. 0-7808-0222-5. $78.

"Particularly useful because it brings much of this information together in one volume." — *Medical Reference Services Quarterly, Fall '98*

"The layout of the book is particularly helpful as it provides easy access to reference material. A most useful addition to the vast amount of information about health insurance. The use of data from U.S. government agencies is most commendable. Useful in a library or learning center for healthcare professional students." — *Doody's Health Sciences Book Reviews, Nov '97*

Healthy Aging Sourcebook

Basic Consumer Health Information about Maintaining Health through the Aging Process, Including Advice on Nutrition, Exercise, and Sleep, Help in Making Decisions about Midlife Issues and Retirement, and Guidance Concerning Practical and Informed Choices in Health Consumerism; Along with Data Concerning the Theories of Aging, Different Experiences in Aging by Minority Groups, and Facts about Aging Now and Aging in the Future; and Featuring a Glossary, a Guide to Consumer Help, Additional Suggested Reading, and Practical Resource Directory

Edited by Jenifer Swanson. 536 pages. 1999. 0-7808-0390-6. $78.

Heart Diseases & Disorders Sourcebook, 2nd edition

Basic Consumer Health Information about Heart Attacks, Angina, Rhythm Disorders, Heart Failure, Valve Disease, Congenital Heart Disorders, and More, Including Descriptions of Surgical Procedures and Other Interventions, Medications, Cardiac Rehabilitation, Risk Identification, and Prevention Tips; Along with Statistical Data, Reports on Current Research Initiatives, a Glossary of Cardiovascular Terms, and Resource Directory

Edited by Karen Bellenir. 600 pages. 1999. 0-7808-0238-1. $78.

Immune System Disorders Sourcebook

Basic Information about Lupus, Multiple Sclerosis, Guillain-Barré Syndrome, Chronic Granulomatous Disease, and More, Along with Statistical and Demographic Data and Reports on Current Research Initiatives

Edited by Allan R. Cook. 608 pages. 1997. 0-7808-0209-8. $78.

Infant & Toddler Health Sourcebook

Basic Consumer Health Information about the Physical and Mental Development of Newborns, Infants, and Toddlers, Including Neonatal Concerns, Nutritional Recommendations, Immunization Schedules, Common Pediatric Disorders, Assessments and Milestones, Safety Tips, and Advice for Parents and Other Caregivers; Along with a Glossary of Terms and Resource Listings for Additional Help

Edited by Jenifer Swanson. 600 pages. 1999. 0-7808-0246-2. $78.

Kidney & Urinary Tract Diseases & Disorders Sourcebook

Basic Information about Kidney Stones, Urinary Incontinence, Bladder Disease, End Stage Renal Disease, Dialysis, and More, Along with Statistical and Demographic Data and Reports on Current Research Initiatives

Edited by Linda M. Ross. 602 pages. 1997. 0-7808-0079-6. $78.

Learning Disabilities Sourcebook

Basic Information about Disorders Such as Dyslexia, Visual and Auditory Processing Deficits, Attention Deficit/Hyperactivity Disorder, and Autism, Along with Statistical and Demographic Data, Reports on Current Research Initiatives, an Explanation of the Assessment Process, and a Special Section for Adults with Learning Disabilities

Edited by Linda M. Shin. 579 pages. 1998. 0-7808-0210-1. $78.

"Readable . . . provides a solid base of information regarding successful techniques used with individuals who have learning disabilities, as well as practical suggestions for educators and family members. Clear language, concise descriptions, and pertinent information for contacting multiple resources add to the strength of this book as a useful tool." — *Choice, Feb '99*

"Recent and recommended reference source."
— *Booklist, Sept '98*

Liver Disorders Sourcebook

Basic Consumer Health Information about the Liver and How It Works; Liver Diseases, Including Cancer, Cirrhosis, Hepatitis, and Toxic and Drug Related Diseases; Tips for Maintaining a Healthy Liver; Laboratory Tests, Radiology Tests, and Facts about Liver Transplantation; Along with a Section on Support Groups, a Glossary, and Resource Listings

Edited by Joyce Brennfleck Shannon. 600 pages. 1999. 0-7808-0383-3. $78.

Medical Tests Sourcebook

Basic Consumer Health Information about Medical Tests, Including Periodic Health Exams, General Screening Tests, Tests You Can Do at Home, Findings of the U.S. Preventive Services Task Force, X-ray and Radiology Tests, Electrical Tests, Tests of Blood and Other Body Fluids and Tissues, Scope Tests, Lung Tests, Genetic Tests, Pregnancy Tests, Newborn Screening Tests, Sexually Transmitted Disease Tests, and Computer Aided Diagnoses; Along with a Section on Paying for Medical Tests, a Glossary, and Resource Listings

Edited by Joyce Brennfleck Shannon. 691 pages. 1999. 0-7808-0243-8. $78.

Men's Health Concerns Sourcebook

Basic Information about Health Issues That Affect Men, Featuring Facts about the Top Causes of Death in Men, Including Heart Disease, Stroke, Cancers, Prostate Disorders, Chronic Obstructive Pulmonary Disease, Pneumonia and Influenza, Human Immunodeficiency Virus and Acquired Immune Deficiency Syndrome, Diabetes Mellitus, Stress, Suicide, Accidents and Homicides; and Facts about Common Concerns for Men, Including Impotence, Contraception, Circumcision, Sleep Disorders, Snoring, Hair Loss, Diet, Nutrition, Exercise, Kidney and Urological Disorders, and Backaches

Edited by Allan R. Cook. 738 pages. 1998. 0-7808-0212-8. $78.

"Recent and recommended reference source."
— *Booklist, Dec '98*

Mental Health Disorders Sourcebook, 1st Edition

Basic Information about Schizophrenia, Depression, Bipolar Disorder, Panic Disorder, Obsessive-Compulsive Disorder, Phobias and Other Anxiety Disorders, Paranoia and Other Personality Disorders, Eating Disorders, and Sleep Disorders, Along with Information about Treatment and Therapies

Edited by Karen Bellenir. 548 pages. 1995. 0-7808-0040-0. $78.

"This is an excellent new book . . . written in easy-to-understand language."
— *Booklist Health Science Supplement, Oct '97*

". . . useful for public and academic libraries and consumer health collections."
— *Medical Reference Services Quarterly, Spring '97*

"The great strengths of the book are its readability and its inclusion of places to find more information. Especially recommended." — *RQ, Winter '96*

". . . a good resource for a consumer health library."
— *Bulletin of the MLA, Oct '96*

"The information is data-based and couched in brief, concise language that avoids jargon. . . . a useful reference source." — *Readings, Sept '96*

"The text is well organized and adequately written for its target audience." — *Choice, Jun '96*

". . . provides information on a wide range of mental disorders, presented in nontechnical language." — *Exceptional Child Education Resources, Spring '96*

"Recommended for public and academic libraries." — *Reference Book Review, '96*

Mental Health Disorders Sourcebook, 2nd Edition

Basic Consumer Health Information about Anxiety Disorders, Depression and Other Mood Disorders, Eating Disorders, Personality Disorders, Schizophrenia, and More, Including Disease Descriptions, Treatment Options, and Reports on Current Research Initiatives; Along with Statistical Data, Tips for Maintaining Mental Health, a Glossary, and Directory of Sources for Additional Help and Information

Edited by Karen Bellenir. 600 pages. 1999. 0-7808-0240-3. $78.

Ophthalmic Disorders Sourcebook

Basic Information about Glaucoma, Cataracts, Macular Degeneration, Strabismus, Refractive Disorders, and More, Along with Statistical and Demographic Data and Reports on Current Research Initiatives

Edited by Linda M. Ross. 631 pages. 1996. 0-7808-0081-8. $78.

Oral Health Sourcebook

Basic Information about Diseases and Conditions Affecting Oral Health, Including Cavities, Gum Disease, Dry Mouth, Oral Cancers, Fever Blisters, Canker Sores, Oral Thrush, Bad Breath, Temporomandibular Disorders, and other Craniofacial Syndromes, Along with Statistical Data on the Oral Health of Americans, Oral Hygiene, Emergency First Aid, Information on Treatment Procedures and Methods of Replacing Lost Teeth

Edited by Allan R. Cook. 558 pages. 1997. 0-7808-0082-6. $78.

"Unique source which will fill a gap in dental sources for patients and the lay public. A valuable reference tool even in a library with thousands of books on dentistry. Comprehensive, clear, inexpensive, and easy to read and use. It fills an enormous gap in the health care literature." — *Reference and User Services Quarterly, Summer '98*

"Recent and recommended reference source." — *Booklist, Dec '97*

Osteoporosis Sourcebook

Basic Consumer Health Information about Primary and Secondary Osteoporosis, Juvenile Osteoporosis, Related Conditions, and Other Such Bone Disorders as Fibrous Dysplasia, Myeloma, Osteogenesis Imperfecta, Osteopetrosis, and Paget's Disease; Along with Information about Risk Factors, Treatments, Traditional and Non-Traditional Pain Management, and Including a Glossary and Resource Directory

Edited by Allan R. Cook. 600 pages. 1999. 0-7808-0239-X. $78.

Pain Sourcebook

Basic Information about Specific Forms of Acute and Chronic Pain, Including Headaches, Back Pain, Muscular Pain, Neuralgia, Surgical Pain, and Cancer Pain, Along with Pain Relief Options Such as Analgesics, Narcotics, Nerve Blocks, Transcutaneous Nerve Stimulation, and Alternative Forms of Pain Control, Including Biofeedback, Imaging, Behavior Modification, and Relaxation Techniques

Edited by Allan R. Cook. 667 pages. 1997. 0-7808-0213-6. $78.

"The text is readable, easily understood, and well indexed. This excellent volume belongs in all patient education libraries, consumer health sections of public libraries, and many personal collections." — *American Reference Books Annual, '99*

"A beneficial reference." — *Booklist Health Sciences Supplement, Oct '98*

"The information is basic in terms of scholarship and is appropriate for general readers. Written in journalistic style . . . intended for non-professionals. Quite thorough in its coverage of different pain conditions and summarizes the latest clinical information regarding pain treatment." — *Choice, Jun '98*

"Recent and recommended reference source." — *Booklist, Mar '98*

Pediatric Cancer Sourcebook

Basic Consumer Health Information about Leukemias, Brain Tumors, Sarcomas, Lymphomas, and Other Cancers in Infants, Children, and Adolescents, Including Descriptions of Cancers, Treatments, and Coping Strategies; Along with Suggestions for Parents, Caregivers, and Concerned Relatives, a Glossary of Cancer Terms, and Resource Listings

Edited by Edward J. Prucha. 587 pages. 1999. 0-7808-0245-4. $78.

Physical & Mental Issues in Aging Sourcebook

Basic Consumer Health Information on Physical and Mental Disorders Associated with the Aging Process, Including Concerns about Cardiovascular Disease, Pulmonary Disease, Oral Health, Digestive Disorders, Musculoskeletal and Skin Disorders, Metabolic Changes, Sexual and Reproductive Issues, and Changes in Vision, Hearing, and Other Senses; Along with Data about Longevity and Causes of Death, Information on Acute and Chronic Pain, Descriptions of Mental Concerns, a Glossary of Terms, and Resource Listings for Additional Help

Edited by Jenifer Swanson. 660 pages. 1999. 0-7808-0233-0. $78.

Pregnancy & Birth Sourcebook

Basic Information about Planning for Pregnancy, Maternal Health, Fetal Growth and Development, Labor and Delivery, Postpartum and Perinatal Care, Pregnancy in Mothers with Special Concerns, and Disorders of Pregnancy, Including Genetic Counseling, Nutrition and Exercise, Obstetrical Tests, Pregnancy Discomfort, Multiple Births, Cesarean Sections, Medical Testing of Newborns, Breastfeeding, Gestational Diabetes, and Ectopic Pregnancy

Edited by Heather E. Aldred. 737 pages. 1997. 0-7808-0216-0. $78.

"A well-organized handbook. Recommended."
— Choice, Apr '98

"Recent and recommended reference source."
— Booklist, Mar '98

"Recommended for public libraries."
— American Reference Books Annual, '98

Public Health Sourcebook

Basic Information about Government Health Agencies, Including National Health Statistics and Trends, Healthy People 2000 Program Goals and Objectives, the Centers for Disease Control and Prevention, the Food and Drug Administration, and the National Institutes of Health, Along with Full Contact Information for Each Agency

Edited by Wendy Wilcox. 698 pages. 1998. 0-7808-0220-9. $78.

"Recent and recommended reference source."
— Booklist, Sept '98

"This consumer guide provides welcome assistance in navigating the maze of federal health agencies and their data on public health concerns."
— SciTech Book News, Sept '98

Rehabilitation Sourcebook

Basic Consumer Health Information about Rehabilitation for People Recovering from Heart Surgery, Spinal Cord Injury, Stroke, Orthopedic Impairments, Amputation, Pulmonary Impairments, Traumatic Injury, and More, Including Physical Therapy, Occupational Therapy, Speech/Language Therapy, Massage Therapy, Dance Therapy, Art Therapy, and Recreational Therapy; Along with Information on Assistive and Adaptive Devices, a Glossary, and Resources for Additional Help and Information

Edited by Dawn D. Matthews. 512 pages. 1999. 0-7808-0236-5. $78.

Respiratory Diseases & Disorders Sourcebook

Basic Information about Respiratory Diseases and Disorders, Including Asthma, Cystic Fibrosis, Pneumonia, the Common Cold, Influenza, and Others, Featuring Facts about the Respiratory System, Statistical and Demographic Data, Treatments, Self-Help Management Suggestions, and Current Research Initiatives

Edited by Allan R. Cook and Peter D. Dresser. 771 pages. 1995. 0-7808-0037-0. $78.

"Designed for the layperson and for patients and their families coping with respiratory illness. . . . an extensive array of information on diagnosis, treatment, management, and prevention of respiratory illnesses for the general reader."
— Choice, Jun '96

"A highly recommended text for all collections. It is a comforting reminder of the power of knowledge that good books carry between their covers."
— Academic Library Book Review, Spring '96

"This sourcebook offers a comprehensive collection of authoritative information presented in a nontechnical, humanitarian style for patients, families, and caregivers."
— Association of Operating Room Nurses, Sept/Oct '95

Sexually Transmitted Diseases Sourcebook

Basic Information about Herpes, Chlamydia, Gonorrhea, Hepatitis, Nongonoccocal Urethritis, Pelvic Inflammatory Disease, Syphilis, AIDS, and More, Along with Current Data on Treatments and Preventions

Edited by Linda M. Ross. 550 pages. 1997. 0-7808-0217-9. $78.

Skin Disorders Sourcebook

Basic Information about Common Skin and Scalp Conditions Caused by Aging, Allergies, Immune Reactions, Sun Exposure, Infectious Organisms, Parasites, Cosmetics, and Skin Traumas, Including Abrasions, Cuts, and Pressure Sores, Along with Information on Prevention and Treatment

Edited by Allan R. Cook. 647 pages. 1997. 0-7808-0080-X. $78.

"... comprehensive easily read reference book."
— Doody's Health Sciences Book Reviews, Oct '97

Sleep Disorders Sourcebook

Basic Consumer Health Information about Sleep and Its Disorders, Including Insomnia, Sleepwalking, Sleep Apnea, Restless Leg Syndrome, and Narcolepsy; Along with Data about Shiftwork and Its Effects, Information on the Societal Costs of Sleep Deprivation, Descriptions of Treatment Options, a Glossary of Terms, and Resource Listings for Additional Help

Edited by Jenifer Swanson. 439 pages. 1998. 0-7808-0234-9. $78.

"Recent and recommended reference source."
— Booklist, Feb '99

Sports Injuries Sourcebook

Basic Consumer Health Information about Common Sports Injuries, Prevention of Injury in Specific Sports, Tips for Training, and Rehabilitation from Injury; Along with Information about Special Concerns for Children, Young Girls in Athletic Training Programs, Senior Athletes, and Women Athletes, and a Directory of Resources for Further Help and Information

Edited by Heather E. Aldred. 624 pages.1999. 0-7808-0218-7. $78.

Substance Abuse Sourcebook

Basic Health-Related Information about the Abuse of Legal and Illegal Substances Such as Alcohol, Tobacco, Prescription Drugs, Marijuana, Cocaine, and Heroin; and Including Facts about Substance Abuse Prevention Strategies, Intervention Methods, Treatment and Recovery Programs, and a Section Addressing the Special Problems Related to Substance Abuse during Pregnancy

Edited by Karen Bellenir. 573 pages. 1996. 0-7808-0038-9. $78.

"A valuable addition to any health reference section. Highly recommended."
— The Book Report, Mar/Apr '97

"... a comprehensive collection of substance abuse information that's both highly readable and compact. Families and caregivers of substance abusers will find the information enlightening and helpful, while teachers, social workers and journalists should benefit from the concise format. Recommended."
— Drug Abuse Update, Winter '96-'97

Women's Health Concerns Sourcebook

Basic Information about Health Issues That Affect Women, Featuring Facts about Menstruation and Other Gynecological Concerns, Including Endometriosis, Fibroids, Menopause, and Vaginitis; Reproductive Concerns, Including Birth Control, Infertility, and Abortion; and Facts about Additional Physical, Emotional, and Mental Health Concerns Prevalent among Women Such as Osteoporosis, Urinary Tract Disorders, Eating Disorders, and Depression, Along with Tips for Maintaining a Healthy Lifestyle

Edited by Heather Aldred. 567 pages. 1997. 0-7808-0219-5. $78.

"Handy compilation. There is an impressive range of diseases, devices, disorders, procedures, and other physical and emotional issues covered ... well organized, illustrated, and indexed."
— Choice, Jan '98

Workplace Health & Safety Sourcebook

Basic Information about Musculoskeletal Injuries, Cumulative Trauma Disorders, Occupational Carcinogens and Other Toxic Materials, Child Labor, Workplace Violence, Histoplasmosis, Transmission of HIV and Hepatitis-B Viruses, and Occupational Hazards Associated with Various Industries, Including Mining, Confined Spaces, Agriculture, Construction, Electrical Work, and the Medical Professions, with Information on Mortality and Other Statistical Data, Preventative Measures, Reproductive Risks, Reducing Stress for Shiftworkers, Noise Hazards, Industrial Back Belts, Reducing Contamination at Home, Preventing Allergic Reactions to Rubber Latex, and More; Along with Public and Private Programs and Initiatives, a Glossary, and Sources for Additional Help and Information

Edited by Helene Henderson. 600 pages. 1999. 0-7808-0231-4. $78.

Health Reference Series Cumulative Index

A Comprehensive Index to 42 Volumes of the Health Reference Series, 1990-1998

1,500 pages. 1999. 0-7808-0382-5. $78.

641